PRIVATE ENFORCEMENT OF EU LAW BEFORE NATIONAL COURTS

The EU Legislative Framework

ELGAR EUROPEAN LAW AND PRACTICE

The *Elgar European Law and Practice* series is a library of reference works by leading practitioners, agency officials and scholars covering discrete areas of substantive law and procedure in the field of European law. Rigorous in their analysis, each title is extensively referenced and shines a spotlight on the legal issues that are most relevant to practice. Designed to be detailed yet focused works, the books in this series offer an in-depth treatment and an authoritative statement on the law, and illuminate key aspects of practice and procedure, relating to topics ranging from Judicial Review to Private Enforcement, from Transport Law to Private International Law and from Public Procurement to Value Added Tax.

Presented in a format that allows for ease of navigation to a particular point of law, each title in the series is written by specialists in their respective fields, often with insight either from private practice or from an enforcement perspective.

PRIVATE ENFORCEMENT OF EU LAW BEFORE NATIONAL COURTS

The EU Legislative Framework

FOLKERT WILMAN

*Member of the Legal Service of the European Commission, Belgium**

* *All views expressed are strictly personal and cannot be ascribed to the European Commission.*

ELGAR EUROPEAN LAW AND PRACTICE

Edward Elgar PUBLISHING

Cheltenham, UK • Northampton, MA, USA

Published by
Edward Elgar Publishing Limited
The Lypiatts
15 Lansdown Road
Cheltenham
Glos GL50 2JA
UK

Edward Elgar Publishing, Inc.
William Pratt House
9 Dewey Court
Northampton
Massachusetts 01060
USA

A catalogue record for this book
is available from the British Library

Library of Congress Control Number: 2015938634

This book is available electronically in the **Elgar**online
Law subject collection
DOI 10.4337/9781784718497

MIX
Paper from responsible sources
FSC® C013056
FSC www.fsc.org

ISBN 978 1 78471 848 0 (cased)
ISBN 978 1 78471 849 7 (eBook)

Typeset by Columns Design XML Ltd, Reading
Printed and bound in Great Britain by TJ International Ltd, Padstow

For Gloria

CONTENTS

EXTENDED TABLE OF CONTENTS

ABBREVIATIONS

ACTA	Anti-Counterfeiting Trade Agreement
BIE	Berichten Intellectuele Eigendom
BR	Tijdschrift voor Bouwrecht
CLJ	Consumer Law Journal
CMLRev	Common Market Law Review
CoJ	Court of Justice
CompLRev	Competition Law Review
CST	Civil Service Tribunal
CWILJ	California Western International Law Journal
EAR	European Antitrust Review
EBLR	European Business Law Review
EC	European Community
ECHR	European Convention for the Protection of Human Rights and Fundamental Freedoms
ECJ	European Competition Journal
ECLR	European Competition Law Review
ECSC	European Coal and Steel Community
ECtHR	European Court of Human Rights
EEC	European Economic Community
EFAR	European Foreign Affairs Review
EFTA	European Free Trade Area
EIPR	European Intellectual Property Review
ELJ	European Law Journal
ELRev	European Law Review
ErLRev	Erasmus Law Review
ERPL	European Review of Private Law
EStAL	European State Aid Law Quarterly
EU	European Union
EuConst	European Constitutional Law Review
FILJ	Fordham International Law Journal
GATT	General Agreement on Tariffs and Trade
GC	General Court
GCLR	Global Competition Litigation Review
GP	Gazette du Palais
GPA	Agreement on Government Procurement
GPRI	Geneva Papers on Risk and Insurance
IBA	International Bar Association
ICLQ	International and Comparative Law Quarterly
IIC	International Review of Intellectual Property and Copyright Law

ILP	International Legal Practitioner
JCLE	Journal of Competition Law and Economics
JCMS	Journal of Common Market Studies
JCP	Journal of Consumer Policy
JDE	Journal de Droit Européen
JECLP	Journal of European Competition Law and Practice
JEPP	Journal of European Public Policy
JESP	Journal of European Social Policy
JIPITEC	Journal of Intellectual Property, Information Technology and E-Commerce
JIPLP	Journal of Intellectual Property Law and Practice
LIEI	Legal Issues of Economic Integration
LPIB	Law and Policy in International Business
MJECL	Maastricht Journal of European and Comparative Law
MLR	Modern Law Review
NiPR	Nederlands Internationaal Privaatrecht
NTER	Nederlands Tijdschrift voor Europees Recht
PLC	Practical Law Company
PPLR	Public Procurement Law Review
RabelsZ	Rabels Zeitschrift für ausländisches und internationales Privatrecht
RDC	Revue des Droits de la Concurrence
REAL	Review of European Administrative Law
REDC	Revue Européenne de Droit de la Consommation
RIDC	Revue Internationale de Droit Comparé
SEW	Sociaal-economische wetgeving: tijdschrift voor Europees en economisch recht
TA	Tijdschrift Aanbestedingsrecht
TEU	Treaty on European Union
TFEU	Treaty on the Functioning of the European Union
TRIPS	Trade-Related Aspects of Intellectual Property Rights
UNIDROIT	International Institute for the Unification of Private Law
WComp	World Competition
WIPO	World Intellectual Property Organization
WTO	World Trade Organization
YLJ	Yale Law Journal

TABLE OF CASES AND OPINIONS

CASE LAW – COURT OF JUSTICE (COJ)

CASE LAW – GENERAL COURT (GC)

CASE LAW – CIVIL SERVICE TRIBUNAL (CST)

CASE LAW – EUROPEAN COURT OF HUMAN RIGHTS (ECTHR)

CASE LAW – EUROPEAN FREE TRADE AREA (EFTA) COURT

CASE LAW – THE NETHERLANDS

OPINIONS – ADVOCATES GENERAL (AG)

TABLE OF LEGISLATION AND OFFICIAL DOCUMENTS

LEGISLATION

Directives

Regulations

Other Legislation

OFFICIAL DOCUMENTS – EU COMMISSION

Commission Decisions, Statements, Guidelines and Notices

Commission Legislative Proposals

Commission Green Papers, White Papers and Reports

Commission Communications

Other Commission Official Documents

OFFICIAL DOCUMENTS – EUROPEAN PARLIAMENT

OFFICIAL DOCUMENTS – EU COUNCIL

Council Official Documents

Council Preparatory Documents (available via an access to documents request to the Council)

OTHER OFFICIAL DOCUMENTS

Part A

INTRODUCTION AND BACKGROUND

1

INTRODUCTION*

> The vigilance of individuals concerned to protect their rights amounts to an effective supervision in addition to the supervision entrusted [...] to the diligence of the Commission and the Member States.[1]

A. THE VIGILANCE OF INDIVIDUALS IN EU LAW

1. The creation of a private enforcement model

In its *Van Gend en Loos* judgment dating from over half a century ago, the Court of Justice of the European Union ("Court of Justice" or "Court") made it clear that the new legal order established through the creation of the European Union[2] ("EU") concerns not only the Member States, on the one hand, and the EU's institutions and other bodies, on the other hand.[3] Rather, the relationship is triangular in nature, in that private parties can also have a legal position under EU law. Not only can this law create obligations for these private parties, it can also confer rights on them, even where that is not expressly stated, provided that the provision in question is sufficiently clear and unconditional. EU law therefore constitutes '*a direct source of rights and duties for all those affected thereby, whether Member States or individuals, who are parties to the legal relationships under [EU] law*'.[4] As is well known, *Van Gend en Loos* thus articulated the principle of direct effect. Equally well known is that shortly afterwards the **1.01**

* The author completed a PhD at the University of Leiden on the same topic, supervised by Professor H.J. Snijders and Professor S.C.G. Van Den Bogaert, and this book draws upon that research.

1 Court of Justice ("CoJ") case 26/62, *Van Gend en Loos*, p. 13.

2 Unless expressly indicated otherwise, in the following reference is consistently made to the current names of the EU, the EU's institutions and other bodies and the relevant acts of EU law. Similarly, the current numbering of the EU Treaties is consistently used throughout this book.

3 CoJ case 26/62, *Van Gend en Loos*, p. 13.

4 CoJ case 106/77, *Simmenthal*, para 15.

Court confirmed the existence of the principle of primacy of EU law over national law.[5] Together these two principles constitute the '*essential characteristics*' of the EU legal order.[6]

By insisting that private parties can in principle directly exercise and enforce the rights that they derive from EU law, the Court laid the foundations for what has become known as the private enforcement model of EU law.[7] This model ensures the possibility for the private parties concerned to initiate legal proceedings for alleged infringements of their rights under EU law.[8] Not only does this serve the interests of those parties themselves, it also adds to the supervision exercised especially by the European Commission ("Commission") as regards compliance with EU law. Indeed, the above quote from *Van Gend en Loos* demonstrates that the notion that legal actions brought by private parties can be instrumental in strengthening compliance with EU law is as old as the very foundations of that law. This implies that private parties can be recruited as the EU's "private attorneys general"[9] or "private policemen".[10] That means in turn that '*the vast potential resources of the general European population [are] enlisted to supplement the Commission in its efforts to secure the uniform and effective application of [EU] law*'.[11] Implicit in this private enforcement model is that these proceedings are to be brought before national courts, that is, the judicial authorities designated by the Member States.[12] All this was and continues to be of considerable importance, for several reasons.

1.02 In the first place, the scope for enforcing EU law at the central, European level (that is, before the EU courts in Luxembourg) is limited for *legal* reasons. The main mechanisms designed to ensure such supervision and enforcement at that level, to which reference was made in *Van Gend en Loos*, are infringement proceedings. The relevant Treaty provisions, Articles 258 and 259 of the Treaty on the Functioning of the EU ("TFEU"), allow both the Member States and

---

5 CoJ case 6/64, *Costa v ENEL*, pp. 593–4.

6 CoJ opinion 1/91, *EEA Agreement*, para 21.

7 Kilpatrick (2000), p. 1.

8 While in the case law of the EU courts reference is typically made to "individuals", the term generally used here to designate the persons that may initiate these private enforcement proceedings is "private parties". This latter term can encompass legal and natural persons and covers the range of terms used in specific legislation and situations, such as undertaking, rightholder or consumer. It includes public authorities where they do not act in a public capacity, that is, where they do not exercise public powers derogating from the rules of law applicable to relations between private individuals but instead act in accordance with these latter rules. Cf. e.g. CoJ case C-167/00, *Henkel*, para 30.

9 Kilpatrick (2000), p. 2.

10 Drake (2006), p. 843, with reference to Weiler (1981), p. 273.

11 Dougan (2004), p. 76.

12 For the present purposes, the term "national court" corresponds, broadly speaking, with the term "court or tribunal of a Member State" within the meaning of Article 267 TFEU on the preliminary reference procedure, discussed in para 1.02 below.

the Commission to bring a case before the Court of Justice when they consider that a Member State has infringed EU law. Private parties can neither initiate these proceedings nor can they be taken to court in this context.[13] Infringement proceedings thus remain an affair from which private parties are largely excluded.[14]

Furthermore, it is of course true that the Treaty on the European Union ("TEU") and the TFEU (collectively "EU Treaties") allow private parties to initiate "direct actions" before the EU courts. But these actions can only be brought in a limited number of circumstances. In particular, in order to have legal standing (*locus standi*, that is, the legal capacity to bring an action before the court) under Article 263 TFEU, a private party must demonstrate that it is directly and individually concerned by the act that is the object of the legal action in question. As construed by the EU courts, this threshold can be notoriously difficult to overcome.[15] The amendment of this article in 2009 (Treaty of Lisbon) has relaxed this test somewhat in certain cases. This has not, however, fundamentally altered the restrictive approach with respect to the private party's possibility of bringing these direct actions before the EU courts.[16] Direct actions are moreover limited to contesting the legality of acts or failures to act of the institutions and other bodies of the EU, as well as claims in connection with the EU's contractual or non-contractual liability.[17] No such actions can be brought against Member States, let alone against other private parties.[18]

In addition, under Article 267 TFEU, the Court of Justice can give preliminary rulings in proceedings that private parties have brought before the courts or tribunals of the Member States in cases where there is uncertainty as to the interpretation or validity of provisions of EU law. The Court has clarified that this term "courts or tribunal" refers to independent and permanent bodies established by law with compulsory jurisdiction, which apply rules of law on the basis of *inter partes* proceedings.[19] Such preliminary rulings clarify EU law as it

---

13 Cf. e.g. General Court ("GC") Order case T-532/12, *Morea*, para 7.

14 See further subsection 2.C.1 below.

15 E.g. CoJ case 25/62, *Plaumann*, pp. 106–7; CoJ case C-50/00 P, *UPA*, para 32–46. See also Opinion AG Jacobs case C-50/00 P, *UPA*, para 36–99. See further e.g. Ward (2009), pp. 343–7.

16 It follows from the fourth subparagraph of Art. 263 TFEU, as amended, that a private party applicant is no longer required to demonstrate individual concern in relation to regulatory acts that do not entail implementing measures. See e.g. CoJ case C-583/11 P, *Inuit*, para 45–62 and 68–77; CoJ case C-456/13 P, *T & L Sugars*, para 29–32 and 43–50. On this amendment, see further e.g. Ward (2009), pp. 357–9; Craig (2010), pp. 129–32; Kornezov (2014), p. 251; Van Malleghem and Baeten (2014), p. 1187.

17 See Articles 263, 265 and 340 TFEU respectively. Cf. e.g. GC Order case T-635/13, *Aćimović*, para 6.

18 E.g. CoJ case 175/84, *Krohn*, para 18; CoJ case C-407/04 P, *Dalmine v*, para 62; GC Order case T-469/11, *Al Qadhafi v France*, para 8; GC Order case T-311/13, *FQ*.

19 E.g. CoJ case 246/80, *Broekmeulen*, para 18; CoJ case C-54/96, *Dorsch Consult*, para 23; CoJ case C-136/11, *Westbahn Management*, para 27; CoJ joined cases C-58/13 and C-59/13, *Torresi*, para 17–19; CoJ case

ought to have been understood from its entry into force and as such they are also of relevance to legal relationships other than those between the parties to the case at hand.[20] The preliminary reference procedure has been held to be '*essential for the preservation of the [EU] character of the law established by the [EU] Treaties*' and an element of the '*complete system of legal remedies and procedures designed to ensure judicial review of the legality of [those] acts*'.[21] These characteristics have led some to call it the '*infringement procedure for private parties*'.[22] However, there are also certain important limits in this case. The preliminary reference system establishes in essence a form of direct cooperation between the national courts and the Court of Justice.[23] Procedurally speaking, such a reference is no more than a sidestep in the proceedings before the former.[24] Where the Court of Justice has issued a preliminary ruling it remains for the national court concerned to apply that ruling to the case at hand.[25] Moreover, while EU law can require the latter to make a preliminary reference, the decision whether or not to do so is, as a matter of EU law, taken independently from the acts or views of the parties to the legal proceedings.[26]

1.03 In the second place, there are *practical* considerations that limit the scope for enforcement of EU law at the central, European level. To begin with, in practice the Member States hardly ever use the above-mentioned powers to initiate infringement proceedings against other Member States.[27] It is therefore, in practice, primarily for the Commission to bring such proceedings. While the Commission, as the "guardian" of the EU Treaties,[28] is generally willing to use its powers in this regard where it deems this necessary, its resources (in terms of information-gathering capacity, manpower as well as financial means) are

---

C-222/13, *TDC*, para 27–32. Although certain arbitration bodies may meet these conditions, alternative dispute resolution bodies normally do not. See e.g. CoJ case 102/81, *Nordsee*, para 9–16; CoJ Order case C-555/13, *Merck Canada*, para 17–25.

20 E.g. CoJ case 61/79, *Denkavit*, para 16; CoJ case C-231/96, *Edis*, para 15.

21 CoJ case C-583/11 P, *Inuit*, para 92. See e.g. also CoJ opinion 2/13, *ECHR*, para 198, where this procedure is called '*the keystone of the judicial system established by the [EU] Treaties*'.

22 Pescatore, cited in Micklitz (2012), p. 393.

23 E.g. CoJ opinion 1/09, *Patent Court Agreement*, para 84; CoJ case C-416/10, *Križan*, para 66.

24 Cf. the standard phrase used by the CoJ in relation to the allocation of costs associated with preliminary references, according to which '*these proceedings are, for the parties to the main proceedings, a step in the action pending before the national court*'. See e.g. CoJ case C-416/10, *Križan*, para 117.

25 E.g. CoJ case 51/74, *Van der Hulst*, para 12; CoJ joined cases C-175/98 and C-177/98, *Lirussi*, para 38.

26 E.g. CoJ case 70/77, *Simmenthal*, para 10; CoJ case C-2/06, *Kempter*, para 41–2; CoJ case C-137/08, *Pénzügi Lízing*, para 28–9; CoJ case C-561/11, *Fédération Cynologique Internationale*, para 30. This is not to say, however, that the parties to the proceedings before a national court may not *suggest* making a preliminary reference, in accordance with the applicable national procedural rules. Some also link the preliminary reference procedure to the principle of effective judicial protection discussed in subsection 2.B below. See e.g. Opinion AG Léger case C-224/01, *Köbler*, para 147; Opinion AG Ruiz-Jarabo Colomer case C-14/08, *Roda Golf*, para 29.

27 Only four such cases have been brought in the period up until 2012. See Lock (2012), p. 1677.

28 Cf. Art. 17 TEU.

limited, however. This was already the case in the early days of the process of European integration, but it arguably carries even more weight today in an EU that has been enlarged to 28 Member States and over 500 million citizens and that is, moreover, involved in many different fields of law.[29] As a consequence, in its own words, the Commission cannot act as *'a kind of "super enforcement authority"'*.[30]

Similar considerations apply to the EU courts.[31] They have over the decades been confronted with a virtually permanently increasing number of cases brought before them. This is illustrated by the fact that the published case law of the Court of Justice for 2001 alone takes up the same shelf space as that for the first 19 years of case law up to 1972.[32] Whereas in 2000 around 900 new cases were brought before the EU courts (with approximately 1450 cases pending), ten years later this number had risen to around 1250 new cases per year (with approximately 2100 cases pending),[33] an increase of almost 40 per cent. As a result the EU courts regularly struggle with their workload. Structural and organisational changes have been enacted, most notably through the creation of the General Court in 1988. More recently the Court of Justice, which is charged *inter alia* with ruling on preliminary references and in infringement proceedings, has been able to cut back the length of the proceedings before it. However, the General Court especially, which acts mainly as the first instance court for direct actions, continues to struggle with its workload and the resulting long delays. Indeed, the length of the proceedings before this latter court has already several times been held to have exceeded a reasonable time period.[34] Discussions on reforms therefore continue.[35]

Lastly, as a general rule, EU law is *implemented by the Member States*.[36] This **1.04**
implementation therefore takes place primarily at national level. It follows that

29 Cf. e.g. recital 6 Directive 2006/123/EC on services in the internal market, OJ 2006, L 376/36 ("Services Directive"), where it is noted that seeking to remove the barriers identified there on a case-by-case basis through infringement procedures under primary EU law *'would, especially following enlargement, be extremely complicated for national and [EU] institutions'*.

30 Commission, Communication on public procurement in the EU, COM(1998) 143, p. 13.

31 The term "EU courts" is used here to refer to the Court of Justice of the European Union, which consists of the Court of Justice and the General Court as well as the Civil Service Tribunal ("CST") as a specialised court.

32 Jacobs (2004a), p. 823.

33 See CoJ, Annual reports 2000 and 2010, respectively.

34 E.g. CoJ case C-40/12 P, *Gascogne*, para 102; CoJ case C-243/12 P, *FLS Plast*, para 142; CoJ case C-467/13 P, *ICF*, para 57–60.

35 On the functioning and workload of the EU courts as well as past and possible future reforms, see further e.g. Rasmussen (2000), p. 1071; Schiemann (2008), p. 3; Forwood (2008), p. 34; Meij (2013), p. 3; Hadroušek and Somlek (2015), p. 188.

36 Cf. Art. 291(1) TFEU. See e.g. also CoJ case C-201/04, *Molenbergnatie*, para 52: *'according to the general principles on which the [EU] is based and which govern the relations between it and the Member States, it is for the Member States, under Article [4(3) TEU], to ensure that [EU] rules are implemented on their territories'*.

there is also considerable potential for the enforcement of EU law at that level, that is, before the competent national courts.[37] The above-mentioned finding in *Van Gend en Loos* that under certain conditions EU law confers rights on private parties on which these parties can rely directly in legal proceedings allowed the unleashing of this potential for decentralised enforcement, particularly in combination with the principle of primacy of EU law.[38] Indeed, after that judgment it did not take the Court of Justice long to clarify that '*every time a rule of [EU] law confers rights on individuals, those rights, without prejudice to the methods of recourse made available by the Treaty, may be safeguarded by proceedings brought before the competent national courts*'.[39] Earlier it had already held that '*it may generally be assumed that a substantive right has as its corollary that it provides the person in whose interest it operates with the means of enforcing it himself by proceedings before the courts rather than the intervention of a third party*'.[40]

Since *Van Gend en Loos*, which concerned a provision of the EU Treaties, it has been made clear that the principle of direct effect extends to potentially all binding EU legal acts. Provided that they are sufficiently clear and unconditional, provisions of regulations and decisions can therefore also be directly effective.[41] The same applies to directives, but only in "vertical" legal relationships, that is, in actions between a private party, on the one hand, and a Member State (including its decentralised entities and semi-public bodies), on the other hand.[42] The Court of Justice has consistently held that directives have no horizontal direct effect. This means that, in and of themselves, provisions of directives cannot impose obligations on private parties and cannot be invoked and enforced in legal relationships between private parties.[43] The effects of this position tend to be moderated somewhat by the fact that the concept of a "state" – and therefore that of a vertical relationship – is a rather wide one in this connection. The capacity in which the latter acts is not of relevance. Provisions of directives that are capable of having direct effect may therefore be relied upon against any body, whatever its legal form, which has been made responsible

37 Cf. CoJ case 294/83, *Les Verts*, para 23.

38 For whereas direct effect can be understood as meaning that EU law is to be considered as the "law of the land", it is the combination with the principle of primacy that ensures that EU law is also the "*higher* law of the land". See Weiler (1991), p. 2415.

39 CoJ case 28/67, *Firma Molkerei*, p. 153.

40 CoJ case 6/60, *Humblet*, pp. 571–2. This case relates to the European Coal and Steel Community ("ECSC") and not to the EU Treaties, but considering its nature in principle and the similarity of the relevant provisions at issue, there appears to be no reason why this statement would not be equally applicable as a matter of EU law. That is confirmed by the reference to this case made in CoJ joined cases C-6/90 and C-9/90, *Francovich*, para 36.

41 CoJ case 9/70, *Grad*, para 5; CoJ case 39/72, *Commission v Italy (slaughtered cows)*, para 17.

42 CoJ case 41/74, *Van Duyn*, para 12.

43 E.g. CoJ joined cases C-397/01 to C-403/01, *Pfeiffer*, para 108; CoJ case C-282/10, *Dominguez*, para 37 and 42.

pursuant to a measure adopted by a Member State for providing a public service under the control of the State and which has for that purpose special powers beyond those which result from the normal rules applicable in relations between private parties.[44] But, for instance, an association governed by private law with a social objective does not meet these conditions.[45] This absence of horizontal direct effect furthermore does not mean that the application of a directly effective provision of EU law in a vertical context cannot, indirectly, have certain adverse repercussions for another private party or have "collateral effects" in horizontal legal relationships.[46] The fact nonetheless remains that the Member States first need to transpose a directive into national law for the rules of EU law in question to have effect in "truly" horizontal legal relationships.[47]

The aforementioned potential is reinforced by other "weapons" that private parties can use in proceedings before national courts where claims based on EU law are at stake. Of particular importance is the principle of consistent interpretation (also known as "harmonious interpretation" or "indirect effect"). Under this principle, as construed by the Court of Justice, national law must be interpreted, in so far as possible, in light of the wording and the purpose of the EU law at issue.[48] This means that national courts must do whatever lies within their jurisdiction, taking the whole body of national law into consideration and applying the interpretative methods recognised by it, with a view to ensuring that the rule of EU law in question is fully effective and to achieving an outcome consistent with the objective pursued by it. The principle of consistent interpretation finds its limits in the general principles of law that form part of the EU legal order, in particular those of legal certainty and non-retroactivity, which can thus constitute a bar to incurring criminal liability and preclude an interpretation *contra legem*. Given the aforementioned absence of horizontal direct effect of directives, the principle of consistent interpretation is particularly relevant in actions between private parties concerning rights and obligations derived from directives, especially where they have not been transposed into national law in a correct and timely manner. Other such "weapons" at the disposal of private parties seeking to assert their rights derived from EU law

44 E.g. CoJ case C-282/10, *Dominguez*, para 38–9; CoJ case C-425/12, *Portgás*, para 24–6.

45 CoJ case C-176/12, *Association de médiation sociale*, para 37.

46 E.g. CoJ case C-443/98, *Unilever*, para 49–51; CoJ case C-201/02, *Wells*, para 57. See further Prechal (2005), pp. 255–70.

47 Cf. Art. 288 TFEU, pursuant to which a directive is '*binding, as to the result to be achieved, upon each Member State to which it is addressed*', while leaving '*to the national authorities the choice of form and methods*'.

48 E.g. CoJ case 80/86, *Kolpinghuis Nijmegen*, para 13–14; CoJ case C-106/89, *Marleasing*, para 8; CoJ joined cases C-397/01 to C-403/01, *Pfeiffer*, para 118; CoJ case C-42/11, *Lopes Da Silva Jorge*, para 54–6; CoJ case C-176/12, *Association de médiation sociale*, para 38–9. See further Prechal (2005), pp. 180–215; Craig and De Búrca (2011), pp. 200–207.

before the courts of the Member States are the principle of Member State liability and the (nascent) principle of private party liability. Pursuant to these latter two principles, infringers must compensate for the harm caused as a consequence of their breaches of EU law.[49]

1.05 National courts are therefore generally the primary venue for private parties to assert their rights vested in EU law.[50] When considering and deciding the resulting cases, those courts do not act in a purely national capacity. They rather act in effect as a judicial organ of a unitary EU judicial power.[51] As the Court of Justice put it, together with the Court itself, the courts of the Member States are the '*guardians of [the EU] legal order and the judicial system of the European Union*', as it is for them to '*ensure that the full application of [EU] law in all Member States and to ensure judicial protection of a [private party's] rights under that law*'.[52] As such these national courts can be seen as the '"*ordinary*" *courts within the European Union legal order*'.[53]

2. EU involvement with private enforcement

1.06 It is remarkable in light of this crucial role in the EU legal order of national courts and the private enforcement proceedings brought before them, as set out above, that there are comparatively few EU rules that regulate the role of those courts and those proceedings. EU law typically defines the rights and obligations of private parties, but it generally does not provide for the remedies (that is, the classes of actions intended to make good infringements of the right at issue) and the procedural rules (that is, the rules governing the exercise of these remedies that are intended to make them operational) that are necessary for their enforcement at national level.[54]

This certainly holds true where *primary* EU law is concerned, that is, the rules laid down in the EU Treaties. While this primary EU law, as interpreted by the EU courts, is often "generous" in conferring rights on private parties,[55] it is largely silent on the remedies and procedures necessary to enforce them.[56] In

---

49 See further section 2.D below.

50 Cf. Tridimas (2006), p. 419.

51 GC case T-51/89, *Tetra Pak*, para 42; Opinion AG Cosmas case C-83/98 P, *France v Ladbroke Racing and Commission*, para 92.

52 CoJ Opinion 1/09, *Patent Court Agreement*, para 66 and 68.

53 Ibid., para 80.

54 Cf. Jacobs and Deisenhofer (2003), p. 214. Regarding these definitions of the terms "remedies" and "procedures", see Van Gerven (2000), p. 502. Note that the term "remedy" is sometimes also understood in a broader sense, namely as corresponding to redress generally. See Prechal (2005), p. 145 (n. 99). Cf. Art. 19(1) TEU.

55 See further para 11.13 and 11.17 below.

56 Cf. Whish (1994), p. 3.

fact, primary EU law contains only one explicit reference to the term "remedies", namely in Article 19(1) TEU.[57] Tellingly, this reference was only introduced in 2009 (Treaty of Lisbon). Even more tellingly perhaps, this provision recalls that it is for the Member States – and therefore in principle not for the EU – to provide '*remedies sufficient to ensure effective legal protection in the fields covered by EU law*'. Article 19(1) TEU thus essentially confirms and formalises the dominant pattern of decentralised judicial review discussed above.[58] As such, it ensures the observance of the fundamental right to effective judicial protection within the EU.[59]

The picture has to a large extent long been comparable if we look at *secondary* EU law, which is the rules laid down in legal acts adopted by the EU legislature on the basis of the EU Treaties, such as regulations and directives.[60] Especially in the early days of EU law, common rules in this regard were almost completely lacking.[61] As is shown in the remainder of this study, significant developments have taken place since. Nonetheless, even today there is no generally applicable set of rules laid down in secondary EU law harmonising the Member States' rules relating to the remedies and procedures that apply to the proceedings initiated by private parties before national courts concerning the enforcement of substantive EU law.

It is important to note that all this is not a matter of mere formalities. While **1.07**
attention may often tend to focus on the substantive provisions conferring rights on the private parties that are subject to EU law, the significance of remedial and procedural rules can hardly be overstated. As the Commission put it, '*rights which cannot be enforced are worthless*'.[62] The European Parliament has similarly noted that '*citizens and companies must not only enjoy rights, but must also be able to enforce those rights effectively and efficiently*'.[63] Formulated somewhat more elegantly, it has been said that (civil) procedural law serves '*to infuse life into all other areas of the law, to bring into actual being and to give reality and effect*

57 Cf. Komninos (2008), p. 149 (n. 52).

58 Tridimas (2006), p. 420 (regarding the corresponding article in the draft EU Constitutional Treaty, which, via the Treaty of Lisbon, later became the current Art. 19(1) TEU). Cf. CoJ Opinion 1/09, *Patent Court Agreement*, para 66; CoJ case C-583/11 P, *Inuit*, para 101. On this provision and its (potential) significance, see also Lenaerts, I Maselis and K Gutman (2014), pp. 117–118.

59 E.g. CoJ case C-418/11, *Texdata*, para 78; CoJ case C-583/11 P, *Inuit*, para 100. On the right to effective judicial protection set out in Art. 47 Charter, see further section 2.B below. Cf. Opinion AG Jääskinen case C-536/11, *Donau Chemie*, para 47, where it is argued that Art. 19(1) TEU supplies a supplementary guarantee to the "*Rewe*-principle" of effectiveness, discussed in subsection 2.A.3 below.

60 Cf. Art. 288 TFEU.

61 For an overview, see subsection 1.B.1 below.

62 Commission, Public consultation towards a coherent approach to collective redress, SEC(2011) 173, p. 2.

63 European Parliament, Resolution, Towards a coherent European approach to collective redress, P7_TA(2012)0021, recital A.

to all the legal rights and duties of every person and body in society'.[64] Remedial and procedural rules may therefore in practice often be at least as important for the private parties concerned as their abstract substantive entitlements under EU law.[65] Without having legal standing, for instance, a private party cannot bring an action before the competent national court in the first place. Similarly, rules on issues such as access to evidence, the burden of proof, causality and legal costs tend to determine to a great extent whether there is any point in bringing such a claim and, when it is brought, whether it will be successful.

The rules on remedies and procedures that apply in private enforcement proceedings can therefore have a substantial impact on the *effectiveness* of the substantive EU law at stake. Particularly at national level issues of enforcement of and compliance with EU law have long been – and continue to be – a matter of particular concern in the EU legal order. The assessment that '*it is not enough to pass laws and simply to hope that they will be applied evenly in all Member States*' seems as valid today as it was over two decades ago.[66] Indeed, two more recent studies found that '*it would be a mistake to hold that the enforcement issue is "solved", far from it*' and that '*much of the evidence [...] suggests that there is a significant problem with enforcement across the Single Market*'.[67] In addition, the predominant reliance on the domestic laws of the Member States to regulate remedial and procedural matters related to the private enforcement of EU law before national courts inherently also implies that differences can and do exist in this respect across the EU, both as regards the manner in which this enforcement takes places and the outcomes to which it may lead. A system of decentralised judicial enforcement that principally relies on national law for the adjudication of private enforcement actions can thus also lead to *inconsistencies* and *unequal treatment*.[68]

Thus, in an EU that has been founded on the rule of law,[69] and that moreover aspires to have a positive impact on the lives of the citizens of its Member States, not least through its extensive "language of rights",[70] ensuring that the applicable rules of substantive EU law are capable of actually having an effect in practice must be a matter of priority. Facilitating private enforcement may be only one of a range of measures that can conceivably be taken to this effect, yet it

64 Jacob (1987), p. 63.
65 Flynn (2008), p. 245.
66 Sutherland Report (1992), p. 5.
67 Study, Pelkmans and Correia de Brito (2012), p. iv; UK Single Market Report (2013), p. 43, respectively.
68 Cf. Bridge (1984), pp. 32–6; Jacobs and Deisenhofer (2003), p. 198.
69 Art. 2 TEU.
70 Wakefield (2009), p. 410. See also para 11.13 below.

is undoubtedly an important one, particularly in light of the characteristics of the EU legal order set out above.

Over the decades significant steps have been taken in the case law of the Court of Justice that mitigate the effects of the general absence of EU rules in the field of remedies and procedures applicable in proceedings before national courts concerning the enforcement of rights vested in EU law.[71] In so doing, that EU institution has corrected to some extent the apparent imbalance referred to above between, on the one hand, the reliance on enforcement of EU law at national level and on the other hand the general lack of common remedial and procedural provisions. However, such intervention can '*by the nature of things only alleviate, but not eliminate the problem*'.[72] Crucial as this case law surely has been and indeed continues to be, for reasons of principle as well as practice there are limits to what can be expected from the judiciary in this respect. While the EU courts are obliged to do justice in the cases brought before them,[73] it is nonetheless primarily for the EU *legislature* to address these issues in a more systematic and general matter.[74] While that holds true generally, it arguably applies even more so in the specific context of EU law. For where the EU courts come close to or are seen as overstepping the line between the resolution of concrete cases and laying down quasi-legislative measures, they become vulnerable to "accusations" of judicial activism.[75] All this applied in 1979 when Advocate General Warner noted that the Court of Justice '*cannot create [EU] law where none exists: that must be left to the [EU]'s legislative organs*'.[76] And it still applies today, as is illustrated by Advocate General Trstenjak's observation thirty years later that the EU courts '*may not assume the role of the [EU] legislature if a gap in the law can be filled by the [EU] legislature*'.[77] **1.08**

While highlighting especially the (potential) differences in treatment of private parties resulting from the lack of uniformity in this respect, the Court of Justice therefore spoke in 1980 of a '*regrettable absence*' of EU law provisions on the

71 See sections 2.A, 2.B and 2.D below.

72 Toth (1978), p. 187.

73 Cf. Art. 19(1) TEU, where it is stipulated that the EU courts '*shall ensure that in the interpretation and application of the [EU] Treaties the law is observed*'. Specifically in relation to the preliminary reference procedure set out in Art. 267 TFEU, it is settled case law that '*where the questions submitted concern the interpretation of [EU] law, the Court [of Justice] is in principle required to give a ruling*'. See e.g. CoJ case C-416/10, *Križan*, para 53.

74 See further subsection 10.C.1 below. References in this book to the EU legislature should, unless specifically indicated otherwise, be understood as references to the European Parliament and the Council acting jointly on the basis of a legislative proposal by the Commission, in accordance with the ordinary legislative procedure (see Art. 289 and 294 TFEU).

75 Cf. Garben (2013), p. 15. Regarding the discussion on judicial activism in relation to the EU courts more generally, see e.g. Tridimas (1996), p. 199; Craig and de Búrca (2011), pp. 63–6; Dougan (2012a), p. 113.

76 Opinion AG Warner case 265/78, *Ferwerda*, p. 640.

77 Opinion AG Trstenjak case C-101/08, *Audiolux*, para 107.

remedies and procedures regarding the enforcement of EU law at national level.[78] It held that '*[i]t is not for the Court to issue general rules of substance or procedural provisions, which only the competent institutions may adopt*'.[79] Particularly from the 1980s onwards and increasingly throughout the 1990s, this barely disguised call for EU legislative action on these matters also started to resonate in the legal literature, often as part of broader concerns relating to the effectiveness and practical effects of EU law in the Member States.[80]

B. THE EU LEGISLATIVE FRAMEWORK

1. Brief overview

1.09 Gradually the EU legislature started responding to the calls for the establishment of EU legislation to facilitate the private enforcement of EU law before national courts referred to at the end of the previous section. Although early examples can be traced back as far as the 1960s,[81] it is appropriate to consider the late 1970s as the period in which the EU legislature took the first, still rather hesitant, steps in this regard.[82] Most notably, in 1976 in the field of gender equality Directive 76/207 was adopted, which has been later recast in Directive

78 CoJ case 130/79, *Express Dairy Foods*, para 12. See e.g. also CoJ case 54/81, *Fromme*, para 4.

79 Ibid. See e.g. also CoJ joined cases 205/82 to 215/82, *Deutsche Milchkontor*, para 24.

80 E.g. Bridge (1984), p. 41; Steiner (1995), p. 60; Neville Brown (1997), p. 71; Himsworth (1997), p. 292. On the above-mentioned broader concerns, see e.g. Snyder (1993), p. 19.

81 E.g. Art. 12 Directive 65/65/EEC on the approximation of provisions laid down by law, regulation or administrative action relating to proprietary medicinal products, OJ 1965, 22/369. This directive has since been replaced by Directive 2001/83/EC on the Community code relating to medicinal products for human use, OJ 2001, L 311/67. Another example is Art. 7 Directive 64/221/EEC on the coordination of special measures concerning the movement and residence of foreign nationals which are justified on grounds of public policy, public security or public health, OJ 1964, 56/850. This directive has since been replaced by Directive 2004/38/EC on the right of citizens of the Union and their family members to move and reside freely within the territory of the Member States, OJ 2004, L 158/77.

82 Apart from the legislation referred to above, see e.g. also the (rather rudimentary) provisions on civil liability in Directive 77/91/EEC on coordination of safeguards which, for the protection of the interests of members and others, are required by Member States of companies within the meaning of the second paragraph of Article 58 of the Treaty, in respect of the formation of public limited liability companies and the maintenance and alteration of their capital, with a view to making such safeguards equivalent, OJ 1977, L 26/1 (Art. 18); Directive 78/855/EEC based on Article 54(3)(g) of the Treaty concerning mergers of public limited companies, OJ 1978, L 295/36 (Art. 20–21). These directives have since been replaced by Directive 2012/30/EU on coordination of safeguards which, for the protection of the interests of members and others, are required by Member States of companies within the meaning of the second paragraph of Article 54 of the Treaty on the Functioning of the European Union, in respect of the formation of public limited liability companies and the maintenance and alteration of their capital, with a view to making such safeguards equivalent, OJ 2012, L 315/74 ("Public Limited Liabilities Companies Directive") and Directive 2011/35/EU concerning mergers of public limited liability companies, OJ 2011, L 110/1, respectively.

2006/54 ("Gender Equality Directive").[83] This directive requires measures to be taken at national level to ensure effective review possibilities through judicial and administrative procedures, touching upon issues such as compensation for damage, legal standing and the burden of proof. Another early example is Directive 85/374 ("Product Liability Directive").[84] In order to protect consumers, this directive establishes the principle of civil liability in damages without fault of producers for defective products. It also addresses a number of related issues, such as the available heads of damages and the limitation periods that apply in legal proceedings brought under this directive.

Especially in the 1990s and the 2000s the EU's legislative involvement with **1.10**
private enforcement-related matters became more intense. The adoption at EU level of specific provisions relating to remedies and procedures available to private parties in proceedings before their national courts became increasingly common. These provisions were – and often still are – typically part of legal acts setting out substantive rules. Examples can be found in fields as diverse as the protection of personal data, e-commerce and the environment. As to the former, Directive 95/46[85] ("Data Protection Directive") and Directive 2002/58[86] ("E-Privacy Directive") follow an approach that is essentially based on establishing a right to effective redress and to reparation in damages for persons having suffered injury. Directive 2000/31 on certain legal aspects of information society services ("E-Commerce Directive") encourages out-of-court settlements, stipulates that rapid court actions, including interim measures, must be available to terminate infringements and prevent further impairment of the interests involved, and contains certain exemptions from liability.[87] And while Directive 2004/35 on environmental liability[88] ("Environmental Liability Directive") is not concerned with civil liability, it nonetheless includes noteworthy rules on legal standing for private parties, including parties not representing strictly individual interests, such as non-governmental organisations.

83 Directive 76/207/EEC on the implementation of the principle of equal treatment for men and women as regards access to employment, vocational training and promotion, and working conditions, OJ 1976, L 39/40. See also Directive 97/80/EC on the burden of proof in cases of discrimination based on sex, OJ 1980, L 14/6. These two directives have since been replaced by Directive 2006/54/EC on the implementation of the principle of equal opportunities and equal treatment of men and women in matters of employment and occupation, OJ 2006, L 204/23.

84 Directive 85/374/EEC on the approximation of the laws, regulations and administrative provisions of the Member States concerning liability for defective products, OJ 1985, L 210/29.

85 Directive 95/46/EC on the protection of individuals with regard to the processing of personal data and of the free movement of such data, OJ 1995, L 281/13.

86 Directive 2002/58/EC concerning the processing of personal data and the protection of privacy in the electronic communications sector, OJ 2002, L 201/37.

87 Directive 2000/31/EC on certain legal aspects of information society services, in particular electronic commerce, in the internal market, OJ 2000, L 178/1.

88 Directive 2004/35/EC on environmental liability with regard to the prevention and remedying of environmental damage, OJ 2004, L 143/56.

With respect to environmental impact assessments, common rules on review were inserted in 2003 in Directive 2011/92 ("Environmental Impact Assessment Directive"), *inter alia* on legal standing and legal costs.[89]

Around the same period the EU legislature also took more ambitious action, in the sense that it adopted broader, free-standing legal acts that are *exclusively* concerned with setting out measures aimed at facilitating the private enforcement of the rules of substantive EU law in a given sector. Prime examples are the twin Directives 89/665 and 92/13 relating to EU public procurement law ("Procurement Remedies Directives").[90] These directives stipulate that effective and rapid remedies should be available to aggrieved private parties. They also contain specific rules on legal standing, forum, interim relief and actions for damages. Similarly Directive 2004/48 ("IPR Enforcement Directive") is dedicated specifically to the private enforcement of intellectual property rights.[91] To this aim it harmonises national remedial and procedural rules on matters such as legal standing, evidence, interim relief, injunctions, damages and legal costs. Furthermore, Directive 98/27, later codified in Directive 2009/22 ("Consumer Injunctions Directive"), seeks to protect consumers' interests by specifying rules on legal standing and providing for certain specific remedies, most notably injunctive relief.[92]

1.11 More recent developments indicate that legislative measures of the type at issue here continue to be considered, proposed and adopted at EU level. Indeed, it is noticeable that many of the pressing current-day EU-level challenges are addressed by an approach that involves a private enforcement element. For instance, the EU's response to the economic crisis included an amendment to Regulation 1060/2009 on credit rating agencies ("Credit Rating Agencies Regulation"), which established a strengthened regime on the civil liability in

89 Directive 2011/92/EU on the assessment of the effects of certain public and private projects on the environment, OJ 2012, L 26/1. This directive is a codification of Directive 85/337/EEC on the assessments of the effects of certain public and private projects on the environment, OJ 1985, L 175/40. It has been amended in 2014, which amendment is to be transposed into national law by May 2017. See Directive 2014/52/EU amending Directive 2011/92/EU on the assessment of the effects of certain public and private projects on the environment, OJ 2014, L 124/1.

90 Directive 89/665/EEC on the coordination of laws, regulations and administrative provisions relating to the application of review procedures to the award of public supply and public works contracts, OJ 1989, L 395/33; Directive 92/13/EEC coordinating the laws, regulations and administrative provisions relating to the application of rules on the procurement procedures of entities operating in the water, energy, transport and telecommunications sectors, OJ 1992, L 76/14.

91 Directive 2004/48/EC on the enforcement of intellectual property rights, OJ 2004, L 195/45.

92 Directive 98/27/EC on injunctions for the protection of consumers' interests, OJ 1998, L 166/51; Directive 2009/22/EC on injunctions for the protection of consumers' interests, OJ 2009, L 110/30.

damages of those agencies.[93] In the area of free movement of persons and employment, Directive 2014/54 ("Free Movement of Workers Enforcement Directive") requires judicial procedures to be made available to EU citizens who exercise their rights in this regard and who are confronted with unjustified restrictions and discrimination.[94] These procedures are also to be made available to certain associations acting on behalf or in support of the private parties concerned. A comparable approach can be found in Directive 2014/67 ("Posting of Workers Enforcement Directive").[95] While this latter directive mainly strengthens public enforcement, it also requires the Member States to ensure that affected private parties as well as certain third parties (for example trade unions) can initiate legal proceedings at national level to safeguard the rights vested in EU law in this domain. Yet another politically charged topic is the protection of personal data. The proposed strengthening of the EU's regime in this regard includes more elaborate provisions on the right of redress of the private parties concerned.[96] Reference can also be made to developments in the area of passengers' rights, where acts such as Regulation 261/2004[97] ("Air Passengers' Rights Regulation") and Regulation 1371/2007[98] ("Rail Passengers' Rights Regulation") require compensation for passengers in certain cases. Last but not least, at the end of 2014, Directive 2014/104 ("Competition Damages Directive"), which provides for common rules on actions for damages in cases of competition law infringements, was adopted.[99] Those rules include specifications on what damage is to be compensated, who can bring such actions, which defences can be raised and the disclosure of evidence.

---

93 Regulation (EC) No 1060/2009 on credit rating agencies, OJ 2009, L 302/1, as amended by Regulation (EU) No 462/2013 amending Regulation (EC) No 1060/2009 on credit rating agencies, OJ 2013, L 146/146. On these liability rules, see further Haar (2014), p. 315.

94 Directive 2014/54/EU on measures facilitating the exercise of rights conferred on workers in the context of freedom of movement for workers, OJ 2014, L 128/8.

95 Directive 2014/67/EU on the enforcement of Directive 96/71/EC concerning the posting of workers in the framework of the provision of services and amending Regulation (EU) No 1024/2012 on administrative cooperation through the Internal Market Information System, OJ 2014, L 159/24.

96 Commission, Proposal for a regulation on the protection of individuals with regard to the processing of personal data and on the free movement of such data, COM(2012) 11.

97 Regulation (EC) No 261/2004 establishing common rules in compensation and assistance to passengers in the event of denied boarding and of cancellation or long delay of flights, OJ 2004, L 46/1. In 2013 the Commission proposed amending this regulation. See Commission, Proposal for a regulation amending Regulation (EC) No 261/2004 establishing common rules on compensation and assistance to passengers in the event of denied boarding and of cancellation or long delay of flights and Regulation (EC) No 2027/97 on air carrier liability in respect of the carriage of passengers and their baggage by air, COM(2013) 130.

98 Regulation (EC) No 1371/2007 on rail passengers' rights and obligations, OJ 2007, L 315/14.

99 Directive 2014/104/EU of the European Parliament and of the Council of 26 November 2014 on certain rules governing actions for damages under national law for infringements of the competition law provisions of the Member States and of the European Union, OJ 2014, L 349/1.

1.12 A final and separate issue that merits attention when discussing EU rules relating to proceedings brought by private parties before national courts concerns another "branch" of EU legislative activity, namely judicial cooperation in civil matters. While historically also this subject matter has received comparatively little attention at EU level, more recently it has been rising up the agenda.[100] Especially in the course of the 2000s, a considerable body of secondary EU law has been established in this domain.[101] Prime examples are Regulation 44/2001 on jurisdiction and the recognition and enforcement of judgments in civil and commercial matters, which has since been replaced by Regulation 1215/2012[102] ("Brussels I Regulation 1215/2012"), Regulation 1206/2001 on cooperation between the courts of the Member States in the taking of evidence in civil or commercial matters[103] ("Evidence Regulation"), Directive 2003/8 concerning legal aid in cross-border disputes[104] ("Legal Aid Directive"), Regulation 861/2007 establishing a European small claims procedure[105] ("Small Claims Regulation") and Regulation 864/2007 on the law applicable to non-contractual obligations[106] ("Rome II Regulation").

1.13 The foregoing overview is by no means meant to be complete and exhaustive. It rather serves to illustrate three main points. First, despite a late and somewhat hesitant start, over the past decades the EU legislature has repeatedly demonstrated its *willingness and ability* to adopt private enforcement-related legislation where this was considered appropriate. Second, the above overview highlights that the relevant provisions are *not limited to specific sectors* or fields of EU law. They can be found scattered across the body of EU law. The need to facilitate legal actions brought by private parties before their national courts to address infringements of EU law can thus be felt in many different areas. Third, even though these legislative measures tend to have certain common characteristics, the *diversity* is significant. The arrangements sometimes consist of only one article, whereas in other instances a more elaborate regime or even a

100 Hodges (2011), p. 448.

101 For an overview of the legislation and other developments in this field, see e.g. Storskrubb (2008); Storskrubb (2011), p. 299.

102 Regulation (EU) No 1215/2012 on jurisdiction and the recognition and enforcement of judgments in civil and commercial matters, OJ 2012, L 351/1. This regulation replaced Regulation (EC) No 44/2001 on jurisdiction and the recognition and enforcement of judgments in civil and commercial matters, OJ 2001, L 12/1, as per January 2015. On this new regulation and the changes it entails, see further Nielsen (2013), p. 502.

103 Regulation (EC) No 1206/2001 on cooperation between the courts of the Member States in the taking of evidence in civil or commercial matters, OJ 2001, L 174/1.

104 Directive 2003/8/EC to improve access to justice in cross-border disputes by establishing minimum common rules relating to legal aid for such disputes, OJ 2003, L 26/41.

105 Regulation (EC) No 861/2007 establishing a European small claims procedure, OJ 2007, L 199/1. In 2013 the Commission proposed an amendment to this regulation. See Commission, Proposal for a regulation amending Regulation (EC) No 861/2007 establishing a European small claims procedure and Regulation (EC) No 1896/2006 creating a European order for payment procedure, COM(2013) 794.

106 Regulation (EC) No 864/2007 on the law applicable to non-contractual obligations, OJ 2007, L 199/40.

free-standing legal act is provided for. The level of detail also tends to vary considerably. These rules, moreover, may or may not contain certain provisions on specific issues such as the burden of proof, legal standing, actions for damages and alternative dispute resolution.

2. Purpose and selection

This book is essentially concerned with the EU's law-making activities of the sort outlined above that are related to facilitating the private enforcement of EU law before national courts. It aims to establish what such legislation[107] entails, particularly in terms of remedies and procedures enacted, and how it is to be understood more generally, notably as regards its typical characteristics and its underlying objectives as well as the advantages and drawbacks of and the limits to the choices made by the EU legislature in this connection. In a nutshell, under consideration are the how, when and why of the EU legislative framework on this subject matter. **1.14**

Whereas the above questions can only be answered having regard to certain EU legislative measures that have been adopted and subsequently applied in a particular context and at a particular point in time, the resulting findings can have broader implications, particularly for any possible future legislative developments relating to the private enforcement of EU law before national courts. For the relevant requirements, limitations and preferences of a legal nature identified in this regard often apply more broadly. Especially where certain issues have been regularly or even consistently encountered in the (recent) past, the same or similar issues can be expected to emerge in the future. Therefore, for legal reasons of an essentially "horizontal" (that is, cross-cutting) nature, certain options that are theoretically conceivable or desirable may have to be discarded or, on the contrary, there may be reasons to apply certain specific law-making approaches more generally. And even apart from these legal considerations, path dependency is a well-documented phenomenon in EU decision-making processes.[108] It implies that already the simple fact that at an earlier stage certain steps were taken in a particular direction may well elicit further moves in that direction along similar lines. Although at every step along the way there remain choices to be made, there can thus be a sort of self-reinforcing mechanism at work at the level of EU policy and law-making.[109] Consciously or not, the actors involved in EU legislative activities on the matters under

107 Here the term "legislation" generally refers to secondary EU law, although it can also include primary EU law (notably Art. 101(2) TFEU).

108 E.g. Kay (2003), p. 405; Ackrill and Kay (2006), p. 113; Greer (2008), p. 219; Giandomenico (2009), p. 89.

109 Kay (2003), p. 406.

consideration here may therefore well be inclined to copy, extend or build on already existing legal measures.

1.15 For the present purposes, four fields of EU law and the EU legislation on private enforcement relating thereto have been selected. The first field is *public procurement law*. As was noted above, the two Procurement Remedies Directives that were adopted in this field provide an early and important example of two (very similar) free-standing EU legal acts that address the issues under consideration here. That makes them obvious candidates for further in-depth analysis. These directives have, moreover, been in force for a considerable period of time. This means that experience has been gained as regards their application in practice and that relevant case law has been generated. Furthermore, these directives were substantially revised in 2007, which means that their analysis does not only offer an insight into the choices at the time of their adoption (that is, around 1990), but also those made roughly a decade and a half later. The Procurement Remedies Directives have over the years also attracted considerable attention in the academic literature.

In the second place, the IPR Enforcement Directive relating to *intellectual property law* has been selected. Also this directive concerns a specialised, free-standing EU legal act that aims to facilitate the private enforcement of EU law before national courts. It sets out a broad range of relatively detailed rules relating to remedies and procedure designed for this purpose. This directive has also been applicable for a number of years, allowing for the generation of practical experience, case law and academic publications. The more recent assessment of the functioning of this directive and reflections on possible amendments reveal the evolution in the thinking in this regard.

The third field addressed below is that of *consumer protection law*. Also in this field can various relevant private enforcement-related provisions of EU law be found. The situation here is somewhat different from the two above-mentioned fields, however, in that there is not one single legal act that is concerned with the issues that are of interest for the present purposes. The relevant provisions are rather mostly spread over a considerable number of directives. This therefore necessitates a somewhat broader assessment. While not overlooking other provisions that may be of interest, attention therefore focuses, to begin with, on the above-mentioned Consumer Injunctions Directive. This is also a stand-alone directive of broader application, even if it is limited in various respects. In addition, the relevant provisions on contractual remedies (that is, private enforcement actions aimed at invalidating or otherwise making ineffective contractual arrangements entered into in violation of EU law), primarily those found in the Directive 93/13 on unfair terms in consumer contracts[110] ("Unfair Terms Directive"), are analysed. That is followed by an assessment of the Product Liability Directive, which focuses on civil liability in damages in relation to defective products. The topic of collective redress is also addressed here.

Fourth and finally, the relevant EU legislation and related developments in the field of *competition law* are assessed. Two types of EU legislative measures are analysed in particular. It concerns in the first place the contractual remedy set out in Article 101(2) TFEU, pursuant to which forbidden anticompetitive agreements are automatically void. In addition, the Competition Damages Directive is an important recent example of an act of secondary EU law relating to private enforcement. While there is at present neither practical experience with nor case law relating to this directive, this is compensated for by the case law of the Court of Justice pre-dating the directive that relates to similar matters, as well as the extensive studies, official documents, consultations, academic publications and debates that preceded and accompanied it and that provide important indications as to the coming into being and the understanding of a directive such as this one.

It is clear that, despite the selection made along the lines set out above, the issues under consideration here are still rather broad and diverse. They relate to a considerable number of legal acts and official documents regarding various fields of EU law and numerous specific issues. It should be noted in this connection that the aim here is not to assess any of these issues for their own sake. The intention is instead to consider them in sufficient detail to come to a meaningful analysis for the purposes of drawing broader conclusions. Making a selection further necessarily implies relegation as much as it implies prioritisation. That is to say, there are certainly also other EU legal acts and developments that can be of interest in the present context, which have nevertheless been mostly left aside here. The Gender Equality Directive, the Environmental Impact Assessment Directive and the principle of Member State liability are but three examples thereof. While the focus here remains firmly on the four selected fields of law, they are occasionally taken into account in the latter parts of this study when this is considered helpful to sketch the broader context or to illustrate a particular point emerging on the basis of the analysis related to the selected fields. Similarly, by means of an illustration, reference is sometimes made to certain relevant developments at national level. In addition, in what follows, account is also taken of several other elements, in particular the EU law principles of national procedural autonomy, equivalence, effectiveness and **1.16**

110 Directive 93/13/EEC on unfair terms in consumer contracts, OJ 1993, L 95/29.

effective judicial protection. The legislation under consideration came into being and continues to operate against the background of a legal environment that is to a large extent shaped by these principles. Not only do they define the *status quo ante*, they also continue to play an important role in the interpretation of this legislation. The applicable public enforcement framework is also considered, as the legislation under consideration co-exists and to some extent interacts with the relevant rules on the enforcement of EU law by the competent EU and national public authorities. Lastly, several key rulings of the Court of Justice related to the enforcement of EU law at national level are examined in some detail, as they establish a number of fundamental concepts in the context of which the EU legislation of the type under consideration should be understood and without which such legislation would arguably hardly be conceivable.

3. Outline

1.17 This book consists of four parts. *Part A* introduces the subject matter under consideration and sketches the relevant background and context. In addition to the present chapter, this first part also consists of Chapter 2. The latter introduces the principles of national procedural autonomy, equivalence, effectiveness and effective judicial protection. It also outlines the general public enforcement context and discusses and analyses five rulings by the Court of Justice that are of particular importance in a private enforcement context.

Part B analyses in turn the EU legislation and other relevant developments relating to the four fields of EU law mentioned above. Accordingly, Chapter 3 is concerned with EU public procurement law and more particularly the Procurement Remedies Directives. Chapter 4 deals with EU intellectual property law, with particular regard to the IPR Enforcement Directive. Chapter 5 focuses on EU consumer protection law, most notably the Consumer Injunctions Directive, the Unfair Terms Directive and the Product Liability Directive. In Chapter 6 attention turns to the relevant developments relating to the private enforcement of EU competition law and especially the Competition Damages Directive.

Part C builds on the findings of the two foregoing parts. It analyses the legislation and other developments that have been considered in Part B in a comparative and contextual manner, with particular emphasis on the relevant provisions on remedies and procedures. More specifically this part consists of three chapters. Chapters 7 and 8 are concerned with the available remedies. In the former, actions for damages and for injunctions are assessed, whereas the latter concentrates on contractual remedies and the other remedies for private enforcement purposes. Chapter 9 analyses the procedural provisions that are of broader interest.

The final *Part D* addresses a number of more general aspects related to EU legislation facilitating the private enforcement of EU law before national courts. Chapter 10 first sets out to answer a set of questions that can be summarised as the how, when and why of this legislation. Chapter 11 then seeks to place in a broader perspective the phenomenon of private enforcement generally and EU legislating thereon specifically. It assesses these matters from two angles, namely those of effectiveness and what is called the "horizontalisation" of EU law. Finally, Chapter 12 summarises the main findings of the foregoing chapters and sets out the conclusions.

2

KEY PRINCIPLES, PUBLIC ENFORCEMENT AND CASE LAW

The EU legislation facilitating the private enforcement of EU law before national courts on which this book concentrates cannot be properly understood without assessing a number of key principles of EU law, as mostly developed in the case law of the Court of Justice. It concerns in the first place the principles of national procedural autonomy, equivalence, effectiveness and effective judicial protection. These principles are therefore introduced and outlined in Sections A and B below. In addition, account should be taken of the relevant public enforcement mechanisms. For that reason the possibilities and obligations under EU law for EU and national public authorities to bring legal actions to ensure compliance with and the enforcement of that law are briefly assessed in Section C. In the last section of this chapter attention turns to five key judgments of the Court of Justice that are of particular importance in connection with the private enforcement of EU law.

A. NATIONAL PROCEDURAL AUTONOMY, EQUIVALENCE AND EFFECTIVENESS

The principle of national procedural autonomy is of obvious importance when discussing issues related to the private enforcement of EU law before national courts. After a general introduction of this principle below a number of more specific remarks are made on the meaning of this principle. This is followed by an assessment of the principles of equivalence and effectiveness that limit the Member States' scope for autonomous decision-making in this regard.

1. Principle of national procedural autonomy

The classic articulation of the principle of national procedural autonomy can be found in the Court of Justice's ruling in *Rewe*, which dates from 1976.[1] This case related to charges for phytosanitary inspection on the importation of apples, which had already been held to be equivalent to customs duties and therefore contrary to EU law. The applicant in the main proceedings had therefore requested a refund, but this was initially rejected because of the non-observance of a time limit provided for under national law. The question then arose whether this was in conformity with EU law. In its preliminary ruling, the Court of Justice ruled as follows: **2.01**

> Applying the principle of [sincere] cooperation laid down in [Article 4(3) TEU], it is the national courts which are entrusted with ensuring the legal protection which citizens derive from the direct effect of the provisions of [EU] law.
>
> Accordingly, in the absence of [EU] rules on this subject, it is for the domestic legal systems of each Member State to designate the courts having jurisdiction and to determine the procedural conditions governing actions at law intended to ensure the protection of the rights which citizens have from the direct effect of [EU] law, it being understood that such conditions cannot be less favourable than those relating to similar actions of a domestic nature.
>
> Where necessary, Articles [114 to 117 and 352 TFEU] enable appropriate measures to be taken to remedy differences between the provisions laid down by law, regulation or administrative action in Member States if they are likely to distort or harm the functioning of the internal market.
>
> In the absence of such measures of harmonization the right conferred by [EU] law must be exercised before the national courts in accordance with the conditions laid down by national rules.[2]

In *Rewe* the central role of national courts in ensuring the legal protection of private parties in cases where their rights derived from EU law are infringed was thus highlighted.[3] The above citation moreover makes it clear that it is in principle for the domestic legal system of each Member State to designate the courts that are competent to rule in those cases and to establish the applicable procedural rules that apply to the legal proceedings in question. The measures

---

1 CoJ case 33/76, *Rewe*. See also CoJ case 45/76, *Comet*. For an earlier reference, see e.g. CoJ case 13/68, *Salgoil*, p. 463.

2 CoJ case 33/76, *Rewe*, para 5.

3 See subsection 1.A.1 above.

needed at national level in order to enforce EU law are thus, as a general rule, to be provided for by *national* law, rather than by EU law. That implies that the Member States have in principle an autonomous choice of means – in relation to both the remedies and the relevant procedural issues[4] – where the enforcement of EU law before national courts is concerned.[5] As the Court of Justice noted in 1981 and has repeated since, the EU Treaties are not intended to create new remedies before national courts to ensure the observance of EU law other than those already provided under national law.[6] This can be otherwise only if the structure of the domestic legal system is such that it is not possible, even indirectly, to ensure respect for the rights that private parties derive from EU law.[7]

2.02 It is important to note at the outset that the resulting predominant reliance on the domestic legal systems of the Member States is the general point of departure in the EU legal order. As was noted earlier, it is in principle for the Member States to implement EU law.[8] When doing so, in so far as EU law does not set out common rules, the Member States are to act in accordance with the substantive and procedural rules of their own national law.[9] Under the broader principle of institutional autonomy, it is primarily for the Member States to decide, within the limits set by EU law, which bodies are charged with fulfilling the obligations that EU law imposes on them and how those bodies are structured and organised, including the means that these bodies have at their disposal and the rules applicable to them.[10]

Several (inter-related) factors are likely to play a role when seeking to explain why this general point of departure remains to a considerable extent intact where remedial and procedural matters relating to proceedings before national courts are concerned, whereas over the decades the EU has adopted common

4 In the specific context of the principle of national procedural autonomy, the term "procedural" is understood in a very broad sense. As is already evident from the above citation from *Rewe* and as is further illustrated below, this term can cover rules relating to the organisation of judicial remedies as well as those on the jurisdiction of the courts. This principle can in effect cover virtually all remedial and procedural rules, mechanisms and arrangements available in legal proceedings before national courts that are concerned with the enforcement of EU law. Cf. Opinion AG Jacobs joined cases C-430/93 and C-431/93, *Van Schijndel*, para 14; Komninos (2009), p. 372. Some distinguish a separate doctrine of "remedial autonomy". See Trstenjak and Beysen (2011), pp. 104–9.

5 Cf. Galetta (2010), p. 12.

6 CoJ case 158/80, *Rewe-Handelsgeschellschaft Nord*, para 44; CoJ case C-432/05, *Unibet*, para 40; CoJ case C-583/11 P, *Inuit*, para 103. This "no new remedies" rule can be traced back to CoJ case 34/67, *Lück*.

7 CoJ case C-432/05, *Unibet*, para 41; CoJ case C-583/11 P, *Inuit*, para 104. See also CoJ case C-562/12, *Liivimaa Lihavei*, para 71.

8 See para 1.04 above.

9 See e.g. CoJ joined cases 205/82 to 215/82, *Deutsche Milchkontor*, para 17; CoJ case C-201/04, *Molenbergnatie*, para 52.

10 See e.g. CoJ case C-389/08, *Base*, para 26. Cf. Prechal (2005), pp. 317–18.

rules on so many issues of substantive law. These factors include considerations of a pragmatic nature. Issues of remedies and procedures were probably not at the forefront of the parties concerned when the foundations were laid of a new legal order that was primarily designed to further economic (and, indirectly, political) integration in Europe. It would indeed seem understandable that at an early stage of the process of European integration attention largely focused on substantive issues, especially reducing the existing barriers to trade and creating an internal market. Deliberate or not, the resulting reliance on national law where remedial and procedural matters are concerned may also have helped further the "embedment" and acceptance of EU law at national level.[11] In addition, while it is not uncommon for courts to apply foreign substantive law, if and when they do so the procedural rules of the forum normally apply.[12] Procedural law thus typically "travels less" and is more territorially grounded than substantive law.[13] Also, from this perspective it is understandable that at least initially matters of remedies and procedures applicable to proceedings before the courts of the Member States were mostly left unregulated. Finally, the principle of national procedural autonomy would also seem to reflect a general assumption that the remedies and procedural rules provided for by national law normally suffice to ensure that EU law is effective and can effectively be enforced at national level by the parties concerned.[14] All Member States are after all subject to the rule of law; according to the EU Treaties, this is a value common to the Member States and one of the central values on which the EU is founded.[15]

Either way, given the resulting lack of any explicit arrangement on remedial and procedural matters concerning the enforcement of EU law at national level in primary and at least initially also in secondary EU law, the EU courts had little choice but to mostly continue to rely on national law in this respect.[16]

---

11 Bridge (1984), p. 31; Prechal (2005), p. 134; Storskrubb (2008), p. 18. On the effects at national level of the EU legislative measures of the type at issue here, see also subsection 10.D.2 below.

12 Cf. Storme (1994), p. 43.

13 Kilpatrick (2000), pp. 17–18.

14 Cf. Opinion AG Jacobs joined cases C-430/93 and C-431/93, *Van Schijndel*, para 29–30. See e.g. also Lindholm (2007), p. 100.

15 Art. 2 TEU. See also CoJ case 294/83, *Les Verts*, para 23. Respecting the rule of law is a precondition for becoming a Member State (Art. 49 TEU), whereas a serious breach thereof by a Member State can lead to the suspension of its rights under the EU Treaties (Art. 7 TEU). In CoJ opinion 2/13, *ECHR*, para 168, reference was made to the '*fundamental premise*' that the Member States share the common values on which the EU is founded, stated in Art. 2 TEU, and that this premise '*implies and justifies the existence of mutual trust between the Member States that those values will be recognised and, therefore, that the law of the EU that implements them will be respected*'.

16 Jacobs (1997), pp. 25–6; Dougan (2004), p. 19.

2.03 The principle of national procedural autonomy has no express basis in the EU Treaties. In *Rewe*, cited above, the Court of Justice identified the principle of sincere cooperation laid down in Article 4(3) TEU as its (primary) legal foundation.[17] Pursuant to that latter principle,

> the [EU] and the Member States shall, in full mutual respect, assist each other in carrying out tasks which flow from the [EU] Treaties. The Member States shall take any appropriate measure, general or particular, to ensure fulfilment of the obligations arising out of the [EU] Treaties or resulting from the acts of the institutions of the [EU]. The Member States shall facilitate the achievement of the [EU]'s tasks and refrain from any measure which could jeopardise the attainment of the [EU]'s objectives.

The term "national procedural autonomy" only entered the Court of Justice's vocabulary at a rather late stage, namely in 2004.[18] It has since used this term rather frequently.[19] This more recent explicit use of this term by the Court does not appear to have had implications for the substance of the Court's rulings, however.[20]

This absence of an express legal basis and its origin in the very broadly formulated principle of sincere cooperation imply that the prerogatives and obligations of the Member States and national courts under this principle are not very clearly described. That means that the Court of Justice is left with a significant margin of discretion in this regard. Some have argued that such discretionary appreciation on the part of the Court brings with it the '*seeds of intrusion*'.[21] Others have rightly noted that it will depend on one's point of view whether the resulting rather obscure delineation of the boundaries between EU and national law in matters relating to remedies and procedures is seen as inevitable, harmful, desirable or simply the lesser of two evils.[22] In any case, it is

---

17 CoJ case 33/76, *Rewe*, para 5. See para 2.01 above. Cf. Temple Lang (2008), p. 76. Other authors have suggested that a (further) basis is to be found in the principle of primacy of EU law (Jacobs and Deisenhofer (2003), p. 217) or the principle of effective judicial protection (Dougan (2004), p. 54).

18 Schebesta (2010), p. 857. See CoJ case C-201/02, *Wells*, para 65. The EU courts tend to refer to "procedural autonomy". As is generally the case in the legal literature, in the following the word "national" is added so as to clarify that it is the Member States that possess this "autonomy".

19 Just to give one example of a phrase typically used in this connection, in 2010 in relation to the question of enforceability obligations provided for in civil law contracts, it was held that '*in the absence of rules provided for under [EU] law, and in accordance with the principle of procedural autonomy, the detailed rules governing implementation of those obligations are a matter for national law*'. CoJ case C-451/08, *Müller*, para 62.

20 In this connection one can also point to the use of the word "detailed" in relation to the national rules that typically accompanies references to the principle of national procedural autonomy in the CoJ's case law, which, however, does not appear to signal a particular willingness to leave the Member States a greater margin of manoeuvre than before.

21 Szyszczak and Delicostopoulos (1997), p. 143.

22 Tridimas (2006), p. 422.

broadly agreed that there is a degree of unpredictability and uncertainty in the case law of the EU courts on these matters.[23]

There is moreover no reason to believe that the insertion into the EU Treaties in 2009 (through the Treaty of Lisbon) of the second subparagraph of Article 19(1) TEU, pursuant to which the Member States must '*provide remedies sufficient to ensure effective legal protection in the fields covered by Union law*', substantially alters any of the foregoing. Quite to the contrary, as was noted above, this provision primarily confirms and formalises the responsibilities of the Member States in ensuring effective judicial protection, without being concerned with the distribution of competences between the EU and the Member States in relation to remedial and procedural matters.[24] Neither the relevant provisions of the EU Treaties themselves nor the relevant case law of the Court of Justice contains any indication that these more recent amendments to the EU Treaties should lead to a reconsideration of the Court's well-established *Rewe* case law.

Another point to notice is that the reference in *Rewe* to '*rights derived from the direct effect*'[25] of the relevant provisions of substantive EU law is not always apparent in the Court's later case law. In its earlier case law, direct effect and the conferral of rights on private parties seemed to be treated as essentially one and the same thing.[26] From the finding that a provision of EU law is directly effective, it was almost automatically deduced that that provision creates rights for private parties.[27] Subsequently both issues "grew apart" to some extent, however.[28] That is to say, the direct effect of a provision of EU law, on the one hand, and the creation of rights through that provision, on the other hand, still often coincide, but that is not necessarily the case.[29] The key difference between both concepts is that '*the question whether a provision creates individual rights is a matter of its* content; *the question whether a provision has direct effect relates to the* qualities ascribed to it, *namely whether it can be invoked by those concerned within* **2.04**

23 See e.g. Prechal (2001), p. 43; Himsworth (1997), p. 310; Dougan (2011), p. 420; Lindholm (2011), p. 482.

24 See para 1.06 above. Cf. Komninos (2008), p. 149; Komninos (2009), pp. 374–5. The issue of distribution of competences has been addressed elsewhere in the EU Treaties, also since 2009. See Title I of Part One TFEU and in particular Art. 3–5 TFEU. Concerning matters relating to the EU's competence to act in this regard, see subsection 7.A.3 below.

25 CoJ case 33/76, *Rewe*, para 5. See para 2.01 above.

26 For an overview of the discussions on the scope and meaning of the principle of direct effect and further references, see Craig and De Búrca (2011), pp. 180–99.

27 E.g. CoJ case 13/68, *Salgoil*, pp. 460–61; CoJ case 33/76, *Rewe*, para 5.

28 Cf. e.g. CoJ joined cases C-6/90 and C-9/90, *Francovich*, discussed in para 2.23 below, which illustrates that a rule of EU law that is not directly effective can still create rights (or at least have been intended to do so).

29 Prechal (2006), p. 305.

the national legal system'.[30] Put differently as it stands the conferment of rights can be a consequence of direct effect, but is not identical to it.[31] More recently reference is often (although by no means in all cases) made in the relevant case law to '*rights which individuals derive from [EU] law*'.[32]

Therefore, the question whether or not a provision of EU law satisfies the conditions for being of direct effect is, in and of itself, not decisive in the present context.[33] Rather, it is the existence of a *right* that is the central element. It has often been noted, however, that the concept of a right is an ambiguous one in EU law.[34] That is probably not in small part due to the significant variations between the domestic legal systems of the Member States in what is understood by this term.[35] For the present purposes, it is understood to refer to a legal position that a person recognised as such by the law may have and which in its normal state can be enforced by that person against others before a court of law.[36]

2. Principle of equivalence

2.05 The phrase '*it being understood that such conditions cannot be less favourable than those relating to similar actions of a domestic nature*' in *Rewe*, cited earlier,[37] contains the essence of the principle of equivalence. As the Court of Justice later clarified, this is '*in fact simply the expression of the principle of equal treatment, which is one of the fundamental principles of [EU] law*'.[38] It essentially requires that the national remedial or procedural rule at issue is to be applied without distinction, regardless of whether the alleged infringement is of EU law or of national law where the purpose, cause of action and essential characteristics are similar.[39] The principle of equivalence applies in relation to all such rules,

30 Ibid. For a more detailed discussion, see Prechal (2005), pp. 99–106. As is noted in this latter contribution (p. 100), should one therefore wish to describe direct effect in terms of rights, it could at most be said that this is a sort of procedural right, namely the "right" to invoke EU law. Cf. CoJ case C-426/05, *Tele2 Telecom*, para 33.

31 Jacobs (2004b), p. 306. See also Prechal (2005), p. 102. An alternative approach that touches essentially upon the same issue is to distinguish between "subjective" and "objective" direct effect, discussed in Van Gerven (2000), p. 506.

32 See e.g. CoJ joined cases C-279/96, C-280/96 and C-281/96, *Ansaldo*, para 27; CoJ case C-224/01, *Köbler*, para 46; CoJ joined cases C-222/05 and C-225/05, *Van der Weerd*, para 28.

33 Lenaerts, Arts and Maselis (2006), p. 83 (n. 385).

34 E.g. Van Gerven (2000), p. 507; Eilmansberger (2004), p. 1199; Prechal (2006), pp. 303–4; Nazzini (2009), pp. 403–4.

35 Jacobs and Deisenhofer (2003), pp. 187–8; Prechal (2005), pp. 98 and 102–4; Van Dam (2006), pp. 129–31.

36 Van Gerven (2000), p. 502.

37 See para 2.01 above.

38 CoJ case C-34/02, *Pasquini*, para 70. Cf. Opinion AG Kokott case C-268/06, *Impact*, para 67.

39 E.g. CoJ case C-326/96, *Levez*, para 41; CoJ case C-78/98, *Preston*, para 49 and 55; CoJ case C-63/08, *Pontin*, para 45; CoJ case C-177/10, *Rosado Santana*, para 90.

irrespective of whether they are judicial or administrative in nature.[40] When applying this principle, national courts must take into account the role played by the allegedly similar provision in the procedure as a whole, as well as the conduct of that procedure and any specific features.[41] The various aspects of these rules should be examined in their general context and not in isolation, in an objective manner rather than subjectively.[42]

Although it can be of considerable importance in individual cases, from the viewpoint of EU law generally the principle of equivalence tends to play a rather modest role.[43] This is in part because of the fact that, as a general rule, it is for the national courts to verify whether this principle has been complied with. The Court of Justice has often noted that only these national courts have after all direct knowledge of the remedial and procedural rules governing actions in the relevant fields.[44] Yet this does not necessarily stop the Court of Justice from issuing '*guidance*' in specific cases.[45] This may involve it, to a varying degree, assessing the relevant national rules and giving its views on what could be considered an equivalent action or what would be likely to violate this principle.[46] Still, this guidance is often far from comprehensive, in that it does not cover the full scope and the precise application of this principle in concrete cases.[47] **2.06**

The principle of equivalence does not mean, however, that the Member States are obliged to extend their most favourable national rules to the EU law-based action concerned.[48] And it cannot be put into effect and will thus be deemed not to have been infringed where no sufficiently similar national action can be established.[49] This conclusion also follows where the situations under consideration are different, to the extent that these differences provide an objective justification for the difference in treatment of the claim at issue.[50]

---

40 CoJ case C-34/02, *Pasquini*, para 62.

41 E.g. CoJ case C-326/96, *Levez*, para 43–4; CoJ case C-63/08, *Pontin*, para 45; CoJ case C-177/10, *Rosado Santana*, para 90.

42 CoJ case C-78/98, *Preston*, para 62; CoJ case C-63/08, *Pontin*, para 46.

43 Cf. Prechal (1998), p. 687.

44 E.g. CoJ case C-326/96, *Levez*, para 43; CoJ case C-78/98, *Preston*, para 49; CoJ case C-177/10, *Rosado Santana*, para 90.

45 CoJ case C-78/98, *Preston*, para 50. See further Craig and De Búrca (2011), p. 238.

46 E.g. CoJ case C-78/98, *Preston*, para 50–53; CoJ case C-147/01, *Weber's Wine World*, para 105–8; CoJ joined cases C-222/05 and C-225/05, *Van der Weerd*, para 29–32; CoJ case C-567/13, *Baczó*, para 43–8.

47 Dougan (2004), p. 25.

48 CoJ case C-326/96, *Levez*, para 42; CoJ case C-63/08, *Pontin*, para 45.

49 CoJ case C-261/95, *Palmisani*, para 39.

50 CoJ case C-132/95, *Jensen*, para 50–51.

3. Principle of effectiveness

2.07 While highlighting in *Rewe* the important role of the Member States' domestic legal systems in remedial and procedural matters, the Court of Justice also noted in that judgment that '*the position would be different only if the conditions and time-limits made it impossible in practice to exercise the rights which the national courts are obliged to protect*'.[51] In so doing it laid the foundation of the principle of effectiveness. The Court later clarified that this principle also covers situations where it is '*virtually impossible or excessively difficult*' – and thus not merely impossible in practice – for a private party to exercise the rights concerned.[52] This widened test not only raised the "effectiveness threshold", it also gave the Court of Justice greater discretion in assessing whether it has been respected in a concrete case.[53]

The principle of effectiveness can be seen as a principle of minimum protection, as it merely lays down the lower limit.[54] But this does not mean that it is necessarily easily complied with. The importance that the Court of Justice attaches to the principle of effectiveness has tended to differ over time. Broadly speaking, one can distinguish: (a) a prudent initial phase in the case law (up to the early 1980s); (b) a significantly bolder period (mid-1980s to early 1990s); and (c) the current period (mid-1990s onwards), which is characterised by a more balanced and selective approach.[55]

2.08 Notwithstanding this evolution over time and its inherent case-by-case character, as compared with the principle of equivalence, the Court of Justice often gives considerably more detailed and "intrusive" guidance where the principle of effectiveness is concerned. While the Court typically refers to both principles in cases that touch upon remedial and procedural issues under national law (pursuant to the principle of national procedural autonomy), it is the principle of effectiveness that tends to receive most attention and that is most likely to lead to the conclusion that the national rule at issue infringes EU law.[56] It has therefore been called '*the most volatile weapon in the Court's armoury*'.[57] The following examples are just three illustrations of the range of situations covered and the impact that this principle can have in individual cases before the courts of the Member States.

---

51 CoJ case 33/76, *Rewe*, para 5.

52 This broader formulation was first used in CoJ case 199/82, *San Giorgio*, para 14.

53 Trstenjak and Beysen (2011), pp. 101–2.

54 Prechal (2001), p. 40.

55 For an overview, see Dougan (2004), pp. 29–30; Craig and De Búrca (2011), pp. 223–37; Dougan (2011), pp. 412–21.

56 Flynn (2008), pp. 245–58.

57 Dougan (2004), p. 27.

To begin with, this principle can come into play in relation to the national rules designed to encourage *out-of-court settlements*. For instance, in *Alassini* the Court of Justice highlighted that a national legal system that entailed mandatory prior recourse to such procedures affected the exercise of the rights of private parties based on EU law.[58] It found that the said principle had not been infringed in light of the specifics of the arrangement in question (no binding outcome, no substantial delay, suspension of time limits, no fees or significant costs), subject to electronic means not being the only means of access to that procedure as well as interim measures being available where necessary. In *Evans*, a situation where the applicable EU law required Member States to establish a simple redress mechanism was assessed.[59] Here the Court held that the national system at issue, which consisted of several phases and concerned a combination of administrative review, arbitration and appellate judicial review, did not as such infringe the principle of effectiveness. Again, the emphasis was on the practical consequences of the procedural arrangement in question for the private party concerned, in particular its advantages in terms of speed and legal costs.[60]

A second example is the impact that the principle of effectiveness can have on the applicable *rules related to evidence*. Even if it is generally for the Member States to establish rules of this kind, those rules may not make the exercise of the rights vested in EU law virtually impossible or excessively difficult.[61] Accordingly, this principle can preclude the application of national rules establishing an unjustified presumption to the applicant's disadvantage or setting out special limitations concerning the form of the evidence to be adduced, such as the exclusion of all evidence other than documentary evidence.[62] It can also have consequences for the question of which party carries the burden of proof.[63] In addition, this principle can imply that a national court must ensure that the applicant can benefit from an exceptional procedure provided for under national law permitting witness evidence.[64] Similarly, the Court of Justice has held that a national court may be required, in light of the burden of proof upon the applicant and the evidence that may not be in the

58 CoJ joined cases C-317/08 to C-320/08, *Alassini*, para 52–60.

59 CoJ case C-63/01, *Evans*, para 44–58.

60 See e.g. also CoJ case C-268/06, *Impact*, para 51–3. In this case it was found that, where a Member State designates specialised courts to rule on certain claims while for other claims separate actions needed to be brought before the ordinary courts, such an arrangement can lead to an infringement of the principle of effectiveness, to the extent that it results in procedural disadvantages for the private parties concerned in terms of *inter alia* costs, duration and rules on representation that make it excessively difficult to exercise their rights.

61 Cf. e.g. CoJ case C-242/95, *GT-Link*, para 25–6; CoJ case C-340/99, *TNT Traco*, para 60–61.

62 CoJ case 199/82, *San Giorgio*, para 11–15; CoJ case C-147/01, *Weber's Wine World*, para 113–14; CoJ case C-129/00, *Commission v Italy*, para 35–40.

63 CoJ case C-72/12, *Altrip*, para 52.

64 CoJ case C-228/98, *Dounias*, para 71.

latter's possession, to order the necessary measures of inquiry provided for under national law, such as obliging the other party to the proceedings or a third party to produce a particular document.[65] It can also entail adjusting or lightening the burden of proof.[66]

Finally, this principle has regularly been applied to national rules setting *limitation periods* for initiating legal proceedings before national courts for alleged infringements of EU law. The question of the admissibility of such time bars was already addressed in the aforementioned *Rewe* judgment itself.[67] There the Court essentially ruled that the principle of effectiveness did not stand in the way of imposing a reasonable limitation period, because this concerns an application of the principle of legal certainty. In subsequent judgments this rule has been repeatedly upheld and applied, while noting, however, that such limitation periods must be reasonable.[68] They should be established in light of *inter alia* the significance for the parties concerned of the decisions to be taken, the complexities of the procedures and of the legislation to be applied, the number of persons who may be affected and any other public or private interests which must be taken into consideration.[69] It follows that whereas in some situations a 15-day period can be sufficient, in other cases it may not.[70] And even when a limitation period is reasonable in and of itself, specific circumstances can lead to the conclusion that its application in a particular case is contrary to the principle of effectiveness.[71] That can occur for instance where there was deceit on the part of the defendant[72] or lack of timely implementation of a directive by a Member State that deprived the private party applicant concerned of any opportunity to rely on its rights.[73]

2.09 The Court of Justice's more recent case law in this regard is characterised by the application in certain cases of a balancing test. This approach was most clearly articulated in its 1995 *Van Schijndel* ruling.[74] This case arose in the context of a

65 CoJ case C-526/04, *Laboratoires Boiron*, para 55. See also CoJ case C-264/08, *Direct Parcel*, para 35.

66 CoJ case C-479/12, *Gautzsch*, para 43.

67 See para 2.01 above.

68 E.g. CoJ case C-30/02, *Recheio*, para 17–22 (regarding the question whether a 90-day period is reasonable); CoJ joined cases C-392/04 and C-422/04, *i-21 Germany*, para 58–64 (regarding the period available for filing an appeal).

69 CoJ case C349/07, *Sopropé*, para 40; CoJ case C-63/08, *Pontin*, para 48; CoJ case C-177/10, *Rosado Santana*, para 93.

70 CoJ case C349/07, *Sopropé*, para 41; CoJ case C-63/08, *Pontin*, para 60–67.

71 CoJ case C349/07, *Sopropé*, para 44.

72 CoJ case C-326/96, *Levez*, para 32.

73 CoJ case C-208/90, *Emmott*, para 23.

74 CoJ joined cases C-430/93 and C-431/93, *Van Schijndel*. See also CoJ case C-312/93, *Petersbroeck*. This balancing approach can be traced back further. See e.g. CoJ case 33/76, *Rewe*, para 5, where the CoJ balanced the need to ensure the effectiveness of EU law with the requirement of legal certainty.

dispute on the compulsory membership of an occupational pension scheme. This led to a preliminary reference asking to what extent there could be an obligation under EU law for a national court to consider of its own motion (*ex officio*) the compatibility of a rule of national law with the EU competition rules. The Court of Justice held that:

> each case which raises the question whether a national procedural provision renders application of [EU] law impossible or excessively difficult must be analysed by reference to the role of that provision in the procedure, its progress and its special features, viewed as a whole, before the various national instances. In the light of that analysis the basic principles of the domestic judicial system [...] must, where appropriate, be taken into consideration.[75]

It has since referred back to this phrase on many occasions.[76]

The Court thus balanced the interests related to the principle of effectiveness, on the one hand, and the aims pursued by certain basic principles of the domestic judicial system at issue, on the other hand. This approach has been called a "procedural rule of reason"[77] or a form of an "objective justification" approach.[78] One of these basic principles is the principle of legal certainty.[79] A specific expression thereof is a rule preventing the re-opening of administrative or judicial decisions that have become final (*res judicata*). In this respect it has been held that '*[EU] law does not require a court to disapply domestic rules of procedure conferring finality on a decision, even if to do so would enable it to remedy an infringement of [EU] law by the decision at issue*'.[80] Other such basic principles include preventing unjust enrichment,[81] the rights of defence[82] and the proper

75 CoJ joined cases C-430/93 and C-431/93, *Van Schijndel*, para 19.

76 E.g. CoJ joined cases C-222/05 and C-225/05, *Van der Weerd*, para 33; CoJ case C-63/08, *Pontin*, para 47; CoJ case C-177/10, *Rosado Santana*, para 92.

77 Prechal (2001), p. 46; Prechal (1998), p. 691.

78 Dougan (2011), p. 419. Considering the particular emphasis that is placed in *Van Schijndel* on the context in which the national rule at issue operates, this is sometimes also referred to as the "contextual approach". See Schebesta (2010), p. 859.

79 E.g. CoJ joined cases C-430/93 and C-431/93, *Van Schijndel*, para 19. See also CoJ case 33/76, *Rewe*, para 5.

80 CoJ case C-234/04, *Kapferer*, para 21. This case concerned judicial decisions. In that connection see e.g. also CoJ case C-2/08, *Olimpiclub*, para 29–30. In relation to arbitration award proceedings, see CoJ case C-126/97, *Eco Swiss*, para 46–7. In relation to administrative decisions, see CoJ case C-453/00, *Kühne & Heitz*, para 24; CoJ joined cases C-392/04 and C-422/04, *i-21 Germany*, para 51 and 57. In this regard the situation concerning the recovery of unlawfully granted state aid is a somewhat special case, in particular in light of the exclusive nature of the Commission's supervisory powers in this domain. See e.g. CoJ case C-24/95, *Alcan*, para 24–5; CoJ case C-199/05, *Lucchini*, para 62–3. See further Nebbia (2008a), p. 427.

81 E.g. CoJ case 199/82, *San Giorgio*, para 13; CoJ case C-309/06, *Marks & Spencer*, para 41.

82 CoJ joined cases C-430/93 and C-431/93, *Van Schijndel*, para 19; CoJ joined cases C-222/05 and C-225/05, *Van der Weerd*, para 33.

conduct of procedure.[83] These latter two principles can find a concrete expression in the passive role of national courts in civil proceedings. In *Van Schijndel* the Court of Justice clarified that the principle of effectiveness does not preclude a national provision which prevents national courts from raising of their own motion the issue of whether a provision of EU law has been infringed, where examination of that issue would oblige them to abandon their passive role by going beyond the ambit of the dispute defined by the parties and relying on facts and circumstances other than those on which the party with an interest in the application of those provisions has based its claim.[84] There are, however, certain exceptions to this rule.[85]

This balancing approach does not mean that a mere abstract reference to any of the above-mentioned basic principles suffices to "counter balance" the working of the principle of effectiveness. In the case law emphasis is often placed on the practical application of these basic principles, on the basis of a case-by-case assessment.[86] That means that the Court's assessment can still be as "intrusive" as was the case under its earlier case law.[87] In its more recent case law the Court of Justice may thus tend to follow an approach that is more nuanced and "respectful" where basic principles of national law truly are at stake, but it also guards against creating a general loophole that would put at risk the interests that it has long sought to protect through the application of the principle of effectiveness.

B. PRINCIPLE OF EFFECTIVE JUDICIAL PROTECTION

After having introduced in the foregoing the principle of national procedural autonomy, as conditioned by the principles of equivalence and effectiveness, the fourth principle that is of particular importance here, namely the principle of effective judicial protection, is introduced below. A general introduction of this principle is followed by an illustration of its practical expression in several private enforcement-related issues.

---

83 CoJ joined cases C-430/93 and C-431/93, *Van Schijndel*, para 21; CoJ joined cases C-222/05 and C-225/05, *Van der Weerd*, para 35.

84 CoJ joined cases C-430/93 and C-431/93, *Van Schijndel*, para 20–22. See also CoJ joined cases C-222/05 and C-225/05, *Van der Weerd*, para 33.

85 E.g. CoJ case C-312/93, *Petersbroeck*, para 16–21; CoJ joined cases C-222/05 and C-225/05, *Van der Weerd*, para 39–40. See subsection 9.D.2 below.

86 Cf. CoJ case C-473/00, *Cofidis*, para 37.

87 Dougan (2004), pp. 31–2.

1. Effective judicial protection: Introduction

The origins of the principle of effective judicial protection as it emerges in EU law can be traced back as far as 1968.[88] It is, however, only since the 1980s that the EU courts properly '*discovered*' this principle,[89] in that it has taken an increasingly prominent position in the case law on matters of remedies and procedures in proceedings both before these EU courts themselves and before national courts in cases involving the enforcement of EU law. This increased prominence of the principle of effective judicial protection is in part due to its having the character of a fundamental right. The Court of Justice has long held that as such it is to be considered a general principle of EU law.[90] It underlies the constitutional traditions common to the Member States and has also been enshrined in the European Convention for the Protection of Human Rights and Fundamental Freedoms ("ECHR"), notably its Articles 6 and 13.[91] These latter two articles provide for a fundamental right to a fair trial and to an effective remedy respectively.[92] In the case law of the European Court of Human Rights ("Court of Human Rights"), the Strasbourg-based court that is charged with interpreting the ECHR, it is Article 6 that typically receives most attention in this connection. This article often "absorbs" Article 13, given that the requirements under the latter article are generally less strict than under the former.[93] **2.10**

In recent years the importance of this principle has been reaffirmed and increased by its inclusion in Article 47 of the Charter of Fundamental Rights of the EU ("Charter"). There it appears in the form of the right to an effective remedy and a fair trial. Since 2009 (Treaty of Lisbon) the Charter expressly has the same legal value as the EU Treaties.[94] It has thus become the main point of **2.11**

88 CoJ case 13/68, *Salgoil*, pp. 462–3.

89 Prechal (2001), p. 40.

90 E.g. CoJ case 222/84, *Johnston*, para 18; CoJ case C-55/06, *Arcor*, para 174.

91 The ECHR and the ECtHR have been established under the auspices of the Council of Europe, an international organisation separate from the EU. On the ECHR and its application by the ECtHR, see further e.g. Mowbray (2012).

92 In this particular context the meaning of the term "remedy" is thus broader than the definition otherwise used in this book, as here it essentially corresponds with redress generally. See para 1.06 above.

93 E.g. ECtHR case 6289/73, *Airey v Ireland*, para 20–35; ECtHR case 12964/87, *De Geouffre de la Pradelle v France*, para 27–37. This does not mean that Art. 13 ECHR cannot have an independent meaning, however. See e.g. ECtHR case 5029/71, *Klass v Germany*, para 61–75; ECtHR case 21987/93, *Aksoy v Turkey*, para 88–100.

94 Art. 6(1) TEU. As was noted in para 1.06 and 2.03 above, from that same moment onwards, Art. 19(1) TEU requires the Member States to '*provide remedies sufficient to ensure effective legal protection in the fields covered by [EU] law*'. As such, both Art. 47 Charter and Art. 19(1) TEU give expression to the *adagio* that each right conferred must be accompanied by a corresponding remedy ensuring its enforcement (*ubi ius, ibi remedium*). The CoJ has clarified that Art. 19(1) TEU serves to ensure the observance of Art. 47 Charter within the EU. See e.g. CoJ case C-418/11, *Texdata*, para 78; CoJ case C-583/11 P, *Inuit*, para 100–101.

reference for the EU courts when assessing the respect for fundamental rights in relation to EU law.

The Court of Justice has held that Article 47 Charter '*secures in EU law the protection afforded by Article 6(1) of the ECHR*', for which reason it can suffice to refer only to this former provision.[95] That is not to say, however, that the ECHR and the corresponding case law of the Court of Human Rights are no longer of relevance. In so far as the Charter contains rights which correspond to rights guaranteed by the ECHR, the meaning and scope of these rights is the same as those laid down in the ECHR.[96] This implies that the Court of Justice has particular regard to the case law of the Court of Human Rights on these matters.[97] The ECHR also remains relevant for two other reasons. First, the EU is to accede to the ECHR.[98] Second, the fundamental rights guaranteed by the ECHR, together with those resulting from the constitutional traditions common to the Member States, continue to constitute general principles of EU law and are as such to be applied by the EU courts.[99]

The field of application of the Charter is not unlimited, however. There can be no doubt that the Charter applies to the acts of the institutions and other bodies of the EU. However, pursuant to its Article 51(1), acts of the *Member States* are only covered where '*they are implementing [EU] law*'.[100] The Court of Justice has made clear that this essentially means that the fundamental rights in question are applicable in all situations governed by EU law, but not outside such

95 CoJ case C-199/11, *Otis*, para 47. In the same sense, see CoJ case C-386/10 P, *Chalkor*, para 51; CoJ case C-439/11 P, *Ziegler*, para 126. See also Opinion AG Cruz Villalón case C-69/10, *Samba Diouf*, para 38–44. The Explanations relating to the Charter of Fundamental Rights, OJ 2007, C 303/2 ("Explanations relating to the Charter"), clarify that the first subparagraph of Art. 47 Charter is based on Art. 13 ECHR (although it is more extensive in that it guarantees an effective remedy before a court), whereas the second subparagraph of Art. 47 Charter corresponds with Art. 6(1) ECHR (although again its scope is wider, as it is not confined to disputes relating to civil law rights and obligations) and the third subparagraph of Art. 47 Charter is based on the ECtHR case law on Art. 6(1) ECHR. See e.g. ECtHR case 6289/73, *Airey v Ireland*. Art. 48 Charter corresponds in turn with Art. 6(2) and (3) ECHR. Pursuant to Art. 6(1) TEU and Art. 52(7) Charter, the Explanations relating to the Charter have to be taken into consideration for the interpretation of the Charter.

96 Art. 52(3) Charter. This is subject to the possibility of providing more extensive protection in EU law.

97 E.g. CoJ case C-506/04, *Wilson*, para 51; CoJ case C-279/09, *DEB*, para 35–37; CoJ case C-399/11, *Melloni*, para 50. See further Douglas-Scott (2006), p. 629.

98 Art. 6(2) TEU. In April 2013 a draft agreement on the accession of the EU to the ECHR was agreed. However, in December 2014 the CoJ ruled that this draft agreement was not compatible with the relevant provisions of EU law. See CoJ opinion 2/13, *ECHR*. See further e.g. Lock (2010), p. 777; Craig (2013), p. 1114; Gragl (2014), p. 13.

99 Art. 6(3) TEU.

100 See also Protocol No 30 TFEU as to the application of the above-mentioned criterion with respect to the United Kingdom ("UK") and Poland, as clarified in CoJ joined cases C-411/10 and C-493/10, *N.S.*, para 119–20. See further Craig (2010), pp. 237–40; Ladenburger (2012), pp. 28–31.

situations.[101] The applicability of EU law thus entails the applicability of the fundamental rights guaranteed by the Charter.[102] Article 47 Charter is likely to be interpreted in such a manner that it covers essentially all situations where rights granted by EU law are affected.[103] As regards the personal scope of the Charter, there may well be a need to differentiate between the various rights set out therein in certain cases.[104] The available case law suggests, however, that Article 47 Charter covers in principle natural as well as legal persons.[105]

As is illustrated by the examples discussed in the following subsection, there can be a noticeable overlap between the principle of effective judicial protection, on the one hand, and the principle of effectiveness that was established in the aforementioned *Rewe* case law, on the other hand.[106] Both principles generally appear to fulfil a similar function in ensuring that rights of private parties vested in EU law can be effectively enforced.[107] The rise to prominence of the former principle is such that it has to some extent eclipsed the principle of effectiveness. Indeed in some respects the latter principle seems to have been entirely "absorbed".[108] Many consider the principle of effective judicial protection as the over-arching principle.[109] This view certainly finds some support, especially in **2.12**

101 CoJ case C-617/10, *Åklagaren*, para 19. See e.g. also CoJ joined cases C-411/10 and C-493/10, *N.S.*, para 64–9; CoJ case C-370/12, *Pringle*, para 179–80; CoJ case C-206/13, *Siragusa*, para 24–34.

102 CoJ case C-617/10, *Åklagaren*, para 21; CoJ case C-418/11, *Texdata*, para 73.

103 This seems implicit in CoJ case C-399/11, *Melloni*, para 49. See the Explanations relating to the Charter, p. 2, where it is stated that '*Article 47 applies to the institutions of the [EU] and of Member States when they are implementing [EU] law and does so for all rights guaranteed by [EU] law*'. In a similar sense, see Opinion AG Cruz Villalón case C-69/10, *Samba Diouf*, para 38–44; Iglesias Sánchez (2012), p. 1586 (n. 111); Ladenburger (2012), pp. 20–21.

104 Certain rights laid down in the Charter are inherently not applicable to legal persons, such as the right to life (Art. 2(1)), whereas certain other rights expressly apply also to legal persons, such as the right to access to documents (Art. 42 Charter). Yet for most rights the situation is less clear. See further Oliver (2011), pp. 2028–37.

105 Cf. e.g. CoJ case C-275/06, *Promusicae*, para 61–70; CoJ case C-279/09, *DEB*, para 36–62; GC case T-496/10, *Bank Mellat*, para 36 (appeal pending; see CoJ case C-176/13, *Bank Mellat).* See also the ECtHR case law cited in Oliver (2011), p. 2030 (n. 29).

106 On the principle of effectiveness, see subsection 2.A.3 above.

107 Cf. Opinion AG Poiares Maduro joined cases C-222/05 to C-225/05, *Van der Weerd*, para 16. For a different view, see Prechal and Widdershoven (2011), p. 46. These authors argue that the main concern underlying the principle of effectiveness is in essence the effective application and enforcement of EU law *per se* rather than the protection of the rights of private parties. On this latter distinction, see subsection 11.A.1 below.

108 E.g. CoJ case C-279/09, *DEB*, para 27–9. Here the referring national court had posed a preliminary question to the CoJ regarding the application of the "*Rewe*-principle" of effectiveness. The CoJ restated the question, however, and answered it as one concerning the application of the principle of effective judicial protection.

109 Van Gerven (2004a), p. 515; Dougan (2004), p. 4; Drake (2005), pp. 332–5; Prechal (2005), p. 144; Tulibacka (2009), p. 1537; Reich (2010), p. 132; Arnull (2011), p. 55; Oliver (2011), pp. 2037–9. See also Opinion AG Trstenjak case C-411/10, *NS*, para 161. Although these authors all essentially identify effective judicial protection as the over-arching concept, their views differ significantly as to why that is the case, which nuances should be acknowledged and which consequences should be drawn therefrom. For another view see e.g. Opinion AG Kokott case C-75/08, *Mellor*, para 28, where it is held that conversely the principle of effective judicial protection is an expression of the "*Rewe*-principle" of effectiveness.

the more recent case law. For instance, the Court of Justice has repeatedly held that '*the requirements of equivalence and effectiveness embody the general obligation on the Member States to ensure effective judicial protection of an individual's rights under [EU] law*'.[110] In this connection it can also be recalled that the principles of equivalence and effectiveness apply only '*in the absence of [EU] rules*'.[111] The granting of legally binding force to the Charter – and thus also to its Article 47 – means that the principle laid down therein is now a rule of (positive) EU law. In addition to its status as a fundamental right, this may help explain why this principle generally obtains most attention.

Having said that, as the law stands it cannot be said with certainty that both principles neatly coincide and that one has "absorbed" the other.[112] There is case law suggesting that, "post-Lisbon", both principles continue to fulfil an independent role, in the sense that the Court of Justice assessed them separately.[113] It is therefore not always evident through which lens a particular question relating to national rules on remedies and procedures will be assessed. Further clarification is needed before firm conclusions can be drawn on the precise relationship and interaction between the two above-mentioned principles. It is moreover uncertain to what extent, if at all, any of this translates into a notable difference in practice. There can be no doubt that the application of the principle of effective judicial protection can have significant consequences for the national rules in question.[114] But the same can be said of the "*Rewe*-principle" of effectiveness.[115] The Court of Justice arguably tends to motivate its more intense scrutiny preferably with reference to the former principle.[116] This may be linked to the positive formulation of that principle (effective judicial protection *must* be ensured), as compared with the negative formulation of the principle of effectiveness (national procedural rules may *not* make the exercise of rights virtually impossible or excessively difficult).[117]

---

110 CoJ joined cases C-317/08 to C-320/08, *Alassini*, para 49. In a similar sense, see CoJ case C-268/06, *Impact*, para 47; CoJ case C-63/08, *Pontin*, para 44. See also CoJ case C-55/06, *Arcor*, para 190, where reference is made to '*the principles of equivalence and effectiveness of judicial protection*'.

111 CoJ case 33/76, *Rewe*, para 5. See para 2.01 above.

112 In a similar sense, see Iglesias Sánchez (2012), p. 1579; Prechal and Widdershoven (2011), p. 31; Parret (2012), p. 159. In the latter two publications it is argued, while acknowledging the overlap and similarities between both principles, that they serve different purposes and are driven by different rationales and should thus be distinguished. On the meaning and significance of the concept of effectiveness in the present context; see also section 11.A below.

113 CoJ case C-12/08, *Mono Car Styling*, para 49; CoJ joined cases C-317/08 to C-320/08, *Alassini*, para 52–66. Cf. also CoJ case C-276/01, *Steffensen*, para 66–80.

114 See subsection 2.B.2 below.

115 See subsection 2.A.3 above.

116 Cf. Prechal (2001), p. 40. See also Prechal and Widdershoven (2011), pp. 38–40.

117 Cf. Dougan (2011), p. 413.

2. Effective judicial protection: Application

The principle of effective judicial protection comprises various elements.[118] One of them is the right of *access to court*. This latter right in turn encompasses a range of more specific issues. It implies, for instance, that the competent court must be independent and impartial. That means that it must be protected against external intervention or pressure liable to jeopardise the independent judgment of its members. It also implies that there must be a "level playing field" for the parties to the proceedings and their respective interests, requiring objectivity and the absence of any interest in the outcome of the proceedings on the part of the members of the courts, apart from the strict application of the rule of law. The applicable rules, for example on the composition of the courts and on the appointment and dismissal of its members, must be such as to dismiss any reasonable doubt in the minds of the parties concerned as to the imperviousness of that body to external factors and its neutrality with respect to the interests before it.[119] This right does not necessarily entail a certain number of levels of jurisdiction, however.[120] **2.13**

The right of access to court also implies certain requirements in terms of the *standard of judicial review* exercised.[121] As the Court of Justice has clarified, for a court to be able to determine a dispute concerning rights or obligations arising under EU law in accordance with Article 47 Charter, (at least) in proceedings where penalties were imposed, it must be empowered to consider all questions of fact and law that are relevant to the case before it.[122] Accordingly, the courts seised must verify among other things whether the evidence relied on is factually accurate, reliable and consistent. They must also establish whether that evidence contains all the information which must be taken into account in order to assess a complex situation and whether it is capable of substantiating the conclusions drawn from it.[123]

The right of access to court can also have implications for rules on *legal standing* and *time limits*. The Court of Justice has held that it is, as a general rule, for

118 CoJ case C-199/11, *Otis*, para 48.

119 CoJ case C-506/04, *Wilson*, para 46–53. In this case the CoJ also clarified that the concept of a "court or tribunal" used here corresponds to that referred to in Art. 267 TFEU on the preliminary reference procedure, discussed in para 1.02 above.

120 CoJ case C-69/10, *Samba Diouf*, para 69.

121 For an overview of the (nuanced) assessment in this regard under Art. 6(1) ECHR, see ECtHR cases 32181/04 and 35122/05, *Sigma Radio Television*, para 126–7 and 147–57.

122 CoJ case C-199/11, *Otis*, para 49.

123 CoJ case C-386/10 P, *Chalkor*, para 53–67. See also CoJ case C-501/11 P, *Schindler*, para 33–8. These rulings relate to the judicial review exercised by the EU courts regarding Commission decisions establishing infringements of EU competition law. On that review, see further Nazzini (2012), p. 971.

national law to determine a private party's standing in initiating legal proceedings, as long as these rules do not undermine the right to effective judicial protection.[124] It is not necessarily required that a direct, free-standing action is available to contest a rule of national law that allegedly infringes EU law. The availability of an indirect remedy may suffice, for instance in the form of a damages claim or the possibility of contesting the measures enacted on the basis of the allegedly infringing provision.[125] In that sense the Court assesses the remedies in their totality.[126] Depending on the circumstances, the right of access to court might, however, be prejudiced where it is made conditional upon a preceding mandatory attempt to settle the dispute in question.[127] As regards the applicable time limits, notably limitation periods for initiating legal proceedings, it has been held that the period prescribed must be sufficient in practical terms to enable the applicant to effectively prepare and bring a case. This does not exclude account being taken of the nature of the procedure at issue.[128]

2.14 Another element of the broader right of effective judicial protection concerns the *rights of defence*. This includes a duty for the competent authorities to state reasons for their decisions in a specific and concrete manner.[129] This should allow the private party concerned to defend its rights in the best possible conditions and ensure that this party has the possibility of deciding, with full knowledge of the relevant facts, whether or not there is any point in applying to the courts.[130] It also serves to ensure that the court is fully in a position to review the lawfulness of the contested decision.[131] The rights of defence in addition imply a right to be heard for the private parties concerned. Thus, in all proceedings that are liable to culminate in a measure adversely affecting a party, every party must be given the opportunity to make known its views effectively before the adoption of a decision, even where the applicable legislation does not expressly provide for such a procedural requirement.[132] It also requires the authorities to pay due attention to the observations submitted by the private party concerned, as well as examining carefully and impartially all the relevant aspects of the individual case.[133]

---

124 E.g. CoJ joined cases C-87/90 to C-89/90, *Verholen*, para 24.

125 CoJ case C-13/01, *Safalero*, para 54–6; CoJ case C-432/05, *Unibet*, para 40–42.

126 This corresponds with the approach followed by the ECtHR under Art. 13 ECHR. See e.g. ECtHR case 9248/81, *Leander v Sweden*, para 84; ECtHR case 46477/99, *Edwards v UK*, para 101.

127 CoJ joined cases C-317/08 to C-320/08, *Alassini*, para 62.

128 CoJ case C-69/10, *Samba Diouf*, para 66–7.

129 CoJ case 222/86, *Heylens*, para 15; CoJ case C-104/91, *Borell*, para 15; CoJ case C-277/11, *M.M.*, para 88.

130 CoJ case C-239/05, *BVBA Management*, para 36; CoJ joined cases C-402/05 P and C-415/05 P, *Kadi*, para 336–7; CoJ case C-75/08, *Mellor*, para 59.

131 CoJ joined cases C-402/05 P and C-415/05 P, *Kadi*, para 337.

132 CoJ case C349/07, *Sopropé*, para 37–38; CoJ case C-277/11, *M.M.*, para 82 and 85–7.

133 CoJ case C-277/11, *M.M.*, para 88.

The rights of defence, including the right to be heard, not only apply in respect of decisions of EU or national administrative authorities. They also apply in relation to decisions by a court in proceedings between private parties, for instance where the court raises an issue of its own motion.[134] This is closely related to the right to adversarial proceedings.[135] That latter right aims to prevent a court from being influenced by arguments that the parties have been unable to discuss.[136] It ensures that the parties to the proceedings have the opportunity to make known any evidence needed for their claims to succeed and to have knowledge of, and comment on, all evidence adduced or observations filed, with a view to influencing the court's decision.[137]

Finally, the principle of *equality of arms* is yet another important element of the broader right of effective judicial protection guaranteed by Article 47 Charter.[138] This principle seeks to ensure a fair balance between the parties to the dispute. It implies that each party is afforded a reasonable opportunity to present its case, including its evidence, under conditions that do not place it at a substantial disadvantage *vis-à-vis* their opponent.[139] The principle of equality of arms (as well as the aforementioned right to adversarial proceedings) can thus for instance have a bearing on national rules of evidence. On the one hand, it is principally for the national courts to assess the evidence brought before them and the relevance of any evidence that a party wishes to produce.[140] On the other hand, at least under Article 6(1) ECHR, the fairness of the proceedings must be considered as a whole, including the manner in which evidence was taken.[141] It must therefore be ensured that a party has a real opportunity to examine and challenge any such evidence, particularly where the evidence pertains to a technical field of which the judges have no knowledge and it is likely to have a preponderant influence on the assessment of the facts by the court.[142] A rule of national law that a particular document issued by the national authorities is to be treated as conclusive evidence can therefore be **2.15**

134 CoJ case C-89/08 P, *Commission v Ireland*, para 51–57; CoJ case C-472/11, *Banif Plus Bank*, para 29.

135 Cf. CoJ case C-89/08 P, *Commission v Ireland*, para 58.

136 CoJ Order case C-17/98, *Emesa Sugar*, para 18.

137 CoJ case C-437/13, *Unitrading*, para 21. See also ECtHR case 21497/93, *Mantovanelli v France*, para 33; ECtHR case 32106/96, *Komanicky v Slovakia*, para 46.

138 E.g. CoJ case C-199/11, *Otis*, para 48; CoJ case C-169/14, *Sánchez Morcillo*, para 48.

139 E.g. CoJ case C-199/11, *Otis*, para 71–2. See e.g. also ECtHR case 14448/88, *Dombo Beheer BV v Netherlands*, para 33; ECtHR case 62543/00, *Gorraiz Lizarraga v Spain*, para 56.

140 CoJ case C-276/01, *Steffensen*, para 75. See e.g. also ECtHR case 21497/93, *Mantovanelli v France*, para 34; ECtHR case 32106/96, *Komanicky v Slovakia*, para 47.

141 ECtHR case 21497/93, *Mantovanelli v France*, para 34; ECtHR case 32106/96, *Komanicky v Slovakia*, para 47.

142 CoJ case C-276/01, *Steffensen*, para 76–7; CoJ case C-199/11, *Otis*, para 72.

contrary to this principle where it deprives a party of the possibility of asserting its rights by judicial process.[143]

C. PUBLIC ENFORCEMENT

Matters related to the private enforcement of EU law cannot be properly understood without having regard to the public enforcement context, that is, the range of coercive measures and mechanisms at the disposal of public authorities of the EU and of the Member States, acting in a public capacity, with a view to ensuring compliance with and the enforcement of EU law. Public enforcement can involve as the case may be the imposition of administrative sanctions such as fines, but also criminal law sanctions such as imprisonment. This section briefly outlines the main public enforcement mechanisms that exist in EU law. Below a distinction is made between infringement proceedings before the Court of Justice and other forms of public enforcement.

1. Infringement proceedings

2.16 One of the most important means of public enforcement in an EU law context is enforcement through infringement proceedings in accordance with Articles 258 and 259 TFEU.[144] These proceedings, which are to be brought before the Court of Justice, can be initiated by either the Commission or a Member State when either of them considers that a Member State has failed to fulfil its obligation under the EU Treaties. Those obligations include compliance with secondary EU law. Not only are the acts and omissions of a Member State's central government concerned here, but also those of its regional or local governments and specific branches, such as the judiciary. These infringement proceedings can result in the Court of Justice declaring that the Member State in question has failed to fulfil its obligations. That Member State is then required to correct the situation so as to ensure conformity with EU law.[145] Where this has been applied for, the Court of Justice can impose a lump sum or a penalty payment on the Member State concerned in case of non-compliance. However, certain special cases aside, under Article 260 TFEU the Commission first needs to initiate additional, separate proceedings before these latter

143 E.g. CoJ case 222/84, *Johnston*, para 20. This case was decided on the basis of the principle of effective judicial protection generally, that is, without any further specification of a particular element thereof.

144 See further e.g. Rawlings (2000), p. 267; Prete and Smulders (2010), p. 9.

145 Art. 260(1) TFEU.

measures can be imposed.[146] As has been noted earlier, in practice, infringement proceedings initiated by the Commission far outnumber the actions brought by Member States.[147] These proceedings are thus principally a matter between the Commission and the Member State allegedly having infringed EU law.

That is not to say, however, that private parties cannot play a role in this context. **2.17** In particular they can file complaints to the Commission on alleged infringements of EU law by the Member States. For these private parties this can be a cheap and easy means of exposing (alleged) non-compliance. One could say that it allows them to enforce their rights in an indirect manner. For the Commission, these complaints are an important means of information-gathering. As is the case with the Commission's own-initiative investigations, only a small minority of all complaints received lead to the Commission actually bringing an infringement action before the Court of Justice. Not only does it not act upon all complaints received, the Commission and the Member State concerned also often prefer negotiating a solution "in the shadow of the law" rather than having the matter settled in court.[148] Nonetheless, a significant amount of the infringement cases that are actually brought before the Court of Justice find their origin in such complaints.[149] In this manner private parties can thus play a significant role in this context.

But that role only goes so far. Whether initiated as a consequence of a complaint or otherwise, infringement proceedings are in essence firmly "public–public" in nature. A private party complainant never becomes a party to these proceedings. The Commission, moreover, enjoys full discretion as to whether or not it wishes to initiate or terminate them. A private party can neither force the Commission to act in a certain manner in this respect nor stop it from acting in the manner that it deems appropriate. Put in legal terms, both an action for the annulment of a Commission decision as to whether or not it wants to initiate infringement proceedings and an action against the Commission for failure to

146 Art. 260(2) TFEU. The above-mentioned special cases concern the situation where the Member States have failed to notify measures transposing a directive into national law within the set time period (see Art. 260(3) TFEU).

147 See para 1.03 above.

148 In 2013 the Commission received more than 3500 complaints, almost 500 of which led to discussions being opened with the Member States concerned, whereas the Commission launched over 1000 own-initiative investigations. In that year more than 900 infringement cases were closed at the informal stage, whereas another 700 cases were closed before or shortly after the stage of litigation before the CoJ. The CoJ delivered around 50 judgments in infringement cases (Art. 258 TFEU). See Commission, 31st Annual report on monitoring the application of EU law (2013), COM(2014) 612, pp. 9–12.

149 Namely 53 per cent in 2009 and 40 per cent in 2010. See Commission, 28th Annual report on monitoring the application of EU law (2010), COM(2011) 588, p. 3 (no such data can be derived from more recent reports).

act upon a complaint received from a private party will normally not succeed.[150] As the Court of Justice has held, '*the Commission is not bound to commence [infringement proceedings], but in this regard has a discretion which excludes the right for individuals to require that institution to adopt a specific position*'.[151] The private party complainants' rights are essentially procedural, particularly with regard to them being kept informed of the decision taken pursuant to their complaint.[152] At most one could therefore speak of "privately triggered public enforcement".[153]

2. Other forms of public enforcement

2.18 EU law also provides for other forms of public enforcement. Unlike the infringement proceedings discussed in the previous subsection, these other forms are "public–private" in nature rather than "public–public". In other words, these latter public enforcement mechanisms essentially entail supervision exercised *by public authorities* concerning the compliance with EU law *by private parties*. In this connection one can distinguish the following two types of situations.

2.19 In the first type of situation, *no explicit provisions* as regards the public enforcement of the applicable rules of substantive EU law have been set out in secondary EU law. This is thus the "default" situation, which is regulated by primary EU law. The EU Treaties do not contain any detailed provisions of a general nature imposing on the Member States an express obligation to ensure the compliance with and enforcement of EU law within their respective jurisdictions. Nonetheless, under the principle of sincere cooperation laid down in Article 4(3) TEU, Member States are required to take all appropriate measures to ensure the fulfilment of the obligations arising out of EU law.[154] The Court of Justice has interpreted this principle in such a manner that it entails not only obligations on the Member States to ensure respect for EU law where their own acts are concerned, but also as regards acts by private parties falling within their jurisdictions.

The Court addressed this issue, most notably, in its 1989 ruling in *Greek maize*.[155] This case concerned fraud to the detriment of the financial interests of

---

150 E.g. CoJ case 48/65, *Lütticke*, p. 27; CoJ case 247/87, *Star Fruit Company*, para 11–12.

151 CoJ case 247/87, *Star Fruit Company*, para 11.

152 Cf. Commission, Communication on updating the handling of relations with the complainant in respect of the application of Union law, COM(2012) 154.

153 Jacobs and Deisenhofer (2003), p. 197.

154 See also para 2.03 above.

155 CoJ case 68/88, *Commission v Greece (Greek maize)*.

the EU in respect of agricultural levies. The Commission brought infringement proceedings in light of the failure by Greece to penalise the persons involved in this fraud. The Court clarified that the principle of sincere cooperation implies that Member States must take '*all measures necessary to guarantee the application and effectiveness of [EU] law*'.[156] To that aim they must ensure that infringements of EU law are penalised:

> under conditions, both procedural and substantive, which are analogous to those applicable to infringements of national law of a similar nature and importance and which, in any event, make the penalty effective, proportionate and dissuasive. Moreover, the national authorities must proceed, with respect to infringements of [EU] law, with the same diligence as that which they bring to bear implementing corresponding national laws.[157]

In this case it was further noted that the above-mentioned obligation to take all necessary measures applies (only) where EU legislation does not specifically provide any penalty for an infringement nor refers for that purpose to national law.[158]

This reference to the absence of specific EU legislation and the requirements to apply analogous conditions, exercise the same diligence and provide for effective, proportionate and dissuasive penalties recalls the requirements elaborated by the Court under the principles of national procedural autonomy, equivalence and effectiveness.[159] Indeed, it has been observed that the Court increasingly tends to treat the Member States' public enforcement-related obligations pursuant to this *Greek Maize* case law as virtually interchangeable with those under its *Rewe* case law concerning legal proceedings brought by private parties for (alleged) infringements of EU law.[160] In subsequent cases, such as *Spanish Strawberries* and *Smidberger*,[161] the Court built on its ruling in *Greek Maize*. It follows from this case law that where EU law does not provide for specific rules, the national public authorities concerned must take the necessary steps against private parties so as to ensure the proper application of the rules of EU law at issue. Yet the Court has also consistently held that in such a case the precise

156 Ibid., para 23.
157 Ibid., para 24.
158 Ibid., para 23.
159 See section 2.A above.
160 Dougan (2010), pp. 106–7. See also Dougan (2004), pp. 39–40.
161 CoJ case C-265/95, *Commission v France (Spanish strawberries)*; CoJ case C-112/00, *Smidberger*.

choice of penalties remains, as a general rule, for the Member States.[162] These penalties can in principle be administrative, civil or criminal in nature.[163]

2.20 The second type of situation is one where secondary EU law does provide for an *explicit obligation* for certain public authorities to enforce the substantive EU rules in question. This is, for instance, the case in the field of competition law. In that field both the Commission and the national competition authorities are charged with ensuring the compliance with the EU competition rules. To this end these authorities are *inter alia* empowered to impose fines on undertakings that have been found to infringe these rules.[164] Although perhaps most well known, this is, however, by no means the only field where public enforcement-related requirements are explicitly provided for as a matter of EU law. Relevant provisions can, for instance, be found in other fields of EU law as diverse as fisheries,[165] the protection of personal data[166] and transport.[167] In those fields the public enforcement obligations at issue are typically on the Member States alone and not (also) on the Commission.

The tasks and powers of the various public authorities concerned under such measures of secondary EU law can differ significantly both between the various fields of EU law and between the Member States. Not one uniform model of public enforcement exists. The degree of detail provided for as a matter of EU law is mostly rather limited, however. This implies also that in these cases considerable discretion tends to be left to the Member States as regards the precise structure, powers and functioning of the national public enforcement authorities in question. For example, under the Railway Passengers' Rights Regulation, the Member States are obliged to designate a body responsible for the enforcement of the rules at issue.[168] It specifies that this body must be independent and that it must take the measures necessary to ensure that the rights of railway passengers are respected. Yet it is further left to the Member States to define the powers of that body.[169] The obligations on the Member

162 E.g. CoJ case 68/88, *Commission v Greece (Greek maize)*, para 24 and 26; CoJ case C-265/95, *Commission v France (Spanish strawberries)*, para 34; CoJ case C-617/10, *Åklagaren*, para 34 and 36.

163 Cf. e.g. CoJ case 14/83, *Van Colson*, para 28; CoJ case C-326/88, *Hansen*, para 15–19; CoJ case C-7/90, *Vandevenne*, para 16–17.

164 See subsection 6.D.2 below.

165 Art. 5 Regulation (EC) No 1224/2009 establishing a Community control system for ensuring compliance with the rules of the common fisheries policy, OJ 2009, L 343/1 ("Fisheries Control Regulation").

166 Art. 28 Data Protection Directive 95/46; Art. 15a(2)–(4) E-Privacy Directive 2002/58.

167 Art. 16(1) Air Passengers' Rights Regulation 261/2004; Art. 30 Railway Passengers' Rights Regulation 1371/2007.

168 Art. 30 Railway Passengers' Rights Regulation 1371/2007.

169 Cf. CoJ case C-509/11, *ÖBB-Personenverkehr*, para 59–66.

States in this respect can also involve providing for a possibility for the private parties concerned to file complaints.[170]

By means of a codification of the aforementioned *Greek maize* case law, the public enforcement obligations on the Member States often also include a requirement to provide for penalties for infringements of the rules of EU law at issue that are effective, proportionate and dissuasive. This has become a standard phrase that can be found in many acts of secondary EU law.[171] The Court of Justice has clarified that it follows from this requirement that the severity of the penalties provided for under national law must be commensurate with the seriousness of the infringement at issue, in particular by ensuring a genuinely dissuasive effect, while respecting the principle of proportionality.[172] This latter principle implies that the competent national authorities must have regard to all the considerations of fact or law specific to each case, including the behaviour of the private party concerned and its good faith or its fraudulent intentions, in order to determine whether a penalty must be imposed and, if so, which one.[173] As is the case under the case law discussed above, these are still rather broad parameters, however. They continue to leave the Member States and the national courts considerable discretion. Although the Court of Justice sometimes gives guidance, it has also emphasised that it is for the national court seised to determine whether the above-mentioned requirements are fulfilled in individual cases.[174] It is only in exceptional cases that the EU legislature goes beyond merely providing for the said standard phrase so as to require, for example, that criminal penalties must be provided for.[175]

D. KEY CASE LAW RELATING TO PRIVATE ENFORCEMENT

In this final section of Chapter 2 attention turns to five rulings of the Court of Justice, namely *Simmenthal*, *Factortame*, *Francovich*, *Courage* and *Muñoz*.[176] Even if they are not all concerned with the private enforcement of EU law before national courts as such, they are of particular importance in this connection, as they set out some key aspects relating to the enforcement of EU

170 E.g. Art. 28(4) Data Protection Directive 95/46; Art. 16(2) Air Passengers' Rights Regulation 261/2004.

171 E.g. Art. 15a(1) E-Privacy Directive 2002/58; Art. 32 Railway Passengers' Rights Regulation 1371/2007; Art. 90(2) Fisheries Control Regulation 1224/2009.

172 E.g. CoJ case C-565/12, *LCL Le Crédit Lyonnais*, para 44–5.

173 E.g. CoJ case C-148/14, *Nordzucker*, para 44.

174 E.g. ibid., para 50–4.

175 Cf. Commission, Communication towards an EU criminal policy, COM(2011) 573. See further Dougan (2012b), p. 74.

176 CoJ case 106/77, *Simmenthal*; CoJ case C-213/89, *Factortame;* CoJ joined cases C-6/90 and C-9/90, *Francovich*; CoJ case C-453/99, *Courage*; CoJ case C-253/00, *Muñoz*.

law at national level. Many will be familiar with these landmark rulings, but their importance for the present purposes justifies recalling and assessing them in some detail here, including certain subsequent case law where relevant. After having introduced first the three former rulings and then the two latter ones, they are also considered jointly.

1. *Simmenthal, Factortame* and *Francovich*

2.21 The Court's ruling in *Simmenthal* dates from 1978. This case concerned a company that had imported beef from France to Italy. A fee had been charged for the veterinary and health inspection of the beef. Earlier it had already been decided that this charge was contrary to EU law.[177] The national court therefore ordered its repayment. The national authorities concerned contested this order, arguing in essence that pursuant to a (subsequent) national law, only the national constitutional court – and not the lower court at issue – could set aside the national law that prevented this repayment.

The Court of Justice did not accept this argument, however. After having recalled the importance of the principles of direct effect and primacy of EU law, it held that the above-mentioned rule of national law would both amount to a denial of the effectiveness of the EU law obligations of the Member State in question and endanger the effectiveness of the preliminary reference procedure.[178] It noted in this connection that:

> every national court must, in a case within its jurisdiction, apply [EU] law in its entirety and protect rights which the latter confers on individuals and must accordingly set aside any provision of national law which may conflict with it, whether prior or subsequent to the [EU] rule. [...] Accordingly, any provision of the national legal system and any legislative, administrative or judicial practice which might impair the effectiveness of [EU] law by withholding from the national court having jurisdiction to apply such law the power to do everything necessary at the moment of its application to set aside national legislative provisions which might prevent [EU] rules from having full force and effect, are incompatible with those requirements which are the very essence of [EU] law.[179]

2.22 A second case that is of particular relevance here is *Factortame*, dating from 1990. The dispute before the national court concerned the compatibility with EU law of a national law which was designed to prevent fishing vessels from

177 See CoJ case 35/76, *Simmenthal*.

178 CoJ case 106/77, *Simmenthal*, para 14–20.

179 Ibid., para 21–2.

other Member States from being registered, where that registration was considered to be merely meant to evade rules on fishing quotas. As in *Simmenthal*, the referral did not concern the question of compatibility as such, but rather the question of which consequences a national court is to draw from the finding that the national law in question is contrary to EU law. More specifically, the central question referred to the Court of Justice was whether a national court must be able to grant interim relief where it considers that a rule of national law is incompatible with EU law, even if under domestic law that remedy is not available in that particular case.

Referring to *Simmenthal* and the principle of sincere cooperation, the Court recalled the need for national courts to ensure the legal protection that private parties derive from the direct effect of provisions of EU law. It also stressed the risks to the effectiveness of EU law if national law were to prevent those courts from setting aside rules of national law '*which might prevent, even temporarily, [EU] rules from having full force and effect*'.[180] It was then added that:

> the full effectiveness would be just as much impaired if a rule of national law could prevent a court seised of a dispute governed by [EU] law from granting interim relief in order to ensure the full effectiveness of the judgment to be given on the existence of the rights claimed under [EU] law. It follows that a court which in those circumstances would grant interim relief, if it were not for a rule of national law, is obliged to set aside that rule.[181]

According to the Court, this interpretation was reinforced by the fact that the preliminary reference system set out in Article 267 TFEU would be endangered if there were no possibility of granting interim relief in attending a preliminary ruling.[182] In subsequent rulings the Court has regularly highlighted the importance of the availability of interim relief in cases where EU law is infringed. The most notable example is *Unibet*.[183] In that case it was clarified that this need not necessarily be a free-standing action. It was also held there that the applicable conditions are to be determined by national law, subject to the principles of equivalence and effectiveness.[184]

A distinct yet related question is whether national courts can grant interim relief where the validity of an act of secondary *EU* law is in question (as opposed to a rule of *national* law, as was the case in *Factortame* and *Unibet*, discussed

180 CoJ case C-213/89, *Factortame*, para 18–20.

181 Ibid., para 21.

182 Ibid., para 22.

183 CoJ case C-432/05, *Unibet*, para 67. See e.g. also CoJ case C-226/99, *Siples*, para 19.

184 Ibid., para 71–3 and 79–82. On the principles of equivalence and effectiveness, see further subsections 2.A.2 and 2.A.3 above. See e.g. also CoJ case C-530/11, *Commission v UK*, para 67.

above), pending a preliminary ruling on the matter. The Court has answered this question essentially in the affirmative. In *Atlanta* it was found that the interim legal protection offered to private parties under national law should not depend on whether a national measure is contrary to EU law or whether an act of secondary EU law is contrary to EU law of a higher order.[185] The Court nonetheless spelled out certain rather strict conditions that must be respected in such cases.[186]

2.23 The third case is the Court's 1991 *Francovich* judgment. This case concerned the lack of timely transposition by Italy into national law of a directive, thus adversely affecting a private party. Although unconditional and sufficiently precise to be directly effective, the rights concerned could nonetheless not be enforced before a national court without the required national measures. The Court of Justice found that under these circumstances a Member State could be held liable by a private party for the *loss and damage* resulting from this breach of the Member State's obligations under EU law. It reached this conclusion after recalling, first, the finding in *Van Gend en Loos* that the EU Treaties had created a new legal order that is also intended to give rise to rights for individuals and, second, the position set out in *Simmenthal* and *Factortame* that national courts must ensure that EU rules take full effect and that they must protect the rights of individuals.[187] On that basis the Court of Justice ruled that the '*full effectiveness of [EU] rules would be impaired and the protection of the rights which they grant would be weakened if individuals were unable to obtain redress when their rights are infringed by a breach of [EU] law for which a Member State can be held responsible*'.[188] Therefore it found that '*it is a principle of [EU] law that the Member States are obliged to make good loss and damage caused to individuals by breaches of [EU] law for which they can be held responsible*'.[189]

This judgment thus articulated the principle of *Member State liability* for breaches of EU law by public authorities. The Court considered this principle to be inherent in the system of the EU Treaties, while finding a further basis in the principle of sincere cooperation set out in Article 4(3) TEU, which implies an obligation to nullify the unlawful consequences of an infringement of EU

185 CoJ case C-465/93, *Atlanta*, para 28.

186 Ibid., para 51. The conditions referred to above are: (a) the existence of serious doubts as to the validity of the act in question; (b) urgency, that is, a necessity with a view to avoiding serious and irreparable damage; (c) due account being taken of the interests of the EU; and (d) respect for earlier decisions by the EU courts on the matter. These conditions are derived from the case law on when interim measures are to be granted in legal proceedings before the EU courts themselves, pursuant to Art. 279 TFEU.

187 CoJ joined cases C-6/90 and C-9/90, *Francovich*, para 31–2.

188 Ibid., para 33.

189 Ibid., para 37.

law.[190] It added in subsequent cases, most notably in *Brasserie du Pêcheur*, that '*the right to reparation is the necessary corollary of the direct effect of the [EU] law provision whose breach caused the damage sustained*' and that there is a '*general principle familiar to the legal systems of the Member States that an unlawful act or omission gives rise to an obligation to make good the damage caused*'.[191] In so doing the Court drew an analogy with the rules on the non-contractual liability of the EU provided for in Article 340 TFEU.[192] Those rules require the EU to make good any damage caused by its institutions and its servants in accordance with the general principles common to the laws of the Member States.

In *Brasserie du Pêcheur* the Court also clarified the *conditions* that must be fulfilled to incur Member State liability.[193] These conditions depend on the nature of the breach of EU law at issue. In principle they also correspond to those applicable to the aforementioned non-contractual liability of the EU. Therefore, in areas where the Member State has a wide discretion, these conditions are that: (a) the rule of law infringed must be intended to confer rights on private parties; (b) the infringement must be sufficiently serious; and (c) there must be a direct causal link between the infringement and the damage sustained by the injured parties. Reparation for the consequences of the loss and damage caused must further be made in accordance with the domestic rules on liability, subject to the principles of equivalence and effectiveness.[194] In subsequent case law the Court has expanded in particular on the application of this principle to the various decentralised or functional bodies of a Member State,[195] the interpretation of the above conditions[196] and the aforementioned analogy with the non-contractual liability of the EU pursuant to Article 340 TFEU.[197]

---

190 Ibid., para 35–6.

191 CoJ joined cases C-46/93 and C-48/93, *Brasserie du Pêcheur*, para 22 and 29.

192 Ibid., para 28–9 and 40–42.

193 Ibid., para 38–51. In *Francovich* the CoJ had already touched upon these conditions, but there no analogy had been drawn with the non-contractual liability of the EU under Art. 340 TFEU. There these conditions had, moreover, been formulated somewhat differently (although this does not entail a difference in substance; see CoJ joined cases C-178/94, C-179/94 and C-188/94 to C-190/94, *Dillenkofer*, para 23).

194 Ibid., para 67. See also CoJ joined cases C-6/90 and C-9/90, *Francovich*, para 41–3. On the principles of equivalence and effectiveness, see further subsections 2.A.2 and 2.A.3 above.

195 E.g. CoJ case C-302/97, *Konle* (regarding Member States with a federal structure); CoJ case C-224/01, *Köbler* (regarding breaches of EU law by the national judiciary).

196 E.g. CoJ case C-4/94, *Hedley Lomas* (regarding situations where there is significantly reduced or no discretion); CoJ case C-222/02, *Paul* (regarding the conferral of rights to private parties); CoJ case C-118/08, *Transportes Urbanos*, para 38 (regarding the fact that no earlier finding by the CoJ in a preliminary ruling procedure of a breach of EU law is required).

197 E.g. CoJ case C-352/98 P, *Bergaderm* (regarding the application of the conditions set out in *Brasserie du Pêcheur* in cases of the non-contractual liability of the EU). On both above-mentioned types of liability and the extent to which these have converted, see further Tridimas (2006), pp. 477–547; Wakefield (2009), p. 390; Gutman (2011), p. 695; Aalto (2011).

2. *Courage* and *Muñoz*

2.24 A fourth judgment that is of particular importance in the present context is *Courage*.[198] This ruling was issued in 2001, roughly a decade after *Francovich*. Two private parties had entered into a contract liable to restrict or distort competition within the meaning of Article 101(1) TFEU. One of these parties later initiated civil proceedings, claiming compensation for damages from its contract partner. Under national law this claim was barred on the basis that a party cannot rely on its own illegal actions to obtain compensation in damages. One of the questions referred to the Court of Justice was whether such an absolute bar is compatible with EU law. In its judgment the Court first restated (with reference to *Van Gend en Loos* and *Francovich*) that the EU Treaties created a new legal order and that EU law is intended to give rise to rights for private parties. In addition, the fundamental importance of the prohibition of Article 101 TFEU was underlined. The Court highlighted that agreements caught by that prohibition are automatically void and that this automatic nullity can be relied on by anyone.[199] It further recalled that the said article produces direct effects in relations between private parties and creates rights that national courts must safeguard.[200]

On the basis of those considerations it was held that '*any individual*' can rely on a breach of Article 101(1) TFEU before a national court, even where he is a party to a contract that is liable to restrict or distort competition within the meaning of that provision.[201] Concerning the possibility of seeking compensation for loss caused by infringements of that article, the Court of Justice repeated, with reference to *Simmenthal* and *Factortame*, that it is the task of the national courts to '*ensure that [the rules of EU law at issue] take full effect and [to] protect the rights which they confer on individuals*'.[202] Accordingly, it was held that:

> [t]he full effectiveness of Article [101 TFEU] and, in particular, the practical effect of the prohibition laid down [therein] would be put at risk if it were not open to any individual to claim damages for loss caused to him by a contract or by conduct liable to restrict or distort competition. Indeed, the existence of such a right strengthens the working of the [EU] competition rules and discourages agreements or practices, which are frequently covert, which are liable to restrict or distort competition. From that point

198 For a more detailed analysis of this ruling, see para 6.14 below.

199 See subsection 6.A.3 below.

200 CoJ case C-453/99, *Courage*, para 19–23.

201 Ibid., para 24.

202 Ibid., para 25.

> of view, actions for damages before the national courts can make a significant contribution to the maintenance of effective competition in the [EU].[203]

The Court thus found that there cannot be an absolute bar to the bringing of such an action by a party that itself might have violated the EU competition rules. As was the case in *Francovich*, reference was made to the domestic legal system of the Member States for the designation of the competent courts and the applicable detailed procedural rules, subject to the principles of equivalence and effectiveness. It was added, however, that EU law does not prevent national courts from taking steps to ensure that the protection of rights guaranteed by EU law does not entail unjust enrichment nor precludes national law from applying the principle that a litigant should not profit from its own unlawful conduct.[204] The Court subsequently expanded on and further refined this landmark judgment in its later case law, most notably in *Manfredi*.[205]

Finally, the ruling in *Muñoz* appeared one year after *Courage*. This case **2.25**
concerned two regulations setting out common quality standards for certain agricultural products. In this preliminary reference also, the point of departure was that a private party had infringed the provisions of these regulations. The question referred to the Court of Justice was, in essence, whether another private party could bring a civil action to address this non-compliance. The Court answered by outlining a number of relatively straightforward steps. It noted that, owing to their very nature and place in the system of sources of EU law, regulations operate to confer rights on individuals. National courts have a duty to protect these rights and to ensure that they take full effect. Furthermore, it was established that the common quality standards at issue served to keep products of unsatisfactory quality off the market, to guide production to meet consumers' requirements and to facilitate trade relations based on fair competition.[206]

The Court therefore concluded in *Muñoz* that the said regulations should be interpreted as meaning that compliance with the provisions concerned must be capable of enforcement by means of civil proceedings instituted by a trader against a competitor.[207] In reaching that conclusion, it held that '*the full effectiveness of the rules on quality standards and, in particular, the practical effect of the obligation laid down [in the provisions of EU law under consideration], imply that it must be possible to enforce that obligation by means of civil proceedings*

203 Ibid., para 25–7.

204 Ibid., para 28–35.

205 CoJ joined cases C-295/04 to C-298/04, *Manfredi*, discussed in para 6.15 below.

206 CoJ case C-253/00, *Muñoz*, para 27–9.

207 Ibid., para 32.

instituted by a trader against a competitor'.[208] Apparently echoing *Courage* (yet without making an explicit reference), the Court further found that:

> [t]he possibility of bringing such proceedings strengthens the practical working of the [EU] rules on quality standards. As a supplement to the action of the authorities designated by the Member States to make the checks required by those rules it helps to discourage practices, often difficult to detect, which distort competition. In that context actions brought before the national courts by competing operators are particularly suited to contributing substantially to ensuring fair trading and transparency of markets in the [EU].[209]

3. Comparison and assessment

2.26 When comparing the five key rulings discussed above, it is clear that the reasoning and concepts used in *Courage* and *Muñoz* resemble to a significant extent the line followed in *Francovich*, whereas the latter builds in turn on *Simmenthal* and *Factortame*. Generally speaking, the importance of ensuring that private parties can effectively enforce their rights based on EU law before their respective national courts emerges as a crucial consideration in the Court's reasoning. Apart from the need to safeguard these rights, the full effectiveness and the practical effects (*effet utile*) of the EU rules at issue typically take centre stage. In respect of these aims all five rulings highlight the importance of the availability of certain remedies in cases of conflicts between EU law and national law, namely the "general" remedy of the setting aside of national law in *Simmenthal*, interim measures in *Factortame*, actions for damages against Member States in *Francovich*, actions for damages against private parties in *Courage* and civil proceedings generally in *Muñoz*.[210] As such, these cases can be seen as exceptions to the "no new remedies" rule formulated by the Court of Justice,[211] although it is also possible to see them as involving extensions of remedies that already existed under national law rather than the actual creation of new remedies.[212] In any case it is evident that the EU's involvement with the remedies and procedures available in private proceedings before national courts that concern rights vested in EU law can be very substantial indeed.

2.27 When zooming in on the three more recent rulings, it is noticeable that – unlike *Courage* and *Muñoz* – *Francovich* is not expressly framed in terms of "dual

208 Ibid., para 30.
209 Ibid., para 31.
210 Cf. Van Gerven (2000), p. 503.
211 See para 2.01 above.
212 See Van Gerven (2000), p. 517; Prechal (2005), pp. 169–70. As the latter author points out, this may also depend on whether the term "remedy" is understood in its wide or rather in its more narrow sense (see para 1.06 above).

vigilance".[213] That is to say, in the two former cases the Court of Justice emphasised that legal actions brought by private parties for breaches of EU law serve a valuable purpose in supplementing public enforcement of EU law. In the latter judgment this was not the case. The Court later clarified that the purpose of Member State liability is not punishment or deterrence, but rather ensuring that the parties having suffered damage are compensated.[214] Nonetheless, the dominant view in the legal literature is that the establishment of the principle of Member State liability should be understood against the background of an "enforcement deficit", originating in the lack of adequate implementation of EU law by the Member States.[215] It is further evident that *Francovich* concerns the liability of a *Member State* for infringements of EU law, while *Courage* and *Muñoz* concern the liability of a *private party* for such infringements. Whereas the former established the principle of Member State liability, the latter thus established a principle of "individual"[216] or "private party" liability.[217] It is common ground that, although the context and certain details may differ, there is an analogy between both principles.[218] This analogy is such that *Courage* has been called a '*private Francovich*'.[219]

Nonetheless, several issues remain to be clarified. One of them is whether this (nascent) principle of private party liability, as articulated in *Courage* and *Muñoz*, is in all respects an autonomous course of action, that is, a remedy that is inherent in the EU Treaties and founded directly on EU law and that as such is not dependent on national law. As was noted above, in relation to the principle of Member State liability, the Court of Justice made clear statements to this effect in *Francovich* and *Brasserie du Pêcheur*. Although less explicitly, similar conclusions have been drawn, for instance, in relation to the remedy of interim relief under the aforementioned *Factortame* and *Atlanta* case law.[220] The question whether the possibility of claiming damages or bringing other civil proceedings for a breach of EU law by a private party is also a proper "EU law remedy" must nonetheless probably be answered in the affirmative. While it could be argued that the rulings in both *Courage* and *Muñoz* are not entirely conclusive in this regard, particularly because they do not contain express

213 Weatherill (2000), p. 92; Tridimas (2006), p. 546.

214 CoJ case C-470/03, *AGM-COS.MET*, para 88. This position seems in line with the case law regarding the non-contractual liability of the EU under Art. 340 TFEU. See Wakefield (2009), p. 398.

215 E.g. Steiner (1995), p. 21; Dougan (2002), pp. 170–71; Tridimas (2006), p. 500; Rebhalm (2008), pp. 184–5; Biondi and Farley (2009), p. 13; Craig and De Búrca (2011), p. 243; Aalto (2011), pp. 154 and 197. See also Lock (2012), p. 1675.

216 Drake (2005), p. 344.

217 Leczykiewicz (2010a), p. 257.

218 E.g. Van Gerven (2004a), p. 522; Komninos (2009), p. 383; Reich (2010), pp. 114–15; Stuyck (2011), p. 524. See e.g. also Opinion AG Kokott case C-557/12, *Kone*, para 24.

219 Dougan (2011), p. 430.

220 See e.g. ibid., pp. 426–7.

statements regarding this principle's foundation directly in EU law, their wording does not appear to allow for too narrow a reading. It is broadly agreed that the principle of private party liability is founded on EU law itself.[221] Therefore, not too much weight should arguably be attached to the absence (at least to date) of express statements to this effect.[222]

This discussion is certainly not without practical relevance. Admittedly it may well be that whether or not the principle of private party liability is based directly on EU law is less crucial in practical terms than was the case with the principle of Member State liability. For, unlike the state of play at the national level "pre-*Francovich*", all Member States already provide for the former possibility under their domestic laws in one form or another.[223] However, recognising a remedy as being based directly on EU law can still have important practical implications, in particular as regards the conditions that apply in this connection. The issue here is especially whether these conditions are (exclusively) a matter of *EU* law or (also) of *national* law.[224] In this connection it has been suggested drawing a distinction between the "constitutive" conditions, which concern the EU remedy as such, and "executive" remedial rules, which concern the applicable procedures to give effect to this remedy.[225] Under this logic these constitutive conditions – being closely related to the underlying right founded in EU law – must be uniform across the EU. They should therefore be set exclusively by EU law. The executive rules could in contrast be left to national law, subject to the principles of equivalence and effectiveness. Appealing as this approach may be for its analytical clarity and logic, it should, however, not be mistaken for an accurate description of the law as it stands. Certainly (but not only[226]) where the principle of private party liability is

---

221 See Opinion AG Jacobs joined cases C-264/01, C-306/01, C-354/01 and C-355/01, *AOB Bundesverband*, para 104; Opinion AG Kokott case C-557/12, *Kone*, para 24. See also e.g. Van Gerven (2003a), p. 407; Drake (2006), pp. 849–50; Eilmansberger (2007), p. 433; Komninos (2009), p. 378; Nazzini (2009), p. 405; Milutinovic (2010), pp. 83, 91 and 93; Dougan (2011), p. 430. Lenaerts, Maselis and Gutman (2014), p. 145, seem somewhat more cautious (in relation to *Courage*).

222 There are other examples where the CoJ only at a later stage acknowledged that a key doctrine of EU law that had already been established earlier was '*inherent in the system of the [EU] Treaties*'. See e.g. CoJ joined cases C-397/01 to C-403/01, *Pfeiffer*, para 114 (concerning the principle of consistent interpretation, discussed in para 1.04 above). Conversely, the CoJ was initially not entirely clear in holding that the principle of Member State liability is founded directly in EU law. See e.g. CoJ case 60/75, *Russo*, para 9; CoJ case 101/78, *Granaria*, para 14.

223 Drake (2006), p. 855. In a similar sense, see Eilmansberger (2007), p. 434.

224 Cf. Komninos (2009), pp. 391–9.

225 Van Gerven (2000), pp. 525–7. Cf. Opinion AG Kokott case C-557/12, *Kone*, para 23.

226 See subsection 2.D.1 above. As was shown there, in its *Francovich* case law the CoJ has set what could perhaps be called the "constitutive" conditions for incurring Member State liability. However, that is not the case in its *Factortame* case law relating to interim relief. In the *Atlanta* case law these conditions were set, but, even if both *Factortame* and *Atlanta* concern interim relief, the situations addressed by both sets of case law are to be distinguished.

concerned, the Court of Justice has to date not set out the applicable ("constitutive") conditions in an unambiguous and detailed manner.[227] Further clarification on this point is therefore awaited.

Finally, different views can be taken as to the respective significance of *Courage* **2.28**
and *Muñoz*. On the one hand, *Courage* can be seen as having the strongest claim to being the main landmark case in this respect, if only because it pre-dates *Muñoz*. The former is, moreover, formulated in a rather sweeping manner, whereas the latter is remarkably short and straightforward.[228] In addition, as was noted above, the rule laid down in *Courage* has at least to some extent been further fleshed out in later case law. That has so far not been the case for *Muñoz*; this latter judgment has in fact been referred to only rarely.[229] Another difference is that in *Courage* it is stated that '*any individual*' can rely on a breach of the provision concerned and can thus claim damages.[230] In contrast, in *Muñoz* the Court of Justice seemed careful to specify that the applicant was a competitor. *Courage* thus seems more ambitious where issues of legal standing are concerned.[231]

On the other hand, in certain other respects *Muñoz* might, at least potentially, have broader implications than *Courage*. The former relies less on the fundamental importance of the provisions of EU law at issue. Most people would probably not consider common quality standards for agricultural products to be of fundamental or otherwise exceptional importance, even if they also affected to some extent the competition between undertakings. Unlike the EU competition rules at issue in *Courage*, the applicable rules were furthermore laid down in secondary EU law and not in the EU Treaties themselves. Those provisions may therefore be difficult to distinguish from other provisions of EU law that seek to ensure fair trading and transparency of the market. That

227 Arguably, a first step in this direction was set in CoJ joined cases C-295/04 to C-298/04, *Manfredi*. Still, this step seems a hesitant one when compared with the considerably more detailed approach set out in in the *Francovich* and *Brasserie du Pêcheur* case law. Indeed, some deduce from this lack of detail that it is as yet too early to speak of a principle of private party liability that is comparable with the principle of Member State liability. See e.g. Leczykiewicz (2010a), p. 257.

228 Cf. by contrast Opinion AG Geelhoed case C-253/00, *Muñoz*, where issues such as the creation of rights for, the direct (economic) interests of and the legal standing of the private party applicants are discussed in much greater detail.

229 Most notably, the private parties in CoJ case C-432/05, *Unibet*, sought to invoke this ruling. This claim was not explicitly addressed by the CoJ, but the AG rejected it, based on a rather narrow reading of *Muñoz*. See Opinion AG Sharpston case C-432/05, *Unibet*, para 53.

230 This statement was subsequently complemented in CoJ joined cases C-295/04 to C-298/04, *Manfredi*, para 61, where it was held that '*any individual can claim compensation for the harm suffered where there is a causal relationship between that harm and an agreement or practice prohibited under Article [101 TFEU]*'. See para 6.15 below.

231 See para 9.08 below.

suggests that the logic of the *Muñoz* ruling might be applied more broadly.[232] At the very least it highlights that the principle of private party liability can also apply outside the field of EU competition law (*sensu stricto*). *Muñoz* also does not merely concern the permissibility of a bar on civil proceedings by a specific party in a situation where such proceedings were generally already possible under national law, as was the case in *Courage*. Rather it provides that such proceedings should be made possible in a situation where they were not possible at all under the national law as it stood. Nor is *Muñoz* limited to actions for damages. It instead concerned the bringing of civil proceedings to address an infringement of EU law by a private party generally. All this implies a substantial step into the realm of the Member States' procedural autonomy. A reference to the principle of national procedural autonomy is indeed notably absent in *Muñoz*.

232 In a similar sense, see Betlem (2003), p. 213.

Part B

SELECTED EU LEGISLATION

3

PUBLIC PROCUREMENT LAW

Part B of this book focuses on the selected EU legislation facilitating the private enforcement of EU law before national courts. It consists of four chapters, each chapter being dedicated to a particular field of EU law and the specific legislative measures adopted in that connection. The present Chapter 3 is concerned with the Procurement Remedies Directives relating to EU public procurement law. The first section below introduces these directives by discussing the relevant substantive rules, their background and a number of general issues. The following two sections then assess in more detail the content of these directives. To that aim the remedies set out therein are first outlined and analysed, followed by a discussion of the most important procedural provisions. In the final section of this chapter attention is paid to certain other issues related to the enforcement of EU public procurement law.

A. INTRODUCTION

The first subsection below outlines the main substantive[1] rules of EU law on public procurement. In the following subsection the Procurement Remedies Directives are introduced, with particular regard to the process leading to their adoption, their objective and scope as well as their revision in 2007. Finally, a

1 The word "substantive" is used here so as to distinguish the rules in question from the enforcement-related rules laid down in Procurement Remedies Directives 89/665 and 92/13. All public procurement rules are, however, in a sense procedural, in that they are in essence concerned with the process of selecting an undertaking for the award of a public contract.

number of additional general remarks are made as regards the broader context in which these directives operate.

1. Substantive EU public procurement law

3.01 The economic importance of public procurement is significant. Spending by public authorities in the EU on the procurement of works, services and supplies has been estimated to account for more than 18 per cent of the EU's accumulated gross domestic product.[2] Traditionally many governments used public procurement, to various degrees and in various manners, to favour domestic undertakings or to achieve certain national policy objectives. This is clearly often difficult to reconcile with the EU's efforts to establish an internal market. The EU has therefore stepped in to regulate this field. In 1971 it adopted a first directive on public work contracts.[3] Over the following decades the EU public procurement regime has been replaced, expanded and updated several times.

3.02 At present there are two general substantive EU directives on public procurement in force. The first is Directive 2004/18 on public procurement in what is known as the "public" sector ("Public Sector Procurement Directive").[4] This directive covers what could be called "regular" public contracts awarded by national, regional or local authorities and semi-public entities of the Member States. Typical examples of the types of contracts covered include the construction of a public library, the supply of computers to a municipality or the provision of accounting services to a national ministry.[5] Since 1990 the substantive EU public procurement regime has been extended so as to also cover the "utilities" sectors. To that effect a separate directive has been adopted, which is now Directive 2004/17 ("Utilities Procurement Directive").[6] The latter covers essentially the same sort of contracts as the Public Sector Procurement Directive, but it applies where these contracts are awarded by entities operating in the water, energy, transport and postal services sectors. In practice the Public Sector Procurement Directive is the more important of the two above-mentioned directives (collectively "Substantive Procurement Directives"), as it accounts for around 80 per cent of the published contract awards, expressed in terms of

2 Commission, Proposal for New Public Sector Procurement Directive 2014/24, COM(2011) 896, p. 2.

3 Directive 71/305/EEC concerning the coordination of procedures for the award of public works contracts, OJ 1971, L 185/5.

4 Directive 2004/18/EC concerning the coordination of procedures for the award of public works contracts, public supplies contracts and public service contracts, OJ 2004, L 134/114.

5 Pursuant to Annex II to Public Sector Procurement Directive 2004/18, not all services are fully covered.

6 Directive 2004/17/EC coordinating the procurement procedures of entities operating in the water, energy, transport and postal services sectors, OJ 2004, L 134/1.

value.[7] Since 2009 the two Substantive Procurement Directives are complemented by a third directive, Directive 2009/81 on public procurement in the fields of defence and security ("Defence Procurement Directive").[8]

In 2014 two new substantive directives were adopted, namely Directive 2014/24 on public procurement ("New Public Sector Procurement Directive") and Directive 2014/25 on procurement by entities operating in the water, energy, transport and postal services sectors ("New Utilities Procurement Directive").[9] These two new directives, which are to be transposed into national law by April 2016, repeal and replace the above-mentioned current Substantive Procurement Directives. While they imply certain significant changes to the substantive rules in question, these new directives leave the main structure and objective of those rules unaltered. At the same time Directive 2014/23 on the award of concession contracts ("Concessions Awards Directive") was also adopted.[10] The latter is an entirely new, additional directive setting out certain substantive rules on public procurement. It covers a specific category of contracts that had hitherto largely remained unregulated as a matter of secondary EU law, namely concessions.[11]

As was noted above, the Substantive Procurement Directives (and also the Concessions Awards Directive) should be understood as part of a broader effort to establish the EU's internal market. These directives give concrete expression to the freedom of establishment and the freedom to provide services set out in the EU Treaties.[12] They have been adopted on the basis of Articles 53, 62 and 114 TFEU. In essence these substantive rules seek to eliminate barriers to the exercise of those freedoms, ensure the development of effective competition in the award of public contracts and in so doing protect the interests of private parties that wish to offer goods or services to contracting authorities established in another Member State.[13] As such the provisions of these directives are in **3.03**

7 Commission, Annual public procurement implementation review 2012, SWD(2012) 342, p. 10.

8 Directive 2009/81/EC on the coordination of procedures for the award of certain works contracts, supply contracts and service contracts by contracting authorities or entities in the fields of defence and security, OJ 2009, L 216/76. On this directive, see further Trybus (2013), p. 3.

9 Directive 2014/24/EU on public procurement, OJ 2014, L 94/65; Directive 2014/25/EU on procurement by entities operating in the water, energy, transport and postal services sectors, OJ 2014, L 94/243. See further Commission, Green paper on the modernisation of EU public procurement policy, COM(2011) 15; Kotsonis (2011a), p. NA51; Williams (2012), p. NA101; Kotsonis (2014), p. 169; Caranta (2015), p. 391.

10 Directive 2014/23/EU on the award of concession contracts, OJ 2014, L 94/1. On this directive, see further Craven (2014), p. 188; Farley and Pourbaix (2015), p. 15.

11 The difference between concessions and "ordinary" public contracts is the method of remuneration and, in particular, that in the former case the holder of the concession bears the risks related to the economic activity at issue. See e.g. CoJ case C-348/10, *Norma*, para 41–4; CoJ case C-269/14, *Kansaneläkelaito*, para 31.

12 Cf. Drijber and Stergiou (2009), p. 805.

13 CoJ case 31/87, *Beentjes*, para 21 and 42; CoJ case C-433/93, *Commission v Germany*, para 19; CoJ joined cases C-20/01 and C-28/01, *Commission v Germany*, para 35; CoJ case C-507/03, *Commission v Ireland*, para 27–8.

many cases directly effective and confer rights on the private parties concerned; they are intended to protect undertakings against arbitrary behaviour on the part of the contracting authority.[14]

The Substantive Procurement Directives are largely similar in terms of content. The basic idea is that the contracting authorities covered must publish a notice, containing information on the contract that they intend to award and inviting interested undertakings to submit a bid. They further lay down rules for the subsequent contract award procedure, relating among other things to the applicable time periods, the selection of tenderers and the criteria to be used for awarding the contract. On the whole the Utilities Procurement Directive tends to leave contracting authorities[15] somewhat more flexibility than its sibling, the Public Sector Remedies Directive.

These directives only apply to contracts the estimated value of which exceeds certain threshold values. These thresholds are adjusted at regular intervals and vary somewhat between both directives. At present the thresholds for awards under the Public Sector Procurement Directive stand at approximately €5 million for public works contracts and approximately €130 000 (central government) or €200 000 (other contracting authorities) for supply and services contracts.[16]

2. Procurement Remedies Directives: General issues

3.04 Having adopted substantive rules on public procurement at EU level at a relatively early stage, over the years it became clear that the compliance with these rules left much to be desired. Infringements of these rules can take many forms. A public contract can for instance be awarded directly, that is, without any prior publication and competition, contrary to what is required, as a general rule, under the Substantive Procurement Directives. Infringements can also consist of the preferential treatment of certain tenderers, for example by providing them with more information, ranking their bids higher without

---

14 See e.g. CoJ case C-433/93, *Commission v Germany*, para 18; CoJ case C-54/96, *Dorsch Consult*, para 44–5. As noted by Prechal (2005), pp. 110 and 122, this appears to come close to a statement that they confer rights. See also Opinion AG Bot case C-19/13, *Fastweb*, para 43. See further Fernández Martín (1996), pp. 200–201; Arrowsmith (2005), pp. 161–2 and 1393; Trepte (2007), p. 537; Pijnacker Hordijk, Van der Bend and Van Nouhuys (2009), pp. 20–21. On the relationship between direct effect and the conferral of rights more generally, see para 2.04 above.

15 "Contracting authority" is the term used in Public Sector Procurement Directive 2004/18 (Art. 1(9)). Utilities Procurement Directive 2004/17 refers to "contracting entities" (Art. 2). For practical reasons, the former term is used here to indicate all bodies covered by the substantive EU procurement rules.

16 Commission Regulation (EU) No 1336/2013 amending Directives 2004/17/EC, 2004/18/EC and 2009/81/EC in respect of the application thresholds for the procedures for the award of contracts, OJ 2013, L 335/17.

objective justification or the unjustified exclusion of an undertaking from the contract award procedure. The Commission's 1985 white paper on completing the internal market observed that the application of substantive EU law on public procurement was '*minimal*'.[17] It also appeared that the private parties affected by such infringements only rarely took legal action to remedy the consequences thereof.[18]

Therefore in 1987 the Commission published a proposal for a directive, which it amended a year later.[19] Here it expanded on the general lack of compliance with the substantive EU public procurement rules. It noted that '*both national and [EU] monitoring arrangements are unable to ensure strict compliance with the [Substantive Procurement Directives], in particular before violation of those rules becomes irreparable*'.[20] The Commission also highlighted the particular challenges encountered in a public procurement context. It stated that: **3.05**

> infringements [...] generally occur before the definitive award of the contract. Since contract award procedures are of short duration – a decision being taken within a few weeks – any failure to comply with the [EU] rules in question needs to be dealt with urgently and rapidly. Further, most such infringements differ from other types in that the irregularity committed is procedural. A procedural irregularity may be enough to exclude an enterprise from a given award procedure, and this encourages discriminatory practices.[21]

In conclusion it was said that, '*with a view to the optimal functioning of the internal market and in order for the [EU] rules on the award of public contracts to have real impact and change mentalities*', it must be ensured that the private parties concerned have easy access to effective remedies at the national level.[22] To this end the proposed directive aimed to '*ensure minimum coordination and strengthen national procedures by the courts [...] so as to ensure that the rules of public contracts are correctly applied*'.[23]

This Commission proposal was not uncontroversial, however. In the course of the law-making process it was the object of rather intense and lengthy discussions in Council (which at the time was the sole legislator) and it underwent

17 Commission, White paper on completing the internal market, COM(85) 310, p. 25.
18 Cf. Cleary Gottlieb, Steen and Hamilton (1988).
19 Commission, Proposal for Public Sector Remedies Directive 89/665, COM(87) 134; Commission, Amended proposal for Public Sector Remedies Directive 89/665, COM(88) 733.
20 Commission, Amended proposal for Public Sector Remedies Directive 89/665, COM(88) 733, p. 6.
21 Ibid., p. 7.
22 Ibid., p. 8.
23 Ibid., p. 10.

considerable modifications.[24] Member States objected in particular to the proposed powers for the Commission to intervene directly at national level to address alleged infringements of the EU procurement rules, further discussed below.[25] Another controversial issue was the concern that the proposed review procedures might lead to abuses by "cowboy tenderers" without a meritorious claim.[26] The proposal nonetheless led to the adoption in 1989 of the Public Sector Remedies Directive.[27] This directive applies to contracts in the public sector, as described above.[28] It was adopted on the basis of Article 114 TFEU, which is the provision of the EU Treaties that allows for the establishment of secondary EU law for the establishment and functioning of the internal market.

3.06 After the adoption of a substantive directive relating to the utilities sector in 1990, it was furthermore clear to the Commission that '*[t]he availability of adequate remedies and control procedures is as important in the hitherto "excluded sectors" as it is in the general field of public procurement*'.[29] In that year it therefore submitted a proposal for a second directive to complement the Public Sector Remedies Directive.[30] This became the Utilities Remedies Directive, which was adopted in 1992, also on the basis of Article 114 TFEU.[31] This directive covers contracts awarded by entities operating in the water, energy, transport and postal services sectors. The Utilities Remedies Directive seeks to take account of the particular characteristics of the entities operating in the utilities sectors that it covers.[32] For that reason it contains a number of specific provisions that generally allow for more flexibility as compared with the Public Sector Remedies Directive.

3.07 These two Procurement Remedies Directives are nonetheless similar in many respects.[33] They are therefore treated jointly here; they are distinguished only where there is a particular reason for doing so.[34] Both directives provide that the existing arrangements at national and EU level for ensuring the '*effective application*' of the Substantive Procurement Directives are '*not always adequate*

---

24 Fernández Martín (1996), p. 206. As regards the legislative history of this directive more generally, see Hebly (2011), pp. 5–262.

25 See para 3.33 below.

26 Gormley (1997), p. 157.

27 Public Sector Remedies Directive 89/665.

28 See para 3.02 above.

29 Commission, Proposal for Utilities Remedies Directive 92/13, COM(90) 297, p. 8.

30 Ibid.

31 Utilities Remedies Directive 92/13.

32 Commission, Proposal for Utilities Remedies Directive 92/13, COM(90) 297, p. 9.

33 Cf. CoJ case C-455/08, *Commission v Ireland*, para 26.

34 For the same reasons, the case law cited in the following, which typically relates to only one of these two directives, is "generalised", in the sense that it is also understood to relate to the other directive. Where the numbering of the articles differs between these two directives, this is specifically indicated.

to ensure compliance', which in turn could deter undertakings from other Member States from participating in contract award procedures.[35] These directives therefore seek to ensure that '*effective and rapid remedies*' are available in case of infringements.[36]

As the Court of Justice has clarified, the objective of the Procurement Remedies Directives is '*to guarantee the existence of effective remedies for infringements of [EU] law in the field of public procurement or of the national rules implementing that law, so as to ensure the effective application of the [Substantive Procurement Directives]*'.[37] On other occasions the Court has formulated this objective somewhat differently, however, namely '*to ensure that unlawful decisions taken by the contracting authorities may be reviewed effectively and as rapidly as possible*'[38] or '*to protect tenderers against arbitrary behaviour on the part of the contracting authority*'.[39]

The scope of the Procurement Remedies Directives essentially coincides with the Substantive Procurement Directive to which they relate.[40] That means that a public contract that is covered by the Public Sector Procurement Directive is also covered by the Public Sector Remedies Directive, while the same parallelism applies as regards the Utilities Procurement Directive and Utilities Remedies Directive in relation to the award of contracts in the utilities sector.[41] In this manner the two Procurement Remedies Directives thus cover in principle all decisions that are taken by contracting authorities concerning contract award procedures falling under the EU's Substantive Procurement Directives. Under the new substantive EU public procurement regime, adopted in 2014, this logic is retained, subject to a widening of the scope of the Procurement Remedies Directive so as to cover also infringements of the substantive rules set out in the new Concessions Awards Directive.[42] However, the Procurement Remedies Directives do not cover infringements of the Defence Procurement Directive. This latter directive contains a set of enforcement-related provisions of its **3.08**

35 Recitals 1, 2 and 4 Public Sector Remedies Directive 89/665. See also recitals 1–3 Utilities Remedies Directive 92/13.

36 Recital 3 Public Sector Remedies Directive 89/665. See also recital 6 Utilities Remedies Directive 92/13.

37 CoJ case C-406/08, *Uniplex*, para 26. See e.g. also CoJ case C-392/93, *British Telecom*, para 26; CoJ case C-314/09, *Stadt Graz*, para 33, 39 and 43; CoJ case C-440/13, *Croce Amica One Italia*, para 42.

38 CoJ case C-455/08, *Commission v Ireland*, para 26; CoJ case C444/06, *Commission v Spain*, para 44; CoJ case C-100/12, *Fastweb*, para 25.

39 CoJ case C-538/13, *eVigilo*, para 50.

40 Art. 1(1) Procurement Remedies Directives 89/665 and 92/13.

41 Cf. CoJ case C-214/00, *Commission v Spain*, para 50 and 79.

42 See Art. 46 and 47 Concessions Awards Directive 2014/23.

own.[43] Although there are certain differences, which generally provide for additional flexibility, those provisions are largely similar to those of the Procurement Remedies Directives.

In this context the term "decision" is to be interpreted broadly.[44] That implies that the scope of the Procurement Remedies is rather wide in this respect. However, only contracts covered by substantive *EU* law on public procurement are covered by these directives. Contracts covered by "purely" *national* public procurement rules (that is, rules of national law other than those transposing the Substantive Procurement Directives) are not covered. The Commission had originally proposed applying the Procurement Remedies Directives also to infringements of these latter rules.[45] This would have meant that these directives could, for instance, also be relied upon in disputes relating to public contracts of a value below the thresholds set out in the Substantive Procurement Directives, but which are nonetheless subject to national public procurement rules. The EU legislature (at the time only the Council) rejected this aspect of the Commission's proposal, however. The Procurement Remedies Directives now stipulate that there should be no discrimination between undertakings claiming harm in the context of a procedure for the award of a contract as a result of the distinction made by these directives between national rules implementing EU law and other ("purely") national rules.[46]

3.09 In 2007 the two Procurement Remedies Directives were substantially revised, which resulted in their amendment through Directive 2007/66 ("Procurement Remedies Amending Directive").[47] This time the legislative process was on the whole relatively swift.[48] This revision generally aimed to '*give greater encouragement to [EU] enterprises to tender in any Member State of the [EU] by providing*

43 Art. 55–64 Defence Procurement Directive 2009/81.

44 In this context a "decision" is any act of a contracting authority adopted in relation to a public contract which falls within the material scope of one of the Substantive Procurement Directives and which is capable of producing legal effects, regardless of whether that act is adopted outside a formal contract award procedure or as part thereof (including therefore a decision *not* to initiate such a procedure). See CoJ C-92/00, *Hospital Ingenieure*, para 48–52; CoJ case C-26/03, *Stadt Halle*, para 34–5.

45 See Commission, Proposal for Public Sector Remedies Directive 89/665, COM(87) 134, p. 6 (Art. 1).

46 Art. 1(2) Procurement Remedies Directives 89/665 and 92/13.

47 Directive 2007/66/EC amending Council Directives 89/665/EEC and 92/13/EEC with regard to improving the effectiveness of review procedures concerning the award of public contracts, OJ 2007, L 335/31. On this revision, see further Wilman (2008), p. 115; Bel (2008), p. 106; Golding and Henty (2008), p. 146; Williams (2008), p. NA19.

48 Agreement between the co-legislators was reached in the first reading of the ordinary legislative procedure. At the outset the Commission had noted that '*virtual consensus*' existed among Member States and interested parties alike at least as regards the main problems to be tackled. See Commission, Proposal for Procurement Remedies Amending Directive 2007/66, COM(2006) 195, p. 4. The Commission's proposal has been criticised in the legal doctrine, however, for imposing an unnecessary and inappropriate degree of uniformity. See e.g.

them with the certainty that they can, if need be, effectively seek effective review if their interests seem to have been adversely affected in procedures for awarding contracts', with a view to '*prompt[ing] awarding authorities to adopt better publication and tendering procedures for the benefit of all involved*'.[49] It follows that the overall objective of the Procurement Remedies Directives remained essentially unchanged after their revision. As was the case when the first of these directives was adopted, the possibility of an increase in "nuisance actions" was also considered in relation to this revision. The Commission considered this risk to be limited, however.[50] The amendments proposed by the Commission as part of this revision were rather narrowly focused. The precise amendments finally adopted are discussed in further detail in the following. Suffice to note here that this amendment essentially sought to address the following two main shortcomings.[51]

The first was the problem of *illegal direct awards*. This refers to the situation where a public contract is awarded to an undertaking without any preceding publication and competition having taken place in violation of the Substantive Procurement Directives. The Court of Justice had earlier identified this as the most serious type of infringement of EU public procurement law.[52] Such infringements are often difficult to detect, both for the Commission and for a private party that might wish to contest the decision to "directly" award the contract. After all, no publication or other form of transparency has taken place. The second main shortcoming identified was what was called the "*race to signature*". This refers to the situation where upon the completion of a contract award procedure an aggrieved private party has brought or intends bringing a case, for instance challenging the decision to award the contract at issue to a competitor, but the contract is concluded anyhow before that dispute is resolved. Before the 2007 revision of the Procurement Remedies Directives, concluded contracts were in principle to be respected in most Member States, even where they were the result of a contract award procedure that was not compliant with EU public procurement law.[53] And even where national law allowed for the setting aside of concluded contracts, claims to this effect were still often found to be rejected on the basis of a balance of convenience test applied by the national court seised. As a consequence, contract award decisions could not be reviewed and annulled where necessary at the pre-contractual

Arrowsmith (2005), p. 1438. As regards the legislative history of this directive more generally, see further Hebly (2011), pp. 543–860.

49 Commission, Proposal for Procurement Remedies Amending Directive 2007/66, COM(2006) 195, p. 2.

50 Commission, Impact assessment report on remedies in the field of public procurement, SEC(2006) 557, p. 30.

51 Ibid., pp. 8–11.

52 CoJ case C-26/03, *Stadt Halle*, para 37.

53 As was, for example, the case in the Netherlands, pursuant to national case law (HR case 16747, *Uneto v De Vliert*).

stage. All that then remained for the aggrieved private party concerned was the possibility of bringing an action for damages.

3. Additional general remarks

3.10 The fact that the Procurement Remedies Directives provide for common rules on review procedures for public procurement disputes inevitably implies that the Member States' scope for autonomous decision-making is reduced. Where necessary, Member States had to amend their existing national laws so as to ensure compliance with these directives. Nevertheless, efforts were made to respect existing national practices as much as possible.[54] As the Commission highlighted in 1990, '*[c]onsiderable flexibility is left for the Member States to implement the directive's requirements in accordance with their particular approaches to administrative and judicial review, including the procedural and other conditions applying to such remedies [so as to] facilitate the insertion of the new remedies into existing national structures*'.[55] Similarly, at the time of the 2007 revision, it stated that '*Member States will retain their power to appoint bodies responsible for the review procedures and to maintain the national procedural rules applicable to such reviews (respect for the Member States' procedural autonomy)*'.[56]

On many points this translates into the wording of the Procurement Remedies Directives. For example, as is discussed in further detail below, a significant number of the measures provided for are merely optional or can be implemented in various manners.[57] Accordingly, as the Court of Justice noted, these directives leave '*Member States discretion in the choice of the procedural safeguards it provides, and the formalities relating thereto*'.[58] The harmonisation established is thus "minimum" (or "partial"); it does not entail "maximum" (or "complete") harmonisation.[59] That means among other things that the Member States are in principle entitled to lay down further-reaching rules on the issues covered by these directives.

---

54 Cf. Commission, Report on the impact and effectiveness of EU public procurement legislation, SEC(2011) 853, p. 73. See also Weiss (1993), p. 104; Bovis (2007), p. 370; Trepte (2007), pp. 530 and 544.

55 Commission, Proposal for Utilities Remedies Directive 92/13, COM(90) 297, p. 15.

56 Commission, Proposal for Procurement Remedies Amending Directive 2007/66, COM(2006) 195, p. 7.

57 See e.g. Art. 1(4), 1(5), 2b, 2d(2) and 2d(3) Procurement Remedies Directives 89/665 and 92/13.

58 CoJ case C-568/08, *Combinatie Spijker*, para 57. See also CoJ case C-440/13, *Croce Amica One Italia*, para. 40, where it is held that these directives do '*no more than coordinate existing mechanisms in member States in order to ensure the full and effective application of the directives laying down substantive rules concerning public contracts*'. In other cases the CoJ has stressed, however, that these directives seek to *reinforce* such existing mechanisms. See e.g. CoJ case C-538/13, *eVigilo*, para 50.

59 CoJ case C-570/08, *Simvoulio*, para 37.

Certain particularities of public procurement law and the disputes relating thereto should also be highlighted here. An obvious point is that, although there are certain limited exceptions,[60] this field of law concerns rules that regulate the relationship between a public or semi-public body, on the one hand, and one or more private parties (undertakings), on the other hand. In many national jurisdictions across the EU such relationships are subject to a particular legal regime. But these regimes differ considerably in terms of content and character.[61] In many Member States, such as Germany, France, Spain and Belgium, this field of law is regulated by a mixture of administrative and civil law. This typically means that decisions up to and including the stage of the award of the contract are subject to review by the administrative courts, while disputes related to the execution of the contract and liability in damages are subject to civil law. But there are also jurisdictions, for instance England and the Netherlands, where review is in principle exercised only by the civil courts. **3.11**

Disputes relating to contract award procedures furthermore generally concern more than two parties. The very aim of these procedures is after all to have several undertakings competing for the public contract at issue. This implies that in many disputes account must also be taken of the legitimate interests of third parties, normally the other (potential) tenderers whose bid was either not successful or who were not allowed to submit a bid in the first place. Speed is often also a key concern.[62] Swift resolution of public procurement disputes, notably before the conclusion of the public contract at issue, means that the aggrieved undertaking or undertakings can still have a chance to win the contract. It also means that the contract award procedure – and consequently the award and execution of the contract – are not too much delayed because of the dispute, which is generally in the interest of all parties concerned.

The EU's Procurement Remedies Directives should further be understood in their international context. This context consists in particular of the Agreement on Government Procurement ("GPA"), concluded under the auspices of the World Trade Organization ("WTO"). The GPA is an international agreement to which, besides countries such as the United States, Canada, South Korea and **3.12**

60 Substantive Procurement Directives 2004/17 and 2004/18 can in certain cases also cover private undertakings. See e.g. Art. 56 Public Sector Procurement Directive 2004/18 on concessionaires and Art. 2(2)(b) Utilities Procurement Directive 2004/17 on undertakings operating on the basis of special or exclusive rights.

61 See further Bovis (2007), pp. 381–97; Hebly, De Boer and Wilman (2007), p. 155; Treumer and Lichère (2011), pp. 105–328. See also Study, Italian Authority for the Supervision of Public Contracts (2010).

62 Cf. CoJ case C-568/08, *Combinatie Spijker*, para 5.

Switzerland, both the EU and its Member States are parties.[63] It is the successor of an earlier agreement concluded in 1979 in the context of the General Agreement on Tariffs and Trade ("GATT").[64] Negotiations on the new agreement started in 1986 and were concluded in 1994.[65] The GPA entered into force in 1996. A revised version of the GPA entered into force in April 2014.[66] The main objectives and means of the substantive public procurement rules set out in the GPA are, broadly speaking, comparable with those of the EU.

Most important for present purposes is that the GPA also contains specific provisions on what are called "domestic review procedures". Through these procedures private parties are given a role in enforcing the substantive rules at issue. This characteristic sets this international agreement apart from its predecessor and most other WTO agreements.[67] This GPA framework for domestic review procedures could be called a slimmed-down version of the EU's regime established in the Procurement Remedies Directives. It leaves the countries concerned significant space to provide for a system that is consistent with their respective legal, constitutional and administrative traditions.[68] Yet it nonetheless lays down a number of key obligations in this regard. Most notably, there is a general obligation to provide for a '*timely, effective, transparent and non-discriminatory administrative or judicial review procedure*' through which private parties that have or have had an interest can challenge breaches of the GPA or the rules implementing it.[69] These parties must be allowed sufficient time to prepare and submit such challenges, with a minimum of ten days. While consensual dispute resolution is to be encouraged, at least one impartial and independent administrative or judicial authority must be designated, which must be competent to rule on these challenges at least on appeal. Where the review bodies are not courts, certain additional requirements apply. Furthermore, '*rapid interim measures [which] preserve the suppliers' opportunities to*

63 Given the diverging range of obligations and its optional nature under WTO law, the GPA is effectively rather a series of bilateral treaties than a single multilateral arrangement. See Arrowsmith (2005), p. 1330.

64 Decision 80/271/EEC concerning the conclusion of the Multilateral Agreements resulting from the 1973 to 1979 trade negotiations, OJ 1980, L 71/1.

65 See Decision 94/800/EC concerning the conclusion on behalf of the European Community, as regards matters within its competence, of the agreements reached in the Uruguay Round multilateral negotiations (1986–1994), OJ 1994, L 336/1.

66 As a consequence of this revision some of the GPA's provisions referred to above were amended, without, however, substantially altering them. On this revision see further Zhang (2011), p. 483; Anderson (2012), p. 83; Williams (2014), p. NA29; Anderson (2014), p. NA160.

67 Arrowsmith (2003), p. 385. These domestic review procedures apply in addition to the "regular" WTO dispute settlement regime, which is essentially an intergovernmental affair, provided for in Art. XX GPA.

68 *Ibid.*

69 Art. XVIII(1) GPA.

participate in the procurement' must be provided for under the GPA.[70] It is added that *'[s]uch interim measures may result in suspension of the procurement process'*, although *'[o]verriding adverse consequences for the interests concerned, including the public interest, may be taken into account in deciding whether such measures should be applied'*.[71] In addition, provision must be made for the possibility of *'corrective action or compensation for the loss or damages suffered, which may be limited to either the costs for the preparation of the tender or the costs relating to the challenge, or both'*.[72]

B. REMEDIES

Having discussed in the foregoing the relevant substantive rules as well as the background of and certain general issues relating to the Procurement Remedies Directives, attention now turns to the content of these directives. As their abbreviated name indicates, a set of remedies lies at the heart of the Procurement Remedies Directives. These remedies can be distinguished by the stage that the contract award procedure is in, especially whether or not that procedure has already led to the conclusion of the public contract put out to tender. The first subsection below concentrates on the remedies relating to the *pre-contractual* stage, namely interim measures and the setting aside of unlawful decisions. The following two subsections subsequently discuss actions for damages and the contractual remedy for which the Procurement Remedies Directives provide, both of which are primarily of relevance in the stage *after* the conclusion of the contract.

1. Interim measures and setting aside injunctions

A first remedy that is of particular relevance at the pre-contractual stage provided for in the two Procurement Remedies Directives is *interim measures*. These directives stipulate that the competent national courts[73] must have the power to take *'at the earliest opportunity and by way of interlocutory procedures, interim measures with the aim of correcting the alleged infringements or preventing further damage to the interests concerned'*. As the Court of Justice has recalled, the measures that may thus be taken do not finally determine the legal situation; they rather provide for a provisional arrangement.[74] The directives specify that **3.13**

70 Art. XVIII(7)(a) GPA.

71 Ibid.

72 Art. XVIII(7)(b) GPA.

73 For reasons of simplicity, reference is made above only to "courts", notwithstanding that under Directives 89/665 and 92/13 other review bodies can also be designated. See para 3.28 below.

74 Cf. CoJ case C-568/08, *Combinatie Spijker*, para 61.

this power must include in any case the possibility for the court seised to suspend ongoing contract award procedures and the implementation of any decision taken by the contracting authority.[75]

The Procurement Remedies Directives further expressly provide that a balance of interests test is permissible in this connection.[76] Accordingly, a national court deciding on an application for interim measures may take account of the probable consequences of these measures for all interests likely to be harmed, including the public interest. Where the negative consequences could exceed the benefits, it may be decided not to grant the measures, without prejudice to any other claim that the private party applicant in question may bring. The application of this test can be problematic in practice, however. For national courts can tend to give greater weight to the public interests related to not endangering or delaying the execution of the public contract in question (for example the timely completion of public infrastructural works or the timely supply of certain goods to a hospital or a school) that may be at stake, than to the individual interests of a private party applicant. In 1996 an EU-wide study found that this could be an important impediment to the availability of this remedy.[77] The Commission noted a similar tendency in the context of the 2007 revision, without, however, proposing to address this concern through legislative amendments.[78]

The Court of Justice has clarified that it is in principle permissible for the national court seised to take account of the chances of success of an action on the merits when deciding an application for interim measures under the Procurement Remedies Directives, in light of the absence of any express EU rules on this matter and the EU law principle of effectiveness.[79] Yet it has also held that an application for interim measures cannot be made dependent on the applicant previously having brought proceedings on the merits, even where that is merely a formality.[80]

3.14 As a second remedy the Procurement Remedies Directives require that the competent national courts are empowered to *set aside* unlawful decisions taken by contracting authorities in the context of a contract award procedure. One

75 Art. 2(1)(a) Procurement Remedies Directives 89/665 and 92/13. Cf. Art. 2(4) Public Sector Remedies Directive 89/665 and Art. 2(3a) Utilities Remedies Directive 92/12, which provide that the initiation of review procedures generally need not necessarily have automatic suspensive effect.

76 Art. 2(5) Public Sector Remedies Directive 89/665; Art. 2(4) Utilities Remedies Directive 92/13.

77 Study, Herbert Smith (1996), pp. 10–11.

78 Commission, Impact assessment report on remedies in the field of public procurement, SEC(2006) 557, p. 15.

79 CoJ Order case C-424/01, *CS Communications*, para 26–33.

80 CoJ case C-214/00, *Commission v Spain*, para 99–100. See also CoJ case C-236/95, *Commission v Greece*, para 11.

could think of a decision to award the contract to a particular party or to exclude a tenderer in violation of the Substantive Procurement Directives.

The Procurement Remedies Directives specify that this power to set aside an unlawful decision includes the possible removal of discriminatory technical, economic or financial specifications in the tender documents.[81] This addition can be of significant relevance in practice, given that the setting of such specifications can be an (indirect) means to prevent undertakings from other Member States from participating or having a fair chance in a contract award procedure. Examples of such unlawful specifications include the specification in the tender documents of the name of a particular product or the requirement of a particular environmental certificate, without making it clear that equivalent products or certificates are also allowed.[82]

Lastly, the Utilities Remedies Directive – but not the Public Sector Remedies Directive – offers the Member States an *alternative* for the two above-mentioned remedies (that is, interim measures and the setting aside of unlawful decisions). Instead of these two remedies, Member States may provide for the power to take '*other measures*' with the aim of correcting any identified infringement and preventing injury to the interests concerned. This could concern ordering the payment of '*a particular sum*' in cases where the infringement has not been corrected or prevented.[83] **3.15**

This arrangement was introduced because the two aforementioned remedies were considered to directly affect the decision-making of the entities operating in the utilities sector covered by this directive. That was seen as unacceptable, given the autonomy that these entities enjoy in the legal systems of certain Member States.[84]

The Commission initially sought to establish a minimum for the amount of this sum. Its proposal for the Utilities Remedies Directive stipulated that this amount should be not less than 1 per cent of the value of the contract at issue, so as to ensure a minimum level of deterrence. However, this suggestion was rejected by the Council.[85] Instead, a more general provision was included. It states that this sum should be set '*at a level high enough to dissuade the contracting*

81 Art. 2(1)(b) Procurement Remedies Directives 89/665 and 92/13.

82 CoJ case C-359/93, *Commission v Netherlands*, para 28; CoJ case C-368/10, *Commission v Netherlands*, para 70.

83 Art. 2(1)(c) Utilities Remedies Directive 92/13.

84 Commission, Proposal for Utilities Remedies Directive 92/13, COM(90) 297, pp. 11–12; Commission, Amended proposal for Utilities Remedies Directive 92/13, COM(91) 158, pp. 6 and 8.

85 Council, doc. 7333/91, p. 5.

entity from committing or persisting in an infringement'.[86] The Member States are entitled to leave it to the judiciary to set this sum on a case-by-case basis.[87]

2. Actions for damages

3.16 The Procurement Remedies Directives also provide for two forms of relief that are of particular relevance at the post-contractual stage, thus after the conclusion of the contested public contract that had been put out to tender. One of these is the possibility for the competent court to award damages. To this end the directives state quite simply that the Member States must ensure that the measures taken concerning the review procedures include provision for powers to '*award damages to persons harmed by an infringement*'.[88] While this provision is common to both directives, there is a difference between them where actions for damages are concerned.

The *Public Sector Remedies Directive* contains no further guidance on issues such as the heads of damages to be awarded, the procedures to be followed or the criteria to be applied. The Commission had made a (modest) suggestion in its initial proposal for this directive in 1987. It mentioned as heads of damages '*costs of unnecessary studies, foregone profits and lost opportunities*'.[89] But this part of the proposal was not retained by the EU legislature (at that time only the Council).

The situation is to some extent different, however, under the *Utilities Remedies Directive*, which was adopted a few years after the Public Sector Remedies Directive. In addition to the above-mentioned general provision on damages claims, it specifies that, where a claim is made for damages representing the costs of preparing a bid or of participating in an award procedure, the applicant shall be required '*only to prove an infringement of [EU] law in the field of procurement or national rules implementing that law and that he would have had a real chance of winning the contract and that, as a consequence of that infringement,*

86 Art. 2(5) Utilities Remedies Directive 92/13. At the time of the adoption of this directive, the Council and the Commission stated that payment of this sum to an entity that is directly or indirectly linked to the contracting authority through a common budget is not to be considered dissuasive. See Council, doc. 7250/91, p. 3.

87 CoJ case C-225/97, *Commission v France*, para 23–8.

88 Art. 2(1)(c) Public Sector Remedies Directive 89/665; Art. 2(1)(d) Utilities Remedies Directive 92/13. Pursuant to Art. 2(6) Public Sector Remedies Directive 89/665 and Art. 2(1) Utilities Remedies Directive 92/13, the Member States may further provide that the contested decision must first be set aside before damages can be claimed on the grounds that that decision was taken unlawfully.

89 Commission, Proposal for Public Sector Remedies Directive 89/665, COM(87) 134, p. 7 (Art. 1(3)). This aspect of the proposal was not explained in the explanatory memorandum. It was not retained in the amended proposal.

that chance was adversely affected'.[90] The industrial and commercial public service character of the utilities sector was deemed to make it more difficult for private parties to obtain the pre-contractual forms of relief discussed in the previous subsection. As the Commission explained in its proposal for this directive, the above provision on bidding costs therefore seeks to ensure that in all Member States claims for damages are a practical proposition and thus a genuine incentive to compliance.[91] The essence is that, in order to receive compensation for their bidding costs, aggrieved private parties need *not* prove that they would have been *awarded* the contract but for the infringement.[92] Providing such proof was considered extremely difficult in many cases. Instead, these private party applicants must "only" demonstrate that they had a *real chance* of winning the public contract at issue for them to obtain such compensation.

Also in this case the Commission had originally proposed going a step further by specifying in its proposal for the Utilities Remedies Directive that the amount of the compensation for these bidding costs would be deemed to be at least 1 per cent of the value of the contract.[93] It had called this '*a limited step designed to ensure that in all Member States claims for damages are a realistic possibility*'. According to the Commission this would be sufficient to meet the EU's immediate objectives in this field. It acknowledged that claims for other losses, such as lost profits, raise '*complex issues*' and would '*for the time being*' continue to be resolved under national law. It further stated that a high level of harmonisation of the quantification of damages would '*certainly encounter difficulties*' and therefore was '*an unrealistic objective*' at least at that stage (that is, in 1990), while adding that in the longer term it would have to be considered whether further action at EU level would be necessary. Even this limited step as regards the *ex ante* quantification of certain damages proved to be a bridge too far, however. It was deleted in the amended Commission proposal at the request of the European Parliament.[94] The latter argued that the amount of damages should be determined in each individual case, as bidding costs cannot be linked to the value of the contract at issue.[95]

In its 1996 green paper on public procurement in the EU the Commission noted certain discrepancies and shortcomings in relation to the provisions of **3.17**

90 Art. 2(7) Utilities Remedies Directive 92/13.

91 Commission, Proposal for Utilities Remedies Directive 92/13, COM(90) 297, pp. 12–13.

92 Cf. the statement made to this effect by the Council and the Commission, laid down in Council, doc. 7250/91, p. 4.

93 Commission, Proposal for Utilities Remedies Directive 92/13, COM(90) 297, pp. 13 and 19.

94 See Commission, Amended proposal for Utilities Remedies Directive 92/13, COM(91) 158, p. 19. Here it is simply stated that the extent of damages payable is to be determined by national law.

95 See European Parliament, Opinion on the proposal for Utilities Remedies Directive 92/13, OJ 1991, C 106/82.

national law implementing the directives' above rules on actions for damages.[96] This green paper pointed to diverging rules and difficulties in practice concerning the provision of proof and the quantification of damages. National courts were said to sometimes only award symbolic damages or compensation for the bidding costs. The Commission therefore floated the idea of making provision for '*liquidated damages of a sufficiently dissuasive sum, exceeding the damage suffered*'. But in its 1998 follow-up communication it did not further elaborate on these issues.[97] That was the case despite the fact that around the same time a study prepared at the Commission's request had found that '*no more than a handful*' of damages cases had arisen in the Member States.[98] This lack of damages litigation was observed to exist even in Member States where other forms of public procurement-related litigation were not unusual. A decade later, in the context of the 2007 revision of the Procurement Remedies Directives,[99] the Commission once more assessed the state of play in the Member States as regards actions for damages for infringements of EU public procurement law. It concluded that the numbers of actions brought remained very low, certainly when compared with the other available remedies.[100] Although there can be notable differences between the various jurisdictions in the EU and although more recently there appears to have been a modest increase, other reports largely confirm this assessment.[101]

Several factors are likely to play a role when seeking to explain this (at best) modest degree of damages litigation for infringements of the EU public procurement rules. The above-mentioned study from 1996 noted that such disputes may be settled out of court. It further pointed to the fact that the legal proceedings tend to be formalised, costly and time-consuming, that uncertainty exists, especially as regards the quantification of damages, and that applicants often have difficulties proving that but for the infringement the applicant would in all likelihood have won the contract, as is required in some jurisdictions as a precondition for damages awards.[102] Subsequent, more recent, assessments, including those carried out for the Commission, have led to similar findings.[103] In addition, it appears that undertakings are mostly

96 Commission, Green paper on public procurement in the EU, COM(96) 583, pp. 15 and 19.
97 Commission, Communication on public procurement in the EU, COM(1998) 143.
98 Study, Herbert Smith (1996), p. 18. See also Brown (1998), p. 93; Treumer (2006), p. 159.
99 On this revision, see also para 3.09 above.
100 Commission, Impact assessment report on remedies in the field of public procurement, SEC(2006) 557, p. 16.
101 Caranta (2011a), pp. 87–8; Fairgrieve and Lichère (2011), p. 192; Treumer (2011a), pp. 149–50. As regards the Netherlands, see also Hebly and Wilman (2010), p. 326.
102 Study, Herbert Smith (1996), pp. 18–19.
103 See in particular Commission, Impact assessment report on remedies in the field of public procurement, SEC(2006) 557, pp. 12 and 16. See also Commission, Responses to the consultation on the operation of national review procedures in the field of public procurement, 2004 (undertakings and lawyers); Fairgrieve and

interested in winning the contract rather than engaging in obtaining awards of damages.[104] Remedies such as interim measures and the setting aside of unlawful decisions discussed in the previous subsection may generally be more attractive from that perspective. Aggrieved private parties may moreover feel (correctly or not) that they would compromise their future business relationship with the contracting authority concerned if they were to initiate legal action ("don't bite the hand that feeds you"; fear of "blacklisting"). The fact that this would evidently be at odds with the EU procurement rules does not necessarily make this fear less real in practice, as is acknowledged in reports based on field research,[105] in the legal literature more generally[106] and by the Commission.[107] It has further been suggested that the generally limited manner in which the Procurement Remedies Directives' provisions on damages claims have been transposed into national law by the Member States also plays a role in this respect.[108]

Against this background, legal scholars and practitioners have over the years called for the inclusion of more detailed provisions in these directives.[109]

While largely acknowledging the above difficulties, amending the Procurement Remedies Directives was, however, not the way forward that the Commission opted for when revising this EU legislation in 2007. It took the view that, for public procurement purposes, actions for damages suffer from certain inherent limits. It pointed among other things to the lack of real corrective effects. This refers to the fact that, even if such a claim is successful, the private party concerned will still not win the contract. The Commission also noted that the above-mentioned fear of private parties of compromising their future business relationship with the contracting authorities concerned limits the deterrent effect of actions for damages. That being so, the Commission considered that '*damages, in the specific context of public procurement procedures, present a less* **3.18**

Lichère (2011), pp. 192–4. Cf. Dahlgaard Dingel (1999), p. 239; Arrowsmith, Linarelli and Wallace (2000), pp. 752 and 759–60; Bovis (2007), pp. 438–9; Trepte (2007), p. 559; Caranta (2011b), p. 175.

104 Cf. Commission, Amended proposal for Utilities Remedies Directive 92/13, COM(91) 158, p. 13. See also Fernández Martín (1996), p. 213; Trepte (2007), pp. 562–3; Bowsher and Moser (2006), p. 196; Caranta (2011a), p. 87; Fairgrieve and Lichère (2011), p. 193.

105 Cf. the study by the UK Department of Trade and Industry, referred to in Arrowsmith, Linarelli and Wallace (2000), pp. 759–60, and the study carried out for the Netherlands' Ministry of Economic Affairs, published as Hebly, De Boer and Wilman (2007), p. 145.

106 Fernández Martín (1996), p. 212; Bovis (2005), pp. 138–9; Arrowsmith (2005), pp. 1435–6; Trepte (2007), p. 553; Brown (1998), pp. 93–4; Treumer (2011b), p. 29; Caranta (2011a), pp. 81–2; Treumer (2011a), p. 157.

107 Commission, Impact assessment report on remedies in the field of public procurement, SEC(2006) 557, p. 16. See also Commission, Amended proposal for Public Sector Remedies Directive 89/665, COM(88) 733, p. 10.

108 Treumer (2006), p. 162. On the situation in several Member States, see Bowsher and Moser (2006), p. 195; Lichère (2006), p. 171; Ruch-Larsen (2006), p. 179; Slavicek (2006), p. 223; Fairgrieve and Lichère (2011).

109 E.g. Fernández Martín (1996), pp. 213–15; Treumer (2006), p. 164; Trepte (2007), p. 558. See also Reich and Shabat (2014), p. 50.

attractive or efficient means of sanction than pre-contractual remedies'.[110] It added that making actions for damages a realistic and deterrent "threat" for contracting authorities would involve a rather far-reaching overhaul of the Procurement Remedies Directives. This could be achieved by removing or relaxing the conditions regarding private parties of proving that they had a serious chance of winning the contract. In the Commission's view '*this would directly touch upon the basic national principles governing contractual liability (i.e. the rules on compensation where loss of a chance has to be proved by the plaintiff) with few benefits (i.e. no corrective effects on the award procedure and the contract signed)*'.[111] It also pointed to the possible costs for taxpayers associated with the payment of damages by contracting authorities (which are generally (semi-)public bodies).

The option of reinforcing private parties' possibilities of claiming damages for infringements of EU public procurement law under the Procurement Remedies Directives was therefore discarded at an early stage of the revision process and no amendments were made in this regard in 2007.[112] The above considerations were at the same time apparently no reason to delete the already existing provisions on damages discussed above; these were left untouched.

3.19 The foregoing does not mean, however, that no damages cases are brought before national courts under the Procurement Remedies Directives. Especially in more recent years, a number of these cases have led to preliminary references to the Court of Justice. The resulting rulings shed light on the relevant provisions of these directives. The first such case is the Court's 2003 ruling in *GAT*, issued pursuant to an Austrian preliminary reference.[113] In this case a tenderer had been excluded, allegedly for unlawful reasons, from a contract award procedure for the supply of road sweeping vehicles. That private party therefore sought compensation in damages. In the following process of judicial review, the national court seised observed, however, that there had been *another* infringement of the applicable public procurement rules. If this court were to raise this point of its own motion (*ex officio*), as it was required to do under national law, this could lead to the conclusion that the applicant would have suffered damage anyway. That would mean in turn that the damage resulting from the allegedly unlawful exclusion would not need to be compensated. The Court of Justice was therefore asked whether the Procurement Remedies Directives precluded a rule of national law providing for an obligation of own-motion judicial review. In its reply it held that it is for the domestic law of each Member State to determine whether and in which circumstances the

110 Commission, Impact assessment report on remedies in the field of public procurement, SEC(2006) 557, p. 12.
111 Ibid., p. 26.
112 Ibid., pp. 26–7.
113 CoJ case C-315/01, *GAT*, para 46–55.

competent court may raise of its own motion an infringement of the applicable EU law. Neither the objective of these directives nor any of their specific provisions was considered to preclude such a rule of national law. The Court added, however, that under the Procurement Remedies Directives an action for damages could nonetheless not be dismissed on the ground, raised by a national court's own motion, that the contract award procedure had in any way been unlawful, for this would be incompatible with the directives' objective of ensuring rapid and effective review for an aggrieved private party.

The second case is the Court's 2010 judgment in *Combinatie Spijker*, which concerned a dispute relating to a public works contract for the renewal of two bridges in the Netherlands.[114] The dispute led to a string of litigation before various national courts regarding both the decision to award the contract to a particular tenderer and a subsequent claim for damages. In relation to the latter claim the Court of Justice was asked whether EU law regulates the criteria for the determination of the damage and, if so, what these criteria are. The Court first observed that the above-mentioned provisions on damages claims laid down in the Procurement Remedies Directives contain no statement either as to the conditions under which a contracting authority may be held liable or the amount of the damages it may be ordered to pay. Second, it clarified that these provisions are an expression of the principle of Member State liability for loss and damage caused as a result of breaches of EU law for which a Member State can be held responsible, as set out in its *Francovich* case law.[115] This means that the conditions for such liability apply in this connection (namely that the rule of EU law infringed must be intended to confer rights on private parties, that the infringement must be sufficiently serious and that there must be a direct causal link between the infringement and the damage suffered). Third, it was noted that, in the absence of EU law provisions in this area, even after the 2007 revision, it is for the domestic legal system of each Member State to determine the applicable criteria once these conditions have been complied with, subject to the principles of equivalence and effectiveness.[116]

Finally, the *Stadt Graz* case, which also dates from 2010 is of relevance.[117] At issue here was a contract award procedure for a public contract to supply asphalt to the city of Graz in Austria. An unsuccessful tenderer alleged that the winning undertaking had not complied with all applicable requirements. The contract

114 CoJ case C-568/08, *Combinatie Spijker*, para 85–92.

115 CoJ joined cases C-6/90 and C-9/90, *Francovich*, discussed in para 2.23 above. Such a link between these two directives and the principle of Member State liability had already been suggested earlier in the legal literature. See e.g. Leffler (2003), p. 154; Arrowsmith (2005), p. 1425; Treumer (2006), pp. 161 and 165.

116 On these two latter principles, see subsections 2.A.2 and 2.A.3 above.

117 CoJ case C-314/09, *Stadt Graz*, para 34–43.

having already been awarded to the latter, the applicant claimed damages from the contracting authority. National law made such claims dependent on the contracting authority being at fault, whereby a rebuttable presumption that this was the case was provided for. In its judgment the Court of Justice started by noting that the implementation of the directives' provision on damages in principle comes under the procedural autonomy of the Member States. However, it found the rule of national law at issue nonetheless to be precluded. It observed that the wording of the directives did not establish a connection between the right to damages and a requirement of fault, a conclusion that it considered to be borne out by the general context and aim of the remedy of damages as provided for in these directives.[118] The Court added that it makes little difference in this respect that in the case at hand national law provided for a rebuttable presumption of fault, as it nonetheless creates the risk that a private party is deprived of the right to damages or at least that it is only belatedly able to obtain such compensation. This was seen as incompatible with the effective and rapid judicial remedies that the Procurement Remedies Directives seek to guarantee.

3. Contractual remedy

3.20 It has been seen in the previous subsection that in the context of the 2007 revision of the Procurement Remedies Directives their provisions on actions for damages were left untouched. By contrast, that revision did lead to the introduction of an entirely new contractual remedy (that is, a class of action intended to make good infringements of EU law by seeking to nullify or to otherwise make ineffective the contractual arrangements entered into by the parties concerned). The introduction of this new remedy should be seen against the background of the case law of the Court of Justice. Initially the Court had held that, under the Procurement Remedies Directives as they stood before the revision, the fate of concluded contracts was essentially a matter for national law.[119] This was in line with an express provision in these directives according to which the effects of the exercise of the powers of the courts after the conclusion of the contract were to be determined by national law and that gave the Member States the possibility of limiting these powers to awarding damages.[120]

---

118 See also CoJ case C-275/03, *Commission v Portugal*, para 37.

119 CoJ case C-314/01, *ARGE*, para 40 and 48–50.

120 Art. 2(7) Public Sector Remedies Directive 89/665 and Art. 2(6) Utilities Remedies Directive 92/13, as they stood before the 2007 amendment. Subsequently, these provisions have been retained in an amended form, clarifying that they are subject to the directives' provisions on ineffectiveness.

Most Member States used this latter possibility.[121] Many believed this to be in conformity with the Procurement Remedies Directives.[122]

This belief appeared to have been put in doubt, however, by subsequent case law, in particular the Court's 2007 ruling in *Commission v Germany*.[123] This case was a follow-up to an earlier decision by the Court in infringement proceedings that Germany had not respected its EU law obligations, because two German local governments had each concluded a contract with an undertaking in violation of EU public procurement law.[124] Subsequently one of the two disputed contracts was not terminated, however. The Commission therefore brought a second case, now seeking a declaration by the Court of Justice that Germany had not complied with the earlier judgment. In the latter case it was held that as long as the disputed contract remains in force, the infringement of EU public procurement law continued. The Court dismissed Germany's arguments based on the aforementioned specific provision of the Procurement Remedies Directives on concluded contracts, the alleged legitimate expectations of the private parties with whom the contract had been concluded and the principles of *pacta sunt servanda* and legal certainty, as they can play no role in infringement proceedings, which are essentially a matter between the Commission and the Member State concerned.[125]

This largely left open the question what importance should be attached, if any, to these kinds of arguments in legal proceedings initiated by a private party before a national court. The introduction of the new contractual remedy of ineffectiveness (discussed in further detail below) is therefore not merely a codification of the above case law.[126] Nonetheless, this case law evidently put the issue of how to deal with contracts concluded in violation of EU public procurement law firmly on the legislative agenda.

In order to address this issue, both Procurement Remedies Directives stipulate **3.21**
since their revision in 2007 that Member States must ensure that '*a contract is considered ineffective*' by the competent national court in certain cases.[127] This

121 See para 3.09 above.

122 See Treumer (2011b), pp. 32–3, with further references.

123 CoJ case C-503/04, *Commission v Germany*, para 33–6. See also CoJ case C-125/03, *Commission v Germany*, para 15. In addition see CoJ case C-81/98, *Alcatel*, discussed in para 3.27 below.

124 CoJ joined case C-20/01 and C-28/01, *Commission v Germany*, para 36–9.

125 See subsection 2.C.1 above.

126 That is illustrated by the timing of the relevant events. The Commission's proposal for the amendment dates from May 2006 and political agreement was reached by June 2007, whereas the above judgment was rendered in July 2007. In a similar sense, see also Pries and Friton (2011), pp. 523–4. For another view, see Caranta (2011a), p. 77.

127 Art. 2d(1) Procurement Remedies Directives 89/665 and 92/13.

remedy must be made available in relation to what are considered the most serious infringements of substantive EU public procurement law.[128] It concerns in particular the illegal direct award of contracts (i.e. without any prior publication and competition in violation of the applicable EU public procurement rules) and the conclusion of a contract during a mandatory standstill period that is meant to allow the other private parties concerned to challenge the contract award decision.[129]

The logic behind this contractual remedy is that the finding that a contract is ineffective normally means that the contract – or at least the part thereof that has not yet been executed – will have to be put out to (re-)tender. That implies that all interested parties in principle have a new and fair chance of winning it. Consequently, competition is restored.[130] This can be an important incentive for private parties to apply for this remedy. As was noted above, they are often more interested in winning contracts than in obtaining damages awards.[131] The risk of a public contract being considered ineffective and the subsequent need to (re-)start a contract award procedure are, moreover, likely to be unattractive for contracting authorities, if only because of the delays that this would involve. As such this remedy can act as a deterrent for those authorities.

3.22 The recitals of the 2007 Procurement Remedies Amending Directive (through which this remedy was inserted in the Procurement Remedies Directives) clarify that this ineffectiveness should not be "automatic". Instead it is to be ascertained by or as the result of a decision by a national court.[132] For that reason the directives' provision in question speaks of the contract being "considered" ineffective rather than it "being" ineffective. The recitals state that this term "ineffectiveness" implies that '*the rights and obligations of the parties under the contract [...] cease to be enforced and performed*'.[133] The Court of Justice has held that in the situations contemplated in this provision on ineffectiveness, the measures that may be taken are to be determined solely by the rules laid down in these directives.[134]

128 Art. 2d(1) Procurement Remedies Directives 89/665 and 92/13. As regards the position of a contract having been concluded pursuant to other infringements of EU public procurement law than the ones mentioned above, see para 8.11 below.

129 Concerning these illegal direct awards and standstill periods, see para 3.09 above and para 3.27 below respectively.

130 Recital 14 Procurement Remedies Amending Directive 2007/66.

131 See para 3.17 above.

132 Recital 13 Procurement Remedies Amending Directive 2007/66.

133 Recital 21 Procurement Remedies Amending Directive 2007/66.

134 CoJ case C-19/13, *Fastweb*, para 42.

Other than that, the Member States have, however, generally been left considerable flexibility as to how to give effect to this provision in their respective domestic legal systems. The Procurement Remedies Directives stipulate expressly that the consequences of a contract being considered ineffective are provided for by national law.[135] They specify that national law may either provide for the retroactive cancellation of all contractual obligations (*ex tunc*) or limit the scope of the cancellation to those obligations which still have to be performed (*ex nunc*). It appears that in practice good use has been made of this flexibility. For instance, German law provides for ineffectiveness "from the beginning", which is presumed to refer to *ex tunc* effects, while Romanian law relies on the concept of nullity, which also presupposes retroactive effects.[136] By contrast, in Denmark the main rule is *ex nunc* with the possibility of imposing *ex tunc* effects in certain specific cases, and in England the national legislature opted instead for "prospective ineffectiveness", which refers to the possibility of nullifying only those contractual obligations that are still to be performed.[137] In Italy and France the competent national court may hold the contract to be ineffective even where the applicant did not make an express request to this effect.[138]

This flexibility is nonetheless limited under the Procurement Remedies Directives in that certain "alternative penalties" must also be imposed where the national legislator opts for *ex nunc* effects. In a separate provision, these directives expand on what these penalties entail.[139] They must be effective, proportionate and dissuasive. The directives moreover stipulate that these alternative penalties can consist of the imposition of fines or the shortening of the duration of the contract. A damages award does not qualify as such, however. It is also explicitly stated in the directives that national courts may be conferred broad discretion to take into account all relevant factors in this regard.

The margin of manoeuvre that is thus left to the Member States is greater than that which the Commission had originally proposed. The latter had proposed using the term "invalid" rather than "ineffective".[140] Under the Commission's proposal it would further have been for the national courts to '*draw all the consequences on the illegal contract, such as those concerning the recovery of any sums*

135 Art. 2d(2) Procurement Remedies Directives 89/665 and 92/13. Cf. CoJ case C-19/13, *Fastweb*, para 52.

136 Burgi (2011), p. 138; Dragos, Neamtu and Veliscu (2011), pp. 191–3.

137 Treumer (2011c), p. 279; Trybus (2011), p. 222.

138 Comba (2011), p. 249; Lichère and Gabayet (2011), p. 319.

139 Art. 2e(2) Procurement Remedies Directives 89/665 and 92/13.

140 Commission, Proposal for Procurement Remedies Amending Directive 2007/66, COM(2006) 195, p. 24 (Art. 2f(2)).

which may have been paid by the awarding authority'.[141] No reference to national law was provided for in this respect. Implicit in this proposed approach was that the contracts at issue would normally not have effects either between the parties concerned or with regard to third parties.[142] The fact that during the legislative process amendments were made on these points can, just as with the limitation of this remedy to only the most serious infringements, largely be ascribed to the reservations of at least some Member States in relation to EU involvement in matters of contract law.[143]

3.23 The Procurement Remedies Directives allow for certain *exceptions* to be made in relation to the foregoing. These come in various forms. One such exception is the possibility for contracting authorities to publish a notice of their intention to "directly" award the contract, including a justification of why this is deemed compatible with the EU public procurement rules,[144] followed by a standstill period of at least ten days before actually concluding the contract in question.[145] The idea is that this allows potentially interested undertakings to be aware of the intended direct award and the underlying reasons, so that they can contest it before the courts should they wish to do so. Where such "voluntary *ex ante* transparency" has been ensured, the resulting contract can, after the expiry of the standstill period and in the absence of a legal challenge, no longer be considered ineffective under these directives. That means that the Member States are precluded from enacting any other rule, pursuant to which the effects of the contract would still not be maintained, even though the above requirements are met.[146]

The Member States further have the option under these directives of providing that the national court seised may decide to dismiss the application for ineffectiveness where there are '*overriding reasons relating to a general interest*'.[147] Also in that case provision must be made for "alternative penalties" of the type discussed in the previous paragraph. The directives stipulate that economic interests in the effectiveness of the contract only qualify as such overriding

141 Ibid., p. 12 (recital 13).

142 Ibid., p. 24 (Art. 2f(3)).

143 See e.g. Council, doc. DS 650/07, where three Member States argue that '*[t]he basis of validity and effectiveness of contracts belong to the sphere of civil law, which belongs exclusively to the competence of the Member States*'. See e.g. also Council, doc. DS 703/06; Council, doc. DS 802/06. Cf. Art. 73 New Public Sector Procurement Directive 2014/24 and Art. 90 New Utilities Procurement Directive 2014/25 on the possible '*termination*' of concluded contracts during their term in certain cases '*under the condition determined by the applicable national law*'.

144 In this respect the contracting authority must act diligently and be able to legitimately hold that such a "direct" award was permissible under the applicable rules. See CoJ case C-19/13, *Fastweb*, para 50. See also Brown (2015), pp. NA15–NA16.

145 Art. 2d(4) Procurement Remedies Directives 89/665 and 92/13.

146 CoJ case C-19/13, *Fastweb*, para 33–54.

147 Art. 2d(3) Procurement Remedies Directives 89/665 and 92/13.

reasons if in exceptional circumstances ineffectiveness would lead to disproportionate consequences. Economic interests directly linked to the contract can in any case not be overriding reasons for the present purposes. Examples of such economic interests directly linked to the contract are cited, namely the costs resulting from the delay of the execution of the contract, the launching of a new procurement procedure, the change of economic operator performing the public contract in question or the legal obligations resulting from that contract. It has been noted that this possibility of exceptions in the general interest might become a loophole.[148] This fear seems, on the one hand, all the more realistic, given the experiences gained concerning the balance of interests test that can be applied in relation to actions for interim measures.[149] On the other hand, it is clear that an attempt has been made to reduce this risk as much as possible through the rather restrictive formulation of this exception. Indeed, it has been argued that this provision now seems to have been formulated so restrictively that it might be difficult to give examples of considerations that could fall under the scope of this exception.[150] All in all the idea has clearly been to leave a degree of flexibility and discretion to the national courts when applying this contractual remedy, while at the same time seeking to minimise the risk of abuse.

Practical experience with the contractual remedy of ineffectiveness is so far limited as a consequence of its relatively recent introduction. There are reasons to believe that this remedy could prove a valuable private enforcement instrument. The possibility of being awarded the contested public contract can act as an important incentive to potential applicants, which are generally undertakings that are interested in that contract. For the contracting authorities concerned it can also have an important deterrent effect, given that the negative consequences of a contract being considered ineffective can be considerable (delays, extra costs, possible political fallout, and so on). **3.24**

Yet there are also several factors that might mean that the system created under these directives will be less frequently and successfully used than intended. Its potential importance appears to be restricted by the aforementioned limitation to the most serious infringements, the considerable leeway left to the Member States as regards the precise effects of this remedy, the various exceptions and the relatively strict limitation periods that can apply in this connection.[151] On a more practical level it remains to be seen, especially in cases of illegal direct awards, whether (potential) applicants will be able to obtain sufficient evidence

148 Cf. e.g. Caranta (2011a), p. 77; Trybus (2011), p. 224.
149 See para 3.13 above.
150 Treumer (2011b), p. 36.
151 On these limitation periods, see para 3.26 below.

and information so as to be in a position to bring a case and, if so, whether the said incentives to sue are sufficient to overcome any hesitations that aggrieved bidders often have.[152] The practical use of this remedy has therefore sometimes been questioned in the legal literature[153] and its application so far seems limited.[154]

C. PROCEDURAL PROVISIONS

The above remedies are complemented by a number of provisions of a procedural nature, the most important of which are assessed below. The rules on legal standing, limitation periods and standstill periods are first discussed. This is followed by an assessment of the directives' provisions on forum and procedure.

1. Legal standing, limitation periods and standstill periods

3.25 Under the Procurement Remedies Directives the Member States must ensure that review procedures are available '*under detailed rules which the Member States may establish, at least to any person having or having had an interest in obtaining a particular contract and who has been or risks being harmed by an alleged infringement*'.[155] It is thus established which private parties have *legal standing* (*locus standi*) to bring proceedings under these directives before the competent national courts. Pursuant to this provision, any – legal or natural[156] – person that has or has had a legitimate interest in the outcome of the award procedure is entitled to bring legal proceedings.[157] The requirement of a (legitimate) interest, which is common to the laws of most Member States, was inserted in this provision by the Council.[158] The Commission had proposed granting legal standing to any person entitled to tender for the award at issue. The eventual, somewhat more restrictive wording has been designed to allow any private party concerned to institute a review procedure under these directives, without, however, '*jeopardising*' the procedural laws of the Member States as they

---

152 See para 3.17 above.

153 E.g. Lichère and Gabayet (2011), p. 317; Trybus (2011), p. 224; Reich and Shabat (2014), p. 65.

154 Brown (2015), p. NA16 (relating in particular to the UK); Halonen (2015), p. 111 (relating to Finland).

155 Art. 1(3) Procurement Remedies Directives 89/665 and 92/13. In addition, at the time of the aforementioned revision, Art. 2a(2) was inserted, clarifying in which cases a private party is '*concerned*' by a particular provision of these directives. This is not a rule on legal standing proper. However, it indirectly establishes which private parties are entitled to contest an alleged infringement, given that a party that is not "concerned" in the above-mentioned sense will normally not have a sufficient interest.

156 CoJ case C236/95, *Commission v Greece*, para 11.

157 Commission, Proposal for Utilities Remedies Directive 92/13, COM(90) 297, p. 17.

158 Cf. Commission, Communication on the Council's position on the proposal for Public Sector Remedies Directive 89/665, SEC(89) 1196, p. 7. See also Fernández Martín (1996), p. 207. As regards developments in England related to legal standing requirements, see Bailey (2015), p. 122.

stood.[159] It follows that the Member States are not required to allow *any* private party to bring legal proceedings under these directives.[160]

The Court of Justice has clarified that the above provision ensures legal standing for aggrieved private parties bringing a claim, but that it does not necessarily extend to the defendants, the latter being the contracting authorities that allegedly infringed the EU procurement rules and which may wish to appeal a decision taken in the first instance (although Member States are not precluded from ensuring legal standing also for these latter parties on the basis of national law).[161] It further appears that persons invoking merely a general or public interest or making an obviously unmeritorious claim can be barred.[162] Similarly, a tenderer that has had its own bid declared invalid, and therefore is no longer a participant in the contract award procedure, can be held to have insufficient interest in having subsequent decisions taken in the context of that procedure reviewed, provided, however, that this party has been in a position to previously contest the decision as regards its own bid.[163]

The Court has further held that the interest of a private party in initiating legal proceedings cannot be made conditional on a prior referral to a non-judicial conciliation committee.[164] Nor can the formal capacity of tenderer or candidate be required. Thus, a private party that did not submit a bid because it found the specifications of the tender documents to be discriminatory will normally have legal standing, in so far as its actions relate to those specifications.[165] Yet, as the Court held in *Grossmann*, that party can be denied access to the review procedures for lack of interest if it did not seek any review of the decision to include these specifications until after the contract had been concluded. In *Grossmann* the Court found that by acting in that manner that party compromised the directives' objective of effective and rapid review.[166] The Court has also repeatedly assessed the conformity with the Procurement Remedies Directives

159 Council, doc. 7834/89 ADD 1, p. 7. See also the statement by the Council and the Commission that '*within the meaning of this Directive any person excluded from participation in a procedure for the award of a public contract owing to an alleged infringement is a person having or having had an interest in obtaining a public contract and who has been harmed or risks being harmed. In particular, the fact of having suffered financial loss shall not be considered a requirement for the admissibility of a review*', laid down in Council, doc. 7490/89, p. 10.

160 CoJ case C-249/01, *Hackermüller*, para 18; CoJ case C-230/02, *Grossmann*, para 26.

161 CoJ case C-570/08, *Simvoulio*, para 35–6.

162 Cf. recital 122 New Public Sector Directive 2014/24; recital 128 New Utilities Procurement Directive 2014/25; Dahlgaard Dingel (1999), p. 228; Trepte (2007), p. 552.

163 CoJ case C-249/01, *Hackermüller*, para 26–9. See also CoJ case C-100/12, *Fastweb*, para 26–30. See further CoJ case C-488/14, *Max Boegl România* (pending), concerning the deposit of a "good conduct guarantee" as a precondition for access to the review procedures referred to in Procurement Remedies Directives 89/665 and 92/13.

164 CoJ case C-410/01, *Fritsch*, para 31–4. See also CoJ case C-230/02, *Grossmann*, para 42.

165 CoJ case C-230/02, *Grossmann*, para 25–30; CoJ case C-26/03, *Stadt Halle*, para 40.

166 CoJ case C-230/02, *Grossmann*, para 34–40.

of national rules on legal standing relating to members of a consortium consisting of several legal persons. In that regard it distinguished between actions for the annulment of the award decision (which cannot be brought by those individual legal persons, but only by the consortium) and actions for damages (which can be brought on an individual basis).[167]

3.26 Provisions on the *limitation periods* applicable to private parties wishing to initiate legal proceedings were inserted in the Procurement Remedies Directives as part of their revision in 2007. The length of these periods varies in light of the remedy sought. In the first place, Member States may set such limitation periods for applications for the *review of decisions* taken by contracting authorities.[168] This provision applies not only to applications for the review of contract award decisions, but also for the review of any other decision taken in the context of a contract award procedure falling within the scope of the Procurement Remedies Directives. These periods must have a length of at least 10 or 15 days, depending on the means of communication used. The fact that these periods are short is related to the predominance of the interest in the rapid resolution of public procurement disputes and consequently the completion of the contract award procedure.[169] In the second place, longer minimum time limits apply for actions seeking to have a concluded contract *considered ineffective*.[170] The latter must be either 30 days, where a contract award notice has been published or the parties concerned have been informed directly, or else six months from the conclusion of the contract. Finally, in all other cases, notably where *actions for damages* are concerned, the limitation periods are to be determined by national law.[171]

The above rules are largely a codification of abundant earlier case law of the Court of Justice on this topic. The general point of departure there is that reasonable limitation periods are in principle acceptable in contract award procedures governed by EU law, provided that the effectiveness of the Procurement Remedies Directives is not compromised and the principles of equivalence and effectiveness are respected.[172] The Court has consistently held that

---

167 CoJ case C-57/01, *Makedoniko Metro*, para 64–73; CoJ case C-129/04, *Espace Trianon*, para 20; CoJ joined cases C-145/08 and C-149/08, *Club Hotel Loutraiki*, para 65–80. Note that this latter case concerned a situation falling outside the scope of Procurement Remedies Directives 89/665 and 92/13, which was examined in particular under the principle of effective judicial protection. On the differences between these two types of actions, see also Opinion AG Sharpston joined cases C-145/08 and C-149/08, *Club Hotel Loutraki*, para 99–125.

168 Art. 2c Procurement Remedies Directives 89/665 and 92/13.

169 See para 3.11 above. As discussed in para 3.12 above, the GPA provides in this respect for a minimum period of 10 days.

170 Art. 2f Procurement Remedies Directives 89/665 and 92/13.

171 Art. 2f(2) Procurement Remedies Directives 89/665 and 92/13.

172 On these two principles, see subsections 2.A.2 and 2.A.3 above.

the full implementation of the objective of these directives to ensure effective and especially rapid review would be undermined if private parties were allowed to initiate legal proceedings at any time during the contract award procedure, thus possibly forcing the contracting authority to restart the entire procedure.[173] However, it has also insisted that limitation periods must be set out expressly and that contracting authorities cannot create uncertainty in this regard.[174] The Court has further clarified that the starting point for these periods is the moment at which the infringement became known (or should have been known) to the private parties concerned.[175] In this connection the importance of adequately informing these parties before any such time period can start to run has also been underlined.[176] The occurrence of new events subsequent to the expiry of the set limitation period of which the private party concerned was not and could not reasonably have been aware can imply that this period will start to run again, as from the date at which that party was adequately informed by the contracting authority or otherwise became aware of the events in question.[177]

Also introduced in 2007 were three new articles concerning *standstill periods.* **3.27**
These provisions should also be understood against the background of earlier case law of the Court of Justice. Of particular relevance is its 1999 landmark ruling in *Alcatel.*[178] This case concerned a contract award procedure initiated by an Austrian ministry for the supply of automatic data transmission systems. Having completed the procedure, on the same day the contract award decision was taken and the contract was concluded with the successful tenderer. The other tenderers were only informed afterwards. Upon application by one of these other tenderers the national court seised established that EU public procurement law had been infringed in the course of the contract award procedure. However, the contract having already been concluded, in the circumstances of the case at hand national law only allowed for an action for damages. The Court of Justice essentially found this to be incompatible with the Procurement Remedies Directives, even if at that time they did not provide expressly for a standstill period to be respected between the contract award decision and the conclusion of the contract. For this would in effect render

173 CoJ case C-470/99, *Universale Bau*, para 77; CoJ case C-327/00, *Santex*, para 50–52; CoJ case C-241/06, *Lämmerzahl*, para 50–51; CoJ case C-456/08, *Commission v Ireland*, para 51–2; CoJ case C-314/09, *Stadt Graz*, para 37.

174 CoJ case C-327/00, *Santex*, para 61; CoJ case C-241/06, *Lämmerzahl*, para 57; CoJ case C-456/08, *Commission v Ireland*, para 57–8 and 74–5.

175 CoJ case C-470/99, *Universale Bau*, para 78; CoJ case C-538/13, *eVigilo*, para 52.

176 E.g. CoJ case C-406/08, *Uniplex*, para 30–32; CoJ case C-251/09, *Commission v Cyprus*, para 57–8. See also CoJ case C-19/13, *Fastweb*, para 48.

177 CoJ case C-161/13, *Idrodinamica*, para 47.

178 CoJ case C-81/98, *Alcatel*, para 29–43.

meaningless the directives' remedies that are meant to be exercised at the pre-contractual stage (that is, interim measures and the setting aside of unlawful decisions).[179] The Court stressed that these directives seek to guarantee the availability of effective and rapid review at a stage where infringements can still be rectified. The Commission subsequently launched a string of infringement cases against Member States that did not provide for such a standstill period in their national law. In one of those cases, *Commission v Austria*, the Court of Justice highlighted in this connection the objective of complete legal protection.[180] This presupposes that prior to the conclusion of the contract all private parties concerned must have sufficient time to examine the validity of the contract award decision. The Court also underlined that this implies that those parties must be informed of that decision.[181] In other cases it ruled that, even where the possibility of judicial review can lead to a concluded contract being annulled *ex post*, this is in principle not sufficient to compensate for the impossibility for a private party to challenge the contract award decision before the conclusion of the contract.[182]

The Commission found that there were significant differences in the manner in which the Member States had given effect to this earlier case law, leading to loopholes and uncertainties.[183] It therefore proposed codifying it at EU level as part of the 2007 revision of the Procurement Remedies Directives. The rules in question in essence seek to ensure that the pre-contractual stage is prolonged where necessary, so as to give the private parties concerned a realistic possibility of initiating proceedings for interim measures or the setting aside of allegedly unlawful decisions. Before this revision, lack of sufficient time was thought to have been an important reason why during the pre-contractual stage it could prove difficult to successfully bring a case. As was explained above, contracting authorities sometimes concluded the contract at issue as quickly as possible, in particular before any legal proceedings challenging a contract award decision could be brought or completed, given that such concluded contracts were normally left unaffected by the review (the "race to signature").[184] The resulting articles in the revised Procurement Remedies Directives essentially provide for a standstill period, which is to be respected by the contracting authority, of at

179 See subsection 3.B.1 above. The CoJ's ruling in *Alcatel* concerned only the setting aside of unlawful decisions, but it would appear to apply also to the granting of interim relief. See Trepte (2007), pp. 555 and 564.
180 CoJ case C-212/02, *Commission v Austria*, para 21–4.
181 See also CoJ case C-455/08, *Commission v Ireland*, para 30–34; CoJ case C-406/08, *Uniplex*, para 30–31.
182 CoJ case C-444/06, *Commission v Spain*, para 45; CoJ case C-327/08, *Commission v France*, para 58.
183 Commission, Impact assessment report on remedies in the field of public procurement, SEC(2006) 557, p. 10.
184 See para 3.09 above.

least either 10 or 15 days (depending on the means of communication used). Subject to certain exceptions, the contract may not be concluded during this period.[185]

These rules are complemented by similar provisions providing for the automatic suspension of ongoing contract award procedures pending the decision by the national court, at least where review at first instance is concerned.[186] Obviously during this latter period the contract may not be concluded either, so as not to make the pending review largely meaningless in practice. The above-mentioned provision on the Member States being able to provide that, after the conclusion of the contract, the powers of the national courts under the directives are limited to merely awarding damages, was retained, subject to the directives' other provisions in this respect, notably those on ineffectiveness.[187]

2. Forum and procedure

The Procurement Remedies Directives further contain rules on *forum*, that is, **3.28**
on the court or other review body designated by the Member States to rule on the cases brought under these directives. On the whole the Member States are left considerable freedom to make their own choices in this respect. The term generally used in these directives is "review body", which is a very broad term indeed. As such the directives leave it in principle to the Member States to decide whether the claims brought are to be decided by a body that is judicial in character, thus a civil or administrative court, or by another body, such as a non-judicial administrative body. In certain cases the directives moreover specifically require these review bodies to be '*independent of the contracting authority*'.[188]

Where a Member State chooses the first option and designates a *judicial* body, no further requirements apply. But specific requirements are set out for the situation where the designated bodies are *not judicial* in nature.[189] These requirements aim to ensure that these bodies nonetheless offer equivalent guarantees in terms of independence and impartiality.[190] They entail in a nutshell the following. First, the body concerned must provide reasons for its

185 Art. 2a and Art. 2b Procurement Remedies Directives 89/665 and 92/13.

186 Art. 1(5) and 2(3) Procurement Remedies Directives 89/665 and 92/13; Art. 2(4) Public Sector Remedies Directive 89/665; Art. 2(3a) Utilities Remedies Directive 92/13.

187 Art. 2(7) Public Sector Remedies Directive 89/665; Art. 2(6) Utilities Remedies Directive 92/13.

188 Art. 2d and 2e Procurement Remedies Directives 89/665 and 92/13 (relating to the contractual remedy, discussed in subsection 3.B.3 above).

189 Art. 2(9) Procurement Remedies Directives 89/665 and 92/13.

190 Commission, Communication on the Council's position on the proposal for Public Sector Remedies Directive 89/665, SEC(89) 1196, p. 9.

decisions in writing. Second, it is required that an appeal can be lodged before a body that is not only independent from the contracting authority, but that is also empowered under the EU Treaties to refer a preliminary question to the Court of Justice.[191] Third, the members of this independent appeal body must be appointed and leave office under the same conditions of the members of the judiciary as regards the authority responsible for their appointment, their period in office and their removal. And at least the president of this body must have the same legal and professional qualifications as members of the judiciary. Finally, this appeal body must take its decisions following procedures in which both sides are heard and those decisions must be legally binding. These rules thus do not exclude review by administrative or specialised arbitration bodies. But where a Member State decides to designate such a non-judicial body, at least the possibility of a review on appeal by a body of a quasi-judicial nature and through a quasi-judicial procedure is to be ensured, so as to guarantee an independent, impartial and fair review of the contracting authorities' decisions at least at second instance and to ensure that preliminary questions can be referred where necessary.

The Procurement Remedies Directives further provide that the power to grant the remedies set out therein may be conferred on separate bodies responsible for different aspects of the review procedures.[192] This provision is meant to accommodate the Member States that require that an unlawful decision is first set aside by an administrative court, after which damages claims can be brought before a civil court.[193] At the time of the adoption of the first of these two directives, the Member States represented in the Council considered it '*not [...] advisable to amend [their] general system of administrative law for the public procurement sector alone*'.[194]

Considering the flexibility resulting from the above provisions, it is unsurprising that in practice the Member States' review systems differ considerably. For review at first instance, most have established some form of specialised non-judicial or quasi-judicial public procurement review body, generally of an administrative nature. This can for example take the form of a special complaints board (Denmark), certain designated public procurement chambers (Germany), a competition office (Czech Republic) or a public procurement commission (Estonia). The decisions taken by these bodies are normally subject to appeal before the – civil or administrative – courts of the Member States in

---

191 On the conditions for qualifying as a "court or tribunal" within the meaning of Art. 267 TFEU on the preliminary reference procedure, see para 1.02 above.

192 Art. 2(2) Procurement Remedies Directives 89/665 and 92/13.

193 See para 3.11 above.

194 Council, doc. 7834/89 ADD 1, p. 7.

question.[195] Yet in several Member States public procurement disputes covered by the Procurement Remedies Directives are to be brought immediately before the ordinary courts. These are mostly either exclusively or partially administrative courts, as is the case for instance in Italy, France and Portugal. Where Member States opted for a "mixed" system of review by administrative as well as civil courts, the latter tend to be competent to consider actions for damages, whereas the administrative courts are to rule in the other cases. By contrast, in Member States such as the United Kingdom, Sweden and the Netherlands, civil courts are in principle competent to hear all public procurement disputes brought under these directives.[196]

Turning to the relevant rules of procedure set out in the Procurement Remedies Directives, most noticeable are their provisions on *pre-trial contacts*. These provisions entitle the Member States to require a private party wishing to initiate proceedings to first notify the contracting authority of the alleged infringement and its intention to seek review.[197] A considerable number of Member States have made use of this option, including Germany, Greece and Poland.[198] Such pre-trial contacts may help to facilitate an amicable settlement, which can be attractive from the point of view of costs and speed. But it can also lead to delays. The directives therefore specify that this possibility should not lead to the limitation periods or standstill periods discussed in the previous subsection being affected. In other words, the delay that such pre-trial contacts involve should not be such that the private party complainant is time-barred should it subsequently wish to bring legal proceedings and nor should the contested public contract be concluded with another party in the meantime. **3.29**

Along similar lines but going a step further is the possibility of requiring a private party to first *seek review* with the contracting authority itself.[199] Only a limited number of Member States have made use of this possibility. One of them is Spain, where reportedly over 90 per cent of the disputes are settled pursuant to such a request for internal review by the authority concerned.[200] Also in this case the directives seek to ensure that there are no serious adverse consequences for the private party seeking review. They do so, notably, by providing that such an application to the contracting authority must result in

195 Commission, Report on the impact and effectiveness of EU public procurement legislation, SEC(2011) 853, pp. 69–70.
196 Commission, Annual public procurement implementation review 2012, SWD(2012) 342, p. 34.
197 Art. 1(4) Procurement Remedies Directives 89/665 and 92/13.
198 Commission, Report on the impact and effectiveness of EU public procurement legislation, SEC(2011) 853, p. 69.
199 Art. 1(5) Procurement Remedies Directives 89/665 and 92/13.
200 Commission, Annual public procurement implementation review 2012, SWD(2012) 342, p. 33.

the immediate suspension of the possibility of concluding a contract. Afterwards a minimum standstill period must be respected before the disputed contract can be awarded so as to ensure that the private party concerned has an opportunity to apply to the courts.[201]

Lastly, the directives require it to be ensured that the decisions taken by the competent national courts (and other review bodies) can be effectively *enforced*.[202]

D. OTHER ENFORCEMENT ISSUES

Apart from the measures facilitating the private enforcement of EU law before national courts discussed in the foregoing, other means of ensuring the compliance with and the enforcement of substantive EU public procurement law are not entirely absent. Below two alternative compliance mechanisms that are peculiar to the Utilities Remedies Directive and the scope for alternative dispute resolution are first discussed. Attention then turns to the role of public enforcement in the present context.

1. Alternative compliance mechanisms and alternative dispute resolution

3.30 Up until 2007 the Utilities Remedies Directive contained two specific alternative mechanisms to ensure compliance with the relevant rules of substantive EU public procurement law. It included, in the first place, the "attestation mechanism".[203] This entailed a voluntary system under which contracting authorities had the possibility of having the conformity of their contract award procedures assessed through periodic audits. The second mechanism is the "conciliation procedure".[204] The latter allowed aggrieved private parties to request the Commission to appoint an independent conciliator. If the Commission agreed, this conciliator was then to be drawn from a list established by the former in consultation with the representatives of the Member States. This procedure could only be used with the agreement of the contracting authority and would not result in any legally binding decisions.

At the time of the adoption of the Utilities Remedies Directive (1992) considerable attention was paid to these two innovative forms of dispute

201 On these standstill periods, see also para 3.27 above.

202 Art. 2(8) Procurement Remedies Directives 89/665 and 92/13.

203 Art. 3–7 Utilities Remedies Directive 92/13, as they stood before the 2007 amendment.

204 Art. 9–11 Utilities Remedies Directive 92/13, as they stood before the 2007 amendment.

prevention and resolution.[205] This suggests that they were thought to be able to play an important role in practice. In the context of the 2007 revision the Commission observed, however, that they had failed to generate any significant interest on the part of the parties concerned. Having regard also to the administrative costs associated with keeping them in place, it was decided that these mechanisms should no longer be retained.[206] The provisions in question were therefore deleted from these directives.

Furthermore, although the provision on the above-mentioned centralised "conciliation procedure" was deleted in 2007, alternative dispute resolution can nonetheless play a role in resolving disputes relating to the application of EU public procurement law at national level. In fact, many Member States have set up bodies that aim to find extrajudicial solutions to public procurement disputes, such as an arbitration panel or an ombudsman.[207] In particular, aggrieved private parties generally tend to prefer settling disputes amicably whenever possible, in light *inter alia* of the aforementioned fears of harming the business relationship with the contracting authority and of the length and costs of legal proceedings.[208] Field research carried out in England and the Netherlands reveals, for example, a clear preference on the part of those parties for non-judicial forms of dispute resolution in one form or another.[209] **3.31**

However, neither the Procurement Remedies Directives nor the other EU rules currently in force in this domain expressly address the issue of alternative dispute resolution, other than these directives' rules of forum allowing for the possibility of the claims in question being decided on by certain alternative dispute resolution bodies (at least at first instance) mentioned earlier.[210] That means that this issue is in principle left to be regulated by the Member States. It has already been seen that the Court of Justice has at times marked the limits to the leeway thus left to the Member States by holding that rules of national law,

205 As a rough illustration, 12 of the 18 articles of the initial Commission proposal for this directive related to these two mechanisms. The importance attached to these mechanisms is moreover illustrated by the attention paid to them in the explanatory memoranda to the initial and amended Commission proposal. See Commission, Proposal for Utilities Remedies Directive 92/13, COM(90) 297; Commission, Amended proposal for Utilities Remedies Directive 92/13, COM(91) 158.

206 Recitals 29 and 30 Procurement Remedies Amending Directive 2007/66. See also Commission, Impact assessment report on remedies in the field of public procurement, SEC(2006) 557, pp. 13–14.

207 Commission, Report on the impact and effectiveness of EU public procurement legislation, SEC(2011) 853, p. 69.

208 See para 3.17 above. See also Commission, Report on the impact and effectiveness of EU public procurement legislation, SEC(2011) 853, pp. 71–3.

209 See Wood Report (2004), p. 54; study carried out on behalf of the Netherlands' Ministry of Economic Affairs, published as Hebly, De Boer and Wilman (2007), p. 147.

210 See para 3.28 above.

which make prior recourse to non-judicial reconciliation a mandatory requirement for a private party to be allowed to bring legal proceedings under the Procurement Remedies Directives, are incompatible with their rules on legal standing.[211]

2. Public enforcement

3.32 In the introduction to this chapter it was noted that over the decades serious shortcomings have been identified as regards compliance with EU public procurement law.[212] Despite the adoption and subsequent revision of the Procurement Remedies Directives, these difficulties are not a thing of the past. Indeed, in 2014 the EU legislature noted that '*there is still considerable room for improvement*' in this regard.[213] One conceivable response to these shortcomings would be to require as a matter of EU law that effective public enforcement structures are in place.[214] At central, EU level this could entail granting the Commission particular powers to investigate and address (alleged) infringements. As regards public enforcement at national level, one could further think in particular of the establishment of authorities charged with supervising and enforcing the correct application of the EU's substantive rules on public procurement. Generally speaking, no such requirements apply at present, however. As is set out below, with respect to the enforcement of the rules in question, public enforcement in effect plays only a modest role as a matter of EU law. This might well be related to the fact that the addressees – and therefore the potential infringers – of those rules are typically (semi-)public authorities themselves. It appears that the EU legislature is rather hesitant to make those authorities subject to significant public enforcement powers entrusted to other public authorities, regardless of whether the latter are EU or national authorities, thus leaving the burden of enforcement instead to the private parties concerned.

3.33 Concerning the possibilities *at EU level* it is noticeable that, especially in its 1987 proposal for the Public Sector Remedies Directive, the Commission placed considerable emphasis on certain innovative forms of public enforcement.[215] There it sought to obtain for itself rather far-reaching powers to intervene directly at national level. This took two forms. First, it was proposed to empower the Commission to intervene in national review procedures, as a sort of *amicus curiae*, regarding matters of EU law. Second, this proposal

211 CoJ case C-410/01, *Fritsch*, para 31–4. See para 3.25 above.
212 See para 3.04–3.05 above.
213 Recital 121 New Public Sector Directive 2014/24; recital 127 New Utilities Procurement Directive 2014/25.
214 See also subsection 2.C.2 above.
215 See Commission, Proposal for Public Sector Remedies Directive 89/665, COM(87) 134. See also Commission, Amended proposal for Public Sector Remedies Directive 89/665, COM(88) 733.

included a provision that would have allowed the Commission to suspend ongoing contract award procedures in certain cases. Arguably for the Commission these two proposed forms of centralised public enforcement were at least as important as the proposed measures that sought to facilitate the private enforcement of EU public procurement law discussed in the foregoing.[216] But the EU legislature (at that time only the Council) judged these proposed forms of direct intervention to be '*foreign to the system for the application of [EU] law provided for in the [EU] Treaties [and] to the legal systems of the Member States*' and it did not wish '*to introduce so fundamental a change in the procedural law of the Member States and to apply it only to one sphere of [EU] law*'.[217] This aspect of the proposal was therefore rejected. In the case of the proposed powers for the Commission to suspend ongoing contract award procedures, this rejection was even unanimous.[218] When discussing the proposal for the Utilities Remedies Directive a few years later, the European Parliament argued in favour of granting the Commission similar powers to intervene directly in national proceedings. However, this time the Commission itself decided against proposing such an arrangement. It argued that, given its limited resources, it could not verify the compliance of each and every entity with the applicable EU public procurement rules and that more cost-effective alternatives existed.[219]

The Commission was not left entirely empty-handed, however. Both Procurement Remedies Directives contain a "corrective mechanism".[220] This empowers the Commission to notify a Member State when it considers that a '*serious infringement*' of EU procurement law has been committed and request its correction. Within 21 days the Member State concerned must then confirm that the infringement has been corrected, explain why no such correction has been made or inform the Commission that the contract award procedure in question has been suspended. But the directives contain no provisions as to possible subsequent steps. The Court of Justice has clarified that in this regard the Member State concerned is not obliged to "automatically" comply with the Commission's request.[221] When a Member State refuses to do so this effectively leaves the Commission only the option of initiating regular infringement

216 Again, by means of a rough illustration, in the initial Commission proposal only one article concerned the remedies available to private parties, whereas three articles related to the proposed Commission's powers. The importance that the Commission attached to these powers is, moreover, evident from the attention paid thereto in the explanatory memoranda to its initial and amended proposals.

217 Council, doc. 7834/89 ADD 1, p. 5.

218 Commission, Communication on the Council's position on the proposal for Public Sector Remedies Directive 89/665, SEC(89) 1196, p. 10. See Fernández Martín (1996), p. 221.

219 Commission, Amended proposal for Utilities Remedies Directive 92/13, COM(91) 158, pp. 4–6 and 14.

220 Art. 3 Public Sector Remedies Directive 89/665; Art. 8 Utilities Remedies Directive 92/13.

221 Cf. CoJ Order case C-387/08 P, *VDH*, para 23–5.

proceedings.[222] As the Court has confirmed, this corrective mechanism can evidently neither derogate from nor replace the system established by the EU Treaties in this respect.[223]

In 2007 the Commission observed that this corrective mechanism had not been used since the early 1990s. It cited difficulties in acting swiftly before the conclusion of the contract and in gathering convincing evidence of the alleged infringement.[224] As part of the revision, amendments were made so as to "refocus" this mechanism on serious infringements of EU public procurement law.[225] However, these amendments seem unlikely to substantially alleviate the said difficulties. Neither do they alter the fact that, as was explained above, the Commission's powers under this mechanism are actually rather limited. It remains to be seen therefore whether this mechanism will be used more frequently and with more success in time to come.

3.34 As regards what could be called the more "classic" forms of public enforcement in the EU legal order, namely through the involvement of *national authorities* charged with supervising and enforcing the application of EU public procurement law,[226] the EU's approach in relation to public procurement law has been somewhat ambivalent. In its 1996 green paper on public procurement, the Commission noted that the establishment of such authorities might have advantages, arguing that their very existence could already help prevent infringements. The Member States were therefore '*invited*' to consider this option.[227] In its communication of two years later, the Commission underlined that it did not have the resources to act itself as '*a kind of "super enforcement authority"*'.[228] It therefore instead '*encouraged*' setting-up of independent authorities by the Member States as contact points for rapid, informal solution of public procurement-related problems and for authorities from other Member States and the Commission.[229] Neither the Procurement Remedies Directives nor the Substantive Procurement Directives at present set out an obligation to this effect, however. The latter directives merely provide (since 2004) that the Member States *may* establish national public procurement authorities of this

222 On these infringement proceedings, see subsection 2.C.1 above.

223 CoJ case C-359/93, *Commission v Netherlands*, para 13; CoJ case C-79/94, *Commission v Greece*, para 11. As is illustrated by these two cases, in practice the Commission tends to consider the notification issued under the corrective mechanism as a letter of formal notice initiating the infringement proceedings.

224 Commission, Impact assessment report on remedies in the field of public procurement, SEC(2006) 557, p. 13.

225 Recital 28 Procurement Remedies Amending Directive 2007/66.

226 See subsection 2.C.2 above.

227 Commission, Green paper on public procurement in the EU, COM(96) 583, p. 17.

228 Commission, Communication on public procurement in the EU, COM(1998) 143, p. 13.

229 Ibid.

kind.[230] This seems little more than stating the obvious. Most Member States have actually established a public supervision authority of some sort, although this is often only an *ex post* audit body or a non-independent procurement office with limited powers.[231]

The more recent amendments to the EU's public procurement rules did not fundamentally alter this situation. In the context of the 2007 revision of the Procurement Remedies Directives, the possibility of including an EU law obligation to establish an independent national authority, empowered to notify alleged infringements to contracting authorities and if necessary bring cases before national courts, was again raised.[232] The Commission acknowledged that this could help solve disputes quickly and in an informal manner. An important further advantage is that enforcement measures would not necessarily depend on the decision of an undertaking whether or not to initiate legal proceedings. As was noted above, apart from possible legal constraints, in practice private parties are often deterred from doing so for fear of repercussions and financial constraints.[233] But in 2007 a majority of Member States took an unfavourable view of this option. Invoked were fears of being "overwhelmed" by nuisance cases, as well as the costs of setting up and operating the authorities.[234] The option of requiring the establishment of public enforcement mechanisms was therefore discarded, despite its having received strong support from interested parties from the private sector.[235] What remains as a matter of EU law at present is the Public Procurement Network. This is an informal forum for the exchange of information and best practices between the public authorities concerned.

This issue later re-emerged in the context of the aforementioned revision of the EU's substantive public procurement rules in 2014.[236] In that context the Commission proposed an obligation for the Member States to designate a

230 Art. 81 Public Sector Procurement Directive 2004/18; Art. 72 Utilities Procurement Directive 2004/17.

231 Commission, Report on the impact and effectiveness of EU public procurement legislation, SEC(2011) 853, pp. 63–5.

232 On this revision, see para 3.09 above.

233 See para 3.17 above.

234 Commission, Impact assessment report on remedies in the field of public procurement, SEC(2006) 557, pp. 25, 26 and 39–42; Commission, Proposal for Procurement Remedies Amending Directive 2007/66, COM(2006) 195, pp. 4–5.

235 In the consultation preceding the 2007 revision, over 85 per cent of the undertakings expressed a preference for obliging the Member States to set up such an independent authority. Of the consulted lawyers and professional and non-governmental organisations, around 60 per cent and almost 70 per cent, respectively, held this view. See Commission, Responses to the consultation on the operation of national review procedures in the field of public procurement, 2004. Similar strong support has been found during field research carried out in the Netherlands. See Hebly, De Boer and Wilman (2007), p. 147.

236 See para 3.02 above.

single, independent "oversight body", which would be charged *inter alia* with monitoring the application of the relevant rules, issuing own-initiative opinions and helping to settle complaints.[237] These already not very ambitious proposals were watered down further during the legislative process. The new substantive public procurement directives now only provide for an obligation to designate '*one or more authorities, bodies or structures*' that are responsible for "monitoring" the application of the relevant rules and for "indicating" possible problems to '*national auditing authorities, courts or tribunals or other appropriate authorities or structures, such as the ombudsman, national parliaments or committees thereof*'.[238] This seems a very modest step indeed.

It is therefore clear that in this field, EU law does not provide for "proper" public enforcement at national level, in that neither under the rules that are currently in force nor under the new substantive public procurement directives that were adopted in 2014 and that are to be transposed into national law by April 2016 are the Member States required to designate a public authority with significant powers to investigate and effectively address (alleged) infringements of EU public procurement law.

237 See Commission, Proposal for New Utilities Procurement Directive 2014/25, COM(2011) 895, pp. 107–8 (Art. 93); Commission, Proposal for New Public Sector Procurement Directive 2014/24, COM(2011) 896, pp. 101–2 (Art. 84).

238 Art. 83 New Public Sector Directive 2014/24; Art. 99 New Utilities Procurement Directive 2014/25. See also Art. 45 Concessions Awards Directive 2014/23. As regards the possibility for interested parties to bring possible infringements to the attention of the competent national authorities see recital 122 New Public Sector Directive 2014/24 and recital 128 New Utilities Procurement Directive 2014/25.

4

INTELLECTUAL PROPERTY LAW

This chapter focuses on EU intellectual property law and, in particular, on the IPR Enforcement Directive. The outline of this chapter largely mirrors that of the foregoing chapter. Accordingly, the first section below discusses the relevant substantive rules and the background and context of this directive. The next sections then analyse its main content. In the latter context the remedies which this directive provides are discussed, whereby a distinction is made between measures of a preliminary, provisional and precautionary nature, actions for damages and other decisions on the merits under this directive. Attention then turns to the most relevant procedural provisions. The final section of this chapter is dedicated to other enforcement-related issues concerning infringements of intellectual property rights, in particular the public enforcement dimension.

A. INTRODUCTION

This section introduces the IPR Enforcement Directive. To this aim the first subsection below briefly outlines the EU's involvement with substantive intellectual property law and the infringements thereof that this directive seeks to address. Subsequently the background and a number of general issues relating to this directive are discussed, followed by some additional general remarks on the context in which it is applied.

1. Substantive law and infringements

4.01 Intellectual property rights are the rights given to persons over the creations of the mind, usually giving those persons an exclusive right over the use of their creations for a certain period of time. The term "intellectual property" in its classic sense encompasses two main categories. To begin with, it covers copyright and related rights, which are rights granted to authors of literary or artistic works and rights of performers, producers of phonograms and broadcasting organisations. It further covers industrial property, thus including distinctive signs protected by trade marks and geographic indications, as well as inventions protected by patents and industrial designs. When understood in a wider sense, intellectual property also includes trade secrets. Trade secrets are typically used as a complement or alternative to protection under intellectual property law strictly speaking, either because the latter is legally not possible or because this is simply seen as a preferable form of protecting know-how and business information in a given situation. They thus result primarily from a policy decision of the undertaking concerned; they are not statutory rights. On a broader understanding of this term, internet domain names can also be considered a form of intellectual property.

4.02 Over the years many acts of secondary EU law concerning substantive intellectual property law have been adopted, in particular with a view to levelling the playing field for undertakings operating on the EU's internal market. At present virtually all types of intellectual property rights are to a greater or lesser extent affected by EU law.[1] These substantive EU rules are all based on internal market-related provisions of the EU Treaties, namely Articles 53, 62, 114 and/or 352 TFEU. Only in 2009 (through the Treaty of Lisbon) was a specific legal basis inserted in the EU Treaties for the creation of European intellectual property rights in the context of the internal market, Article 118 TFEU.

A distinction can be made between two forms of EU legislative activity on matters of substantive intellectual property law. First, there is EU legislation *harmonising* the relevant rules of national law. Such harmonisation has taken place, for instance, concerning national laws on trade marks,[2] designs,[3] and copyright and related rights, the latter leading *inter alia* to the adoption of Directive 2001/29 concerning copyright and related rights in the information

---

1 Cf. recital 3 IPR Enforcement Directive 2004/48: '*the substantive law on intellectual property [...] is nowadays largely part of the acquis communautaire*'.

2 Directive 2008/95/EC to approximate the laws of the Member States relating to trade marks, OJ 2008, L 299/25 ("Trade Marks Directive"). In 2013 the Commission proposed recasting this directive. See Commission, Proposal for a directive to approximate the laws of the Member States relating to trade marks, COM(2013) 162.

3 Directive 98/71/EC on the legal protection of designs, OJ 1998, L 289/28.

society[4] ("Infosoc Directive"). Second, the EU has adopted legislation that creates *EU unitary rights*. This latter legislation is not concerned with the harmonisation of national laws, but instead creates new, free-standing intellectual property rights at EU level, which offer direct protection in all Member States. Examples include Regulation 207/2009 on the Community trade mark[5] ("Community Trade Mark Regulation"), Regulation 6/2002 on Community designs[6] ("Community Designs Regulation") and Regulation 2100/94 on Community plant variety rights[7] ("Community Plant Variety Rights Regulation").

Furthermore, in 2012 a patent package was adopted. It consists of two regulations,[8] complemented by an Agreement on a Unified Patent Court[9] ("Patent Court Agreement"). This agreement has been signed (but for the time being not yet ratified) by almost all Member States.[10] After several earlier attempts over the past decades,[11] this package creates an EU regime on unitary rights for patents. It differs from the above-mentioned regimes providing for EU unitary intellectual property rights, however, as it creates the possibility of giving unitary effect to European patents granted pursuant to the European Patent Convention, rather than an EU unitary right proper. Procedurally this regime came into being as a form of "enhanced cooperation".[12] That implies that it does not (or at least not necessarily) involve all Member States. The Patent Court Agreement is an intergovernmental agreement, which is not part of EU law strictly speaking.[13] This agreement not only designates the competent courts, as its name already indicates, but it also sets out the applicable rules on remedies

4 Directive 2001/29/EC on the harmonisation of certain aspects of copyright and related rights in the information society, OJ 2001, L 167/10. See also Directive 93/83/EEC on the coordination of certain rules concerning copyright and rights related to copyright applicable to satellite broadcasting and cable retransmission, OJ 1993, L 248/15; Directive 2006/116/EC on the term of protection of copyright and certain related rights, OJ 2006, L 372/12; Directive 2009/24/EC on the legal protection of computer programmes, OJ 2009, L 111/16.

5 Regulation (EC) No 207/2009 on the Community trade mark, OJ 2009, L 78/1.

6 Regulation (EC) No 6/2002 on Community designs, OJ 2002, L 3/1.

7 Regulation (EC) No 2100/94 on Community plant variety rights, OJ 1994, L 227/1.

8 Regulation (EU) No 1257/2012 implementing enhanced cooperation in the area of the creation of unitary patent protection, OJ 2012, L 361/1; Regulation (EU) No 1260/2012 implementing enhanced cooperation in the area of the creation of unitary patent protection with regard to the applicable translation arrangements, OJ 2012, L 361/89. In 2013 Spain filed actions for the annulment of these two regulations, which were rejected, however. See CoJ case C-146/13, *Spain v Parliament and Council*, CoJ case C-147/13, *Spain v Council.*

9 Council, Notice Agreement on a Unified Patent Court, OJ 2013, C 175/1. See also CoJ Opinion 1/09, *Patent Court Agreement.*

10 For the most recent state of play as regards the signature and ratification of the Patent Court Agreement, see http://ec.europa.eu/internal_market/indprop/patent/ratification/index_en.htm. See also Ullrich (2015), p. 1.

11 See e.g. Commission, Proposal for a regulation on the Community patent, COM(2000) 412.

12 Art. 20 TEU; Art. 326–34 TFEU. See CoJ joined cases C-274/11 and C-295/11, *Spain and Italy v Council.* See further e.g. Pistoa (2014), p. 247.

13 Cf. Opinion AG Bot case C-146/13, *Spain v Parliament and Council*, para 163.

and procedures for the private enforcement of the rights in question.[14] In this respect it thus constitutes, as it were, a form of "harmonised transposition" of the IPR Enforcement Directive by the Member States concerned regarding the enforcement of this specific intellectual property right.

4.03 Infringements of intellectual property rights can take many forms. One could think of the production and sale of clothing containing a protected brand name without the authorisation of the trade mark proprietor or the reproduction of a film in violation of copyright law. It is generally acknowledged that intellectual property right infringements of this kind take place on a very significant and probably increasing scale. In its 1998 green paper on this subject matter, the Commission called this a '*widespread phenomenon with a global impact*'.[15] Precise and undisputed figures about the scale of these infringements are scarce, however. Worldwide trade in counterfeit and pirated products[16] has been estimated to represent a value of $250 billion in 2007, up from $100 billion in 2000.[17]

More specifically, regarding the EU the Commission has held that these infringements are detrimental to the proper functioning of the internal market, as they give rise to a deflection of trade and distort competition, leading to a loss of confidence and less investment and outlay on innovation and creativity.[18] They are also said to have negative consequences in terms of consumer protection, as "fake" products may not offer the same quality as "real" ones. It has been estimated that infringements of intellectual property rights could lead to losses reducing the EU's cumulative gross domestic product by €8 billion per year.[19] In 2000 the Commission found that its concerns were largely shared by the respondents to the consultation that it had initiated through the 1998 green paper.[20] In this connection it noted that '*[c]ounterfeiting and piracy, which were once craft activities, have become almost industrial-scale activities*'.[21] It appears that

14 See Art. 56–82 Patent Court Agreement.

15 Commission, Green paper on combating counterfeiting and piracy in the single market, COM(98) 569, p. 4.

16 The term "counterfeiting and piracy" is sometimes used as an alternative for infringements of intellectual property rights, without there being a material difference (at least as these terms are used by the Commission). See Commission, Green paper on combating counterfeiting and piracy in the single market, COM(98) 569, pp. 6–7; Commission, Communication on enhancing the enforcement of intellectual property rights in the internal market, COM(2009) 467, p. 3 (n. 1).

17 Commission, Communication on a single market for intellectual property rights, COM(2011) 287, p. 17.

18 Commission, Green paper on combating counterfeiting and piracy in the single market, COM(98) 569, p. 5.

19 Commission, Communication on a single market for intellectual property rights, COM(2011) 287, p. 17.

20 Commission, Communication on the follow-up to the green paper on combating counterfeiting and piracy in the single market, COM(2000) 789.

21 Commission, Proposal for IPR Enforcement Directive 2004/48, COM(2003) 46, p. 12.

these activities regularly involve organised crime.[22] As the Commission observed in 2014, such commercial-scale infringements are '*both insidious and a moving target*'.[23]

2. IPR Enforcement Directive: General issues

In light of the EU's involvement with substantive intellectual property law and the scale and possible consequences of the infringements of this law, as discussed in the foregoing, the question arose as to whether legislative measures should be taken at EU level as regards the remedies and procedures applicable in proceedings before national courts relating to the enforcement of the rights in question by the private parties concerned. In January 2003 the Commission essentially answered this question in the affirmative by adopting a proposal for a new directive on this subject matter.[24] **4.04**

In the explanatory memorandum to this proposal, the Commission called EU involvement with the enforcement of intellectual property rights a '*logical extension*' of the EU's involvement with substantive intellectual property law.[25] There it also expanded on the scale and consequences of these infringements. This was called '*a constantly growing phenomenon*' that constitutes '*a serious threat to national economies and governments*'.[26] According to the Commission, disparities between national laws in the EU had a '*major impact, in particular on the effectiveness and costs of procedures, time scales and the amounts of damages granted*'.[27] This was said to have direct repercussions on trade between the Member States and a direct impact on the conditions governing competition in the market. The Commission found this '*difficult to reconcile with guaranteeing rights holders an equivalent level of protection in the internal market*'.[28] Other negative effects of intellectual property rights infringements were also noted, such as their impact on innovation and competitiveness, the cultural sector, employment, tax revenues and market stability, consumer protection and public order.[29] Combating such infringements was therefore seen as being of '*vital*

22 Commission, Communication towards a renewed consensus on the enforcement of intellectual property rights, COM(2014) 392, p. 2. Here a UK study is cited, according to which 81 per cent of intellectual property rights-infringing products are estimated to be associated with organised crime.

23 Ibid.

24 Commission, Proposal for IPR Enforcement Directive 2004/48, COM(2003) 46.

25 Ibid., p. 5. Cf. Reinbothe (2010), p. 6, where the provisions on the enforcement of intellectual property rights are called '*a corollary*' of harmonisation of EU Member States' intellectual property rights.

26 Ibid., p. 3.

27 Ibid., p. 15.

28 Ibid., p. 5. On these differences between national enforcement systems, see further e.g. Vandermeulen (2005), p. 30.

29 Ibid., pp. 4–12.

importance' and a directive was proposed '*to tackle this situation by harmonising national legislation on the enforcement of intellectual property rights*'.[30]

4.05 After a relatively speedy legislative process, this Commission proposal led to the adoption by the EU legislature of the IPR Enforcement Directive in April 2004.[31] Agreement between the EU's two co-legislators, the European Parliament and the Council, was reached little more than a year after the publication of the Commission proposal. The imminent "eastern" enlargement of the EU with ten new Member States in May 2004 is believed to have acted as an important incentive to reach an agreement beforehand.[32]

Whereas the adoption process may have been rather smooth, the same cannot be said of the process of transposition. The Member States were obliged to transpose the directive into national law by April 2006.[33] Only five Member States did so on time, however.[34] The overall transposition process was not fully completed until 2009, Germany, Sweden and Luxemburg being the last Member States to ensure transposition.[35] This also means that to date the rules set out in this directive have been applicable at national level and available to aggrieved private parties for a relatively modest period of time. As a consequence, the experiences with its practical application and the case law generated in this regard are somewhat limited.

4.06 The IPR Enforcement Directive's legal basis is the EU Treaties' provision that allows for the adoption of measures for the approximation of national laws having as their object the establishment and functioning of the internal market, Article 114 TFEU. This link between the legislative measures in question and the internal market is extensively explained in the directive's recitals. There the protection of intellectual property is called an essential element of the success of the internal market.[36] The negative consequences of an absence of '*effective means of enforcing intellectual property rights*' are also highlighted.[37] It is said to be necessary, therefore, to ensure that the substantive law on intellectual property is '*applied effectively*' in the EU. The recitals further note the '*major*

30 Ibid., p. 3.

31 IPR Enforcement Directive 2004/48. For an overview of the process leading to the directive's adoption, see Kur (2004), p. 821.

32 Kur (2004), p. 821; Reinbothe (2010), p. 8; Lakits-Josse (2011), p. 520.

33 Art. 20 IPR Enforcement Directive 2004/48.

34 Commission, Staff working document accompanying the report on IPR Enforcement Directive 2004/48, SEC(2010) 1589, p. 27.

35 Commission, Report on IPR Enforcement Directive 2004/48, COM(2010) 779, p. 4; Commission, Staff working document accompanying the report on IPR Enforcement Directive 2004/48, SEC(2010) 1589, p. 27.

36 Recital 1 IPR Enforcement Directive 2004/48.

37 Recital 3 IPR Enforcement Directive 2004/48.

disparities' between the Member States concerning the means of enforcing intellectual property rights, for instance as regards provisional measures, the preservation of evidence, the calculation of damages and injunctive relief.[38] This was seen as:

> prejudicial to the proper functioning of the internal market and [making] it impossible to ensure that intellectual property rights enjoy an equivalent level of protection throughout the [EU] [and leading] to a weakening of the substantive law on intellectual property rights and to a fragmentation of the internal market in this field.[39]

The directive's objective is, in the words of its recitals, '*to approximate legislative systems so as to ensure a high, equivalent and homogeneous level of protection in the internal market*'.[40] This has also been identified as its objective in the case law of the Court of Justice.[41] In other rulings the Court has, however, referred in this respect to ensuring the '*effective protection of intellectual property*'[42] or '*the enforcement of intellectual property rights by means of the introduction, for that purpose, of various measures, procedures and remedies within the Member States*'.[43] The provisions of this directive thus govern the aspects of intellectual property rights related to the enforcement of those rights and their infringements by requiring that there must be effective legal remedies designed to prevent, terminate or rectify any such infringement.[44]

In this connection mention can also be made of what can be called the directive's "general rules". This refers to its broadly formulated provisions concerning the manner in which the directive is to be understood and applied in general. It stipulates that the measures, procedures and remedies set out therein must be '*fair and equitable and [...] not be unnecessarily complicated or costly, or entail unreasonable time-limits or unwarranted delays*'.[45] It is added that they must also be '*effective, proportionate and dissuasive*' and be applied in such a manner as to avoid the creation of barriers to legitimate trade and to provide for safeguards against their abuse.[46] While these general rules might be of limited significance as independent rules, they may well provide useful guidance when interpreting the other, more detailed provisions of this directive or when deciding matters that are not expressly addressed therein.

38 Recital 7 IPR Enforcement Directive 2004/48.
39 Recitals 8–9 IPR Enforcement Directive 2004/48.
40 Recital 10 IPR Enforcement Directive 2004/48.
41 CoJ case C-406/09, *Realchemie*, para 49.
42 CoJ case C-324/09, *L'Oréal v eBay*, para 131.
43 CoJ case C-180/11, *Bericap*, para 73; CoJ case C-435/12, *ACI Adam*, para 60.
44 CoJ case C-180/11, *Bericap*, para 75; CoJ case C-435/12, *ACI Adam*, para 61.
45 Art. 3(1) IPR Enforcement Directive 2004/48.
46 Art. 3(2) IPR Enforcement Directive 2004/48.

4.07 During the law-making process the EU legislature extended the scope of the proposed directive in two ways. In the first place, the general restriction to infringements of intellectual property rights committed for *commercial purposes or causing significant harm* that the Commission had proposed was considered too limited.[47] This general limitation was therefore dropped at an early stage of the legislative deliberations, although a similar restriction has been retained in a number of specific provisions.[48] A second extension of the scope of the directive concerned the inclusion of a provision specifying that this directive not only relates to infringements of intellectual property rights established or harmonised by *EU* law, as the Commission had proposed,[49] but also to "purely" *national* laws (that is, national laws other than those transposing obligations stemming from the relevant EU directives on substantive intellectual property law). One could think of acts involving unfair competition such as parasitic copying or similar activities.[50]

The Commission had further proposed listing the relevant instruments of substantive EU law on intellectual property in an annex to the directive.[51] The IPR Enforcement Directive as finally adopted does not list the legal instruments or rights concerned, however. It stipulates instead in a general manner that the directive applies to '*any infringement of intellectual property rights as provided for by [EU] law and/or by the national law of the Member State concerned*'.[52] In the recitals it is added that the scope of the directive should be defined as widely as possible.[53] In 2005 the Commission published a statement listing the intellectual property rights that it considers to be covered by the directive.[54] This list is not legally binding, however, and neither is it exhaustive. If and when the aforementioned possible revision of this directive takes place, a list might be annexed to it for clarification purposes.[55] For the time being, the current arrangement means, however, that the scope of the IPR Enforcement Directive is not always entirely clear.

Not included in the above-mentioned Commission list are trade secrets, which are not intellectual property rights in a classic sense but which can be considered

47 Council, doc. 11107/03; Council, doc. 12450/03; European Parliament, Report on the proposal for IPR Enforcement Directive 2004/48, A5_0468/2003, p. 6. See also Massa and Strowell (2004), pp. 247–53.
48 See Art. 6(2), 8(1) and 9(2) IPR Enforcement Directive 2004/48. See also its recital 14.
49 Commission, Proposal for IPR Enforcement Directive 2004/48, COM(2003) 46, pp. 18 and 32 (Art. 2).
50 Cf. recital 13 IPR Enforcement Directive 2004/48.
51 Commission, Proposal for IPR Enforcement Directive 2004/48, COM(2003) 46, pp. 44–5 (annex).
52 Art. 2(1) IPR Enforcement Directive 2004/48.
53 Recital 13 IPR Enforcement Directive 2004/48.
54 Commission, Statement concerning Article 2 IPR Enforcement Directive 2004/48, OJ 2005, L 94/37.
55 Commission, Report on IPR Enforcement Directive 2004/48, COM(2010) 779, p. 7.

as such when this term is understood more broadly.[56] Rather than amending the IPR Enforcement Directive so as to clarify that trade secrets are also covered and to insert certain complementary rules, in 2013 the Commission published a proposal for a separate directive on the protection of trade secrets, however.[57] At the heart of this draft directive lie a set of remedial and procedural rules meant to ensure the availability of civil redress against unlawful acquisition, use and disclosure of trade secrets.[58] These rules are to a large extent similar to the rules set out in the IPR Enforcement Directive, without, however, being exactly the same. In the recitals of this draft directive it is said that, should the scope of these two directives overlap, the proposed trade secret directive takes precedence as a *lex specialis*.[59]

Both in its 2010 report on the application of the IPR Enforcement Directive and in several subsequent (consultation) documents, the Commission discussed the possibility of revising this directive. For now it remains uncertain, however, whether a legislative amendment will actually be proposed in the near future. The available documents suggest that if and when such an amendment were to be proposed, it would in all likelihood address a limited number of specific issues, such as the directive's application in an online environment, a clarification of its scope, the involvement of third-party intermediaries and the difficulties that small and medium-sized enterprises are said to experience when trying to enforce their intellectual property rights.[60] These issues are further discussed below, where relevant. **4.08**

3. Additional general remarks

The first additional remark to be made here concerns the directive's impact on the domestic laws of the Member States. On the one hand, the IPR Enforcement Directive evidently seeks to harmonise the relevant rules of national law. It obliges the Member States to amend those laws, albeit to varying degrees and in various manners, where they relate to the remedies and procedures for the **4.09**

56 See para 4.01 above. Trade secrets constitute intellectual property within the meaning of the TRIPS Agreement (see its Art. 1(2) and 39). On this agreement, see para 4.12 below.

57 Commission, Proposal for a trade secrets directive, COM(2013) 813. On this proposal, see further Grassie (2014), p. 677; Saias (2014), p. 721. See also Bronckers and McNelis (2012), p. 673.

58 Ibid., pp. 19–24 (Art. 5–15).

59 Ibid., p. 16 (recital 28).

60 Commission, Report on IPR Enforcement Directive 2004/48, COM(2010) 779, pp. 5–9. See also Commission, Responses to the report on IPR Enforcement Directive 2004/48, July 2011; Commission, Communication on a single market for intellectual property rights, COM(2011) 287, p. 19; Commission, Consultation on the civil enforcement of intellectual property rights, 2012; Commission, Responses to the public consultation on the civil enforcement of intellectual property rights, July 2013; Commission, Communication towards a renewed consensus on the enforcement of intellectual property rights, COM(2014) 392, p. 7.

enforcement of intellectual property rights.[61] On the other hand, efforts have been made to ensure that the pre-existing national legal regimes are respected as much as possible. The Commission has stressed that '*account should be taken of the legal traditions and situation of each Member State*' and that '*the question is to ensure that intellectual property rights are enforced in an equivalent fashion throughout the [EU], but within the existing national frameworks*'.[62] The directive explicitly allows Member States to retain or adopt further-reaching national legislation, in so far as such measures are more favourable for holders of intellectual property rights.[63] Some of its provisions are, moreover, merely optional.[64] The Commission has described the directive as '*a minimum but standard toolbox*' to combat infringements of intellectual property rights in legal proceedings before national courts.[65]

4.10 It can further be noted that the (draft) directive was on the whole rather critically received by academics and other interested parties. Some criticised it for not going far enough in harmonising the laws of the Member States.[66] Others questioned, in contrast, the justification for amending those laws.[67] The latter doubted especially the underlying assessment by the Commission that infringers of intellectual property rights exploited disparities in the domestic laws of the Member States.[68] It was argued that the matters at issue should be left to national law, pursuant to the principle of subsidiarity. The "fragmenting" effects that the directive would have on national laws were also noted. The latter refers to the fact that the directive applies only to infringements of intellectual property rights, whereas the national laws that it affects are typically designed to apply across the board and therefore also in relation to infringements of other rules of law. Other commentators found several of the directive's provisions too vague and elastic.[69]

4.11 A third remark is that other rules of EU law may also be of relevance in relation to infringements of EU intellectual property law. To begin with, substantive EU intellectual property law can be of importance, not only for the relevant substantive rules it lays down, but also for the enforcement-related provisions it

61 Cf. Speyart (2005), p. 271; Norrgård (2005), p. 507; Harbottle (2006), p. 721; Schaffner (2010), p. 178.

62 Commission, Proposal for IPR Enforcement Directive 2004/48, COM(2003) 46, p. 15.

63 See in particular Art. 2(1) and recitals 13 and 14 IPR Enforcement Directive 2004/48. Cf. Commission, Staff working document accompanying the report on IPR Enforcement Directive 2004/48, SEC(2010) 1589, p. 5.

64 E.g. Art. 12 and Art. 13(2) IPR Enforcement Directive 2004/48.

65 Commission, Report on IPR Enforcement Directive 2004/48, COM(2010) 779, p. 5.

66 Massa and Strowell (2004), p. 246.

67 Cornish et al. (2003), p. 448.

68 See also Massa and Strowell (2004), p. 244.

69 Kur (2004), p. 830; Gielen (2005), p. 10. In a similar sense, see Geiger, Raynard and Rodà (2011), p. 546; Norrgård (2005), p. 503.

occasionally contains. The Infosoc Directive, for instance, sets out some (rather rudimentary) rules on sanctions and remedies in respect of infringements, including on actions for damages, prohibitive injunctions and the seizure of infringing material.[70] The above-mentioned legislation establishing EU unitary rights typically contains rather detailed rules on the designation of specialised national courts, applicable law, jurisdiction, sanctions and provisional and protective measures. Such rules can, for example, be found in the Community Design Regulation and the Community Trade Mark Regulation.[71] The Community Plant Variety Rights Regulation also includes rules on civil law claims.[72] Those rules specify that infringers may be sued to enjoin such infringements or pay reasonable compensation and make good any further damage. Restitution of unlawfully made profits by the infringer may take place in accordance with national law. Pursuant to the implementing rules, there is, moreover, an obligation to pay damages covering at least a lump sum calculated on the basis of the quadruple average amount charged for the licensed production of a corresponding quantity in certain cases of repeated and intentional non-compliance.[73]

The IPR Enforcement Directive should further be understood against the background of certain other provisions of EU law that can have an impact on the enforcement of intellectual property rights. Regulation 608/2013 ("Customs Enforcement Regulation") provides, for instance, the basis for cooperation between private parties holding intellectual property rights and the customs authorities of the Member States.[74] This regulation (and its predecessor) is seen as an important means to fight intellectual property right infringements where customs matters are concerned.[75] The E-Commerce Directive also contains rules that can be relevant in the present context, especially in relation to liability of online intermediaries in relation to infringements of intellectual property rights.[76] Intellectual property rights-related disputes can further have a fundamental rights dimension, which means that the Charter can be of importance

70 Art. 8 Infosoc Directive 2001/29.

71 See e.g. Art. 80, 88–90 and 93 Community Designs Regulation 6/2002; Art. 95, 101–3 and 109 Community Trade Mark Regulation 207/2009.

72 Art. 94 and 97 Community Plant Variety Rights Regulation 2100/94. See e.g. also its Art. 101, 103, 104 and 107 concerning jurisdiction, rules of procedure, legal standing and penalties, respectively.

73 Art. 18(2) Commission Regulation (EC) No 1768/95 implementing rules on the agricultural exemption provided for in Article 14(3) of Council Regulation (EC) No 2100/94 on Community plant variety rights, OJ 1995, L 173/14.

74 Regulation (EU) No 608/2013 concerning customs enforcement of intellectual property rights, OJ 2013, L 181/15.

75 See e.g. Daele (2004), p. 214. See further Vrins and Schneider (2006).

76 Art. 12–15 E-Commerce Directive 2000/31. Pursuant to Art. 2(3)(a) IPR Enforcement Directive 2004/48, the rules of the IPR Enforcement Directive are without prejudice to those rules set out in the E-Commerce Directive.

too.[77] The provisions of the Charter that can come into play, depending on the case at hand, include its Article 47 on the right to effective judicial protection,[78] its Article 17(2) stipulating that intellectual property shall be protected[79] and its Articles 7 and 8 on the right to respect for private life and protection of personal data, respectively.[80]

4.12 Finally, the IPR Enforcement Directive's international law context should not be overlooked.[81] Of particular importance is the Agreement on Trade-Related Aspects of Intellectual Property Rights ("TRIPS Agreement"), concluded in the context of the WTO.[82] This agreement, which came into effect on 1 January 1995, applies to all WTO members, including all EU Member States and the EU itself.[83] It sets out general obligations, such as most-favoured nation treatment, national treatment of non-nationals and intergovernmental dispute resolution,[84] as well as certain substantive rules on the protection of intellectual property rights.[85] Most importantly for the present purposes, the TRIPS Agreement lays down rules on the enforcement of these rights by private parties.[86] The IPR Enforcement Directive is one of the measures through which the EU has given effect to its obligations under the TRIPS Agreement[87] and, in many respects, the former builds on the latter. In the explanatory memorandum to its proposal for this directive, the Commission repeatedly highlighted this kinship, while noting that on various points the obligations

77 Cf. recitals 2 and 32 IPR Enforcement Directive 2004/48.

78 See further para 2.11 above.

79 See Geiger (2009), p. 113, with further references.

80 Concerning the protection of personal data Art. 2(3)(a) IPR Enforcement Directive 2004/48 provides explicitly that it does not affect Data Protection Directive 95/46. In addition, Art. 16 Charter on the freedom to conduct a business and Art. 11 Charter on the freedom of expression and information can, for example, be of relevance. See also para 4.18 below.

81 On the external dimension of intellectual property rights enforcement from an EU perspective, see further Matthews (2010), p. 104.

82 See recitals 4 and 5 IPR Enforcement Directive 2004/48.

83 See Decision 94/800/EC concerning the conclusion on behalf of the European Community, as regards matters within its competence, of the agreements reached in the Uruguay Round multilateral negotiations (1986–94), OJ 1994, L 336/1.

84 Parts I and V TRIPS Agreement.

85 Part II TRIPS Agreement. In many instances these rules reproduce and extend provisions of pre-existing international conventions established under the aegis of a specialised agency of the United Nations, the World Intellectual Property Organization ("WIPO"). The main WIPO conventions are the Paris Convention for the protection of industrial property ("Paris Convention") and the Berne Convention for the protection of literary and artistic works ("Berne Convention"). Both conventions also contain certain (rather rudimentary) provisions relating to enforcement. See Art. 2(1) and 9–10 Paris Convention; Art. 15–16 Berne Convention.

86 Part III TRIPS Agreement.

87 CoJ case C-180/11, *Bericap*, para 73.

contained in this directive go beyond those set out in the agreement.[88] Consequently, the relevant provisions of EU law are, as far as possible, to be interpreted in accordance with the TRIPS Agreement.[89]

The parties to the TRIPS Agreement must '*permit effective action*' against any act of infringement, including expeditious and deterrent remedies.[90] The relevant procedures must be '*fair and equitable [...] and not be unnecessarily complicated or costly, or entail unreasonable time-limits or unwarranted delays*'.[91] Civil judicial procedures must be available, fulfilling certain minimum requirements as regards the course of proceedings.[92] The TRIPS Agreement further stipulates that the competent judicial authorities must have the authority to order the defendant to produce evidence lying within its control, where the applicant has presented reasonable available evidence sufficient to support its claims.[93] Similarly, but on an optional basis, these authorities may be authorised to order infringing parties to provide information on third parties involved in the production or distribution of the goods or services concerned.[94] Specific remedies are also provided for, including actions for injunctions (aimed at obtaining an order for the opposing party to desist from an infringement) and actions for damages (which must be adequate to compensate for the injury suffered because of the infringement).[95] It must further be possible to order the disposal or destruction of the infringing goods, as well as prompt and effective provisional measures.[96] Lastly, the parties to the TRIPS Agreement are under an obligation to provide for criminal sanctions, at least in cases of wilful trade mark counterfeiting or copyright piracy on a commercial scale.[97]

Apart from the foregoing, in 2010 agreement was reached at international level on the Anti-Counterfeiting Trade Agreement ("ACTA"). This international agreement was negotiated on an *ad hoc* multilateral basis, outside existing structures such as the WTO. In essence, ACTA seeks to strengthen the possibilities to enforce intellectual property rights worldwide. It builds on the TRIPS Agreement, but it contains further-reaching provisions on various

88 Commission, Proposal for IPR Enforcement Directive 2004/48, COM(2003) 46, p. 12. See also Commission, Communication on the follow-up to the green paper on combating counterfeiting and piracy in the single market, COM(2000) 789, p. 6.
89 CoJ case C-53/96, *Hermès International*, para 28.
90 Art. 41(1) TRIPS Agreement.
91 Art. 41(2) TRIPS Agreement.
92 Art. 42 TRIPS Agreement.
93 Art. 43(1) TRIPS Agreement.
94 Art. 47 TRIPS Agreement.
95 Art. 44 and 45 TRIPS Agreement, respectively.
96 Art. 46 and 50 TRIPS Agreement, respectively.
97 Art. 61 TRIPS Agreement.

points, including on enforcement via civil law procedures and criminal law.[98] ACTA has been signed by countries such as the US, Canada, Japan and South Korea, as well as by the EU and most of its Member States. The Commission took the view that ACTA's provisions are fully in line with the currently existing EU *acquis*.[99] It proposed finalising the process of ratification that follows signature.[100] However, within the EU this international agreement proved to be very controversial. From various sides criticism was voiced, relating *inter alia* to the non-transparent manner in which ACTA had (allegedly) been negotiated, the correctness of the Commission's above assessment, the impact it might have on the right to privacy and protection of personal data and, more generally, the absence of a sufficiently balanced approach.[101] In the end the European Parliament refused to give its consent, which is required for an international agreement such as this one to be ratified at EU level.[102] As a consequence, the EU did not ratify ACTA and it is therefore not bound by it.

B. REMEDIES

The core of the IPR Enforcement Directive consists of a set of specific private enforcement remedies, which for the present purposes can be divided into five categories. To begin with, there are measures related to obtaining and preserving evidence and information relevant to intellectual property disputes. These measures, which take an important place under this directive, are largely of a preliminary nature, in that they normally precede any assessment of the merits of the case. Second, the directive sets out a number of measures of a provisional and precautionary nature. It concerns in particular interlocutory injunctions, to be issued by means of interim measures. Third, as regards possible decisions on the merits, the directive provides for the possibility for a national court to order certain corrective measures and "permanent" injunctions. The fourth remedy concerns actions for damages, which is another possible decision on the merits.

---

98 Art. 7–12 and 23–6 ACTA. See also Art. 27 ACTA, which lays down specific provisions relating to enforcement in the digital environment.

99 E.g. Commission, Communication on a single market for intellectual property rights, COM(2011) 287, p. 20.

100 See Commission, Proposal for a decision on the conclusion of ACTA, COM(2011) 380.

101 E.g. European Parliament, Resolution on the transparency and the state of play of ACTA negotiations, P7_TA(2010)0058; European Data Protection Supervisor, Opinion on the current negotiations by the EU of an Anti-Counterfeiting Trade Agreement (ACTA), OJ 2010, C 147/1; European Parliament, Resolution on the Anti-Counterfeiting Trade Agreement (ACTA), P7_TA(2010)0432. See also European academics (2011), p. 65; Commission, Comments on the "opinion of European academics on ACTA", April 2011. For a further explanation from the side of the Commission officials involved in the ACTA negotiations, see Devigne, Velasco-Martins and Iliopoulou (2010), pp. 33–42.

102 European Parliament, Legislative resolution on the draft Council decision on the conclusion of ACTA, P7_TA-PROV(2012)0287. The European Parliament's consent was required pursuant to Art. 218(6) TFEU. See further Matthews and Žikovská (2013), p. 626.

Finally, a national court seised can order two complementary measures under this directive, namely the payment of legal costs and publicity measures. These five categories are discussed in the following sections.

1. Measures on the disclosure of evidence

The recitals of the IPR Enforcement Directive state that '*evidence is an element of paramount importance for establishing the infringement of intellectual property rights*'.[103] This view is widely shared by academics, practitioners and other stakeholders alike.[104] The EU legislature also considered it of importance, with a view to ensuring a high level of protection, to allow a rightholder to obtain precise information on the origin of infringing goods or services, relevant distribution channels or the identity of any third parties involved in the infringement.[105] Against this background the IPR Enforcement Directive lays down three sorts of measures relating to the disclosure of evidence and information. **4.13**

First, the directive provides in a general manner that the competent national court must be able to order the defendant to *present* evidence lying within the latter's control, subject to the protection of confidential information. However, this can only be done upon the private party initiating the proceedings having first presented '*reasonably available evidence sufficient to support its claims, and has, in substantiating those claims, specified evidence which lies in the control of the opposing party*'.[106] Thus a court order is required and confidential information is protected, while it is for the applicant to establish a *prima facie* case and specify the evidence concerned. This provision is modelled on the TRIPS Agreement.[107] The directive adds that on an optional basis Member States may provide that '*a reasonable sample of a substantial number of copies of a work or any other protected object*' is considered to constitute reasonable evidence.[108] **4.14**

Apart from this general provision, the Member States must also ensure more specifically that under the same conditions their national courts can order, where appropriate, the communication of banking, financial or commercial

103 Recital 20 IPR Enforcement Directive 2004/48.

104 See e.g. Gielen (2005), p. 8; Bonadio (2008), p. 321; Hess (2008), pp. 289–90; Cornish, Llewelyn and Aplin (2010), pp. 88–9; Lakits-Josse (2011), pp. 529 and 531. See also Study, European Observatory on Counterfeiting and Piracy (undated a), p. 2.

105 Recital 21 IPR Enforcement Directive 2004/48.

106 Art. 6(1) IPR Enforcement Directive 2004/48.

107 Art. 43 TRIPS Agreement. Cf. Commission, Proposal for IPR Enforcement Directive 2004/48, COM(2003) 46, p. 20.

108 Art. 6(1) IPR Enforcement Directive 2004/48.

documents under the control of the opposing party.[109] This latter measure is limited, however, to cases of infringements committed on a commercial scale. In the recitals it is clarified that this refers to acts carried out for direct or indirect commercial advantage, and that this would normally exclude acts carried out by end consumers acting in good faith.[110] In this manner the directive seeks to ensure a degree of proportionality between (the scale of) the infringements and the measures imposed as a consequence thereof.

4.15 Secondly, particularly when confronted with the possibility of having to present evidence lying within its control discussed above, a party having infringed intellectual property rights might be inclined to destroy or otherwise dispose of relevant evidence.[111] It must therefore be ensured under the IPR Enforcement Directive that, even before proceedings on the merits of the case are initiated, a court can order '*prompt and effective*' provisional measures to *preserve* evidence.[112] The applicable conditions are essentially similar to the ones mentioned in the previous paragraph as regards the presentation of evidence. The directive specifies that these preservation measures may take the form of the detailed description (with or without taking samples) or the physical seizure of the infringing goods or the production or distribution of those goods or of documents relating thereto. This thus entails the possibility of issuing *ex parte* search orders, allowing a private party to enter the premises of another party for the preservation of evidence of alleged infringements of intellectual property rights.

The IPR Enforcement Directive indicates that in certain cases this remedy may be granted without the other party having been heard. On the one hand, such an approach is understandable, because hearing that party might mean that the latter is given an opportunity to destroy the evidence before a court order is issued. On the other hand, this obviously goes rather far, as it denies that party its right to contest the claims made by the applicant. Therefore, this measure can only be ordered where it is necessary, '*in particular where any delay is likely to cause irreparable harm to the rightholder or where there is a demonstrable risk of evidence being destroyed*'.[113] A set of additional procedural safeguards are also provided, including an obligation to inform the party that is subject to this measure afterwards, the possibility of an *ex post* review and hearing, the lodging of adequate security by the applicant, revocation if no proceedings on the merits

109 Art. 6(2) IPR Enforcement Directive 2004/48.
110 Recital 14 IPR Enforcement Directive 2004/18.
111 Cf. Study, European Observatory on Counterfeiting and Piracy (undated a), p. 2.
112 Art. 7(1) IPR Enforcement Directive 2004/48.
113 Art. 7(1) IPR Enforcement Directive 2004/48.

are initiated within a set time period and compensation to be paid where it turns out that the measure was incorrectly applied for.[114]

This provisional measure to preserve evidence has been modelled upon arrangements that already existed in various Member States, in particular what used to be known as "Anton Pillar orders" under English law and the French *saisie-contrefaçon* procedure.[115] This English law equivalent has been said to have greatly contributed to the speed and effectiveness of the civil process in dealing with infringers of intellectual property rights.[116] Its inclusion in the IPR Enforcement Directive means that this measure has been "generalised", in that it must be made available in all Member States and in relation to all intellectual property rights covered by the directive. In some cases this "generalisation" has gone even further, for instance in the Netherlands, where the rules in question have also occasionally been applied by analogy to cases that do not concern (alleged) infringements of intellectual property rights.[117]

Thirdly, the IPR Enforcement Directive also provides for what it calls the *right of information* of the private parties affected by infringements.[118] This provision has been modelled on the pre-existing laws of certain Member States, notably the Benelux countries and Germany.[119] According to the Commission its "elevation" to the European level, upon a suggestion by the European Parliament, found unanimous support in interested circles.[120] This right is concerned with information on the origin and the distribution networks of the infringing goods or services, such as names and addresses of producers or suppliers. It can also concern information on quantities produced and prices obtained. Whereas the former information can be of obvious importance to determine whether and how an infringement has been committed, the latter information can *inter alia* be of relevance to determine its scale and the damage it may have caused. In response to a '*justified and proportionate request*', a national court must under this directive be able to order the disclosure of the aforementioned information. **4.16**

114 Art. 7(1)–(4) IPR Enforcement Directive 2004/48.

115 Commission, Proposal for IPR Enforcement Directive 2004/48, COM(2003) 46, pp. 13 and 20; Commission, Staff working document accompanying the report on IPR Enforcement Directive 2004/48, SEC(2010) 1589, p. 8.

116 Cornish, Llewelyn and Aplin (2010), pp. 89–90.

117 HR case 12/05529, *UGH*.

118 Art. 8 IPR Enforcement Directive 2004/48.

119 Commission, Proposal for IPR Enforcement Directive 2004/48, COM(2003) 46, p. 20. See also Art. 47 TRIPS.

120 Ibid.

One possibility is that this order is addressed to the (alleged) infringer. However, the directive also provides for the possibility that the order is addressed to certain *third parties*, namely where the latter were found to be in possession of the infringing goods, using the infringing services or providing services used in the infringing activities. Covered also are third parties that have been indicated by any of the aforementioned persons as being involved in the production, manufacture or distribution of the goods and services in question. In each of these cases the third party in question can only be involved if its activities take place on a commercial scale. Consumers acting in good faith are consequently in principle excluded.[121] The providers of services used in the infringing activities are known as intermediaries.[122] One can think of undertakings transporting the goods concerned or, in an online environment, providers of Internet access or of services for online marketplaces. This extension of the right of information so as also to cover certain third parties is an example of a situation where the directive goes beyond the regime of the TRIPS Agreement, as the latter provides for this measure only on an optional basis.[123]

4.17 The Commission's 2010 assessment of the application of the IPR Enforcement Directive suggests that the overall picture is rather positive where the functioning in practice of the above measures is concerned. The possibility of using samples as evidence is, for instance, said to have been on the whole considered favourably by stakeholders.[124] Even though the provision in question is only optional, it has been introduced in many Member States. This was found to have led to a general improvement in the enforcement possibilities. The above-mentioned provisional measures for the preservation of evidence were also highlighted as having helped render the enforcement of intellectual property rights more effective.[125] By contrast, the possibility of description orders, included on an optional basis in the directive, was reported to have been little used by the Member States. Many found this to be more common in a criminal law context than in a civil law context.[126] Concerning the above-mentioned right of information, the possibility of requiring information from third-party intermediaries was reported to be novel to most Member States. It was said to have significantly increased the ability to trace and obtain knowledge of parties

121 See recital 14 IPR Enforcement Directive 2004/48.

122 Cf. recital 23 IPR Enforcement Directive 2004/48.

123 Art. 47 TRIPS Agreement.

124 Commission, Report on IPR Enforcement Directive 2004/48, COM(2010) 779, p. 3; Commission, Staff working document accompanying the report on IPR Enforcement Directive 2004/48, SEC(2010) 1589, pp. 7–8.

125 Commission, Report on IPR Enforcement Directive 2004/48, COM(2010) 779, p. 3.

126 Commission, Staff working document accompanying the report on IPR Enforcement Directive 2004/48, SEC(2010) 1589, p. 8.

infringing intellectual property rights and to have facilitated the calculation of damages.[127]

That is not to say that no critical comments were made in this context. The collection of evidence in cross-border cases reportedly remains difficult, for example.[128] This refers to situations where the applicant and the defendant are not established in the same Member State or where an element relevant to the dispute falls within the jurisdiction of another Member State. In addition, gathering evidence in relation to infringements committed via the internet was singled out as a particular difficulty, both in light of the anonymity that this medium can offer and the formal requirements in terms of acceptable evidence that apply in some national jurisdictions.[129] Lastly, some stakeholders considered several specific issues to be in need of clarification, including the *prima facie* evidence needed in order to obtain a court order, the degree to which applicants must specify the information to which their request for disclosure relates, the requirement that the evidence must be under the control of the other party and the scope of the protection offered to confidential information.[130] As regards the aforementioned *ex parte* search orders, while rightholders asked for a further strengthening, academics and consumer organisations warned against risks of abuse.[131]

The involvement of *third-party intermediaries* in the context of the afore- **4.18**
mentioned right of information has proven to be particularly controversial, especially in online situations. This possibility regularly leads to litigation where, besides the IPR Enforcement Directive, various other acts of secondary EU law as well as a number of fundamental rights are involved.[132] One such case is *Promusicae*, which was decided by the Court of Justice in 2008 on the basis of a Spanish preliminary reference.[133] Promusicae, a non-profit organisation of holders of intellectual property rights, applied for a court order addressed to an internet access provider to disclose the identities and addresses of some of the latter's clients. The persons in question had allegedly infringed

127 Ibid., p. 11. On actions for damages, including issues of quantification, see subsection 4.B.4 below.

128 Commission, Report on IPR Enforcement Directive 2004/48, COM(2010) 779, p. 9; Commission, Staff working document accompanying the report on IPR Enforcement Directive 2004/48, SEC(2010) 1589, p. 8. See also Commission, Responses to the report on IPR Enforcement Directive 2004/48, July 2011, p. 18. See further Hess (2008), p. 289.

129 Commission, Staff working document accompanying the report on IPR Enforcement Directive 2004/48, SEC(2010) 1589, p. 8.

130 Commission, Report on IPR Enforcement Directive 2004/48, COM(2010) 779, p. 9; Commission, Staff working document accompanying the report on IPR Enforcement Directive 2004/48, SEC(2010) 1589, p. 9. See also Commission, Responses to the report on IPR Enforcement Directive 2004/48, July 2011, pp. 18–19.

131 Commission, Responses to the report on IPR Enforcement Directive 2004/48, July 2011, p. 19.

132 See further Van Eecke (2011), p. 1455.

133 CoJ case C-275/06, *Promusicae*. See also CoJ Order case C-557/07, *LSG*.

intellectual property rights held by Promusicae's members by using a "peer-to-peer" file exchange programme. Promusicae needed this information to be able to initiate legal proceedings against those persons. The Court of Justice held that, although this is not excluded, the IPR Enforcement Directive's aforementioned right of information does not mean that the Member States are *obliged* to provide for the disclosure of personal data, which are protected *inter alia* under the E-Privacy Directive,[134] in the context of civil proceedings.[135] In terms of the fundamental rights at issue were, on the one hand, the right to protection of intellectual property and the right to an effective remedy on the side of the rightholders and, on the other hand, the right to privacy and protection of personal data of the persons concerned.[136] The Court ruled that *a fair balance* needs to be struck between these various fundamental rights, taking account also of the principle of proportionality.[137] In subsequent case law it added that national legislation that provides for such a possibility of disclosure of personal data is likely to ensure the required fair balance, where it enables the national court seised to weigh the conflicting interests involved on the basis of the facts of each case and taking due account of the requirements of proportionality.[138]

In 2010 the Commission limited itself in this respect to the statement that '*[f]urther evaluations could be needed*' regarding the extent to which the Member States complied with the requirements resulting from the above case law.[139] The fate of ACTA, where similar concerns played an important role, underlines the sensitivity of this matter.[140] This is confirmed by the responses to the consultations on the function and future of the IPR Enforcement Directive, including from the side of several Member States.[141] This possible involvement of third-party intermediaries in the context of civil proceedings between holders of intellectual property rights and alleged infringers has been justified essentially on the basis of the central role of these (online) intermediaries as

134 See in particular Art. 5(1) E-Privacy Directive 2002/58.

135 CoJ case C-275/06, *Promusicae*, para 57–8. See Art. 8(3)(e) IPR Enforcement Directive 2004/48.

136 Art. 17(2), 47, 7 and 8 Charter respectively.

137 CoJ case C-275/06, *Promusicae*, para 68.

138 CoJ case C-461/10, *Bonnier*, para 57–60.

139 Commission, Report on IPR Enforcement Directive 2004/48, COM(2010) 779, pp. 7–8. Commission, Staff working document accompanying the report on IPR Enforcement Directive 2004/48, SEC(2010) 1589, pp. 12–13.

140 See para 4.12 above.

141 Commission, Responses to the report on IPR Enforcement Directive 2004/48, July 2011, pp. 4–7 and 11–14. See also Commission, Responses to the public hearing on IPR Enforcement Directive 2004/48, June 2011; Commission, Responses to the public consultation on the civil enforcement of intellectual property rights, July 2013, p. 14.

"gatekeepers" and the information that they often possess in that capacity.[142] The Court of Justice seems receptive to this view.[143] Rightholders tend to be in favour of such an approach involving third-party intermediaries. But organisations concerned with the protection of online freedoms, consumer organisations and intermediaries themselves speak of a "privatisation" of enforcement and stress the risk of "private censorship". These opponents argue that intermediaries should not act as a sort of "internet police", forcing them to take arbitrary decisions with respect to their customers based on allegations, and that in this connection personal data should only be disclosed to the competent public authorities and not to other private parties.

2. Interlocutory injunctions and seizures

The IPR Enforcement Directive specifies a number of provisional and precautionary measures that national courts must be able to take. In all cases the measures in question, further discussed below, are to be ordered at the applicant's request. The applicable requirements to be fulfilled before such an order can be made are essentially similar to those discussed in the foregoing subsection as regards the preservation of evidence.[144] Accordingly, the applicant must submit reasonably available evidence and there must be a possibility for these orders to be made in appropriate cases without having heard the opposing party, subject to a set of specific safeguards.[145] **4.19**

A first type of measure of this kind is an *interlocutory injunction*. In its 2003 proposal for the IPR Enforcement Directive, the Commission took the view that provisional measures are of paramount importance in the event of an infringement of intellectual property rights.[146] Under this directive this remedy entails preventing any imminent infringement as well as provisionally forbidding the continuation of an alleged infringement.[147] This being an interim measure, there is no need to await a decision on the merits of the case, as is clarified in the corresponding recital.[148] There it is further said that these measures are particularly justified where any delay would cause irreparable harm to the private party holding the intellectual property right. They can therefore **4.20**

142 Commission, Staff working document accompanying the report on IPR Enforcement Directive 2004/48, SEC(2010) 1589, p. 16. See also Frabboni (2010), p. 119.

143 See e.g. CoJ case C-314/12, *UPC Telekabel Wien*, para 27, where it is held (in connection with the injunctions referred to in Art. 8(3) Infosoc Directive 2001/29) that '*such intermediaries are, in many cases, best placed to bring such infringing activities to an end*'.

144 See para 4.15 above.

145 Art. 9(3)–(7) IPR Enforcement Directive 2004/48.

146 Commission, Proposal for IPR Enforcement Directive 2004/48, COM(2003) 46, p. 21.

147 Art. 9(1)(a) IPR Enforcement Directive 2004/48.

148 Recital 22 IPR Enforcement Directive 2004/48.

even be taken in certain cases without the defendant having been heard.[149] This remedy is thus meant for cases where rapid interference is required by means of the establishment of interim measures. The definitive legal situation can subsequently be determined in an action on the merits. However, this recital also recalls that this should not come at the expense of the defendant's rights of defence and the requirements of proportionality.

In this connection the directive sets out several complementary rules. It is specified, for instance, that this remedy may also entail making the continuation of the allegedly infringing activity subject to the lodging of a guarantee. That guarantee can then be used to ensure that the rightholder is compensated, should it later emerge that he is entitled thereto. The directive also specifies that under the same conditions these interlocutory injunctions can also be issued against intermediaries, which are third parties whose services are used to infringe intellectual property rights. In those cases the relevant conditions and procedures are to be determined by national law.[150] As was the case with the extension of the right of information to intermediaries,[151] in this case also the coverage of these third parties marked a step beyond the regime of the TRIPS Agreement.[152] This approach was novel to most Member States.[153] Lastly, it is stipulated that the above injunctions can be made subject to a recurring penalty payment, where provided for by national law. That is, for instance, the case in the Netherlands, where these payments are due to the applicant, as well as in Slovakia and Germany, where they are instead to be paid to the court that imposed this measure.[154]

4.21 It appears that the functioning in practice of the above remedy is mostly considered rather positively. Interlocutory injunctions are said to be granted relatively quickly.[155] These injunctions, being interim measures, reportedly often lead to a settlement between the parties, thus making legal proceedings on the merits unnecessary. The Commission therefore called this the '*main enforcement remedy*' for most private parties concerned.[156] The possibility of issuing such injunctions against third-party intermediaries was also reported to be relatively frequently used, once again especially in relation to alleged online

149 Art. 9(4) IPR Enforcement Directive 2004/48.

150 See recital 22 IPR Enforcement Directive 2004/48.

151 See para 4.16 above.

152 Art. 50 TRIPS Agreement. On this agreement see para 4.12 above.

153 Commission, Staff working document accompanying the report on IPR Enforcement Directive 2004/48, SEC(2010) 1589, p. 15.

154 Ibid., p. 13.

155 Ibid., pp. 13–15.

156 Ibid., p. 14. See also Commission, Responses to the public consultation on the civil enforcement of intellectual property rights, July 2013, p. 15.

infringements.[157] This can, for instance, lead to the blocking of a website or taking down specific information. This generally rather favourable assessment of this remedy is echoed in other studies and in the legal literature.[158] This is consistent with the finding that stopping the infringing activity is, together with dissuading future infringements, typically the prime objective of private parties that are confronted with infringements of their intellectual property rights.[159]

Yet in the context of the said assessment certain complaints were also observed. These include the level of evidence required in some Member States, such as Finland, among other things as regards the level of certainty that an infringement has actually taken place before these provisional measures are granted.[160] Other sources suggest, however, that evidence is generally not a major concern in this respect.[161] The Commission further reported that the legal costs (lawyers, court fees, experts, and so on) involved in obtaining this remedy can be a concern.[162] However, again there are other reports suggesting that the amounts involved are on the whole comparatively modest.[163] In the legal literature this remedy is in fact mostly seen as relatively cheap to obtain.[164] An arguably more substantial – or at least seemingly more widely shared – concern, especially with respect to interlocutory injunctions, is their functioning in cross-border situations.[165] That applies especially where the intellectual

157 As regards the issues related to the involvement of third-party intermediaries under IPR Enforcement Directive 2004/48, see in particular para 4.18 above and 4.24 below.

158 See e.g. Study, European Observatory on Counterfeiting and Piracy (undated b), p. 4. As regards the legal literature, see e.g. Bonadio (2008), p. 322; Cornish, Llewelyn and Aplin (2010), p. 75. See also Reinbothe (2010), p. 7 (concerning Art. 8(3) Infosoc Directive 2001/29). Note that interlocutory injunctions have often already played an important role before the entry into force of this directive. See e.g. Kur (2004), p. 825; Meier-Beck (2004), pp. 113–14.

159 Commission, Responses to the public consultation on the civil enforcement of intellectual property rights, July 2013, p. 7.

160 Commission, Staff working document accompanying the report on IPR Enforcement Directive 2004/48, SEC(2010) 1589, p. 14.

161 Study, European Observatory on Counterfeiting and Piracy (undated b), p. 5. According to this study, in most Member States rightholders encounter no difficulties in providing the required evidence as regards the applicant being the rightholder and the imminent infringement of this party's right.

162 In Commission, Staff working document accompanying the report on IPR Enforcement Directive 2004/48, SEC(2010) 1589, p. 14 (n. 35), amounts ranging from €3500 to €25 000, and up to €40 000 in patent infringement cases are cited. These amounts appear to be based on the study by the European Observatory on Counterfeiting and Piracy (undated b), pp. 6–7. However, the relevant section in this latter report relates specifically to measures to preserve evidence, and not to interlocutory injunctions.

163 Study, European Observatory on Counterfeiting and Piracy (undated b), pp. 6–7. Here it is reported that obtaining interlocutory injunctions (and other provisional and precautionary remedies) can be rather costly in some Member States, but much less so in other Member States. The amounts cited entail at most a few thousands euros and often less.

164 Bonadio (2008), p. 322; Cornish, Llewelyn and Aplin (2010), p. 75.

165 These concerns generally apply in much the same way to the "permanent" injunctions discussed in para 4.24 below. For practical reasons both issues are discussed jointly here. See Commission, Responses to the public

property right at issue is not an EU unitary right.[166] In the latter case, pursuant to the relevant EU regulations, both the jurisdiction of the national court seised and the territorial scope of the right granted cover in principle the entire EU.[167] Although in these cases also stakeholders have reported difficulties in practice in obtaining cross-border interlocutory injunctions,[168] these difficulties are typically considerably greater in relation to intellectual property rights based on national law (notably patents[169]). For here the general rule is that jurisdiction and territorial scope are limited to national borders.[170]

4.22 The IPR Enforcement Directive also provides for two other types of provisional and precautionary measures, both of which involve the *seizure* of certain goods. To begin with, there is the possibility for the court to order the seizure or delivery of the goods suspected of infringing an intellectual property right.[171] This serves to prevent their entry into or movement within the channels of commerce. The idea is thus to create a possibility of intervening before the goods in question disappear out of sight or become difficult to trace for the private party wishing to initiate private enforcement proceedings. In addition, the competent national court must be able to order the precautionary seizure of movable and immovable property of the alleged infringing party, including the blocking of bank accounts and other assets.[172] This latter provision has been modelled on an arrangement found in English law, known as a "freezing" (or "Mareva") injunction.[173] Under the directive it can only be ordered in cases of infringements committed on a commercial scale and where the applicant has demonstrated that there are circumstances likely to endanger the recovery of damages. It is specified that to this end the competent authorities may order the communication of bank, financial or commercial documents or appropriate

---

consultation on the civil enforcement of intellectual property rights, July 2013, p. 8. See further Kur (2006), p. 844; Joseph (2006), p. 850; Döring and Van Velsen (2006), p. 858. As regards EU unitary rights see Fields (2011), p. 597; Schnell (2011), p. 210.

166 See para 4.02 above.

167 Art. 103(2) Community Trade Mark Regulation 207/2009; Art. 90(3) Community Design Regulation 2006/6. See e.g. CoJ case C-235/09, *DHL Express*, para 50.

168 Commission, Staff working document accompanying the report on IPR Enforcement Directive 2004/48, SEC(2010) 1589, p. 18.

169 In particular, before the patent package, referred to in para 1.02 above, had entered into force.

170 In the late 1990s certain national courts (especially in the Netherlands, but later also in other Member States such as Germany) issued injunctions which also had effects beyond the borders of the jurisdiction in question. This can obviously be attractive for rightholders, for example where various infringers belonging to the same group infringe a patent in several jurisdictions in an identical manner. However, in 2006 the CoJ marked certain clear limits to these practices. It did so on the basis of Brussels I Regulation 1215/2012 (see its Art. 24). See in particular CoJ case C-539/03, *Roche Nederland*, para 41. See also CoJ case C-4/03, *GAT v LUK*, para 31. Cf. Nuyts (2008); Commission, Staff working document accompanying the report on IPR Enforcement Directive 2004/48, SEC(2010) 1589, p. 18.

171 Art. 9(1)(b) IPR Enforcement Directive 2004/48.

172 Art. 9(2) IPR Enforcement Directive 2004/48.

173 Commission, Proposal for IPR Enforcement Directive 2004/48, COM(2003) 46, pp. 13 and 21.

access to the relevant information. It follows that here the emphasis is not so much on the prevention of the infringement or limiting the damage that may emerge as a result thereof, but that this latter remedy rather aims to ensure that any such damage, if and when it emerges, can actually be compensated as much as possible.

3. Corrective measures and "permanent" injunctions

Turning to the various remedies which the IPR Enforcement Directive provides as a result of a decision by the competent national court on the merits of the case, a first type concerns what the directive calls *corrective measures*. This refers to the '*appropriate measures*' that must be available with regard to the infringing goods or the materials principally used in their creation.[174] These measures can take (at least) three forms, namely: (a) recall from the channels of commerce; (b) definitive removal from those channels; and (c) destruction of the goods and materials in question. These measures are to be taken in principle at the expense of the infringing party.[175] Proportionality as well as respect for the interests of third parties must be ensured when requests for these measures are considered.[176] The measures referred to here can in a sense be seen as the "permanent" version of the possibilities of seizure on a provisional basis discussed in the previous subsection.[177] **4.23**

The possibility of recall and definitive removal of infringing goods from the channels of commerce, developed in the national laws of the Netherlands and Belgium, was new to most other Member States.[178] These measures appear to be generally little used in practice, something that is said to be due largely to the fact that they are difficult to enforce where the goods are no longer in the infringer's possession.[179] The possibility of having infringing goods destroyed, based on the TRIPS Agreement,[180] has been reported to be the most common corrective measure.[181] Nonetheless, the costs of these measures are often seen as a particular problem. Even if the directive makes it clear that these costs are to be borne by the defendant, in practice they are often first incurred by the

174 Art. 10(1) IPR Enforcement Directive 2004/48.
175 Art. 10(2) IPR Enforcement Directive 2004/48.
176 Art. 10(3) IPR Enforcement Directive 2004/48.
177 See para 4.22 above.
178 Commission, Proposal for IPR Enforcement Directive 2004/48, COM(2003) 46, p. 22.
179 Commission, Staff working document accompanying the report on IPR Enforcement Directive 2004/48, SEC(2010) 1589, p. 19.
180 Art. 46 TRIPS Agreement. Cf. Commission, Proposal for IPR Enforcement Directive 2004/48, COM(2003) 46, p. 22.
181 Commission, Staff working document accompanying the report on IPR Enforcement Directive 2004/48, SEC(2010) 1589, p. 20. See also Study, European Observatory on Counterfeiting and Piracy (undated c), p. 1.

applicant. Having these costs reimbursed may then prove difficult, for instance because the former is unknown or insolvent.[182]

4.24 On the whole, of greater practical importance is the possibility under the IPR Enforcement Directive for a private party to apply for *injunctions* aimed at prohibiting the continuation of an infringement.[183] This is also, as it were, the permanent version of the possibility of issuing interlocutory injunctions discussed earlier.[184] According to the directive, non-compliance with these "permanent" injunctions shall, where appropriate, be subject to a recurring penalty payment with a view to ensuring compliance where provided for by national law. As was the case with those interlocutory injunctions, these permanent injunctions are also regularly used in practice.[185] The remarks made in the foregoing as regards the functioning of this remedy in cross-border situations also apply here *mutatis mutandis*.[186] The IPR Enforcement Directive further expressly stipulates that these permanent injunctions may also be addressed to intermediaries.[187] For most Member States this was a novelty.[188] The Commission has singled out this remedy as one of the elements that has helped render the enforcement of intellectual property rights in the EU more effective.[189] However, this possible involvement of these third parties in civil disputes has once more led to legal complexities and controversies. This debate is to some extent similar to the one on their involvement in relation to the right of information; reference is therefore again made to the foregoing.[190] In 2010 the Commission stated its intention to explore how to involve intermediaries more closely.[191]

In the meantime the Court of Justice has clarified a number of issues related to the issuing of injunctions against (online) intermediaries.[192] Of particular importance is the 2011 judgment in *L'Oréal v eBay*.[193] In this case, an English

182 Commission, Report on IPR Enforcement Directive 2004/48, COM(2010) 779, p. 8; Commission, Staff working document accompanying the report on IPR Enforcement Directive 2004/48, SEC(2010) 1589, p. 20.

183 Art. 11 IPR Enforcement Directive 2004/48. See also Art. 8(3) Infosoc Directive 2001/29.

184 See para 4.20 above.

185 Commission, Staff working document accompanying the report on IPR Enforcement Directive 2004/48, SEC(2010) 1589, p. 17.

186 See para 4.21 above.

187 See the last sentence of Art. 11 IPR Enforcement Directive 2004/48.

188 Commission, Staff working document accompanying the report on IPR Enforcement Directive 2004/48, SEC(2010) 1589, p. 17.

189 Commission, Report on IPR Enforcement Directive 2004/48, COM(2010) 779, p. 3.

190 See para 4.18 above.

191 Commission, Report on IPR Enforcement Directive 2004/48, COM(2010) 779, p. 7.

192 On the concept of an (online) "intermediary", see CoJ case C-314/12, *UPC Telekabel Wien*, para 30–39 (relating to Art. 8(3) Infosoc Directive 2001/29).

193 CoJ case C-324/09, *L'Oréal v eBay*.

preliminary reference, a number of persons had sold products protected by intellectual property rights held by an undertaking (L'Oréal) on an online marketplace (eBay). Before the competent national court the rightholder applied for an injunction under the IPR Enforcement Directive against the online marketplace in its capacity as intermediary in the form of a court order to prevent future infringements occurring on its website. The Court of Justice held that, while a "permanent" injunction is limited to prohibiting the *continuation* of an infringement when an infringing party is the addressee,[194] when used in connection with intermediaries, it can also entail measures to *prevent* future infringements from occurring.[195] It also clarified that the rules for the operation of these injunctions, such as the conditions to be met and the procedures to be followed, are a matter for *national* law, provided that these rules allow the directive's objective to be achieved and its limitations are respected.[196] In particular, an online marketplace cannot be obliged to actively monitor all the data of each of its customers, as this would be against both the express prohibition laid down in the E-Commerce Directive and the IPR Enforcement Directive's rules that state that any measure to be taken must be fair and proportionate and not be excessively costly.[197] The Court further highlighted the need to strike a *fair balance* between the various fundamental rights and interests at stake when imposing any of the measures at issue here.[198] Implicit in the *L'Oréal v eBay* ruling is also that there is no need for the *liability* of the intermediary to be established before injunctions can be imposed under this directive. This is in line with the position of the Commission, which had stressed that injunctions are not intended as penalties and that the IPR Enforcement Directive contains no such liability requirement.[199] Several Member States nonetheless provided for such a requirement.[200]

194 See the first sentence of Art. 11 IPR Enforcement Directive 2004/48.

195 CoJ case C-324/09, *L'Oréal v eBay*, para 128–34. See also CoJ case C-70/10, *Scarlet Extended*, para 31; CoJ case C-360/10, *SABAM*, para 29.

196 Cf. recital 23 IPR Enforcement Directive 2004/48. See also CoJ case C-314/12, *UPC Telekabel Wien*, para 43–4 (relating to the injunctions referred to in Art. 8(3) Infosoc Directive 2001/29).

197 CoJ case C-324/09, *L'Oréal v eBay*, para 135–9. See Art. 15(1) E-Commerce Directive 2000/31; Art. 3(1) IPR Enforcement Directive 2004/48. See also CoJ case C-70/10, *Scarlet Extended*, para 32–36; CoJ case C-360/10, *SABAM*, para 30–34.

198 CoJ case C-324/09, *L'Oréal v eBay*, para 143. Here a reference was made to CoJ case C-275/06, *Promusicae*, discussed in para 4.18 above. See also CoJ case C-70/10, *Scarlet Extended*, para 41–6; CoJ case C-360/10, *SABAM*, para 39–51; CoJ case C-314/12, *UPC Telekabel Wien*, para 46.

199 Commission, Staff working document accompanying the report on IPR Enforcement Directive 2004/48, SEC(2010) 1589, p. 16. See also Commission, Report on IPR Enforcement Directive 2004/48, COM(2010) 779, p. 7.

200 Commission, Staff working document accompanying the report on IPR Enforcement Directive 2004/48, SEC(2010) 1589, p. 16. This issue is of particular relevance in light of the liability exemptions for online intermediaries laid down in Art. 12–15 E-Commerce Directive 2001/31 (see in particular its Art. 12(3), 13(3) and 14(3)). Cf. Study, European Observatory on Counterfeiting and Piracy (undated b), pp. 5 and 9. Cf. CoJ case C-484/14, *McFadden* (pending). See further Husovec and Peguera (2015), p. 10.

4.25 As a final point it should be noted that the IPR Enforcement Directive offers the Member States the possibility to provide for certain *alternative measures*.[201] These measures are meant as an alternative to the corrective measures and the permanent injunctions discussed above. This possibility entails, in appropriate cases and at the request of the person liable to be subject to the measure in question, a court order for the defendant to pay *pecuniary compensation* to the injured party. Where a Member State has given effect to this optional provision it thus allows the defendant to "buy off" for instance an imminent order to recall infringing goods or a particular injunction. The underlying idea is to prevent disproportionate outcomes from occurring.[202] The IPR Enforcement Directive makes this possibility subject to certain conditions, however. The defendant must have acted unintentionally and without negligence, it must be established that the execution of the measure in question would cause the defendant disproportionate harm and the compensation to be paid to the injured party must appear reasonably satisfactory. In 2010, less than half of the Member States, including Denmark, Poland, Romania, Sweden and Germany, had made use of this option.[203]

4. Actions for damages

4.26 The provision of the IPR Enforcement Directive on actions for damages was one of the issues that was controversial during the legislative process leading to its adoption. This aspect of the Commission's proposal was hotly debated and underwent significant changes.[204] A key issue was the means of qualifying and quantifying the damages due. The point of departure was that private parties holding intellectual property rights were reported to generally encounter difficulties establishing and proving the precise level of damages suffered.[205] As was noted above, the TRIPS Agreement provides that damages should be '*adequate*' to compensate for the injury suffered in cases of wilful or negligent infringements.[206] At the level of the Member States at least three different methods were in use before the adoption of the directive, whereby the details of each of them varied widely and some Member States also allowed for combining

201 Art. 12 IPR Enforcement Directive 2004/48.

202 Cf. recital 25 IPR Enforcement Directive 2004/48. See also Commission, Proposal for IPR Enforcement Directive 2004/48, COM(2003) 46, p. 22.

203 Commission, Staff working document accompanying the report on IPR Enforcement Directive 2004/48, SEC(2010) 1589, pp. 20–21.

204 Cf. Reinbothe (2010), p. 19.

205 Cf. Commission, Green paper on combating counterfeiting and piracy in the single market, COM(98) 569, pp. 20–21.

206 Art. 45(1) TRIPS Agreement. In its Art. 45(2) it is added that the parties to this agreement *may* authorise their judicial authorities to order recovery of profits and/or payment of pre-established damages even where the infringer did not knowingly, or without reasonable grounds to know, engage in infringing activity. See para 4.12 above.

several of these methods. These three methods entailed calculating the amount of damages due on the basis of: (a) the actual loss suffered by the applicant; (b) the infringer's unlawful profits made in connection with the infringement; or (c) the royalties or fees that would have been due had the infringer requested authorisation from the rightholder.[207]

In its *proposal* the Commission sought to supplement the TRIPS Agreement and to tackle the above-mentioned disparities.[208] It proposed taking this agreement's "adequate damages" criterion as the starting point in cases of wilful or negligent infringements. On that basis it then specified this further through two – alternative – methods of calculating the damages due. The first of these methods was the establishment of fixed-rate damages, amounting to *double the royalties or fees* that would have been due. The second method entailed the award of damages corresponding to the *actual prejudice suffered*, including lost profits. On an optional basis it was proposed that this latter method would also encompass elements other than economic factors (that is, non-material damage), such as the moral prejudice caused. It would also include the recovery for the benefit of the rightholder of all the profits made by the infringer attributable to the infringement in question. In the Commission's view the latter was meant to act as a deterrent, particularly with respect to intentional infringements perpetrated on a commercial scale.[209] Regarding these "unfair profits", it also proposed including a rule of evidence, pursuant to which it would be for the rightholder to submit evidence only with regard to the amount of the gross income achieved by the infringer. It would then be for the latter to provide evidence of its deductible expenses and profits attributable to factors other than the protected object.[210] **4.27**

This first proposed method, in particular, was critically received by the Member States represented in Council, however.[211] No clear single reason for this opposition emerges from the available preparatory documents; this is likely to have varied by Member State. The above-mentioned diversity at national level probably played a role, in that most Member States may well have been keen to avoid having to amend their national laws as they stood. Another probable factor is that – even if the Commission had argued the contrary[212] – many understood the proposed fixed-rate "double royalties" arrangement as constituting, or at least coming (too) close to, a form of punitive damages, which are

207 Commission, Proposal for IPR Enforcement Directive 2004/48, COM(2003) 46, p. 14.
208 Ibid., pp. 14 and 23.
209 Ibid., p. 23.
210 Ibid., pp. 23 and 38–9 (Art. 17(2)).
211 Council, doc. 12055/03, pp. 9–10.
212 Commission, Proposal for IPR Enforcement Directive 2004/48, COM(2003) 46, p. 23.

damages that are not so much aimed at compensating the injury suffered, but rather at punishing and deterring infringers.[213]

4.28 The *final text* of the IPR Enforcement Directive therefore does not include the provision on the doubling of the royalties or fees referred to above. Instead, the directive's damages regime builds on the second method proposed by the Commission. It takes as the central criterion, for wilful and negligent infringements, the award of damages '*appropriate to the actual prejudice suffered*'.[214] Two more detailed methods of setting these damages are then provided for. These somewhat resemble, but nonetheless differ from, the ones initially proposed by the Commission.

The first method is based on taking into account '*all appropriate aspects*', including lost profits of the rightholder, unfair profits made by the infringer and, '*in appropriate cases*', non-economic factors such as moral prejudice. In deviation from the Commission's proposal, no rule of evidence has been included as regards the extent of these unfair profits. The second, alternative method provided for in the IPR Enforcement Directive is the setting of damages as '*a lump sum on the basis of elements such as at least the amount of royalties or fees which would have been due*'. Thus, the Commission proposal to provide for compensation of twice the royalties has been reduced to (at least) once. In the recitals of this directive it is clarified that the aim is not to introduce an obligation to provide for punitive damages. Rather the idea is to allow for compensation based on objective criteria, while taking account of the expenses incurred by the rightholder.[215]

On an optional basis the Member States may furthermore provide that in cases other than wilful or negligent infringements the competent national court is empowered to order '*the recovery of profits or the payment of damages, which may be pre-established*'.[216]

4.29 The EU legislature thus rejected the Commission's relatively innovative suggestions to provide for pre-fixed "double royalties" damages as well as the proposed rule of evidence. The provision that was finally adopted is in fact rather modest. The damages regime seems to add little of substance to the TRIPS Agreement. It follows from the foregoing that several elements are either rather vaguely worded or only addressed on an optional basis. As a consequence, considerable

213 Cf. Kur (2004), p. 827; Meier-Beck (2004), p. 122; Benhamou (2009), p. 147; Cohen and Mottet Haugaard (2010), p. 376–7; Lakits-Josse (2011), p. 545.

214 Art. 13(1) IPR Enforcement Directive 2004/48.

215 Recital 26 IPR Enforcement Directive 2004/48.

216 Art. 13(2) IPR Enforcement Directive 2004/48.

leeway continues to be left to the Member States when transposing the above provision into their respective national laws. The Commission reported in 2010 that most Member States had found it unnecessary to amend their pre-existing national laws, as these were deemed to be already compatible with the damages regime of the IPR Enforcement Directive.[217] Having said that, the IPR Enforcement Directive's provision on damages nonetheless appears to have had some impact at national level, even if this may not always be a direct consequence. For instance, the possibilities for claiming unfair profits made by the defendant reportedly improved in France and Italy.[218] In the Netherlands, the possibility of setting damages as a lump sum was made explicit,[219] whereas Swedish law was amended so as to clarify that non-material damage can be compensated as well.[220] In Spain, provision has been made in certain cases for the recovery of a lump sum equal to 1 per cent of the infringer's relevant turnover.[221]

It should further probably not be assumed too readily that the directive's provision on damages is not very "demanding". On various points its wording is such that a more extensive reading is also possible.[222] For example, '*all appropriate aspects*', account of which must be taken when setting the damages, is not an unequivocal term. An argument could be made that this does not include either the negative economic consequences or the unfair profits made by the infringer, but rather both in accumulation.[223] Different views can also be taken as to who is to decide (and on which basis) what is '*an appropriate case*' where non-material damages are to be made available. The directive similarly makes it clear that when quantifying the damages due, its "all appropriate aspects" and the "lump sum" methods are alternatives. It is less evident, however, whether these two alternatives should be available to the private party applicant and the national court or that – instead – it is for the national legislature to select and impose one of these two methods.[224] There thus remains scope for debate and interpretation on several points. It is therefore not excluded that the Court of Justice will

---

217 Commission, Staff working document accompanying the report on IPR Enforcement Directive 2004/48, SEC(2010) 1589, p. 5.

218 Urbanchuk and Tumbridge (2008), pp. 578–9; Benhamou (2009), p. 125; Hassan (2010), pp. 756–7; Schaffner (2010), p. 184.

219 Brinkhof, Van Gardingen and Hermans (2010), p. 179.

220 Lundgren and Ulfsdotter (2010), p. 218.

221 Study, European Observatory on Counterfeiting and Piracy (undated d), p. 2; Adamov, Fazekas and Tivadar (2009), p. 344; Pérez, Rabadán and Serano (2010), p. 201.

222 That may apply even more so when the provision is read in conjunction with the "general rules", laid down in Art. 3 IPR Enforcement Directive 2004/48, discussed in para 4.06 above.

223 Cf. Rognstad (2011), p. 50. On this issue in relation to English law, see Fitzgerald and Firth (2014), p. 737.

224 Commission, Staff working document accompanying the report on IPR Enforcement Directive 2004/48, SEC(2010) 1589, p. 23.

interpret this provision more extensively than is currently sometimes presumed.[225]

4.30 In 2010 damages awarded for intellectual property right infringements were said to remain rather low, with only a few Member States reporting an increase as a result of the directive.[226] The Commission observed that '*damages awards in intellectual property cases are not requested by rightholders as a matter of course*'.[227] Various legal and practical difficulties were reported, including lengthy procedures, high costs and difficulties in assessing and demonstrating the amount of loss allegedly suffered, resulting in low amounts awarded.[228] It appears that as a consequence actions for damages are generally not the preferred remedy in cases of infringements of intellectual property rights.[229]

The Commission has therefore floated several ideas for the directive's possible amendment on this point. These include granting damages commensurate with the infringer's unfair profits even where they exceed the actual damage suffered so as to prevent unjust enrichment and claiming damages from managing directors in case of insolvent legal-person infringers.[230] Particularly this latter suggestion has, however, generally not been received favourably by respondents. More generally rightholders tend to favour legislative change, arguing *inter alia* for lump sums to be included.[231] By contrast, potential defendants tend to oppose it, invoking the risk of non-professionals and intermediaries being sued and the possible chilling effects on innovation and the sharing of cultural expressions. The latter parties insist on the determination of damages on the basis of concrete data regarding the material loss suffered. Most respondents, including all Member States that reacted to the 2010 report in which the Commission made these suggestions, argued against punitive damages. Provisions of this kind were held to be inconsistent with the European legal tradition, even if the 2010 Commission report and other reports indicate that such measures are available in certain cases under the domestic laws of the Member States.[232] Most Member States generally argued against amending

---

225 Cf. CoJ case C-99/15, *Liffers* (pending).

226 Commission, Report on IPR Enforcement Directive 2004/48, COM(2010) 779, p. 8.

227 Ibid., p. 21.

228 Ibid., pp. 21–3. See also Study, European Observatory on Counterfeiting and Piracy (undated d); Commission, Responses to the public consultation on the civil enforcement of intellectual property rights, July 2013, p. 20; Roland (2014), p. 297.

229 Ibid., p. 21.

230 Commission, Report on IPR Enforcement Directive 2004/48, COM(2010) 779, p. 8.

231 Cf. Study, European Observatory on Counterfeiting and Piracy (undated d), p. 11.

232 Commission, Staff working document accompanying the report on IPR Enforcement Directive 2004/48, SEC(2010) 1589, p. 24. This report indicates that under Slovenian law provision is made for punitive damages. Punitive damages are further reported to be available in certain cases in Bulgaria and Ireland as well as in Austria and in the UK. See, respectively, Cohen and Mottet Haugaard (2010), p. 376; Study, European

the IPR Enforcement Directive's current damages regime.[233] This would appear to make substantial changes in this regard unlikely in the near future.

5. Legal costs and publicity measures

As regards the last two remedies to be discussed here, the IPR Enforcement Directive contains, in the first place, a provision on the allocation of *legal costs*. It stipulates that '*reasonable and proportionate legal costs and other expenses incurred by the successful party shall, as a general rule, be borne by the unsuccessful party, unless equity does not allow this*'.[234] As the Court of Justice has clarified, this provision aims to strengthen the level of protection of intellectual property rights by avoiding the situation in which an injured party is deterred from initiating legal proceedings in order to protect its rights. In the Court's view it follows that the infringer '*must generally bear all the financial consequences of his conduct*'.[235] This broadly corresponds with the Commission's original intention, which was to ensure that the legal costs, lawyers' fees and any other expenses incurred by the successful party are in principle borne in full by the other party.[236] **4.31**

This provision on legal costs has led to several concerns, however. To begin with, at the time of the adoption of the IPR Enforcement Directive, several Member States initially wished to delete it altogether, because in their perception it did not respect the principle of subsidiarity and the EU lacked competence to legislate on this subject matter.[237] The European Parliament objected to the explicit reference to lawyers' fees that the Commission's proposal originally contained.[238] It pointed in this connection to the particularities of the laws of various Member States in this regard.[239] This reference was therefore eventually deleted. This article has been formulated in such a broad manner that most Member States did not deem it necessary to amend their pre-existing national rules in order to comply with this provision of the directive.[240] There are exceptions, however. Most notably in the Netherlands,

Communities Trade Mark Association (undated); Beetz and Tremmel (2010), pp. 21–2; Cornish, Llewelyn and Aplin (2010), pp. 81–2; Till (2010), pp. 131 and 133. On the potential disadvantages of punitive damages in the present context, see also Geiger, Raynard and Rodà (2011), p. 547.

233 Commission, Responses to the report on IPR Enforcement Directive 2004/48, July 2011, pp. 14–16.

234 Art. 14 IPR Enforcement Directive 2004/48.

235 CoJ case C-406/09, *Realchemie*, para 48–9.

236 Commission, Proposal for IPR Enforcement Directive 2004/48, COM(2003) 46, p. 23.

237 Council, doc. 13027/03, p. 5. See also Council, doc. 16289/03, p. 16.

238 See Commission, Proposal for IPR Enforcement Directive 2004/48, COM(2003) 46, p. 41 (Art. 18). Here reference was made to '*legal costs, lawyers' fees and any other expenses*', while including a sentence stating that '*[t]he responsible authorities shall determine the sum to be paid*'.

239 European Parliament, Report on the proposal for IPR Enforcement Directive 2004/48, A5_0468/2003, p. 29.

240 Commission, Staff working document accompanying the report on IPR Enforcement Directive 2004/48, SEC(2010) 1589, p. 24.

an amendment to the national rules of civil proceedings was introduced, which has in turn led to a judicial practice whereby the legal costs are typically deemed to be recoverable in their entirety in intellectual property cases, in a deviation from the ordinary rules in civil law proceedings. In the legal literature it has been questioned whether this is in all respects in accordance with the requirements of the directive, in particular where the rather rigid application of this rule is concerned, which appears to leave little or no space for taking account of the particular circumstances of the case at hand.[241] It can be noted in this connection that, seemingly different from the comparable provision in the TRIPS Agreement,[242] the IPR Enforcement Directive's rule on legal costs allows any '*successful party*' – and therefore not just a successful rightholder, but also a defendant – to claim compensation for its legal costs. This can make certain rightholders hesitant to bring a claim for fear of the financial consequences if it is dismissed. That in turn would seem at odds with the objective pursued by both this particular provision and by this directive more generally.

Another concern is that after the adoption of the IPR Enforcement Directive, stakeholders continue to complain that the legal costs reimbursed in the cases covered by it are in practice often far below the costs actually incurred.[243] Estimates of the recoupable percentage of the legal costs incurred differ considerably between the Member States, ranging from, for instance, 30 per cent in Italy to 80 per cent in Ireland.[244] Adequate rules on the compensation of legal costs are considered to be of considerable importance, as litigation costs in intellectual property cases are said to be often high.[245] Such costs can, for example, be incurred for using technical experts or for making test purchases in order to gather evidence and substantiate a claim. That applies even more so in cross-border situations. Also in light of the seemingly diverging interpretation of the directive's provision on legal costs across the EU, calls have therefore been made for its clarification.[246] The Commission has seemed inclined to act upon

241 For an overview, discussion and further references see Vrendenbarg (2013), p. 160. The fact that all preliminary references relating to this provision of the directive to date were made by Dutch national courts should probably be seen in light of this legislative change and the resulting case law and discussions at national level (which have since led to reforms). See CoJ case C-406/09, *Realchemie*; CoJ case C-180/11, *Bericap*; CoJ case C-435/12, *ACI Adam*. See also CoJ case C-681/13, *Diageo Brands* (pending). In addition, see CoJ case C-57/15, *United Video Properties* (pending), which is a Belgian case concerning the interpretation of Art. 14 IPR Enforcement Directive 2004/48.

242 Art. 45(2) TRIPS Agreement. Cf. Commission, Proposal for IPR Enforcement Directive 2004/48, COM(2003) 46, p. 24.

243 Commission, Staff working document accompanying the report on IPR Enforcement Directive 2004/48, SEC(2010) 1589, p. 24. Cf. Study, European Observatory on Counterfeiting and Piracy (undated d), p. 9.

244 Study, European Observatory on Counterfeiting and Piracy (undated d), p. 10.

245 Commission, Staff working document accompanying the report on IPR Enforcement Directive 2004/48, SEC(2010) 1589, p. 24.

246 Geiger, Raynard and Rodà (2011), p. 548.

these concerns, at least where the enforcement of intellectual property rights by small and medium-sized enterprises is concerned.[247] However, it remains for now uncertain whether any such action will involve proposing amendments to the directive.

A final remedy to be mentioned here is *publicity measures*. In this connection the IPR Enforcement Directive requires the Member States to ensure that a national court may order '*appropriate measures for the dissemination of the information concerning the decision, including displaying the decision and publishing it in full or in part*'.[248] It adds that Member States may also allow for other additional publicity measures, including prominent advertising. In its proposal for this directive, the Commission had stated that the publication of judicial decisions is generally considered an effective measure for informing the public and a deterrent against infringements of intellectual property rights.[249] The recitals clarify accordingly that this measure is meant to act as '*a supplementary deterrent to future infringers and to contribute to the awareness of the public at large*'.[250] In some jurisdictions, for instance in Ireland and the United Kingdom, the introduction of this remedy implied a notable innovation, which is occasionally used in practice.[251] However, on the whole this provision of the IPR Enforcement Directive tends to receive only limited attention.[252] **4.32**

C. PROCEDURAL PROVISIONS

Having introduced the IPR Enforcement Directive and having discussed the remedies laid down therein in the foregoing sections, attention now turns to the directive's most important procedural provisions. The first subsection below discusses the rules on the legal standing of private parties wishing to initiate legal proceedings under this directive. The subsequent subsection then concentrates on issues of forum and procedure.

---

247 Commission, Communication towards a renewed consensus on the enforcement of intellectual property rights, COM(2014) 392, p. 7.

248 Art. 15 IPR Enforcement Directive 2004/48.

249 Commission, Proposal for IPR Enforcement Directive 2004/48, COM(2003) 46, p. 23.

250 Recital 27 IPR Enforcement Directive 2004/48.

251 Gibbons (2014), p. 23.

252 Cf. e.g. Commission, Staff working document accompanying the report on IPR Enforcement Directive 2004/48, SEC(2010) 1589, p. 24, where this provision is not mentioned at all. Neither does it appear to have been raised by the respondents to the ensuing consultation. See Commission, Responses to the report on IPR Enforcement Directive 2004/48, July 2011.

1. Legal standing

4.33 The IPR Enforcement Directive lays down common rules on legal standing, which are the rules determining which private parties have the legal capacity to bring proceedings for (alleged) infringements of the intellectual property rights covered by the directive before the competent national courts. The directive lists four categories of persons that have this capacity.[253] The first category is made up of the *holders* of the intellectual property rights in question. The second category consists of all other persons *authorised to use* these rights, such as licensees. And intellectual property *collective rights management bodies* that are regularly recognised as having a right to represent rightholders are also mentioned. The fourth and last category consists of *professional defence bodies* that are regularly recognised as having a right to represent rightholders.

In all four cases the directive contains certain further specifications. As regards the rightholders, it has been added that these private parties have legal standing '*in accordance with the provisions of the applicable law*'. That same specification also applies to all three other categories mentioned above. In addition, for these latter categories of persons, the further specification has been included that they have legal standing '*in so far as permitted by and in accordance with the provisions of the applicable law*'. The precise meaning of these phrases remains to be clarified by the Court of Justice. A likely reading appears to be that these latter three categories of persons *can* have a sufficiently direct interest and (therefore) legal standing under the IPR Enforcement Directive, but *only in so far as* permitted by the applicable (presumably national) law.[254] In contrast, the first category – the rightholders – *must* have legal standing as a matter of EU law. In all cases the further detailed rules in this respect remain in principle to be determined by the applicable national law. Presuming that this reading is correct, it implies a step back from the Commission's proposal, which was more ambitious in this regard. According to this proposal, all the above-mentioned categories of person would essentially have had legal standing as a matter of EU law, including the specification that the collective rights management bodies and the professional defence bodies were to have legal standing regardless of the Member State in which they are established.[255]

253 Art. 4 IPR Enforcement Directive 2004/48.

254 See also recital 18 IPR Enforcement Directive 2004/48.

255 Commission, Proposal for IPR Enforcement Directive 2004/48, COM(2003) 46, pp. 19 and 33 (Art. 5).

2. Forum and procedure

No detailed rules on the forum competent to rule on the actions brought pursuant to it have been laid down in the IPR Enforcement Directive. At various places throughout the directive reference is simply made to '*the competent judicial authorities*'.[256] This appears to imply that the cases brought under this directive are to be decided by a body that is judicial in character, thus a national court and not a non-judicial dispute resolution body. Although this is neither made explicit nor necessarily the case,[257] the assumption is that these actions are normally to be brought before a national *civil* court. This is implicit in the statement in the recitals that the directive does not aim to establish harmonised rules for judicial cooperation, jurisdiction, the recognition and enforcement of decisions in civil and commercial matters or deal with applicable law, there being other instruments of EU law governing such matters which apply equally to intellectual property cases.[258] This assumption also finds expression in the Commission's statement that '*[t]he Directive's provisions (only) relate to civil law measures to enforce intellectual property rights*', incorporating the TRIPS Agreement's civil law measures.[259] **4.34**

The IPR Enforcement Directive is even less detailed regarding the rules of procedure that apply in legal proceedings under the IPR Enforcement Directive that have been brought before national courts. In fact, no such rules are provided for. That means that issues such as the possibility of pre-trial contacts between the parties to the dispute or the limitation periods for initiating legal proceedings remain unregulated in so far as this directive is concerned. **4.35**

D. OTHER ENFORCEMENT ISSUES

This final section briefly addresses a number of other issues relating to the enforcement of intellectual property law generally and the IPR Enforcement Directive in particular, namely alternative dispute resolution and public enforcement. It is shown that as a matter of EU law these two issues play, at present, at most a very limited role in the enforcement of intellectual property law.

256 See e.g. Art. 6(1), 7(1) and 8(1) IPR Enforcement Directive 2004/48.
257 Cf. recital 28 IPR Enforcement Directive.
258 Recital 11 IPR Enforcement Directive 2004/48.
259 Commission, Report on IPR Enforcement Directive 2004/48, COM(2010) 779, pp. 4–5.

1. Alternative dispute resolution

4.36 In settling intellectual property-related conflicts, alternative dispute resolution certainly can play some role in practice.[260] This applies in particular where such disputes emerge in situations where the parties have a contractual relationship of some sort, for instance relating to licences or research and development activities. Concerning disputes founded on non-contractual liability of a private party resulting from (alleged) infringements of intellectual property rights, beyond direct negotiations between the parties before initiating legal proceedings, alternative dispute resolution is generally used to a rather limited extent, however.[261] Generally speaking, in this field no EU-level mechanisms aimed at encouraging this manner of resolving the intellectual property-related disputes at issue here exist at present. A notable exception is, however, the alternative dispute resolution procedure for disputes relating to the registration of ".eu" top-level internet domain names provided for by Commission Regulation 874/2004.[262] Disputes of this kind are to be brought before the Czech Arbitration Court, which has settled many of them since its designation in 2005.[263]

2. Public enforcement

4.37 The IPR Enforcement Directive does not contain any provisions on the public enforcement of the relevant substantive rules. The directive limits itself to requiring the designation of Member States' correspondents for questions on the implementation of the measures set out in the directive.[264] These national correspondents are meant to create between them a network for administrative cooperation and exchange of information.[265] The directive further includes a very general reference to Member States being entitled (but not obliged) to apply '*other proportionate sanctions*'.[266] This refers especially to sanctions of a criminal nature. For in the corresponding recital it is clarified that, in addition to the civil and administrative procedures and remedies provided under the

---

260 Cf. e.g. Commission, Responses to the public consultation on the civil enforcement of intellectual property rights, July 2013, p. 6. See e.g. also Gardner (2014), p. 565.

261 Cf. Vitoria (2006), p. 398; Hanotiau (2010), p. 155; Jabaly (2010), p. 730; Theurich (2010), p. 175.

262 Art. 22 and 23 Commission Regulation (EC) No 874/2004 laying down public policy rules concerning the implementation and functions of the .eu top-level domain and the principles governing registration, OJ 2004, L 162/40.

263 On this type of dispute resolution more generally, see De Werra (2012), p. 39.

264 Art. 19 IPR Enforcement Directive 2004/48.

265 Recital 30 IPR Enforcement Directive 2004/48. See also Commission, Communication towards a renewed consensus on the enforcement of intellectual property rights, COM(2014) 392, pp. 8–10, where the Commission discusses ways to improve the cooperation between the various national authorities concerned and announces the establishment of a Member State export group on this subject matter.

266 Art. 16 IPR Enforcement Directive 2004/48.

directive, '*criminal sanctions also constitute, in appropriate cases, a means of ensuring the enforcement of intellectual property rights*'.[267]

It follows that under the IPR Enforcement Directive Member States are not required to establish a particular public enforcement mechanism or authority that seeks to ensure the effective application and enforcement of substantive intellectual property law. More particularly, although this is not precluded, under this directive the Member States are not obliged to provide for *criminal* sanctions for infringements of that law. Quite to the contrary, it is stipulated that the directive does not affect any national provisions relating to criminal procedures or penalties in respect of IPR infringements.[268]

It is noticeable that on the point of criminal sanctions, the IPR Enforcement Directive thus deviates from the Commission's proposal. Already in its 1998 green paper the Commission had argued that sanctions of this kind have certain advantages over civil law actions, in particular '*greater dissuasive effect [and] more effective gathering of evidence*'.[269] When the Commission adopted its proposal for the IPR Enforcement Directive, all Member States actually already provided for criminal sanctions, as is required under the TRIPS Agreement.[270] However, according to the Commission, there were considerable differences in the level of punishment and the method of calculating fines.[271] It therefore held that '*although this directive does not aim to harmonise criminal penalties as such, the effective application of genuinely deterrent sanctions in all Member States would help greatly in combating counterfeiting and piracy*'.[272] In concrete terms the Commission proposed stipulating that all infringements committed intentionally and for commercial purposes should be treated as criminal offences. It also proposed including a rule that the available sanctions should consist of imprisonment, fines and the confiscation of goods.[273] In appropriate cases certain further sanctions would also have to be provided for, such as the destruction of infringing goods, the closure of the establishment concerned, a ban on engaging in commercial activities and judicial winding-up.[274] 4.38

267 Recital 28 IPR Enforcement Directive 2004/48.

268 Art. 2(3) IPR Enforcement Directive 2004/48.

269 Commission, Green paper on combating counterfeiting and piracy in the single market, COM(98) 569, p. 18. See also Commission, Communication on the follow-up to the green paper on combating counterfeiting and piracy in the single market, COM(2000) 789, p. 9.

270 Art. 61 TRIPS Agreement. See e.g. also Study, Westkamp (2007), pp. 75–8.

271 Commission, Proposal for IPR Enforcement Directive 2004/48, COM(2003) 46, p. 15.

272 Ibid., p. 15.

273 Cf. Framework Decision 2005/212/JHA on confiscation of crime-related proceeds, instrumentalities and property, OJ 2005, L 86/49.

274 Commission, Proposal for IPR Enforcement Directive 2004/48, COM(2003) 46, p. 40 (Art. 20).

However, as has been observed elsewhere, the reaction of the Member States to this aspect of the proposal '*could not have been more negative*'.[275] They unanimously rejected it, mainly on grounds related to the proposal's legal basis. The Member States considered – unlike the Commission – that Article 114 TFEU on measures related to the internal market, which was part of the then so-called "first pillar",[276] did not allow for the adoption of measures relating to criminal law.[277] By implication, in the Member States' view such measures could only be adopted under the then "third pillar", which concerned matters related to justice and home affairs. The provision concerned was consequently deleted from the draft. All that currently remains, by means of a compromise with the European Parliament,[278] is the aforementioned provision that Member States may apply other proportionate sanctions.

At the time, the Commission announced that it was sticking to its views that criminal sanctions were required to effectively fight infringements of intellectual property law and that this could be done under Article 114 TFEU.[279] Therefore it soon presented a new proposal based on that article.[280] This proposal is largely similar to the 2003 one, but it goes further by proposing to include minimum levels of maximum penalties (four years' imprisonment, fines up to €300 000).[281] The proposal also includes rules on powers of confiscation, rightholders being allowed to form "joint investigation teams" with the competent Member States' authorities and the *ex officio* initiation of criminal proceedings.[282] Yet this new proposal also proved to be very controversial,

275 Reinbothe (2010), p. 21.

276 Before the entry into force of the Lisbon Treaty in 2009, the EU edifice rested on three so-called "pillars". The first pillar consisted of the Treaty establishing the European Community ("EC") and encompassed *inter alia* internal market-related provisions. The "third pillar" concerned justice and home affairs, as provided for under the (then) EU Treaty.

277 Council, doc. 6052/04, pp. 2–3.

278 Cf. European Parliament, Report on the proposal for IPR Enforcement Directive 2004/48, A5_0468/2003, p. 30

279 Council, doc. 8285/04, p. 2.

280 Initially, in 2005, the Commission had submitted two new proposals, namely a draft directive and a Council framework decision based on the (then) first and third pillars, respectively. In 2006 it replaced these two proposals by a single proposal. In the Commission's view the ruling in CoJ case C-176/03, *Commission v Council*, on criminal measures in the field of environmental law, another former first pillar matter, implied that provisions of criminal law required for the effective implementation of first pillar instruments of EU law could be established under that pillar. See Commission, Proposal for a directive on criminal measures for the enforcement of intellectual property rights, COM(2006) 168, p. 2. On the Commission's reading of the said ruling more generally, see Commission, Communication on the implications of the Court's judgment of 13 September 2005 (Case C-176/03, Commission v Council), COM(2005) 583.

281 Commission, Proposal for a directive on criminal measures for the enforcement of intellectual property rights, COM(2006) 168, p. 10 (Art. 5).

282 Ibid., p. 11 (Art. 6, 7 and 8 respectively).

especially in the Council.[283] Not only did certain doubts as to its legal basis remain, some Member States also doubted the necessity of an EU instrument on this matter in light of the nature and scale of the problem, noting that the effects of the IPR Enforcement Directive could not be properly assessed at that stage.[284] This proposal therefore did not lead to the adoption of a directive.

283 Seville (2009), p. 413. Cf. Hilty, Kur and Peukert (2006), p. 970; Geiger (2010), p. 629. See however also Schneider and Vrins (2006), p. 173.

284 Council, doc. 10329/06.

5

CONSUMER PROTECTION LAW

This chapter is concerned with selected legislative developments in the field of EU consumer protection law. Contrary to the fields assessed in the foregoing two chapters, in this case no one single, free-standing EU legal act exists that is exclusively concerned with private enforcement and that covers in principle all substantial rules at issue. That is not to say, however, that there is no legislation in force that is relevant for the present purposes. Quite to the contrary, consumer protection law may well be one of the fields of EU law with the greatest regulatory focus on remedial and procedural issues, even if in this case the relevant provisions are mostly embedded in and interlinked with the substantive regulatory activity.[1] With some notable exceptions, the measures related to enforcement (be it private or public) are typically not restricted to specific legislative acts. Instead many of the legal acts that mainly contain substantive rules also contain certain enforcement-related provisions. These measures, moreover, tend to be rather diverse. Without being exhaustive, a number of legal acts and other legislative developments that are particularly relevant for the present purposes are assessed below, in particular the Consumer Injunctions Directive, the Unfair Terms Directive and the Product Liability Directive. When discussing these and a number of related directives, the focus is each time especially on the three main (substantive) private enforcement remedies provided for therein, namely actions for injunctions, contractual

1 Cf. Storskrubb (2008), p. 27.

remedies and actions for damages, respectively. The field of EU consumer protection law generally is first briefly introduced, however. At the end of this chapter the relevant developments related to three other enforcement-related issues are discussed.

A. INTRODUCTION

By means of an introduction, this section first briefly sketches the background of EU consumer protection law. Subsequently an overview is given of the most important substantive rules applicable in this field of law. The early developments as regards consumers' rights of redress are also sketched.

1. Background

Consumer protection is one of various fields of action that developed at EU level in the "slipstream" of the drive towards establishing and completing the EU's internal market. This drive implied the disapplication of national rules seeking to protect consumers where those rules had the (incidental or deliberate) side effect of '*crystallising given consumer habits so as to consolidate an advantage acquired by national industries*' and where, as such, they especially constituted an obstacle to the free movement of goods and services within the EU.[2] In the case law of the Court of Justice it has been clarified that consumer protection can be a justified reason to restrict such free movement, but only under certain relatively strict conditions, notably non-discrimination and proportionality.[3] Establishing the EU's internal market thus led to a degree of deregulation at national level ("negative harmonisation"). Partially as a consequence, the need was felt for a degree of re-regulation at EU level ("positive harmonisation").[4] As the European Parliament stated in 1987, '*the protection of the interest of the consumer [...] must be considered a corollary of the free movement of goods and services*'.[5] Consumer protection is thus also seen as a means to increase the credibility of the project of European integration in the public eye and to bring that project "closer to the citizens".[6] **5.01**

2 CoJ case 178/84, *Commission v Germany*, para 32.

3 E.g. CoJ case 120/78, *Cassis de Dijon*, para 8; CoJ case 178/84, *Commission v Germany*, para 28; CoJ case C-76/90, *Säger*, para 15; CoJ joined cases C-105/12 to C-107/12, *Essent*, para 58.

4 See further Unberath and Johnston (2007), p. 1237; Weatherill (2011), pp. 838–46.

5 European Parliament, Resolution on consumer redress, OJ 1987, C 99/203, recital B.

6 See e.g. Commission, Green paper on access of consumers to justice and the settlement of consumer disputes in the single market, COM(93) 576, p. 7.

5.02 EU activity related to consumer protection can be traced back to the 1970s, when the rights of the European consumers were stressed in several "soft law" instruments (that is, non-legally binding acts, such as resolutions and recommendations). These rights include the right to protection of health and safety and the right to information and education.[7] By the mid-1980s, the EU legislature adopted the first "hard law" consumer protection measures (that is, legally binding instruments, such as directives or regulations).[8] Yet it was not until 1993 (Treaty of Maastricht) that consumer protection was recognised as an EU competence in its own right. Under the current EU Treaties, this competence is shared by the EU and the Member States.[9] Article 12 TFEU requires that account is taken of consumer protection requirements when defining and implementing EU policies and activities, whereas, pursuant to Article 38 Charter, EU policies must ensure a high level of consumer protection.[10] This means that consumer protection has a "cross-cutting" dimension.

More specifically, Article 169(1) TFEU states that '*in order to promote the interests of consumers and to ensure a high level of consumer protection, the [EU] shall contribute to protecting the health, safety and economic interests of consumers, as well as promoting their right to information, education and to organise themselves in order to safeguard their interests*'. The following paragraphs of this article provide for two legal bases for the adoption of secondary EU law in this field. Reference is made in the first place to Article 114 TFEU for the adoption of measures in the context of the completion of the internal market so as to contribute to the attainment of the aforementioned consumer protection objectives.[11] In addition, a proper free-standing legal basis for the adoption of measures to support, supplement and monitor the consumer protection policies pursued by the Member States is provided for.[12] The latter measures cannot prevent the Member States from maintaining or introducing more stringent protective measures.[13] Unlike under the former legal basis, the measures adopted on the basis of the latter are thus necessarily limited to "minimum harmonisation". That means that Member States remain at liberty to retain or adopt further-reaching rules of national law. The latter provision has hardly been used to

7 Cf. Council, Resolution on a preliminary programme of the EEC for a consumer protection and information policy, OJ 1975, C 92/1.

8 See e.g. Directive 84/450/EEC relating to the approximation of the laws, regulations and administrative provisions of the Member States concerning misleading advertising, OJ 1984, L 250/17.

9 Art. 4(2)(f) TFEU.

10 On the Charter more generally, see para 2.11 above.

11 Art. 169(2)(a) TFEU.

12 Art. 169(2)(b) and (3) TFEU.

13 Art. 169(4) TFEU.

date.[14] As is discussed in further detail below, instead, Article 114 TFEU tends to be the preferred legal basis when adopting secondary EU law in this field.

2. Substantive EU consumer law and consumers' rights of redress

Since the mid-1980s a relatively broad and diverse range of EU legal acts related to consumer protection have been adopted.[15] In many cases this legislation has since been updated and replaced by more recent acts. Generally speaking, the EU legislation can be taken to confer rights on the private parties concerned, as the Court of Justice has had occasion to confirm expressly in several cases.[16] The traditional core of the EU's body of consumer protection law consists of rules that regulate *pre-contractual* sales practices. In this context particular emphasis is typically placed on the provision of information so as to allow consumers to take informed decisions. As the Court of Justice has held, '*information, before concluding a contract, on the terms of the contract and the consequences of concluding it is of fundamental importance for a consumer*'.[17] Examples of this approach can be found in Directive 2005/29 on unfair commercial practices[18] ("Unfair Commercial Practices Directive"), Directive 2008/48 on consumer credit agreements[19] ("Consumer Credit Directive") and Directive 2011/83 on consumer rights[20] ("Consumer Rights Directive"). **5.03**

A number of other consumer protection directives regulate, at least to some degree, the actual *content* of consumer contracts. Examples of the latter include the aforementioned Unfair Terms Directive and Directive 99/44 on certain aspects of the sale of consumer goods and associated guarantees ("Consumer Sales Directive").[21] Elements of both of these two regulatory approaches can be

14 Stuyck (2009), p. 68. The only example cited of a legal act adopted on this basis is Directive 98/6/EC on consumer protection in the indication of the prices of products offered to consumers, OJ 1998, L 80/27.

15 For an overview and a general discussion, see Weatherill (2005); Micklitz, Reich and Rott (2009); Weatherill (2011), pp. 837–67.

16 See e.g. CoJ case C-91/92, *Faccini Dori*, para 28 (regarding what is now Consumer Rights Directive 2011/83); CoJ joined cases C-178/94, C-179/94 and C-188/94 to C-190/94, *Dillenkofer*, para 33–46 (regarding Art. 7 Package Travel Directive 90/314); CoJ case C-144/99, *Commission v Netherlands*, para 18 (regarding Unfair Terms Directive 93/13).

17 CoJ case C-92/11, *RWE Vertrieb*, para 44.

18 Directive 2005/29/EC concerning unfair business-to-consumer commercial practices in the internal market, OJ 2005, L 149/22.

19 Directive 2008/48/EC on consumer credit agreements for consumers, OJ 2008, L 1333/66.

20 Directive 2011/83/EU on consumer rights, OJ 2011, L 304/64.

21 Unfair Terms Directive 93/13; Directive 1999/44/EC on certain aspects of the sale of consumer goods and associated guarantees, OJ 1999, L 171/12.

found in Directive 90/314 on package travel, package holidays and package tours ("Package Travel Directive").[22]

Understood in a wider sense, EU consumer protection law also includes *advertising law*, notably Directive 2006/114 on misleading and comparative advertising[23] ("Misleading Advertising Directive") and Directive 2003/33 on tobacco advertising[24] ("Tobacco Advertising Directive"). There is further a considerable body of EU *product safety law*, such as Directive 2001/95 on general product safety[25] ("Product Safety Directive") and Directive 2009/48 on toy safety[26] ("Toy Safety Directive"). The Product Liability Directive can also be included in this latter category, even if it is somewhat of an outlier, in that it seeks to protect consumers by laying down certain rules on civil liability in case of defects rather than by setting out certain specific prohibitions or prescriptions.[27]

Although this may vary to some extent depending on the legal act at issue, in EU consumer protection law the term "consumer" is normally understood to refer to a natural person acting for purposes falling outside his trade, business, craft or profession.[28]

5.04 From the outset considerable emphasis has been placed on the importance of the consumers' right of redress. This was already the case in the aforementioned "soft law" instruments dating from the 1970s, where this was identified as one of the basic consumer rights. The Council held in this respect that '*consumers are [...] entitled to proper redress for [...] injury or damage [resulting from purchase or use of defective goods or unsatisfactory services] by means of swift, effective and inexpensive procedures*'.[29] The Commission specified, however, that '*this right [of redress] will not be applied at [EU] level but remains within the jurisdiction of each*

22 Directive 90/314/EEC on package travel, package holidays and package tours, OJ 1990, L 158/59. In 2013 the Commission proposed replacing this directive. See Commission, Proposal for a new package travel directive, COM(2013) 512. In May 2015 political agreement on this proposal was reached between the two co-legislators.

23 Directive 2006/114/EC concerning misleading and comparative advertising, OJ 2006, L 376/12.

24 Directive 2003/33/EC on the approximation of the laws, regulations and administrative provisions of the Member States relating to the advertising and sponsorship of tobacco products, OJ 2003, L 152/16.

25 Directive 2001/95/EC on general product safety, OJ 2002, L 11/4. In 2013 the Commission proposed replacing this directive. See Commission, Proposal for a regulation on consumer product safety, COM(2013) 78.

26 Directive 2009/48/EC on the safety of toys, OJ 2009, L 170/1.

27 Product Liability Directive 85/374.

28 See e.g. Art. 2(1) Consumer Rights Directive 2011/83; Art. 2(b) Unfair Terms Directive 93/13; Art. 2(a) Unfair Commercial Practices Directive 2005/29.

29 Council, Resolution on a preliminary programme of the EEC for a consumer protection and information policy, OJ 1975, C 92/1, p. 8.

Member State. Only where the situation requires it, will the Commission present proposals for improving existing systems and putting them to better use'.[30]

In this context the difficulties involved in dealing with minor claims (in monetary terms) were acknowledged early on. As the Commission noted in its 1984 memorandum on consumer redress, such difficulties can result from comparatively high legal costs, lengthy proceedings and psychological barriers.[31] Already in the late 1970s and early 1980s especially, the European Parliament therefore called for the adoption of secondary EU law to improve and harmonise legal procedures available in consumer cases, ensuring among other things that consumer associations have legal standing to initiate proceedings and facilitating alternative dispute resolution.[32] More generally, the European Parliament considered that '*the substantive rights conferred by [EU] legislation on the consumer must be supplemented by appropriate procedural mechanisms to ensure their enforcement*'.[33] Initially the Commission maintained that enacting EU legislation of this kind would be difficult and time-consuming.[34] But by 1987 it announced its intention to examine the opportunity of drafting a directive introducing a general right for consumer associations to act in the courts of the Member States in the general interest of consumers.[35] In the Commission's subsequent green paper on consumers' access to justice, dating from 1993, the idea of facilitating actions for injunctions brought by bodies representing consumer interests was further outlined. This document also identified several other issues in respect of which further steps could possibly be taken at EU level, such as the granting of legal aid, the simplified settlement of cross-border disputes, the promotion of self-regulation by industry and cooperation between the competent authorities of the Member States.[36]

---

30 Commission, Information memo on the adoption by the Council of a preliminary programme for a consumer protection and information policy, P-19/75, p. 2.

31 Commission, Memorandum on consumer redress, COM(84) 629 final, p. 7.

32 Cf. the 1977 report and resolution by the European Parliament and the 1979 opinion by the Economic and Social Committee, cited in Commission, Memorandum on consumer redress, COM(84) 629 final, p. 7.

33 European Parliament, Resolution on consumer redress, OJ 1987, C 99/203, recital C.

34 Commission, Memorandum on consumer redress, COM(84) 629 final, pp. 11–12. The annex to this document sets out several options that exist in the laws of certain Member States and third countries.

35 Commission, Supplementary communication on consumer redress, COM(87) 210, p. 3. This statement should be seen especially against the background of the European Parliament's insistence on the adoption of legislative measures. Cf. European Parliament, Resolution on consumer redress, OJ 1987, C 99/203.

36 Commission, Green paper on access of consumers to justice and the settlement of consumer disputes in the single market, COM(93) 576, pp. 77–86. See also Commission, Communication on an action plan on consumer access to justice and the settlement of consumer disputes in the internal market, COM(96) 13.

B. CONSUMER INJUNCTIONS DIRECTIVE: INJUNCTIONS

This subsection concentrates on the Consumer Injunctions Directive. Exceptionally in EU consumer protection law, this is a free-standing legal act that is exclusively concerned with enforcement-related issues. It concentrates on facilitating injunctive relief, to be granted in the collective interest of consumers. In the first subsection below the directive is introduced. Its system of mutual recognition as regards legal standing to bring a case and the remedies available under the directive are also outlined. In the following subsection attention turns to the directive's other provisions, its functioning in practice and other EU legislation that is relevant in connection with actions for injunctions to address infringements of certain rules of substantive consumer protection law.

1. Introduction, mutual recognition and remedies

5.05 As was observed in the foregoing section, the idea of adopting secondary EU law facilitating the bringing of actions for injunctions by bodies representing the interests of consumers dates back to the very beginning of EU consumer protection law. Although provisions on this subject matter can also be found elsewhere, the most prominent example of EU legislation of this kind is the Consumer Injunctions Directive.[37] This directive was originally adopted in 1998 after a comparatively smooth legislative process.[38] It was codified in 2009 so as to incorporate the amendments made to its annex.[39] Its legal basis is Article 114 TFEU on the EU's internal market.[40]

According to its recitals, the directive was adopted in light of '*an urgent need for some degree of approximation of national provisions*' on the matters covered by it.[41] At the same time the Commission underlined in its proposal that '*historical and legal traditions will be in no way compromised*' by the adoption of this directive.[42] There it was added that '*the proposed text in no way prejudices established remedies*

37 Consumer Injunctions Directive 2009/22.

38 See Commission, Proposal for Consumer Injunctions Directive 2009/22, COM(95) 712. See also Commission, Amended proposal for Consumer Injunctions Directive 2009/22, COM(96) 725. The European Parliament was mostly supportive of the Commission proposal. See European Parliament, Report on the proposal for Consumer Injunctions Directive 2009/22, A4–0354/96. Although on a number of issues the Member States represented in the Council introduced amendments (discussed below), an agreement between the co-legislators was reached relatively quickly. The final text of this act resembles to a great extent that of the Commission's original proposal.

39 In the EU's legislative terminology, the term "codification" refers to the adoption of a new legal act that incorporates amendments made to the initial legal act, without, however, making any substantive changes.

40 On the function of Art. 114 TFEU in a consumer protection context, see also para 5.02 above.

41 Recital 7 Consumer Injunctions Directive 2009/22. On the background of this directive, see further Rott (2001), p. 401.

42 Commission, Proposal for Consumer Injunctions Directive 2009/22, COM(95) 712, p. 8.

at national level: these rights may be far broader in certain Member States [...] than in others, but their harmonisation does not seem warranted given the current state of [EU] law'.[43]

5.06 At the basis of the Consumer Injunctions Directive lies the notion that most Member States had already designated one or more entities qualified to take legal action in the *collective* interests of consumers.[44] Its recitals explain that this does not include the cumulation of interests of individual private parties that have been harmed by an infringement.[45] At stake are thus rather the interests of the consumers as a whole and not the interests of individual consumers, regardless of whether the latter are pursued individually or "bundled" in a collective claim.

The directive leaves it in principle to the Member States to determine which entities are qualified to bring these kinds of claims under their respective national laws. The central concept of a "qualified entity" is defined broadly. It encompasses '*any body or organisation which, being properly constituted under the law of a Member State, has a legitimate interest in ensuring that the provisions [of substantive consumer protection law at issue] are complied with*'.[46] These entities may in particular be either independent *public bodies* specifically responsible for protecting the aforementioned interests or *private organisations*, such as consumer associations, whose purpose it is to protect those interests in accordance with the criteria laid down by the national law.[47] The Member States can either choose between or combine these two options.[48]

This implies that the Member States have considerable leeway when determining which entities they wish to regard as qualified and thus as having legal standing for the purposes of this directive. That reflects the diversity across the EU as regards the responsibility for enforcing consumer protection law. Historically Member States such as France and Belgium have tended to rely on actions brought by consumer associations, whereas for instance in the United Kingdom, Ireland, Denmark and Sweden, specific public authorities were responsible, and in Germany, the Netherlands and Italy this was left open to any

43 Ibid., p. 8.
44 Cf. ibid., p. 10.
45 Recital 3 Consumer Injunctions Directive 2009/22.
46 Art. 3 Consumer Injunctions Directive 2009/22.
47 Art. 3 Consumer Injunctions Directive 2009/22. Note that organisations representing firms or federations of firms are not mentioned here. In this regard this provision deviates from the Commission's proposal and from certain other consumer protection directives, such as Art. 23(2)(c) Consumer Rights Directive 2011/83. Cf. Council, doc. 11674/96.
48 Recital 11 Consumer Injunctions Directive. See also its recitals 9 and 10.

entity meeting certain predetermined criteria.[49] In practice also after the adoption of the Consumer Injunctions Directive, the Member States continue to retain widely diverging criteria in force for the recognition of such entities.[50] That said, virtually all Member States now grant legal standing to consumer associations.[51] Facilitating actions brought by these latter parties is one of the main purposes of this directive.[52] Although less common, many Member States also empower certain specialised national consumer authorities, an ombudsman or another public authority to take legal action under this directive.[53]

5.07 The Consumer Injunctions Directive concentrates on *cross-border* situations, where infringements of substantive EU consumer protection law produce effects in other Member States. Before its adoption most Member States reserved the right to take legal action to address such infringements to entities that they had expressly recognised.[54] A situation could therefore, for instance, occur whereby an undertaking established in Member State A sold a product to a consumer in Member State B, while imposing a contract term that is considered unfair under the Unfair Terms Directive.[55] An entity qualified to take legal action in this Member State A might then well be unaware, unwilling or legally unable to act against such an infringement. After all, the infringement had its effects in Member State B. As it stood, a qualified entity from Member State B would often not be qualified to take legal action in Member State A.[56] As a consequence the effectiveness of the EU consumer protection rules was considered to be at risk. Against this background the Consumer Injunctions Directive essentially seeks to ensure that '*the effectiveness of national measures transposing the [substantive EU consumer protection directives concerned] [...] is [not] thwarted where the [unlawful] practices produce effects in a Member State other than that in which they originate*'.[57] This is done with a view to avoiding disruptions to the smooth functioning of the internal market and distortions of competition, as well as ensuring that consumer confidence in the internal market is not diminished.[58]

---

49 Commission, Proposal for Consumer Injunctions Directive 2009/22, COM(95) 712, pp. 6 and 10.

50 Study, University of Bielefeld (2008), p. 611.

51 Study, University of Leuven (2007), p. 331.

52 Cf. Cafaggi and Micklitz (2009), pp. 408–9.

53 Study, University of Leuven (2007), pp. 331–2.

54 Commission, Proposal for Consumer Injunctions Directive 2009/22, COM(95) 712, pp. 5–11.

55 Unfair Terms Directive 93/13 is one of the directives listed in Annex I to Consumer Injunctions Directive 2009/22 (see point 5 of this annex).

56 The applicable rules of private international law can of course also be of relevance in this regard. Cf. Art. 2(2) and recital 7 Consumer Injunctions Directive 2009/22.

57 Recital 4 Consumer Injunctions Directive 2009/22.

58 Recitals 5 and 6 Consumer Injunctions Directive 2009/22.

The directive seeks to tackle these above-mentioned so-called "intra-EU infringements" essentially by providing for a system of mutual recognition.[59] It works as follows. The Member States must inform the Commission of the entities that, pursuant to their respective national laws, are qualified to initiate legal proceedings under this directive. On that basis the Commission publishes a list of notified qualified entities.[60] The Member States must then ensure that, in the case of an infringement originating in their territory, '*any qualified entity from another Member State where the interests protected by that entity are affected by the infringement, may apply to the [competent] court or administrative authority*'.[61] The list must be accepted as proof of the entity's legal capacity to bring a case. However, the competent national court[62] retains the right '*to examine whether the purpose of the qualified entity justifies its taking action in a specific case*'.[63] This latter provision thus restricts to some extent the application of the above-mentioned principle of mutual recognition by allowing for further verifications in individual cases. It was not part of the Commission's proposal; it was inserted at the insistence of the Member States in the course of the legislative process leading to the adoption of this directive.[64]

The Consumer Injunctions Directive lists three remedies. The main one is an **5.08** action for the '*cessation or prohibition*' of the infringement at issue.[65] As is already evident from the title of this legal act, this directive is thus primarily concerned with actions for (prohibitive) *injunctions*.[66] It is added in the directive that this measure is to be ordered '*with all due expediency, where appropriate by way of summary procedure*'.

Two other remedies are also provided for. Where appropriate, an applicant may seek the imposition of *publicity measures*, which entails the publication of the decision in question in full or in part or of a corrective statement with a view to eliminating the continuing effects of the infringement. In addition, the directive refers to the availability of *penalty payments*, which are to be paid into the public purse or to any other designated beneficiary. These payments are to be

59 Art. 4 Consumer Injunctions Directive 2009/22. See also its recital 12.

60 See e.g. OJ 2012, C 97/1. In 2006 276 qualified entities had been notified, whereby two Member States (Germany and Greece) together accounted for over half of these. See Study, University of Bielefeld (2008), p. 632.

61 Art. 4(1) Consumer Injunctions Directive 2009/22.

62 For the sake of brevity, reference is made here only to national courts, even if this directive also allows for cases being brought before a national administrative authority. See para 5.10 below.

63 Art. 4(1) Consumer Injunctions Directive 2009/22.

64 Cf. Council, doc. 5382/1/97.

65 Art. 2(1)(a) Consumer Injunctions Directive 2009/22.

66 This limitation to injunctions does not imply, however, that other remedies, such as actions for damages, cannot be available under national law in relation to the infringements in question. Several Member States provide for this possibility. See Study, University of Leuven (2007), p. 340.

made in the event of a failure to comply with the decision rendered within a set time limit, so as to ensure compliance. At the insistence of the Member States represented in Council, this latter measure only applies, however, '*in so far as the legal system of the Member State concerned so permits*'.[67] A majority of Member States nonetheless provide for this possibility.[68]

2. Other provisions, practical effects and other legislation

5.09 The aforementioned remedies must be made available in relation to infringements, which are defined in the Consumer Injunctions Directive as any act contrary to the consumer protection directives listed in Annex I to the directive as transposed into the internal legal orders of the Member States that harms the collective interests of consumers.[69] After several additions over the years, this annex currently lists 13 consumer protection directives. According to the Commission this means that '*a large proportion*' of the substantive EU rules in this domain are now within the scope of the Consumer Injunctions Directive.[70]

In the recitals it is suggested that this directive applies not only to infringements of the national measures transposing the directives listed in its Annex I, but also the protective measures that go beyond the level required by those directives.[71] Although this is not expressly stated, it thus appears that where those directives provide only for "minimum" harmonisation and a Member State chooses to also enact further-reaching consumer protection measures, infringements of the latter can also be covered by the Consumer Injunctions Directive. In any case, the directive does not prevent Member States from granting qualified entities or other persons concerned more extensive rights to bring actions at national level.[72] Poland and the Netherlands apply, for instance, the directive to *any* practice harming the collective interests of consumers, whereas Portugal and Latvia also permit action where the interest of an *individual* consumer is at stake.[73]

---

67 Cf. Council, doc. 11674/96.

68 Study, University of Bielefeld (2008), pp. 611 and 622–4.

69 Art. 1(2) Consumer Injunctions Directive 2009/22. As from January 2016, this provision no longer refers to "directives" but instead to "EU acts", given that Annex I also includes a regulation. See Art. 20 and 22 Regulation (EU) No 524/2013 on online dispute resolution for consumer disputes, OJ 2013, L 165/1 ("Consumer ODR Regulation").

70 Commission, First report on Consumer Injunctions Directive 2009/22, COM(2008) 756, p. 4.

71 Recital 4 Consumer Injunctions Directive 2009/22.

72 Article 7 Consumer Injunctions Directive 2009/22.

73 Commission, First report on Consumer Injunctions Directive 2009/22, COM(2008) 756, p. 5; Study, University of Bielefeld (2008), pp. 610 and 638–40.

5.10 The above provisions are complemented by certain rules on the *forum* before which proceedings under this directive are to be brought. These rules are formulated in a very general manner. The Consumer Injunctions Directive provides that the Member States must designate '*the courts or administrative authorities competent to rule on proceedings commenced by qualified entities*'.[74] No further requirements are set out, other than the statement in the recitals that the courts or administrative authorities concerned should have the '*right to examine the effects of previous decisions*'.[75] There it is also stated in general terms that the specific features of national legal systems must be taken into account to the full extent possible by leaving Member States free to choose between different options having equivalent effect. Presumably that means that Member States are in principle free to designate either a court or a (non-judicial) administrative authority to rule on the actions brought under this directive. Arguably it also means that where an administrative authority is competent, safeguards must be provided for that ensure a degree of independence and impartiality equivalent to those of the national judicial authorities. A clear majority of the Member States has opted for designating a national court and not an administrative authority.[76]

5.11 The directive further contains a separate article on *prior consultation*.[77] It allows the Member States to require a private party that intends to apply for an injunction to first try to achieve the cessation of the infringement at issue with the alleged infringer and, if the Member State concerned so decides, also with the qualified entity of the Member State in which the injunction would be sought, before it can initiate legal proceedings. This is meant to give the defendant an opportunity to "spontaneously" bring the infringement to an end.[78] This possibility of requiring such pre-trial contacts between the parties is subject to a time limit; if the consultation does not lead to the cessation of the infringement within two weeks, an action may be brought without delay. A considerable number of Member States, including Italy, Romania, Sweden and the United Kingdom, made use of the option offered by this provision.[79]

---

74 Art. 2 Consumer Injunctions Directive 2009/22.

75 Recital 9 Consumer Injunctions Directive 2009/22.

76 Commission, First report on Consumer Injunctions Directive 2009/22, COM(2008) 756, p. 3.

77 Art. 5 Consumer Injunctions Directive 2009/22. See also Notice from the Member States, Rules governing prior consultation adopted pursuant to Article 5 of Consumer Injunctions Directive 2009/22, OJ 2009, C 181/6.

78 Recital 14 Consumer Injunctions Directive 2009/22. Cf. Commission, Proposal for Consumer Injunctions Directive 2009/22, COM(95) 712, p. 12.

79 Commission, First report on Consumer Injunctions Directive 2009/22, COM(2008) 756, p. 4. See also Study, University of Leuven (2007), p. 336; Study, University of Bielefeld (2008), pp. 609 and 634–6.

5.12 The Commission observed in 2008 that the directive's effects in practice were '*disappointing*' in so far as tackling cross-border infringements of the relevant rules of substantive EU consumer protection law were concerned.[80] It could only point to two (successful) cases where the above-mentioned system of mutual recognition had been used. Subsequent reports suggest that there may have been an increase since then; stakeholders reported 70 cases with a cross-border dimension over the 2008–11 period. However, this is still only a fraction of the total number of actions for injunctions reportedly brought during that latter period (namely 5632 cases, thus slightly over 1 per cent).[81] Moreover, this reported increase seems mainly due to a broader understanding of what constitutes a cross-border case. Also included are situations where a qualified entity initiates legal proceedings in its "home" Member State against an (alleged) infringer that is established in another Member State but that operates in that "home" Member State. The above-mentioned mutual recognition mechanism that is meant to allow qualified entities to act outside their "home" Member State continues to be '*rarely used*'.[82]

The view is widely shared that an important explanation for this limited use of this remedy with respect to cross-border infringements lies in the difficulties relating to costs and funding, especially where consumer associations are concerned.[83] The costs of the legal proceedings were mentioned as an obstacle when assessing the use of actions for injunctions under this directive more generally. This appears to concern not necessarily the legal costs of the applicant themself, but rather the potential costs associated with the risk of having to pay the opponents' costs under the "loser pays" principle. Some Member States therefore provide for financial support for qualified entities.[84] Likewise, complexities of the legal proceedings, real or perceived, are seen as a general concern, which is, however, aggravated in cross-border situations.[85] Other concerns mentioned are the length of proceedings and the limited effects that judgments typically have, namely only in the jurisdiction concerned and in principle only between the parties to the dispute (and not *erga omnes*).[86] The effectiveness of the directive's rules on penalty payments has also been questioned, whilst the possibility of ordering the publication of the court or

80 Ibid., p. 5.

81 Commission, Second report on Consumer Injunctions Directive 2009/22, COM(2012) 635, p. 4.

82 Ibid., p. 6.

83 See e.g. Study, University of Leuven (2008), pp. 612–13, 641 and 644; Cafaggi and Micklitz (2009), p. 422; Poncibò (2009), pp. 297–8; Rott (2001), p. 410. See also Commission, First report on Consumer Injunctions Directive 2009/22, COM(2008) 756, p. 6.

84 Commission, Second report on Consumer Injunctions Directive 2009/22, COM(2012) 635, p. 11.

85 Ibid., p. 12.

86 Ibid., pp. 12–13. See also Commission, First report on Consumer Injunctions Directive 2009/22, COM(2008) 756, pp. 6–8; Study, University of Leuven (2007), pp. 342–8.

authority's decision or a corrective statement appears not be used frequently in practice.[87] More generally, while acknowledging that it marks an important step, the directive has been widely criticised for addressing '*but very few of the complex legal questions involved in cross-border litigation with a view to private enforcement of [EU] law*'.[88] One of the suggestions made in this connection covers not only injunctive relief, but also actions for damages.[89]

Yet these continuing difficulties with respect to cross-border infringements and the fact that certain obstacles remain should not distract from the fact that actions for injunctions are a widely used remedy in consumer cases. It is, generally speaking, moreover, a rather effective one, as the success rate tends to be high.[90] Injunctions have been held to be '*a successful tool for policing markets*'.[91] Presumably in this light in 2008 and again in 2012 the Commission decided against proposing amendments to this directive.[92] Specifically in relation to the difficulties encountered in cross-border cases it appears that other EU legislative measures that have a broader scope of application, such as in particular the Brussels I Regulation on jurisdiction and the recognition and enforcement of judgments and the Rome II Regulation on the law applicable to non-contractual obligations,[93] are expected to have a positive effect. One could also think of the increased cooperation between consumer protection authorities under the EU's rules relating to public enforcement.[94]

Finally, many *other* consumer protection directives also contain provisions that **5.13**
aim to facilitate the bringing of actions for injunctions. These provisions are typically part of directives that principally set out certain substantive rules. A common element tends to be the requirement for the Member States to ensure that '*adequate and effective means*' exist to enforce compliance with the rules at

87 Study, University of Leuven (2007), pp. 341–2. In relation to these penalties and the enforcement of court decisions, see also Commission, Second report on Consumer Injunctions Directive 2009/22, COM(2012) 635, pp. 13–14.

88 Betlem (2007), p. 703. For comparable criticism, see Bogdan (1998), p. 374; Micklitz (2001), p. 867; Storskrubb (2008), pp. 29–30; Azar-Baud (2010), p. 199. See also Study, University of Leuven (2007), pp. 347–8.

89 Study, University of Bielefeld (2008), pp. 613 and 644. At the time of its adoption, the European Economic and Social Committee had also argued in favour of making provision for actions for damages. See Economic and Social Committee, Opinion on the proposal for a directive on injunctions for the protection of consumers' interests, OJ 1997, C 30/112. For a discussion of this option, see Poncibò (2009), p. 283.

90 Commission, First report on Consumer Injunctions Directive 2009/22, COM(2008) 756, p. 4.

91 Commission, Second report on Consumer Injunctions Directive 2009/22, COM(2012) 635, p. 7. See also Study, University of Leuven (2007), pp. 346–7.

92 Commission, First report on Consumer Injunctions Directive 2009/22, COM(2008) 756, p. 8; Commission, Second report on Consumer Injunctions Directive 2009/22, COM(2012) 635, p. 16.

93 Brussels I Regulation 1215/2012 and Rome II Regulation 864/2007. See para 1.12 above.

94 See subsection 5.E.4 below.

issue.[95] In some cases it is then merely added that these means shall include provisions whereby public bodies and consumer and professional organisations having a legitimate interest may take action under national law before the courts or before the competent administrative authorities.[96]

In other cases more detailed rules are provided for, such as in the Unfair Terms Directive. This directive specifies that persons or organisations that have a legitimate interest under national law in protecting consumers must be allowed to initiate legal action before a national court or administrative authority. The purpose of these actions is to obtain '*a decision as to whether contractual terms drawn up for general use are unfair, so that they apply appropriate and effective means to prevent the continued use of such terms*'.[97] Also here the idea is to facilitate some form of "representative" action, in particular (but not necessarily) by consumer associations.[98] While these actions are typically aimed at obtaining injunctive relief, under national law they can also take other forms, such as a contractual remedy.[99] These actions can be brought even where the unfair term has not (yet) been used in a specific contract, in light of the deterrent nature and dissuasive purpose of these measures and their independence of any particular dispute.[100] In terms of forum, although many Member States also provide for a system of administrative control in one form or another, the above actions are normally to be brought before their civil courts, whereby many provide for what the Commission called in its 2000 report on this directive a '*substantial "administrative" admixture*'.[101] The latter refers to the possibility of certain public authorities (such as a national consumer authority or an ombudsman) bringing a case before the competent national civil courts. More generally, the introduction of the above-mentioned rules is said to have led to a significant increase in the number of cases brought, even if its effects vary considerably by

95 E.g. Art. 23 Consumer Rights Directive 2011/83. Further specifications are sometimes added, e.g. '*in the interest of consumers, competitors and the general public*', '*in the interests of traders and competitors*' or '*in the interests of consumers*' in Art. 7 Unfair Terms Directive 93/13, Art. 5 Misleading Advertising Directive 2006/114 and Art. 11 Unfair Practices Directive 2005/29 respectively.

96 E.g. Art. 23 Consumer Rights Directive 2011/83.

97 Art. 7(2) Unfair Terms Directive 93/13. On this directive, see also section 5.C below.

98 Cf. Commission, First amended proposal for Unfair Terms Directive 93/13, COM(92) 66, p. 3. See also CoJ joined cases C-240/98 and C-244/98, *Océano Grupo*, para 27; CoJ case C-372/99, *Commission v Italy*, para 14; Study, University of Bielefeld (2008), pp. 430–31.

99 Cf. e.g. CoJ case C-472/10, *Invitel*, para 35–40. See also Opinion AG Trstenjak case C-472/10, *Invitel*, para 39 (n. 12); Study, University of Bielefeld (2008), pp. 428–9.

100 CoJ case C-372/99, *Commission v Italy*, para 15–16; CoJ case C-472/10, *Invitel*, para 37. Such independence of a specific dispute also implies, however, that these associations are not entitled to intervene in individual cases under this directive. See CoJ case C-470/12, *Pohotovost*, para 43–57.

101 Commission, Report on Unfair Terms Directive 93/13, COM(2000) 248, p. 21. See also Study, University of Bielefeld (2008), pp. 423–32.

Member State.[102] The shortcomings in its application broadly resemble those identified in relation to the Consumer Injunctions Directive discussed above.[103]

The Unfair Commercial Practices Directive provides for rather detailed rules that are comparable to the aforementioned ones set out in the Unfair Terms Directive, but that go further in that they specify that the competent courts or administrative authorities must be empowered to order the cessation of the infringement and to prohibit imminent infringements '*even where there is no proof of actual loss or damage or of intention or negligence*'.[104] An accelerated procedure, either with interim or with definitive effect, must further be made available to decide on these actions.[105] Under the Unfair Commercial Practices Directive, Member States may also provide for the possibility of the publication of the decisions or of corrective statements to be ordered.[106] Where a Member State designates an administrative authority as the competent forum, the latter must be composed so as not to cast doubts on its impartiality, have adequate powers to monitor and enforce the observance of their decisions, give reasons for its decisions and be subject to judicial review.[107] Also in this case the Member States remain free to require prior recourse to other means of dealing with complaints.[108] Finally, the competent national courts or authorities must be able to require the defendant where appropriate to furnish evidence to underpin any factual claims made in relation to a commercial practice and to consider these claims inaccurate if the evidence is deemed to be insufficient.[109]

C. UNFAIR TERMS DIRECTIVE: CONTRACTUAL REMEDIES

In this section attention turns to contractual remedies, which are measures affecting the validity or effectiveness of contractual arrangements concluded in breach of EU law. Of particular importance in this respect is the Unfair Terms Directive. This directive is therefore first briefly introduced, after which its provision laying down a contractual remedy is assessed. The second subsection then discusses the obligation of the competent national courts to raise of its own motion the unfairness of a contract term and its possible consequences for the

102 Ibid., p. 32. See also Study, University of Bielefeld (2008), pp. 433–4.

103 Ibid., pp. 22–3. Here the length of proceedings and the general lack of *erga omnes* effect of decisions taken are cited in particular. See also para 5.12 above.

104 Art. 11(2), first subparagraph Unfair Commercial Practices Directive 2005/29. See also Art. 5–7 Unfair Advertising Directive 2006/114; Art. 7 Tobacco Advertising Directive 2003/33.

105 Art. 11(2), second subparagraph Unfair Commercial Practices Directive 2005/29.

106 Art. 11(2), third subparagraph Unfair Commercial Practices Directive 2005/29.

107 Art. 11(3) Unfair Commercial Practices Directive 2005/29.

108 Art. 11(1) Unfair Commercial Practices Directive 2005/29.

109 Art. 12 Unfair Commercial Practices Directive 2005/29.

contract, the effects of this contractual remedy in practice and the other EU legislation that is relevant in this connection.

1. Introduction and contractual remedy

5.14 The Unfair Terms Directive,[110] which was adopted in 1993 on the basis of the EU's main internal market provision, Article 114 TFEU,[111] has been called '*a first incursion of EU law into the heartland of national contract thinking*'.[112] The process of drafting and adopting it took almost two decades, considering that early drafts were discussed as far back as 1975, although it was not until 1990 that the Commission actually submitted a proposal.[113] In this proposal the Commission was careful to underline that '*the time is not ripe for approximating or unifying the national laws relating to the whole field of contractual and quasi-contractual obligations or even to the limited sphere of the sale of goods and provision of services*'.[114] Nevertheless, heated debates took place in the Council before the directive was eventually adopted, not least concerning the provision discussed below.[115] The Commission has described the end result as '*a delicate compromise*'.[116]

5.15 This directive essentially seeks to harmonise the laws of the Member States as regards the prevention of the use of unfair terms in "standard" contracts concluded between consumers and undertakings (sellers or suppliers).[117] Under the directive a term is qualified as "unfair" if it has not been individually negotiated and causes, contrary to the requirements of good faith, a significant imbalance in the parties' rights and obligations arising under the contract, to the detriment of the consumer.[118] Its annex contains an indicative and non-exhaustive list of such terms.[119] Examples include contract terms obliging the consumer concerned to pay a disproportionately high compensation where he fails to fulfil his obligations, allowing the undertaking concerned to terminate a

---

110 Unfair Terms Directive 93/13.

111 On the use of Article 114 TFEU in a consumer protection context, see also para 5.02 above.

112 Weatherill (2005), p. 115.

113 See Commission, Proposal for Unfair Terms Directive 93/13, COM(90) 322, pp. 9–12. See also Commission, Communication on unfair terms in contracts concluded with consumers, COM(84) 55.

114 Commission, Proposal for Unfair Terms Directive 93/13, COM(90) 322, p. 13.

115 See further Weatherill (2005), pp. 115–16; Micklitz, Reich and Rott (2009), pp. 123–6.

116 Commission, Report on Unfair Terms Directive 93/13, COM(2000) 248, p. 5.

117 Art. 1(1) Unfair Terms Directive 93/13. See also its recital 4. On matters falling outside the scope of this directive pursuant to its Art. 1(2), see e.g. CoJ case C-92/11, *RWE Vertrieb*, para 25–31; CoJ case C-280/13, *Barclays*, para 38–45. Regarding the capacity of the persons concerned, see CoJ case C-488/11, *Asbeek Brusse*, para 24–30.

118 Art. 3 Unfair Terms Directive 93/13.

119 Cf. e.g. CoJ case C-472/10, *Invitel*, para 25.

contract without reasonable notice or excluding or hindering the consumer's right to take legal action.

Against the background of the aim of progressively establishing the EU's internal market, the directive seeks to avoid or lessen the '*many disparities*' and '*marked divergences*' that were observed to exist in this respect.[120] In the recitals it is further held that '*more effective protection of the consumer can be achieved by adopting uniform rules*',[121] while also noting that '*as they now stand, national laws allow only partial harmonisation to be envisaged*'.[122]

Of particular importance for the present purposes is Article 6(1) Unfair Terms **5.16**
Directive, which states that the Member States must provide that unfair terms '*shall, as provided for under their national law, not be binding on the consumer*'.[123] This provision further stipulates that the contract shall continue to bind the parties upon those terms if it is capable of continuing in existence without the unfair terms. The Court of Justice has clarified that this is a mandatory provision that aims to replace the formal balance that the consumer contract in question establishes between the rights and obligations of the parties concerned with an effective balance that re-establishes equality between them.[124]

The Commission had proposed laying down an obligation for the Member States to prohibit the use of unfair terms in combination with a provision stipulating that such contracts would be "void" if used nonetheless.[125] However, the Council deleted this prohibition as it was seen as partially redundant and excessive, while also replacing the term "void" by "not binding", as this latter term was considered legally more appropriate.[126] The latter term is a more neutral legal concept, thus allowing the Member States a wider margin of manoeuvre, in light of diverging legal systems and traditions in respect of civil law.[127] This is underlined by the explicit reference to national law that the Council also inserted. The addition of the words "on the consumer" furthermore makes it explicit that this remedy can be invoked only to the benefit of the

---

120 Recitals 1–3 Unfair Terms Directive 93/13.

121 Recital 10 Unfair Terms Directive 93/13.

122 Recital 12 Unfair Terms Directive 93/13.

123 Art. 6(1) Unfair Terms Directive 93/13.

124 E.g. CoJ case C-618/10, *Banco Español de Crédito*, para 40; CoJ case C-169/14, *Sánchez Morcillo*, para 23.

125 Commission, Proposal for Unfair Terms Directive 93/13, COM(90) 322, p. 69 (Art. 3); Commission, First amended proposal for Unfair Terms Directive 93/13, COM(92) 66, p. 11 (Art. 7).

126 See Council, doc. 8406/1/92; Council, doc. 8406/1/92, p. 5. See also Commission, Communication on the Council's position on the proposal for Unfair Terms Directive 93/13, SEC(92) 1944, p. 6; Commission, Second amended proposal for Unfair Terms Directive 93/13, COM(93) 11, p. 2.

127 Opinion AG Trstenjak case C-472/10, *Invitel*, para 48.

consumer and not (also) of the undertaking concerned.[128] The Commission explained that the intention of the resulting provision is '*to ensure that no unfair term may be enforced to the detriment of a consumer*', while leaving the precise legal classification to the domestic legal system of each Member State.[129] It suggested that this could be done through legal concepts of national law such as relative or absolute nullity, non-existence or "voidance".[130]

5.17 Seen against this background, it is not surprising that the relevant provision of the Unfair Terms Directive has been transposed into national law in many different ways. Effect has been given to the term "not binding on the consumer" through national law concepts such as non-existence, nullity, revocability, voidability and unenforceability.[131] Under Bulgarian, German and Spanish law, for instance, an unfair term within the meaning of the directive is automatically null and void.[132] A largely similar concept of non-existence is applied in France.[133] The laws of the Czech Republic and the Netherlands provide for relative nullity, whereby the unfair term can be declared void upon application.[134] In Italy provision is made for a somewhat comparable concept of "protective nullity", allowing the consumer to rely on the term so long as it suits him, as only this party can invoke the nullity.[135] Under the laws of certain Member States, such as Hungary and Poland, a court ruling establishing the unfairness of a term can in certain cases have effects *erga omnes*. This means that the ruling applies in respect of all consumers that concluded a contract containing this term with that particular undertaking or even with other undertakings.[136]

5.18 This raises the issue of what, from an EU law perspective, the limits are to the leeway that the above provision leaves to the Member States. In 2000 the Commission took the view that it should at least be ensured that the consumer in question is free to refuse to honour the contractual obligation imposed by the unfair term before the competent national court has adjudicated on the matter.[137] In addition, it argued that any court judgment finding a term to be

128 Cf. Micklitz, Reich and Rott (2009), p. 144 (see also p. 207).

129 Commission, Second amended proposal for Unfair Terms Directive 93/13, COM(93) 11, p. 2.

130 Ibid., p. 2. See also Council, doc. 4884/93, p. 2, where the Council expressed the view that this term can imply *inter alia* that the relevant part of the contract is void.

131 Commission, Report on Unfair Terms Directive 93/13, COM(2000) 248, pp. 19–20.

132 Study, University of Bielefeld (2008), pp. 357, 361, 373 and 407.

133 Ibid., pp. 360 and 407.

134 Ibid., pp. 358, 368 and 407. Under Netherlands' law an unfair term can also not be applied on the basis of the principles of reasonableness and equity (*redelijkheid en billijkheid*; Art. 6:248 BW).

135 Ibid., p. 365.

136 Ibid., pp. 431–2. See also Keirsbilck (2013), pp. 1468–9. As such, these rules address some of the concerns noted in Commission, Report on Unfair Terms Directive 93/13, COM(2000) 248, pp. 22–3.

137 Commission, Report on Unfair Terms Directive 93/13, COM(2000) 248, p. 19.

unfair should take effect from the time of conclusion of the contract, thus with retroactive effect (*ex tunc*).[138] This would significantly limit the possibilities available under national law.

It appears, however, that the Court of Justice is inclined to take more of a "hands-off" approach. It mostly respects the Member States' leeway under this provision, while at the same time seeking to ensure that the aim of this provision is achieved. The Court has confirmed that the Member States have '*a certain degree of autonomy so far as concerns the definition of the legal arrangements applicable to unfair terms*'.[139] In line with the wording of the Unfair Terms Directive, the key issue is that the Member States must ensure that these terms are not binding on the consumer.[140] The Court has left it to the national court seised to draw all the necessary consequences under national law so as to achieve this result, and to assess whether the contract in question can continue to exist without that term.[141] To this aim that court must '*do whatever lies within its jurisdiction, taking the whole body of domestic law into consideration and applying the interpretative methods recognised by domestic law, with a view to ensuring that [Article 6(1) Unfair Terms Directive] is fully effective and achieving an outcome consistent with the objective pursued by it*'.[142] This also applies with regard to the future.[143] For the Court of Justice, the key is therefore that a national court does not apply a term that it considers to be unfair, without such non-application being qualified further as a matter of EU law.[144]

The Court has further ruled that, at least in cases where a contract term is found to be unfair pursuant to a "representative" action brought under this directive,[145] that term should generally not be binding on consumers who have concluded a contract containing this term with that particular undertaking, regardless of whether these consumers were party to the proceedings in question.[146] Yet whilst this result can be achieved through a ruling having effects *erga omnes*,[147] it also noted that this does not exclude the possibility of other types of national

138 For a similar view, see Opinion AG Trstenjak case C-472/10, *Invitel*, para 47.
139 CoJ case C-618/10, *Banco Español de Crédito*, para 62.
140 Ibid., para 62.
141 CoJ case C-40/08, *Asturcom*, para 57–8; CoJ Order case C-76/10, *Pohotovost*, para 61–2; CoJ case C-453/10, *Pereničová*, para 30.
142 CoJ case C-618/10, *Banco Español de Crédito*, para 72.
143 CoJ case C-472/10, *Invitel*, para 43.
144 CoJ case C-243/08, *Pannon*, para 35; CoJ case C-488/11, *Asbeek Brusse*, para 49.
145 Pursuant to Art. 7(2) Unfair Terms Directive 93/13. See para 5.13 above.
146 CoJ case C-472/10, *Invitel*, para 38. See also Opinion AG Trstenjak case C-472/10, *Invitel*, para 59–60, where it was argued that serious doubts from the viewpoint of proportionality and protection of fundamental rights would arise, however, if the effects of such a ruling were to extend also to *other* undertakings that use the same term in their contracts but that are not party to the proceedings in question.
147 See para 5.12 above.

measures.[148] Concerning the remainder of the contract (that is, its terms other than the unfair ones), it has been held that, although national law may provide otherwise, the directive itself does not imply that a national court could or should annul the *entire* contract containing an unfair term where this would be advantageous for the consumer concerned.[149] Neither does it allow the national court to *amend* the contract other than by deleting the unfair term to the extent that such continuity is legally possible under national law.[150] That does not preclude, however, that in certain cases, notably where the alternative is the annulment of the entire contract thereby exposing the consumer to disadvantageous consequences, the national court substitutes, upon such deletion, a supplementary provision of national law for the unfair term.[151]

2. Own-motion judicial review, practical effects and other legislation

5.19 The Court of Justice has shown considerably less restraint on another issue relating to the contractual remedy set out in the Unfair Terms Directive discussed above. This concerns the question of whether a national court should verify *of its own motion* (*ex officio*) – thus without any of the parties to the proceedings having raised the issue – whether a given term is unfair and therefore not binding on the consumer. Of particular importance in this regard is its 2000 judgment in *Océano Grupo*.[152] This case concerned a preliminary reference by a Spanish court. Several consumers had bought certain products (encyclopaedias), but they failed to pay the sums due. The undertakings that had sold them the products then initiated legal proceedings. By application of the relevant term of the contract, these cases were brought before the court located at the undertakings' principal place of business rather than at the place where the consumers were domiciled, as is the general rule. The national court seised doubted whether it had jurisdiction, considering the possible unfairness of the term in question. It was also unsure as to whether it could raise the issue of the possible unfairness of its own motion.

In its judgment the Court of Justice confirmed that a term such as the one at issue had the object or effect of excluding or hindering the consumers' right to take legal action and was therefore unfair. It was noted that the Unfair Terms Directive is founded on the idea that the consumer is in a weak position

---

148 CoJ case C-472/10, *Invitel*, para 39–40.

149 CoJ case C-453/10, *Pereničová*, para 31–5.

150 CoJ case C-618/10, *Banco Español de Crédito*, para 64–71. See also CoJ C-26/13, *Kásler*, para 77–9.

151 CoJ case C-26/13, *Kásler*, para 80–5. See also CoJ joined cases C-482/13, C-484/13, C-485/13 and C-487/13, *Unicaja Banco*, para 32–3.

152 CoJ joined cases C-240/98 and C-244/98, *Océano Grupo*, para 22–9. On this case and subsequent case law, see further Stuyck (2001), p. 719; Ebers (2010), p. 823; Stuyck (2010), p. 879; Schebesta (2010), p. 847; Trstenjak and Beysen (2011), pp. 119–21; Keirsbilck (2013), p. 1467.

vis-à-vis the undertaking concerned as regards both his bargaining power and his level of knowledge. The Court found that the aim of the contractual remedy for which it provides would not be achieved if the consumer were himself obliged to raise the unfair nature of the term. Especially where the amounts involved are limited, the consumer may be deterred by the lawyers' fees. In the Court's view there is thus a real risk that the consumer does not challenge the unfair term himself, particularly because of ignorance of the law. It was therefore found that the effective protection of the consumer could be attained only if the national court acknowledges that it has power to evaluate terms of this kind of its own motion.

In *Océano Grupo* the Court also noted that the system of protection laid down in this directive is based on the notion that the imbalance between the consumer and the undertaking concerned may only be corrected by positive action unconnected with the actual parties to the contract. In that context it referred to the aforementioned possibility of "representative" actions being brought under this directive by certain third parties, such as consumer associations, provided for in Article 7 Unfair Terms Directive.[153] In conclusion it was held that:

> the [national] court's power to determine of its own motion whether a term is unfair must be regarded as constituting a proper means both of achieving the result sought by Article 6, namely, preventing an individual consumer from being bound by an unfair term, and of contributing to achieving the aim of Article 7, since if the court undertakes such an examination, that may act as a deterrent and contribute to preventing unfair terms in contracts concluded between consumers and sellers or suppliers.[154]

In subsequent cases the Court of Justice has ruled that the competent national **5.20**
court should not only be *empowered* to act of its own motion, but that it is in principle *obliged* to do so.[155] In this manner it went further than the position initially taken by the Commission in this respect.[156] In the context of the possible annulment of an arbitration award, the Court found that, in light of the nature and importance of the public interest underlying this directive, Article 6(1) Unfair Terms Directive must be regarded as having standing equal to national rules of public policy (*d'ordre public*).[157] As a general rule, provided that

153 Art. 7(2) Unfair Terms Directive 93/13. See para 5.13 above.

154 CoJ joined cases C-240/98 and C-244/98, *Océano Grupo*, para 28.

155 In addition to the cases mentioned above and below, see also CoJ case C-473/00, *Cofidis*; CoJ case C-137/08, *Pénzügyi Lízing*. Note that the CoJ has since applied essentially the same reasoning to other consumer protection directives also, namely Consumer Credit Directive 2008/48 and Consumer Rights Directive 2011/83. See CoJ case C-429/05, *Rampion*; CoJ case C-227/08, *Martín Martín*.

156 See Commission, Report on Unfair Terms Directive 93/13, COM(2000) 248, pp. 19–20.

157 CoJ case C-168/05, *Mostaza Claro*, para 35–8; CoJ case C-40/08, *Asturcom*, para 52–3. For an alternative approach, rejecting an extensive interpretation of the concept of "public policy" and concentrating instead on an infringement of the right to a fair hearing, see Opinion AG Tizzano case C-168/05, *Mostaza Claro*,

the necessary legal and factual elements are available to it, a national court is therefore under an obligation to assess whether a term is unfair within the meaning of the Unfair Terms Directive and therefore not binding on the consumer, as a means to compensate for the imbalance between the private parties concerned.[158]

Although broad and far-reaching, this obligation is not unqualified, however. The Court has clarified for instance that where this own-motion assessment leads to the finding that the term is unfair, the national court should normally inform the parties to the dispute and invite them to comment.[159] When the consumer then still does not wish to assert the unfairness of the term, the national court is not obliged to consider it unfair.[160] Neither does such an obligation necessarily exist in the context of the enforcement of a previous arbitration award which has since become final (*res judicata*).[161] In addition, this obligation does not apply in cases brought by consumer protection associations, given that here the same imbalance between the parties is not presumed to exist.[162]

In this line of case law the EU law principles of equivalence and effectiveness have been repeatedly applied.[163] This provision of the Unfair Terms Directive having been held to be of equal standing as a national rule of public policy, the former principle implies that the effects of earlier, final judgments may still need to be reassessed where national law provides for this possibility in cases of breaches of national rules of public policy. Here the Court underlined that in case national law gives the competent national court the *discretion* to do so, this must be taken to imply an *obligation*.[164] It has further held that specific national proceedings for the simplified and rapid recovery of uncontested claims can be incompatible with the principle of effectiveness, where such procedures completely prevent the court from considering of its own motion whether a term is unfair. Here the risk that a consumer would not lodge his objections because of the short time period, associated costs or his unawareness, was stressed once more.[165] On similar grounds, interim relief must be available against

para 55–61. On the term "public policy" within the meaning of Brussels I Regulation1215/2012, see e.g. CoJ case C-7/98, *Krombach*, para 37; CoJ case C-394/07, *Gambazzi*, para 27.

158 E.g. CoJ case C-618/10, *Banco Español de Crédito*, para 42–3; CoJ case C-415/11, *Aziz*, para 46–7; CoJ case C-169/14, *Sánchez Morcillo*, para 24.

159 CoJ case C-472/11, *Banif Plus Bank*, para 31. See also CoJ case C-488/11, *Asbeek Brusse*, para 52.

160 CoJ case C-243/08, *Pannon*, para 33.

161 CoJ case C-40/08, *Asturcom*, para 34–8.

162 CoJ case C-413/12, *ACICL*, para 49–50.

163 On these two principles, see subsections 2.A.2 and 2.A.3 above.

164 E.g. CoJ case C-40/08, *Asturcom*, para 51–4; CoJ case C-488/11, *Asbeek Brusse*, para 46.

165 CoJ case C-618/10, *Banco Español de Crédito*, para 53–5.

enforcement proceedings in certain cases.[166] Yet the Court has also ruled that in this context the principle of effectiveness cannot be '*stretched*' so far as to mean that the national court must compensate not only for a procedural omission on the part of the consumer, but also his '*total inertia*'.[167]

Apart from the rules on actions for injunctions discussed earlier,[168] the Unfair Terms Directive contains no further provisions in respect of the remedies and procedures applicable in proceedings before national courts under this directive. No provision is made, for example, for actions for damages. In respect of the contractual remedy at issue here, the directive also leaves it open which body is to rule on the actions in question.[169] Neither does it touch upon the issue of limitation periods for actions brought under the directive. **5.21**

Doubts have been expressed as to whether the current system of protection that the Unfair Terms Directive offers to private parties is adequate.[170] In its report on this directive, dating from 2000, the Commission was critical, observing that unfair terms continue to be used on a wide scale and calling the said system '*very ineffective*'.[171] It noted that the situation where a term has been held to be non-binding differs little from the situation where the term had not been used in the first place, which implies that the undertakings using those terms in effect run little risk. The Commission further argued that its effectiveness depends also on the ease of the consumers' access to justice and, perhaps primarily, on sufficient information being available to them. This report therefore raised the options of reinforcing this "civil penalty" or complementing it by providing for criminal sanctions or actions for damages. **5.22**

The above-mentioned *Océano Grupo* case law, which dates from after the publication of the Commission's report, appears to have helped to address its latter concern about consumers being insufficiently informed. However, to a large extent the former concern about undertakings in effect running hardly any risk still seems equally valid today. A more recent study also warned against the possible lack of effectiveness as a consequence of the rather rudimentary regulation of the legal consequences of a finding that a contract term is unfair as well as consumers' lack of knowledge in this respect.[172] Nonetheless, when in

166 CoJ case C-415/11, *Aziz*, para 57–63. CoJ case C-34/13, *Kušinová*, para 66.

167 CoJ case C-40/08, *Asturcom*, para 47. See also CoJ case C-34/13, *Kušinová*, para 56.

168 See para 5.13 above.

169 Cf. CoJ case C-567/13, *Baczó*, para 40–59.

170 Cf. CoJ case C-144/99, *Commission v Netherlands*, para 18; CoJ case C-478/99, *Commission v Sweden*, para 16 and 18; CoJ case C-243/08, *Pannon*, para 21. Here it is clarified that Art. 6(1) Unfair Terms Directive 93/13 is intended to accord rights to citizens in their role of consumers.

171 Commission, Report on Unfair Terms Directive 93/13, COM(2000) 248, p. 35 (see also p. 20).

172 Study, University of Bielefeld (2008), pp. 347 and 434.

2008 the Commission proposed replacing the Unfair Terms Directive, its intended successor contained a provision that is essentially the same as the one discussed above.[173] The EU legislature eventually decided against repealing this directive, however.[174] The aforementioned provision consequently remains in force today, without its having been integrated into the Consumer Rights Directive, as the Commission had proposed.[175]

5.23 Finally, several *other* directives in the domain of consumer protection also contain certain provisions on contractual remedies designed to address infringements of the applicable rules. For example, the Consumer Sales Directive provides that a consumer may have the contract "rescinded" where the consumer goods to which the contract relates are not in conformity.[176] In the recitals of this directive it is specified that the detailed arrangements whereby the recession of the contract is effected may be laid down in national law.[177] The consequences of exercising this right of rescission are sometimes seen as unclear.[178] In addition, under this directive any contract term or agreement concluded before the lack of conformity is brought to the seller's attention that waives or restricts the rights resulting from the directive '*shall, as provided for by national law, not be binding on the consumer*'.[179] The similarity in wording between this latter provision and Article 6(1) Unfair Terms Directive is evident. In the absence of any relevant indications in the preparatory documents, the case law of the Court of Justice or otherwise, it remains for now an open question, however, as to whether it should be understood in the same manner.[180]

Another example of contractual remedies in the field of EU consumer protection law can be found in the Package Travel Directive, which allows consumers to '*withdraw from the contract*' without penalty in case the undertaking concerned does not honour its primary commitments under the contract in question.[181] It has been held that this is to be understood as a right for the consumer to cancel the contract, similar to the right of rescission as provided in the Consumer Sales Directive.[182] The Commission's 2013 proposal to replace

173 Commission, Proposal for Consumer Rights Directive 2011/83, COM(2008) 614, p. 34 (Art. 37).

174 See e.g. Council, doc. 8992/11, pp. 5–6.

175 Consumer Rights Directive 2011/83.

176 Art. 3(2), (5) and (6) Consumer Sales Directive 1999/44.

177 Recital 15 Consumer Sales Directive 1999/44.

178 Study, University of Bielefeld (2008), p. 706. Some clarity is provided by CoJ case C-404/06, *Quelle*, para 39; CoJ joined cases C-65/09 and C-87/09, *Weber*, para 72. Regarding the implementation of this directive, see also Commission, Report on Consumer Sales Directive 1999/44, COM(2007) 210.

179 Art. 7 Consumer Sales Directive 1999/44.

180 Cf. Commission, Proposal for Consumer Sales Directive 1999/44, COM(95) 520, p. 16. As regards the transposition into national law, see Study, University of Bielefeld (2008), p. 692.

181 Art. 4(5) Package Travel Directive 90/314. See also its Art. 4(6).

182 Study, University of Bielefeld (2008), pp. 213 and 298–9.

the Package Travel Directive speaks in this regard of the right to "terminate" the contract.[183] This suggests that this right is to be distinguished from the right of "withdrawal" that can be found in several other consumer protection directives.[184] In these latter cases this concept relates primarily to a "cooling-off period", meaning that a consumer can withdraw from a concluded contract under certain conditions and within a limited time period.[185]

D. PRODUCT LIABILITY DIRECTIVE: DAMAGES

A third, quite different approach from the ones discussed in the foregoing two subsections has been laid down in the Product Liability Directive. This directive seeks to facilitate the private enforcement of the relevant substantive rules of EU law by focusing on another remedy, namely civil liability for damages. After a brief general introduction of this directive, its central principle of no-fault liability is outlined below. There it is also explained what is understood in this context by the term "damage". Subsequently the manner in which this liability is limited and the other relevant legislation are discussed.

1. Introduction, no-fault liability and damage

The Product Liability Directive dates from 1985.[186] This directive is considered not only a cornerstone of the EU's consumer protection *acquis*, but also as an important step on the path towards the gradual harmonisation of the law on non-contractual liability and private law generally.[187] It was adopted on the basis of Article 115 TFEU, which also relates to the EU's internal market.[188] This directive aims to address divergences between national laws on product liability, so as to ensure undistorted competition between economic operators, facilitate the free movement of goods and avoid differences in levels of consumer protection.[189] The Court of Justice has described this directive as **5.24**

183 Commission, Proposal for a new package travel directive, COM(2013) 512, p. 24 (Art. 9(2)(b) and 10).

184 E.g. Art. 6 Distance Marketing Directive 2002/65; Art. 14 Consumer Credit Directive 2008/48; Art. 9 Consumer Rights Directive 2011/83.

185 On the effects of such a withdrawal, cf. CoJ case C-481/99, *Heininger*, para 35; CoJ case C-350/03, *Schulte*, para 66–9 and 92; CoJ case C-229/04, *Crailsheimer*, para 46–9. Note that these cases relate to Directive 85/577/EEC to protect the consumer in respect of contracts negotiated away from business premises, OJ 1985, L 372/31 ("Doorstep Selling Directive"), which has since been replaced by Consumer Rights Directive 2011/83. Different from its predecessor, Consumer Rights Directive 2011/83 contains a relatively detailed harmonised arrangement concerning this right of withdrawal and its effects and uses somewhat different terminology (see its Art. 9–16).

186 Product Liability Directive 85/374.

187 E.g. Izquierdo Peris (1999), p. 331; Weatherill (2005), p. 137; Fairgrieve and Howells (2007), pp. 692–3.

188 On the relationship between Art. 114 and 115 TFEU, see para 10.21 below.

189 Cf. recital 1 Product Liability Directive 85/374.

reflecting '*a complex balancing of different interests, [including] guaranteeing that competition will not be distorted, facilitating trade within the common market, consumer protection and ensuring the sound administration of justice*'.[190] The directive aims to ensure a fair apportionment of the risks inherent in modern technological production between the injured person and the producer.[191] The Court has also held that the directive confers rights on the injured private parties concerned.[192]

5.25 The Commission initially published its proposal for this directive in 1976, followed by an amended version in 1979.[193] This proposal proved to be controversial.[194] Certain Member States, in particular Germany, feared that extended liability for damages would harm industry.[195] There was also a fear of excessive litigation, especially regarding small claims.[196] No less than nine years of discussions by the EU legislature (at that time only the Council[197]), numerous statements at the time of its adoption as well as various exceptions, limitations and merely optional provisions (discussed below) were required before agreement could finally be reached. As imposed by its legal basis, Article 115 TFEU, this agreement was unanimous.

In a sense controversies continued after its adoption. France, for instance, did not transpose the directive into national law until more than a decade later, after having been condemned by the Court of Justice for not having done so earlier.[198] Whereas some Member States were concerned that the liability regime would be too harsh on businesses, France's reluctance related rather to the higher level of consumer protection for which its national law provided.[199] Particularly problematic from this perspective is the Court's ruling that the directive provides for "maximum" (or "complete") harmonisation (as opposed to "minimum" or "partial" harmonisation) of the matters regulated by it.[200] This means that Member States remain at liberty to retain or establish their domestic

190 CoJ case C-52/00, *Commission v France*, para 29.

191 CoJ joined cases C-503/13 and C-504/13, *Boston Scientific Medizintechnik*, para 42. See recitals 2 and 7 Product Liability Directive 85/374.

192 Cf. CoJ case C-177/04, *Commission v France*, para 49 (regarding Art. 3(3) of the directive).

193 Commission, Proposal for Product Liability Directive 85/374, COM(76) 372; Commission, Amended proposal for Product Liability Directive 85/374, COM(79) 415.

194 Commission, Third report on Product Liability Directive 85/374, COM(2006) 496, p. 6. See also Study, Lovells (2003), p. 135; S. Weatherill (2005), p. 135; Micklitz, Reich and Rott (2009), pp. 220–21.

195 Reich (1986), p. 137. See e.g. Council, doc. 5555/80, pp. 4 and 13.

196 Van Doorn (1989), p. 11. See e.g. Council, doc. 7020/81, p. 19; Council, doc. 7413/84, p. 9.

197 At the time, the European Parliament only had a consultative role. For its opinion, see European Parliament, Opinion on the proposal for Product Liability Directive 85/374, OJ 1979, C 127/61.

198 CoJ case C-52/00, *Commission v France*.

199 Van Dam (2006), pp. 371 and 374–5.

200 E.g. CoJ case C-52/00, *Commission v France*, para 14–24; CoJ case C-154/00, *Commission v Greece*, para 10–20; CoJ case C-495/10, *Dutrueux*, para 20–22; CoJ case C-310/13, *Novo Nordisk Pharma*, para 23.

regimes on product liability only for matters not regulated by this directive, such as liability based on other grounds or concerning other products.[201] But other national rules, such as those on the liability of suppliers, which existed *inter alia* in France, cannot be maintained, because this matter is exhaustively covered by the directive.[202]

The Product Liability Directive starts by providing that '*the producer shall be liable for damage caused by a defect in his product*'.[203] It defines what constitutes a "product" and which undertakings qualify as "producers" for the purposes of this directive.[204] It also explains when a product is defective, that is, when it does not provide the safety which a person is entitled to expect, taking into account all circumstances.[205] The directive continues by specifying its central principle of *liability without fault*. It stipulates in this regard that '*the injured person shall be required to prove the damage, the defect and the causal relationship between defect and damage*'.[206] By implication a private party applicant does *not* need to prove (and presumably does not even need to submit) that the producer was *at fault* for the latter's liability for damage to be incurred.[207] **5.26**

The Product Liability Directive thus establishes no-fault ("strict") liability of the producer for any defects in the products covered. This approach relies on the view that it is extremely difficult or even impossible for a consumer to provide proof of fault on the part of the producer, meaning that imposing such a requirement would leave consumers unprotected.[208] According to its recitals the no-fault liability provided for is the '*sole means*' of adequately solving the perceived problem related to product liability, namely the fair apportionment of risks inherent in modern technological production.[209] Even so, this approach was new to most Member States.[210]

The directive adds that where two producers are liable for the same damage, they are *jointly and severally liable*.[211] The rights of contribution or recourse in such a case are expressly left to be regulated by national law. It is further made **5.27**

---

201 E.g. CoJ case C-183/00, *González Sánchez*, para 30–31; CoJ case C-285/08, *Moteurs Leroy Somer*, para 25.

202 Art. 3(3) Product Liability Directive 85/374.

203 Art. 1 Product Liability Directive 85/374.

204 Art. 2 and 3(1) Product Liability Directive 85/374 respectively. Pursuant to its Art. 3(3), the liability established under this directive extends in certain cases to the supplier of the product in question.

205 Art. 6(1) Product Liability Directive 85/374. See CoJ joined cases C-503/13 and C-504/13, *Boston Scientific Medizintechnik*, paras 37–8.

206 Art. 4 Product Liability Directive 85/374.

207 Cf. CoJ case C-402/03, *Skov*, para 19.

208 Commission, Proposal for Product Liability Directive 85/374, COM(76) 372, p. 1.

209 Recital 2 Product Liability Directive 85/374.

210 Cf. Van Gerven, Lever and Larouche (2000), p. 674 (concerning the legal systems of England, France and Germany). See also e.g. Council, doc. 10512/81, p. 2.

211 Art. 5 Product Liability Directive 85/374.

explicit that the producer cannot limit or exclude its liability under this directive.[212] The rules in question are thus mandatory in nature.

5.28 Another important provision is the Product Liability Directive's description of what is understood in this connection by the concept of "damage".[213] This was another controversial issue during the legislative process.[214] Two heads of damage have been specified in the directive, namely: (a) damage *caused by death or by personal injuries*; and (b) damage to or the destruction of any *item of property*, with a lower threshold of €500, provided that the item of property is of a type ordinarily intended for private use and that it was used by the injured person mainly for his own private use or consumption. Claims for compensation in respect of damage to or the destruction of the defective product itself are not covered, which implies that these claims are to be settled under national law.[215] Issues relating to *non-material damage*, such as compensation for pain and suffering, are expressly left to be dealt with by the laws of the Member States.[216] This is in line with the Commission's initial proposal.[217] However, its amended proposal did include this head of damage, further to a suggestion to this effect by the European Parliament.[218] The Council nonetheless decided to exclude this head of damage from the final text of the directive in light of the differing understandings of this concept in the Member States and because it was felt inappropriate to harmonise this aspect only for this particular domain.[219] In relation to the above-mentioned threshold of €500, the recitals of the Product Liability Directive clarify that this is meant to '*avoid litigation in an excessive number of cases*'.[220] This threshold was introduced as part of an overall compromise on the contentious issue of what damage is to be covered by the directive.[221]

The Court of Justice has since further clarified what is to be understood by this concept of "damage" within the meaning of this directive. It did so particularly in *Veedfald*.[222] This case, dating from 2001, was referred by a Danish court. It concerned a defective perfusion fluid used for kidney transplants. In the context

212 Art. 12 Product Liability Directive 85/374.
213 Art. 9 Product Liability Directive 85/374.
214 Taschner (2002), p. 390.
215 Cf. Commission, Proposal for Product Liability Directive 85/374, COM(76) 372, p. 13.
216 Art. 9, last subparagraph Product Liability Directive 85/374. See also its recital 9.
217 Commission, Proposal for Product Liability Directive 85/374, COM(76) 372, p. 12.
218 Commission, Amended proposal for Product Liability Directive 85/374, COM(79) 415, p. 6.
219 Council, doc. 7669/85, pp. 4–5.
220 Recital 9 Product Liability Directive 85/374. Note that some uncertainty exists as to whether this is a proper threshold or rather that this is a deductible amount (which may in part be due to the differences between the various language versions of this directive). See Fairgrieve and Howells (2007), pp. 674–975.
221 Taschner (2002), p. 390.
222 CoJ case C-203/99, *Veedfald*, para 23–33.

of the resulting litigation, the question arose how the above-mentioned provision was to be interpreted. In its reply the Court began by pointing out that, while two heads of damage are specified, the term "damage" itself is not defined in the directive. It also held that the directive exhaustively sets out the heads of damage that may be possible. Thus, a national court may not decline to award any damages at all under the directive on the ground that, where the other conditions of liability are fulfilled, the damage incurred is not such as to fall under any of the above-mentioned heads mentioned in the directive. The Court ruled that, although it is left to the national legislatures to determine the precise content of these two heads of damage, it must be ensured that '*full and proper compensation*' is available for damage resulting from death or personal injury or from damage to or destruction of an item of property. A Member State can therefore not restrict these types of material damage which are to be made good. By contrast, the Court found that the reparation of non-material damage is governed solely by national law, meaning that this latter type of damage may or may not be recoverable. The Court subsequently built on this ruling in *Boston Scientific Medizintechnik*, where it emphasised that this notion of "damage" must be interpreted broadly and held that "*[c]ompensation for damage thus relates to all that is necessary to eliminate harmful consequences and to restore the level of safety which a person is entitled to expect*" in accordance with the relevant provisions of the directive.[223] It has also held that the above-mentioned threshold of €500 is not to be regarded as unduly affecting injured parties' rights of access to court, as despite this exclusion of minor material damage from the scope of this directive's special liability regime, these parties can still bring an action for damages under the ordinary national laws of contractual or non-contractual liability.[224]

2. Limits, practical effects and other legislation

The Product Liability Directive limits and moderates the effects of the afore- **5.29**
mentioned no-fault liability in various ways. In fact, it does so to the extent that it has been held that the provisions in question '*fail to live up to the ideal*' of no-fault liability.[225] An important element in this connection is that a producer cannot be held liable under the directive if he proves the existence of certain *exonerating circumstances*. These are set out in an exhaustive list included in the directive.[226] These circumstances include the defence that the state of science

223 CoJ joined cases C-503/13 and C-504/13, *Boston Scientific Medizintechnik*, para 47 and 49, respectively.

224 CoJ case C-52/00, *Commission v France*, para 29–32. See also CoJ case C-154/00, *Commission v Greece*, para 29–32.

225 Van Gerven, Lever and Larouche (2000), p. 678.

226 Art. 7 Product Liability Directive 85/374. This possibility was largely absent in the Commission's proposals. Cf. CoJ case C-203/99, *Veedfald*, para 15; CoJ case C-127/04, *O'Byrne*, para 25.

and technological knowledge when the product was put into circulation was not such as to enable the existence of the defect to be discovered, known as the "development risk defence".[227] The provision making this defence available is optional, in that the directive entitles Member States not to include it in their national laws.[228] Only very few Member States (Finland, Luxembourg) decided, however, to completely exclude this defence.[229]

5.30 The Product Liability Directive also provides for certain time bars applicable to damage claims brought under this directive. These come in two forms. First, there is a *limitation period* of three years as from the day the injured party becomes aware or should reasonably have become aware of the damage, the defect and the identity of the producer.[230] Setting such a uniform period was seen as being in the interest of both the injured private party and the producer.[231] The suspension and interruption of this period is left to be settled by national law.[232] Second, the directive specifies a time period of ten years as from the moment the product was put into circulation, at the expiry of which the consumer's rights under this directive are *extinguished*, unless legal proceedings have been instituted in the meantime.[233] This latter provision rests on the thought that it would be unreasonable to make the producer liable for an unlimited period.[234]

5.31 Pursuant to the directive, liability may further be reduced or disallowed when, having regard to all the circumstances, the damage is caused by a defect in the product and by the fault of the injured person or any person for whom the injured person is responsible.[235] This thus covers the situation of *contributory negligence* by the private party concerned.[236] By contrast, under the directive the act or omission of a *third party* may not be a reason to reduce the liability of the producer. In the latter case any right of contribution or recourse for the producer *vis-à-vis* that third party is to be determined in accordance with the applicable national law.[237]

---

227 Art. 7(e) Product Liability Directive 85/374. On the development risk defence, see CoJ case C-300/95, *Commission v UK*, para 25–9. See also Study, Fondazione Rosselli (2004).

228 Art. 15(1)(b) Product Liability Directive 85/374.

229 Howells (2008), p. 126.

230 Art. 10(1) Product Liability Directive 85/374.

231 Recital 10 Product Liability Directive 85/374.

232 Art. 10(2) Product Liability Directive 85/374.

233 Art. 11 Product Liability Directive 85/374. On the application of this ten-year period, see CoJ case C-127/04, *O'Byrne*; CoJ case C-358/08, *Aventis Pasteur*.

234 Recital 11 Product Liability Directive 85/374.

235 Art. 8(2) Product Liability Directive 85/374.

236 Cf. recital 8 Product Liability Directive 85/374.

237 Art. 8(1) Product Liability Directive 85/374.

A last measure that limits the effects of the no-fault liability for which the directive provides is that it leaves the Member States the option to "*cap*" the producer's liability for damage resulting from death or personal injury and caused by identical items with the same defect at an amount not lower than €70 million.[238] The fact that this provision is accompanied by an express requirement for the Commission to report after ten years on the effects of this provision and the statement that on that basis the Council shall decide whether or not to repeal this cap illustrates that this issue was also contentious.[239] The recitals explain that in most Member States it was seen as inappropriate to set such a financial ceiling, but that legal traditions in this regard differ and that therefore the possibility of a derogation from the principle of unlimited liability should be provided for.[240] 5.32

The picture that emerges on the basis of various reports and studies regarding the practical effects of the Product Liability Directive is that the relevant national regimes on product liability continue to differ significantly.[241] That is the case, for instance, as regards the assessment of damages, group actions, rules on evidence, pre-trial discovery of evidence and recovery of legal costs. Many stakeholders reportedly consider these procedural differences of more importance than differences in the applicable substantive law. It further appears that on the whole under this directive only limited numbers of cases are brought before national courts, in part because many disputes are thought to be settled.[242] In this light it has been held that the Product Liability Directive has been more debated than utilised in litigation.[243] While a modest increase in litigation has been observed in more recent years, the Product Liability Directive is reported to have played only a limited role in this regard. More important factors are thought to have been greater consumer awareness and access to information as well as increased media attention.[244] 5.33

The Commission appears to find neither the above-mentioned legal differences nor the low level of litigation problematic, at least not to such a degree that it proposed or seems to intend proposing legislative change. The only amendment made to the Product Liability Directive dates from 1999 when, in the aftermath

238 Art. 16(1) Product Liability Directive 85/374.
239 Art. 16(2) Product Liability Directive 85/374.
240 Recital 17 Product Liability Directive 85/374.
241 See in particular Study, Lovells (2003), pp. 9–23.
242 Commission, First report on Product Liability Directive 85/374, COM(95) 617, p. 2; Commission, Second report on Product Liability Directive 85/374, COM(2000) 893, p. 10; Commission, Fourth report on Product Liability Directive 85/374, COM(2011) 547, p. 4. See also Study, McKenna (1994), p. 14; Weatherill (2005), p. 146; Howells (2008), p. 130; Micklitz, Reich and Rott (2009), p. 247.
243 Howells (2008), p. 121.
244 Study, Lovells (2003), pp. 31–8.

of the "mad cow" crisis, primary agricultural products were brought within its scope.[245] Various possible, more profound, amendments were discussed in a Commission green paper dating from the same year, further to suggestions from the European Parliament.[246] These included measures relating to the following issues: (a) the relaxation of the burden of proof on consumers, for instance by inferring a causal relationship, establishing a lower standard of proof or imposing obligations on producers to disclose certain documentation or to bear the costs of an expert opinion; (b) the possibility of abolishing the above-mentioned development risk defence; (c) reducing or abolishing the financial threshold of €500; (d) extending the concept of "damage" so as to cover non-material damage too; and (e) improving access to justice for private parties by making provision for injunctions and/or collective redress mechanisms such as the type known in the United States as class actions. But in 2001 and again in 2006 and 2011 the Commission decided against proposing any amendments.[247] It did so despite the persistent pressure in favour of amendments from consumer associations and certain national authorities, generally (if cautiously) supported by the European Parliament.[248] The Commission argued that there was insufficient proof of major problems and that the differences in the application of the directive did not affect the functioning of the internal market.[249] It also recalled the controversies that existed at the time of the adoption of this directive, arguing that the resulting compromise constitutes a delicate balance between the various interests concerned, which it did not wish to upset.

5.34 Looking beyond the Product Liability Directive to other relevant EU legislation, it can be noted that in 1990 the Commission proposed a directive on the liability of *suppliers of services*.[250] The Commission explained in its proposal that here it had originally intended to propose a no-fault liability system similar to that of the Product Liability Directive. But this approach had encountered

245 Directive 1999/34/EC amending Council Directive 85/374/EEC on the approximation of the laws, regulations and administrative provisions of the Member States concerning liability for defective products, OJ 1999, L 141/20 ("Product Liability Amending Directive").

246 Commission, Green paper on liability for defective products, COM(1999) 396. See also Commission, Communication on the Council's position on the proposal for Product Liability Directive 85/374, SEC(1998) 2232. See further Izquierdo Peris (1999), pp. 339–44; Whittaker (2005), pp. 440–50.

247 Commission, Second report on Product Liability Directive 85/374, COM(2000) 893, p. 28; Commission, Third report on Product Liability Directive 85/374, COM(2006) 496, pp. 11–12; Commission, Fourth report on Product Liability Directive 85/374, COM(2011) 547, p. 4.

248 European Parliament, Resolution on the Commission green paper on liability for defective products, A5–0061/2000.

249 Cf. Study, Lovells (2003), pp. 15–28.

250 Commission, Proposal for a services liability directive, COM(90) 482. See further Pfenningstorf (1991), p. 493. On the liability of undertakings under Product Liability Directive 85/374 and the liability of service providers, see CoJ case C-495/10, *Dutrueux*.

strong resistance from interest groups and was considered to deviate too much from the national laws in force. Therefore, the Commission instead proposed a fault-based liability regime, subject to a reversal of the burden of proof to the advantage of the injured private party.[251] This proposal was rather negatively received by the European Parliament, the Economic and Social Committee and interests groups, however. The Commission concluded that the proposal stood no chance of being adopted and withdrew it in 1994.[252] It follows that, despite certain subsequent efforts by the Commission in this regard,[253] civil liability for damage of service providers is in principle regulated by the laws of the Member States.

Furthermore, the Package Travel Directive contains provisions that are to some extent comparable to those of the Product Liability Directive.[254] It provides in essence that the Member States must ensure that undertakings organising or offering package holidays are liable for damage resulting from the failure to properly perform the contract at issue. This liability is subject to an exception in case of *lack of fault* of that undertaking, because of failures in the performance attributable to the consumer or a third party or to *force majeure*. As such, the Package Travel Directive can be said to be based on an approach that is somewhere in between no-fault and fault-based liability.[255] In the context of its currently ongoing revision, the option of moving towards clear no-fault liability received considerable support from Member States.[256] The Commission's 2013 proposal for a directive replacing the Package Travel Directive does not address this matter expressly, however.[257]

Finally, the 2002 *Leitner* ruling of the Court of Justice is noteworthy in this connection.[258] This case concerned an Austrian preliminary reference that arose as a result of salmonella poisoning during an all-inclusive package holiday.

---

251 Commission, Proposal for a services liability directive, COM(90) 482, p. 8.

252 Commission, Communication on new directions on the liability of suppliers of services, COM(94) 260.

253 See e.g. Study, View (2004). See also Commission, Proposal for Services Directive 2006/123, COM(2004) 2. Here it was proposed to stipulate that contractual liability of service providers would be covered by the country of origin principle, whereas non-contractual liability would not (see its Art. 16–17). This aspect of the proposal was not retained by the EU legislature, however. Recital 51 Services Directive 2006/123 now states that '*[i]ssues such as liability for providing incorrect or misleading information should be determined by Member States*'.

254 Art. 5 Package Travel Directive 90/314.

255 Cf. European Parliament, Study on safety and liability issues relating to package travel, January 2008, p. 4. See also Study, University of Bielefeld (2008), p. 321. Whether or not a fault requirement applies is left to the Member States, according to the latter study.

256 Commission, Responses to the consultation on Package Travel Directive 90/314, March 2010, p. 5.

257 Commission, Proposal for a new package travel directive, COM(2013) 512, p. 26 (Art. 12). Here mention is no longer made of the absence of fault as a reason for not incurring liability, but there are other exonerating circumstances. According to the Commission's proposal (p. 9), the underlying principles remain unaltered, while certain clarifications are provided for and certain gaps are closed.

258 CoJ case C-168/00, *Leitner*, para 20–24.

Austrian law did not provide for compensation for non-material damage (in this case: loss of holiday enjoyment). The Package Travel Directive does not expressly address this issue. But it does stipulate that Member States may limit compensation for damage other than personal injury. The Court ruled that the type of damage at issue is covered by this directive. It pointed first to its objective, which is to eliminate disparities. It held that divergences as to whether non-material damage is covered would cause significant distortions of competition, given that non-material damage is a frequent occurrence in relation to package holidays. It recalled that the directive and especially its provision on liability are designed to protect consumers and that compensation for non-material damage arising from the loss of enjoyment of the holiday is of particular importance to consumers. While noting that the directive refers in a general manner to "damage", the Court took the above-mentioned possibility of limiting compensation for damage other than personal injury as an implicit recognition of the right to compensation of non-material damage too.

E. OTHER ENFORCEMENT ISSUES

After a general remark on the more recent developments relating to the enforcement of EU consumer protection law at national level, three specific issues are discussed in more detail below, namely collective redress, alternative dispute resolution and public enforcement.

1. General

5.35 Notwithstanding the range of legislative measures discussed in the preceding sections, the Commission held in 2007 that enforcement and redress remained priority areas for further action in the field of EU consumer protection law.[259] Generally speaking, what appears to be emerging is a partial move away from the dominant "corporatist" approach that underlies the reliance on actions for injunctions brought by representative organisations, as provided for in the Consumer Injunctions Directive and numerous other directives.[260] In 2006 the Commission suggested providing for a set of general contractual remedies, including a right to terminate the contract, and a general right to damages.[261] These suggestions proved controversial, however. The European Parliament argued against any such further-reaching EU measures, submitting that these

259 Commission, Communication on the EU consumer policy strategy 2007–2013, COM(2007) 99, pp. 8 and 10–11.

260 Poncibò (2009), pp. 293 and 306, respectively. See section 5.B above.

261 Commission, Green paper on the review of the consumer acquis, COM(2006) 744, pp. 22–3 and 30.

issues are generally best left to be settled under national law, whereas Member States proved to be divided.[262] The rather modest provisions on these points that the Commission eventually included in its subsequent proposal for the Consumer Rights Directive were deleted by the EU legislature.[263] More recent developments tend to concentrate mainly on the specific issues of facilitating collective redress actions by private parties, promoting alternative dispute resolution and ensuring stronger public enforcement.[264] These three topics are discussed in some further detail below.

2. Collective redress

It has already been seen that in the 1980s collective redress in consumer cases was identified as an area where EU legislative action might need to be taken.[265] However, only in more recent years did this topic reappear on the EU's law-making agenda, in particular through the Commission's 2008 green paper on collective redress.[266] At the heart of this discussion lies the concern that certain infringements of EU law – notably, but certainly not exclusively, consumer protection law – may lead to harm that on the individual level is comparatively modest in monetary terms, but that taken together may have significant negative consequences, including the distortion of the market. Without specific measures, in such a case a typical individual consumer is likely to decide against initiating legal proceedings, considering the effort, litigation costs, complexities and uncertainties involved in doing so, which are likely to outweigh the possible gains even if those proceedings result in a favourable outcome. This is known as the "*rational apathy*" of the private parties concerned. As a consequence the infringement in question can remain unaddressed, the ("scattered") damage uncompensated and the infringed provision ineffective, thus leading to "under-enforcement".[267] Where the aggrieved individual private parties nevertheless do decide to bring legal proceedings, reasons of procedural efficiency and consistency may also argue in favour of treating these claims collectively, rather than adjudicating each of them separately. **5.36**

The (perceived) problem of rational apathy can be tackled in various ways. Public enforcement could be strengthened, for example.[268] One could also seek

262 Commission, Report on the outcome of the public consultation on the review of the consumer acquis, 2007, pp. 10–11; Study, Civic Consulting (2007), pp. 14–15 and 85–90.

263 Commission, Proposal for Consumer Rights Directive 2011/83, COM(2008) 614, in particular pp. 30–32 (Art. 25 and 27).

264 Cf. Commission, Communication on the enforcement of the consumer acquis, COM(2009) 330, p. 3.

265 See para 5.04 above.

266 Commission, Green paper on consumer collective redress, COM(2008) 794.

267 Cf. Loos (2011), p. 487.

268 See subsection 5.E.4 below.

to reduce the costs, risks and complexities to the private parties concerned when they act individually. Certain measures to this effect have already been taken at EU level, notably through ensuring the availability of legal aid and simplified small claims procedures.[269] Another possible manner is facilitating *collective redress*. This encompasses any mechanism that may accomplish the cessation or prevention of unlawful business practices that affect a multitude of applicants or the compensation for the harm caused by such practices.[270] Accordingly, the focus is typically on two remedies, namely (prohibitive) injunctions and actions for damages. In the EU's terminology the term "collective redress" generally covers cases where several individual claims are bundled in one single claim (known as "collective action") as well as actions brought by certain third parties, such as consumer associations, other non-governmental organisations, or an ombudsman, on behalf of the parties that actually suffered harm without the latter being party to the proceedings themselves (known as "representative action").[271]

5.37 Two studies conducted in 2008 indicated that at national level the relevant legal environment tends to be very dynamic and very diverse where collective redress is concerned.[272]. While roughly half of the Member States had some form of collective redress mechanism in place, a total of 326 "consumer-relevant" collective redress cases were documented.[273] The existing collective redress mechanisms were found to have improved consumers' access to justice, while not entailing disproportionate negative consequences for business. Costs, formal requirements and lack of awareness were identified as obstacles to litigation in group actions, which were said to lead to significant adverse immediate economic consequences for consumers and structural effects on consumer markets, particularly in cross-border situations. At the same time it was found that the lack of collective redress mechanisms in certain Member States led only to a very modest loss in consumer welfare (in total €2.1 million per year). In case of large-scale low-value damage, consumers were further found to be generally not motivated to participate in opt-in group actions, whereby they expressly need to signal their willingness to participate in the collective redress proceedings. No significant deterrent effect was observed as a result of collective redress

269 Legal Aid Directive 2003/8; Small Claims Regulation 861/2007.

270 Commission, Public consultation towards a coherent approach to collective redress, SEC(2011) 173, p. 3.

271 See e.g. Commission, Staff working paper accompanying the white paper on damages actions for breach of the EC antitrust rules, SEC(2008) 404, pp. 18–22. Actions by qualified entities under Consumer Injunctions Directive 2009/22, discussed in subsection 5.B.1 above, are therefore representative actions.

272 Study, Civic Consulting (2008a); Study, Civic Consulting (2008b). See also European Parliament, Study on collective redress in antitrust, June 2012.

273 The period under consideration covered roughly the decade up to 2008. A clear majority of these cases came from just one Member State (namely France: 196 cases). The three most "productive" Member States (France, Germany and Spain) together accounted for almost 85 per cent of all documented cases.

mechanisms, except where collective actions received particular media attention. The amount of awarded damages appeared a less important factor in this regard. Finally, the impact on trade and competition between Member States of the differing national approaches was said to remain very modest, although this might change depending on future developments.

The Commission found this situation unsatisfactory.[274] It therefore embarked on a consultation process with a view to establishing whether and, if so, which measures ought to be taken at EU level in relation to collective redress. The areas of particular attention identified in the 2008 green paper included the financing of procedures, the issue of legal standing, whether collective redress procedure should have an opt-in or rather an opt-out character (in the latter case, the consumer's participation is presumed, unless he expressly indicates otherwise) and how to distribute the compensation obtained.[275] Here it was further stated that '*elements which are said to encourage a litigation culture such as is said to exist in some non-European countries, such as punitive damages, contingency fees and other elements*' should be avoided.[276] In 2011 a second round of consultation aimed at identifying common legal principles on collective redress and examining how these principles could fit into the EU legal system and the domestic legal orders of the Member States so as to '*guide any possible initiative for collective redress in legislation*'.[277] This second consultation sought to ensure a "coherent" (or "horizontal") approach. This refers to a possible initiative that is not limited to infringements of EU consumer protection law, but that would instead apply across the board in principle in any field of EU law. Infringements of EU competition law, which had initially been excluded, would therefore also be covered.[278] This is in line with the situation in most Member States that provide for collective redress mechanisms.[279]

274 Commission, Green paper on consumer collective redress, COM(2008) 794, pp. 3–7.

275 On the issues that can arise in relation to opt-in and opt-out models of collective redress as well as collective redress generally, see also para 11.12 below.

276 Commission, Green paper on consumer collective redress, COM(2008) 794, pp. 12–14. The term "contingency fees" refers to lawyers' fees that are granted as a percentage of the damages awarded. Cf. Study, Civic Consulting (2008b), p. 54.

277 Commission, Public consultation towards a coherent approach to collective redress, SEC(2011) 173, p. 5. The following principles were mentioned: (a) effective and efficient redress; (b) the importance of information and the role of representative entities; (c) need to take account of collective consensual resolution as a means of alternative dispute resolution; (d) strong safeguards to avoid abusive litigation; (e) appropriate financing mechanisms, notably for citizens and small and medium-sized enterprises; and (f) effective enforcement across the EU. See also Commission, Responses to the collective redress benchmark consultation, 2008.

278 Commission, Public consultation towards a coherent approach to collective redress, SEC(2011) 173, p. 12. On the initial exclusion of competition law infringements, see Commission, Green paper on consumer collective redress, COM(2008) 794, p. 3.

279 See European Parliament, Study on collective redress in antitrust, June 2012, p. 19; Buccirossi and Carpagnano (2013), p. 4. Galvin (2015), p. 2.

The responses to these consultations indicated that views on the possibility of EU legislative action relating to collective redress tend to differ considerably.[280] *Consumer associations* mostly expressed their support for such an initiative. They pointed to the difficulties that consumers were said to encounter in obtaining effective redress and the expected positive effects in terms of compliance and equal treatment. Representatives of *business*, in contrast, generally took a negative view. These parties submitted that the existence of an enforcement problem with a European dimension had not been demonstrated and warned against creating a "US-style" litigation culture. Many *legal practitioners and academics* expressed doubts as to whether a sufficient legal basis could be found in the EU Treaties, in particular if such action were to extend to situations without a clear cross-border dimension. The positions taken by the *public authorities* that responded largely echoed these diverging views. A majority supported introducing new EU-level mechanisms for collective redress, as these were expected to have beneficial effects on the enforcement of substantive law, the protection of consumers' rights, the right to equal access to justice and legal certainty. Some also thought that such measures could serve as a deterrent. Other respondents expressed doubts, however, as regards the need and added value of EU action. Concerns related to legal basis and subsidiarity issues were also voiced, in particular in the case of a horizontal approach. At the same time many noted that a sector-specific approach would be detrimental to the internal cohesion of the national legal systems of civil procedure. A great majority of public authorities also cautioned against creating a "claims culture". Making provision for punitive damages or contingency fees was almost unanimously opposed. The "loser pays" principle for the allocation of legal costs and discretion for the judge on points such as admissibility were mentioned as important safeguards in this respect. The European Parliament found that possibilities for injunctive relief should be improved, arguing that any possible legislative initiative should be of horizontal application and be based on an opt-in approach, that there should not be an obligation for defendants to disclose relevant evidence and information ("discovery"), that punitive damages should be prohibited and that the allocation of legal costs should be left to be settled in accordance with the applicable national law.[281]

280 See Commission, Responses to the consultation on consumer collective redress, 2009; Commission, Responses to the hearing on collective redress, October 2011; Commission, Responses to the consultation and hearing on collective redress, October 2011.

281 European Parliament, Resolution, Towards a coherent European approach to collective redress, P7_TA(2012)0021.

In 2013 the foregoing culminated in the adoption by the Commission of Recommendation 2013/396 on common principles for injunctive and compensatory collective redress mechanisms in the Member States concerning violations of rights granted under Union law ("Collective Redress Recommendation").[282] Its aim is to facilitate access to justice, stop illegal practices and enable injured private parties to obtain compensation in mass harm situations caused by violations of rights granted under EU law, while ensuring appropriate procedural safeguards to avoid abusive litigation.[283] The scope of this recommendation is consequently truly horizontal, in that the recommendation covers in principle all fields of EU law. Expressly mentioned are, besides consumer protection law, EU law on competition, environmental protection, protection of personal data, financial services and investor protection.[284] It moreover sets the threshold for something being considered a "mass harm situation" rather low, as this is understood to cover any situation where two or more persons claim to have suffered harm causing damage resulting from the same illegal activity.[285] **5.38**

The Collective Redress Recommendation states that all Member States should have collective redress mechanisms at national level for both injunctive and compensatory relief in accordance with the basic principles laid down therein.[286] Such mechanisms can cover group actions as well as representative actions.[287] In the latter case actions can be brought by (non-profit) representative entities, either designated in advance or certified on an *ad hoc* basis, or by certain public authorities.[288] In cross-border situations the bringing of a single action in a single forum should not be prevented and representative entities designated in advance should also have legal standing in other Member States.[289] Other recommendations relate to the allocation of legal costs ("loser pays" principle; contingency fees in principle prohibited) and funding (transparency; conditions for third-party financing; as a general rule, no remuneration related to a damages award).[290]

---

282 Commission, Recommendation 2013/396/EU on common principles for injunctive and compensatory collective redress mechanisms in the Member States concerning violations of rights granted under Union law, OJ 2013, L 201/60. See also Commission, Communication towards a European horizontal framework for collective redress, COM(2013) 401. For a (critical) discussion of this recommendation, see Hodges (2013), p. 67. See also Stadler (2013a), p. 483; Benöhr (2014), p. 243; Tzakas (2014), p. 225.

283 Point 1 Collective Redress Recommendation 2013/396.

284 Recital 7 Collective Redress Recommendation 2013/396.

285 Point 3(b) Collective Redress Recommendation 2013/396.

286 Point 2 Collective Redress Recommendation 2013/396.

287 Recital 17 Collective Redress Recommendation 2013/396.

288 Points 4, 6 and 7 Collective Redress Recommendation 2013/396.

289 Points 17 and 18 Collective Redress Recommendation 2013/396.

290 Points 13–16, 29–30 and 32 Collective Redress Recommendation 2013/396. The latter points only relate to compensatory collective redress.

Particularly concerning *injunctive* collective redress, the recommendation states that such actions should be treated with all due expediency, where appropriate by way of summary proceedings.[291] Sanctions are recommended against the losing defendant with a view to ensuring compliance with the court's order, including the payment of a fixed amount per day's delay.[292] The recommendations that particularly relate to *compensatory* collective redress include applying an opt-in approach as a general rule.[293] Alternative dispute resolution and out-of-court settlements are to be encouraged, but not imposed.[294] Limitation periods should be suspended during any attempt to resolve the dispute consensually, whilst it is also said that the binding outcome thereof should be verified by the courts.[295] It is further recommended that punitive damages should be prohibited and that collective redress actions should normally only start after the conclusion of any public enforcement proceedings.[296]

5.39 The Collective Redress Recommendation specifies that the Member States should implement the principles set out therein by June 2015.[297] Whereas this legal act can certainly have an influence in practice, it is important to note, however, that in the EU legal order a recommendation has no binding force.[298] The Court of Justice has clarified that recommendations are not capable of creating rights on which private parties can rely before national courts.[299] But it also insists that recommendations '*are not without any legal effect*' and that '*national courts are bound to take them into consideration in order to decide disputes brought before them, in particular where such recommendations cast light on the interpretation of national measures adopted in order to implement them or where they are designed to supplement binding provisions of EU law*'.[300] Recommendations are thus a "soft law" instrument of a particular sort. That being so, it remains to be seen to what extent the Collective Redress Recommendation will help to achieve the aforementioned objectives. The Commission committed to evaluating its impact after four years and assessing whether any further measures – including legally binding legislative measures – should be proposed.[301]

291 Point 19 Collective Redress Recommendation 2013/396.
292 Point 20 Collective Redress Recommendation 2013/396.
293 Points 21–4 Collective Redress Recommendation 2013/396.
294 Points 25–6 Collective Redress Recommendation 2013/396.
295 Points 27–8 Collective Redress Recommendation 2013/396.
296 Points 31 and 33–4 Collective Redress Recommendation 2013/396.
297 Point 38 Collective Redress Recommendation 2013/396.
298 Art. 288 TFEU. Art. 292 TFEU empowers the Commission to adopt recommendations.
299 See e.g. CoJ joined cases C-317/08 to C-320/08, *Alassini*, para 40.
300 Ibid.
301 Point 41 and recital 26 Collective Redress Recommendation 2013/396.

3. Alternative dispute resolution

Another more recent enforcement-related development concerns efforts to facilitate alternative dispute resolution in consumer protection cases. This refers to the out-of-court resolution of disputes arising between consumers and undertakings through the intervention of an external entity of some sort. It encompasses mediation procedures as well as non-judicial procedures of an adjudicatory nature, such as procedures before complaint boards, arbitration and conciliation. In this context direct negotiations between the parties and internal complaint-handling are not covered by the term "alternative dispute resolution".[302] This development overlaps in part with the one discussed in the previous subsection, given that, as was noted above, alternative dispute resolution is seen as one of the means to facilitate collective redress. **5.40**

Studies carried out in the second half of the 2000s found that alternative dispute resolution can offer a low-cost and speedy means for settling consumer disputes.[303] In practice, this often does not cost more than €50, while taking on average 90 days to conclude. It was also observed in these studies that the vast majority of existing arrangements at national level are voluntary in nature. Alternative dispute resolution tends to be often and increasingly used across the EU, but only to a limited extent for collective or cross-border cases. The diversity of existing mechanisms was found to be high, however, *inter alia* as regards the composition of the external entity involved and the effects of the positions it takes. The shortcomings identified include the generally very limited awareness of the availability of such mechanisms and gaps in their coverage. Funding was also found to be a sensitive issue. Consultations of stakeholders revealed that, certainly as compared with the issue of collective redress discussed in the previous subsection, the facilitation of alternative dispute resolution in consumer cases is not particularly controversial.[304] According to the Commission, the need to further develop it was generally acknowledged, a majority of the respondents also supporting the idea of the EU taking action on this point.[305] **5.41**

Over the years certain measures to encourage and facilitate alternative dispute resolution have already been enacted at EU level, including several Commission **5.42**

302 Commission, Proposal for Consumer ADR Directive 2013/11, COM(2011) 793, pp. 2 and 4.

303 Study, University of Leuven (2007); Study, Civic Consulting (2009). See also European Parliament, Study on cross-border alternative dispute resolution in the EU, June 2011.

304 Commission, Consultation paper on the use of alternative dispute resolution, 2011.

305 Commission, Proposal for Consumer ADR Directive 2013/11, COM(2011) 793, p. 3. On the legal effects of recommendations, see para 5.39 above.

recommendations.[306] Legislative measures have also been taken, such as Directive 2008/52 on certain aspects of mediation in civil and commercial matters[307] ("Mediation Directive") and the inclusion of specific provisions in several consumer protection directives, although the latter tend to be limited in scope and detail.[308] On the back of the aforementioned studies and consultations and as part of an effort to improve the functioning of the internal market at retail level, the Commission considered it necessary, however, to address this issue in a more general manner.[309] It explained that, considering that consumers tend to be concerned about difficulties relating to the resolution of disputes when buying across borders and that a majority of consumer complaints currently remain unresolved, alternative dispute resolution procedures can be a means to empower consumers and put them at the heart of the EU's internal market.[310]

In 2013 the EU legislature therefore adopted Directive 2013/11 on alternative dispute resolution for consumer disputes ("Consumer ADR Directive").[311] This directive seeks to ensure that EU-wide, in all economic sectors, alternative dispute resolution procedures are available for consumer disputes. These procedures are to be used in principle on a voluntary basis.[312] At the heart of these procedures are alternative dispute resolution entities which seek to propose or impose a solution or to bring together the parties concerned with the aim of facilitating a solution to both domestic and cross-border consumer disputes.[313] The directive provides that these procedures should be easily accessible and that certain common quality requirements are to be respected, in terms of expertise,

306 Commission, Recommendation 98/257/EC on the principles applicable to the bodies responsible for out-of-court settlement of disputes, OJ 1998, L 115/31; Commission, Recommendation 2001/310/EC on the principles for out-of-court bodies involved in the consensual resolution of consumer disputes, OJ 2011, L 109/56. See also Commission, Recommendation 2010/304/EC on the use of a harmonised methodology for classifying and reporting consumer complaints and enquiries, OJ 2010, L 136/1. Reference can further be made to the existence of ECC-Net, an EU-wide network of European consumer centres that seek to inform consumers about their rights and assist them in the resolution of disputes in cross-border cases. See further http://ec.europa.eu/consumers/ecc/about_ecc_en.htm. FIN-Net does something similar in relation to financial services. See further http://ec.europa.eu/consumers/ecc/about_ecc_en.htm.

307 Directive 2008/52/EC on certain aspects of mediation in civil and commercial matters, OJ 2008, L 136/3.

308 See e.g. Art. 24 Consumer Credit Directive 2008/48.

309 Cf. Commission, Communication on a digital agenda for Europe, COM(2010) 245, p. 13; Commission, Communication on a Single Market Act, COM(2011) 206, p. 9.

310 Commission, Communication on alternative dispute resolution for consumer disputes in the single market, COM(2011) 791, pp. 2–3.

311 Directive 2013/11/EU on alternative dispute resolution for consumer disputes, OJ 2013, L 165/63. For a (critical) assessment of this directive see Wagner (2014), p. 165. Together with this directive a complementary act was adopted, which is specifically concerned with the resolution of consumer disputes in the online sphere, namely Consumer ODR Regulation 524/2013. In this connection, see also the draft procedural rules on online dispute resolution for cross-border electronic commerce transactions established in the context of the UN Commission on International Trade Law (Uncitral).

312 Art. 1 Consumer ADR Directive 2013/11.

313 Art. 2(1) Consumer ADR Directive 2013/11.

independence, impartiality, transparency and effectiveness.[314] Any applicable limitation and prescription periods for initiating legal proceedings are to be suspended during an attempt to settle a dispute out of court.[315] Rules are further set out on informing and, where necessary, assisting consumers and as regards the cooperation between the above-mentioned entities amongst themselves and with the competent public enforcement authorities that the Member States must designate under this directive.[316] The latter have as their main task the supervision of those entities, including the verification of compliance with the said quality requirements and the creation of a list of compliant entities.[317] The directive is to be transposed into national law by July 2015.[318]

4. Public enforcement

Although there are significant differences between Member States, EU-wide public enforcement has traditionally not occupied a central position in relation to consumer protection law. By 2003 several Member States had still not established any form of public authority with specific consumer protection enforcement responsibilities.[319] They were not obliged to do so under EU law. Most EU consumer protection legislation only sets out the general and rather rudimentary obligation for the Member States to ensure the availability of effective, proportionate and dissuasive penalties to address infringements.[320] It has been seen earlier that under the Consumer Injunctions Directive public bodies can act as a qualified entity and initiate legal proceedings in that capacity.[321] Yet this does not concern what is normally understood by public enforcement properly speaking, as it involves these bodies acting before a court in the same capacity as certain private parties, such as consumer associations. Moreover, under EU law it is only a possibility and not an obligation to provide for the involvement of public authorities in this respect, even if this possibility has reportedly contributed to public bodies playing an increasingly important role in the enforcement of consumer protection law.[322] **5.43**

314 Art. 5–11 Consumer ADR Directive 2013/11.
315 Art. 12 Consumer ADR Directive 2013/11.
316 Art. 13–18 Consumer ADR Directive 2013/11.
317 Art. 19–20 Consumer ADR Directive 2013/11.
318 Art. 25(1) Consumer ADR Directive 2013/11.
319 Commission, Proposal for CPC Regulation 2006/2004, COM(2003) 443.
320 E.g. Art. 11 Distance Marketing Directive 2002/65; Art. 13 Unfair Practices Directive 2005/29; Art. 24 Consumer Rights Directive 2011/83. See also subsection 2.C.2 above.
321 See para 5.06 above.
322 Cf. Study, University of Leuven (2007), p. 331.

5.44 Especially from the early 2000s onwards, the above picture began to change, however. Since then stronger emphasis has been placed on the public enforcement of the EU consumer protection rules. The Commission's overall policy is now said to be to push Member States to establish public enforcement authorities charged with enforcing EU consumer protection law.[323] This is illustrated by the fact that the Commission's 2009 communication on the enforcement of the EU consumer protection rules is concerned almost exclusively with public enforcement. There it is stated that action by public authorities '*occupies a central role, because it underpins all other strategies and is a prerequisite for their success*'.[324] This increased attention at EU level for the public enforcement of EU consumer protection law is illustrated by the following two specific developments.

In the first place, measures related to public enforcement can be found in certain specific EU legal acts, especially those relating to product safety. Most notably, the 2001 Product Safety Directive specifies not only that Member States must ensure that producers and distributors comply with the substantive rules at issue. It also stipulates that public authorities must be established at national level to monitor compliance.[325] These public authorities are charged with taking certain specified measures where necessary, such as checks, warnings or product recalls. The Commission must be informed when these measures are taken. Under this directive a network has also been established to facilitate cooperation between all public authorities involved. In addition, subject to certain conditions, the Commission has been empowered to intervene directly by requiring the national authorities concerned to take one of the said specified measures.[326] This system is supplemented by the framework established under Regulation 765/2008 setting out the requirements for accreditation and market surveillance relating to the marketing of products.[327] As part of this framework Member States must establish public authorities charged with certain market

323 Micklitz and Reich (2009), p. 514. See also Micklitz (2011a), p. 581.

324 Commission, Communication on the enforcement of the consumer acquis, COM(2009) 330, p. 2. See e.g. also Commission, Green paper on European consumer protection, COM(2001) 531. The chapter of this latter document dealing with enforcement (pp. 16–18) is dedicated almost exclusively to public enforcement. See also Commission, Communication on the follow-up to the green paper on EU consumer protection, COM(2002) 289. Cf. Cafaggi and Micklitz (2009), p. 405.

325 Chapters IV and V Product Safety Directive 2001/95. See also chapter IV Toy Safety Directive 2009/48.

326 These conditions include that there must be a serious risk to the health or safety of consumers in various Member States. Three specific (cumulative) conditions must further have been met, in effect providing that Commission intervention is a last resort in cases with an EU dimension. In addition, the Member States and, where relevant, an EU scientific committee must be consulted before any decision can be taken. See further Weatherill (2005), pp. 209 and 212–13. See also CoJ case C-359/92, *Germany v Council*, para 37.

327 Regulation (EC) No 765/2008 setting out the requirements for accreditation and market surveillance relating to the marketing of products and repealing Regulation (EEC) No 339/93, OJ 2008, L 218/30 (see its chapter III).

surveillance and intervention tasks. These measures are considered to have had a mostly positive effect, although certain shortcomings have also been observed.[328] The Commission's 2013 "product safety and market surveillance package" includes a proposal for a new regulation that would in effect merge the above-mentioned regimes, so as to simplify the applicable market surveillance rules.[329]

In the second place, of broader importance is Regulation 2006/2004 on consumer protection cooperation ("CPC Regulation").[330] Just as with the aforementioned Consumer Injunctions Directive, this regulation seeks to address infringements of EU consumer protection legislation with a cross-border dimension.[331] The CPC Regulation relies, however, primarily on "classic" public enforcement means. It obliges the Member States to designate public authorities with specific responsibilities to enforce the consumer protection rules set out in its annex.[332] It also specifies which powers these authorities must possess, including the possibility of requesting information from any person, carrying out on-site inspections and requiring the cessation or prohibition of infringing activities.[333] The CPC Regulation also seeks to facilitate cooperation between these authorities, for instance as regards the exchange of information and the provision of assistance in enforcement actions. The Commission has certain tasks at the central level, including maintaining a

328 Cf. Commission, Report on Product Safety Directive 2001/95, COM(2008) 905; Commission, Responses to the consultation on Product Safety Directive 2001/95, November 2010. These shortcomings include a lack of resources on the part of the competent national authorities, difficulties related to the cooperation between these authorities and regulatory fragmentation.

329 Commission, Proposal for a regulation on market surveillance of products, COM(2013) 75. See Commission, Communication on more product safety and better market surveillance in the single market for products, COM(2013) 74. This package includes Commission, Proposal for a regulation on consumer product safety, COM(2013) 78.

330 Regulation (EC) No 2006/2004 on cooperation between national authorities responsible for the enforcement of consumer protection laws, OJ 2004, L 364/1. On the functioning of this regulation, see Study, Civic Consulting, Van Dijk and ICF GHK (2012).

331 Accordingly, the provisions of CPC Regulation 2006/2004 on mutual assistance (chapters II and III) cover "intra-EU infringements", that is, acts or omissions contrary to the legislation covered that harms or is likely to harm the collective interests of consumers residing in a Member State other than the one where the act or omission took place or originated, where the infringing undertaking is established or where relevant evidence or assets can be found. Cf. Art. 2(1) and 3(b) CPC Regulation 2006/2004. On Consumer Injunctions Directive 2009/22, see section 5.B above. Recital 14 and Art. 2(5) CPC Regulation 2006/2004 clarify that this directive and this regulation are meant to apply in parallel.

332 Art. 3(a) and (c) and Art. 4(1) CPC Regulation 2006/2004. During the legislative process the flexibility left to the Member States was considerably increased, however. E.g., pursuant to Art. 4(2) and (4) CPC Regulation 2006/2004, other public or non-public bodies may also be designated in certain cases and the competent national authorities may exercise their powers either directly under their own authority or under the supervision of the judicial authorities, or by application to the competent courts. Cf. Commission, Proposal for CPC Regulation 2006/2004, COM(2003) 443; Council, doc. 7073/04; European Parliament, Resolution on the proposal for CPC Regulation 2006/2004, P5_TA(2004)0296.

333 Art. 4(3) and (6) CPC Regulation 2006/2004.

database with information concerning the various actions taken under this regulation.[334] Provision is made for more general coordination and cooperation activities between all public authorities concerned in the CPC Network.[335]

5.45 The Toy Safety Directive stipulates, in addition to the "standard" clause on the Member States providing for effective, proportionate and dissuasive penalties to address infringements of the EU rules at issue,[336] that these penalties '*may include criminal sanctions for serious infringements*'.[337] Provisions of this kind have also been included in the aforementioned Commission proposals relating to product safety.[338] However, beyond these rather basic references – which still leave it to the Member States to decide whether or not they wish to provide for penalties of this kind – no provision is made under EU law regarding criminal sanctions for infringements of the EU consumer protection rules. Some Member States (for example France) nonetheless provide for criminal sanctions for certain infringements of consumer protection legislation.[339]

334 Art. 10 CPC Regulation 2006/2004.

335 Art. 16–17 CPC Regulation 2006/2004. Implementing rules concerning this cooperation have been laid down in Commission Decision 2007/76/EC implementing Regulation (EC) 2006/2004 on cooperation between national authorities responsible for the enforcement of consumer protection laws as regards mutual assistance, OJ 2007, L 32/192.

336 See further para 2.20 above.

337 Art. 51 Toy Safety Directive 2009/48.

338 E.g. Commission, Proposal for a regulation on consumer product safety, COM(2013) 78, p. 21 (Art. 18(2)).

339 Study, University of Bielefeld (2008), p. 610; Cafaggi and Micklitz (2009), p. 408; Azar-Baud (2010), p. 204.

6

COMPETITION LAW

This final chapter of Part B is concerned with the private enforcement-related developments regarding EU competition law.[1] In this field both the oldest and the most recent EU legislative measures of the type under consideration here can be found. Since the very beginning of EU law, the EU Treaties have contained an important contractual remedy, laid down in Article 101(2) TFEU, while at the end of 2014 the Competition Damages Directive was adopted. A discussion of these two measures and in particular this directive lies at the heart of this chapter. In the following section this field of law is first introduced. Attention then turns to the Competition Damages Directive. First the road towards the adoption of this directive is outlined in some detail, considering its long history and the insights that this offers as regards the coming into being of this recent private enforcement-related act of secondary EU law. Next the content of this directive is analysed. In the final section of this chapter, several other issues relevant to the enforcement of EU competition law are discussed, particularly the applicable public enforcement mechanisms.

1 The term "competition law" is used here in a narrow sense, covering the substantive rules laid down in Articles 101 and 102 TFEU and the corresponding rules of national law. As such, this term is used interchangeably with the term "antitrust law". It excludes, most notably, the rules of EU law on state aid and merger control set out in Art. 107–9 TFEU and Regulation (EC) No 139/2004 on the control of concentrations between undertakings, OJ 2004, L 24/1, respectively. On the private enforcement of these latter rules, see e.g. Bailey (2007), p. 101; Grzeszick (2011), p. 907; Honoré and Eram Jensen (2011), p. 265; Hohler (2012), p. 369.

A. INTRODUCTION

This section begins with a brief outline of the main rules of substantive EU competition law and the rules of secondary EU law that regulate their application. It then discusses some of the typical sorts of competition law infringements that are of relevance here and the damage that these infringements cause to individual parties and to society as a whole. In the last subsection the contractual remedy laid down in Article 101(2) TFEU is discussed.

1. Substantive EU competition law and its application

6.01 The main provisions of EU competition law, set out in Articles 101 and 102 TFEU, have always played an important role in the EU legal order. The Court of Justice has held that Article 101 TFEU constitutes a fundamental provision that is '*essential for the accomplishment of the tasks entrusted to the [EU] and, in particular, the functioning of the internal market*'.[2] Already at an early stage the Court clarified, notably in its ruling in *BRT*, that Articles 101 and 102 TFEU produce direct effects in relations between private parties and create rights in respect of the parties concerned that national courts must safeguard.[3] The primary function of EU competition law is generally understood to be protecting the competitive process and, in so doing, consumer welfare, against the background of the EU's internal market imperative.[4] Subject to these substantive EU competition rules are "undertakings", which are understood to mean any entity, regardless of its legal status or the way it is financed, engaged in economic activity, meaning that it is offering goods or services in a given market.[5]

6.02 The first pillar of substantive EU competition law, Article 101 TFEU, prohibits in its first paragraph agreements between undertakings, decisions by associations of undertakings and other concerted practices that may affect trade between Member States and that have as their object or effect the prevention, restriction or distortion of competition within the internal market. This article thus prohibits in particular *cartels*. In more concrete terms, it is, for instance, in

2 CoJ case 126/97, *Eco Swiss*, para 36. This statement was made with reference to Art. 3(1)(g) EC, as it stood before the entry into force of the Treaty of Lisbon in 2009. Cf. Art. 3(1)(b) TFEU, where it is stipulated that the EU has exclusive competence as regards the establishment of the competition rules necessary for the functioning of the internal market.

3 CoJ case 127/73, *BRT*, para 16; GC case T-458/04, *Au Lys de France*, para 70.

4 Commission, Guidelines on the application of Article 81(3) EC, OJ 2004, C 101/97, para 13. See e.g. also Monti (2003), p. 3; Ehlermann (2008), p. x; Komninos (2008), p. 190; Whish and Bailey (2012), pp. 19–24. This does not mean, however, that opinions cannot differ as to how "consumer welfare" is to be understood in this connection. See e.g. Ottervanger (2010).

5 E.g. CoJ case C-41/90, *Höfner*, para 21; CoJ joined cases C-180/98 to C-184/98, *Pavlov*, para 75.

principle illegal under this provision for competing undertakings to agree between them to set prices at a certain level or to divide the market by restricting their respective activities to certain territories or segments.

Article 101 TFEU also reflects the thought that agreements, decisions or concerned practices that would normally be prohibited under its first paragraph can in some cases have overall positive effects. One could think of certain forms of cooperation between undertakings in the field of research and development, the training of personnel or the distribution of their products or services. Article 101(3) TFEU therefore stipulates that the prohibition set out in the first paragraph may be '*declared inapplicable*'. This possibility is subject to the conditions that the cooperation in question leads to efficiency gains, that consumers get a fair share of the resulting benefits, that the restriction of competition is indispensable to achieve those benefits and that competition is not entirely eliminated.[6]

The second cornerstone of substantive EU competition law is Article 102 TFEU. Whereas Article 101 typically covers coordinated behaviour between several undertakings, Article 102 covers *unilateral* anticompetitive behaviour by one undertaking alone.[7] It prohibits more specifically undertakings from abusing a dominant position within the internal market or a substantial part thereof, in so far as this may affect trade between Member States. This article is thus concerned with undertakings having a particularly strong position in the relevant market, possibly (but not necessarily) a monopoly. Having such a dominant position is in and of itself not prohibited; what is not allowed under Article 102 TFEU is the *abuse* of such a position. **6.03**

Article 102 TFEU does not include a provision that is equivalent to Article 101(3) TFEU, mentioned above. In this case the prohibition cannot therefore be declared inapplicable where the behaviour in question is deemed to have overall beneficial effects. Despite the absence of such an "Article 102(3)", the Court of Justice has made it clear, however, that there is scope for an undertaking that infringed the prohibition set out in Article 102 to argue that its conduct is objectively necessary or that it produces substantial efficiencies that outweigh any anticompetitive effects on consumers.[8]

6 Cf. Commission, Guidelines on the application of Article 81(3) EC, OJ 2004, C 101/97.

7 Exceptionally, Art. 102 TFEU can also cover cases of "collective dominance" by more than one undertaking. See e.g. CoJ joined cases C-395/96 P and C-396/96 P, *Compagnie Maritime Belge*.

8 E.g. CoJ case 311/84, *Centre belge d'etudes de marché*, para 26; CoJ case C-95/04 P, *British Airways*, para 69 and 86. See also Commission, Guidance on the Commission's enforcement priorities in applying Article 82 EC to abusive exclusionary conduct by dominant undertakings, OJ 2009, C 45/7, para 28–30.

6.04 While the above-mentioned rules of primary EU law on competition have in substance been left unaltered since the very beginning of EU law, the same cannot be said of the rules of secondary EU law that regulate the application of Articles 101 and 102 TFEU. Regulation 1/2003 on the implementation of the EU competition rules ("Competition Regulation") is of particular importance in this regard.[9] This regulation, adopted in 2003 and applicable as from May 2004, is the result of a fundamental reform of the previously existing supervision and enforcement structure.[10] This '*legal and cultural revolution*'[11] sought to modernise and decentralise the application of EU competition law. At the heart of this reform lay the manner in which Article 101(3) TFEU is applied. Under the old system only the Commission was empowered to grant exemptions under this provision.[12] It did so upon prior notification by the undertakings concerned. Undertakings could also ask the Commission to certify that an agreement, decision or concerted practice did not violate the EU competition rules. All this led to an extensive system of notifications of intended actions to the Commission, with a view to obtaining such exemptions and clearances. In practice, a parallel system of informal guidance by the Commission also developed.

The Competition Regulation takes a radically different approach. Under the reformed regime the Commission no longer has the exclusive power to grant the exemptions referred to in Article 101(3) TFEU.[13] Instead, each undertaking must in principle make its own assessment as to the compliance of its behaviour with the EU competition rules, including the conditions set out in this third paragraph. National competition authorities as well as the competent national courts are empowered to assess whether these rules and conditions have been complied with.[14] In this respect it is provided that, whereas the burden of proving an infringement of Articles 101 and 102 TFEU rests on the party or authority alleging the infringement in question, undertakings that claim the benefit of Article 101(3) must prove that the conditions set out therein have been met.[15] Similarly, under the aforementioned case law relating to possible defences under Article 102 TFEU, it is for the undertaking

9 Regulation (EC) No 1/2003 on the implementation of the rules on competition laid down in Articles 81 and 82 EC, OJ 2003, L 1/1.

10 Cf. Commission, White paper on modernisation of the rules implementing Articles 85 and 86 EC, OJ 1999, C 132/1.

11 Ehlermann (2000), p. 537.

12 See Council Regulation No 17 First Regulation implementing Articles 85 and 86 of the Treaty, OJ 1962, 13/204.

13 Art. 1(2) Competition Regulation 1/2003.

14 Cf. Art. 5 and 6 Competition Regulation 1/2003.

15 Art. 2 Competition Regulation 1/2003.

concerned to raise this defence and to demonstrate the existence of the facts and circumstances on which it seeks to rely in this connection.[16]

Particularly in light of the decentralisation that it brought about, the Competition Regulation contains several rules on the application and enforcement of EU competition law at national level. Three such rules are of particular relevance here. First, where the competition authorities or the courts of the Member States apply national competition law to agreements, decisions or concerted practices covered by Article 101(1) TFEU that may affect trade between Member States or to any abuse prohibited by Article 102 TFEU, they must also apply this EU law provision *in parallel*.[17] Second, the Commission and national competition authorities each have the possibility of submitting, upon request or on their own initiative, *amicus curiae observations* in proceedings before national courts relating to EU competition law.[18] The Commission is entitled to do so where the coherent application of Articles 101 and 102 TFEU so requires, regardless of whether the proceedings in question are of an administrative, civil or criminal nature.[19] Third and finally, the Competition Regulation stipulates that national courts cannot take decisions in respect of agreements, decisions and concerted practices that *run counter* to earlier decisions adopted by the Commission and that these courts must avoid giving decisions that would conflict with a decision contemplated by the Commission in proceedings it has initiated.[20]

Subject to the applicable rules of EU law such as the ones referred to above, the application of Articles 101 and 102 TFEU at national level is in principle governed by the procedural rules of the Member States.[21] Accordingly, as confirmed in the Court of Justice's 1995 landmark ruling in *Van Schijndel*, as a general rule EU law does not require national courts to abandon the passive role assigned to them in civil proceedings in order to raise a point of EU competition law of their own motion (*ex officio*).[22] **6.05**

16 E.g. GC case T-201/04, *Microsoft*, para 688. See also Commission, Guidance on the Commission's enforcement priorities in applying Article 82 EC to abusive exclusionary conduct by dominant undertakings, OJ 2009, C 45/7, para 30.

17 Art. 3(1) Competition Regulation 1/2003.

18 Art. 15 Competition Regulation 1/2003. See also Commission, Cooperation notice, OJ 2004, C 101/54.

19 Recital 21 Competition Regulation 1/2003; Commission, Cooperation notice, OJ 2004, C 101/54, para 4. Cf. CoJ case C-429/07, *Inspecteur van de Belastingdienst v X*.

20 Art. 16(1) Competition Regulation 1/2003. Cf. CoJ case C-344/98, *Masterfoods*, para 60. On the interpretation of the resulting rule, see also Opinion AG Cruz-Villalon case C-199/11, *Otis*, para 46–7.

21 Cf. e.g. CoJ case C-60/92, *Otto v Postbank*, para 14.

22 CoJ joined cases C-430/93 and C-431/93, *Van Schijndel*, para 13–14 and 22. See also para 2.09 above.

But this rule is not without exceptions. As was held in *Van Schijndel* itself, pursuant to the principle of equivalence, an obligation of own-motion judicial review can exist where the court seised has an obligation or discretion to raise comparable points of law under national law.[23] In *Eco Swiss*, a subsequent case that concerned proceedings for the annulment of an arbitration award whereby national law required the court seised to raise certain issues of public policy (*d'ordre public*) of its own motion, such an obligation was also found to exist.[24] In that case the Court pointed to the above-mentioned fundamental importance attached to EU competition law, meaning that it should be seen as a matter of public policy. It also noted that own-motion judicial review ensured that preliminary questions could be referred to the Court of Justice, given that arbitration panels are in principle not allowed to do so in so far as they are not courts or tribunals within the meaning of Article 267 TFEU.[25]

More recently, the Court has at times also stated in proceedings that did not concern the possible annulment of arbitration awards that Articles 101 and 102 TFEU are '*a matter of public policy which must be automatically applied by national courts*'.[26] For now it remains to be clarified what precisely is meant by this statement. In particular in light of the earlier *Van Schijndel* judgment and the fact that, as the Court later confirmed on another occasion,[27] the application of the principle of equivalence was central to the outcome reached in *Eco Swiss*, it is uncertain whether this more recent case law should be understood as implying an obligation on national courts to raise of their own motion rules of EU competition law wherever relevant, including in situations where domestic law does not provide for such a possibility even for matters of public policy.[28]

2. Infringements and damage

6.06 Infringements of EU competition law can take many forms. Some infringements are the result of *bona fide* unawareness or misunderstanding of the

23 On the principle of equivalence, see subsection 2.A.2 above.

24 CoJ case C-126/97, *Eco Swiss*, para 40–41.

25 On Art. 267 TFEU and the term "court or tribunal" used therein, see also para 1.02 above.

26 CoJ joined cases C-295/04 to C-298/04, *Manfredi*, para 31. See also CoJ case C-8/08, *T-Mobile Netherlands*, para 49.

27 CoJ joined cases C-222/05 and C-225/05, *Van der Weerd*, para 40.

28 See also recital 1 Competition Damages Directive 2014/104, where it is stated that '*Articles 101 and 102 [TFEU] are a matter of public policy*'. While this statement appears to echo the above-mentioned CoJ rulings in *Manfredi* and *T-Mobile Netherlands*, no further explanation is provided in this directive. Notably, contrary to those rulings, in this recital it is not stated that these provisions '*must be automatically applied*'; instead it is said that these articles '*should be applied effectively throughout the [EU]*'.

applicable rules. Yet in many other instances the illegal anticompetitive behaviour is deliberate and considerable efforts are made to conceal it.[29] Article 102 TFEU itself expressly lists various forms of forbidden abuses of a dominant position. This includes the undertaking concerned charging excessive prices, differentiating its prices between trading partners without objective justification or refusing to supply its products or services to certain customers. Article 101 TFEU in contrast does not itself cite any examples of forbidden behaviour. Various sorts of anticompetitive acts can be covered by the prohibition set out in its first paragraph. Such behaviour can take place in a "vertical" context, thus between undertakings that do not operate – and compete – at the same level of the supply chain. By means of an example, one could think of a "beer tie" agreement. Many pubs are owned by beer brewers and subsequently leased to a tenant. Yet it can be contrary to Article 101 TFEU for the lease agreement to stipulate that the tenant is obliged to purchase all the beer served in the pub from that brewer, thus excluding other brewers.

A typical example of an infringement of Article 101 TFEU for the present purposes is, however, a "horizontal" cartel, whereby several undertakings supplying a particular product or service coordinate their market behaviour. Take for instance the elevator cartel that was discovered in 2007.[30] Instead of competing, the four major European manufacturers of elevators and escalators were found to have allocated tenders and other contracts between them in several Member States, thus sharing markets and fixing prices in violation of the prohibition set out in Article 101(1) TFEU. These undertakings had also exchanged information on sales volumes and prices, operated a mutual compensation scheme, participated in regular meetings and established other contacts in order to decide on these competition restrictions and the implementation thereof. With a view to concealing their illegal anticompetitive behaviour, the meetings in question mostly took place in hotels and restaurants instead of at the premises of the undertakings concerned. For the same reason, the employees concerned regularly used their private and prepaid mobile phones instead of their company phones.

Infringements of the kind referred to above can cause considerable harm. **6.07**
Although the amounts at issue may vary considerably, there is research suggesting that nine out of ten cartels lead to an overcharge, that is, an amount that is higher than the customers of the conspiring undertakings would have had to

29 Cf. e.g. CoJ case C-453/99, *Courage*, para 27, where anticompetitive behaviour is observed to be '*frequently covert*'.

30 See Commission, Decision C(2007) 512, *Elevators and escalators cartel*; GC joined cases T141/07, T142/07, T145/07 and T146/07, *Otis*; CoJ Order case C-493/11 P, *United Technologies*; CoJ case C-199/11, *Otis*.

pay under normal competitive conditions.[31] At macro-level the damage caused by price-fixing and other particularly serious "hard-core"[32] cartels alone has been estimated to amount to somewhere from €25–69 billion per year EU-wide, which corresponds to a negative impact on consumer welfare of around 0.2–0.55 per cent of EU GDP.[33] At the same time, the chances of detecting such illegal cartels are generally rather low, as it stands, probably no more than 10–20 per cent.[34] Acknowledging, on the one hand, that not all infringements are detected and, on the other hand, that infringements of Articles 101 and 102 TFEU other than by such hard-core cartels also incur damage, forgone amounts of compensation for these competition law infringements have been estimated to amount to a total of between €5.7 billion and €23.3 billion each year across the EU.[35]

3. Article 101(2) TFEU: Contractual remedy

6.08 From the very beginning of EU law an important private enforcement remedy was laid down in the EU Treaties. It concerns the contractual remedy provided for in Article 101(2) TFEU. This provision stipulates that any agreement or decision prohibited under that article shall be '*automatically void*'. This is in fact the only instance where primary EU law provides for such a measure. Article 102 TFEU does not contain a similar provision regulating the contractual consequences of an infringement of the prohibition of the abuse of a dominant position set out in that article.[36] Neither do the EU Treaties expressly provide for a comparable remedy for infringements of other rules of substantive EU law.

The Court of Justice has clarified that this term "automatically void" is an autonomous concept of EU law, which is intended to ensure compliance with the relevant substantive rules prohibiting anticompetitive cartels.[37] It is absolute, the agreement or decision concerned having no effect either between the parties concerned or *vis-à-vis* third parties, with retroactive effect (*ex tunc*).[38]

---

31 Commission, Proposal for Competition Damages Directive 2014/104, COM(2013) 404, p. 18. See further Study, Oxera Consulting (2009), p. 91.

32 On "hard-core" restrictions in the context of Art. 101(1) TFEU, see Commission, *De minimis* notice, OJ 2001, C 368/13, para 11.

33 Commission, Impact assessment report on damages actions for breach of the EU antitrust rules, SWD(2013) 203, p. 22 (relating to EU GDP in 2011).

34 Ibid., p. 23.

35 Ibid.

36 That does not necessarily mean, however, that there cannot be such consequences as a matter of EU law. See para 8.10 below.

37 CoJ case 56/65, *Société Technique Minière*, p. 250.

38 CoJ case 319/82, *Société de Vente de Ciments*, para 11; CoJ case 48/72, *Brasserie de Haecht*, para 26–7; CoJ case C-453/99, *Courage*, para 22; CoJ joined cases C-295/04 to C-298/04, *Manfredi*, para 57.

Under the Court's case law the further consequences of a finding of an agreement or decision being void within the meaning of Article 101(2) TFEU are, however, in principle to be determined in accordance with national law. This includes the question to what extent other provisions of the agreement, or of related agreements, that do not in themselves imply a breach of the prohibition set out in this article, can be severed and can continue to apply.[39]

The practical importance of the above contractual remedy lies especially in the fact that the agreements in question cannot be enforced in court. This can lead to uncertainty for the infringing undertakings concerned, which in turn can act as a strong disincentive for undertakings to conclude agreements that may not be in conformity with the prohibition set out in this article.[40] Accordingly, it '*intensifies the conflicts of interests and the internal centrifugal force among the participants of a cartel*'.[41] There is, for instance, little point in including a beer tie provision in a lease agreement for a pub of the kind referred to above when the brewer knows that he cannot enforce that provision if the pub tenant refuses to respect that contractual obligation. Likewise, undertakings operating a cartel comparable to the aforementioned elevator cartel may sometimes be able to secretly divide the market, fix prices and operate a compensation scheme between them. But the moment one of the cartel members no longer respects the agreement, none of the other members can (threaten to) bring legal proceedings to enforce what had been agreed in violation of EU competition law. **6.09**

This remedy also has its limitations, however. As the above examples already illustrate, Article 101(2) TFEU tends to be used mainly as a "defensive" instrument in litigation between private parties.[42] That means that it is typically invoked by one of the parties to the agreement with a view to avoid being bound by a particular obligation resulting from the agreement in question (for example to purchase beer exclusively from one brewer or to respect agreed market shares). Third parties may generally have little incentive to bring private enforcement proceedings relying on this remedy, as they are not a party to the agreement and they are therefore at most only indirectly affected. The foregoing also illustrates that the relevance of this contractual remedy especially for the most serious (hard-core) infringements of Article 101(1) TFEU can be limited. For instance, given the evident illegality of the scheme operated by the elevator

39 CoJ case 56/65, *Société Technique Minière*, p. 250; CoJ case 319/82, *Société de Vente de Ciments*, para 11; CoJ case 10/86, *VAG France*, para 14–15. See further Cauffman (2012), p. 95.

40 Wils (2003a), p. 474.

41 Möschel (2013), p. 2.

42 Wils (2003a), pp. 474–5; Eilmansberger (2007), p. 433; Komninos (2008), p. 149; Milutinovic (2010), p. 144; Peyer (2012), p. 350.

cartel members, normally none of the undertakings concerned would consider enforcing the agreement in court anyway.[43]

This contractual remedy is therefore of considerable practical importance, but it is generally not very well suited as an "offensive" tool for private parties wishing to address these most serious infringements of EU competition law.

B. TOWARDS THE COMPETITION DAMAGES DIRECTIVE

The thought that the aforementioned contractual remedy laid down in Article 101(2) TFEU might need to be supplemented by other private enforcement-related measures provided for as a matter of secondary EU law is far from new. In many respects, the road towards the Competition Damages Directive had been long and winding indeed. This section sketches the main developments that eventually led to the adoption of this directive in 2014. Four stages are distinguished. First, an overview is given of the early developments in this regard (1960–2000). Second, two subsequent developments – one legislative and one jurisprudential – are discussed, which go a long way in explaining why this subject matter then reappeared on the EU's law-making agenda (2000–2005). Third, the Commission's green paper and white paper outlining possible EU legislative measures in this respect are analysed, together with its subsequent aborted initiative to propose a directive (2005–10). Lastly, attention is paid to subsequent jurisprudential developments and the Commission's proposal for this directive (2010–13).

1. Early developments (1960–2000)

6.10 As early as the 1960s a study was carried out that looked into the possibilities for what is now known as the private enforcement of EU competition law.[44] It concluded that in all of the then six Member States, private parties affected by a violation of the EU competition rules could take legal action before national courts to obtain civil law remedies such as damages, injunctions, periodic penalty payments and the publication of court judgments.[45] A few years later the Commission added that actions for damages brought by private parties

43 Whish and Bailey (2012), p. 320.

44 European Parliament, '*Rapport fait au nom de la commission du marché intérieur ayant pour objet la consultation demandée à l'Assemblée parlementaire européenne par le Conseil de la Communauté économique européenne sur un premier règlement d'application des articles 85 et 86 du traité de la C.E.E.*', doc. 104/1960–1961, cited in Milutinovic (2010), pp. 27–8.

45 Study, '*La réparation des conséquences dommageables d'une violation des articles 85 et 86 du traite instituant la CEE*', p. 5, cited in Temple Lang (1981), p. 338.

could provide '*useful support*' for the public enforcement of these rules, while noting that the civil law consequences, other than those resulting from the application of Article 101(2) TFEU, '*are generally considered as being governed by the national laws of the Member States*'.[46]

In the following decades this issue resurfaced repeatedly. In particular in the 1980s, the Commission floated the idea of adopting secondary EU law on the private enforcement of the EU competition rules. The Commission's 1983 report on competition policy noted that, while '*[s]cant use has yet been made of the possibility of actions for damages for breaches of the [EU] competition rules*', '*[t]he Commission believes it desirable that the judicial enforcement of Articles [101 and 102 TFEU] should also include the award of damages to injured parties, because this would render [EU] law more effective*'.[47] This report indicated that the Commission was therefore looking at what steps could be taken to facilitate damages actions of this kind.[48] **6.11**

In the same period, a similar point was made in various academic publications (many of them written by a Commission official).[49] These publications not only set out the legal framework and highlighted some successful examples of such actions that had been brought before national courts. It was also suggested here that the EU should adopt a directive with the purpose of '*[making] it clear that actions for compensation, declarations and injunctions could be brought in national courts, harmonising national law remedies for breaches of [EU] antitrust law, [which] would substantially improve the general level of compliance with [EU] antitrust law*'.[50] In these publications the deterrent effect of these measures and the scarce manpower of the Commission and national authorities charged with the public enforcement of this law were emphasised, noting that such a "decentralisation" of EU competition law enforcement to the national courts would allow the Commission to focus on the more complex and particularly serious and cross-border cases.[51]

In the second half of the 1980s, the Commission reportedly considered the possibility of proposing a regulation on the application of EU competition law

46 Reply to European Parliament question 519/72, OJ 1973, C 67/54, cited in Temple Lang (1981), p. 339.
47 Commission, Thirteenth report on competition policy, 1984, p. 136. Cf. Komninos (2008), p. 163.
48 Ibid.
49 Temple Lang (1981), p. 335; Jacobs (1983), p. 353; Temple Lang (1983), p. 219; Temple Lang (1985), p. 29; Steiner (1987), p. 102. Mr Temple Lang worked at the time for the Commission's legal service (only one of these publications states that the opinions expressed there are personal).
50 Temple Lang (1983), pp. 302. See also Temple Lang (1981), pp. 341–2.
51 On the public enforcement of EU competition law, see subsection 6.D.2 below.

by national courts. But it eventually decided against doing so, in light of negative reactions by legal experts of the Member States.[52]

6.12 In the early 1990s some further relevant statements were made, this time in particular in relation to cases brought before the EU courts. The General Court touched upon this issue in passing in 1992. It held that:

> among the consequences which an infringement of [Article 101(1) TFEU] may have in civil law, only one is expressly provided for in Article [101(2)], namely the nullity of that agreement. The other consequences attaching to an infringement of Article [101 TFEU], such as the obligation to make good the damage caused to a third party or a possible obligation to enter into a contract [...], are to be determined under national law.[53]

Here the emphasis was thus still firmly on the private enforcement possibilities under *national* law, as was the case in the aforementioned Commission statements made in the 1960s.

In 1993 Advocate General Van Gerven suggested, however, an altogether different approach in his opinion in the *Banks* case.[54] Building on the Court's 1991 *Francovich* ruling relating to the liability of Member States for infringements of EU law,[55] he argued that – even in the absence of any specific rules of secondary EU law – such actions for damages are primarily a matter of *EU* law. In an extensive opinion it was said that '*the general basis established by the Court in the Francovich judgment for [Member] State liability also applies where an individual infringes a provision of [EU] law to which he is subject, thereby causing loss and damage to another individual*'. It was added that '*in a field such as competition law*' there are two '*powerful additional arguments*' that mitigate in favour of private parties having the possibility under EU law of obtaining reparation for loss and damages caused by these infringements, namely that this would be the logical conclusion of the horizontal direct effect of the EU competition rules and that it would help make these rules more operational.[56]

In the slipstream of the *Francovich* ruling and the *Banks* opinion, calls were made in the legal literature for EU legislative intervention on this matter.[57]

52 Komninos (2008), p. 163 (n. 131).

53 GC case T-24/90, *Automec*, para 50.

54 Opinion AG Van Gerven case C-128/92, *Banks*, para 36–54. The fact that this case concerned the ECSC Treaty appears to be of little relevance here (cf. para 36 of the opinion). In its judgment the CoJ did not rule on the issue raised by the AG. See CoJ case C-128/92, *Banks*.

55 CoJ joined cases C-6/90 and C-9/90, *Francovich*. See para 2.23 above.

56 Opinion AG Van Gerven case C-128/92, *Banks*, para 43–4.

57 E.g. Smith (1992), p. 129; Benedict (1995), p. 247.

However, apart from the publication of an additional report assessing the situation at national level,[58] at this stage still no concrete steps were taken in the direction of the adoption of secondary EU law facilitating the private enforcement of EU competition law.

2. Legislative reform and *Courage* case law (2000–05)

The first of the two subsequent developments that go a long way in explaining why possible EU legislative intervention in this domain re-emerged more recently has already been touched upon earlier. It concerns the *fundamental reform* of the rules on the application of Articles 101 and 102 TFEU that led to the adoption of the Competition Regulation in 2003.[59] This reform, which in effect amounted to a significant decentralisation from the EU to the national level, was mainly meant to allow the Commission to focus on actively uncovering particularly serious and covert infringements of EU competition law rather than handling the routine notifications and clearances that were typical of the pre-existing system.[60] It is to be noted that the Competition Regulation contains no provisions that directly relate to the private enforcement of EU competition law. As the discussion of the early developments in the previous subsection illustrates, this reform was not a *conditio sine qua non* for private enforcement to take place.[61] It has been argued that, if anything, the reform mainly helped to facilitate "defensive" actions by private parties,[62] as opposed to the "offensive" type whereby, for instance, a claim for damages is brought by a third party.[63] However, the resulting devolution of powers to the national level is still thought to have helped create the conditions under which private enforcement could take off, notably by forcing undertakings to think and act more independently on competition law issues and by empowering the national courts.[64] The energy and resources required to conceive, draft, adopt and implement this reform further probably explain in large part why EU legislative **6.13**

58 Commission, The application of Articles 85 and 86 EC by national courts in the Member States, July 1997.

59 See para 6.04 above.

60 Cf. recital 3 Competition Regulation 1/2003. See also Commission, White paper on modernisation of the rules implementing Articles 85 and 86 EC, OJ 1999, C 132/17. Note that although the solutions enacted differ, this reasoning is comparable to that invoked in relation to the pleas for encouraging private enforcement in the 1980s, referred to in para 6.11 above.

61 For an extensive discussion of the "pre-modernisation" and the "modernised" system in relation to private enforcement, see Komninos (2008), pp. 24–139.

62 Cf. para 6.09 above.

63 Wils (2003a), p. 475; Eilmansberger (2007), p. 434.

64 Cf. e.g. recital 7 Competition Regulation 1/2003; Opinion AG Geelhoed joined cases C-295/04 to C-298/04, *Manfredi*, para 30; Commission, Staff working paper accompanying the green paper on damages actions for breach of EC antitrust rules, SEC(2005) 1732, p. 11.

action on private enforcement was not properly discussed until after the completion of this reform.[65]

6.14 The second development is the Court of Justice's *Courage* case law.[66] The 2001 *Courage* ruling has already been introduced earlier,[67] but its importance in the present context justifies assessing it in further detail here. Courage Ltd, a brewery, and Mr Crehan, a pub tenant, had agreed on a "beer tie" as part of a lease agreement for the pub in question. As was explained above, this means that the latter was contractually obliged to purchase the beer sold in that pub exclusively from this particular brewer.[68] When Courage sued Mr Crehan for unpaid deliveries of beer, the latter argued that the beer tie contract was contrary to Article 101(1) and thus automatically void under Article 101(2) TFEU.[69] In addition, Mr Crehan made a counterclaim for damages. He argued that he had been forced to buy its beers at prices higher than those that Courage charged to independent pub tenants. However, under English law this latter claim was barred even if an infringement of competition law was to be found, because it does not allow a party to rely on its own illegal actions to obtain damages. The question referred to the Court of Justice by the English court seised was essentially whether such an absolute bar is compatible with EU law.

In its reply the Court first recalled three general points, namely that EU law constitutes its own legal order intended to give rights to private parties; that Article 101 TFEU is a fundamental provision, as is underlined by the principle of automatic nullity laid down in Article 101(2) that can be relied on by anyone and that has absolute consequences; and that Article 101(1) produces direct effects in relations between private parties and creates rights for the parties concerned that national courts must safeguard.[70] It follows according to the Court that '*any individual can rely on a breach of Article [101(1) TFEU] before a national court even where he is a party to a contract that is liable to restrict or distort competition within the meaning of that provision*'.[71] Specifically in relation to the action for damages, it added that:

---

65 As the then Commissioner for competition policy, Mr Monti, noted in 2001 in relation to the Commission's proposal for what was to become the Competition Regulation, '*[o]ur reform proposal already introduces substantial changes [and] [w]e should not try to achieve too much all at once if we want to obtain real progress in reasonable time*'. See Monti (2003), p. 8.

66 Earlier the CoJ had already touched upon private enforcement-related aspects, yet without being particularly clear in this respect. See CoJ case C-282/95 P, *Guérin*, para 39; CoJ case C-242/95, *GT-Link*, para 58–61.

67 CoJ case C-453/99, *Courage*. See also para 2.24 above.

68 See para 6.06 above.

69 See subsection 6.A.3 above.

70 CoJ case C-453/99, *Courage*, para 19–23.

71 Ibid., para 24.

> [t]he full effectiveness of Article [101 TFEU] and, in particular, the practical effect of the prohibition laid down [therein] would be put at risk if it were not open to any individual to claim damages for loss caused to him by a contract or by conduct liable to restrict or distort competition. Indeed, the existence of such a right strengthens the working of the [EU] competition rules and discourages agreements or practices, which are frequently covert, which are liable to restrict or distort competition. From that point of view, actions for damages before the national courts can make a significant contribution to the maintenance of effective competition in the [EU].[72]

It was therefore found that there should not be an absolute bar to the actions at issue here.

The Court continued by recalling that, subject to the principles of equivalence and effectiveness, it is for the domestic legal system of each Member State to designate the competent courts and to lay down the detailed procedural rules governing such actions. It held that EU law does not prevent national courts from taking steps to ensure that the protection of rights guaranteed by that law does not entail the unjust enrichment of those who enjoy them. Similarly, EU law does not in principle preclude national law from denying a party who is found to bear significant responsibility for the distortion of competition the right to obtain damages from the other contracting party, as a litigant should not profit from their own illegal conduct. In that regard account is to be taken according to the Court of the economic and legal context in which the parties find themselves and of their respective bargaining power and conduct and, in particular, whether the party claiming damages was in a markedly weaker position such as to seriously compromise or even eliminate their freedom to negotiate the terms of the contract and their capacity to avoid the loss or reduce its extent.[73]

In 2006 the Court of Justice returned to this topic in *Manfredi*.[74] This case, an Italian preliminary reference, concerned a "follow-on" action, meaning that the competent national competition authority had already found that the defendants (several undertakings offering civil liability auto insurance) had entered into an unlawful price-fixing agreement. Subsequently Mr Manfredi and a number of other clients of these undertakings demanded to be compensated for the increase in the premiums that they had paid as a consequence of this coordinated anticompetitive behaviour. The questions referred to the Court of **6.15**

72 Ibid., para 26–7.
73 Ibid., para 29–35.
74 CoJ joined cases C-295/04 to C-298/04, *Manfredi*.

Justice in this case concerned not so much the existence of the right to compensation as such, but rather the more detailed rules that apply in this respect.

In its judgment the Court started by confirming what it had already held in *Courage*. In particular, it recalled that the full effectiveness and practical effect of the prohibition laid down in Article 101(1) TFEU would be at risk if such damages claims could not be brought, pointing to the discouraging effect thereof on possible infringements and the significant contribution that these claims can make to the maintenance of effective competition.[75] On this basis the Court clarified that *any party* can claim compensation where there is a *causal relationship* between the harm suffered and the infringement at issue. In the absence of rules of EU law on this subject matter, subject to the principles of equivalence and effectiveness, it is for the Member States to lay down the detailed rules on the application of the concept of "causal relationship".[76] Under the same conditions it also for them to designate the courts before which these cases are to be brought, to provide for the limitation periods that may apply to the bringing of these actions for damages and to set the criteria for determining the extent of the damages.[77]

On these latter two points the Court also offered further clarification, however. In respect of the applicable *limitation periods*, it held that when under national law such a period begins to run from the day of the establishment of the agreement or concerted practice, this makes it practically impossible to exercise the right to seek compensation, particularly if this is combined with a short limitation period that is not capable of being suspended. For in such a situation, where there are continuous or repeated infringements, it is possible that this period expires even before the infringement is brought to an end. This would mean that it is impossible for a private party that suffered harm after the expiry of that period to initiate legal proceedings.[78] Concerning the *extent of the damages* due, the Court first held that, pursuant to the principle of equivalence, it must be possible to award punitive damages for infringements of EU competition law if the award of such damages is available for infringements of similar actions founded on national law. It added that EU law does not prevent national courts from taking steps to prevent unjust enrichment. The Court further ruled that in cases of infringements of EU competition law, injured private parties must be able to seek compensation not only for actual loss

75 Ibid., para 60 and 90–91.
76 Ibid., para 61–4.
77 Ibid., para 71, 77 and 92.
78 Ibid., para 78–9.

(*damnum emergens*), but that it must also be possible for them to be compensated for loss of profit (*lucrum cessans*). A total exclusion of this latter head of damage cannot be accepted according to the Court. Interest must also be paid, this being called an essential component of the compensation due.[79]

The above line of case law has since been confirmed on many occasions.[80] It has been instrumental for the present purposes particularly in two respects. To begin with, in line with what Advocate General Van Gerven had already argued in his opinion in *Banks*,[81] this case law confirmed that private parties injured by infringements of Article 101 TFEU have *as a matter of EU law* the right to claim damages. Unlike what had sometimes been assumed earlier,[82] this is therefore not something that is left primarily to national law. Rather, in the absence of any specific EU rules, only the more detailed rules are to be determined by national law, pursuant to the principle of national procedural autonomy and subject to the principles of equivalence and effectiveness.[83] At the same time, the above rulings still leave many questions unanswered, such as whether the same reasoning applies to Article 102 TFEU, which conditions apply precisely in relation to these private enforcement actions and whether they may also encompass other remedies than actions for damages. Without in itself necessitating any further measures to be taken by the EU legislature, the *Courage* case law thus placed the issue of private enforcement firmly in the spotlight.[84] **6.16**

In addition, the above case law underlines the significant contribution that private enforcement proceedings can make to the maintenance of *effective competition* in the EU. These actions are therefore not only about a private party's right to obtain compensation for the harm suffered. They also fulfil an important role in contributing to the achievement of one of the EU's key policy objectives, the maintenance of effective competition, thus supplementing the public enforcement efforts in this field. Thus, '*[w]hile pursuing his private interest, a plaintiff in such proceedings contributes at the same time to the protection of the public interest*'.[85] This highlights, on the one hand, the general interest

79 Ibid., para 93–6.

80 E.g. CoJ case C-421/05, *City Motors*, para 33; CoJ case C-360/09, *Pfleiderer*, para 28; CoJ case C-199/11, *Otis*, para 40–43; CoJ case C-536/11, *Donau Chemie*, para 21–7; CoJ case C-557/12, *Kone*, para 20–24.

81 Opinion AG Van Gerven case C-128/92, *Banks*. See para 6.12 above.

82 See e.g. para 6.10 and 6.12 above.

83 On these principles, see section 2.A above.

84 See e.g. Komninos (2002), p. 447; Ehlermann and Atanasiu (2003); Wils (2003a), p. 473; Andreangeli (2004), p. 758; Jones (2004), p. 13.

85 EFTA Court case E-14/11, *Schenker*, para 132.

associated with private enforcement actions, while, on the other hand, it leaves unaddressed the question of precisely how both forms of enforcement relate to each other.

3. Green paper, white paper and draft proposal (2005–10)

6.17 On the back of this legislative reform and the *Courage* case law, the Commission judged the time ripe to renew its thinking on a possible legislative initiative. Therefore, in 2005 it published a green paper on damages actions for infringements of the EU's competition rules.[86] This document aimed to identify obstacles to a more efficient system for bringing such actions and to outline various options for solving these problems. It reflected the view that there is a state of '*total underdevelopment*' where actions for damages for infringements of EU competition law under the laws of the Member States are concerned.[87] This assessment rested largely on the findings of an external study that was published in 2004, which spoke in this connection of '*astonishing diversity and total underdevelopment*'.[88] It observed that by 2004 there were, EU-wide, only around 60 judged cases for damages actions for infringement of EU or national competition law, around half of which had led to an award of damages.[89] It identified a number of obstacles to bringing successful claims and suggested possible ways to tackle them.

6.18 Building on this assessment and the comments received, in 2008 the Commission published a white paper on the same subject matter.[90] It acknowledged that since the publication of the green paper three years earlier, specific legislation had been adopted in some Member States, such as Germany, Italy and the United Kingdom, and that generally awareness and the number of cases brought (and probably also the number of out-of-court settlements reached) had increased.[91] Indeed, a subsequent study identified 96 damages actions in

---

86 Commission, Green paper on damages actions for breach of the EC antitrust rules, COM(2005) 672. See also Commission, Staff working paper accompanying the green paper on damages actions for breach of EC antitrust rules, SEC(2005) 1732.

87 Ibid., p. 4.

88 Study, Ashurst (2004), p. 1.

89 Ibid.

90 Commission, White paper on damages actions for breach of the EC antitrust rules, COM(2008) 165. See also Commission, Staff working paper accompanying the white paper on damages actions for breach of the EC antitrust rules, SEC(2008) 404; Commission, Impact assessment relating to the white paper on damages actions for breach of the EC antitrust rules, SEC(2008) 405.

91 For an overview of these developments at national level, see e.g. Komninos (2008), pp. 183–6; Nazzini (2009), pp. 402–3.

the 2004–07 period.[92] But that study also found that these cases were restricted to only ten Member States and that it mainly concerned groups of "follow-on" actions initiated following findings of infringements by the competition authorities. Proper "stand-alone" actions, which are cases brought independently of a preceding finding of an infringement by a competition authority, were found to make up only a relatively small part of the total. Here it was therefore submitted that the aforementioned state of total underdevelopment had only marginally changed.[93] On that basis, the Commission considered that the problems identified earlier essentially remained unchanged and that victims of infringements of EU competition law were still only rarely compensated for the harm suffered.[94] It pointed to the amount of compensation forgone and it argued that a great deal of legal uncertainty existed.

While the main line thus remained unchanged, there are, however, certain notable differences in emphasis between this white paper and the green paper that preceded it.[95] Initially, public and private enforcement of competition law had been said to be part of a common enforcement system and to serve the same aims, namely to deter forbidden anticompetitive practices and to protect undertakings and consumers.[96] Actions for damages were thus seen as serving the twin purposes of compensation and deterrence. In the white paper, allowing for the full compensation of the harm caused by competition law infringements was by contrast held to be the '*first and foremost guiding principle*'.[97] This was said to '*inherently*' also produce beneficial effects in terms of deterrence of future infringements and greater compliance with the substantive rules at issue.[98] In this later document the importance of following a '*genuinely European approach*' was also reinforced, involving '*balanced measures that are rooted in European legal culture and traditions*'.[99] The importance of preserving strong public enforcement was also underlined.[100] Another difference in emphasis can be found in the Commission highlighting that the intended legislative exercise would on

92 Study, CEPS, Erasmus University Rotterdam and LUISS (2007), p. 39. Unlike the aforementioned 2004 study by Ashurst, this later study concerns only claims for damages as a consequence of breaches of *EU* competition law, thus excluding cases concerning infringements of *national* competition law.

93 Ibid., pp. 28 and 39–40.

94 Commission, Staff working paper accompanying the white paper on damages actions for breach of the EC antitrust rules, SEC(2008) 404, p. 9.

95 This occurred presumably in response to the comments made on the preceding green paper. Cf. Cauffman (2011a), pp. 182–3; Wils (2013), p. 6.

96 Commission, Green paper on damages actions for breach of the EC antitrust rules, COM(2005) 672, p. 3.

97 Commission, White paper on damages actions for breach of the EC antitrust rules, p. 3.

98 Ibid.

99 Ibid.

100 Ibid.

various points concern (merely) a codification of the relevant case law of the Court of Justice.[101]

In the 2008 white paper the Commission did not expand on the concrete form or legal basis of any legislative measures that it might propose.[102] Nonetheless, several specific measures were outlined that could be taken to address the obstacles that private parties wishing to bring actions for damages for alleged infringements of EU competition law were said to encounter.[103] These measures included rules on collective redress; the disclosure of evidence; the binding effect of infringement decisions taken by national competition authorities; fault requirements; the qualification and quantification of damage; limitation periods; and legal costs. They also included possible rules on the interaction between public and private enforcement in this domain, in particular the non-disclosure of "leniency" statements, which are documents in which undertakings confess to the competent public enforcement authorities their infringements of the competition rules in the hope of obtaining immunity from or a reduction of the fines that these authorities can impose, and the limitation of the successful leniency applicants' civil liability in damages.[104]

6.19 The two above-mentioned official documents generated a lively debate. In academic circles they set many pens in motion.[105] Many stakeholders, academics, practitioners and public authorities also used the possibility offered to comment on these documents.[106] The reactions from the side of the *business* community were largely negative.[107] These parties voiced objections in principle and in practice against using actions by private parties to further the

101 See ibid., p. 7, and in particular Commission, Staff working paper accompanying the white paper on damages actions for breach of the EC antitrust rules, SEC(2008) 404, pp. 90–91. On this proposed codification exercise, see further Milutinovic (2010), p. 301.

102 Cf. Commission, White paper on damages actions for breach of the EC antitrust rules, p. 2. See also Commission, Staff working paper accompanying the white paper on damages actions for breach of the EC antitrust rules, SEC(2008) 404, pp. 97–8.

103 Commission, White paper on damages actions for breach of the EC antitrust rules, pp. 4–10. See also Commission, Green paper on damages actions for breach of the EC antitrust rules, COM(2005) 672, pp. 5–11.

104 On these leniency programmes, see para 6.48 below.

105 See e.g. Hodges (2006), p. 1381; Komninos (2006), p. 5; Riley and Peysner (2006), p. 748, Wilsher (2006), p. 27; Eilmansberger (2007), p. 431; Komninos (2008); Nebbia (2008b), p. 23; Andreangeli (2009), p. 229; Wils (2009), p. 3; Komninos (2009), p. 363; Zippro (2009b); Milutinovic (2010); Nazzini (2011), p. 131; Basedow, Terhechte and Tichý (2011); Peyer (2011), p. 627; Frese (2011), p. 397.

106 For the responses submitted to the green paper and the white paper, see http://ec.europa.eu/competition/antitrust/actionsdamages/index.html.

107 See e.g. the comments on the green paper submitted by Association of French undertakings (MEDEF); Internal Chamber of Commerce (ICC); American Chamber of Commerce to the EU (Amcham EU); European Chemical Industry Council (Cefic); Confederation of Finnish Industries (EK); association of the European insurance industry (CEA); the association of German industry (BDI); UK business lobby CBI; Union of Industrial and Employers Federation of Europe (UNICE; now called BusinessEurope).

general interest associated with the effective application of EU competition law and concerns that the contemplated EU private enforcement rules might create a "US-style" litigation culture. Most *consumer associations* spoke out in favour of taking action at EU level.[108] The *lawyers and academics* that responded were on the whole rather nuanced.[109] These latter respondents mostly recognised that there was room for improvement. But they also cautioned against a litigation culture, stressed the primacy of public enforcement and expressed doubts as to whether the obstacles identified indeed explained the relatively low number of damages claims brought, considering for instance that many cases are settled out of court. The logic of treating competition cases differently from other civil litigation was also questioned. Some further recalled that in certain Member States private competition litigation was already rather well developed and that more recently there had been a significant increase in the number of cases brought.

Reactions from the side of *public authorities* were rather mixed. Many stressed the compensatory – and not punitive – nature of damages awards.[110] Several public authorities also highlighted the risks posed to the coherence of their respective domestic legal systems if specific action with regard to competition cases were to be taken. Arguments against a litigation culture were again voiced. The German and French governments were among those that took a rather negative stance.[111] They essentially contested the need for EU legislation, raised questions as to its legal basis and submitted that, in accordance with the principles of national procedural autonomy and subsidiarity, the aforementioned issues should be left to be regulated by the Member States. It was argued that, if any legislative action were to be taken, those issues would fall under the rules of the EU Treaties on judicial cooperation in civil matters.[112]

---

108 See e.g. the comments on the green paper submitted by the European Consumer's Organisation (*Bureau européen des Unions de consommateurs*, BEUC); and the UK-based consumer organisation, Which?

109 See e.g. comments on the green paper submitted by law firms Clifford Chance, Freshfields Bruckhaus Deringer, Linklaters and CMS; UK bars and law societies; Europa Instituut Leiden University; Max Planck Institute; Dutch Bar Association; International Bar Association.

110 See e.g. the comments on the green paper submitted by the French government and *Cour de cassation*; Danish Ministry for Economic and Business Affairs; Netherlands government and national competition authority; competent German federal ministry; UK government and national competition authority; Irish Competition Authority. Cf. Study, Ashurst (2004), p. 84, where it is observed that punitive damages are only available in certain cases for infringements of the competition rules in three Member States, namely the UK, Ireland and Cyprus.

111 Apart from the submissions by the competent German ministries and *Bundesrat* and the French government, see e.g. also the comments on the white paper submitted on behalf of Ireland, Luxembourg, Austria and Denmark.

112 Cf. Art. 81 TFEU on judicial cooperation in civil matters, discussed in para 10.49 below. At the time these latter matters were part of the "third pillar", which implied that different requirements for the adoption of any secondary EU law applied as compared with the "first pillar" provisions of the EU Treaties on competition

Many other public authorities generally did not respond outright negatively, however, and some spoke out in favour of an EU legislative initiative.[113] The European Parliament also expressed certain hesitation.[114] It requested clarification on the legal basis of any future legislative action and insisted on the use of the ordinary legislative procedure, meaning that it decides on a par with the Council on the proposed EU legislation.[115] Just like several other public authorities, it argued in favour of a consistent and horizontal approach on collective redress,[116] whereas it looked unfavourably upon the suggestion of giving binding effect to decisions by national competition authorities. The European Parliament further considered that rules on limitation periods (for stand-alone actions), quantification of damages and legal costs should be left to be regulated by national law. Notably, while it had initially urged the Commission to publish a white paper, in response to this latter document it did not expressly invite or encourage the Commission to submit a legislative proposal. Only in 2011 did it make a suggestion to this effect.[117]

6.20 In 2009 the Commission services set out to draft a directive on damages claims for infringements of EU competition law.[118] However, the resulting draft proposal for a directive never made it past the internal hurdles. That is to say, while this draft also circulated informally outside the Commission, it was never adopted by its College of Commissioners. Consequently, neither was it formally published, let alone discussed or adopted by the EU legislature. It is therefore important to note that, although it offers an interesting insight into the thinking of the Commission services at that point in time, this draft proposal is non-existent in formal terms.

In terms of content, the approach set out in this draft proposal was largely in line with the 2008 white paper. Its main objective would be to ensure that

---

(Art. 103 TFEU) or the internal market (Art. 114 TFEU). Since the entry into force of the Treaty of Lisbon in 2009, this pillar structure has been abolished, however.

113 See e.g. the comments on the white paper submitted by the Netherlands government as well as the Belgian, UK, Czech and Romanian competition authorities.

114 European Parliament, Resolution on the green paper on damages actions for breach of the EC antitrust rules, P6_TA(2007)0152; European Parliament, Resolution on the white paper on damages actions for breach of the EC antitrust rules, P6_TA(2009)0187. See also Economic and Social Committee, Opinion on the green paper damages actions for breach of EC antitrust rules, OJ 2006, C 324/1; Economic and Social Committee, Opinion on the white paper on damages actions for breach of the EC antitrust rules, OJ 2009, C 228/40.

115 Art. 289 TFEU.

116 On collective redress, see also subsection 5.E.2 above.

117 European Parliament, Resolution on the report on competition policy 2009, P7_TA(2011)0023, para 15.

118 Commission, Draft Proposal for a Council directive on the rules governing damages actions for infringements of Articles 81 and 82 of the Treaty. The text of this draft proposal has been published in Lowe and Marquis (2014) (see its Annex III). On this draft proposal, see also Alfaro and Reher (2010), p. 43; Cupa (2012), p. 524.

private parties could obtain full compensation for harm suffered as a consequence of infringements of Articles 101 and 102 TFEU. Punishing and deterring infringers would not be a primary objective, although deterrence would remain a welcome side effect. The draft further contained specific measures on the concept of full compensation (covering actual loss, loss of profit and interests); collective redress (either as a group action or as a representative action by a qualified entity, without that entity being required to individually identify the parties it represents but with a right of opt-out); the disclosure of evidence (by the parties to the proceedings and third parties, to be ordered by a national court upon the presentation of reasonably available facts and evidence and subject to certain conditions and exceptions, including for leniency statements); the argument that the applicant did not suffer any harm because the overcharge resulting from the anticompetitive behaviour was passed on to the applicant's own customers, known as the passing-on defence (permitted); the binding effect across the EU of final decisions by competition authorities (and review courts) finding an infringement; fault (rebuttable presumption of fault upon the establishment of an infringement); and limitation periods (which would not begin to run before the end of the infringement and which would not end until two years after the final decision by a national competition authority in follow-on cases).

The draft proposal was abandoned in the autumn of 2009, reportedly shortly before it was due to be adopted by the Commission. The reasons for this last-minute change of course remain unclear. The above-mentioned hesitation and opposition expressed by business organisations and certain Member States, in particular Germany, are widely believed to have played a role in this decision.[119] The same can probably be said of the potential for inter-institutional conflicts relating to the choice of legal basis, Article 103 TFEU, which implied that the European Parliament would only have had a consultative role in the legislative process,[120] as well as the need felt by many of the parties involved not to endanger the central role of public enforcement mechanisms.[121] Personnel changes within the College of Commissioners in 2009 may also have been a relevant factor.[122] In any case, after this aborted attempt, plans for such a directive were shelved for several years.

119 Cf. Chellel (2009); Milutinovic (2010), pp. 324–7; Vrcek (2010), pp. 277–8; Siragusa (2014), pp. 237–8.

120 Cf. e.g. Boylan (2009). On the legal basis issues arising in this connection, see para 6.27 below.

121 See e.g. Reich (2010), p. 119.

122 Then Commission president Mr Barroso was re-elected for a second term in office in September 2009. It has been suggested that this re-election was linked to developments (or rather the lack thereof) in respect of the present subject matter. See e.g. Micklitz (2011b), p. 102; Beumer and Karpetas (2012), p. 143 (n. 143); Hodges (2013), p. 72. Subsequently portfolios were redistributed within the Commission, including the nomination of a new Commissioner for competition policy (Mr Almunia replacing Ms Kroes). The new Commission formally took up its tasks on 1 February 2010.

4. *Pfleiderer* case law and proposal (2010–13)

6.21 Yet another important jurisprudential development – this time relating not so much to the right to claim damages as such, but rather to the interaction between public and private enforcement in this field – was arguably required to reanimate the project. For in 2011 the Court of Justice issued its ruling in *Pfleiderer*.[123] In this case, a German preliminary reference, the competent national competition authority had imposed fines on several undertakings for infringements of Article 101 TFEU. In the context of those public enforcement proceedings, some of these undertakings had submitted a leniency application to this authority. Pfleiderer AG was a customer of one of the infringing undertakings. With a view to preparing a claim for damages, it applied to the competition authority requesting full access to the case file, including the said leniency applications. After access had been refused, this private party appealed to the national court. The latter essentially asked the Court of Justice whether EU law precluded the granting of such access.

In its judgment the Court started by observing that there are no binding EU rules in respect of national leniency programmes or the right of access to documents related thereto. It is therefore in principle for the Member States to establish and apply such rules.[124] But these rules may not render the implementation of EU law impossible or excessively difficult and it must be ensured that the effective application of Articles 101 and 102 TFEU is not jeopardised. The Court noted in this connection that leniency programmes are useful tools to uncover and end competition law infringements that serve the objective of effective application of the said articles. It acknowledged that the effectiveness of these programmes could be compromised if documents related thereto were to be disclosed, because the possibility of such disclosure could deter undertakings from participating.[125] However, with reference to its *Courage* case law,[126] it also recalled that any private party has the right to claim damages for loss caused to him by an infringement of EU competition law and that the resulting actions for damages can make a significant contribution to the maintenance of effective competition.[127]

---

123 CoJ case C-360/09, *Pfleiderer*. Cf. Commission, Impact assessment report on damages actions for breach of the EU antitrust rules, SWD(2013) 203, pp. 13–14.

124 Ibid., para 19–23.

125 Ibid., para 24–7.

126 See para 6.14 and 6.15 above.

127 CoJ case C-360/09, *Pfleiderer*, para 28–9.

In this light the Court held that, apart from the application of the principles of equivalence and effectiveness,[128] it is necessary '*to weigh the respective interests in favour of disclosure of the information and in favour of the protection of that information provided voluntarily by the applicant of leniency*' and that '*[t]hat weighing exercise can be conducted by the national courts and tribunals only on a case-by-case basis, according to national law, and taking into account all the relevant factors in the case*'.[129] In so doing it chose a different route to the one outlined by Advocate General Mazák, who had essentially argued that self-incriminating statements made by leniency applicants should be protected from disclosure.[130] The Court instead found that EU law does not preclude giving access to the documents in question, but that it is for the national courts, on the basis of their national law, to determine the relevant conditions by weighing the interests protected under EU law.[131]

Two years later the Court of Justice built on this judgment in *Donau Chemie*.[132] **6.22**
This latter case also concerned a request by certain private parties to be granted access to the file of a national competition authority so as to gather the evidence needed to bring a damages claim. The applicable national (Austrian) legislation did not allow the national court seised to weigh the interests at stake. The national legislature had in effect itself decided to give priority to the interest associated with keeping documents relating to public enforcement proceedings confidential, making the disclosure subject to the consent of all parties concerned. The referring court's question to the Court of Justice was whether this legislation was to be considered compatible with EU law and in particular the principle of effectiveness.

The Court of Justice answered this question in the negative. It insisted that, pursuant to the principle of effectiveness, a national court must have the possibility of weighing up the respective interests in favour of and against disclosure. This weighing-up was held to be necessary because '*any rule that is rigid, either by providing for absolute refusal to grant access to the documents in question or for granting access to those documents as a matter of course, is liable to undermine the effective application of, inter alia, Article 101 TFEU and the rights that provision confers on individuals*'.[133] On the one hand, where the parties adversely affected by the infringement have no other way of obtaining the evidence needed to establish their claim, in the Court's view a refusal to grant

128 On these two principles, see subsections 2.A.2 and 2.A.3 above.
129 CoJ case C-360/09, *Pfleiderer*, para 30–31.
130 Opinion AG Mazák case C-360/09, *Pfleiderer*, para 44.
131 CoJ case C-360/09, *Pfleiderer*, para 32.
132 CoJ case C-536/11, *Donau Chemie*.
133 Ibid., para 31.

them access renders nugatory the right to compensation under EU law. On the other hand, it held that generalised access is not necessary and could harm the legitimate interests of the undertakings concerned (for example relating to their right to protection of business secrets) and the general interest (by deterring undertakings from cooperation with public enforcement authorities).[134] Specifically as regards documents relating to leniency programmes, the Court acknowledged both the importance of these programmes and the possibility that undertakings will be deterred by the possibility of disclosure. But this was not seen as sufficient to systematically refuse all access to such documents. Given the importance of actions for damages, a mere abstract risk of undermining the effectiveness of leniency programmes was found not to suffice. Instead it was held that for non-disclosure to be justified there must be overriding reasons relating to each specific document, that is, a risk that disclosure of that particular document would actually undermine the public interest relating to the effectiveness of leniency programmes.[135]

6.23 Just a few days after the Court issued its ruling in *Donau Chemie*, the Commission published its proposal for the Competition Damages Directive.[136] Whilst the content of this proposal is discussed, where relevant, in the following section together with the text of the directive, it merits being noted at this stage that in many respects this proposal is a continuation of the line that was set out in the aforementioned documents.[137] It aims to ensure that parties having suffered harm as a consequence of infringements of the EU competition rules can obtain full compensation.[138] The Commission acknowledged that there had been '*some recent signs of improvement in a few Member States*'.[139] For several Member States had adopted specific rules or were contemplating (further) amendments to their national laws relating to actions for damages for competition law infringements. For example, Hungarian competition law now provides for a rebuttable presumption that (hard-core) cartels lead to an illegal overcharge of 10 per cent.[140] A rise in the number of damages actions brought was also observed, while noting, however, that the vast majority of large actions of this kind are brought in just three Member States, namely the United Kingdom,

134 Ibid., para 32–3.
135 Ibid., para 40–48.
136 Commission, Proposal for Competition Damages Directive 2014/104, COM(2013) 404. See also Commission, Impact assessment report on damages actions for breach of the EU antitrust rules, SWD(2013) 203.
137 That is, the 2005 green paper, the 2008 white paper and the 2009 draft proposal, discussed in subsection 6.B.3 above.
138 Commission, Proposal for Competition Damages Directive 2014/104, COM(2013) 404, p. 3.
139 Ibid., p. 4.
140 Commission, Impact assessment report on damages actions for breach of the EU antitrust rules, SWD(2013) 203, p. 17 (and its Annex 3). On this Hungarian law, see further Nagy (2011), p. 63. Note that this law establishes a (rebuttable) presumption of a price increase as a consequence of the competition law infringement in question, which is not necessarily the same as the amount of harm suffered.

Germany and the Netherlands.[141] The Commission therefore found that the situation had not significantly changed in this respect since 2005.[142] In its view '*a clear deficit in terms of compensatory justice*' remained.[143] This was attributed to the obstacles resulting from the applicable national laws that were mentioned earlier.[144]

Yet there are certain noticeable differences in the general approach followed by the Commission. In particular, apart from the aforementioned obstacles that private party applicants are said to encounter, the proposal also emphasised the *diversity* in the rules of national law that regulate actions for damages for infringements of the EU competition rules. This diversity was said to lead to legal uncertainty and "uneven enforcement" of the EU right to compensation and therefore to competitive advantages for some undertakings and distortions of the internal market.[145] The proposal thus aims not only to shift the costs away from the victims and to act as an incentive for better compliance, but it also seeks to contribute to a more level playing field.[146] In addition, optimising the *interaction between public and private enforcement* was no longer one issue to be addressed among several others in the context of the overall objective of ensuring full compensation for injured parties, as was the case earlier. The proposal instead identified this as a second objective in its own right, on a par with ensuring full compensation for aggrieved private parties.[147] This was said to be due to '*a new issue*' that showed that '*the EU right to compensation can sometimes be at odds with the effectiveness of public enforcement of the EU*'.[148] This refers to the aforementioned *Pfleiderer* ruling.[149] Whilst admitting that there was no evidence that this ruling has had or will have a negative impact on the functioning of leniency programmes operated by the competent public enforcement authorities, it was thought to have led to uncertainty. For where there is a case-by-case assessment on questions of disclosure, an undertaking does not know in advance with certainty whether or not its leniency application will be

141 Ibid., p. 19.

142 Commission, Proposal for Competition Damages Directive 2014/104, COM(2013) 404, p. 4; Commission, Impact assessment report on damages actions for breach of the EU antitrust rules, SWD(2013) 203, p. 18. On these earlier documents and the above-mentioned obstacles, see subsection 6.B.3 above.

143 Commission, Impact assessment report on damages actions for breach of the EU antitrust rules, SWD(2013) 203, p. 15.

144 Commission, Proposal for Competition Damages Directive 2014/104, COM(2013) 404, p. 4.

145 Ibid.; Commission, Impact assessment report on damages actions for breach of the EU antitrust rules, SWD(2013) 203, pp. 18–20.

146 Commission, Proposal for Competition Damages Directive 2014/104, COM(2013) 404, p. 4. See also Commission, Impact assessment report on damages actions for breach of the EU antitrust rules, SWD(2013) 203, pp. 15–20.

147 Ibid., pp. 3–4.

148 Commission, Impact assessment report on damages actions for breach of the EU antitrust rules, SWD(2013) 203, p. 5.

149 CoJ case C-360/09, *Pfleiderer*. See para 6.21 above.

disclosed. According to the Commission, this could negatively affect the willingness of undertakings to cooperate with the competent public enforcement authorities in the context of the leniency programmes and thus the effectiveness of public enforcement of EU competition law as such.[150]

It is noticeable that many observers considered that the degree of damages litigation for infringements of competition law (predominantly follow-on actions) has been increasing over the past years, not only in the few Member States to which the Commission referred but also in the EU more generally.[151] The view was further broadly shared that "post-*Pfleiderer*" the tension between actions for damages for competition law infringements and leniency programmes indeed needed to be addressed at EU level so as to preserve the effectiveness of these programmes.[152] The Commission proposal itself was on the whole received in cautiously favourable terms in the legal literature; criticism concerned mainly the generally rather modest degree of detail and the related concerns that some uncertainty and divergences might persist after its adoption.[153]

C. COMPETITION DAMAGES DIRECTIVE

In this section the Competition Damages Directive is discussed. The first subsection below addresses a number of general (and interrelated) issues concerning its adoption, objectives, scope and legal basis. The following subsection concentrates on the directive's principal (substantive) remedy, namely actions for damages, and the rules directly relating thereto regarding the qualification and quantification of the harm caused by the infringements at issue. Attention then turns to the measures related to the disclosure of evidence,

150 Commission, Impact assessment report on damages actions for breach of the EU antitrust rules, SWD(2013) 203, pp. 12–15 and 28.

151 See e.g. Barone and Amore (2010), p. 346; Jalabert-Doury (2010), p. 316; Milutinovic (2010), p. 346; Danov and Becker (2013), p. 77; Danov and Dnes (2013), p. 51; Kammin and Becker (2013), p. 61; Hodges (2013), p. 71; Wils (2013), p. 6; Guttuso (2014), p. 12; Laurila and Kalliokoski (2014), p. 519; Ratliff (2014), p. 272.

152 See e.g. Nascimbene (2013), p. 269; Campbell and Feunteun (2014), pp. 34 and 38; Burrichter and Ahlenstiel (2014), p. 103; Hummer and Cywinski (2014), pp. 117–18; Kumar Singh (2014), p. 117; Milutinovic (2014), p. 363; Pietrini (2014), p. 262; Ratliff (2014), p. 287; Silva Morais (2014), p. 128. See also Heads of the European competition authorities, Resolution on the protection of leniency materials in the context of civil damages actions, 23 May 2012. See, however, also Danov and Dnes (2013), pp. 56 and 59, where it is suggested that the possible friction between increasing numbers of actions for damages and leniency programmes may be overstated to some degree.

153 See e.g. Batchelor, Pike and Ghiorghies (2013), p. 165; Gamble (2013), pp. 619–20; Babirad (2013), p. 160; Bentley and Henry (2014), p. 271; Guttuso (2014), pp. 20–22; Howard (2014), pp. 53 and 55; Louis (2014), p. 90; Milutinovic (2014), p. 376; Nordlander and Abenhaïm (2014), pp. 7–8; Silva Morais (2014), pp. 137–8; Stauber (2014), p. 38; Wisking, Dietzel and Herron (2014), p. 185. For a critical assessment, see in particular Kumar Singh (2014), pp. 120–22; Weidt (2014), p. 438.

followed by a discussion of the rules on joint and several liability, the passing-on defence and the position of indirect purchasers. The last subsection examines the directive's relevant provisions of a procedural nature.

1. General issues

Even when excluding the discussions on a possible legislative initiative on the private enforcement of EU competition law that took place in the 1980s and 1990s,[154] the Competition Damages Directive has been a long time in the making.[155] But after an incubation time of almost a decade (taking the 2005 green paper as the starting point), the actual law-making process was relatively speedy. Less than a year elapsed between the publication of the Commission proposal in June 2013 and the political agreement that was reached in March 2014, which was followed by the adoption of the directive in November 2014. The Member States are required to transpose the directive into national law by the end of December 2016.[156] Although several important changes were made in the course of the legislative process (discussed in further detail below), the main features of the Commission's proposal remained unaltered. The end result has been described as '*a finely-tuned compromise that goes to the limits of the flexibility of the co-legislators*'.[157] **6.24**

Although a range of factors is likely to have played a role, three elements stand out when seeking to explain the fact that, after having proved controversial at an earlier stage, the Competition Damages Directive was in the end adopted rather speedily.[158] First, there is the 2011 *Pfleiderer judgment*, which led to the protection of the effectiveness of public enforcement (especially leniency programmes) being elevated as an objective in its own right on a par with the actual facilitation of private enforcement.[159] This meant that those that consider the public enforcement of EU competition law to be of particular importance now also had a stake in seeing this directive adopted. The second factor relates to the *position of the European Parliament*. As is explained below, a solution was found for the question relating to the involvement of this institution in the legislative process, ensuring that it could co-decide together with the Council.[160] The upcoming elections for the European Parliament in May 2014 probably gave the negotiations on the draft directive an (extra) sense of urgency.

154 See subsection 6.B.1 above.
155 Competition Damages Directive 2014/104.
156 Art. 21(1) Competition Damages Directive 2014/104.
157 Council, doc. 8088/14.
158 Cf. Hodges (2013), pp. 74–5.
159 CoJ case C-360/09, *Pfleiderer*. See para 6.21 above.
160 See para 6.27 below.

Lastly, the Commission and with it the EU legislature *moderated their ambitions*. Several issues that had earlier been identified as obstacles but that had also proved controversial were excluded from this legislative initiative, especially, for example, possible EU rules on collective redress, which are instead addressed in a more horizontal (and not legally binding) manner in the Collective Redress Recommendation.[161] But the same can be said of fault requirements, which are only briefly mentioned in the recitals,[162] and legal costs, which had already been excluded at an earlier stage.[163] The issue of the causal relationship between the infringement and the harm is also left unaddressed in the directive.[164]

6.25 In line with the Commission's proposal the Competition Damages Directive has two objectives.[165] Its first objective is to ensure that anyone who has suffered harm caused by an infringement of the relevant rules of competition law can effectively exercise the right to claim *full compensation* for that harm and to ensure the proper functioning of the internal market by ensuring equivalent protection throughout the EU for anyone who has suffered such harm.[166] In addition, in the aftermath of the aforementioned *Pfleiderer* case law, the directive seeks to *coordinate the public and private enforcement* of the competition rules in so far as actions for damages before national courts are concerned.[167] Speaking of "coordination" (or "interaction"[168]) between public and private enforcement seems in fact somewhat of a euphemism. The measures taken in connection with this second objective essentially determine the degree to which the private enforcement possibilities provided for are to be limited so as to safeguard the effectiveness of the existing public enforcement mechanisms.[169]

---

161 See recital 13 Competition Damages Directive 2014/104: '*This Directive should not require Member States to introduce collective redress mechanisms for the enforcement of Articles 101 and 102 [TFEU]*'. See further Commission, Impact assessment report on damages actions for breach of the EU antitrust rules, SWD(2013) 203, p. 55. On Collective Redress Recommendation 2013/396 see subsection 5.E.2 above. This exclusion of collective redress from Competition Damages Directive 2014/104 has been perceived as the Commission '*bend[ing] to the will of industry*'. See Marquis (2014), p. xx.

162 See recital 11 Competition Damages Directive 2014/104, which states that '*[w]here Member States provide other conditions for compensation under national law, such as imputability, adequacy or culpability, they should be able to maintain such conditions in as far as they comply with the case law of the Court of Justice, the principles of effectiveness and equivalence, and this Directive*'. See para 7.06 and 7.07 below.

163 Already in its 2008 white paper the Commission had limited itself to "inviting" Member States to "reflect" on their rules on legal costs and the allocation thereof between the parties to the proceedings. See Commission, White paper on damages actions for breach of the EC antitrust rules, pp. 9–10. See also para 8.31 below.

164 See recital 11 Competition Damages Directive 2014/104.

165 See para 6.23 above. See also recital 54 Competition Damages Directive 2014/104.

166 Art. 1(1) Competition Damages Directive 2014/104.

167 Art. 1(2) Competition Damages Directive 2014/104. On the above-mentioned case law, see para 6.21 and 6.22 above.

168 Cf. recital 6 Competition Damages Directive 2014/104. See also Commission, Proposal for Competition Damages Directive 2014/104, COM(2013) 404, p. 3.

169 See in particular Art. 6 and 11 Competition Damages Directive 2014/104, discussed in para 6.33 and 6.36 below, concerning the non-disclosure of certain documents and the limits to the joint and several liability of

It might therefore be more accurate to speak of the "protecting" or "preserving the central role" of public enforcement, as the Commission did earlier.[170] In any case it follows from this second objective that the directive does not wholeheartedly seek to facilitate private enforcement, but that it also restricts the possibilities to do so in some respects.

The main point to note as regards the scope of the Competition Damages Directive is that it covers not only infringements of substantive *EU* competition law, that is, Articles 101 and 102 TFEU, but that it also covers certain rules of substantive *national* competition law. Not all rules of national competition law are covered, however. The measures set out in the directive relate to only those provisions of national competition law that '*predominantly pursue the same objective as Articles 101 and 102 TFEU and that are applied to the same case and in parallel to [EU] competition law pursuant to Article 3(1) of [the Competition Regulation]*'.[171] **6.26**

This inclusion of certain rules of national competition law, which is in line with the Commission's proposal, can be seen as somewhat of a surprise.[172] For the 2005 green paper, the 2008 white paper and the 2009 draft proposal were all concerned only with the private enforcement of *EU* competition law.[173] Not even the possibility of such an extension to also cover national law had been suggested there; neither was this issue raised in the subsequent comments by stakeholders on these earlier documents.[174] Neither does this extended scope seem immediately evident in light of the fact that the Court's *Courage* case law, on which the directive builds in many respects,[175] linked a private party's right to compensation under EU law only to the effectiveness of the EU competition rules. The directive's recitals explain this approach by pointing out that otherwise the position of applicants would be adversely affected by the application in the same case of diverging rules on civil liability for infringements of EU and national competition law, which is seen as constituting an obstacle to the proper

infringers, respectively. See also its Art. 9, discussed in para 6.41 below, on the effects of infringement decisions by national competition authorities in proceedings before national courts (but not *vice versa*). See also Milutinovic (2015), pp. 6–11.

170 See Commission, Impact assessment report on damages actions for breach of the EU antitrust rules, SWD(2013) 203, p. 25; Commission, Work programme 2012 (annex), COM(2011) 777, p. 3.

171 Art. 2(3) Competition Damages Directive 2014/104. There it is added that this does not include national laws which impose criminal penalties on national persons except to the extent that such penalties are the means whereby competition rules applying to undertakings are enforced. As regards this parallel application pursuant to Art. 3(1) Competition Regulation 1/2003, see also para 6.04 above.

172 Cf. Milutinovic (2014), pp. 368 and 374.

173 As is, for example, evident from the titles of these three documents, which all refer only to the EU (then: EC) competition rules. On these documents, see further subsection 6.B.3 above.

174 See para 6.19 above.

175 On the *Courage* case law and its relevance in this connection, see further para 6.14–6.16 above.

functioning of the internal market.[176] According to the Commission, this would have made it unworkable for judges to handle a case and it would have led to legal uncertainty and possibly conflicting results, depending on whether the case is considered as relating to an infringement of the EU or of national competition law.[177] Actions for damages for infringements of national competition law that do not affect trade between the Member States within the meaning of Articles 101 and 102 TFEU remain unaffected, however.[178]

6.27 The Competition Damages Directive rests on a *dual* legal basis, namely Articles 103 and 114 TFEU. The choice of Article 103 TFEU seems unsurprising. This provision allows in its first paragraph for the adoption of '*appropriate regulations or directives to give effect to the principles set out in Articles 101 and 102 [TFEU]*'. Although private enforcement is not among the possible measures specifically mentioned in its second paragraph, both the broad formulation of the first paragraph and the non-exhaustive character of its second paragraph appear to make this provision in principle a sufficient legal basis. Before the adoption of this directive, it was widely agreed that this provision seemed the most appropriate legal basis for a legislative initiative on the private enforcement of EU competition law.[179] It was also the legal basis cited in the draft proposal for a directive that the Commission services prepared in 2009.[180] By contrast, adding Article 114 TFEU, which empowers the EU to legislate when necessary for the purposes of its internal market, seems less obvious. For one thing, it is settled case law that a dual legal basis is only to be used exceptionally, and even then only on the condition that the legislative procedures for the adoption of the act in question prescribed by the articles concerned are not incompatible.[181] For another thing, the "internal market dimension" of the private enforcement of competition law was a theme that received only comparatively little attention in the Commission's earlier official documents and the associated consultations.[182] It was only in the Commission's 2013 proposal that this issue was given emphasis.[183] In line with the reasoning set out in this proposal, the recitals of the Competition Damages Directive explain that the divergences between

176 Recital 10 Competition Damages Directive 2014/104.

177 Commission, Proposal for Competition Damages Directive 2014/104, COM(2013) 404, pp. 12–13.

178 Recital 10 Competition Damages Directive 2014/104.

179 Van Gerven (2003a), p. 410; Eilmansberger (2007), pp. 440–41; Komninos (2008), pp. 180–81; Milutinovic (2010), pp. 315–19. Specifically in relation to collective redress for competition law infringements, see also Leskinen (2011), p. 113; European Parliament, Study on collective redress in antitrust, June 2012, p. 60; Buccirossi and Carpagnano (2013), p. 9.

180 See para 6.20 above.

181 E.g. CoJ case C-155/07, *Parliament v Council*, para 35–7 and 76–85; CoJ case C-130/10, *Parliament v Council*, para 43–7.

182 See subsection 6.B.3 above.

183 See para 6.23 above.

the pre-existing rules of the Member States in this regard lead to uncertainty, an uneven playing field and uneven enforcement of the right to compensation.[184]

The explanatory memorandum accompanying the proposal for this directive goes to considerable length in further explaining this choice for this dual legal basis. It is said there that the directive pursues '*two equally important goals which are inextricably linked*', namely: (a) giving full effect to Articles 101 and 102 TFEU; and (b) ensuring a more level playing field for undertakings operating in the internal market and making it easier for citizens and businesses to make use of the rights that they derive from the internal market.[185] Article 103 TFEU alone was considered not to be sufficient, in particular because, while that provision only allows for the adoption of measures giving effect to *EU* competition law, the directive also covers certain rules of *national* competition law, as was noted above. According to the Commission, the latter above-mentioned objective is not merely ancillary to the former and there is an indissociable link between them and the measures that they entail. On that basis, the view is taken that the directive is to be based on Article 114 as well as on Article 103 TFEU.[186]

This explanation for the choice of legal basis for the Competition Damages Directive seems reasonable enough in itself.[187] Yet there may also be an additional element that helps explain this choice. For the legal basis chosen for an act of secondary EU law also determines which *legislative procedure* is to be followed when adopting that act, and therefore the degree of involvement of the European Parliament in that procedure. In the present context the European Parliament had long insisted on its being allowed to decide on a par with its co-legislator, the Council, under the ordinary legislative procedure.[188] Article 103(1) TFEU prescribes that the Council acts alone and gives the European Parliament only a consultative role. Article 114(1) TFEU, in contrast, provides for the use of the ordinary legislative procedure. Adding this latter article as a second legal basis thus provided a justification for using the ordinary legislative procedure when adopting the Competition Damages Directive. The aforementioned somewhat surprising extension of the initiative's scope so as also to cover certain rules of national competition law, which in turn necessitated the use of Article 114 and the ordinary legislative procedure that it prescribes, should therefore perhaps (also) be seen in this light.[189] None of this necessarily

184 See recitals 7–9 Competition Damages Directive 2014/104.
185 Commission, Proposal for Competition Damages Directive 2014/104, COM(2013) 404, p. 8.
186 Ibid., pp. 9–10.
187 Cf. e.g. Cauffmann (2013), p. 634.
188 See para 6.19 above.
189 In a similar sense, see Milutinovic (2014), p. 375; Milutinovic (2015), p. 12.

leads to the conclusion that this choice of legal basis is incompatible with the EU Treaties.[190] However, it does mean that the directive's legality in this respect relies on the correctness of the assumptions that this is indeed a case where: (a) exceptionally a dual legal basis can be used, because the two cited objectives and the measures corresponding thereto are inseparably linked, without one being ancillary to the other; and (b) the two distinct legislative procedures prescribed by the two above-mentioned articles are not incompatible. The fact that legal basis issues were a matter of debate in the course of the legislative process, in particular in the Council, suggests that there is scope for debate on these points, even if the Council eventually concluded that the dual legal basis proposed by the Commission could be retained.[191]

2. Actions for damages, qualification and quantification

6.28 Much of the discussion over the past decade on what was to become the Competition Damages Directive took place under the broad banner of the "private enforcement" of EU competition law generally. However, this directive concentrates on only one main (substantive) private enforcement remedy, namely actions for damages. Its recitals confirm that this remedy is an '*example*' and '*only one element of an effective system of private enforcement*'.[192] This focus on actions for damages was not always apparent when the possible facilitation of private enforcement of EU competition law was discussed at an earlier stage.[193] Only more recently have actions for damages become the '*legal and political fashion*' in this domain.[194] Indeed, all of the documents discussed above – ranging from the Commission's 2005 green paper up to its 2013 proposal – acknowledged, on the one hand, that other remedies could also play a role in this respect, but concentrated, on the other hand, solely on this particular remedy.[195]

190 The EU legislature generally has considerable scope in determining the aim and content of an act of secondary EU law in light of which the choice of legal basis for that act is to be assessed. See para 10.01 below.

191 See Council, doc. 16176/13, which concerns an opinion of the Council's legal service on the choice of legal basis of the draft directive (which was at the time of writing only partially accessible to the public). On this opinion see also Crofts (2013), p. 1. See e.g. also Council, doc. 15979/13, p. 2; Council, doc. 15983/13, p. 2. See also European Parliament, Study on collective redress in antitrust, June 2012, p. 60, where doubts are expressed with regard to the compatibility of the two legislative procedures at hand.

192 Recitals 3 and 5 Competition Damages Directive 2014/104 respectively.

193 See subsection 6.B.1 above.

194 Milutinovic (2010), p. 143.

195 See Commission, Green paper on damages actions for breach of the EC antitrust rules, COM(2005) 672, p. 3; Commission, Staff working paper accompanying the green paper on damages actions for breach of EC antitrust rules, SEC(2005) 1732, p. 9 Commission, Staff working paper accompanying the white paper on damages actions for breach of the EC antitrust rules, SEC(2008) 404, p. 7 (n. 5); Commission, Impact assessment report on damages actions for breach of the EU antitrust rules, SWD(2013) 203, p. 12. In Commission, Proposal for Competition Damages Directive 2014/104, COM(2013) 404, p. 2, it is simply said

The Competition Damages Directive expressly lays down and details further the right to "full compensation". It is stated that the Member States must ensure that '*any natural or legal person who has suffered harm caused by an infringement of competition law is able to claim and obtain full compensation for that harm*'.[196] Here it is also explained that such full compensation entails placing the person concerned in the position that that person would have been in had the infringement not been committed. According to the directive, three heads of damages are '*therefore*' covered, namely compensation for actual loss, loss of profit and interest.[197] The recitals explain that this is meant as a "reaffirmation" of the case law of the Court of Justice.[198] The Commission had held earlier that such a codification increases legal certainty and awareness.[199] Specifically as regards the obligation to compensate interest, the recitals add that this is without prejudice to the qualification of such interest as compensatory or default interest and to whether the effluxion of time is taken into account as a separate category or rather as part of the actual loss or loss of profit.[200] The clarification proposed by the Commission that it concerns '*interest from the time the harm occurred until the compensation in respect of that harm has actually been paid*'[201] was not retained by the EU legislature, however. Although the directive does not mention this expressly, the Commission appears to consider that non-material damage is compensable as well.[202] 6.29

The directive further stipulates that full compensation under this directive shall not lead to overcompensation, whether by means of punitive, multiple or other types of damages.[203] This too is a deviation from the proposal, which contained no such provision. The Commission had agreed that certain safeguards ought to be provided for, but it had also held that no risk of "overcompensation" had occurred in the Member States.[204] This provision is in line with the position expressed by many respondents to the earlier consultations and by the European

that damages claims are '*an important area of private enforcement of EU competition law*'. On the possibilities of injunctive relief in a competition law context, see para 7.33 below.

196 Art. 3(1) Competition Damages Directive 2014/104.

197 Art. 3(2) Competition Damages Directive 2014/104.

198 Recital 12 Competition Damages Directive 2014/104. Presumably this refers in particular to CoJ joined cases C-295/04 to C-298/04, *Manfredi*, para 95–7, discussed in para 6.15 above. Cf. Commission, Proposal for Competition Damages Directive 2014/104, COM(2013) 404, pp. 4 and 13; Commission, Staff working paper accompanying the white paper on damages actions for breach of the EC antitrust rules, SEC(2008) 404, pp. 56–9.

199 Commission, White paper on damages actions for breach of the EC antitrust rules, COM(2008) 165, p. 7.

200 Recital 12 Competition Damages Directive 2014/104.

201 Commission, Proposal for Competition Damages Directive 2014/104, COM(2013) 404, p. 31 (Art. 2(2)).

202 Ibid., p. 13.

203 Art. 4(3) Competition Damages Directive 2014/104.

204 Commission, Impact assessment report on damages actions for breach of the EU antitrust rules, SWD(2013) 203, p. 18. See also its p. 26, where it is noted that a trade-off exists between a higher chance of full compensation and a risk of overcompensation.

Parliament.[205] It appears that accordingly this provision was inserted particularly at the insistence of this latter institution.[206]

The directive also codifies the principles of equivalence and effectiveness in relation to the damages actions covered by the directive.[207]

6.30 The Competition Damages Directive states that *quantifying* the harm caused to the private parties concerned as a result of the infringements covered is '*a very fact-intensive process and may require the application of complex economic models*', which is said to be '*often very costly*' and the cause of '*difficulties [for claimants] in obtaining the necessary data to substantiate their claims*' and therefore a '*substantial barrier preventing effective claims for compensation*'.[208] The view that such quantification is in practice often both difficult and important in the present context is widely shared.[209] Against this background the Competition Damages Directive sets out the following four specific measures in an attempt to address the difficulties that aggrieved private parties might experience when attempting to obtain full compensation for competition law infringements.

In the first place, the Member States must ensure that the *burden and the standard of proof* required for the quantification of the harm caused are not such as to render the exercise of the right to damages practically impossible or excessively difficult.[210] This is in effect a restatement of the EU law principle of effectiveness that would otherwise have applied anyway in the absence of more specific EU rules.[211] The second measure is that the national court must be empowered to *estimate* the amount of this harm.[212] This is meant to take account of the fact that the quantification of the harm is by definition a hypothetical exercise which cannot be made with complete accuracy.[213] Most (although not all) national jurisdictions already provided for the possibility of *ex aequo et bono* determination or similar ways of leaving the national court seised

205 See para 6.19 above.

206 European Parliament, Report on the proposal for Competition Damages Directive 2014/104, A7–0089/2014, p. 17 (Art. 2(2a)). Cf. Milutinovic (2015), p. 15.

207 Art. 4 Competition Damages Directive 2014/104. On these two principles, see further subsections 2.A.2 and 2.A.3 above.

208 Recital 45 Competition Damages Directive 2014/104. On issues of quantification, see also Commission, White paper on damages actions for breach of the EC antitrust rules, COM(2008) 165, p. 7; Commission, Staff working paper accompanying the white paper on damages actions for breach of the EC antitrust rules, SEC(2008) 404, pp. 60–61.

209 See e.g. Komninos (2008), p. 210; Whish and Bailey (2012), p. 311; Calisti and Haasbeek (2013), p. 5; Danov and Becker (2013), p. 79; Butz (2014), p. 331. See, however, also Wisking, Dietzel and Herron (2014), p. 190, who note that experience in the UK shows that damages can be assessed without significant issues.

210 Art. 17(1) Competition Damages Directive 2014/104.

211 On this principle, see subsection 2.A.3 above. See also recital 46 Competition Damages Directive 2014/104.

212 Art. 17(1) Competition Damages Directive 2014/104.

213 Recital 46 Competition Damages Directive 2014/104.

some leeway in determining the amount of damages.[214] Different from the Commission's proposal,[215] this obligation under the directive is qualified in two ways, however, as it is to take place in accordance with national procedures and it must be practically impossible or excessively difficult to precisely quantify the harm suffered.

In the third place, the directive provides for a *rebuttable presumption* that cartel infringements cause harm.[216] This provision rests on findings that in practice the great majority of these infringements do indeed lead to harm being caused.[217] From the side of the European Parliament, it had initially been criticised for being '*a generalisation of reality which is not entirely accurate*',[218] but this provision was in the end retained nonetheless. The reference made to cartels implies that this rule is not applicable in relation to other competition law infringements covered by this directive.[219] This is in fact not a rule on quantification properly speaking, as it merely provides *that* harm was caused rather than that it relates to the question *how much* harm was caused.[220] Crucially, neither does it indicate *to whom* the harm was caused. That seems to imply that each individual applicant must still demonstrate that it suffered harm.[221] The fourth and last measure on quantification provided for in the directive is new as compared with the Commission's proposal, although it had been suggested earlier in the legal literature.[222] It concerns the possibility for *national competition authorities* to *assist* national courts regarding the determination of the quantum of damages.[223] While the directive obliges the Member States to create this possibility, it also specifies that this is to occur upon request by the court and only where the authority concerned deems this appropriate. Somewhat similar arrangements already existed in some Member States, such as Spain and Finland.[224]

214 Commission, Staff working paper accompanying the green paper on damages actions for breach of EC antitrust rules, SEC(2005) 1732, p. 40. See also Study, Ashurst (2004), pp. 70–71; Study, CEPS, Erasmus University Rotterdam and LUISS (2007), pp. 451–2.

215 Commission, Proposal for the Competition Damages Directive 2014/104, COM(2013) 404, p. 39 (Art. 16(2)).

216 Art. 17(2) Competition Damages Directive 2014/104.

217 See para 6.07 above.

218 European Parliament, Draft report on the proposal for Competition Damages Directive 2014/104, 2013/0185(COD), p. 47. See also Batchelor, Pike and Ghiorghies (2013), p. 164.

219 The term "cartel" is defined in Art. 2(14) Competition Damages Directive 2014/104. Its recital 47 explains that this limitation to cartels is considered justified in light of the secretive nature of cartels, which makes it more difficult for applicants to obtain the necessary evidence.

220 Cf. recital 47 Competition Damages Directive 2014/104. Cf. Calisti and Haasbeek (2013), p. 5.

221 Cf. Council, doc. 8088/14, p. 12.

222 See e.g. Rüggeberg and Schinkel (2006), pp. 407–18. See also Study, CEPS, Erasmus University Rotterdam and LUISS, pp. 200–201.

223 Art. 17(3) Competition Damages Directive 2014/104.

224 Komninos (2014), p. 155 (describing this as a '*well-intended but flawed idea*').

The above four measures should, moreover, be understood in their broader context. In particular, the directive's measures on the disclosure of evidence (discussed below[225]) can be of importance in relation to the quantification of the harm caused by a competition law infringement. This can allow an applicant to obtain the information necessary for him to be able to adequately substantiate his claim where issues of quantification are concerned. Furthermore in 2013, together with its proposal for the Competition Damages Directive, the Commission issued non-legally binding guidance.[226] This includes a practical guide that aims to assist national courts and parties involved in actions for damages for competition law infringements by outlining economic and practical insights that may be of use when quantifying the harm caused by competition law infringements.[227] The guide sets out various methods and techniques that can be used to establish as precisely as possible what would probably have happened had the infringement not occurred, for instance in terms of the development of prices. On the basis of such a counterfactual scenario, a comparison can be made with what actually happened. The difference can thus possibly serve as a yardstick to determine the extent of the harm caused that needs to be compensated.

3. Measures on the disclosure of evidence

6.31 One of the key elements of the Competition Damages Directive is a set of measures relating to the disclosure, preservation and use of evidence in the context of the actions for damages covered. Before the adoption of the directive the great majority of the Member States already provided for the possibility of some form of disclosure of evidence in private enforcement proceedings.[228] But these rules were often interpreted in a restrictive manner, making disclosure difficult in practice, as reportedly occurred, for instance, in Italy, the Netherlands and Spain.[229] Moreover, in many Member States, such as Germany, France and the Czech Republic, only specifically designated pieces of evidence (as opposed to entire categories of evidence) were disclosable.[230] Rules on the involvement of third parties and the disclosure of evidence included in the file

---

225 See subsection 6.C.3 below.

226 Cf. recital 46 Competition Damages Directive 2014/104, where it is said that the Commission should provide general guidance at EU level in order to ensure coherence and predictability.

227 Commission, Practical guide on quantifying harm in actions for damages based on breaches of Article 101 and 102 TFEU, SWD(2013) 205. See also Commission, Communication on quantifying harm in actions for damages based on breaches of Articles 101 and 102 TFEU, OJ 2013, C 167/19.

228 Ibid., p. 17. See also Study, Ashurst (2004), pp. 61–5; Study, CEPS, Erasmus University Rotterdam and LUISS (2007), pp. 345–57.

229 Barone and Amore (2010), p. 355; Callol (2010), p. 388; Lunsingh Scheurleer *et al.* (2010), p. 372; Siragusa (2014), p. 254.

230 See e.g. Jalabert-Doury (2010), pp. 318 and 338; Uřičař (2011), p. 144; Stauber (2014), p. 32.

of competition authorities also differed across the EU. According to the Commission, this thus constituted '*the primary example of divergence*', while holding that many of these national rules are inadequate to guarantee effective access to evidence.[231] The directive's disclosure regime could only be agreed after '*intense negotiations*' between the two EU co-legislators.[232] While the main features of the Commission's proposal remain intact, it was considerably altered during the legislative process.[233]

In essence this regime reflects an effort to reconcile two conflicting considerations, leading to what has been called a '*Faustian dilemma*'.[234] On the one hand, the litigation at issue here is said to typically require a complex factual and economic analysis, notably as regards establishing the infringement, quantifying the damage caused and establishing causality, and to be characterised by an "information asymmetry".[235] This refers to much of the relevant evidence often being in the possession of the defendant and third parties, without its being sufficiently known or accessible to the private party applicant. The crucial importance of adequate access to evidence is widely agreed.[236] All this thus points to a need to provide for rules on the disclosure of evidence that are, seen from the point of view of the (potential) applicant, generally *permissive*. On the other hand, the disclosure of certain items of evidence included in the file of a competition authority (that is, the Commission or a national authority[237]) is considered to be potentially harmful for the public enforcement of the rules at issue.[238] That applies in particular for leniency statements and settlement submissions, in which undertakings confess or agree not to contest their infringements with a view to obtaining immunity from fines or ending the public enforcement proceedings respectively.[239] This thus corresponds to the directive's second objective, coordinating public and private enforcement. As

231 Commission, Practical guide on quantifying harm in actions for damages based on breaches of Article 101 and 102 TFEU, SWD(2013) 205, p. 19.

232 Council, doc. 8088/14, p. 5.

233 See Commission, Proposal for Competition Damages Directive 2014/104, COM(2013) 404, pp. 33–5 (Art. 5–8).

234 Völcker (2012), p. 695. On this tension, see further e.g. Canenbley and Steinvorth (2011), p. 315; Cauffman (2011a), p. 181; Rizzuto (2012), p. 1; Beumer and Karpetas (2012), p. 123; Ortega González (2014), p. 117. For a (critical) analysis of how the balance between these two conflicting considerations has in the end been struck, see Cauffman (2015), pp. 136–137.

235 See in particular recitals 14–15 Competition Damages Directive 2014/104. See e.g. also Commission, Staff working paper accompanying the white paper on damages actions for breach of the EC antitrust rules, SEC(2008) 404, pp. 28–9; Commission, Proposal for Competition Damages Directive 2014/104, COM(2013) 404, pp. 13–14.

236 See e.g. Bruns (2011), p. 130; Batchelor, Pike and Ghiorghies (2013), p. 161; Danov and Dnes (2013), p. 43; Kammin and Becker (2013), p. 67; Howard (2014), p. 53; Calisti and Haasbeek (2015), p. 3.

237 Cf. Art. 2(8) Competition Damages Directive 2014/104.

238 See in particular recital 21 Competition Damages Directive 2014/104.

239 On these leniency and settlement programmes, see para 6.48 and 6.49 below, respectively.

the Court of Justice made clear in its aforementioned *Pfleiderer* case law, in the absence of specific rules of EU law, it cannot simply be presumed that this type of evidence is barred from being disclosed.[240] This thus corresponds to what could be called the *restrictive* element of the directive's disclosure regime.

6.32 The main rule for which the Competition Damages Directive provides against this background is that, upon request of the applicant, the competent national court must be able to order the defendant or a third party to *disclose* relevant evidence that lies in their control.[241] To this aim the private party requesting the disclosure must present '*a reasoned justification containing reasonably available facts and evidence sufficient to support the plausibility of its claim for damages*'.[242] For reasons of equality of arms between the parties concerned, the defendant can also make such a request.[243] In the latter case the same conditions presumably apply.

The directive aims to give a central function to the national courts that are to decide on these requests for disclosure.[244] They are expected to exercise strict control.[245] That is consistent with the legal tradition in the great majority of Member States.[246] The national courts must be able to order the disclosure of specified pieces of evidence or of relevant categories of evidence circumscribed as precisely and as narrowly as possible, while ensuring that any disclosure is limited to what is proportionate in light of the legitimate interests of all parties concerned.[247] In that connection, these courts must consider in particular three explicitly mentioned factors, namely: (a) the extent to which the claim or defence is supported by available facts and evidence justifying the request; (b) the scope and cost of the disclosure, especially for any third parties concerned, also to avoid non-specific searches of information which is unlikely to be of relevance (known as "fishing expeditions"[248]); and (c) whether the evidence in question contains confidential information, especially concerning any third parties, and the arrangements for the protection of such information.

240 CoJ case C-360/09, *Pfleiderer*. See para 6.21 and 6.22 above. See also CoJ case C-557/12, *Kone*, para 36.
241 Art. 5(1) Competition Damages Directive 2014/104.
242 Art. 5(1) Competition Damages Directive 2014/104.
243 Cf. recital 15 Competition Damages Directive 2014/104.
244 Commission, Proposal for Competition Damages Directive 2014/104, COM(2013) 404, p. 14.
245 Recital 16 Competition Damages Directive 2014/104.
246 Commission, Proposal for Competition Damages Directive 2014/104, COM(2013) 404, p. 14. See also Bruns (2011), p. 129.
247 Art. 5(2) and (3) Competition Damages Directive 2014/104. See also its recital 16. Its Art. 5(4) stipulates that the interest of an undertaking to avoid actions for damages does not constitute an interest that warrants protection.
248 Cf. recital 23 Competition Damages Directive 2014/104. See also Council, doc. 8088/14, p. 5; European Parliament, Report on the proposal for Competition Damages Directive 2014/104, A7–0089/2014, p. 21 (Art. 5(3)(b)).

As is already implicit in this last factor, confidential information can in principle be disclosed under the directive, where the court considers this relevant. However, Member States must ensure that effective measures are available to protect this information.[249] Full effect must further be given to applicable legal professional privileges under EU or national law.[250]

Turning to the more restrictive part of the rules at issue, additional requirements apply where the possible disclosure concerns evidence consisting of *documents included in the file* of a competition authority.[251] Three points stand out in this regard. First, several *additional factors* are spelled out that national courts must take into account in the context of the above-mentioned proportionality assessment. In these cases these courts must also consider: (a) the specificity of the request for disclosure as regards the nature, object or content of the document submitted to the competition authority; (b) whether the party requesting disclosure is doing so in relation to an action for damages; and (c) the need to safeguard the effectiveness of the public enforcement of the rules of competition law concerned.[252] **6.33**

Second and most importantly, the directive distinguishes several categories of evidence. For certain categories there is a *temporal ban* on disclosure, namely until the moment the competition authority concerned has closed its proceedings. This "grey list" covers information that the undertaking in question specifically prepared for those public enforcement proceedings, information drawn up and sent by these authorities as well as any withdrawn settlement submissions.[253] This is meant to avoid undue interference with ongoing investigations by public enforcement authorities.[254] Leniency statements and settlement submissions are, by contrast, on a "black list", meaning that these pieces of evidence cannot be disclosed at any time.[255] This *absolute protection* reflects the

249 Art. 5(5) Competition Damages Directive 2014/104. See also its recital 18.

250 Art. 5(6) Competition Damages Directive 2014/104.

251 The directive does not specify, however, which documents precisely are referred to and how the national courts and the parties to the proceedings are to know precisely which documents have been included in such a file. Cf. Cauffman (2015), p. 130. Further, pursuant to Art. 6(2) Competition Damages Directive 2014/104, the above rules are without prejudice to the rules and practices on public access to documents under Regulation (EC) No 1049/2001 regarding public access to European Parliament, Council and Commission documents, OJ 2001, L 145/43 ("Transparency Regulation"). On the possible disclosure of documents in the Commission's file under Transparency Regulation 1049/2001, see in particular CoJ case C-365/12 P, *EnBW Energie*. On this latter line of case law more generally, see Kellerbauer (2014), p. 56. According to Bentley and Henry (2014), p. 277, the directive leaves this case law intact and reaffirms that the route to disclosure via that regulation is effectively barred.

252 Art. 6(4) Competition Damages Directive 2014/104.

253 Art. 6(5) Competition Damages Directive 2014/104. Pursuant to its Art. 6(8), partial disclosure of evidence covered by the grey list is to be ordered where possible.

254 Recital 25 Competition Damages Directive 2014/104.

255 Art. 6(6) Competition Damages Directive 2014/104.

thought that leniency and settlement procedures are important public enforcement tools and that undertakings could be deterred from participating if these self-incriminating documents were disclosed, thus exposing them to civil liability.[256] The disclosure of evidence in a competition authority's file that is not covered by either of these two lists can in principle be ordered at any time.[257]

Third and finally, there are limits to the *use* of evidence that is obtained solely through *access to the file* of a competition authority. Such access is given to undertakings so as to allow them to exercise their rights of defence in public enforcement proceedings.[258] But this information could also be used in private enforcement proceedings. Blacklisted evidence obtained in this manner is therefore to be deemed inadmissible in legal proceedings covered by the directive.[259] The same applies for grey-listed evidence for as long as the public enforcement proceedings in question have not been closed.[260] For all other pieces of evidence obtained through access to the file, there is also a restriction as to its use, namely that it can only be used in an action for damages by the party concerned or its legal successor, including a party that acquired this party's claim.[261] This latter rule is meant to prevent the information in question from becoming the object of trade.[262]

6.34 For the time being it remains an open question how – if and when asked – the Court of Justice would assess the above regime in light of its earlier rulings in *Pfleiderer* and especially *Donau Chemie*.[263] It will be recalled that in those

256 Recital 26 Competition Damages Directive 2014/104.

257 Art. 6(9) Competition Damages Directive 2014/104.

258 Cf. Art. 27(2) Competition Regulation 1/2003.

259 Art. 7(1) Competition Damages Directive 2014/104. Instead of being deemed inadmissible, the evidence in question may also be '*otherwise protected under the applicable national rules to ensure the full effect of the limits on the disclosure of evidence*' set out in Art. 6 Competition Damages Directive 2014/104.

260 Art. 7(2) Competition Damages Directive 2014/104.

261 Art. 7(3) Competition Damages Directive 2014/104.

262 Recital 32 Competetion Damages Directive 2014/104.

263 CoJ case C-360/09, *Pfleiderer*; CoJ case C-536/11, *Donau Chemie*. See para 6.21 and 6.22 above. For the sake of brevity, it is presumed here that, despite the legal and factual differences, the logic underpinning this case law is also applicable to the situations covered by Competition Damages Directive 2014/104, including where evidence in the Commission's file is concerned. Cf. Cauffman (2011b), pp. 608 and 611. It can further be noted that the EU legislature is not bound by the principle of effectiveness, discussed in subsection 2.A.3 above, which was at issue in the above-mentioned rulings. Any possible assessment by the CoJ would therefore probably rather concern compliance with the principle of proportionality and the principle of effective judicial protection guaranteed under Art. 47 Charter. On the relationship between the principles of effectiveness and effective judicial protection, see para 2.12 above. On the CoJ's review of compliance by the EU legislature with the principle of proportionality and the fundamental rights set out in the Charter, see subsection 10.A.2 below. Lastly, as this case law did not relate to settlement programmes, and considering the differences between these programmes and leniency programmes (see para 6.49 below), it remains for now an open question how the CoJ would rule on the absolute and temporal protection of the documents relating to these latter programmes.

rulings the Court essentially refused – on the basis of the law as it stood prior to the directive – to prioritise the interest associated with public enforcement and in particular the protection of leniency programmes over the interests of private parties having suffered harm. It instead stressed the importance of both interests and insisted on a case-by-case weighing by the judiciary. On the one hand, a legislative rule providing for absolute non-disclosure precludes by definition such a weighing exercise. This could be understood to mean that therefore (also) the EU legislature cannot provide for such a rule. Concerns of this kind arose during the legislative process leading to the adoption of the Competition Damages Directive, especially on the part of the European Parliament,[264] and in the legal literature.[265] Considering the approach eventually chosen, some scope for discussion on this point therefore still remains after the adoption of this directive.[266]

Yet it must be acknowledged, on the other hand, that the above-mentioned black list is limited to the documents that touch upon the very essence of these public enforcement tools, namely leniency applications and settlement submissions. The directive allows applicants to request the national court seised to verify whether a particular document indeed qualifies as such.[267] The temporal non-disclosure of the documents on the more extensive grey list is moreover compensated for by the extension of the applicable limitation periods.[268] Arguably the above regime does not leave a private party applicant worse off as compared with a situation where no such public enforcement mechanisms exist at all, as is the case elsewhere in EU law and in civil litigation generally. That party is thus "merely" denied a weapon that it would not have had anyway in an "ordinary" tort case. There seems no reason to believe that a private enforcement action in a competition case can generally only succeed where the

264 See European Parliament, Draft report on the proposal for Competition Damages Directive 2014/104, 2013/0185(COD), p. 26; Council, doc. 6493/14, p. 3. See also the suggestion to provide for the non-disclosure of these documents '*as a general rule*' (thus allowing exceptions in certain cases) set out in European Parliament, Report on the proposal for Competition Damages Directive 2014/104, A7–0089/2014, p. 22 (Art. 6(2a)).

265 E.g. Cauffmann (2013), p. 632; Gamble (2013), pp. 619–20; Guttuso (2014), p. 20; Kersting (2014), p. 2; Murphy (2014), p. 224; Nordlander and Abenhaïm (2014), p. 5; Stauber (2014), p. 26; Weidt (2014), pp. 440 and 444; Wisking, Dietzel and Herron (2014), p. 188; Gamble (2014), pp. 478–479; Cauffman (2015), p. 132. On this question, see also Opinion AG Jääskinen case C-536/11, *Donau Chemie*, para 52–69.

266 As noted by Kumar Singh (2014), p. 118, the approach chosen by the EU legislature is in effect closer to the one suggested by Advocate General Mazák in *Pfleiderer* than to the Court's ruling in that case. See Opinion AG Mazák case C-360/09, *Pfleiderer*, referred to in para 6.21 above.

267 Art. 6(7) Competition Damages Directive 2014/104. In this connection a national court can ask (only) the competent competition authority for assistance, while the author of the document in question may also be heard.

268 Art. 10(5) Competition Damages Directive 2014/104. See para 6.42 below.

applicant has access to the documents concerned.[269] That applies even more so when this disclosure regime is assessed in light of the other measures provided for in this directive, which are often favourable to private party applicants.[270]

6.35 The Competition Damages Directive further provides for several *complementary rules* relating to the above measures on the disclosure and non-disclosure of evidence. One of these is that the party from whom disclosure is sought must be provided with an opportunity to be heard before the order is granted.[271] Furthermore, a competition authority may on its own initiative state its views on the proportionality of a disclosure request concerning evidence included in its file.[272] Under the directive, that authority is to be addressed itself by a disclosure order only as a last resort, that is, only where the parties to the proceedings or a third party cannot reasonably do so.[273] There seems something to be said for instead turning to the competition authorities first, given the availability of these documents in their files and the associated reduced costs, efforts and intrusion on the part of the private parties concerned.[274] This was, however, considered too much of a burden on these authorities.[275]

Penalties are to be provided for in case of non-compliance with a disclosure order, the destruction of evidence, non-compliance with an obligation to protect confidential information and breaches of the above-mentioned limits on the use of evidence.[276] These penalties must be effective, proportionate and dissuasive and they must include the possibility for the national court seised to draw adverse inferences (for example presuming something to be proven or the dismissal of the claim or defence) and to order the payment of costs.[277] Lastly, the directive stipulates that the Member States may provide for rules that lead to wider disclosure, without prejudice, however, to the aforementioned rules on

269 Cf. CoJ case C-536/11, *Donau Chemie*, para 33; CoJ case C-365/12 P, *EnBW Energie*, para 132. See also recital 22 Competition Damages Directive 2014/104.

270 See e.g. the relatively broad disclosure regime set out in Art. 5 Competition Damages Directive 2014/104, discussed in para 6.32 above, but also the rules of evidence set out in its Art. 9, 14(2) and 17(1) and (2), discussed in para 6.41 and 6.38 below and para 6.30 above, respectively. As is discussed in para 9.15 below, there is evidently a relationship between the rules on the *access* to evidence (or the lack thereof) and the rules on the *burden and the standard of proof*.

271 Art. 5(7) Competition Damages Directive 2014/104.

272 Art. 6(11) Competition Damages Directive 2014/104. See also its recital 30.

273 Art. 6(10) Competition Damages Directive 2014/104.

274 Cf. Rosch (2014), p. 192; Siragusa (2014), p. 254.

275 Council, doc. 6493/14, p. 4. Cf. European Parliament, Report on the proposal for Competition Damages Directive 2014/104, A7–0089/2014, p. 20 (Art. 5(1a)).

276 Art. 8(1) Competition Damages Directive 2014/104.

277 Art. 8(2) Competition Damages Directive 2014/104. Cf. recital 33 Competition Damages Directive 2014/104. Penalties of this kind are of little relevance, however, where third parties fail to comply with disclosure orders addressed to them. See Bruns (2011), pp. 136–7.

the disclosure of confidential information, the right to be heard and the (non-)disclosure of evidence included in the file of a competition authority.[278]

4. Joint and several liability and passing-on

Under the Competition Damages Directive the undertakings that committed an infringement through joint behaviour, such as a cartel, are *jointly and severally liable* for the harm caused. This means that each of those undertakings is bound to compensate the harm in full and that a private party having suffered harm can require full compensation from any of them until it is fully compensated.[279] Where relevant it is then for the undertaking concerned to recover a contribution from its co-infringers. The amount of that contribution is to be determined in light of the undertakings' relative responsibility for the harm in question, in accordance with the applicable rules of national law.[280] Specific rules apply in certain cases where the infringing undertaking is a small or medium-sized enterprise.[281] **6.36**

Whereas the above rules clearly seek to further the objective of ensuring full compensation, the objective of coordinating public and private enforcement also plays a role here. Undertakings that have been granted immunity from fines under a leniency programme are protected from '*undue exposure to damages claims*'.[282] This was deemed necessary because the competition authority's decision finding an infringement is likely to become final at an earlier stage with respect to these undertakings than with respect to the co-infringing undertakings that were not granted leniency (and which may therefore contest that decision). This could mean that the immunity recipient becomes the most likely target in a ("follow-on") action for damages, where he would risk being required to compensate the applicant in full.[283] For that reason the directive relieves immunity recipients in principle from joint and several liability for the full damage caused. That undertaking remains jointly and severally liable only *vis-à-vis* its direct or indirect purchasers or providers, whereas other injured parties can only claim damages from this undertaking where they cannot obtain full compensation from the other infringing undertakings.[284] These co-infringers can similarly only recover a contribution from that undertaking

278 Art. 5(8) Competition Damages Directive 2014/104.

279 Art. 11(1) Competition Damages Directive 2014/104.

280 Art. 11(5) Competition Damages Directive 2014/104. See also its recital 37.

281 Art. 11(2) and (3) Competition Damages Directive 2014/104. See also its recital 33.

282 Recital 38 Competition Damages Directive 2014/104.

283 Cf. Commission, Proposal for Competition Damages Directive 2014/104, COM(2013) 404, pp. 16–17.

284 Art. 11(4) Competition Damages Directive 2014/104. See also its recital 33.

that does not exceed the amount of harm caused to the latter's direct or indirect purchasers or providers.[285]

6.37 A separate issue is the *passing-on defence*, in respect of which considerable divergences were observed to exist at national level before the directive's adoption.[286] The Competition Damages Directive harmonises these national rules by expressly permitting this defence. This means that a defendant can argue that the private party claiming damages under this directive in effect passed on in whole or in part the alleged harm resulting from the infringement to its own customers in the form of higher prices (known as the overcharge).[287] After all, if and when such passing-on occurred, it was these customers, as indirect purchasers, that suffered the harm, and not the initial applicant.[288] Compensating the latter in such a case would thus result in overcompensation, which is expressly precluded under the directive.[289]

The directive provides that it is for the defendant who wishes to rely on this passing-on defence to prove not only the existence, but also the extent of the passing-on.[290] The competent national courts must be empowered to estimate which share of this overcharge resulting from the infringement was passed on, in accordance with the applicable rules of national law.[291] The directive requires the Commission to issue guidelines on how to make such estimates.[292]

6.38 The availability of the passing-on defence logically leads to the question whether these *indirect purchasers* can themselves claim damages for the harm suffered lower down the supply chain as a consequence of this passing-on. The directive answers this question in the affirmative.[293] In this case the burden of proving the existence and scope of the passing-on rests in principle with this

---

285 Art. 11(5) Competition Damages Directive 2014/104. See also its Art. 11(6). The Council initially considered that this contribution regime proposed by the Commission went further than necessary to neutralise the negative effects of actions for damages on leniency programmes described above. But at the insistence of the European Parliament it later accepted the Commission proposal on this point, as this was considered to increase the efficiency of enforcement. See Council, doc. 15983/13, p. 3; Council, doc. 6493/14, p. 5.

286 Commission, Impact assessment report on damages actions for breach of the EU antitrust rules, SWD(2013) 203, pp. 16–17. On issues related to passing-on, see further Bulst (2011), p. 67.

287 Art. 13 Competition Damages Directive 2014/104. See also its recital 41.

288 Note that the higher prices resulting from the passing-on of an overcharge can result in reduced sales and thus a loss of profit for the applicant. The right to claim compensation for such loss of profit remains unaffected by the availability of the passing-on defence. See Article 12(3) and recital 40 Competition Damages Directive 2014/104.

289 Art. 12(1) and (2) Competition Damages Directive 2014/104. See also its Art. 3(3).

290 Art. 13 Competition Damages Directive 2014/104.

291 Art. 12(5) Competition Damages Directive 2014/104.

292 Art. 16 Competition Damages Directive 2014/104.

293 Art. 12(1) Competition Damages Directive 2014/104.

applicant, however.[294] Apart from the above-mentioned possibility for the national court to estimate the share of the overcharge that was passed on, which also applies here, the directive also seeks to alleviate this burden on the indirect purchaser in another manner. For it is provided that this private party is deemed to have proven that the passing-on to it occurred where it can make a *prima facie* case to this effect.[295] This means that the indirect purchaser must show that the defendant committed an infringement resulting in an overcharge and that it purchased the goods or services that were the subject of this infringement. It is then for the defendant to rebut this presumption.[296]

When assessing whether the burden of proof relating to actions by indirect purchasers is satisfied, national courts must, by means available under EU and national law, take due account of actions for damages and judgments relating to the same infringement brought by applicants from other levels in the supply chain as well as relevant information in the public domain resulting from public enforcement cases.[297] The same applies as regards the burden of proof relating to the aforementioned passing-on defence. The underlying aim here is to ensure consistency and to avoid both undue multiple liability and an undue absence of liability for damage caused by the infringements at issue, without disregarding the rights of defence and right to effective judicial protection of the parties concerned.[298]

5. Procedural provisions

The first of the five remaining issues of a procedural nature to be discussed here **6.39** is that of *legal standing*. The Competition Damages Directive contains no specific provision that outlines which private parties are entitled to bring legal proceedings under this directive. But that does not mean that this subject matter is not regulated with a degree of detail. Several provisions contain relevant indications. Most important is the provision that the directive seeks to ensure that '*[a]nyone who has suffered harm caused by an infringement of competition law*' can exercise the right to obtain full compensation that the directive seeks to guarantee.[299] This is a reaffirmation of earlier case law.[300] This wording makes it clear that a wide category of private parties is to have legal standing

294 Art. 14(1) Competition Damages Directive 2014/104.
295 Cf. recital 41 Competition Damages Directive 2014/104.
296 Art. 14(2) Competition Damages Directive 2014/104.
297 Art. 15(1) Competition Damages Directive 2014/104.
298 See recital 44 Competition Damages Directive 2014/104. See also Commission, Proposal for Competition Damages Directive 2014/104, COM(2013) 404, pp. 17–18.
299 Art. 1(1) Competition Damages Directive 2014/104.
300 See recital 12 Competition Damages Directive 2014/104. See in particular CoJ case C-453/99, *Courage*, para 24, discussed in para 6.14 above.

under the directive. That is confirmed elsewhere in the directive, where reference is made to '*any natural or legal person who has suffered harm*'[301] and where it is, moreover, clarified that this applies '*irrespective of whether they are direct or indirect purchasers from an infringer*'.[302] The recitals explain that this term "anyone" includes consumers, undertakings and public authorities alike, irrespective of the existence of a direct contractual relationship with the infringing undertaking and regardless of whether or not a competition authority has previously found an infringement to exist.[303] The directive furthermore indicates that actions for damages can also be brought by a third party acting on behalf of the allegedly injured party where EU or national law provides for such a possibility or by a party that succeeded in the right of the allegedly injured party, including where the former acquired the claim from the latter.[304]

6.40 The second issue is the *forum* before which the actions for damages at issue are to be brought. In this regard the directive simply refers to "national courts".[305] This term has been defined as '*any court or tribunal of a Member State within the meaning of Article 267 [TFEU]*'.[306] This latter article sets out the preliminary reference procedure. In this manner it is ensured that the national court seised by an action for damages under the directive can refer preliminary questions to the Court of Justice. This reference to Article 267 TFEU, moreover, means that these national courts must meet the conditions set in the Court's case law on this Treaty article.[307] Thus while the competent body need not necessarily be judicial in character, account is taken among other things of whether it has a basis in law, it is independent and the proceedings are *inter partes*. Although this is not required under the directive, the presumption is that it is normally for the national *civil* courts to rule on the damages claims in question.[308] As the Commission noted in its proposal, '*[a]warding compensation is [...] within the domain of national courts and of civil law and procedure*'.[309] In several Member States a degree of specialisation is nonetheless ensured with respect to competition-related private enforcement actions, for instance in England and

---

301 Art. 3(1) Competition Damages Directive 2014/104.

302 Art. 12(1) Competition Damages Directive 2014/104.

303 Recital 13 Competition Damages Directive 2014/104. See also its recital 3. For an example of a private enforcement action brought by a public authority (namely the Commission), see CoJ case C-199/11, *Otis*.

304 See Art. 2(4) Competition Damages Directive 2014/104.

305 See e.g. Art. 1(2) Competition Damages Directive 2014/104.

306 Art. 2(9) Competition Damages Directive 2014/104.

307 See para 1.02 above.

308 See e.g. recital 6 Competition Damages Directive 2014/104, where reference is made to '*private enforcement actions under civil law*'. See e.g. also the reference to Evidence Regulation 1206/2001, laid down in Art. 5(1) Competition Damages Directive 2014/104. Evidence Regulation 1206/2001 only applies to the taking of evidence on civil and commercial matters (see its Art. 1(1)).

309 Commission, Proposal for Competition Damages Directive 2014/104, COM(2013) 404, p. 2.

Wales (Competition Appeal Tribunal) and France (specialised chambers in a limited number of courts).[310]

Pursuant to the Competition Regulation, national courts cannot take decisions in private enforcement proceedings that run counter to the decisions taken by the *Commission*.[311] The question therefore arose whether or not the Competition Damages Directive should include a rule that treated decisions by *national* competition authorities in the same manner. The relevant national rules pre-dating the directive varied considerably. While such binding effect in private enforcement proceedings for infringement decisions by the "home" competition authority was not uncommon, only very few Member States (notably Germany) also extended this rule to decisions taken by "foreign" authorities.[312] Providing for such a rule at EU level would clearly be helpful to applicants seeking to obtain compensation in damages. It could also help avoid diverging rulings across the EU. But it would also mean that a national court would no longer be free to make its own judgment on the important point of whether or not an infringement occurred. Instead, that court would be bound by a finding to this effect by a public authority of another Member State, notwithstanding the fact that the standards and procedural safeguards applicable in national public enforcement proceedings vary between the Member States. This was therefore '*one of the more controversial issues*' at the stage of the consultations preceding the directive and it also proved to be controversial in the legal literature.[313] **6.41**

This controversy continued during the legislative process. The Commission had proposed that a national court seised in an action for damages under the directive would be categorically barred from taking a decision running counter to a finding of an infringement by a national competition authority (or by a national court reviewing the decision establishing such a finding), regardless of whether it concerned a finding by the "home" or a "foreign" competition authority.[314] In light of the diverging views both between the Member States and between the two co-legislators, in the end, however, a different compromise

310 Jalabert-Doury (2010), p. 320; Smith, Maton and Cambell (2010), pp. 301–2. See also Study, Ashurst (2004), pp. 31–6.

311 Art. 16(1) Competition Regulation 1/2003. See para 6.04 above.

312 Commission, Impact assessment report on damages actions for breach of the EU antitrust rules, SWD(2013) 203, pp. 16 and 57. See also Buccirossi and Carpagnano (2013), p. 5; Esteva Mosso (2013), p. 51. Here it is reported that Sweden also provides for such a rule under its national law, whereas Austria was said to be in the process of implementing one.

313 Commission, Impact assessment report on damages actions for breach of the EU antitrust rules, SWD(2013) 203, p. 57. As to the legal literature, see Komninos (2007), p. 1387; Milutinovic (2010), pp. 281–301; Bruns (2011), p. 140; Komninos (2014), pp. 147–9; Milutinovic (2014), pp. 357–60.

314 Commission, Proposal for Competition Damages Directive 2014/104, COM(2013) 404, p. 36 (Art. 9).

was struck.[315] Under the Competition Damages Directive such a finding of an infringement is now deemed to be '*irrefutably established*' for the purposes of an action for damages covered by the directive only in so far as it does not concern a decision given in another Member State.[316] In the latter case the decision may, in accordance with national law, '*be presented before [the] national courts as at least prima facie evidence that an infringement of competition law has occurred and, as appropriate, may be assessed along with any other evidence adduced by the parties*'.[317] While it remains to be seen what this entails in concrete terms, it has been argued that this comes close to a rebuttable presumption.[318]

6.42 The fourth issue concerns rules on *limitation periods* for initiating legal proceedings under the Competition Damages Directive. According to the Commission the fact that a vast majority of the Member States did not provide for limitation periods specifically for "follow-on" actions constituted an important obstacle to successfully bringing actions for damages.[319] The directive therefore requires Member States to lay down rules in this regard, without these rules being restricted to follow-on actions only, however. The Member States are to specify when the limitation period begins to run, its duration and the circumstances under which it can be suspended or interrupted.[320] On each of these three points further precision is provided for, in a manner that partly builds on earlier case law by the Court of Justice.[321] These rules boil down to the following.

First, as regards the starting point it is specified that the limitation period for bringing actions for damages under the directive shall not begin to run before the injured party knows or can reasonably be expected to know three elements, namely: (a) the behaviour and that it constitutes an infringement; (b) that that infringement caused harm to the applicant; and (c) the identity of the infringer.[322] Second, the directive specifies that the *duration* of the limitation period must be at least five years.[323] Although hardly spectacular in itself, this

---

315 Council, doc. 15983/13, p. 3; Council, doc. 6493/14, p. 3. See also European Parliament, Report on the proposal for Competition Damages Directive 2014/104, A7–0089/2014, p. 25 (Art. 9), from which it follows that this institution essentially supported the Commission's proposal on this point.

316 Art. 9(1) Competition Damages Directive 2014/104.

317 Art. 9(2) Competition Damages Directive 2014/104.

318 Calisti and Haasbeek (2015), p. 5.

319 Commission, Impact assessment report on damages actions for breach of the EU antitrust rules, SWD(2013) 203, pp. 16 and 57. Cf. recital 36 Competition Damages Directive 2014/104.

320 Art. 10(1) Competition Damages Directive 2014/104.

321 See in particular CoJ joined cases C-295/04 to C-298/04, *Manfredi*, para 77–82, discussed in para 6.15 above.

322 Art. 10(2) Competition Damages Directive 2014/104. The Commission had proposed also stipulating that limitation periods cannot begin to run before the day on which a continuous or repeated infringement ends, but this provision was not retained by the EU legislature. See Commission, Proposal for Competition Damages Directive 2014/104, COM(2013) 404, p. 36 (Art. 10(3)).

323 Art. 10(3) Competition Damages Directive 2014/104.

provision is notable for being one of the few instances where the Commission's proposal and subsequently the directive itself goes further than the 2008 white paper. For in that document the focus was squarely on follow-on actions only where this aspect was concerned.[324] Third, Member States are to ensure that the applicable limitation periods are *suspended* (or interrupted) if a competition authority initiates an investigation or proceedings in respect of the infringement at issue. That suspension shall end not earlier than one year after the termination of these public enforcement proceedings.[325] This latter provision can be expected to be of significant importance in practice. It implies that "follow-on" actions can sometimes be brought many years after the moment at which the infringement was committed, considering that it can take a long time for public enforcement proceedings to be concluded with a final decision.

Finally, the Competition Damages Directive contains rules that have been designed to encourage *consensual dispute resolution*, which term includes out-of-court settlements directly negotiated between the parties, arbitration and mediation as well as conciliation.[326] A first measure to this effect is the requirement that limitation periods must be suspended for the duration of the consensual dispute resolution process in so far as the participants to that process are concerned.[327] This is meant to give these parties sufficient time to reach an out-of-court settlement.[328] Likewise, there may be reason for the national court seised to suspend legal proceedings when they have already been initiated. The directive requires the court to be empowered to do the latter, without this being an obligation for the court, however, and subject to a maximum of two years.[329] **6.43**

Consensual dispute resolution is further facilitated by the rule that, in case of several infringing undertakings that would normally be jointly and severally liable, the remaining claim of an injured party that agreed a settlement with one of those undertakings is reduced by the latter's share of the harm inflicted and that its remaining claim can only be exercised against the other, non-settling undertakings, whereas the latter cannot recover contribution from the undertaking that settled.[330] This rule prevents settling undertakings from being worse

324 See Commission, White paper on damages actions for breach of the EC antitrust rules, COM(2008) 165, pp. 8–9.

325 Art. 10(4) Competition Damages Directive 2014/104.

326 See Art. 2(21) and recital 48 Competition Damages Directive 2014/104.

327 Art. 18(1) Competition Damages Directive 2014/104.

328 See recital 49 Competition Damages Directive 2014/104.

329 Art. 18(2) and (3) Competition Damages Directive 2014/104. This requirement is without prejudice to provisions of national law in matters of arbitration. See also its recital 50, where reference is made to the interest in an expeditious procedure.

330 Art. 19(1) and (2) Competition Damages Directive 2014/104. Its Art. 19(3) provides for an exception to the rule on the recovery of contributions set out in Art. 19(2) in cases where the non-settling co-infringers cannot

off as a consequence of the rules on joint and several liability discussed earlier.[331] Also more generally national courts are to take due account of any damages paid pursuant to a prior consensual settlement when determining the amount of contribution that co-infringers can recover from each other.[332]

A last measure prescribed by the directive in this connection is that competition authorities may consider that compensation paid as a result of a consensual settlement prior to their decision to impose a fine is a mitigating factor in the setting of that fine.[333] This measure had not been included in the Commission's proposal; it was inserted at the request of the European Parliament.[334] This latter institution had initially sought the inclusion of a "voluntary compensation mechanism" as part of the relevant public enforcement proceedings, in the form of a provision on the suspension of those proceedings so as to allow for the conclusion of an out-of-court settlement and an obligation for the competition authority concerned to consider this a mitigating factor when establishing the level of the fine.[335] Suggestions along these lines were also raised in the legal literature, noting that this approach has actually at times already been put in practice both at EU and national level.[336] The provision finally agreed upon is considerably less stringent, however, considering especially that the directive merely provides for a possibility for these authorities to do so and not an obligation.

D. OTHER ENFORCEMENT ISSUES

This final section concentrates on the role of alternative dispute resolution and out-of-court settlements as well as on the applicable public enforcement regime that has traditionally been of particular importance in this domain.

---

pay the damages corresponding to the remaining claim, subject, however, to the possibility of expressly excluding this possibility in the settlement agreement.

331 Cf. recital 51 Competition Damages Directive 2014/104. See para 6.36 above.

332 Art. 19(4) Competition Damages Directive 2014/104.

333 Art. 18(3) Competition Damages Directive 2014/104.

334 Cf. Council, doc. 6493/14, p. 4; European Parliament, Report on the proposal for Competition Damages Directive 2014/104, A7–0089/2014, p. 29 (Art. 17(2b)).

335 European Parliament, Draft report on the proposal for Competition Damages Directive 2014/104, 2013/0185(COD), p. 43.

336 See Neruda (2011), pp. 245–7; Rivas and Eclair-Heath (2012), p. 1; Ratliff (2014), pp. 291–3; Silva Morais (2014), pp. 131–2.

1. Alternative dispute resolution and settlements

As in many other fields of law, alternative dispute resolution can certainly be of relevance for resolving disputes concerning EU competition law.[337] Indeed, it has been argued that the growing importance of arbitration in settling competition law disputes is too often ignored and underestimated and that there may well be grounds for regulating certain aspects thereof at EU level.[338] However, for the time being it appears that especially out-of-court settlements directly negotiated between the parties to the dispute play an important role in practice, at least where competition disputes of the type under discussion here are concerned. Even if it is hard to obtain concrete data, many private enforcement disputes are thought to be settled out of court before a final judgment is rendered or even before a case is brought.[339] Indeed, it may well be that at least in certain jurisdictions a majority of these disputes are settled, as is, for example, reportedly the case in the United Kingdom.[340] **6.44**

The EU law measures in this regard are on the whole rather modest, however. As was set out above, the Competition Damages Directive contains several rules that are expressly meant to encourage consensual dispute resolution.[341] This illustrates that this manner of resolving disputes between private parties relating to infringements of EU competition law is generally looked upon favourably by the Commission and the EU legislature. The Commission has pointed to its potential to provide for a speedy solution, reduce costs for the parties concerned and avoid overburdening the courts.[342] Of the two co-legislators, the European Parliament especially tends to take a favourable view of this form of dispute resolution, as do many stakeholders.[343] But the rules set out in this directive essentially do no more than *encourage and facilitate* consensual dispute resolution, for instance by suspending limitation periods and by removing disincentives resulting from rules on joint and several liability. The directive contains no rules on the circumstances or the manner in which **6.45**

---

337 Cf. e.g. CoJ case 126/97, *Eco Swiss*.

338 Silva Morais (2014), pp. 115–17 and 134.

339 See also para 6.19 above.

340 Study, CEPS, Erasmus University Rotterdam and LUISS (2007), p. 44; Danov and Dnes (2013), p. 49. See also Komninos (2008), p. 187, where a study is cited that suggests that in the US more than 80 per cent of private enforcement cases in this domain are settled before the courts award any damages.

341 See para 6.43 above.

342 Commission, Impact assessment report on damages actions for breach of the EU antitrust rules, SWD(2013) 203, pp. 27–8. See e.g. also Commission, White paper on damages actions for breach of the EC antitrust rules, COM(2008) 165, p. 3; Commission, Staff working paper accompanying the white paper on damages actions for breach of the EC antitrust rules, SEC(2008) 404, pp. 75–6.

343 See e.g. European Parliament, Resolution on the white paper on damages actions for breach of the EC antitrust rules, P6_TA(2009)0187, para 7. As regards the view of stakeholders, see Commission, Impact assessment report on damages actions for breach of the EU antitrust rules, SWD(2013) 203, p. 18.

these alternative dispute resolution procedures *themselves* are to take place. In this context the Commission expressly rejected the option of introducing an obligation to engage in an effort at consensual dispute resolution before a private party would be able to bring an action for damages under the directive.[344]

2. Public enforcement

6.46 The private enforcement-related developments discussed earlier in this chapter notwithstanding, public enforcement has traditionally been and seems likely to continue to be the dominant manner in which the competition rules are enforced in the EU. At EU level as well as in most Member States, this public enforcement is generally primarily ensured by public authorities governed by administrative law.[345]

6.47 Concerning public enforcement *at EU level* the Competition Regulation grants the Commission far-reaching powers to investigate and punish (alleged) infringements of EU competition law. It can among other things make unannounced visits (known as "dawn raids") in order to investigate business and private premises.[346] When an infringement is established, it can impose a range of penalties, including injunctions, structural remedies and fines of up to 10 per cent of the undertaking's annual turnover.[347] These powers of the Commission are subject to review by the EU courts.[348]

Private parties that have a sufficient interest can play a role in this connection by bringing alleged infringements of the EU competition rules to the Commission's attention.[349] They can use what could be called a "reinforced" complaint procedure, as compared with (and in addition to) the "general" possibility for private parties to file complaints with the Commission regarding alleged infringements of EU law in the context of the latter's power to bring infringement proceedings against Member States.[350] This complaint procedure plays

---

344 Commission, Impact assessment report on damages actions for breach of the EU antitrust rules, SWD(2013) 203, p. 35.

345 Cf. e.g. Opinion AG Geelhoed joined cases C-295/04 to C-298/04, *Manfredi*, para 29; Whish and Bailey (2012), p. 295.

346 Art. 20 and 21 Competition Regulation 1/2003.

347 Art. 104 TFEU; Art. 7, 17–21 and 23–4 Competition Regulation 1/2003. Regarding these fines, see also Commission, Guidelines on fines, OJ 2006, C 210/2.

348 Cf. Art. 31 Competition Regulation 1/2003, where it is specified that the EU courts have unlimited jurisdiction to review decisions whereby the Commission has fixed a fine or periodic penalty payments.

349 Cf. Art. 7 Competition Regulation 1/2003; Art. 6–7 Commission Regulation (EC) No 773/2004 relating to the conduct of proceedings by the Commission pursuant to Articles 81 and 82 EC, OJ 2004, L 123/18 ("Competition Proceedings Regulation"); Commission, Complaints notice, OJ 2004, C 101/5.

350 See subsection 2.C.1 above.

an important role in practice. As such, it sometimes functions as an alternative for private parties that otherwise might have brought a private enforcement action against the alleged infringing undertaking before national courts.[351] Yet the fact remains that under this mechanism, private party complainants essentially have only certain procedural rights, such as being kept informed.[352] The public enforcement proceedings themselves that may (or may not) be initiated upon the submission of a complaint remain firmly public in nature. In particular, filing such a complaint cannot lead to the award of damages by the Commission or the EU courts to the private party that filed the complaint. The amounts raised by any fines that the Commission might eventually impose flow to the EU budget.

As has already been touched upon in the foregoing, *leniency programmes* play an important role in connection with public enforcement in this field of law. The Competition Damages Directive defines a leniency programme as: **6.48**

> a programme concerning the application of Article 101 TFEU or a corresponding provision under national law on the basis of which a participant in a secret cartel, independently of the other undertakings involved in the cartel, cooperates with an investigation of the competition authority, by voluntarily providing presentations of his knowledge of the cartel and his role therein, in return for which the participant receives, by decision or a discontinuation of proceedings, immunity from any fine to be imposed for the cartel or a reduction of such fine.[353]

The Commission's leniency programme was introduced in 1996.[354] The EU courts have held that, for the undertakings concerned to qualify for a reduction of the fine under this programme, they must demonstrate '*a genuine spirit of cooperation*'.[355] Undertakings wishing to blow the whistle can do so by submitting "leniency statements" to the Commission in which they describe their knowledge of the cartel and their role therein.[356]

Especially considering that the fines imposed by the Commission can be very high, this programme thus creates an important incentive for undertakings to turn in their fellow cartel participants, while they themselves might escape punishment entirely. This incentive is increased by the rule that only the *first*

351 Cf. Jacobs and Deisenhofer (2003), p. 197.

352 Cf. GC case T-24/90, *Automec*, para 71–98; GC case T-306/05, *Scippecercola*, para 66 and 91–7; GC case T-432/05, *EMC Development*, para 55–60 (upheld on appeal in CoJ Order case C-367/10 P, *EMC Development*).

353 Art. 2(15) Competition Damages Directive 2014/104.

354 Cf. Commission, Impact assessment report on damages actions for breach of the EU antitrust rules, SWD(2013) 203, pp. 70–71; Commission, Leniency notice, OJ 2006, C 298/17.

355 CoJ case C-301/04 P, *SGL Carbon*, para 68.

356 Cf. Art. 2(16) Competition Damages Directive 2014/104.

leniency applicant can qualify for full immunity, provided that the Commission did not already have sufficient incriminating evidence and that the leniency applicant concerned is also actually the first to provide such evidence. One of the key aspects of leniency programmes is therefore that they create distrust between the cartel members.[357] For the undertakings concerned cannot be certain that one of them will not turn to the competent competition authorities so as to obtain immunity, in which case the others could be confronted with hefty fines. In this manner leniency programmes allow the unravelling of cartels, which are otherwise generally difficult to detect. In the words of the Court of Justice, '*leniency programmes are useful tools if efforts to uncover and bring to an end infringements of competition rules are to be effective and serve, therefore, the objective of effective application of Articles 101 TFEU and 102 TFEU*'.[358] The practical importance of the Commission's leniency programme for its public enforcement activities in this field can indeed hardly be overstated. The vast majority of the cartels it discovers come to light after one or more undertakings concerned have applied for leniency. In the 2008–11 period, no less than 21 of the Commission's 24 decisions in cartel cases (that is, 88 per cent) resulted from applications made under its leniency programme.[359]

6.49 Since 2008 the Commission's competition policy has also included the possibility of reaching *settlements* in the context of public enforcement proceedings.[360] Under this settlement procedure, undertakings that infringe EU competition law, having seen the evidence against them in the Commission's file, may choose to cooperate rather than to contest the finding of an infringement and the imposition of a fine by the Commission. In that case they must file a "settlement submission" in which they voluntarily acknowledge their participation in and responsibility for the infringement.[361] In return the undertaking concerned can receive a reduction (by 10 per cent) of the fines to be imposed.

The main aim of this settlement procedure is to simplify the public enforcement proceedings, reduce public enforcement litigation before the EU courts and in so doing free up Commission resources. It thus serves the effectiveness of the procedure dealing with cartels and is to be distinguished from the adversial, standard administrative procedure to address alleged infringements of the rules

357 Cf. Study, CEPS, Erasmus University Rotterdam and LUISS (2007), pp. 493–9.

358 CoJ case C-360/09, *Pfleiderer*, para 25.

359 Commission, Impact assessment report on damages actions for breach of the EU antitrust rules, SWD(2013) 203, p. 21.

360 Cf. Art. 10a Competition Proceedings Regulation 773/2004; Commission, Settlement notice, OJ 2008, C 167/1. On the EU's settlement regime generally, see GC case T-456/10, *Timab Industries*, para 58–74; Hinds (2014), p. 292. These "public enforcement settlements" are not to be confused with the "private enforcement settlements" between private parties amongst themselves, referred to in subsection 6.D.1 above.

361 Cf. Art. 2(18) Competition Damages Directive 2014/104.

at issue.[362] As such, the settlement policy differs from the above-mentioned leniency policy, in that the former is initiated by an undertaking and is primarily focused on *improving detection*, whereas the decision to initiate the latter is exclusively a matter for the Commission and it mainly serves the aim of *efficient prosecution*. According to the Commission, the practical importance of its settlement programme has been increasing, with five cartel cases having been settled in the 2008–11 period.[363] The Commission considers that this too is an important tool for the public enforcement of EU competition law.[364]

In addition, *national* competition authorities also have an important role to play in the public enforcement of EU competition law. In fact, in quantitative terms (thus in light of the number of decisions taken), these authorities have been said to have become '*the primary public enforcers of Articles 101 and 102 TFEU*'.[365] The Competition Regulation obliges the Member States to designate such authorities and it empowers them to apply Articles 101 and 102 TFEU and to take decisions *inter alia* requiring an infringement to be brought to an end, ordering interim measures or imposing fines and periodic penalty payments.[366] These national competition authorities are also empowered to carry out inspections.[367] Although there are notable differences between the various national public enforcement systems in the EU, the competition authorities designated by the Member States thus generally possess powers that are similar to those of the Commission.[368] The national competition authorities cooperate among themselves and with the Commission in the context of the European Competition Network (ECN).[369] In virtually all Member States, leniency programmes are in place, which are largely similar to the Commission's programme, described above.[370] As is the case with the latter, these national leniency programmes also tend to play an important role where public enforcement at national level is concerned.[371] **6.50**

362 Cf. GC case T-456/10, *Timab Industries*, para 65 and 73.

363 Commission, Impact assessment report on damages actions for breach of the EU antitrust rules, SWD(2013) 203, p. 21.

364 Commission, Proposal for the Competition Damages Directive 2014/104, COM(2013) 404, p. 25 (recital 19).

365 Wils (2013), p. 4.

366 Art. 5 and 35 Competition Regulation 1/2003.

367 Art. 22 Competition Regulation 1/2003.

368 Cf. recital 35 of Competition Regulation 1/2003. See e.g. also Study, European Competition Network (2012a); Study, European Competition Network (2012b).

369 Art. 11–15 and 22 Competition Regulation 1/2003. See also Council and Commission, Joint statement on the functioning of the network of competition authorities, 2002; Commission, Network notice, OJ 2004, C 101/43.

370 Commission, Impact assessment report on damages actions for breach of the EU antitrust rules, SWD(2013) 203, p. 71. See e.g. also Wils (2008), p. 121.

371 Cf. ibid., p. 21.

6.51 Furthermore, it has already been seen that *coordinating* public and private enforcement of competition law is an important objective of the Competition Damages Directive.[372] Under the rules pre-dating the directive, any leniency granted by the Commission does not affect the undertaking's situation before national courts in private enforcement actions.[373] The same applies where public enforcement settlements of the type discussed above are concerned. It is important to note that this also remains the general rule after the entry into force of the Competition Damages Directive and the rules of national law transposing it (which are due to be adopted by the end of 2016). However, with a view to safeguarding the effectiveness of the above-mentioned public enforcement instruments, this directive limits the effects of the private enforcement-facilitating measures laid down therein on two main points. It provides for the temporal and (for leniency statements and settlement submissions) absolute non-disclosure of documents in the file of a competition authority in private enforcement proceedings brought under the directive and it limits the joint and several liability of undertakings that have been granted immunity from fines under a leniency programme.[374]

It is further worth recalling that the Competition Damages Directive establishes a degree of integration in legal-procedural terms over and above the aforementioned already existing possibility under the Competition Regulation for competition authorities to make *amicus curiae* interventions in proceedings before national courts.[375] Under the directive these authorities may intervene in pending private enforcement proceedings, by submitting observations on the proportionality of a disclosure request and by providing assistance on the determination of the quantum of damages.[376] In addition, findings of infringements by national public enforcement authorities (and the courts reviewing these decisions) constitute either binding evidence or at least *prima facie* evidence in actions for damages under the directive.[377] The effect of this latter rule can be reinforced by the suspension of limitation periods until after the termination of the public enforcement proceedings.[378] Under the directive, competition authorities may also consider any compensation payments made as part of consensual settlements as a mitigating factor when they set fines for the infringements in question.[379]

---

372 See in particular para 6.25 above.

373 Cf. Commission, Leniency notice, OJ 2006, C 298/17, para 39.

374 Art. 6 and 11 Competition Damages Directive 2014/104, respectively. See para 6.33 and 6.36 above, respectively.

375 Art. 15 Competition Regulation 1/2003. See para 6.04 above.

376 Art. 6(11) and 17(3) Competition Damages Directive 2014/104. See para 6.35 and 6.30 above, respectively.

377 Art. 9 Competition Damages Directive 2014/104. See para 6.41 above.

378 Art. 10(4) Competition Damages Directive 2014/104. See para 6.42 above.

379 Art. 18(3) Competition Damages Directive 2014/104. See para 6.43 above.

Finally, there is also another form of public enforcement of competition law, namely through *criminal* law. In competition cases criminal sanctions can, for example, take the form of imprisonment of directors of undertakings having been found guilty of prohibited anticompetitive behaviour. Over the past years the feasibility and desirability of such measures has regularly been discussed and it has increasingly been put into practice at national level.[380] Several Member States, including Ireland and the United Kingdom, provide under their national laws for criminal sanctions for competition law infringements. The sanctions imposed by the Commission itself are not of a criminal nature.[381] Yet the EU could conceivably still play a role in this respect, especially by establishing an EU law obligation on the Member States to make provision for this type of sanction at national level and by setting certain common rules in this regard.[382] To date no such EU legislative measures have, however, been adopted or proposed. **6.52**

380 See e.g. Wils (2003b), pp. 409–40; Zuleeg (2003), p. 451–61; Cseres, Schienkel and Vogelaar (2006); Wils (2008), pp. 155–201; Zippro (2009b), pp. 147–59; Baker (2014), pp. 41–62.

381 Cf. Art. 23(5) Competition Regulation 1/2003.

382 Cf. Wils (2003b), pp. 448–9; Zuleeg (2003), pp. 455–7. See also Wils (2005), pp. 156–9.

Part C

COMPARISON AND CONTEXTUALISATION: REMEDIES AND PROCEDURES

7

ACTIONS FOR DAMAGES AND ACTIONS FOR INJUNCTIONS

In Part A above the most important EU law principles and case law relating to private enforcement were assessed, together with the relevant public enforcement mechanisms. Part B subsequently outlined and analysed on an individual basis selected EU legislation relating to private enforcement before national courts in four fields of EU law. Building on the foregoing, Part C essentially seeks to analyse this legislation in a comparative and contextual manner, with a particular emphasis on the remedies and procedural rules provided for therein. Where appropriate, the findings that thus emerge are placed in their broader context, especially by taking account of legislation and case law concerning other fields of EU law. To this aim the present Chapter 7 concentrates on two of the three "main" (substantive) remedies that can be identified in this context, namely actions for damages and actions for injunctions. Chapter 8 continues this assessment by analysing the third "main" class of action for private enforcement purposes, contractual remedies, as well as the other remedies. Chapter 9 then discusses the most relevant procedural provisions.

A. ACTIONS FOR DAMAGES

In the foregoing chapters it has been seen that the Procurement Remedies Directives, the IPR Enforcement Directive, the Product Liability Directive and the Competition Damages Directive all aim to facilitate the bringing of actions for damages. These actions for damages are therefore evidently an important remedy when discussing EU legislation facilitating the private enforcement of

EU law. The particularities of each of the aforementioned fields of law notwithstanding, in the first subsection below four general observations are made on this remedy as it has been provided for in the EU legislation under consideration, followed by an interim conclusion. Next, five more specific issues are addressed in each of the following subsections, namely: fault; causality; quantification of the harm; qualification of damages, including joint and several liability; and damages awards going beyond mere compensation of the injury suffered, in particular punitive damages.

1. General: Contradictions and paradoxes

7.01 The first general observation regarding the EU legislative measures on actions for damages discussed in Part B is that the relevant provisions laid down in the EU legislation concerned are often only *modestly prescriptive.*

That is, to begin with, evidently the case under the Procurement Remedies Directives. Here the relevant provision says in fact little more than that Member States should ensure that damages can be awarded to persons harmed by an infringement of the substantive rules at issue.[1] It is thus not specified whether or not the infringer must be at fault for liability in damages to be incurred; there is at best only an implicit causality requirement and it is not specified what the damages to be awarded should entail. Only one of these two directives, the Utilities Remedies Directive, contains some further details on one particular issue. This latter directive specifies that, where bidding costs are claimed, the applicant '*only*' needs to prove the existence of an infringement, that he had a '*real chance*' of winning the contract and that as a consequence of the infringement that chance was adversely affected.[2] This implies that this provision alleviates the burden on the applicant in that he does *not* need to demonstrate that he would have won the contract put out to tender but for the infringement.

The IPR Enforcement Directive provides that infringers that acted knowingly or with reasonable grounds to know are to be ordered to pay '*damages appropriate to the actual harm suffered by him/her as a result of the infringement*'.[3] It clarifies that these damages can be set in two ways. One option is setting them on the basis of '*all appropriate aspects*'. Mentioned in this connection are the negative economic consequences, including lost profits on the side of the injured party,

1 Art. 2(c) Public Sector Remedies Directive 89/665; Art. 2(d) Utilities Remedies Directive 92/13. See subsection 3.B.2 above.

2 Art. 2(7) Utilities Remedies Directive 92/13.

3 Art. 13(1) IPR Enforcement Directive 2004/48. See subsection 4.B.4 above. A largely similar regime has been set out in Commission, Proposal for a trade secrets directive, COM(2013) 813, p. 24 (Art. 13).

unfair profits made by the infringer and in appropriate cases elements other than economic factors such as the moral prejudice caused. The alternative is setting these damages as a lump sum, to be determined on the basis of elements such as (at least) the amount of royalties or fees that would have been due had authorisation been requested from the holder of the intellectual property right in question. It follows that, on the one hand, the rules on actions for damages applicable in intellectual property cases are on the whole somewhat more detailed than those applicable in public enforcement cases. On the other hand, the fact remains, however, that these rules are still formulated in rather general and non-committal terms. Several relevant elements are touched upon (causality, extent of damages), but often by means of an illustration or as an option rather than in a specific and prescriptive manner.

The picture concerning the Product Liability Directive's provisions on actions for damages is to some extent similar.[4] Here also is a degree of detail provided for. But at the same time several relevant issues are left either unaddressed or to be decided on an optional basis by the Member States. Central to this directive is the principle of no-fault liability of the producer of a defective product. It specifies that an injured party must prove the damage, the defect and the causal relationship between the defect and the damage. Hence there is no requirement to prove that the producer was at fault. It is further stipulated what the term "damage" entails in this connection, namely damage caused by death or personal injuries or damage to property, while non-material damage is expressly left to be regulated by national law.[5] The Product Liability Directive further contains provisions on contributory negligence by the injured party and on the producer not being able to limit or exclude its liability.[6] But issues such as causality or the quantification of the harm are not addressed. Furthermore, under this directive a party that risks being held liable has a number of defences at its disposal, but one of the most important of these, the development risks defence, is only provided for on an optional basis.[7] Similarly, Member States may or may not decide to cap the producer's liability.[8] Consequently, as the Commission acknowledged, the directive is '*only an initial step towards establishing a genuine producer liability policy at [EU] level*'.[9]

Finally, in many respects the Competition Damages Directive goes furthest in setting out common EU rules on damages claims. It stipulates that anyone who

4 Art. 4 Product Liability Directive 85/374. See section 5.D above.
5 Art. 9 Product Liability Directive 85/374.
6 Art. 8(2) and 12 Product Liability Directive 85/374.
7 Art. 7 and 15(1)(b) Product Liability Directive 85/374.
8 Art. 16 Product Liability Directive 85/374.
9 Commission, Green paper on liability for defective products, COM(1999) 396, p. 11.

has suffered harm has a right to full compensation for the harm caused, while specifying how the harm caused is to be qualified and quantified as well as how to deal with situations where the harm may have been "passed on".[10] It also contains rules on related matters such as the disclosure of evidence, the effects of infringement decisions taken by national competition authorities (and the courts reviewing those decisions), limitation periods and the joint and several liability of certain infringers.[11] However, on several points the directive does in fact little more than codify the case law of the Court of Justice. This is to a greater or lesser extent the case with respect to these rules on the qualification of the harm, legal standing and limitation periods.[12] And also the directive's provision on the quantification of harm seems in fact somewhat less substantial than might appear at first glance.[13] Moreover, several issues that had been initially identified as obstacles to the effective bringing of actions for damages, such as collective redress, fault requirements and legal costs, remain unaddressed in this directive.[14]

7.02 A second point is that for the EU legislature it has often been particularly *difficult to agree* on the above EU legislative measures. Almost without exception the provisions on damages claims in question were only adopted after lengthy and intense discussions and several amendments. While that applies to some extent for the Procurement Remedies Directives and the IPR Enforcement Directive,[15] it may be no coincidence that the two legal acts that are exclusively concerned with this substantive remedy, namely the Product Liability Directive and the Competition Damages Directive, proved to be particularly controversial. As regards the former, the Commission had taken years to prepare its proposal and the directive was subsequently eventually only adopted after a legislative process that lasted no less than another nine years.[16] As regards the latter, it is true that the law-making process itself was relatively speedy. But this should not distract from the fact that the Competition Damages Directive only came into being after an incubation time of almost a decade, during which this initiative proved to be highly controversial and the Commission aborted at the last moment an earlier attempt to adopt and submit

10 Art. 1(1), 3(1) and (2), 17 and 12–15 Competition Damages Directive 2014/104, respectively. See section 6.C above.

11 Art. 5–6, 9, 10 and 11 Competition Damages Directive 2014/104, respectively.

12 See also its Art. 4, which provides for a codification of the EU law principles of equivalence and effectiveness, discussed in subsections 2.A.2 and 2.A.3 above.

13 See para 7.15 below.

14 See para 6.24 above. On fault and causality under this directive, see also subsections 7.A.2 and 7.A.3 below, respectively. On collective redress and legal costs, see also subsections 5.C.2 above and 8.B.5 below, respectively.

15 See in particular para 3.05 and 3.16 above (concerning Procurement Remedies Directives 89/665 and 92/12) and para 4.05 and 4.27–4.29 above (concerning IPR Enforcement Directive 2004/48).

16 See para 5.25 above.

a proposal.[17] There is furthermore a case to be made that the fact that this directive was eventually proposed and adopted can be ascribed as much to a desire to protect the existing public enforcement mechanisms from possible negative consequences from increased private enforcement as to the ambition to facilitate private enforcement.[18]

The third general observation concerns the *practical importance* of this remedy. The Commission has over the years regularly observed that private party applicants wishing to bring actions for damages under the Procurement Remedies Directives, the IPR Enforcement Directive and the Product Liability Directive are typically confronted with many obstacles.[19] These obstacles include the length of the proceedings, high legal costs and difficulties in obtaining evidence and meeting the required standard of proof, as well as problems when seeking to quantify the harm caused by the infringement. Successful actions for damages for infringements of the relevant substantive rules of EU law brought under these directives are therefore rather scarce. In 1996 a study found, for instance, that EU-wide there had been '*no more than a handful*' of damages cases for infringements of EU public procurement law.[20] Since then there may have been a modest increase, but the overall level of damages litigation remains low.[21] The situation is largely similar where the Product Liability Directive is concerned. Roughly a decade after its adoption, a study noted that '*almost no cases have been reported under this directive*'.[22] Here also has an increase been observed more recently, but again the overall numbers of damages actions remain modest and the directive is moreover thought to have hardly contributed to this increase.[23] In relation to the IPR Enforcement Directive, the Commission observed in 2010 that '*damages awards in intellectual property cases are not requested by rightholders as a matter of course*'.[24] **7.03**

---

17 See subsection 6.B.3 above.

18 See para 6.23 and 6.24 above.

19 E.g. Commission, Green paper on public procurement in the EU, COM(96) 583, pp. 15 and 19; Commission, Second report on Product Liability Directive 85/374, COM(2000) 893, pp. 13–27; Commission, Impact assessment report on remedies in the field of public procurement, SEC(2006) 557, pp. 12–14; Commission, Staff working document accompanying the report on IPR Enforcement Directive 2004/48, SEC(2010) 1589, pp. 21–3; Commission, Responses to the public consultation on the civil enforcement of intellectual property rights, July 2013, p. 20.

20 Study, Herbert Smith (1996), p. 18. See also Brown (1998), p. 93.

21 Commission, Impact assessment report on remedies in the field of public procurement, SEC(2006) 557, pp. 16–17. See para 3.17 above.

22 Study, McKenna (1994), p. 45.

23 Study, Lovells (2003), pp. 31–8. See para 5.33 above.

24 Commission, Staff working document accompanying the report on IPR Enforcement Directive 2004/48, SEC(2010) 1589, p. 21.

This suggests that the much-discussed picture of '*astonishing diversity and total underdevelopment*' identified in a study dating from 2004 relating to actions for damages for infringement of EU competition law,[25] which was subsequently echoed by the Commission and provided the basis for its initiative in this field,[26] is not exceptional. It rather seems to be in line with the state of play in EU law generally, certain variations between the different fields of law and between the different national jurisdictions notwithstanding. That such a situation exists in the above-mentioned fields other than competition law is all the more striking, given that in those fields EU legislative measures that aim to facilitate the bringing of these actions were enacted years or even decades ago. That this is a more general phenomenon seems to be confirmed by the fact that the situation seems to a great extent comparable to where actions for damages brought pursuant to the principle of Member State liability are concerned.[27]

It consequently appears that the secondary EU law at issue here has on the whole been at best only modestly successful where it seeks to facilitate the bringing of actions for damages by private parties before national courts. It remains to be seen whether the situation will be fundamentally different in relation to competition law infringements once the Competition Damages Directive has been transposed into national law (which is due by the end of 2016) and can thus be relied upon by private parties wishing to claim damages for competition law infringements. In this field, the number of damages actions brought appears already to be increasing, even in the absence of applicable EU legislative measures.[28]

7.04 That leads to the fourth general observation. Across the different fields of law at issue here, there appears to be a *discrepancy in the conclusions drawn*, especially by the Commission, on the basis of the findings referred to in the previous paragraph. The observation that generally few actions for damages are brought, that the relevant national laws differ and that private parties wishing to bring such actions tend to encounter various obstacles has been reason for intense activities in the field of EU competition law. These activities include the

25 Study, Ashurst (2004), p. 1.

26 Commission, Green paper on damages actions for breach of the EC antitrust rules, COM(2005) 672, p. 4. See subsection 6.B.3 above.

27 See Van Dam (2006), p. 40, where it is noted that the applicants bringing actions for damages pursuant to the principle of Member State liability often '*entered the hall of fame, but lost the case*'. This refers to the fact that in landmark cases such as *Francovich*, *Brasserie du Pêcheur* and *Köbler*, the applicants were ultimately unsuccessful in their efforts to obtain compensation in damages. See also Lock (2012), p. 1675. On the principle of Member State liability generally, see para 2.23 above. The situation might well be comparable where the liability of the EU under Art. 340 TFEU is concerned. See e.g. Kaleda (2014), p. 193 (regarding actions for damages in the context of public procurement by the EU institutions and other bodies).

28 See para 6.23 above.

publication of official documents, the commissioning of studies, the consultation of stakeholders, an attempt to propose a directive that was aborted at the last moment and eventually the submission of a proposal for and the adoption of the Competition Damages Directive.[29] During this period this remedy has thus clearly been the '*legal and political fashion*' in this field.[30]

In contrast, similar activities are notably absent in relation to the three other fields mentioned above, where the relevant directives have already been in place for years, if not decades. Take the Product Liability Directive. As noted above, relatively few damages claims have been brought under this directive. Having published a green paper in 1999 with possible measures aimed at facilitating the bringing of such claims,[31] the Commission observed in 2001 that '*[i]n practice it may be difficult to prove that a product was defective and/or that a causal link exists*'.[32] It also noted that the legal situation in the Member States differed, including for instance national rules on the disclosure of evidence.[33] However, neither at that time nor at a later stage has this led to any amendments to the directive or other legislative measures being proposed to increase the effectiveness of this remedy. The Commission maintains that there is a lack of evidence that the identified divergences cause significant trade barriers or distortions of competition.[34] Yet it seems to have made little effort to obtain such evidence.[35] Its references to the controversies that existed when adopting this directive and the delicate balance that it establishes between the various interests at stake give the impression that this inaction is at least in part motivated by political considerations.[36]

This contrast between the shortcoming observed and the lack of even an attempt at a legislative response is arguably most striking in the field of EU public procurement law. Facilitating actions for damages was originally an important element of the EU's private enforcement-facilitating approach in

29 See subsections 6.B.3, 6.B.4 and 6.C.1 above.

30 Milutinovic (2010), p. 143.

31 Commission, Green paper on liability for defective products, COM(1999) 396.

32 Commission, Second report on Product Liability Directive 85/374, COM(2000) 893, p. 13. See also Commission, Fourth report on Product Liability Directive 85/374, COM(2011) 547, pp. 7–8.

33 Ibid., pp. 14–15.

34 Commission, Fourth report on Product Liability Directive 85/374, COM(2011) 547, p. 11. See para 5.33 above.

35 Note that the officially commissioned study by Lovells (2003), pp. 15–28, dates from almost a decade earlier.

36 Cf. e.g. Commission, Second report on Product Liability Directive 85/374, COM(2000) 893, p. 12; Commission, Third report on Product Liability Directive 85/374, COM(2006) 496, p. 6. See European Parliament, Resolution on the Commission green paper on liability for defective products, A5-0061/2000; Council, Resolution on amendment of the liability for defective products directive, OJ 2002, C 26/2. These latter documents suggest opposing views by the two branches of the EU legislature.

this field.[37] It seems, however, that this remedy has over the years become particularly unfashionable. For when the Procurement Remedies Directives were revised in 2007, it was expressly decided not to concentrate on this remedy.[38] The Commission explained this choice by arguing that damages awards had '*little deterrent effect on [contracting] authorities, especially because [private parties] who feel that their interests have been harmed must prove that they had serious chances of being awarded the contract*'.[39] In this connection it pointed to the '*inherent limits*' of damages actions, notably the (alleged) absence of real corrective effects, practical difficulties and the length and costs of the legal proceedings.[40] In this case the above-mentioned obstacles typically encountered by injured private parties seeking compensation (costs, burden of proof, quantification, and so on) were thus cited as reasons *not* to take legislative action on this point, whereas essentially the same obstacles were seen precisely as reasons to *act* where infringements of competition law were concerned. The particularities of a given field of EU law can of course justify a policy choice to concentrate for instance on other remedies. Nonetheless, the contrast in the approach followed by this same institution at around the same time in these two fields of law is striking. That applies all the more so in light of the (at best) questionable explanation given for this difference in approach.[41]

---

37 Cf. e.g. Commission, Proposal for Utilities Remedies Directive 92/13, COM(90) 297, p. 19: '*the possibility of claims for damages will be a particularly important part of the system*'.

38 Instead a new contractual remedy was introduced. See subsection 3.B.3 above.

39 Commission, Proposal for Procurement Remedies Amending Directive 2007/66, COM(2006) 195, p. 2.

40 Commission, Impact assessment report on remedies in the field of public procurement, SEC(2006) 557, p. 12. See also its p. 20 and pp. 26–7.

41 See Commission, Impact assessment report on remedies in the field of public procurement, SEC(2006) 557, p. 27 (n. 32). Here it is argued that the situation in procurement law is substantially different from the one existing in relation to competition law, because in the former case the damages are paid from the public purse whereas in the latter case compensation is paid by an undertaking. As a matter of fact, this observation generally seems correct. However, this appears to overlook the fact that private undertakings can in certain cases be subject to EU public procurement law, just as public bodies can be subject to EU competition law. More importantly, from the perspective of the private party having suffered damage, *any* damages award will serve to compensate the harm caused, regardless from which purse it is paid. As such, this award does have a corrective effect. Furthermore, the underlying suggestion that exposing contracting authorities to the risk of financial consequences in cases of infringements does not have a corrective or deterrent effect is debatable. It is at odds with the logic underlying the principle of Member State liability for infringements of EU law (discussed in para 2.23 above), even if the provision on actions for damages set out in Procurement Remedies Directives 89/665 and 92/13 gives concrete expression to precisely this principle of Member State liability (see CoJ case C-568/08, *Combinatie Spijker*, discussed in para 3.19 above). This suggestion also seems internally inconsistent, given that Art. 2(1)(c) and (5) Utilities Remedies Directive 92/13 provides for the possibility of a payment by the contracting authorities of a "dissuasive sum" and, moreover, that during the very same 2007 revision the possibility of imposing a fine on contracting authorities was introduced (see Art. 2e(2) Procurement Remedies Directives 89/665 and 92/13). See also Commission, Staff working paper accompanying the green paper on damages actions for breach of EC antitrust rules, SEC(2005) 1732, p. 9 (n. 3).

By means of a concluding remark concerning the above general issues, it appears that EU legislative involvement in actions for damages for infringements of EU law is a topic that is not without contradictions. This remedy is provided for in most of the legislation at issue here. It generally also receives considerable attention from stakeholders, academics and institutional actors alike. But the degree of harmonisation provided for is all in all typically rather modest. Moreover, in practice this remedy often functions in a manner that leaves much to be desired. Whereas the shortcomings observed do not tend to vary much across the various fields of law at hand, these findings are in some cases reason for putting a lot of energy into trying to address them through the EU legislative measures (competition law), while in other fields the more recent legislative response has been largely muted (product liability law, intellectual property law) or this remedy even seems to have largely been given up altogether (public procurement law). In this light, one may thus be inclined to agree with Advocate General Sharpston's description of damages claims as being '*generically awkward*'.[42] **7.05**

Having said that, the above observation relating to the difficulties that the EU legislature often experiences in trying to agree on measures to facilitate the bringing of actions for damages for infringements of EU law probably goes a long way in explaining this, at first sight, perhaps somewhat confusing state of affairs. Most of the aforementioned contradictions may in effect rather be *paradoxes*. At the risk of oversimplification, those difficulties probably explain in large part the generally only modestly prescriptive character of the EU law provisions in question. For where a particular issue proves controversial, a (political) solution may well be found in addressing it only in vague terms, leaving the matter in question entirely unaddressed or by inserting an optional provision.[43] Such solutions in turn might well provide at least a partial explanation for the practical problems that injured parties often continue to encounter when seeking to obtain compensation in damages. It might also explain the tendency in situations where EU legislation on this remedy exists to either not propose further amendments to that legislation or to concentrate on other remedies instead. Seen against this background, it also seems hardly surprising that the initiative leading to the Competition Damages Directive proved to be controversial, just as the observed state of "diversity" and "total underdevelopment" at national level that provided the thrust for this initiative seems considerably less exceptional and therefore perhaps also considerably less "astonishing" than sometimes seems to be presumed.

42 Opinion AG Sharpston case C-432/05, *Unibet*, para 49.

43 See para 10.13 below.

2. Fault

7.06 The first of five more specific issues relating to the secondary EU law on actions for damages under consideration here concerns fault requirements. The Procurement Remedies Directives do not expressly address this subject matter at all. The IPR Enforcement Directive's provision on actions for damages refers to the infringing party having acted knowingly or with reasonable grounds to know.[44] This is normally understood as a fault requirement of sorts.[45] By contrast, the absence of a fault requirement is central to the "strict" liability approach set out in the Product Liability Directive.[46] Finally, concerning EU competition law, after having considered a number of options, including no-fault liability, in its 2008 white paper and in its 2009 unofficial draft proposal, the Commission initially suggested opting for a sort of middle way in the form of a rebuttable presumption of fault.[47] But in its subsequent proposal for the Competition Damages Directive, this issue was in the end entirely left out, in light of the criticism that those earlier suggestions received, particularly from the side of businesses.[48] As a result this directive does not address issues of fault other than through a statement in its recitals that the Member States should be able to maintain a requirement of this kind '*in as far as they comply with the case law of the Court of Justice, the principles of equivalence and effectiveness, and this directive*'.[49]

The foregoing shows that the question whether, and if so to what extent, an applicant must demonstrate that the defendant was at fault when infringing the applicable rules of EU law in order to obtain compensation in damages is answered *very differently* in the four fields of law under consideration. The more general picture of EU law being '*extremely heterogeneous*'[50] on this point therefore also holds true where these four fields of law are concerned. In several other acts of secondary EU law, a range of approaches on fault-related matters can be found. This can involve an express fault requirement,[51] something in between

44 Art. 13(1) IPR Enforcement Directive 2004/48. Its Art. 13(2) contains an optional rule for cases where the infringer did not act knowingly or with reasonable grounds to know.

45 Cf. e.g. Lukas (2008), p. 82.

46 Art. 4 Product Liability Directive 85/374.

47 Commission, White paper on damages actions for breach of the EC antitrust rules, COM(2008) 165, pp. 6–7. On the above-mentioned unofficial draft proposal, see para 6.20 above.

48 Commission, Impact assessment report on damages actions for breach of the EU antitrust rules, SWD(2013) 203, p. 35.

49 Recital 11 Competition Damages Directive 2014/104.

50 Lukas (2008), p. 101.

51 Art. 35a(1) Credit Rating Agencies Regulation 1060/2009, which refers to the committing of infringements '*intentionally or with gross negligence*'. Cf. recital 33 Regulation 462/2013, which inserted this Art. 35a into Credit Rating Agencies Regulation 1060/2009. Note, however, that, pursuant to its Art. 35(4), the terms "intention" and "negligence" are to be interpreted and applied in accordance with the applicable national law.

an express fault requirement and the express absence of such a requirement,[52] or a rebuttable presumption of fault.[53]

7.07 The case law of the Court of Justice is also to be considered. Of particular relevance is the Court's 2010 ruling in *Stadt Graz*.[54] In that case it was clarified that the Procurement Remedies Directives *preclude* a fault requirement established on the basis of national law in relation to actions for damages brought under these directives, even where national law provides for a presumption of fault that it is for the defendant to rebut. The Court noted that the wording of the relevant provisions of those directives do not indicate that the infringement giving rise to a right to damages is to be connected to fault. It also took account of the function that this remedy plays under these directives. It noted that a fault requirement means that an injured party runs the risk of not, or only belatedly, being compensated. This was deemed to be contrary to the objective of these directives, which is ensuring effective and rapid review. This ruling is of evident importance for public procurement cases, but it may also be of broader relevance. The question is then whether by analogy to the Court's reasoning in *Stadt Graz* a more general argument can be made that EU law precludes fault requirements established on the basis of national law in relation to actions for damages for infringements of EU law. It is submitted that in this respect a distinction should be made between the following two situations.

In the first place, there is the situation where *specific EU legislation* concerning liability in damages applies, but does not expressly deal with issues of fault. In such cases, reasoning similar to *Stadt Graz* may well be applied. Indeed in *Dekker*, a case dating from 1990 relating to the Gender Equality Directive, the Court of Justice came to a similar conclusion to the one formulated in *Stadt Graz*.[55] In *Dekker* it was also found that this directive did not allow for a fault requirement. Also, this conclusion was based on the absence of any explicit reference in the directive, combined with the need to safeguard the practical effect of the principles underlying it. The Court added in a subsequent case that this applies '*no matter how easy it would be to adduce proof of fault*'.[56] This case law thus suggests that, where the applicable specific EU legislation provides for civil liability in damages without the issue of fault being expressly addressed therein, a fault requirement established under national law for the award of damages for

---

52 Art. 5 Package Travel Directive 90/314. See para 5.34 above.

53 E.g. Art. 6(1) and (2) Directive 1999/93/EC on a Community framework for electronic signatures, OJ 2000, L 13/12 ("Electronic Signatures Directive"); Art. 20(3) Public Limited Liabilities Companies Directive 2012/30.

54 CoJ case C-314/09, *Stadt Graz*, para 30–45. See para 3.19 above.

55 CoJ case C-177/88, *Dekker*, para 22–5. See Gender Equality Directive 2006/54.

56 CoJ case C-180/95, *Draehmpaehl*, para 21.

infringements of the relevant substantive rules of EU law may well be precluded, no matter how low the threshold to prove fault actually is. It is for now an open question as to how the Competition Damages Directive is to be assessed in this light. The fact that it does not contain an express fault requirement could be understood to imply that the above logic is also applicable here and that therefore such a requirement is precluded. However, in this particular case this view seems to be contradicted by the above-mentioned statement in the recitals of this directive that the Member States should in principle continue to be able to impose fault-related conditions. While the latter therefore appears to be the better view, there is certainly some scope for debate in this respect, especially in light of the not unequivocal reference in these recitals to the need to comply with the Court's case law, the principles of equivalence and effectiveness and the directive itself.[57]

All this is to be distinguished from the second situation, where *no specific EU legislation* of the type at issue in *Stadt Graz* and *Dekker* applies. This thus concerns cases where there is no specific rule of secondary EU law regulating the possibility of bringing actions for damages for infringements of EU law. Then the logic followed in those rulings is probably not applicable. After all, as was explained above, the outcome in *Stadt Graz* and in *Dekker* was based on two key considerations. In the first place, arguably the main point was the absence of an explicit provision on fault in the specific EU legislation at issue. The Court of Justice essentially seemed to reason that the decision by the EU legislature not to address this issue explicitly as a matter of EU law should be taken to mean that there cannot be a requirement of fault under national law. In the second place, the result reached was closely tied to the need to ensure the effectiveness of the applicable EU legislation regulating damages claims. That seems to imply that there are no grounds for drawing comparable conclusions where no such EU legislation applies. Put differently, the interests associated with safeguarding the effectiveness of the applicable rules of *substantive* EU law alone are unlikely to be sufficient to justify the conclusion that a fault requirement established in national law is as such unacceptable.[58] This suggests that the above-mentioned case law does not imply that EU law generally precludes a

57 Note that in CoJ joined cases C-295/04 to C-298/04, *Manfredi*, para 61–3, discussed in para 6.15 above, no explicit reference was made to a fault requirement. On that basis it was suggested in Commission, Staff working paper accompanying the white paper on damages actions for breach of the EC antitrust rules, SEC(2008) 404, p. 51, that no such requirement can apply in respect of actions for damages for infringements of EU competition law. This view has been contested, however. See Eilmansberger (2007), p. 458.

58 Admittedly this may be somewhat less clear from *Dekker*, because that ruling can be read as indicating that the CoJ was (also) concerned with the effectiveness (practical effect) of the *substantive* rules in question, and not (only) with the relevant provisions on enforcement (see its para 22–5). However, in CoJ case C-180/95, *Draehmpaehl*, para 21, the absence of an express fault requirement in the relevant directive is highlighted, rather than this effectiveness argument.

fault requirement in relation to actions for damages for infringements of that law.[59] It follows that as the law stands, in cases where EU law does not expressly address this issue, it is to be determined in accordance with the applicable national law whether or not such a requirement applies (and if so what it entails), subject to the principles of equivalence and effectiveness.[60]

Another potentially relevant line of case law relates to the principle of *Member State liability*.[61] In this context the Court of Justice has repeatedly addressed the issue of fault. It has held that one of the three conditions for incurring Member State liability in damages is the existence of '*a sufficiently serious breach*' of the applicable rule of EU law.[62] Relevant factors in this respect include the clarity and precision of the rule in question, the measure of discretion, whether there was any intention and whether the error of law was excusable.[63] The Court has noted that such factors may well be connected with the concept of fault as it exists in a national legal system.[64] This test seems to come close to a test of negligence.[65] However, the Court has also held that beyond the condition of a sufficiently serious breach, there is no scope for any requirement based on fault, whether intentional or negligent, for Member State liability to be incurred.[66] It further appears that the requirement of a sufficiently serious breach applies only where the Member State that infringed EU law did so in relation to an issue where it had discretion, notably where it exercises its legislative function.[67] There is case law suggesting that a *mere* infringement may be sufficient to incur liability where there is only reduced or no discretion.[68] In the legal literature a **7.08**

59 See also the discussion in para 2.27 above on the EU law principle of private party liability and the "constitutive" conditions for incurring such liability set by EU law.

60 Cf. e.g. CoJ case C-348/98, *Mendes Ferreira*, para 28–9. On the principles of equivalence and effectiveness, see subsections 2.A.2 and 2.A.3 above.

61 On the principle of Member State liability generally, see para 2.23 above. Note that in CoJ case C-568/08, *Combinatie Spijker*, para 87, it was held that the provision on actions for damages set out in Procurement Remedies Directives 89/665 and 92/13 gives expression to this principle of Member State liability. In that case, reference is also made to the requirement of a sufficiently serious breach. That raises some questions as to how this ruling relates to the aforementioned *Stadt Graz* ruling (CoJ case C-314/09, *Stadt Graz)*. For the present purposes, it suffices to note that there are no indications that this link with Member State liability made in *Combinatie Spijker* played any role in the Court's ruling in *Stadt Graz* in respect of fault requirements. For a discussion of these two rulings, see para 3.19 above.

62 CoJ joined cases C-46/93 and C-48/93, *Brasserie du Pêcheur*, in particular para 51 and 55–7. It has been observed that for an applicant it is in practice often particularly difficult to demonstrate that this condition has been met. See Lock (2012), pp. 1693–7.

63 Ibid., in particular para 56.

64 Ibid., para 78.

65 Cf. Van Dam (2006), p. 254.

66 CoJ joined cases C-46/93 and C-48/93, *Brasserie du Pêcheur*, para 75 and 79. See e.g. also CoJ joined cases C-178/94, C-179/94 and C-188/94 to C-190/94, *Dillenkofer*, para 28.

67 Ibid., in particular para 38 and 46. See e.g. also CoJ case C-224/01, *Köbler*, para 51–6. In this latter case it was clarified that where breaches of EU law by the *judiciary* are concerned, this requirement should be understood as meaning that a *manifest* infringement of EU law is required in order to incur Member State liability.

68 E.g. CoJ case C-4/94, *Hedley Lomas*, para 28.

parallel has regularly been drawn in this respect between the liability in damages of Member States and of private parties. In particular, it is widely agreed that in disputes between private parties there is hardly any scope (if at all) to require a sufficiently serious breach.[69] After all, private parties normally do not have the "State-type" discretion referred to here, as Member States do when they exercise their law-making functions.

On that basis it is sometimes suggested that therefore *any* infringement of a rule of EU law *by a private party* could lead to an obligation to compensate the damage caused, without there being scope for any requirement of fault.[70] It is, however, submitted that this view is contestable. For one thing, the above case law on Member State liability can probably not be simplified to the point that it necessarily implies "automatic" (that is, no-fault) liability in the absence of discretion.[71] The formulation used by the Court of Justice on this issue tends to be rather cautious, indicating that a mere infringement '*may*' be sufficient. Discretion, moreover, seems less and less the only decisive criterion in the relevant case law. Instead, account can also be taken of other factors, including a duty of care, complexity and intention.[72] Indeed, it has been held that '*illegality as such never leads automatically to liability*' where the non-contractual liability of the EU under Article 340 TFEU is concerned, while '*[t]he convergence [of Member State liability and EU non-contractual liability] argument can also be used to set aside the idea that no-fault liability might exist in Member State liability*'.[73] There is no reason to believe that such other factors are inherently inapplicable in situations where a private party infringed EU law. For another thing, even while there is certainly a degree of parallelism between Member State and private party liability for breaches of EU law, it is as yet still largely an open question as to precisely what extent the above-mentioned case law on the former can and should be transposed to the context of the latter.[74] There are certain differences that may well argue against a "one-to-one" transplant, the

69 E.g. Dougan (2004), pp. 37 and 242; Van Gerven (2004a), p. 522; Tridimas (2006), p. 544; Komninos (2009), p. 398; Milutinovic (2010), p. 112. For a different approach, see e.g. Reich (2010), pp. 126–7.

70 In this sense see e.g. Opinion AG Van Gerven case C-128/92, *Banks*, para 53; Commission, Staff working paper accompanying the white paper on damages actions for breach of the EC antitrust rules, SEC(2008) 404, p. 51.

71 In a similar sense, see Eilmansberger (2007), pp. 458–9.

72 That applies in particular (but not exclusively) as regards the case law on the non-contractual liability of the EU. See e.g. CoJ case C-47/07 P, *Masdar*, para 90–91; GC case T-437/10, *Gap SA granen & producten*, para 15 and 28; GC case T-333/10, *ATC*, para 61–3; GC case T-384/11, *Safa Nicu Sepahan*, para 50–55. As regards Member State liability, see e.g. Opinion AG Léger case C-224/01, *Köbler*, para 138–9; CoJ case C-424/97, *Haim*, para 42–3. See further Hilson (2005), p. 677; Van Dam (2006), pp. 500–504; Biondi and Farley (2009), p. 130; Wakefield (2009), p. 406; Gutman (2011), p. 723.

73 Aalto (2011), p. 204. On the said convergence, see also para 2.23 above.

74 See also para 2.27 above.

issue of discretion not being the least among them.[75] It follows that the case law on Member State liability may well be of some relevance in the present context, but it does not necessarily imply that there is no scope for a fault requirement in relation to damages claims for infringements of EU law brought by one private party against another.

As a final point, it is worthwhile to consider the *effects* of the EU rules on fault discussed above. The first observation in this regard concerns their effects on the *national laws* of the Member States. It is true that, in the words of the Court of Justice, '*the concept of fault does not have the same content in the various legal systems*' of the Member States.[76] Nonetheless, almost all legal orders of the Member States have in common that, as a general rule, they perceive a fault requirement, in one form or another, as a criterion for the imputation of damages liability.[77] That means that, where EU law precludes such a requirement, the consequences for national law can be significant indeed. It has been seen above that this is the case under the Product Liability Directive as well as (as construed by the Court of Justice) the Procurement Remedies Directives and the Gender Equality Directive and arguably any other comparable act of secondary EU law. Accordingly, national law often needs to be amended where secondary EU law precludes a fault requirement. Where this has not (yet) been done, national courts must disapply any such national fault requirements in concrete cases. **7.09**

The second observation concerns the effects *in practice* of the EU rules under consideration here. It was noted above that many different approaches in relation to fault requirements can be found in the legislation under consideration, ranging from an (almost) explicit fault requirement to an (almost) explicit lack of such a requirement, with certain intermediate approaches. One would logically presume that where a private party has to demonstrate fault for liability to be incurred, it will normally be more difficult to successfully bring an action for damages. This presumption was central to the adoption of the Product

75 In the words of CoJ joined cases C-46/93 and C-48/93, *Brasserie du Pêcheur*, para 42, even when assuming that the conditions under which a private party may incur liability for damages cannot differ from those governing the liability of a Member State, this only applies in '*like circumstances*' and '*in the absence of a particular justification*' for any such difference.

76 CoJ joined cases C-46/93 and C-48/93, *Brasserie du Pêcheur*, para 76 (in the context of Member State liability in damages). See also e.g. Van Gerven, Lever and Larouche (2000), pp. 300–306; Van Dam (2006), pp. 113–16.

77 Lukas (2008), p. 81; Kellner (2009), p. 139. See e.g. also Opinion AG Cosmos case C-348/98, *Mendes Ferreira*, para 50; Commission, Staff working paper accompanying the white paper on damages actions for breach of the EC antitrust rules, SEC(2008) 404, p. 50. There are exceptions, however, for example in relation to intellectual property rights. See Study, European observatory on counterfeiting and piracy (undated d), pp. 1 and 6. In some Member States the issue of fault is addressed primarily through the concept of attribution.

Liability Directive.[78] It was also an important element in the reasoning of the Court of Justice in *Stadt Graz* and *Dekker*.[79] However, as was noted earlier, in each of the fields of law at issue here, successful actions for damages are generally rather scarce.[80] That applies for actions brought on the basis of EU legislation that imposes a fault requirement (for example the IPR Enforcement Directive) as much as it does for actions brought under EU legislation that insists on the absence of such a requirement (for example the Product Liability Directive). Therefore, contrary to what one might expect, there seems to be no clear relationship between the degree of (successful) damages litigation, on the one hand, and the existence or absence of a fault requirement as a matter of EU law, on the other hand. Even if this does not necessarily mean that it is *irrelevant* whether or not the relevant secondary EU law provides for a fault requirement, the foregoing suggests that in and of itself this is unlikely to be a *decisive* factor. In that sense, the effects of EU legislative intervention in relation to fault should probably not be overstated.

This latter finding can be explained at least in part by the fact that the differences between fault and no-fault approaches referred to above are often not as clear-cut as this terminology might suggest.[81] The transition between the two approaches rather tends to be more fluent.[82] Take for instance the apparently most "extreme" no-fault ("strict") liability provided for by the Product Liability Directive. Its effects are in fact significantly limited and moderated through a range of specific provisions, such as particular defences, time bars, financial ceilings and limited heads of damages to be compensated.[83] Similarly, the phrase '*knowingly or with reasonable grounds to know*' laid down in the IPR Enforcement Directive allows for a range of nuanced approaches. Paradoxically, in practice the most "extreme" result may well emerge where issues of fault have not been dealt with at all in the EU legislation at hand. As has been seen above, this absence of explicit rules was one of the reasons for the Court of Justice to rule that the Procurement Remedies Directives preclude a fault requirement. These directives thus in effect also establish no-fault liability

78 See e.g. Commission, Proposal for Product Liability Directive 85/374, COM(76) 372, p. 13, where it is stated that it is '*extremely difficult or even impossible*' to prove fault on the part of the producer.

79 See para 7.07 above. See e.g. also CoJ joined cases C-46/93 and C-48/93, *Brasserie du Pêcheur*, para 79: '*[i]mposition of such a supplementary condition [of fault, beyond a sufficiently serious breach] would be tantamount to calling in question the right to reparation founded on the [EU] legal order*'.

80 See in particular para 7.03 above.

81 There are in all likelihood several other factors that are of relevance when explaining the lack of a clear correlation between the number of successful damages claims and the presence or absence of a fault requirement as a matter of EU law, including other applicable rules of EU or national law on issues such as legal standing, limitation periods, quantification of harm, etc., as well as "unwritten obstacles" such as cultural attitudes towards litigation. On the latter, see para 10.34 below.

82 Lukas (2008), p. 81. See also Van Dam (2006), p. 12.

83 See para 5.29–5.32 above.

in damages, as is the case in the Product Liability Directive, but given that the issue of fault is not expressly addressed, they do not contain limiting or moderating measures of the sort found in the Product Liability Directive.

3. Causality

Most of the secondary EU law considered in Part B goes at least some way in making it explicit that, for liability in damages to be incurred, it needs to be demonstrated that there is a causal link between the infringement at issue and the harm suffered. Both the IPR Enforcement Directive and the Product Liability Directive expressly require such a causal link, be it in somewhat different wording. Whereas the former speaks of prejudice suffered '*as a result*' of the infringement,[84] the latter expressly refers to the requirement of a '*causal relationship*' between the defect in the product and the damage.[85] The Procurement Remedies Directives are less explicit, but it is beyond doubt that in this connection too, a causality requirement applies.[86] Neither can there be any doubt in relation to the Competition Damages Directive, which establishes a right to compensation for anyone who has suffered harm '*caused by*' the infringements at issue.[87] This latter rule is essentially a codification of the Court's ruling in *Manfredi*, where it was held that a private party wishing to claim damages for a competition law infringement must demonstrate the existence of a '*causal relationship*' between the harm suffered and that infringement.[88] **7.10**

A similar picture emerges when we look beyond the EU legislation assessed in Part B above. For instance, the Gender Equality Directive refers (much like the IPR Enforcement Directive) to compensation for the loss or damage sustained by a person injured '*as a result of*' discrimination on grounds of sex.[89] And in relation to the principle of Member State liability in damages for infringements of EU law, the Court of Justice has furthermore long made it clear that a

84 Art. 13(1) IPR Enforcement Directive 2004/48.

85 Art. 4 Product Liability Directive 85/374.

86 A causality requirement is inherent in these directives' provisions on damages, which speak of the '*award of damages to persons injured by the infringement*' (see Art. 2(c) Public Sector Remedies Directive 89/665 and Art. 2(d) Utilities Remedies Directive 92/13). See also Art. 2(7) Utilities Remedies Directive 92/13 on compensation for bidding costs, discussed in para 3.16 above, where it is stipulated that the applicant must demonstrate that its chance of winning the contract in question was adversely affected '*as a consequence*' of the infringement. See also CoJ case C-568/08, *Combinatie Spijker*, para 87, where reference is made to the requirement of a '*direct causal link*'.

87 See Art. 1(1) and 3(1) Competition Damages Directive 2014/104. See also its Art. 3(2), pursuant to which a private party that has suffered harm must be placed in a position in which that party would have been had the infringement not been committed.

88 CoJ joined cases C-295/04 to C-298/04, *Manfredi*, para 61. See para 6.15 above.

89 Art. 18 Gender Equality Directive 2006/54.

causality requirement applies. It is settled case law that in this connection a '*direct causal link*' must be demonstrated between the damage and the infringement.[90] The Court has called this an '*indispensable condition governing the right to compensation*'.[91] In most national jurisdictions, a causality requirement also applies in relation to actions for damages, even if there can be considerable differences in what precisely is understood by this concept.[92] All in all, it therefore seems safe to say that causation is inherent in damages liability.[93]

7.11 However, *providing* for a causality requirement is one thing; clarifying how the concept of causality is to be precisely *understood* can be quite another matter. In practice there are many acts or events that can "break the causality chain" and can thus prevent (full) liability from being incurred. Just to give one example, it may not always be easy to prove that the existence of an anti-competitive cartel agreement within the meaning of Article 101(1) TFEU caused damage to a particular party that purchased the products to which the cartel relates. An applicant having suffered harm may need to convincingly address a number of issues when seeking to demonstrate that the cartel caused or contributed to the harm, and not certain other factors, such as the acts or omissions of third parties (subcontractors, intermediaries, and so on) or the behaviour of the applicant himself. This can be challenging, especially where the commercial and economic context is complex.

It can therefore be of particular importance precisely how, legally speaking, the concept of causation is understood. Yet only the Product Liability Directive goes some way in specifying this and then only on one particular point. This directive provides for the possibility of the liability to be reduced or even disallowed entirely where there is contributory negligence on the part of the party claiming damages (while excluding this possibility where the damage is also caused by a third party).[94] Apart from that, none of the legal acts considered in Part B specifies in any detail precisely what is meant by the requirement of causality. In its recitals the Competition Damages Directive

---

90 E.g. CoJ joined cases C-46/93 and C-48/93, *Brasserie du Pêcheur*, para 51; CoJ case C-118/08, *Transportes Urbanos*, para 30. As regards the use of the word "direct" in this connection, although some uncertainty exists, it is not immediately evident that this is meant to point to any significant difference in substance as compared to the causality test applied in the above-mentioned EU legislation or the *Manfredi* judgment. Note that in CoJ case C-557/12, *Kone*, which builds on *Manfredi*, the CoJ refers to the existence of '*a direct causal link*' (see its para 33).

91 CoJ case C-420/11, *Leth*, para 45.

92 See further e.g. Study, Ashurst (2004), pp. 72–4; Van Dam (2006), pp. 270–79; Kellner (2009), pp. 142–9.

93 Cf. Durant (2008), p. 47.

94 Art. 8 Product Liability Directive 85/374. The issue of contributory negligence is not always assessed in the context of causality, but these two issues seem in any case closely connected. This connection is such that it has been held that it is impossible to divorce any theory of contributory negligence from the concept of causation. See Van Dam (2006), p. 268.

states that this is a matter not dealt with in that directive, which implies that this is in principle left to be regulated by the applicable rules of national law.[95]

Not only the EU *legislature*, but also the EU *courts* seem mostly to take something of a "hands-off" approach in respect of causality. Rulings that go into detail on the requirement of causality that applies in the context of the principle of *Member State liability* are rather scarce.[96] In this connection the Court of Justice has at times applied a requirement of reasonable diligence on the part of the injured party in limiting the extent of the loss or damage, holding that a failure to do so can break the causality chain in whole or in part.[97] This entails a particular form of contributory negligence, whereby the negligence of the applicant does not relate to the *occurrence of the act* leading to liability being incurred, but rather to the *extent of the damage* resulting from that act. The Court's finding that this requirement of due diligence on the part of the applicant constitutes a general principle common to the legal systems of the Member States suggests that it can be applied more broadly.[98] It can therefore probably also be invoked in relation to the EU legislation discussed in Part B. Other than that the Court has, however, restricted itself to clarifying that the applicable test is whether the damage claimed '*flows sufficiently directly from the breach of [EU] law to render the [Member] State liable to make it good*'.[99] This provides only limited further precision as to the precise meaning of the concept of causality.[100] Indeed it has been noted that, while the Court tends to maintain control over the other conditions that apply in this regard, it seems to have "decentralised" this aspect of the Member State liability test by typically leaving it to the national courts to determine the question of causation.[101] **7.12**

95 Recital 11 Competition Damages Directive 2014/104.

96 On the principle of Member State liability generally, see para 2.23 above.

97 E.g. CoJ joined cases C-46/93 and C-48/93, *Brasserie du Pêcheur*, para 84–5; CoJ case C-445/06, *Danske Slagterier*, para 61.

98 This principle has also been applied in relation to the non-contractual liability of the EU under Art. 340 TFEU. See e.g. CoJ case 145/83, *Adams*, para 53–4; CoJ joined cases C-104/89 and C-37/90, *Mulder*, para 26 and 33; GC case T-437/10, *Gap SA granen & producten*, para 81. Cf. e.g. also Study, Expert group on European contract law (2011) (Art. 166–7).

99 CoJ case C-446/04, *Test Claimants*, para 218. See also CoJ case C-319/96, *Brinkmann*, para 29. In this respect the CoJ's case law on the non-contractual liability of the EU, with which the case law on Member States has converged (as discussed in para 2.23 above), occasionally offers more clarification. See e.g. GC case T-384/11, *Safa Nicu Sepahan*, para 71. For a discussion see Gutman (2011), pp. 725–34. See also Durant (2008), pp. 56–79.

100 Even if this is rather broadly formulated as well, more helpful may be the following description that the requirement of causality has been met where '*the damage arises directly from the conduct of the wrongdoer and does not depend on the intervention of other causes, whether positive or negative. That means that the cause may not be too remote or too broad and unspecific. It also means that intervening causes, such as contributory negligence of the applicant, may break the chain of causation*'. See Van Gerven (2004b), p. 238.

101 Biondi and Farley (2009), p. 55. See e.g. also Lock (2012), pp. 1697–8.

Furthermore in *Manfredi*, which concerned the liability of *private parties* for infringements of competition law, the Court held that – in the absence of EU rules governing this matter – it is for the domestic legal system of each Member State to prescribe the detailed rules on the application of the concept of a causal relationship, provided that the principles of equivalence and effectiveness are observed.[102] In other words, while in this case the existence of a causality requirement was established as a matter of EU law, the precise meaning of this concept was left to be determined in principle in accordance with the applicable rules of national law. Subsequent case law seems to indicate that the standard set by national law might only be incompatible with EU law in rather "extreme" cases, such as where in certain circumstances the causal link is *by definition* considered to have been broken under that law, without allowing for any assessment of the circumstances of the case at hand.[103] Considering the general lack of precision on this subject matter in the above-mentioned EU legislation, it therefore seems not unlikely that the Court will take a comparable stance where questions of causality under that legislation are concerned.

7.13 It follows that under the secondary EU law at issue, as well as in EU law more generally, the concept of causality tends to be somewhat of a "black box" in legal terms. This is not the same, however, as saying that it has no meaning whatsoever. Given that the aforementioned EU legislation expressly provides for such a requirement, it cannot simply be disregarded. That being so, arguably the *condition sine qua non* should be seen as a minimum standard.[104] Yet apart from that – and its importance in practice notwithstanding – it may well be that there is actually only limited need and scope for providing further details as regards the causality test at EU legislative level. For while submitting the required proof that the applicable causality requirement has been met can be problematic in practice and "decentralising" this aspect to the national level inevitably leads to some divergences, to date there generally seems to be no clear evidence that the *legal notion* of causality is problematic from an EU law viewpoint. That is to say, it appears not to constitute a serious and structural bar to successfully bringing actions for damages against a private party that infringed EU law where the other applicable conditions have been met and neither is it clear that the said divergences substantially affect trade or distort competition.[105]

---

102 CoJ joined cases C-295/04 to C-298/04, *Manfredi*, para 64. See para 6.15 above.

103 CoJ case C-557/12, *Kone*, para 33.

104 Cf. Opinion AG Kokott case C-557/12, *Kone*, para 33–6.

105 Cf. e.g. Study, European observatory on counterfeiting and piracy (undated d), p. 4, where difficulties as regards the legal notion of causality were not singled out as a particular practical difficulty in intellectual property cases. Neither was further action on this point considered necessary in the field of competition law. See Commission, Staff working paper accompanying the green paper on damages actions for breach of EC antitrust rules, SEC(2005) 1732, p. 77. In respect of Member State liability, cf. Biondi and Farley (2009), pp. 55–7; Lock (2012), pp. 1697–9.

Moreover, the concept of causality might generally not lend itself well to being further pinned down by means of legislative measures. An assessment of whether the condition of causality has been met may be principally legal in nature, but it is often particularly closely connected to the facts of the case at hand. The broad range of circumstances that may be of relevance in a particular case are often difficult to "catch" in a general rule. It therefore seems legitimate – if not inevitable – to leave the national courts some discretion in this respect so as to allow for a proper case-by-case assessment, as generally tends to be the case under the domestic legal systems of the Member States.[106] It would appear that any possible concerns from an EU law perspective can normally be addressed by either reasoning on the basis of the objective and the effectiveness of the EU legislation at issue or the principles of equivalence, effectiveness and effective judicial protection.[107]

4. Quantification of damages

In order to be compensable, the harm suffered as a consequence of the infringement of EU law at issue must be assessable in monetary terms.[108] The issue of quantification of the extent of the damage is therefore of considerable practical importance. But private parties harmed by infringements of rules of substantive EU law at issue often encounter difficulties in substantiating to the satisfaction of the competent national court the full extent of the harm that they claim to have suffered.[109] This issue is among the key bottlenecks for successfully bringing actions for damages. The practical use made of this remedy is therefore likely to increase significantly if the applicable EU rules could somehow help to reduce the burden on the applicant in this regard. **7.14**

The Competition Damages Directive states that quantification is a '*substantial barrier*' for effectively bringing actions for damages.[110] This directive is noteworthy in this regard for containing a range of measures to address this issue.[111] These measures relate to the standard and burden of proof that apply in this regard, the empowerment of national courts to estimate the extent of the **7.15**

106 Van Dam (2006), p. 266 (regarding the French, German and English legal systems); Kadner Graziono and Oertel (2008), p. 465 (regarding the German legal family); Tichý (2008), p. 533 (regarding the Eastern-European legal family); Troiano (2008), p. 413 (regarding the Romanic legal family). See also Study, Ashurst (2004), p. 73.

107 On these three principles see subsections 2.A.2 (equivalence) and 2.A.3 (effectiveness) and section 2.C (effective judicial protection) above.

108 Cf. e.g. Rebhahn (2008), p. 206; Vaquer (2008), p. 30.

109 See e.g. Study, Herbert Smith (1996), p. 18; Commission, Proposal for IPR Enforcement Directive 2004/48, COM(2003) 46, p. 15; Commission, Proposal for the Competition Damages Directive 2014/104, COM(2013) 404, p. 18.

110 Recital 45 Competition Damages Directive 2014/104.

111 Art. 17 Competition Damages Directive 2014/104. See para 6.30 above.

damage, a rebuttable presumption that harm is caused and assistance by the competent public enforcement authorities. In addition, in 2013 the Commission issued a guidance document to assist the parties to the proceedings and the courts seised when they are being confronted with quantification issues in a competition law context.[112]

These measures can certainly be helpful for an applicant trying to quantify the harm suffered, particularly when they are considered collectively and in combination with the measures on the disclosure of evidence for which this directive also provides.[113] Yet on closer inspection they may be somewhat less impressive than might appear at first sight. For instance, the rule that the burden and standard of proof that apply in this respect may not render the right to damages practically impossible or excessively difficult is no more than a restatement of the principle of effectiveness that applies anyway under the Court's case law.[114] The obligation for the Member States to empower the courts to estimate the harm is further significantly qualified by the fact that – differing from what the Commission had proposed – it applies only where it is established that the applicant suffered harm and where a precise quantification thereof is practically impossible or excessively difficult. Most Member States, moreover, already provided for such a power in one form or another. The directive's rebuttable presumption that harm is caused furthermore only applies in relation to cartels and it leaves open the key questions *to whom* and *how much* harm was caused. This is therefore not a rule of quantification properly speaking. Finally, the possibility for national competition authorities to assist the courts upon the latter's request may be an interesting innovation, but its effects in practice will largely depend on the assertiveness and available resources of the authorities concerned. This is for them, after all, a possibility and not an obligation.

7.16 As regards the EU legislation assessed earlier relating to fields other than competition law, it can be observed that neither the Procurement Remedies Directives nor the IPR Enforcement Directive nor the Product Liability Directive contain any specific provision that seeks to address the quantification-related difficulties that applicants also experience in these fields. This is not for lack of trying on the part of the Commission, however. Take the proposal for the Utilities Remedies Directive, dating from 1990. There the Commission proposed setting the compensation for bidding costs at 1 per cent of the value of the contract put out to tender, as '*a limited step designed to ensure that in all*

112 See in particular Commission, Practical guide on quantifying harm in actions for damages based on breaches of Article 101 and 102 TFEU, SWD(2013) 205.

113 On these measures on the disclosure of evidence, see subsections 6.C.3 above and 8.B.2 below.

114 On the principle of effectiveness, see subsection 2.A.3 above.

Member States claims for damages are a realistic possibility'.[115] This step was limited in that it was not concerned with the issue of compensation for lost profits. The Commission considered that '*[a] high level of harmonisation of the quantification of damages is an unrealistic objective at this stage*'.[116] Even this modest suggestion was seen as too far-reaching, however. The European Parliament (which then only had a consultative role in the legislative process) insisted that these costs had to be determined on a case-by-case basis. The Commission therefore decided to drop this aspect of its proposal.

Over a decade later the Commission made a comparable suggestion in its proposal for the IPR Enforcement Directive. There it proposed making provision for the payment of damages consisting of a lump sum equal to twice the royalties or fees that would have been due had proper authorisation been requested from the rightholder instead of the illegal use.[117] The EU legislature considerably watered down this aspect of the proposal, however, resulting in the current (optional) provision on lump sum payments, which refers to the amount of the royalties or fees only by means of an example and which does not entail a doubling of that amount.[118] Worth mentioning also is another rule that the Commission included in this proposal, meant specifically to lighten the burden on the applicant wishing to claim the "unfair profits" made by the infringer. It concerned a rule of evidence that the applicant would only have to prove the amount of the gross income achieved by the defendant, after which it would be for the latter to provide evidence of their deductible expenses and profits attributable to factors other than the protected object.[119] But the EU legislature also struck out this aspect of the Commission's proposal.

The foregoing underlines the Commission's awareness of the difficulties that applicants experience when seeking to quantify the harm suffered. Yet it also illustrates the challenges encountered when trying to address them through EU legislative measures. The overall picture that thus emerges is that the EU legislature is generally rather averse to rules that aim to tackle these difficulties in a straightforward, but (therefore) also rather rigid and inaccurate manner, **7.17**

---

115 Commission, Proposal for Utilities Remedies Directive 92/13, COM(90) 297, pp. 13 and 19. See para 3.16 above. The Commission also proposed setting at the same level the penalty payment for which Member States can make provision under Art. 2(1)(c) Utilities Remedies Directive 92/13 by means of an alternative for interim measures or the order to set aside contested decisions. Also this suggestion was rejected by the EU legislature, however. See para 3.15 above.

116 Commission, Proposal for Utilities Remedies Directive 92/13, COM(90) 297, pp. 13 and 19.

117 Commission, Proposal for IPR Enforcement Directive 2004/48, COM(2003) 46, p. 40 (Art. 17(1)). See para 4.27 above.

118 Art. 13(1)(b) IPR Enforcement Directive 2004/48. See para 4.28 above.

119 Commission, Proposal for IPR Enforcement Directive 2004/48, COM(2003) 46, p. 40 (Art. 17(2)). See para 4.27 above.

namely by providing for some kind of predetermined and simplified standard or mechanism to calculate what is presumed to be the harm caused to an individual applicant. The Competition Damages Directive suggests that, subject to certain limitations, rules allowing for somewhat more flexibility – such as rules providing for certain rebuttable presumptions or the possibility for national courts to estimate the harm caused – may stand a better chance of being adopted. This is probably due to the fact that overly rigid rules can lead to overcompensation, which is generally seen as something that is to be avoided both at EU and at national level.[120]

It is somewhat ironic, therefore, that the only instance under consideration where the EU legislature did adopt a rule of sorts involving the rigid *ex ante* quantification of damages is the possibility of setting a financial ceiling (of €70 million) for the amount of damages that may be due under the Product Liability Directive.[121] This thus entails what is essentially a "negative" rule, that is, a rule that protects the defendant by setting an absolute limit for the amount of damages due rather than helping the applicant in a "positive" manner to quantify the harm caused. In the recitals of this directive it is explained that in the legal traditions of most Member States it is inappropriate to set such an absolute ceiling, but that these traditions differ. It was therefore considered to be '*possible to derogate from the principle of unlimited liability*'.[122] This ceiling should probably be seen in light of the fact that the Product Liability Directive provides for no-fault liability. The "stricter" the liability in damages, the more justification there arguably is for moderating its effects by capping the amount of damages to be paid. Such an absolute ceiling may well be seen as inappropriate in cases of less strict, fault-based liability.[123] That applies all the more so given that in other fields of EU law the Court of Justice has generally shown itself to be critical of absolute ceilings of this kind, at least in so far as they are established under national law.[124]

5. Qualification of damages and joint and several liability

7.18 Whereas the EU legislature can thus be said to be generally somewhat hesitant as to the adoption of rules on quantification, the picture in relation to the

120 See subsection 7.A.5 below.

121 Art. 16(1) Product Liability Directive 85/374. See e.g. also Art. 30(2) of Annex I to Rail Passengers' Rights Regulation 1371/2007.

122 Recital 17 Product Liability Directive 85/374.

123 Cf. Art. 35a Credit Rating Agency Regulation 1060/2009, which does not cap the civil liability of infringers but nonetheless allows limiting it in advance, provided that the limitation is reasonable and proportionate and allowed under the applicable national law.

124 E.g. CoJ case 14/83, *Von Colsen*, para 24; CoJ case C271/91, *Marshall*, para 34; CoJ case C-180/95, *Draehmpaehl*, para 40. See also Art. 18 Gender Equality Directive 2006/54.

qualification of damages is quite different. The issue here is not *how much* damage is to be compensated, but rather *which type* of damage is compensable under the applicable EU legislation facilitating the private enforcement of EU law before national courts. In respect of this latter issue, it did prove possible to adopt EU rules that provide for a degree of precision, even if the Commission has not always succeeded in having its more ambitious proposals adopted and the rules in question tend to differ considerably between them.

Each of the directives under consideration in Part B is characterised by a distinct approach in this regard. First, the approach set out in the Procurement Remedies Directives can be best described as *unspecific*. The Commission's 1987 proposal for the Public Sector Remedies Directive was comparatively ambitious, in that it specified that the compensation due should include the costs of unnecessary studies, forgone profits and lost opportunities.[125] However, this aspect of the proposal was left out of the text finally adopted. This directive does not now contain any further qualification of the term "damage". The same applies to its sibling, the Utilities Remedies Directive. While this latter directive does contain a specific arrangement for compensation for bidding costs,[126] in this case the more sensitive – and arguably also more important – issue of compensation for lost profits is not addressed. When proposing this latter arrangement in 1990, the Commission had deliberately not included a rule on compensation for lost profits, in anticipation of difficulties in the legislative process.[127] **7.19**

Second, the Product Liability Directive's rules on the qualification of damages are rather *selective*. Here two heads of damages are specified, namely damage caused by death or personal injuries and damage to property.[128] This directive does not provide any further details on what is understood precisely by these terms. It further leaves the issue of non-material damage expressly to be settled in accordance with national law. This is in line with what the Commission had originally proposed (even if, at the suggestion of the European Parliament, it later suggested bringing also this latter head of damage within the directive's scope).

Third, the position under the IPR Enforcement Directive in respect of the qualification of damages is *mixed*. The main rule laid down here is that the

125 Commission, Proposal for Public Sector Remedies Directive 89/665, COM(87) 134, p. 7 (Art. 1(3)). See para 3.16 above.
126 Art. 2(7) Utilities Remedies Directive 92/13. See para 3.16 above.
127 Commission, Proposal for Utilities Remedies Directive 92/13, COM(90) 297, pp. 13 and 19.
128 Art. 9 Product Liability Directive 85/374. See para 5.28 above.

damages must be '*appropriate to the actual prejudice suffered*'.[129] This provision then continues by stipulating that when setting these damages, account is to be taken of '*all appropriate aspects, such as the negative economic consequences, including lost profits which the injured party has suffered, any unfair profits made by the infringer and, in appropriate cases, elements other than economic factors, such as the moral prejudice caused to the rightholder by the infringement*'.[130] Yet the directive also provides for the possibility of a lump sum approach as an alternative to the aforementioned rule.[131] Thus the IPR Enforcement Directive mentions several elements that can be relevant to the setting of damages, but it tends to do so in a seemingly somewhat loose manner.

Lastly, the Competition Damages Directive is *relatively detailed* as regards the heads of damages that are compensable. It expressly seeks to ensure that "full compensation" can be awarded, while stipulating that this means placing the private party having suffered harm in the position in which that party would have been had the infringement in question not been committed. It specifies that this therefore covers the right to compensation for actual harm and loss of profit, plus payment of interest.[132] With respect to the interest due, the directive leaves the Member States a degree of flexibility, however.[133]

7.20 Looking beyond these legislative provisions, the case law of the Court of Justice suggests that EU law requires, as a general rule, that any loss or damage caused by an infringement of EU law can be compensated *in full*. This follows, for instance, from *Veedfald*, a case relating to the Product Liability Directive.[134] The Court of Justice clarified here that, although it is for national law to determine the precise content thereof, under the above-mentioned heads of damages for which this directive provides, '*full and proper compensation*' must be available. It later added that compensation for damage under this directive '*thus relates to all that is necessary to eliminate harmful consequences and to restore the level of safety*

129 Art. 13(1)(a) IPR Enforcement Directive 2004/48. See para 4.28 above.

130 Cf. Art. 68 Patent Court Agreement, where a similar rule is provided for, while adding, however, that to the extent possible the injured party must be placed in the position it would have been in if no infringement had taken place and that the infringer should not benefit from the infringement. On this agreement, see further para 4.02 above.

131 Art. 13(1)(b) IPR Enforcement Directive 2004/48. See para 4.28 above and para 7.22 below. On an optional basis, its Art. 13(2) further allows Member States to provide for the recovery of profits or the payment of damages (possibly pre-established) in cases of infringements where the infringer did not knowingly or with reasonable grounds to know engage in infringing activity.

132 Art. 3(1) and (2) Competition Damages Directive 2014/104. See para 6.29 above.

133 See recital 12 Competition Damages Directive 2014/104.

134 CoJ case C-203/99, *Veedfald*, para 25–8. See para 5.28 above. In Opinion AG Ruiz-Jarabo Colomer case C-203/99, *Veedfald*, it had been argued that this term "damage" is an autonomous concept of EU law, but in its ruling the CoJ did not touch upon this point.

which a person is entitled to expect'.[135] This is broadly in line with earlier rulings in other fields of EU law. Most notably in *Marshall*, a case relating to the Gender Equality Directive, the Court held that financial compensation must be '*adequate, in that it must enable the loss and damage actually sustained as a result of the discriminatory dismissal to be made good in full in accordance with the applicable national rules*'.[136] Interestingly, the situation may not be fundamentally different where no rules of secondary EU law on damages liability apply. This was the case in the 2006 *Manfredi* ruling relating to actions for damages for infringements of EU competition law.[137] Here the Court held that in the absence of specific EU rules (given that the Competition Damages Directive did not yet exist at that time), it was in principle for national law to set the criteria for determining the extent of the damages. It added, however, that, pursuant to the principle of effectiveness and the right of any individual to seek compensation for loss caused by infringements of the competition rules, such compensation must cover actual loss and loss of profit as well as interest. This thus seems to boil down to a requirement for full compensation. As such, it has subsequently been codified in the Competition Damages Directive.[138]

It further seems likely that full compensation in principle also covers *non-material damage*, such as pain and suffering.[139] It has been said to be an '*almost universally accepted principle*' that compensable harm may in principle also include damage which goes beyond mere pecuniary loss, at least where natural persons are concerned.[140] This can be different, however, where EU law expressly provides otherwise. Therefore, pursuant to the express wording to this effect of the Product Liability Directive, in *Veedfald* it was found that this matter is to be determined by national law.[141] By contrast in *Leitner*, a case relating to the Package Travel Directive, which does not touch upon the issue of non-material damage expressly, the Court held that the term "damage" as used in that directive implies that it must be possible for non-material damage to be compensated.[142] This latter ruling is in line not only with what, despite

135 CoJ joined cases C-503/13 and C-504/13, *Boston Scientific Medizintechnik*, para 49.

136 CoJ case C271/91, *Marshall*, para 26. See also e.g. CoJ case C-63/01, *Evans*, para 68, where a similar line was followed in relation to Directive 2009/103/EC relating to insurance against civil liability in respect of the use of motor vehicles, and the enforcement of the obligation to insure against such liability, OJ 2010, L 263/11 ("Motor Vehicle Insurance Directive").

137 CoJ joined cases C-295/04 to C-298/04, *Manfredi*, para 92–7. See para 6.15 above.

138 Cf. recital 12 Competition Damages Directive 2014/104. See also Commission, Proposal for Competition Damages Directive 2014/104, COM(2013) 404, pp. 4 and 13.

139 Cf. Reich (2010), p. 149. Generally speaking, the term "non-material damage" refers to damage that is not assessable in monetary terms on the basis of any standard financial yardstick and that affects personal feelings, such as pain and suffering or loss of reputation. See Vaquer (2008), p. 39.

140 Opinion AG Wahl case C-371/12, *Petillo*, para 39.

141 CoJ case C-203/99, *Veedfald*, para 33.

142 CoJ case C-168/00, *Leitner*, para 21–3 (concerning Package Travel Directive 90/314). See para 5.34 above.

considerable variations, generally applies under the laws of the Member States.[143] It is also consistent with case law relating to other fields of EU law, such as Article 340 TFEU on the non-contractual liability of the Union,[144] the Motor Vehicle Insurance Directive[145] and the Air Passengers' Rights Regulation.[146] The Court of Justice has also held that in international law the ordinary meaning of the term "damage" includes material as well as non-material damage.[147] In this light the Commission may therefore be correct in considering that non-material damage can also be compensable under the Competition Damages Directive.[148]

7.21 By means of a last comment, it is noticeable that the two legal acts under consideration that specifically concentrate on damages liability, namely the Product Liability Directive and the Competition Damages Directive, in a sense take the general objective of full compensation a step further. Both directives provide that when two or more undertakings are liable for the same damage, they are *jointly and severally liable* for that damage.[149] This appears to be in line with the general rule provided for in the national laws of the Member States where non-contractual liability (tort) is concerned.[150] The Competition Damages Directive specifies that this means that the co-infringing undertakings are bound to compensate the damage in full and that the injured party has the right to require full compensation from any of them. The same essentially follows from the recitals of the Product Liability Directive.[151]

Also, on two other points the regime on joint and several liability laid down in the Competition Damages Directive is more elaborate than the one set out in the Product Liability Directive. To begin with, subject to certain conditions the former directive *limits* the joint and several liability of three categories of

143 See e.g. Van Gerven, Lever and Larouche (2000), p. 140; Opinion AG Tizzano case C-168/00, *Leitner*, para 30 and 40–42; Study, Expert group on European contract law (2011) (Art. 2(12)); Opinion AG Wahl case C-371/12, *Petillo*, para 40; Study, European observatory on counterfeiting and piracy (undated d), p. 4.

144 E.g. CoJ case C-308/87, *Grifoni*, para 37; GC case T-384/11, *Safa Nicu Sepahan*, para 85. In the context of EU personnel disputes, see also e.g. CoJ joined cases 169/83 and 136/84, *Leussink*, para 18–20; CoJ case C-343/87, *Culin*, para 29. See further Oliphant (2008), pp. 264–70; Basedow (2010a), p. 459.

145 Motor Vehicle Insurance Directive 2009/103. See CoJ case C-22/12, *Haasová*, para 39–50; CoJ case C-371/12, *Petillo*, para 35. See also EFTA Court case E-8/07, *Nguyen*, para 26.

146 Air Passengers' Rights Regulation 261/2004. See CoJ case C-83/10, *Sousa Rodríguez*, para 47.

147 CoJ case C-63/09, *Walz*, para 27–9. See also Opinion AG Tizzano case C-168/00, *Leitner*, para 39.

148 Commission, Proposal for Competition Damages Directive 2014/104, COM(2013) 404, p. 13.

149 Art. 5 Product Liability Directive 85/375; Art. 11 Competition Damages Directive 2014/104. See para 5.27 and 6.36 above, respectively.

150 See e.g. Vrcek (2010), p. 283.

151 Recital 5 Product Liability Directive 85/375.

undertakings, namely: (a) small and medium-sized enterprises; (b) undertakings having received leniency in the context of public enforcement proceedings; and (c) undertakings that reached a consensual settlement with the injured private party.[152] The Product Liability Directive leaves the issue of *contribution* (that is, the right for the undertaking that was held to be jointly and severally liable and thus had to compensate for the damage in full to recover part of this damages award from the other co-infringing undertakings) to national law.[153] The Competition Damages Directive in contrast expressly provides for a right to recover a contribution. It specifies that the amount of that contribution is to be determined in light of the relative responsibility of the parties concerned for the damage caused, although it is left to national law how this is to be determined precisely.[154]

6. Punitive damages and other damages going beyond compensation

A last issue to be assessed in connection with actions for damages is the possibility of providing for damages awards that go beyond mere compensation for the harm suffered, in particular punitive damages.[155] In this respect it should be underlined at the outset that none of the legal acts considered in Part B make provision for the award of this type of damages. That is not to say, however, that no discussions have taken place on this matter in the fields of law concerned. **7.22**

As was noted above, the Commission's 2003 proposal for the IPR Enforcement Directive included a provision that set the damages due at lump sum of *twice* the royalties or fees that would have been due had the infringer asked for authorisation from the rightholder.[156] The Commission's 1996 green paper on public procurement further contained a suggestion to make provision for '*liquidated damages of a sufficiently dissuasive sum, exceeding the damage suffered*'.[157] And in the Commission's 2005 green paper on actions for damages for infringements of EU competition law, the option of *doubling* the damages in

152 Art. 11(2)–(4) and Art. 19(2) and (3) Competition Damages Directive 2014/104. See also para 6.43 above.

153 Most national legal systems provide for such a right of contribution. See Study, CEPS, Erasmus University Rotterdam and LUISS (2007), p. 516.

154 Recital 37 Competition Damages Directive 2014/104.

155 For the present purposes, the term "punitive damages" also covers what are sometimes called "exemplary damages". On punitive damages, see also para 11.10 and 11.39 below. The "flip-side", as it were, of the issue discussed above is the award of *nominal or symbolic* damages. The award of such damages is generally not precluded under EU law (at least under Art. 340 TFEU), but that does not relieve the applicant of the obligation to provide conclusive proof of the damage suffered. See CoJ case 26/74, *Roquette frères*, para 24; GC case T-652/11, *Sabbagh*, para 65. See further Vaquer (2008), pp. 26–8.

156 Commission, Proposal for IPR Enforcement Directive 2004/48, COM(2003) 46, p. 40 (Art. 17(1)). See para 4.27 and 7.16 above.

157 Commission, Green paper on public procurement in the EU, COM(96) 583, p. 15.

certain cases was raised.[158] Each of these suggestions was met with mostly negative responses, however. Therefore, while the final text of the IPR Enforcement Directive does provide for an (optional) provision on damages awards in the form of lump sums, unlike the Commission's proposal, there is no longer a mention of the doubling of the sum in question.[159] This directive's recitals, moreover, emphasise that here the aim is not to introduce an obligation to provide for punitive damages.[160] The Commission furthermore did not pursue the suggestions made in relation to public procurement and competition law, in light of the negative reactions from interested parties.[161] Quite to the contrary, in its 2008 white paper on competition damages, the Commission stressed that damages awards primarily serve a compensatory function rather than a punitive one.[162] The same view underlies the Commission proposal for the Competition Damages Directive.[163]

Therefore, more recently virtual consensus seems to have emerged that punitive damages are not to be provided for by EU law.[164] It can thus be said that, '*[s]een from the perspective of [EU] law, compensation for harm suffered as a result of the infringement of [EU] law should be appropriate to the harm suffered*'.[165]

7.23 It is important to note, however, that the foregoing does not mean that punitive damages are necessarily *precluded* under EU law. The IPR Enforcement Directive's provision on lump sums mentioned above includes, for instance, the words "at least".[166] That implies that Member States that wish to do so are not barred from making provision for further-reaching measures under national law.[167] In the Procurement Remedies Directives and the Product Liability Directive, the

---

158 Commission, Green paper on damages actions for breach of the EC antitrust rules, COM(2005) 672, p. 7.

159 Art. 13(1)(b) IPR Enforcement Directive. See also its Art. 13(2). See para 4.27 and 4.28 above.

160 Recital 26 IPR Enforcement Directive 2004/48.

161 See para 3.17 and 6.19 above.

162 See para 6.18 above.

163 See e.g. Commission, Impact assessment report on damages actions for breach of the EU antitrust rules, SWD(2013) 203, pp. 39–40, where it is said that increasing deterrence is not a primary objective of this initiative. Cf. Esteva Mosso (2013), p. 52.

164 Note, however, that in many national laws provision is made for the award of interest on the sum due during the period preceding the trial and the judgment. The practical effect of such provisions has been compared with the availability of punitive damages. See Jones (2003), pp. 102–5.

165 Opinion AG Geelhoed joined cases C-295/04 to C-298/01, *Manfredi*, para 69. In the context of EU non-contractual liability under Art. 340 TFEU see e.g. GC case T-260/97, *Camar*, para 97 and 101, where it is held that: '*[i]t is settled case law that compensation for loss in the context of non-contractual liability is intended so far as possible to provide restitution for the victims*' and that '*compensation for loss must in principle allow the applicant to be placed in the position, financially, in which it would have been if the [EU institution or body concerned] had refrained from the unlawful conduct which caused the loss*'.

166 Art. 13(1)(b) IPR Enforcement Directive 2004/48.

167 Similarly, the statement in its recital 26 that the IPR Enforcement Directive 2004/48 does not aim to *introduce* an obligation to provide for punitive damages does not exclude Member States from doing so under national law.

issue of punitive damages is simply left unaddressed. This can be taken to mean that the question of whether or not they are available is in principle left to national law. The Court of Justice has so far not expressed any objections in principle to the availability of punitive damages under national law. It has rather assessed this subject matter primarily under the principle of equivalence.[168] Neither can it be said that there is consensus in the legal doctrine on the unacceptability *per se* of punitive damages as a matter of EU law.[169]

More generally it would appear that the argument that punitive damages are to be rejected as being incompatible with the European legal traditions, as is sometimes maintained in the context of the above-mentioned discussions, is incorrect or at least incomplete. There is in fact EU legislation that contains provisions that would appear to provide for compensation going beyond the harm actually suffered.[170] More significantly, perhaps, when the Commission proposed in 2003 to provide in the Rome II Regulation on the law applicable to non-contractual obligations that punitive damages are against EU public policy, this was rejected by the EU legislature.[171] And whilst it is true that in the domestic legal systems of the Member States damages awards serve first and foremost to compensate a party for the injury suffered, this is by no means an absolute rule.[172] In many national jurisdictions it is acknowledged that damages liability can at least to some extent also fulfil a (secondary) function in deterring and punishing infringers.[173] A significant number of Member States actually have provisions in place that allow for the award of damages that are or at least can be considered punitive in nature.[174]

---

168 CoJ joined cases C-295/04 to C-298/04, *Manfredi*, para 99. See also CoJ joined cases C-46/93 and C-48/93, *Brasserie du Pêcheur*, para 90; CoJ case C-174/12, *Hirmann*, para 40. On the principle of equivalence, see subsection 2.A.2 above.

169 Cf. e.g. Van Gerven (2003b), p. 92.

170 See e.g. Art. 18(2) Plant Variety Rights Implementing Regulation 1768/1995. Here it is stipulated that compensation equal to *four times* the normal licence fee can be due. It is not explicitly stated that this arrangement aims to punish and deter infringers, but both the high amount and the limitation to cases of repeated and intentional infringements appear to point in that direction. Cf. also Art. 2(6) Directive 2011/7/EU on combating late payment in commercial transactions, OJ 2011, L 48/1, where provision is made for a legal interest rate for late payment which is at least *eight percentage points* above the rate applied by the European Central Bank.

171 Commission, Proposal for Rome II Regulation 864/2007, COM(2003) 427, p. 40 (Art. 24). Recital 32 of Rome II Regulation 864/2007 provides in essence only that *excessive* punitive damages *could be* held to be contrary to the public policy *of the forum*, depending on the legal order of the Member State concerned.

172 Cf. e.g. Van Gerven, Lever and Larouche (2000), p. 740; Study, Ashurst (2004), p. 80; Study, View (2004), p. 7; Opinion AG Geelhoed joined cases C-295/04 to C-298/04, *Manfredi*, para 68; Study, CEPS, Erasmus University Rotterdam and LUISS (2007), p. 417; Komninos (2008), pp. 160 and 211; Kellner (2009), p. 138; Milutinovic (2010), p. 119; Hazelhorst (2010), p. 767.

173 Cf. Van Gerven, Lever and Larouche (2000), pp. 25–6, 69 and 741; Van Dam (2006), pp. 12 and 302–3; Kelliher (2008), pp. 10–11.

174 Namely the UK, Ireland, France, Cyprus, Slovenia, Bulgaria and Austria. See para 4.30 and 6.19 above. See also Kelliher (2008), pp. 10–11.

It follows that as it stands EU law is largely neutral in respect of punitive damages; they are generally not required as a matter of EU law (other than possibly in application of the principle of equivalence), but neither are they necessarily precluded.

7.24 Having said that, there appears to be a more recent trend towards taking a more restrictive stance as a matter of EU law in relation to punitive damages and other damages awards that go beyond mere compensation for the harm caused. Most notably, the 2014 Competition Damages Directive expressly states that '*[f]ull compensation under this directive shall not lead to over-compensation, whether by means of punitive, multiple or other types of damages*'.[175] This provision, which did not feature in the Commission's proposal for this directive, appears to have been inserted mainly at the insistence of the European Parliament.[176] Similarly, in line with an earlier suggestion to this effect from the side of the European Parliament,[177] the Commission's 2013 Collective Redress Recommendation states that '*punitive damages [...] should be prohibited*'.[178] The 2012 Patent Court Agreement also provides that the damages to be awarded in the cases covered by the rules in question '*shall not be punitive*'.[179]

Thus where earlier discussions were mainly concerned with opposition against *requiring* the availability of such damages at EU level, which led to the largely neutral position referred to above, there now appears to be a trend (or at least some first steps in that direction) towards actively *prohibiting* them under EU law. This development can probably be ascribed to the fact that punitive damages are often associated with the "litigation culture", which many seek to avoid in the EU.[180]

7.25 A last – related yet distinct – observation is that, even apart from the aforementioned virtual consensus and the said more recent trend, in several respects scope for discussion remains. That is in large part related to the fact that there is not always a uniform understanding of precisely what is meant by the term "punitive damages". One understanding is that whether or not damages awards are to be qualified as punitive is to be determined on the basis of their *objective*,

175 Art. 3(3) Competition Damages Directive 2014/104. See also its Art. 12(1) and (2).

176 See para 6.29 above.

177 European Parliament, Resolution, Towards a coherent European approach to collective redress, P7_TA(2012)0021.

178 Point 31 Collective Redress Recommendation 2013/396. See para 5.38 above.

179 Art. 68(2) Patent Court Agreement. On this agreement, see para 4.02 above. A similar rule had already been included in Commission, Proposal for a regulation on the Community patent, COM(2000) 412, p. 56 (Art. 44(2)).

180 See para 11.26 below.

that is, whether or not the aim is to punish and deter infringers. This view finds broad support.[181] When understood in such an "objective-based" manner, there indeed appears to be a virtual consensus as to the undesirability of punitive damages under EU law. However, others appear to have a somewhat different understanding of this term. The emphasis is then not so much on the objective pursued, but rather on the *effects* in practice of the damages awards. On this latter understanding the key issue is whether or not the amount awarded is greater than the damage actually suffered by the party receiving it.

This distinction can be of particular relevance where matters of quantification and qualification of the harm caused are concerned.[182] One example of a situation where this can come to light relates to the possibility of setting damages as a predetermined lump sum. As has been seen, this can be done for instance either as a percentage of the value of the public contract at issue in public procurement cases or by reference to the fees or royalties that would have been due had authorisation been requested in intellectual property cases. In competition cases, one could think of a certain percentage of the total price charged, which is presumed to be the overcharge caused by the cartel.[183] Another example relates to the possibility of providing for the award of restitutory or gain-based damages (disgorgement). Put briefly, the latter are damages awarded on the basis of the profit made by the defendant as a result of the infringement. These "unfair profits" are an element that can be taken into account when setting the damages in various Member States, especially for intellectual property-related infringements but sometimes also in competition cases.[184] In respect of these two fields of law, the Commission has suggested establishing or further elaborating on this possibility as a matter of EU law.[185] When the focus is on the *objective* of the measure in question, it seems evident that none of the above measures are to be considered as punitive damages. These rules on lump sums are after all essentially meant to reduce the burden on the applicant in terms of the quantification of the harm so as to make this

181 See e.g. Study, Ashurst (2004), p. 80; Commission, Staff working paper accompanying the green paper on damages actions for breach of EC antitrust rules, SEC(2005) 1732, p. 36; Zippro (2009b), p. 432; Milutinovic (2010), p. 119; Hazelhorst (2010), p. 764. See, however, also Kellner (2008), p. 580.

182 On these matters generally, see subsections 7.A.4 and 7.A.5 above.

183 See e.g. the rule of Hungarian competition law, referred to in para 6.23 above.

184 As regards intellectual property law, see Commission, Proposal for IPR Enforcement Directive 2004/48, COM(2003) 46, p. 14; Study, European observatory on counterfeiting and piracy (undated d), pp. 1–4. As regards competition law see Study, Ashurst (2004), p. 80; Study, CEPS, Erasmus University Rotterdam and LUISS (2007), p. 427. See also Commission, Staff working paper accompanying the green paper on damages actions for breach of EC antitrust rules, SEC(2005) 1732, pp. 35–6; Milutinovic (2010), p. 118.

185 Commission, Green paper on damages actions for breach of the EC antitrust rules, COM(2005) 672, p. 7; Commission, Report on IPR Enforcement Directive 2004/48, COM(2010) 779, p. 8. Note that under Art. 13(1)(a) IPR Enforcement Directive 2004/48 unfair profits are already one of the relevant aspects to be taken into account when setting damages. See also subsection 8.B.6 below.

remedy more effective. This leaves the main (compensatory) objective of the damages award itself unaffected. Likewise, the objective of gain-based damages is principally to compensate the injured party as well as to prevent the wrongdoer's unjust enrichment, rather than to punish the latter.[186] Providing for these kinds of measures could, however, be seen as objectionable if one focuses on their possible *effects*. For in all of the above cases, irrespective of the objective pursued, it cannot be excluded that in certain instances the sum paid will be higher than the harm actually suffered. Part of the objections expressed in relation to the aforementioned Commission's proposal for the provision on lump sums in the IPR Enforcement Directive seem to be attributable to these differences in understanding as to what constitutes punitive damages.[187] In relation to the possibility of taking account of unfair profits, it has similarly been argued that this should not entail a "camouflaged" form of punitive damages.[188]

B. ACTIONS FOR INJUNCTIONS

This section is concerned with the second "main" (substantive) remedy for private enforcement purposes that emerges on the basis of the foregoing, namely injunctive relief. It is shown below that this remedy is of considerable importance, even if it tends to receive less attention than actions for damages in discussions on the private enforcement of EU law. The first subsection in the following contains a comparative analysis of the provisions regarding injunctions laid down in the legislation discussed in Part B above. Subsequently, the functioning of this remedy in practice and the applicable conditions are considered. The final subsection discusses two specific issues, namely the possible implications of the foregoing for the private enforcement of competition law and the functioning of actions for injunctions in cross-border situations.

---

186 See further e.g. Van Gerven, Lever and Larouche (2000), p. 872; Kelliher (2008), p. 11.

187 See e.g. Meier-Beck (2004), p. 122; Kur (2004), p. 827; Cohen and Mottet Haugaard (2010), pp. 376–7; Lakits-Josse (2011), p. 545. See Commission, Proposal for IPR Enforcement Directive 2004/48, COM(2003) 46, p. 23, where the Commission held that this aspect of its proposal did not entail punitive damages but rather a provision that '*allows for compensation based on an objective criterion while taking account of the expenses incurred by the rightholder*'.

188 Meier-Beck (2004), p. 121; Till (2010), p. 136. See also Commission, Responses to the collective redress benchmark consultation, 2008, p. 7, where various stakeholders argue against providing for gain-based damages in a collective redress context on the grounds that this would entail a form of punitive damages.

1. Comparative overview and general remarks

Injunctive relief can essentially take two forms, namely the award of *prohibitive* and *mandatory* injunctions.[189] In its first form it entails an order by a court or an administrative authority for the defendant to *refrain from acting* in a particular manner that has already led or that would lead to an infringement of a legal norm. In its second form it refers to a court order to *act* in a certain manner. In that case the order thus entails a positive obligation on the defendant, as opposed to a negative one. **7.26**

Prohibitive injunctions are a particularly important remedy for the enforcement of EU consumer protection law. This remedy is central to the Consumer Injunctions Directive, as its name already indicates.[190] Under this directive judicial or administrative authorities must be empowered to order '*the cessation or prohibition of any infringement*' of the substantive consumer protection rules covered by this legal act, set out in its annex.[191] Several other consumer protection directives also provide for this remedy.[192] For instance, under the Unfair Terms Directive it must be possible to '*prevent the continued use*' of unfair terms in consumer contracts.[193] A comparable arrangement has been laid down in the Unfair Commercial Practices Directive in connection with the cessation or the prohibition of unfair commercial practices.[194]

EU rules on prohibitive injunctions can also be found in EU intellectual property law. The IPR Enforcement Directive stipulates that it must be possible for national courts to issue interlocutory as well as "permanent" injunctions.[195] These interlocutory injunctions serve to prevent an imminent infringement of an intellectual property right, to provisionally forbid the continuation of an alleged infringement or to make such continuation subject to the lodging of a guarantee.[196] These permanent injunctions aim to prohibit the continuation of

189 See e.g. Chisholm (1997), p. 73; Van Dam (2006), p. 301; Komninos (2008), p. 215; Peyer (undated), p. 7. Note, however, that in practice the distinction between the two forms of injunction need not be a fundamental one, as this can depend in part on the manner in which the applicant formulates its claim and the national court seised formulates the operative part of its judgment.

190 See subsection 5.B.1 above. As discussed in para 5.08 above, Consumer Injunctions Directive 2009/22 also provides for penalty payments and publicity measures. On these two latter remedies, see subsections 8.B.3 and 8.B.4 below, respectively.

191 Art. 2(1)(a) Consumer Injunctions Directive 2009/22. As discussed in para 5.09 above, this annex covers most of the body of substantive EU consumer protection law.

192 See para 5.13 above.

193 Art. 7(1) Unfair Terms Directive 93/13.

194 Art. 11(2) Unfair Commercial Practices Directive 2005/29. See e.g. also Art. 5(3) Misleading Advertising Directive 2006/114.

195 See subsections 4.B.2 and 4.B.3 above.

196 Art. 9(1)(a) IPR Enforcement Directive.

infringements on a permanent basis.[197] In addition, even if in this directive itself the term "injunction" is only used in its narrow, prohibitive sense, it also provides for mandatory injunctions.[198] In this respect the IPR Enforcement Directive requires in particular the possibility for a court to order the seizure, delivery up, recall, definitive removal from the channels of commerce or destruction of goods infringing intellectual property law.[199] The Infosoc Directive and the Commission's proposal for a trade secrets directive contain comparable provisions.[200]

The Procurement Remedies Directives do not expressly refer to the possibility of granting injunctive relief. The possibility of applying for an order to set aside an unlawful decision taken in the course of a contract award procedure set out in these directives can nonetheless be seen as a mandatory injunction, as it concerns the granting of a court order for the defendant to act in a certain manner.[201] These directives specify that such an order can entail the removal of discriminatory specifications in the tender documents. On an interim basis, the Procurement Remedies Directives also refer to the possibility of ordering measures to correct infringements or to prevent further damage to the interests concerned.[202] One could think of the revocation by the contracting authority of a decision to exclude a tenderer from the contract award procedure taken in violation of the applicable EU public procurement rules.

Finally, concerning the field of EU competition law, suffice it to note that the Competition Damages Directive does not make provision for actions for injunctions. In terms of substantive remedies, this directive is only concerned with actions for damages.[203] Neither is Article 101(2) TFEU of relevance here, as it contains only a contractual remedy.[204]

7.27 The foregoing indicates that the EU legislative provisions on injunctive relief at issue here have two key characteristics. In the first place, there is a great deal of *variety*. At the most general level there is the aforementioned distinction

197 Art. 11 IPR Enforcement Directive 2004/48.

198 In the Commission's proposal for this directive the term "injunction" was used also in its broader sense, encompassing also mandatory injunctions. See Commission, Proposal for IPR Enforcement Directive 2004/48, COM(2003) 46, p. 14.

199 Art. 9(b) and Art. 10 IPR Enforcement Directive 2004/48.

200 Art. 8(2) and (3) Infosoc Directive 2001/29; Commission, Proposal for a trade secrets directive, COM(2013) 813, pp. 21–4 (Art. 9–12).

201 Art. 2(1)(b) Procurement Remedies Directives 89/665 and 92/13. See subsection 3.B.1 above. As was noted in para 2.26 above, the setting aside of an act or decision contrary to EU law can also be seen as a "general" remedy in its own right.

202 Art. 2(1)(a) Procurement Remedies Directives 89/665 and 92/13.

203 See para 6.28 above.

204 See para 6.08 above.

between prohibitive and mandatory injunctions, both of which are provided for. And there is also considerable variety within these two broad categories. To begin with, neither the above-mentioned prohibitive injunctions nor the mandatory ones are formulated in the same manner. Moreover, the substance of what precisely can be ordered under the provisions of EU law in question also tends to differ. In fact, even within one and the same field of law, what appears to be the same sort of injunction can be provided for in diverging terms. This is best illustrated by the provisions set out in the various consumer protection directives referred to above.

A second characteristic is the *flexibility* that the provisions in question tend to leave. With the partial exception of the IPR Enforcement Directive, those provisions tend to be worded in rather broad terms. Terms such as "to order the cessation or prohibition", "to prevent the continued use" or "to set aside or to ensure the setting aside" leave it largely to the Member States and to the competent national courts precisely how effect is to be given to these rules of EU law. Apart from that, there are two instances where an additional degree of diversity can emerge in relation to the question whether the remedy for which EU law makes provision applies in the first place. For both the Utilities Remedies Directive and the IPR Enforcement Directive contain an optional clause that essentially allows for the defendant to "buy off" the specific obligation that may be imposed on the defendant by means of an injunction. The former directive provides for the possibility of ordering the payment of '*a particular sum*', which must be dissuasive and ensure effectiveness in preventing injury being caused, instead of the setting aside of an unlawful decision.[205] The latter directive allows for the aforementioned permanent injunctions to be replaced by the payment of '*pecuniary compensation to be paid to the injured party*', subject to a number of conditions, including that the infringer acted unintentionally and without negligence.[206]

A first factor that helps explain the state of affairs described above is that injunctions are inherently to a large extent a *tailor-made remedy*. Even though there can also be considerable variety in relation to other remedies such as actions for damages, as has been shown in the previous section, their essence is rather straightforward: the loss and damage caused by an infringement of EU law must be compensated through the payment of a certain sum. Measures aimed at halting or preventing such infringements, by contrast, tend to be more closely linked to that infringement itself. Given that – certainly across various 7.28

205 Art. 2(1)(c) and 2(5) Utilities Remedies Directive 92/13.

206 Art. 12 IPR Enforcement Directive 2004/48. See also Commission, Proposal for a trade secrets directive, COM(2013) 813, pp. 23–4 (Art. 12(3)).

fields of law but also with each field – these infringements of the applicable substantive rules can take many forms, this will often also apply to the injunctive relief being ordered to address them. Hence the diverging formulation of the provisions and the leeway that is typically left, both of which serve to allow for the tailoring of the measure to be imposed as much as possible to the infringement at issue. The nature, effect and formulation of these measures thus depend to a great extent on the specifics of the situation at hand.

A second factor is that the *national legal environments* in which the abovementioned EU legislative measures are to be embedded *differ* significantly from each other. Consider for instance the field of consumer protection law. As was noted earlier, injunctive relief tends to play an important role here. Whereas under certain national legal systems actions for injunctive relief for infringements of this law are to be brought before an administrative authority, in other systems the civil courts are competent to rule on these disputes.[207] A similar situation exists in relation to public procurement law.[208] These divergences as regards the nature of the applicable law and the competent national courts add an extra "layer" of diversity in addition to the diversity that often already exists between the various domestic legal systems within the EU. These divergences can be a reason for formulating the relevant provisions of EU law in such a manner that a minimum degree of "fit" is ensured between the EU legislative measures and the legal environments in which they are to be embedded and function after the transposition of the directives in question.

A third factor that may also play a role in this connection, especially in relation to mandatory injunctions, is that it can sometimes be seen as *inappropriate* for a court to prescribe *in detail* how a defendant is to act. That applies particularly (but not exclusively) where the defendant is a state entity of some sort. This factor can be particularly relevant in relation to the Procurement Remedies Directives, where the defendants are normally public or semi-public bodies.[209] This is why the (mandatory) injunction for which these directives provide is formulated in such a broad manner ("to set aside or to ensure the setting aside"). The wish not to unduly affect the autonomy of the bodies in question also lies behind the possibility under the Utilities Remedies Directive referred to in the previous paragraph of "buying off" any such court order by paying a dissuasive sum.[210] Where the defendants are typically private parties, as is the case under the IPR Enforcement Directive, the issue is not so much one of autonomy, but rather one of avoiding disproportionate outcomes. That was the reason behind

207 See para 5.10 and 5.13 above. On the rules on forum generally, see also subsection 9.C.1 below.
208 See para 3.11 and 3.28 above.
209 See para 3.11 above.
210 See para 3.15 above.

the insertion of the possibility of paying pecuniary compensation instead of awarding a permanent injunction that was also discussed in the previous paragraph.[211] Elsewhere in EU law, other illustrations of this potential sensitivity of mandatory injunctions can be found. For example, while an EU institution must take the necessary measures to comply with a judgment annulling one of its acts, the EU courts tend to leave it to the institution concerned to decide how to do so.[212] To some extent comparably, perhaps, under the EU law principle of Member State liability, the obligation on the latter to make good the consequences of their infringements of EU law normally consists of paying pecuniary compensation and not a (positive) court order for the Member State in question to take certain specific measures.[213]

2. Injunctions: Practice and applicable conditions

In relation to the practical functioning of the EU legislative provisions on actions for injunctions at issue here, it appears that actions of this kind are brought rather frequently and successfully under consumer protection directives such as the Consumer Injunctions Directive, the Unfair Terms Directive and the Unfair Commercial Practices Directive.[214] The experiences with the actions for injunctions provided for in the IPR Enforcement Directive are on the whole also positively assessed by the Commission, stakeholders, practitioners and legal scholars alike.[215] The Commission has called this the directive's '*main enforcement remedy*'.[216] With respect to the Procurement Remedies Directives, the situation seems less clear. Yet it nonetheless appears that at least by comparison it generally is a rather attractive means to address alleged infringements of EU law. In this domain actions for injunctions tend to be initiated more frequently and with more success than the other remedies for which these directives provide.[217] **7.29**

211 See para 4.25 above.

212 Art. 266 TFEU. See e.g. GC case T-342/11, *CEEES*, para 43, where it is noted that *'the case-law does indeed make clear that it is not for the [EU] judicature, when exercising the jurisdiction to annul acts conferred on it by Article 263 TFEU, to issue directions to the [EU] institutions'*.

213 Cf. Dougan (2004), pp. 256–8; Prechal (2005), pp. 296–7; Tridimas (2006), p. 539; Granger (2007), p. 190; Rebhalm (2008), p. 183; Biondi and Farley (2009), p. 83. Note that the *retroactive application* of national law transposing a directive has at times been held to be an acceptable solution, unless the applicants suffered complementary losses due to them not being able to benefit at the appropriate time from the rights granted to them under the belatedly transposed directive. See e.g. CoJ case C-94/95, *Bonifaci*, para 51–3. On the principle of Member State liability generally, see para 2.23 above.

214 See para 5.12 and 5.13 above.

215 See para 4.21 above. This observation concerns prohibitive injunctions; the aforementioned mandatory injunctions for which this directive makes provisions generally appear to be used less frequently.

216 Commission, Staff working document accompanying the report on IPR Enforcement Directive 2004/48, SEC(2010) 1589, p. 14 (regarding interlocutory injunctions).

217 See para 3.13, 3.14 and 3.17 above.

Therefore injunctions are on the whole often not only an important private enforcement remedy on paper, but also in practice. As such, the contrast with the actions for damages discussed in the previous section is particularly striking.[218] When seeking to explain this relative success, it is important to note at the outset that this depends always to some extent on the applicable detailed national rules. That applies all the more so given that, as was indicated above, the provisions in question tend to leave considerable leeway to the Member States. That said, it seems that – seen from a legal perspective and in so far as EU law is concerned – the applicable *conditions* for obtaining injunctive relief are especially likely to play a crucial role in explaining this relative success. To be more precise, it seems that the conditions that do *not* apply under the above-mentioned EU legislation are of particular importance. This can be further explained as follows.

7.30 To begin with, whereas in order to be able to obtain compensation in damages an applicant must demonstrate that he *suffered harm*, it is widely assumed that such a requirement does *not* apply in the case of actions for injunctions.[219] At first sight this may seem obvious enough. Injunctions typically seek to prevent or terminate unlawful conduct, with a view to preventing (further) harm from occurring.[220] If no compensation in damages is claimed, why would there be a need to demonstrate the occurrence of damage? Yet the EU legal acts on which this book concentrates do not address this matter expressly. Only the Unfair Commercial Practices Directive and the Misleading Advertising Directive stipulate that the injunctions provided for therein must be available even in cases where there is no proof of actual loss or damage.[221]

That leads to the question what the legal consequences are, if any, of this absence of such an express statement. The question is in particular whether this implies that a requirement to demonstrate harm could be imposed on the basis of national law, should a Member State wish to do so. It is submitted that this question is in all likelihood to be answered in the negative. The express statement to this effect in the two above-mentioned directives should probably be seen as a mere confirmation, and not as giving rise to an argument *a contrario* that there is scope to apply such a requirement under national law where no such express statement is made in the directive in question. This view rests on

218 See in particular para 7.03 above.

219 E.g. Jacobs and Deisenhofer (2003), p. 196; Eilmansberger (2007), p. 433; Cauffman (2010), p. 59. In several Member States account is taken, however, of the *potential* harm occurring in the absence of this remedy being granted, particularly in relation to the award of interim relief. See e.g. Commission, Responses to the public consultation on the civil enforcement of intellectual property rights, July 2013, pp. 15–16.

220 Cf. CoJ case C-167/00, *Henkel*, para 39 and 48.

221 Art. 11(2) Unfair Commercial Practices Directive 2005/29; Art. 5(3) Misleading Advertising Directive 2006/114.

the absence of an express requirement as a matter of EU law, in combination with the fact that the application of such a requirement would probably prevent the objective of the EU rules in question from being achieved, as it would considerably raise the threshold for an applicant to obtain an injunction. In other words, it would appear that the Court's reasoning relating to a fault requirement in the context of actions for damages, set out in the above-mentioned rulings such as *Stadt Graz* and *Dekker*, can be "transplanted" to the present context.[222]

It might appear that in *L'Oréal v eBay* the Court of Justice took a different view. For in that case it was held that '*the rules for the operation of the injunctions for which the Member States must provide under the third sentence of Article 11 [IPR Enforcement Directive], such as those relating to the conditions to be met and the procedure to be followed, are a matter of national law*'.[223] However, this statement only relates to the directive's provision on actions for injunctions against *third parties*. As the Court recalled in its ruling, the recitals of the IPR Enforcement Directive specify that the conditions for this specific form of injunctive relief should be left to be set by national law.[224] The directive does not contain any similar provisions in relation to the *other* forms of injunctive relief set out in this directive. Already on this basis it would seem that the above statement by the Court cannot be generalised so as to apply to all provisions of secondary EU law on actions for injunctions. Moreover, in *L'Oréal v eBay* the Court also underlined that the relevant rules of national law must respect a number of EU law requirements, including that they allow for the directive's objective to be achieved and that they respect the applicant's right to an effective remedy.[225] Although this issue was not further addressed in this judgment, a national law requirement to prove damage for an injunction to be granted may well be seen as being incompatible with these EU law requirements. It is submitted, therefore, that on closer reading this judgment does not generally invalidate the view set out above; it may actually rather confirm it. Nonetheless, it provides a useful reminder that each situation must be assessed on its own merits and that the starting point of each analysis remains the wording of the EU legislation at issue.

---

222 CoJ case C-314/09, *Stadt Graz*; CoJ case C-177/88, *Dekker*. See para 7.07 above.

223 CoJ case C-324/09, *L'Oréal v eBay*, para 135. See para 4.24 above.

224 Recital 23 IPR Infringement Directive 2004/48. See CoJ case C-324/09, *L'Oréal v eBay*, para 135. Cf. also CoJ case C-314/12, *UPC Telekabel Wien*, para 43 (relating to the injunctions referred to in Art. 8 Infosoc Directive 2001/29).

225 CoJ case C-324/09, *L'Oréal v eBay*, para 136 and 142. Cf. CoJ case C-314/12, *UPC Telekabel Wien*, para 44. On the fundamental right to an effective remedy under Art. 47 Charter, see para 2.11 above.

7.31 A further issue is whether in relation to actions for injunctions the said directives allow for a *fault requirement*, in one form or another, to be set under national law.[226] Of the above-mentioned EU legal acts containing provisions on injunctive relief, the Consumer Injunctions Directive, the Unfair Terms Directive, the Procurement Remedies Directives and the IPR Enforcement Directive are largely silent on this matter. Again, only the Unfair Commercial Practices Directive and the Misleading Advertising Directive deal with this issue expressly. These two latter directives stipulate that no proof of intention or negligence on the part of the defendant is required for this form of relief to be granted.[227] It would appear, however, that, following essentially the same reasoning as the one set out in the foregoing paragraph, this is unlikely to point to any difference in substance between any of the above-mentioned directives.

The resulting conclusion that, for injunctions to be granted under the EU law provisions at issue, the applicant cannot be required to demonstrate that the defendant was at fault, finds further support in the Court's ruling in *Stadt Graz* discussed earlier.[228] It will be recalled that in this case it was held that the Procurement Remedies Directives preclude a fault requirement in relation to actions for damages. Here the Court also implied, however, that these directives equally preclude such a requirement in relation to the *other* remedies set out therein and therefore also for actions for injunctions.[229] In addition, unlike for actions for damages, it appears that most national legal systems do not require proof of fault for injunctions to be granted.[230] This would seem to make the conclusion all the more likely that the above-mentioned directives are not to be understood as implying such a requirement. It also suggests that the view that the said directives actually preclude the application of such a requirement is unlikely to lead to significant controversies.

Once again it could conceivably be argued that the IPR Enforcement Directive is different in this respect. As was noted earlier, this directive includes an (optional) arrangement on pecuniary compensation as an "alternative measure" to be imposed instead of the permanent injunctions provided for in this

226 For a more elaborate assessment of the issue of fault in relation to actions for damages, see subsection 7.A.2 above. That assessment would appear to be also largely applicable here, *mutatis mutandis and* subject to the above comments.

227 Art. 11(2) Unfair Commercial Practices Directive 2005/29; Art. 5(3) Misleading Advertising Directive 2006/114.

228 CoJ case C-314/09, *Stadt Graz*. See para 3.19 and 7.07 above.

229 CoJ case C-314/09, *Stadt Graz*, para 39. In a similar sense, see Kotsonis (2011b), p. NA62.

230 Van Dam (2006), p. 301 (regarding English, French and German law). See also Peyer (undated), p. 20 (regarding German law in a competition context).

directive.[231] This alternative is only available where the infringer acted '*unintentionally or without negligence*'. From this one could deduct *a contrario* that for those injunctions themselves to be granted, normally a requirement of the infringing party having acted intentionally or negligently applies, or at least that the application of such a requirement is not necessarily precluded. Yet then again one could also argue on the basis of the presence in this directive of an express provision on fault in relation to actions for damages,[232] and the absence of such an express provision in relation to actions for injunctions, that in the latter instance no such requirement can apply. Consequently, while some uncertainty might exist, with respect to the IPR Enforcement Directive also the better view appears to be that there is in principle no scope for a fault requirement in relation to actions for injunctions.

The absence of an obligation on the applicant to demonstrate that he suffered loss or damage or that the defendant was at fault for injunctive relief to be granted makes this remedy easier to obtain, not only in the sense that the legal threshold is lower in respect of these two points, as discussed above. This normally also has *indirect* repercussions that are beneficial to private party applicants. For instance, when such a party does not need to demonstrate harm, there can be no discussion on the qualification or quantification thereof. It also follows that there is no requirement of a causal link between the infringement and the damage. As a consequence of the absence of all of these requirements, proceedings for injunctions will also, moreover, mostly be less lengthy and less costly as compared with, in particular, actions for damages.[233] It has already been seen that these legal and practical factors are often important thresholds in relation to the latter remedy.[234] Finally, again in contrast to damages awards, injunctive relief can normally be granted by means of interim measures, that is, in proceedings that can lead to a decision with provisional effects and which are normally (relatively) speedy, uncomplicated and not overly costly.[235] In that sense, the relative success referred to above is probably partially a shared success of the remedy discussed here and of that of interim measures. **7.32**

3. Competition law and cross-border litigation

A first further specific issue to be discussed here is the question of what the foregoing implies specifically for the discussions on the private enforcement of EU *competition* law. As was observed earlier, while Article 101(2) TFEU only **7.33**

231 Art. 12 IPR Enforcement Directive 2004/48. See para 4.25 and 7.27 above.
232 Art. 13 IPR Enforcement Directive 2004/48. See para 4.28 and 7.06 above.
233 Cf. Jacobs and Deisenhofer (2003), p. 196; Eilmansberger (2007), p. 433; Cauffman (2010), p. 59.
234 See in particular para 7.03 above.
235 On interim relief more generally, see subsection 8.B.1 below.

provides for a contractual remedy, in terms of substantive remedies the Competition Damages Directive is exclusively focused on ensuring compensation in damages. Actions for damages have long had the Commission's particular attention in this context.[236] In terms of EU legislative involvement, actions for injunctions therefore do not play a role in this field. Yet it would be wrong to presume that this choice not to include measures on injunctive relief in the Competition Damages Directive is somehow obvious or inevitable. Both the directive itself and the Commission's official documents preceding it acknowledge that (in this field of law as in any other) private enforcement can also take place through the bringing of actions for injunctions.[237] The important role that this latter remedy can also play with respect to competition law infringements is in fact widely acknowledged in the legal literature.[238] This is not surprising, especially in light of the aforementioned relative attractiveness of injunctive relief for potential applicants when compared with actions for damages. Practical experience in Germany suggests, for instance, that especially the (relatively) low costs and flexibility associated with injunctive relief make this the preferred private enforcement remedy for private parties affected by competition law infringements, although few such actions are brought in England.[239] This remedy has also been reported to have a significantly higher success rate than actions for damages.[240] It further appears that private parties are, in practice, generally often more interested in bringing an end to infringements than in obtaining compensation for the damage suffered as a consequence thereof. This has been observed to be the case, for instance, in relation to infringements of EU intellectual property law.[241] There seems little reason to believe that this would be fundamentally different where infringements of EU competition law are concerned.[242]

It is therefore remarkable not only that the Commission decided to exclude from its initiative on the private enforcement of EU competition law remedies other than actions for damages and especially injunctions, but also – and in

236 See para 6.10, 6.11 and 6.28 above.

237 See Commission, Green paper on damages actions for breach of the EC antitrust rules, COM(2005) 672, pp. 3–4; Commission, Staff working paper accompanying the white paper on damages actions for breach of the EC antitrust rules, SEC(2008) 404, p. 7 (n. 5). See also recital 3 Competition Damages Directive 2014/104, where actions for damages are said to be merely an '*example*' of private enforcement.

238 E.g. Komninos (2008), p. 215; Eilmansberger (2007), p. 437; Cauffman (2010), p. 60; Whish and Bailey (2012), p. 301; Hjelmeng (2013), p. 1011; Louis (2014), p. 87; Ottervanger (2014), p. 18; Ratliff (2014), p. 272; Wisking, Dietzel and Herron (2014), p. 187.

239 Peyer (undated). See also Peyer (2012), p. 350.

240 Peyer (2012), p. 353.

241 Commission, Responses to the public consultation on the civil enforcement of intellectual property rights, July 2013, p. 7.

242 Cf. Cauffman (2010), p. 59; Whish and Bailey (2012), p. 301.

particular – that this choice has never been properly explained.[243] One can therefore only speculate as to the reasons that underlie the current *'shadowy existence'* and *'[astonishing] neglect of this remedy on the policy level'*.[244] A factor may have been the influence of the approach to the private enforcement of competition law taken in the United States, where damages claims tend to play a central role. This may in particular have had an effect on the academic debate.[245] Another factor could be that landmark rulings of the Court of Justice, such as *Courage*, on which the Commission's initiative built,[246] related only to the possibilities for the private parties concerned to claim damages. However, it is submitted that this latter factor would provide a largely unsatisfactory explanation in legal terms. For the Court's reasoning in *Courage* may well be applicable beyond the narrow confines of actions for damages. Indeed, back in 2003 Advocate General Jacobs argued that this reasoning is essentially equally applicable to actions for injunctions.[247] Also, the Court's ruling in *Muñoz*, which related to the field of EU agricultural law, would seem to point in that direction.[248] The Court's reasoning in this latter case is very similar to the one followed in *Courage*, but the question at issue concerned not actions for damages but civil proceedings more generally. Another relevant element could lie in the underlying objective, for instance in terms of which types of infringements are to be addressed, the sorts of difficulties experienced by private parties or the anticipated deterrent or corrective effects of such actions. However, it seems uncertain whether clear conclusions could be drawn on any of these points.[249] In any case there are at present no indications that an in-depth assessment of any of these aspects underpins the choice to concentrate the

243 In Commission, Staff working paper accompanying the green paper on damages actions for breach of EC antitrust rules, SEC(2005) 1732, pp. 9–11, this issue is discussed in some detail, without, however, actually explaining the choice made to concentrate exclusively on actions for damages.

244 Peyer (undated), pp. 1 and 51.

245 Cf. Opinion AG Van Gerven case C-128/92, *Banks*, para 44. See e.g. Jones (1999); Jones (2003), p. 94.

246 CoJ case C-453/99, *Courage*. The same applies for CoJ joined cases C-295/04 to C-298/04, *Manfredi*. On these two cases and their relevance in the present context, see para 6.14–6.16 above. Similarly, in Opinion AG Van Gerven case C-128/92, *Banks*, discussed in para 6.12 above, attention concentrated on actions for damages. Cf. Commission, Staff working paper accompanying the green paper on damages actions for breach of EC antitrust rules, SEC(2005) 1732, p. 9, where reference is made to the *Courage* judgment as well as the AG's opinion in *Banks*.

247 Opinion AG Jacobs joined cases C-264/01, C-306/01, C-354/01 and C-355/01, *AOB Bundesverband*, para 105. In Commission, Staff working paper accompanying the green paper on damages actions for breach of EC antitrust rules, SEC(2005) 1732, p. 9 (n. 2), reference was made to this opinion seemingly in a concurring manner. In a similar sense, see Peyer (undated), pp. 10–14.

248 CoJ case C-253/00, *Muñoz*. For a discussion of this case and a comparison with *Courage*, see para 2.25 and 2.28 above, respectively.

249 For example, it has been suggested that damages actions might be more suitable in relation to cartels, whereas injunctive relief may be more suitable with respect to abuse of market power and anticompetitive vertical constraints. See Peyer (2011), p. 655; Peyer (undated), p. 46. Others have argued for concentrating efforts regarding the facilitation of private enforcement not on hard-core competition law infringements but rather on "grey area" cases. See Eilmansberger (2007), p. 478.

Commission's legislative initiative that resulted in the adoption of the Competition Damages Directive solely on actions for damages. This directive's narrow scope in terms of private enforcement remedies might therefore well be seen as a missed opportunity.

7.34 A second specific point relating to actions for injunctions constitutes essentially an important qualification of the aforementioned relative success thereof as a private enforcement remedy. Very little use tends to be made of this remedy in *cross-border* situations, where the applicant and the defendant reside or are established each in a different Member State. A prime example relates to the provision on "intra-EU infringements" laid down in the Consumer Injunctions Directive.[250] Under this directive a qualified entity from one Member State may in certain cases bring an action for an injunction in another Member State. One could say that the very essence of this directive is to facilitate precisely these kinds of actions. But in 2008 the Commission concluded that the effect given to this provision has so far been '*disappointing*'.[251] This seems somewhat of an understatement, given that at the time the mechanism had been used in no more than two instances EU-wide. It appears that since then this situation has hardly improved, if at all.[252] Another example is the IPR Enforcement Directive. The Commission has observed that the relative success of this directive's provisions on injunctive relief does not seem to extend to cross-border situations,[253] while stakeholders identify cross-border infringements as a significant and increasing concern.[254] Concerning the Procurement Remedies Directives, applications for cross-border reviews in procurement cases, of which actions for injunctions typically make up a considerable share, have been found to be scarce.[255]

It is important to note that these findings probably do not stand on their own. Within the EU generally, only a relatively limited amount of cross-border litigation takes place, regardless of what form of relief is sought precisely.[256] The above observations are therefore likely to reflect a broader issue. Arguably this

250 Art. 4 Consumer Injunctions Directive. See para 5.07 above.

251 Commission, First report on Consumer Injunctions Directive 2009/22, COM(2008) 756, pp. 5–9.

252 Commission, Second report on Consumer Injunctions Directive 2009/22, COM(2012) 635, p. 6. See para 5.12 above.

253 Commission, Staff working document accompanying the report on IPR Enforcement Directive 2004/48, SEC(2010) 1589, p. 18.

254 See e.g. Commission, Responses to the public consultation on the civil enforcement of intellectual property rights, July 2013, p. 8. See para 4.21 and 4.24 above.

255 See e.g. Commission, Responses to the consultation on the operation of national review procedures in the field of public procurement, 2004 (economic operators and lawyers).

256 See e.g. Rosas and Armanti (2010), pp. 172–3; Loos (2011), p. 499–502. This finding also extends to alternative dispute resolution mechanisms. See European Parliament, Study on cross-border alternative dispute resolution in the EU, June 2011, p. 9.

difference between "domestic" and "cross-border" litigation is only more striking where injunctions are concerned, because these actions are comparatively successful in situations that are confined to one Member State. This generally limited degree of cross-border litigation is often explained by pointing to the (anticipated) extra costs, delays and complications connected to bringing an action for an injunction before a court in another Member State.[257] To some extent this may say as much about the perceptions and expectations in this regard as it does about actual experiences in practice. Actual experiences with cross-border litigation are after all limited. It also does not seem self-evident that cross-border litigation is necessarily overly complex, in an age where all domestic legal systems of the Member States are influenced by EU law and many law firms have branches in several Member States or are part of international networks. But fully justified or not, perceptions and expectations of this kind still matter, as they can play an important role in a private party's decision as to whether or not to initiate private enforcement proceedings in another Member State. Linguistic differences can obviously be a relevant factor too.[258]

That being so, the Commission seems to prefer addressing the above issues through measures of broader application rather than in the sectoral legislation under consideration here.[259] It seems to have largely vested its hopes in improvements that may result from EU legislation applicable to litigation in civil and commercial matters, such as the Brussels I Regulation on jurisdiction and the recognition and enforcement of judgments and the Rome II Regulation on the law applicable to non-contractual obligations.[260] These regulations contain several specific rules for the fields of law under consideration here.[261] Supplementary measures have also been taken, such as the establishment of the

257 Cf. e.g. Eurobarometer, Consumer redress in the EU, August 2009, p. 39: '*Consumers anticipate that the difficulties they would experience in their home countries would be multiplied if they were to seek out information on redress mechanisms and the processes consumers need to follow in order to seek compensation for cross-border complaints. As a result, consumers are even less likely to pursue these complaints.*'

258 Cf. Commission, Second report on Consumer Injunctions Directive 2009/22, COM(2012) 635, p. 13; Stadler (2013b), p. 151.

259 See in particular Commission, Staff working paper accompanying the white paper on damages actions for breach of the EC antitrust rules, SEC(2008) 404, p. 9; Commission, First report on Consumer Injunctions Directive 2009/22, COM(2008) 756, pp. 8–9; Commission, Second report on Consumer Injunctions Directive 2009/22, COM(2012) 635, p. 12.

260 Brussels I Regulation 1215/2012; Rome II Regulation 864/2007.

261 Concerning Brussels I Regulation 1215/2012, see in particular its Art. 17–19 (regarding consumer contracts), Art. 24(4) (regarding certain intellectual property rights) and Art. 35 (regarding provisional measures). Its recital 25 clarifies that the concept of "provisional measures" includes the orders referred to in Art. 6 and 7 IPR Enforcement Directive 2004/48. Specifically in relation to the Unified Patent Court, referred to in para 4.02 above, see De Miguel Asensio (2014), p. 868. As regards competition cases, see CoJ case C-352/15, *CDC Hydrogen Peroxide*. Concerning Rome II Regulation 864/2007, see in particular its Art. 5 (regarding product liability), 6(3) (regarding restrictions of competition) and 8 (regarding intellectual property rights).

European judicial network in civil and commercial matters.[262] An important objective of this network is the dissemination of information with a view to facilitating effective access to justice. While all these measures can, generally speaking, undoubtedly be helpful for a private party who is considering bringing a case before a court in another jurisdiction,[263] it would seem that there are limits to what can be expected in this regard. These measures are, for example, mostly limited to litigation in civil and commercial matters.[264] They will therefore be of little help in proceedings under administrative law. Neither have they been designed to address collective redress situations.[265] These measures further tend to help clarify certain legal aspects that are relevant to cross-border litigation (which court is competent, which law applies, and so on), but they do little to address the aforementioned practical concerns that are often cited to explain the limited degree of cross-border litigation (perceptions, costs, linguistic issues, and so on).[266]

262 Cf. Decision 2001/470/EC establishing a European Judicial Network in civil and commercial matters, OJ 2001, L 168/35.

263 However, the rules set out in Brussels I Regulation 1215/2012 can also lead to unintended (and what many would consider undesirable) consequences. The most well-known example is the possible pre-emptive exercise of jurisdiction in application of the *lis pendens* rule (see its Art. 29), known as "torpedo" actions. This entails bringing a case before a national court that may not have jurisdiction (typically seeking a declaration of non-infringement) in a Member State where legal proceedings can take a long time to be completed. In this manner the jurisdiction of another national court in the EU can be pre-empted. See Commission, Report on Brussels I Regulation 44/2001, COM(2009) 174, pp. 6–7. See also e.g. Gardella (2008), p. 181. On this subject matter specifically in relation to the "new" Brussels I Regulation 1215/2012, see Nielsen (2013), pp. 518–22.

264 As such, they do not apply to actions brought by or against public authorities acting in the exercise of their powers or situations otherwise regulated by administrative law. See Art. 1(1) Brussels I Regulation 1215/2012; Art. 1(1) Rome II Regulation 864/2007. See e.g. CoJ case C-292/05, *Lecouritou*, para 28–34; CoJ case C-406/09, *Realchemie*, para 38–44.

265 See Stadler (2013a), pp. 484–8.

266 For example, Small Claims Regulation 861/2007 may be of some help in this respect, but its practical use is limited due to its covering claims with a monetary value of no more than €2000. Reference can further be made to Consumer ADR Directive 2013/11, discussed in para 5.42 above. But this directive essentially provides for an alternative to litigation before the courts, while it is moreover limited to consumer disputes only.

8

CONTRACTUAL AND OTHER REMEDIES

In the previous chapter the relevant EU rules on actions for damages and actions for injunctions have been considered. By means of a continuation of the comparative and contextual analysis set out there, the present chapter turns to the remaining remedies for private enforcement purposes laid down in the selected EU legislation discussed in Part B above. To that end this chapter consists of two sections. In the first section, the third and final "main" (substantive) class of actions distinguished here, namely contractual remedies, is analysed. The following section then discusses the other remedies laid down in that legislation.

A. CONTRACTUAL REMEDIES

This section concentrates on actions intended to make good infringements of EU law by seeking to nullify or to otherwise make ineffective the contractual arrangements entered into by the parties concerned, which are referred to here as contractual remedies. After a brief overview, the terminology used in the legislation at issue as well as the nature and practical functioning of this remedy are discussed. The following subsection then assesses in further detail, first, the flexibility left to the Member States in relation to this remedy and, second, the position of the parts of the contract that are not incompatible with EU law. In the third and final subsection attention turns to the regime applicable to what are called "excluded" contracts, which refers to contracts that fall entirely outside the scope of the EU rules at issue here but that are covered by primary EU law.

1. Terminology, nature and functioning in practice

8.01 Contractual remedies can be found in three of the four fields of law under consideration in Part B, namely EU public procurement, consumer protection and competition law. Each time this remedy has been set out in different terms, however. Since their revision in 2007, whereby the relevant provision was introduced, the Procurement Remedies Directives speak of the possible "ineffectiveness" of concluded contracts.[1] By contrast, the main provision in the field of consumer protection law, laid down in the Unfair Terms Directive, refers to contracts that are "not binding" on the private party concerned.[2] In other consumer protection directives different terms are used, such as contracts being "rescinded" or the possibility of "withdrawal" from a contract (this latter term is, moreover, used in different legal acts with two apparently distinct meanings).[3] Finally, in relation to competition law infringements, Article 101(2) TFEU speaks of contracts being "automatically void".[4]

This evidently raises the question of what explains this divergent terminology. Departing from the presumption that it is preferable to use consistent terminology across the entire body of EU law wherever possible, the question also emerges as to what extent there may be scope for a more coherent approach in this respect.[5] These questions are answered below by subsequently considering the terms used in each of the three above-mentioned provisions of EU law.

8.02 An appropriate starting point is the term "automatically void" within the meaning of Article 101(2) TFEU. This seems the most obvious candidate for broader application in acts of secondary EU law providing for contractual remedies. This term has after all been in use since the entry into force of the Treaty establishing the European Economic Community ("EEC") in 1958. It is, moreover, the only concept to have primary law status.[6] The Court of Justice

---

1 Art. 2d(2) Procurement Remedies Directives 89/665 and 92/13. See subsection 3.B.3 above.

2 Art. 6(1) Unfair Terms Directive 93/13. See subsection 5.C.1 above.

3 Art. 3(2), (5) and (6) Consumer Sales Directive 1999/44; Art. 4(5) and (6) Package Travel Directive 90/314. See para 5.23 above. Cf. the use of "withdrawal" e.g. in Art. 6 Distance Marketing Directive 2002/65, Art. 14 Consumer Credit Directive 2008/48 and Art. 9 Consumer Rights Directive 2011/83. There this term appears to have a different meaning than in Art. 4(5) and (6) Package Travel Directive 90/314.

4 See subsection 6.A.3 above. Art. 101(2) TFEU relates to '*agreements and decisions*' that are prohibited under that article. For reasons of simplicity and ease of comparison, the emphasis is here only on the effects of this provision on contracts.

5 On issues of coherence and fragmentation more generally, see section 10.04 below.

6 See also Art. 264 TFEU. There it is stated that if an act of an EU institution or other body is annulled pursuant to Art. 263 TFEU, the EU courts shall declare that act to be '*void*'. Note that this latter provision speaks of acts being *declared* void, whereas the former refers to prohibited anticompetitive agreements or decisions being *automatically* void.

has over the course of the years had the opportunity to clarify the meaning of this term.[7] It has held in particular that this term is an autonomous concept of EU law. As such it has a particular meaning, independent from the laws of the Member States. It has retroactive effects (*ex tunc*), meaning that it is as if there had never been a contract in the first place when this provision is successfully invoked. These effects are also absolute; they apply in principle with respect to all parties to the contract in question as well as third parties.

It is interesting to note in this connection that the Commission's proposal for the Unfair Terms Directive, dating from 1990, also contained the term "void".[8] However, the Member States represented in the Council subsequently changed this to the current term "not binding".[9] Already in itself the latter is a more neutral legal term than "void". Especially in combination with the express reference to national law for which the Unfair Terms Directive provides in this connection, which was also inserted by the EU legislature, this leaves the Member States more scope when transposing this provision into national law. Although there can be some debate on this point, it would appear that, unlike the term "automatically void" within the meaning of Article 101(2) TFEU, this allows, for instance, for the possibility of leaving the past application of the contract intact (*ex nunc*). In any case at national level a wide range of concepts are currently used to give effect to this provision, such as non-existence, revocability, voidability, unenforceability.[10] **8.03**

It can further be noted that the absolute effect associated with the term "void" could lead to evidently undesirable outcomes when applied here. Such an effect may generally be appropriate pursuant to, say, a price-fixing agreement between two undertakings caught by the prohibition laid down in Article 101(1) TFEU. However, in cases covered by the Unfair Terms Directive, the "standard" consumer contract at issue is in effect imposed on the consumer, who finds himself generally in a weak position *vis-à-vis* his contracting party (the latter being a seller or supplier acting in a professional capacity). It would then be contrary to the aim of protecting consumers if the latter could also free himself from his contractual obligations by invoking the consequences of the unfairness of a term, for the drafting of which he himself is responsible. In these cases this remedy should thus only be invoked for the benefit of the consumer. Put

7 E.g. CoJ joined cases C-295/04 to C-298/04, *Manfredi*, para 57. See para 6.15 above.

8 Commission, Proposal for Unfair Terms Directive 93/13, COM(90) 322, p. 69 (Art. 3); Commission, First amended proposal for Unfair Terms Directive 93/13, COM(92) 66, p. 11 (Art. 7).

9 See para 5.16 above.

10 See para 5.17 above.

differently, the desired result under this directive is relative and not absolute.[11] This is reflected in the use of the words not binding "on the consumer".

8.04 The story behind the use of the term "ineffectiveness" set out in the Procurement Remedies Directives is not dissimilar. In this case also, the Commission proposal was significantly more prescriptive than the text of the legal act eventually adopted. The Commission had suggested using the term "invalid". It had also proposed including a certain precision as regards the meaning of this term under EU law, providing in principle for absolute effects.[12] However, once more the EU legislature and in particular the Member States represented in the Council decided to use a less precise term, namely "ineffectiveness".[13] Differing from the Commission's proposal, the Procurement Remedies Directives now also stipulate expressly that the consequences of a contract being considered ineffective are provided for by national law. These directives further state that this national law may either provide for retroactive cancellation of all contractual obligations (that is, *ex tunc*) or limit the scope of the cancellation to those obligations which still have to be performed (that is, *ex nunc*). As a result, the domestic laws of the Member States give effect to this EU law provision in diverging manners.[14] In this case there is no "automatic" effect, in the sense that a preceding finding by a court or another review body is required for the contract to be considered ineffective. The latter is in line with the Commission's proposal.[15]

Furthermore, in this case there are also certain particular characteristics that to a certain extent set a typical public procurement case apart from a typical competition case. Most notably, in contrast to Article 101 TFEU, under the EU public procurement rules the conclusion of the contract as such does not constitute an infringement. In this case the infringement rather relates to the *pre-contractual* stage, that is, the selection of the private party contractor by the contracting authority. This is connected to the fact that the former is not subject to these rules in the first place. That said, it is questionable whether these differences justify granting the private party concerned particular protection in this respect, as essentially occurs under the Unfair Terms Directive. For one thing, in public procurement cases both parties to the contract operate on a professional basis. It seems not unreasonable to expect from the private party

---

11 Cf. Van Gerven (2003b), p. 57.

12 Commission, Proposal for Procurement Remedies Amending Directive 2007/66, COM(2006) 195, p. 24 (Art. 2f(2) and (3)).

13 See para 3.21 above.

14 See para 3.22 above.

15 Ibid.

contractor a degree of knowledge and diligence as regards the correct application of the law by the contracting authority.[16] That applies all the more so because the cases covered by the Procurement Remedies Directives concern public contracts with a significant value and the infringements in question are by definition very serious.[17] For another thing, in these cases any such protection would necessarily come at the expense of third parties, namely the private party's (potential) competitors.[18] For having the contract considered ineffective normally results in the contracting authority putting the contract out to (re-)tender, allowing these parties a (renewed) possibility to compete.[19] All in all in this case there would thus seem to be considerably less convincing legal or factual reasons for not opting for an approach similar to Article 101(2) TFEU.[20]

In contrast to the above-mentioned legal acts, no contractual remedy has been included in the IPR Enforcement Directive. This illustrates that this remedy is somewhat *more selective* than the two remedies discussed in the previous chapter. Whereas actions for damages and actions for injunctions are (or at least can be) relevant in principle in relation to *any* infringement of EU law, providing for a contractual remedy obviously only makes sense where the relevant infringements have "contractual dimension" of some sort. In the field of intellectual property law this dimension of the infringements in question is normally limited. Under the IPR Enforcement Directive (and under rules of EU intellectual property law more generally[21]), disputes can of course arise in respect of which certain contractual elements can be of relevance. However, the infringements of intellectual property law that the IPR Enforcement Directive seeks to address do not typically – and certainly not necessarily – result from or relate to a contractual relationship.[22] **8.05**

In the three other aforementioned fields of law under consideration, the situation is different. In public procurement cases the conclusion of a contract

16 Pursuant to the case law of the CoJ, aggrieved private parties can be expected to be diligent in bringing actions for review and in obtaining information in this connection. See CoJ case C-456/08, *Commission v Ireland*, para 73; CoJ case C-161/13, *Idrodinamica*, para 43. See also CoJ case C-19/00, *SIAC*, para 43. Cf. CoJ case C-24/95, *Alcan*, para 25, concerning the diligence required on the part of the undertakings concerned in state aid cases.

17 As regards the value of the contracts in question, certain threshold values must be exceeded for the substantive rules in question to apply. See para 3.03 above. As regards this limitation to the most serious infringements, see para 3.21 above.

18 That is, where such protection relates to the validity of the contract entered into. Whether or not the private party concerned is entitled to damages is a distinct matter. See Halonen (2015), p. 113.

19 Cf. recital 14 Procurement Remedies Amending Directive 2007/66, where it is observed that this is '*the most effective way to restore competition and to create new business opportunities*'.

20 In a similar sense, see Clifton (2009), p. 170.

21 See Art. 15 Directive 96/9/EC of the European Parliament and of the Council of 11 March 1996 on the legal protection of data bases, OJ 1996, L 77/20, pursuant to which certain contractual provisions are '*null and void*'.

22 See para 4.03 above.

between the contracting authority and the selected tenderer is both the very objective and the logical conclusion of the preceding contract award procedure. The fact that public procurement law has been infringed in the course of this procedure will often imply that the contract should not have been concluded with the tenderer in question or at least that not all interested private parties have had a fair chance of winning it. As was noted earlier, the continuous application of the contract also means that it will not be put out to tender again. As regards the Unfair Terms Directive, the relevance of contractual issues is somewhat different in nature, but no less evident. After all, this directive seeks to prevent the use of unfair terms used in "standard" consumer contracts. Where such terms are used nonetheless, it is not illogical to provide for a contractual remedy to address their continuous application. Finally, in relation to the EU competition rules, the very fact that two or more undertakings concluded an anticompetitive (cartel) agreement can constitute a violation of Article 101(1) TFEU. Also, in this case the importance of contractual remedies is therefore almost a given.

The selective character of this remedy is not only evident from a comparison between the various aforementioned fields of law. It often also applies *within* the above-mentioned fields. This can be best illustrated with reference to the field of EU competition law. The importance of contractual remedies may almost be a given in relation to certain types of infringements of this law, but this by no means applies for *all* such infringements. The prohibition set out in Article 101(1) also covers anticompetitive concerted practices that do not involve the conclusion of a contract. Moreover, substantive EU competition law also entails the prohibition of abuse of a dominant position set out in Article 102 TFEU. Yet the contractual remedy provided for in Article 101(2) does not extend to contracts concluded in violation of Article 102 TFEU, whereas this latter article itself does not contain an equivalent provision.[23] And also the scope of the contractual remedy laid down in the Procurement Remedies Directives is limited. It applies only to the contracts concluded pursuant to what the EU legislature considered to be the most serious infringements.[24] This implies that many other infringements of the substantive EU public procurement rules cannot lead to this provision being invoked.[25] Only under the Unfair Terms Directive (and many other consumer protection directives) does the

23 See para 6.08 above. For a discussion of the possible contractual consequences of violations of Art. 102 TFEU, see para 8.10 below.

24 See para 3.21 above.

25 For a discussion of the possible contractual consequences of other violations of EU public procurement law, see para 8.11 below.

remedial provision at issue here coincide with the relevant substantive rules, both of which have been laid down in the same legal act.[26]

When the use of the aforementioned contractual remedies *in practice* is considered, the situation appears to be somewhat mixed. The aforementioned diversity and selectivity also come to light here. To begin with, Article 101(2) TFEU tends to be used rather frequently and effectively in litigation between private parties. But this use is mainly "defensive", thus by one of the parties to the contract that seeks to avoid being bound by an obligation set out in the contract concerned. This remedy is little used in an "offensive" manner. Third parties may generally have little incentive to do so. And at least where particularly serious (hard-core) violations of Article 101(1) TFEU are at issue, the same mostly goes for the undertakings that are party to the contract, as this would evidently expose their illegal behaviour.[27] **8.06**

Concerning the contractual remedy provided for in the Unfair Terms Directive, its use is by contrast necessarily "offensive", in that it can only lead to the consumer concerned (and not the infringing undertaking) not being bound. Nonetheless in 2000 the Commission called the system thus established '*very ineffective*'.[28] It noted that the undertakings that include unfair terms in their contracts typically stand to lose little where this remedy is applied. This has been linked to the aforementioned flexibility that the directive leaves to the Member States in this respect.[29] Moreover, as the Commission also observed, its effectiveness relies to a large extent on consumers being aware of their rights, which is in practice often not the case.[30] The Court of Justice has picked up on the latter point. In particular, central to its *Océano Grupo* case law discussed earlier is the thought that the objective of this contractual remedy would not be achieved if it were left to the consumer himself to raise the unfair nature of a term in a consumer contract.[31] The Court pointed in this connection to the deterrent effect that high lawyers' fees may have on consumers and the fact that these consumers themselves may not be aware of their rights. It thus seems to consider that this remedy could only properly function in practice if a third party, including a national court acting of its own motion, actively intervenes.[32]

---

26 This does not mean that the scope of the contractual remedy set out in this directive is particularly wide. Rather the scope of the substantive rules is relatively narrow. Given that here the substantial and the remedial rules of EU law coincide, the same then consequently applies for this remedy.

27 See para 6.09 above.

28 Commission, Report on Unfair Terms Directive 93/13, COM(2000) 248, p. 35. See para 5.22 above.

29 Study, University of Bielefeld (2008), p. 347.

30 See also ibid., p. 434.

31 CoJ joined cases C-240/98 and C-244/98, *Océano Grupo*. See para 5.19 and 5.20 above.

32 On own-motion judicial review generally, see subsection 9.D.2 below. Another option can be a third party, such as a consumer association, bringing a "representative" action under Art. 7(2) Unfair Terms Directive

In any case the considerable number of preliminary references made over the past years suggests that there seems to be no shortage of litigation relating to this provision.[33]

Finally, it is for now too early to adequately assess the functioning in practice of the contractual remedy of ineffectiveness set out in the Procurement Remedies Directives, given the relatively recent introduction of this remedy. On the one hand, it seems to have considerable potential as an "offensive" private enforcement instrument. The typical private parties concerned (that is, rejected bidders or other undertakings that might be interested in the contract at issue) will often have the knowledge, the means and also an incentive to bring legal proceedings seeking to have the contract in question declared ineffective. It can also have an important deterrent effect for the contracting authorities that are subject to the EU's system for public procurement. On the other hand, there are also several factors that imply that this remedy might well be used less frequently in practice. These factors are both legal (for example, limitation to most serious infringements, flexibility as to the precise legal effects, multiple exceptions, limitation periods[34]) and practical (for example, possible absence of evidence and information concerning illegal direct awards, general hesitance to sue[35]) in nature. While it may well be that the use of this remedy will increase over time and that it already has a certain impact in practice through the deterrent effect referred to above, the (limited) experience to date indicates that, at least for now, it is generally little applied in practice.[36]

All this suggests that, although contractual remedies of the type at issue here can certainly have a role to play in practice, particularly as they are currently provided for in the above-mentioned provisions of primary and secondary EU law, they are not without limitations as a remedy in private enforcement proceedings.

2. Member States' flexibility and non-infringing provisions

8.07 It has been noted in the previous subsection that in relation to the contractual remedies provided for in the EU legislation assessed in Part B above, the Unfair Terms Directive and the Procurement Remedies Directives, in particular leave

93/13. Read together with Art. 7(1) and 6(1) of this directive, an action of this kind could lead to a finding of a term being unfair and therefore not binding with certain *erga omnes* effects. See CoJ case C-472/10, *Invitel*, para 38–40.

33 See in particular para 5.20 above.

34 See in particular para 3.22 and 3.23 above.

35 See para 3.17 above.

36 See para 3.24 above.

considerable flexibility to the Member States. That facilitates the "embedment" of these provisions of EU law in their respective domestic legal systems. This applies both with regard to the transposition of the relevant provisions of the aforementioned directives into national law and the subsequent application of the resulting national laws by all parties concerned more generally. There can thus be good reasons for allowing for a degree of flexibility. As Advocate General Ruiz-Jarabo Colomor observed in relation to the more general question of which legal consequences are to be drawn at the national level from the fact that EU law has been infringed:

> [t]he Court's case law could, in theory, have had recourse to some of the legal categories well known in the general theory of law (such as, for example, "non-existence", "invalidity", "nullity", "ineffectiveness", "loss of force", "illegitimacy" or other similar categories) in order to identify the defect which affects national provisions where they are incompatible with the [EU] legal order. [...] However, the Court has carefully avoided employing such concepts in its decisions, no doubt because it is aware that the choice of any of these concepts – whose meaning, moreover, varies from one legal system to another – is more a matter for the individual legal systems.[37]

Considerations of this type arguably carry particular weight in relation to contractual remedies given that contract law has mostly been left to be regulated by the Member States. Indeed, the Court of Justice has held that:

> the question of the conclusions to be drawn in the main proceedings [...] as regards the severity of the sanction under the applicable national law, such as nullity or unenforceability of the contract [...], is a question governed by national law, in particular as regards the rules and principles of contract law which admit or adjust that sanction in order to render its severity proportionate to the particular defect found.[38]

But this flexibility can still have important downsides. It is important to note that the above statements by the Advocate General and the Court of Justice related to situations where no specific rules of EU law applied. In such a situation recourse is had, by default as it were, to national law.[39] The same need not apply where EU law does address this issue specifically, as is the case in the situations under consideration here. The very point of providing for a contractual remedy in the EU legislation at issue is, after all, to harmonise, at least to some extent, the relevant national laws and to specify as a matter of EU law the

37 Opinion AG Ruiz-Jarabo Colomer joined cases C-10/97 and C-22/97, *IN.CO.GE '90*, para 18–19. This statement was made in connection with the case law of the CoJ holding that in case of an infringement of EU law, the relevant provision of national law must be disapplied, as set out in particular in CoJ case 106/77, *Simmenthal*, discussed in para 2.21 above.

38 CoJ case C-159/00, *Sapod*, para 52.

39 In relation to contractual remedies specifically, see also subsection 8.A.3 below. On the relationship between the EU legislation at issue here and national law more generally, see subsection 10.A.3 below.

consequences for a concluded contract of an infringement of EU law.[40] In those cases the desire to ensure a degree of flexibility can seem to be as much related to a (political) desire to "shield" the field of contract law as much as possible from EU legislative intervention, than that it is related to any inherent (legal or factual) imperative. Either way, this flexibility may put at risk the objectives of the very harmonisation that the EU legislative measures in question seek to achieve. It is one thing to leave Member States with flexibility as to *how* a certain result is to be achieved in their respective legal systems.[41] But it is quite another thing where this flexibility relates to the *result itself*. It follows from the discussion in the previous subsection that the latter (also) appears to have occurred here. For instance, whether a contractual remedy has effects *ex nunc* or rather *ex tunc* is evidently not merely a matter of form or details. It rather touches upon the essence of the EU law measure in question. It might be too far-reaching to speak of purely "fictitious harmonisation" that allows the Member States to pursue '*fundamentally divergent approaches under the camouflage of a platitudinous framework measure*', but it certainly sometimes seems not too far off either.[42]

The Procurement Remedies Directives offer a good illustration of the complex compromises that may be required when seeking to balance the potentially conflicting desires for an effective EU law remedy, on the one hand, and retaining a certain margin of manoeuvre at national level, on the other hand.[43] As was noted above, these directives stipulate expressly that the consequences of a contract being considered ineffective are determined by national law and that this may entail effects either *ex nunc* or *ex tunc*. But in the recitals the result sought is specified, namely that '*the rights and obligation of the parties under the contract should cease to be enforced and performed*'.[44] These directives also provide that in case of *ex nunc* effects, certain "alternative penalties" (for example fines) must be imposed in addition.[45] That implies that the two options are not treated as fully equivalent. These directives further offer additional flexibility via a provision holding that ineffectiveness need not follow where there are '*overriding reasons relating to the general interest*'.[46] This potential loophole is

40 Cf. e.g. Commission, Proposal for Procurement Remedies Amending Directive 2007/66, COM(2006) 195, p. 2: '*In the absence of legislative action at [EU] level, the very different situations among the Member States with regard to the effectiveness of review procedures available to enterprises would continue to exist or even be aggravated. Situations of legal uncertainty and serious and repeated infringements of the [substantive] public procurement Directives would continue*'.

41 As is generally the case where an EU legal act takes the form of a directive, pursuant to Art. 288 TFEU.

42 Weatherill (2000), p. 96.

43 Unfair Terms Directive 93/13 has similarly been described as being the result of '*a delicate compromise*'. See Commission, Report on Unfair Terms Directive 93/13, COM(2000) 248, p. 5.

44 Recital 21 Procurement Remedies Amending Directive 2007/66.

45 Art. 2d(2) and Art. 2e(2) Procurement Remedies Directives 89/665 and 92/13.

46 Art. 2d(3) Procurement Remedies Directives 89/665 and 92/13.

then in turn narrowed down by specifying in a rather restrictive manner what these reasons are (and are not), while there is also a requirement to impose alternative penalties in that case.[47] Not dissimilarly, the Court of Justice has acknowledged that the Member States have '*a certain degree of autonomy*' when defining the applicable legal arrangements concerning the concept of not binding within the meaning of the Unfair Terms Directive.[48] But it has stressed at the same time the importance of ensuring the full effectiveness of, and achieving an outcome consistent with, the objectives pursued by the provision of EU law in question.[49] This implies that a national court that finds that a contract term is unfair must '*draw all the consequences that follow under national law, so that the consumer is not bound*'.[50] The Court has made similar statements in relation to other contractual remedies in the field of EU consumer protection law.[51]

The assessment thus far has focused on the provisions of the contract that were deemed to violate EU law. A connected issue is the position of what could be called the "non-infringing provisions" of the contract in question. In other words, the question arises as to what is the fate of contractual provisions that *themselves* do not imply a violation of EU law, but that are *part of* a contract that includes other provisions that are deemed not to be compliant. When assessing the provisions under consideration here it becomes clear once more that the approaches followed in the three EU law provisions under consideration differ considerably from each other. **8.08**

First, in relation to the Procurement Remedies Directives, one could speak of an *all-or-nothing* approach. Under these directives it must be ensured that '*a contract*' is considered ineffective where certain serious infringements have been established.[52] This remedy thus seems to relate, as a general rule, to the *entire* contract at issue, and not merely to certain parts thereof or certain terms set out therein.[53] That is not surprising. Public procurement law applies particularly at

47 Art. 2d(3) and Art. 2e(2) Procurement Remedies Directives 89/665 and 92/13.

48 CoJ case C-618/10, *Banco Español de Crédito*, para 62.

49 E.g. ibid., para 72.

50 CoJ case C-453/10, *Pereničová*, para 30.

51 Cf. e.g. CoJ case C-350/03, *Schulte*, para 66–9 and 92. Here the CoJ ruled in a similar manner in relation to the above-mentioned right of "withdrawal" provided for in Consumer Rights Directive 2011/83. It concluded that the result sought must correspond to the restoration of the *status quo ante*.

52 Art. 2d(1) Procurement Remedies Directives 89/665 and 92/13.

53 This rule is not also without an exception, however. Pursuant to Art. 2d(2) Procurement Remedies Directives 89/665 and 92/13, when specifying the precise legal consequences of the ineffectiveness, national law may either provide for the retroactive cancellation of '*all contractual obligations*' or limit this to '*those obligations which still have to be performed*'. In the latter case, "alternative penalties" must be provided for, which include, besides fines, shortening the duration of the contract (see their Art. 2e). Under this latter provision account may be taken of '*the extent to which the contract remains in force*'. It follows that this possible exception does not allow consideration of some provisions of the contract as ineffective and others as effective. Rather, it allows in essence for distinguishing between the parts of the contract that already have been performed and the parts

the pre-contractual stage. That means that the contested contract as such will normally be the result of the earlier defective contract award procedure (or the unjustified absence of such a procedure). There is therefore normally not one particular provision of that contract that violates EU law. It follows that the question of severance between the infringing and the non-infringing provisions of the contract will not arise in a typical public procurement case.

Second, the Unfair Terms Directive approaches this subject matter differently, in a manner that can be described as *restraint*. This directive states expressly that '*the contract shall continue to bind the parties upon those terms if it is capable of continuing in existence without the unfair terms*'.[54] The Court of Justice has clarified this further. It duly noted that the objective pursued consists in '*restoring the balance between the parties while in principle preserving the validity of the contract as a whole, not in abolishing all contracts containing unfair terms*'.[55] This can thus be understood as a preference for leaving the non-infringing provisions of the contract unaffected whenever possible. Whether or not this is possible is principally to be determined at national level. It has further been held that this directive does not imply that the national court could or should annul the *entire* contract containing an unfair term. Nor is the national court allowed to *amend* the contract; all it can do in this respect, in principle, is delete the unfair term.[56] Consequently, here the general rule is that the remainder of the contract is meant to continue to bind the parties. This is also understandable, considering that such unfair terms typically take the form of unbalanced (one-sided) rights in terms of liability, termination, amendment or compliance.[57] These issues thus relate to specific issues that are ancillary to the main subject matter of the contract, namely the purchase of certain goods or services by the consumer.[58]

Third and finally, Article 101(2) TFEU can be said to be largely *neutral* as to the continued application of the non-infringing provisions of the contract in question. It is noticeable that this provision itself does not contain any particular specifications on this point. The Court of Justice has long made clear that the extent to which severance is possible is one of the further consequences of the

that are still to be performed. This dividing line is thus purely factual, and not related to the legal content of the provisions at issue.

54 Art. 6(1) Unfair Terms Directive 93/13. See e.g. also Art. 15 Consumer Rights Directive 2011/83, which provides that the exercise of the rights of "withdrawal" provided for also has the effect that '*any ancillary contracts shall be automatically terminated*'.

55 CoJ case C-453/10, *Pereničová*, para 31. See para 5.18 above.

56 CoJ case C-618/10, *Banco Español de Crédito*, para 64–71. See also CoJ case C-26/13, *Kásler*, para 79–85; CoJ joined cases C-482/13, C-484/13, C-485/13 and C-487/13, *Unicaja Banco*, para 32–3.

57 See the annex to Unfair Terms Directive 93/13. See para 5.15 above.

58 Cf. recital 19 Unfair Terms Directive 93/13.

finding of a contract being void that is to be settled under national law.[59] Further guidance comparable with that provided relating to the Unfair Terms Directive discussed above is so far largely absent. It would appear that the remainder of the contract is in principle simply not of relevance from the perspective of EU competition law. Presumably this "neutrality" nonetheless finds its limits where the effectiveness of this rule of EU law might be at risk.

3. Excluded contracts

Having assessed what the position is of the non-infringing provisions of contracts that fall within the scope of the aforementioned EU rules providing for a contractual remedy, a related yet distinct question is how to assess contracts that fall *entirely outside* the scope of those rules. This question is relevant for several reasons. On the general level an assessment of the position of these "excluded contracts" sheds light on what applies in situations where no specific EU legislative action has (yet) been taken on this point. It may also help clarify the nature of this remedy. Besides and more specifically, this question is of relevance in relation to EU legislation of the type at issue here. It has already been seen earlier that the scope of the rules on contractual remedies set out in this legislation tends to be rather limited. That leaves open the question of how to deal with contracts that have been concluded in violation of the applicable rules of substantive EU law, without this situation being expressly covered by the legislative provisions discussed in the two foregoing subsections. **8.09**

Let us begin once more by considering the situation under EU competition law. It has already been seen that Article 102 TFEU, which prohibits the abuse of a dominant position, does not contain a contractual remedy similar to the one set out in Article 101(2) TFEU.[60] This thus leaves unanswered the question of what the position is as a matter of EU law of contracts concluded in breach of Article 102 TFEU, in particular whether such contracts are also automatically void or whether they can continue to apply. The Court of Justice has so far not expressly addressed this question. **8.10**

It has been argued in the legal literature that the absence of a provision similar to Article 101(2) TFEU is not decisive and that a similar result can and indeed should be achieved through interpretation.[61] One line of reasoning relies on the finding by the Court that Article 102 TFEU, read in conjunction with the principle of sincere cooperation set out in Article 4(3) TEU, '*imposes a duty on*

59 CoJ case 56/65, *Société Technique Minière*, p. 250. See para 6.08 above.
60 See para 6.03 above.
61 E.g. Eklöf and Pehrson (2008), p. 196.

Member States not to adopt or maintain in force any measure which would deprive [Article 102 TFEU] of its effectiveness'.[62] A (slightly) different approach starts by pointing to the particular background and nature of Article 102 TFEU. On this reading the absence of an equivalent to Article 101(2) TFEU can be explained by the fact that – in contrast to cartels and other concerted practices – the abuse of a dominant position does not usually take the form of a contract. The aforementioned absence should therefore not be understood as deliberately differing from Article 101 TFEU in this respect. Where the abuse of a dominant position exceptionally does take the form of a contract, the argument goes, it should still be deemed to be automatically void, by analogy to Article 101(2) TFEU, so as to safeguard the effectiveness of the prohibition concerned.[63]

In both cases it is thus essentially argued that in the situation at issue here, the concluded contract must be terminated.[64] These views largely build on judgments such as *Simmenthal* and *Francovich*. It will be recalled that in the former judgment, it was essentially held that national courts must have the power to '*set aside national legislative provisions which might prevent EU rules from having full force and effect*', so as to safeguard the effectiveness of EU law.[65] In the latter judgment, the Court of Justice ruled that, pursuant to the duty of sincere cooperation, '*Member States must take all appropriate measures, whether general or particular, to ensure fulfilment of their obligation under [EU] law. Among these is the obligation to nullify the unlawful consequences of a breach of [EU] law*'.[66] A broadly similar line of reasoning is also followed in certain more recent rulings relating to other fields of EU law.[67]

8.11 Turning to EU public procurement law, it has already been noted that the relevant contractual remedy is limited to only the *most serious* infringements, notably illegal direct awards of public contracts and awards during a mandatory standstill period.[68] When considering the question of what applies in relation to

62 CoJ case 13/77, *INNO*, para 31. See further Milutinovic (2010), pp. 11 and 148. In a similar sense, see Temple Lang (2008), pp. 101–2.

63 Komninos (2008), p. 159.

64 For reasons of simplicity, in this subsection the term "terminate" is used in a general manner, that is, without implying any particular type of legal effect under EU or national law.

65 CoJ case 106/77, *Simmenthal*, para 22. See para 2.21 above.

66 CoJ joined cases C-6/90 and C-9/90, *Francovich*, para 36. See para 2.23 above. Here reference was made to CoJ case 6/60, *Humblet*, p. 572, where it had been held that '*[i]f the Court rules in a judgment that a legislative or administrative measure adopted by the authorities of a Member State is contrary to [EU] law, that Member State is obliged, by virtue of [the provision of the ECSC Treaty that corresponds with the principle of sincere cooperation set out in Article 4(3) TEU], to rescind the measure in question*'.

67 E.g. CoJ case C-41/11, *Inter-Environnement Wallonie*, para 42–6; CoJ case C-518/11, *UPC Nederland*, para 59–63.

68 See para 3.21 above.

contracts concluded pursuant to *other* infringements, the first point of reference is the Court's ruling in *Commission v Germany*.[69] This case concerned the Procurement Remedies Directives as they stood before the introduction of the contractual remedy of ineffectiveness in 2007. Here the Court of Justice held in essence that neither the possible legitimate expectations of the undertaking with whom the contract had been concluded nor the principles of *pacta sunt servanda* and legal certainty could be relied upon in order to justify the Member State concerned not taking the necessary measures to give effect to the Court's earlier finding that the applicable EU public procurement rules had been infringed in the course of the foregoing contract award procedure. At first sight this case law might thus seem to hint at a general obligation to terminate contracts concluded after a non-compliant contract award procedure. However, this case was decided in the context of infringement proceedings brought by the Commission against a Member State. These proceedings are essentially a matter between the various public authorities concerned, without there being a role for private parties.[70] It is evident from the Court's reasoning that this fact played an important role in this case, as it was on this basis that the Court left aside the aforementioned principles.[71] For this reason one should be careful in drawing general conclusions on the basis of this case.

More enlightening is the Court's ruling in *Wall*, which dates from 2010.[72] This case concerned a contract award procedure that fell entirely outside the scope of the EU's directives on public procurement. It was instead decided on the basis of EU Treaties' fundamental freedoms, in particular the right of establishment and the freedom to provide services, from which the Court of Justice already deduced an obligation of transparency.[73] In *Wall* the Court first observed that, where this latter obligation has not been respected, '*all necessary measures would have to be taken, in accordance with the national legal system of the Member State concerned, to restore the transparency of the procedure, which might extend to a new award procedure*'.[74] Although no explicit reference was made, this wording clearly echoes earlier rulings in cases such as *Francovich*. But in *Wall* the Court had also been asked expressly whether under EU law there is an obligation to terminate the contract at issue. The Court essentially answered this question in the negative. It held that this matter is to be settled on the basis of the domestic legal system of the Member State concerned, subject to the principles of

69 CoJ case C-503/04, *Commission v Germany*. See para 3.20 above.

70 See subsection 2.C.1 above.

71 See CoJ case C-503/04, *Commission v Germany*, para 36.

72 CoJ case C-91/08, *Wall*.

73 Ibid., para 33–6, and the case law cited there. See also Commission, Interpretative communication on the Community law applicable to contract awards not or not fully subject to the provisions of the Public Procurement Directives, OJ 2006, C 179/2.

74 Ibid., para 42.

equivalence and effectiveness.[75] In its view the provisions of the EU Treaties on the fundamental freedoms do not require such termination '*in every case of an alleged breach*'.[76] This ruling evidently leaves several questions unanswered.[77] Yet it nonetheless suggests that there is no unqualified rule under primary EU law to the effect that contracts that were concluded following infringements of the applicable substantive EU law must always be terminated.[78]

It seems unlikely that the insertion in 2007 of the aforementioned provision on ineffectiveness in the Procurement Remedies Directives fundamentally alters this picture in respect of contracts that are covered by these directives but that do not fall within the scope of that provision. There are good reasons to believe that neither these directives nor primary EU law requires those contracts to be terminated. First, only this outcome would appear to do justice to the EU legislature's express decision to restrict the contractual remedy of ineffectiveness to contracts concluded after only the most serious infringements of substantive EU public procurement law. Second, the Procurement Remedies Directives provide for a carefully balanced regime in this respect, including certain exceptions.[79] Therefore, if an obligation to terminate contracts were to be assumed also for situations falling outside the scope of the said provision on ineffectiveness, the paradoxical situation could emerge that the regime applicable to the most serious infringements of EU public procurement law is more lenient than the one that applies to all other – less serious – cases. Third, after their revision the Procurement Remedies Directives (also) explicitly refer to national law to decide the effects of concluded contracts concerning situations falling outside the scope of the provision on ineffectiveness.[80] If anything, these legislative developments thus seem to confirm the aforementioned conclusion that in the situations at issue here there is no "universal" EU law obligation to terminate the contracts in question.

8.12 In EU consumer protection law the scope of the substantive rules and that of the contractual remedy typically coincide, which implies that a contract that is

75 Ibid., para 63–5.

76 Ibid., para 65.

77 For example, the statement that termination is not required "in every case" does not exclude that this may nonetheless be required in *certain* cases. The following question is then of course in which cases there is such an obligation and in which cases there is not.

78 This is all the more noticeable given that *Wall* did not concern a horizontal relationship between two private parties, but rather a situation whereby one of the parties to the contract was a public authority. As such the latter is undoubtedly bound by the above-mentioned provisions of the EU Treaties and the principle of sincere cooperation. See also EFTA Court, case E-24/13, *Casino Admiral*, para 70.

79 See para 3.23 above.

80 Art. 2(7) Public Sector Remedies Directive 89/665 and Art. 2(6) Utilities Remedies Directive 92/13. These provisions also stipulate that on an optional basis Member States may provide that in the situations referred to here, the powers of the review bodies are limited to awarding damages.

covered by the substantive rules of the Unfair Terms Directive will also be covered by the contractual remedy for which this directive provides. It follows that the issue of "excluded" contracts plays less of a role here.[81] Still, issues similar to those discussed above can arise in relation to the *effects* given to the provision constituting the contractual remedy. Take the 2010 judgment of the Court of Justice in *Friz*.[82] This case related to a consumer protection directive on contracts negotiated away from business premises ("doorstep selling"), which has since been incorporated in the Consumer Rights Directive. The former directive granted consumers the right to '*renounce the effects of his undertaking*' by sending a notice within a certain time period, which '*[releases] the consumer from any obligations under the cancelled contract*'.[83] In *Friz* the Court first recalled that the termination by a consumer of a contract normally entails a restoration of the *status quo ante* for all parties to the contract.[84] However, it then added that '*in certain specific cases*' it is not precluded that the consumer has to bear '*certain consequences resulting from the exercise of his right of cancellation*'.[85] The Court reached that conclusion with reference to the rule of national law at issue in this case that intended to ensure, in accordance with '*the general principles of civil law*', a satisfactory balance and a fair division of risks among the various interested parties.[86] Also this ruling leaves several questions unanswered.[87] But it nonetheless underlines that at least in certain cases account can be taken of general principles of (national) civil law when determining the effects to be given to the rule of EU law at issue.[88]

What then is the overall picture that emerges on the basis of the foregoing? To begin with, the issues discussed here are complex, especially where they relate to the relationship and interaction between EU law and national contract law, as is inevitably the case where contractual remedies of the type under consideration **8.13**

81 Cf. however Art. 15 Consumer Rights Directive 2011/83 concerning "ancillary" contracts.

82 CoJ case C-215/08, *Friz*.

83 Art. 5 Doorstep Selling Directive 85/577. This directive further specified that the legal effects of such renunciation are governed by national law (see its Art. 7). This directive has since been replaced by Consumer Rights Directive 2011/83.

84 CoJ case C-215/08, *Friz*, para 45. In this sense, see also CoJ case C-350/03, *Schulte*, para 88.

85 Ibid.

86 CoJ case C-215/08, *Friz*, para 48–9. Here it was also noted that this allowed the consumer in question to recover his holding while taking on a proportion of the risks inherent in any capital investment and enables third parties not to have to bear the financial consequences of a termination which occurs following the signature of a contract to which they were not party.

87 For example, it is uncertain which types of cases qualify as "specific" for the present purposes, what the "certain consequences" entail precisely and to exactly which "general principles of private law" the CoJ actually referred.

88 In other cases the CoJ has come to similar conclusions. See e.g. CoJ case C-412/06, *Hamilton*, para 42; CoJ case C-489/07, *Messner*, para 26. This latter case concerned the provision on "withdrawal" from a contract pursuant to Art. 6 Directive 97/7, which has since also been replaced by Consumer Rights Directive 2011/83. See, however, also CoJ case C-209/12, *Endress*, para 30–31.

here are concerned.[89] Much remains to be clarified, which is a task that typically falls upon the Court of Justice. But the Court too has been criticised for not providing sufficient clarity and coherence when addressing the issues mentioned above.[90]

What does seem clear, however, is that, in contrast to what is sometimes suggested, it should probably not be too readily assumed that the principles of (civil) law, such as *pacta sunt servanda*, the protection of the rights of third parties and legitimate expectations and the freedom of contract, will always and unconditionally be sacrificed at the altar of effectiveness of EU law and sincere cooperation. There can of course be little doubt that the latter considerations generally constitute persuasive and powerful arguments in an EU law context.[91] Rulings such as *Simmenthal* and *Francovich* have long made this clear. But these cases related primarily to *legislative or administrative* measures taken by the *public* authorities of the Member States. It would appear that the reasoning used there does not lend itself to a simple "one-to-one" transfer to situations that are concerned with *contracts* concluded with or between *private parties*, as cases such as *Wall* and *Friz* seem to illustrate. That applies all the more so because the EU courts have equally acknowledged the fundamental importance of the aforementioned principles.[92] For all the issues that remain to be clarified, it would rather seem that the Court is seeking to achieve a sort of balance between the various interests at stake.[93] It may indeed be seen as appropriate to leave the Member States a certain margin of manoeuvre in this connection, to be exercised within relatively broad boundaries set by EU law, so as to provide for a solution that is compatible with their respective domestic legal systems.[94]

Finally, it appears that the precise legal and factual circumstances of the case at hand are likely to determine to a great extent the outcome in an individual case. It may, for instance, make a difference whether the contract in question has

89 For a more in-depth discussion, see e.g. Storme (2007), p. 233; Hartkamp (2010a), p. 527; Reich (2010), p. 142; Safjan and Miklaszewicz (2010), p. 475.

90 See e.g. Clifton (2009), p. 168; Basedow (2010a), pp. 454–60; Harmathy (2010), p. 429; Weatherill (2012), pp. 1298 and 1303–5.

91 On considerations related to effectiveness, see also section 11.A below.

92 In CoJ case C-162/96, *Racke*, para 49, the principle *pacta sunt servanda* was e.g. held to be '*a fundamental principle of any legal order*'. See e.g. also GC case T-154/01, *Distilleria F. Palma*, para 45. The principle that acquired rights must be respected and the principle of legitimate expectations have also been recognised as fundamental principles of EU law. See e.g. CoJ case C-168/09, *Flos*, para 50. On several occasions the CoJ has further underlined the importance of the principle of freedom of contract, as an element of the broader fundamental right to conduct a business guaranteed under Art. 16 Charter. See e.g. CoJ case C-240/97, *Spain v Commission*, para 99–100; CoJ case C-283/11, *Sky Österreich*, para 42–3.

93 Cf. Hartkamp (2010b), p. 256.

94 Cf. Opinion AG Sharpston case C-209/12, *Endress*, para 38–9. Note e.g. also the express reference to the procedural autonomy of the Member States in CoJ case C-41/11, *Inter-Environnement Wallonie*, para 45.

been concluded either between a public and a private party (for example in a public procurement case) or in an entirely horizontal context (that is, between two private parties, for example in a consumer protection or competition case).[95] A connected factor that has already been touched upon is whether or not the infringed rule of EU law imposes obligations on all parties to the contract.[96] Conceivably the behaviour and (relative) strength of the parties concerned can also be of relevance.[97] Yet another relevant factor can be whether the infringed rule of EU law is mandatory in nature,[98] as may be the case in fields such as consumer protection,[99] free movement,[100] competition[101] and gender equality.[102]

B. OTHER PRIVATE ENFORCEMENT REMEDIES

This second section is concerned with the remedies set out in the EU legislation facilitating the private enforcement of EU law before national courts assessed in

---

95 Even if this is not immediately clear from CoJ case C-91/08, *Wall*, as was noted in para 8.11 above. As was also noted there, it may well matter whether or not the questions under consideration here emerge in the context of infringement proceedings.

96 In particular, EU public procurement law imposes in principle obligations only on the contracting authority and not on the latter's private party contractor, whereas all parties to the contested contract can be subject to Art. 101 TFEU.

97 It may matter, for instance, whether one of the parties is a consumer or where the parties are otherwise in an unequal position. As explained in para 8.04 above, there may also be less reason to protect acquired rights pursuant to a public contract concluded with a professional party following a clearly defective contract award procedure. Cf. CoJ case C-209/12, *Endress*, para 30, where it was held that an undertaking cannot rely on reasons of legal certainty in order to redress a situation caused by its own failure to comply with a requirement under EU law. Cf. e.g. also CoJ case C-453/99, *Courage*, para 32–3.

98 Cf. Basedow (2010a), p. 451, who considers that most EU legal acts dealing with issues of substantive private law are mandatory. As regards the issue of EU law being mandatory or of public policy (*d'ordre public*), particularly connected to a court raising that rule of law of its own motion, see also subsection 9.D.2 below.

99 Cf. e.g. Art. 6(2) and recital 22 Unfair Terms Directive 93/13; Art. 12 Product Liability Directive 85/374. For a critical discussion of the ("unilaterally") mandatory nature of EU law on consumer contracts generally, see Eidenmuller et al. (2011), pp. 1079–90.

100 Cf. e.g. CoJ case 58/80, *Dansk Supermarked*, para 17. Note that, even if there may well be a need to differentiate between the various free movement provisions set out in the EU Treaties, this ruling seems difficult to reconcile e.g. with CoJ case C-91/08, *Wall*, discussed in para 8.11 above (concerning the freedom of establishment and the freedom to provide services). See also Opinion AG Sharpston case C-325/08, *Olympique Lyonnais*, para 43 (regarding the free movement of workers), where it was held that '*it is clear from the Court's case law that Article [45 TFEU] does indeed cover restrictions on freedom to contract if they are such as to preclude or deter a national of one Member State from exercising his right to freedom of movement in another Member State, at least as long as they derive from actions of public authorities or rules aimed at regulating gainful employment in a collective manner*'. See also para 11.17 below.

101 Cf. para 6.05 above.

102 Cf. CoJ case 43/75, *Defrenne*, para 39. For an application of the rule set out in the aforementioned *Simmenthal* judgment, discussed in para 2.21 above, to a collective labour agreement, see e.g. CoJ case C-184/89, *Nimz*, para 19–20.

Part B, other than the actions for damages, actions for injunctions and contractual remedies already discussed in the foregoing. These other remedies concern interim relief, measures on the disclosure of evidence, recurring penalty payments, publicity measures and measures related to legal costs. As is shown below, several of these remedies can be of considerable importance to a private party that has initiated or that considers initiating private enforcement proceedings. These latter remedies can nonetheless be distinguished from the "main" (substantive) remedies discussed earlier on several grounds. With the exception of interim relief, these other remedies are generally less broadly provided for in the EU legislation under consideration. They also tend to be concerned with more specific issues and therefore have a more limited scope of application. And they are not "free-standing". That is to say, as is explained below, either as a matter of law or in practice these remedies are essentially all ancillary to a main claim of some sort being brought in the legal proceedings concerned. At the very end of this section it is briefly noted that certain remedies other than the ones mentioned above are notably absent from the legislation at issue, while they can nonetheless be of relevance in the present context.

1. Interim relief

8.14 Of the EU legislation on private enforcement assessed in Part B above, the Procurement Remedies Directives are most elaborate where provisions on interim relief are concerned. Their provision on this subject matter has been formulated in a rather broad and general manner. It speaks of '*interim measures with the aim of correcting alleged infringements and preventing further damage to the interests concerned*'.[103] Further precision is added through three additional clauses. First, it is provided that the said measures must be made available '*at the earliest opportunity and by way of interlocutory procedures*'. Second, these directives stipulate that this includes '*measures to suspend or to ensure the suspension of the procedure for the award of a public contract or the implementation of any decision taken by the contracting authority*'. Third, they contain a separate (optional) provision on the weighing of the various interests at stake, which allows Member States to provide that account is taken of '*the probable consequences of interim measures for all interests likely to be harmed, as well as the public interest*' and '*not to grant such measures when their negative consequences could exceed their benefits*'.[104] None of the directives below contains a similar provision, even if the

103 Art. 2(1)(a) Procurement Remedies Directives 89/665 and 92/13. See para 3.13 above.

104 Art. 2(5) Public Sector Remedies Directive 89/665 and Art. 2(4) Utilities Remedies Directive 92/13.

application of such a balance of interests test is not uncommon in proceedings for interim relief.[105]

Several other directives also require this remedy to be made available to aggrieved private parties. The IPR Enforcement Directive contains two specific references to the granting of interim relief. One of the provisional and precautionary measures provided for concerns the possibility of granting interlocutory injunctions aimed at preventing imminent infringements or prohibiting the continuation thereof.[106] Under this directive the national court seised must further be empowered to '*order prompt and effective provisional measures to preserve relevant evidence*', such as the detailed description or the physical seizure of the allegedly infringing products.[107] And whereas the Product Liability Directive is silent in this respect, most consumer protection directives assessed in Part B above also provide for this remedy. Here the formulation is generally less specific and less committal, however. Under the Consumer Injunctions Directive, the cessation or prohibition of an infringement must be ordered '*with all due expediency*' and '*where appropriate*' by way of summary procedure.[108] The Unfair Commercial Practices Directive specifies that an '*accelerated procedure*' must be made available, while leaving it to the Member States to decide whether that should entail a procedure leading to an outcome with interim or with definitive effects.[109]

It follows that, while the scope and the level of detail provided for may differ, most of the EU legislation at issue provides for the possibility for a national court seised in private enforcement proceedings to grant interim relief in one form or another. Of the fields of EU law under consideration here, only in relation to competition law infringements can no such EU law provisions on interim measures be found, considering that neither Articles 101 and 102 TFEU nor the Competition Damages Directive contains any rule in this regard.

The fact that most legal acts under consideration contain provisions on interim **8.15**
relief is consistent with the *general emphasis* that the Court of Justice tends to

105 For example, a similar weighing of the interests at stake takes place in proceedings for interim measures before the EU courts. See e.g. GC Order case T-392/02 R, *Solvay v Council*, para 120–27; GC Order case T-37/04 R, *Azores v Council*, para 192–5. Cf. e.g. also Art. 62(2) Patent Court Agreement; Commission, Proposal for a trade secrets directive, COM(2013) 813, pp. 21–2 (Art. 10(2)). See also Peyer (undated), pp. 23 and 32–3, concerning interim relief in the German and the English legal systems.

106 Art. 9(1)(a) IPR Enforcement Directive 2004/48. See para 4.20 above.

107 Art. 7(1) IPR Enforcement Directive 2004/48. See para 4.15 above.

108 Art. 2(1)(a) Consumer Injunctions Directive 2009/22. See para 5.08 above.

109 Art. 11(2) Unfair Commercial Practices Directive 2005/29. See e.g. also Art. 5(3) Misleading Advertising Directive 2006/114. See para 5.13 above.

place on the availability of this remedy in the EU legal order. It did so, most notably, in cases such as *Factortame* and *Unibet*.[110] With reference to these two earlier cases, the Court of Justice observed more recently that '*it is apparent from settled case law that a national court seised of a dispute governed by [EU] law must be in a position to grant interim relief in order to ensure the full effectiveness of the judgment to be given on the existence of the rights claimed under [EU] law*'.[111] Essentially the same applies in litigation before the EU courts themselves.[112] In the latter connection it has been held that '*the purpose of interlocutory proceedings is to guarantee the full effectiveness of the final future decision, in order to ensure that there is no lacuna in the legal protection provided by the Court of Justice*'.[113]

These statements not only underline the fundamental importance that is attached to the availability of interim relief in the EU legal order. They also give an indication of *why* this is considered important. These measures serve in essence to safeguard the rights of private parties conferred on them by EU law. Without interim relief being available, pending a definitive ruling in the dispute at hand, the situation "on the ground" may well evolve in such a manner that this latter ruling will prove to be devoid of practical effects. This would, as the Court noted, lead to a *lacuna* in the legal protection of the private parties concerned. The function of interim relief is thus to '*preserve the ability to grant effective relief by final judgment or to maintain or otherwise regulate the status quo*' in situations where this is deemed necessary.[114]

8.16 The issue of interim relief is thus to be distinguished from, but nonetheless closely connected to, the *rapidity* with which the *proceedings on the merits* are being decided. Put simply, the less time that is needed to complete these latter proceedings, the less need there is for the award of interim measures. The "demand" for this remedy will thus typically be greater where proceedings on the merits take a long time to conclude. This is well illustrated by the provisions of the consumer protection directives outlined above. For both the Consumer Injunctions Directive and the Unfair Commercial Practices Directive place the emphasis primarily on the rapid resolution of the dispute. It is only in this context that reference is made to interim relief, which is to be made available '*where appropriate*' or where the Member State concerned decides to do so, respectively. In that sense the availability of interim relief can thus be said to be of secondary importance under these directives, the main issue being ensuring

110 CoJ case C-213/89, *Factortame*; CoJ case C-432/05, *Unibet*. See para 2.22 above.

111 CoJ case C-416/10, *Križan*, para 107.

112 Art. 279 TFEU.

113 CoJ Order case C-278/13 P(R), *Pilkington*, para 36.

114 International Institute for the Unification of Private Law ("UNIDROIT"), Principles of Transnational Civil Procedure (Art. 8(1)).

the speedy conclusion of the proceedings. Whether this rather "loose" approach in consumer protection cases suffices to have the intended effect in practice is, however, another matter.[115] In any case the more recent Collective Redress Recommendation is worded similarly.[116]

The foregoing also explains why this remedy has been most elaborated in the Procurement Remedies Directives. After all, in public procurement cases the speedy resolution of a dispute, if only provisionally, is often particularly important, notably where the review of decisions relating to the contract award procedure is concerned (for example a decision to exclude a tenderer for failure to meet the applicable requirements or a contract award decision). Indeed, one of the key objectives of these directives is to ensure that decisions taken in relation to contract award procedures can be reviewed '*as rapidly as possible*'.[117] Consider for instance the situation where a contracting authority decided to award a public contract for the construction of a building to an undertaking. Where a competitor seeks to have that decision annulled for infringements of the public procurement rules, the award may already have led to the (partial) execution of the contract by the time the court seised takes a decision in the proceedings on the merits. Even if the latter then agrees with the applicant, it is unlikely to order the demolition and subsequent reconstruction of the building. This could thus deprive a private party applicant of their right to effective review. Rapid proceedings generally and the availability of interim measures in particular are therefore often a key concern in a public procurement context.

Compare this with a typical intellectual property dispute covered by the IPR Enforcement Directive. Clearly, as in almost all cases, the speedy conclusion of the proceedings is certainly also of interest here. For that reason this directive stipulates, for example, that there should be no '*unwarranted delays*'.[118] However, there is normally no *general* urgency of the sort that tends to exist in the public procurement cases described above. In typical intellectual property cases brought under the IPR Enforcement Directive, the urgency rather tends to relate to more *specific* issues, such as the halting of an infringement or ensuring that relevant evidence is not being destroyed. The aforementioned provisions on interim measures set out in this directive are therefore more narrowly focused on those specific issues.

115 See the critical comments made in this connection by stakeholders, set out in Commission, Second report on Consumer Injunctions Directive 2009/22, COM(2012) 635, pp. 12 and 15.

116 Point 19 Collective Redress Recommendation 2013/396. See para 5.38 above.

117 Art. 1(1) Procurement Remedies Directives 89/665 and 92/13. See para 3.05, 3.07 and 3.11 above.

118 Art. 3(1) IPR Enforcement Directive 2004/48. See para 4.06 above.

8.17 Interim measures accordingly serve in particular to bridge the period needed to settle the dispute in the case at hand in a definitive manner and to preserve any rights in this respect. This illustrates the *provisional* and *"dependent" character* of this remedy. That is to say, the concept of interim relief refers first and foremost to the *effects* of the relief sought by the applicant, while leaving it open *what* the measures to be ordered might entail in concrete terms. Legally speaking, the granting of interim relief does not lead to a definitive settlement of the dispute. As the Court has held, '*by its nature, an interim measure does not finally determine the legal situation*'.[119] Often an application for interim measures will therefore be preceded or accompanied, or at least followed, by an action on the merits of the case. Interim measures retain their provisional character, even in cases where the parties to the dispute consider that there is no longer a need to bring or to continue the proceedings on the merits.[120] Put differently, while *de facto* the result may well be a final settlement, *de jure* the dispute has then only been settled on a provisional basis.

It is noticeable in this connection that the aforementioned directives are largely silent on the precise relationship between the proceedings for interim relief and the proceedings on the merits. Only the IPR Enforcement Directive addresses this issue in some detail. Here it is said that the provisional measures to preserve evidence provided for in this directive are to be made available '*even before the commencement of proceedings on the merits of the case*'.[121] Although the Procurement Remedies Directives do not address this point expressly, the Court of Justice has held that they preclude making the filing of an application for interim measures dependent on a requirement that proceedings on the merits must first have been brought.[122] That applies even where the latter is a mere formality. Such a requirement would mean, according to the Court, that the system of interim judicial protection offered is inadequate.[123] It follows that the *presumption* may be that an action for interim measures is preceded or accompanied by an action on the merits, but that at least under the above-mentioned directives this cannot be *required* as a matter of EU law. In that sense the "dependent" nature of this remedy therefore only goes so far.

---

119 CoJ case C-568/08, *Combinatie Spijker*, para 61. See e.g. also Peyer (undated), p. 6.

120 Cf. CoJ case C-53/96, *Hermès International*, para 44 (regarding the provisional measures provided for in Art. 50 TRIPS Agreement).

121 Art. 7(1) IPR Enforcement Directive 2004/48. No such statement is made in Art. 9(1)(a) IPR Enforcement Directive 2004/48 however.

122 CoJ case C-214/00, *Commission v Spain*, para 99–100.

123 It is noticeable that this ruling seems to be at odds with the rules applicable in proceedings before the EU courts themselves, which require that an action on the merits is pending for an application for interim measures under Art. 279 TFEU to be admissible. See Art. 160 CoJ Rules of procedure, OJ 2012, L 265/1. Cf. Pijnacker Hordijk, Van der Bend and Van Nouhuys (2009), p. 562.

In terms of material content the interim measures provided for in the EU legislation referred to above tend to involve the granting of *injunctions* on a provisional basis.[124] The IPR Enforcement Directive provides, for instance, for the granting of interlocutory injunctions '*intended to prevent any imminent infringement of an intellectual property right, or to forbid, on a provisional basis [...] the continuation of the alleged infringements of that right*'.[125] The possibility under this directive for a national court to order provisional measures to preserve evidence is also a (specific) form of injunctive relief. The same essentially applies under the aforementioned consumer protection directives and the Collective Redress Recommendation. This is especially evident from the link established under the Consumer Injunctions Directive between interim relief and '*the cessation or prohibition of an infringement*'.[126] The same will normally apply under the Procurement Remedies Directive, even if here the relevant provision has been drafted in a more general manner. All this illustrates that, generally speaking, interim measures lend themselves well to bringing an (alleged) infringement to a (provisional) halt or to prevent the occurrence of damage in one form or another. **8.18**

By contrast, interim relief is normally not available in relation to *actions for damages*.[127] Damages claims are generally not seen as particularly urgent, as no irreparable damage will be done in the absence of interim relief being granted.[128] The objective in those cases is, after all, to obtain monetary compensation. Even if such a claim is upheld only after a considerable time period, the award of damages can still have the effect of compensating the applicant for the injury suffered. Thus, certain exceptions aside, in those cases the "facts on the ground" are not presumed to be evolving in such a manner that the granting of interim relief is justified. Again, this is also the position in legal proceedings before the EU courts.[129] It would seem that for this reason the EU legislation discussed above does not provide for interim relief in relation to actions for damages. This also explains why neither the Product Liability Directive nor the Competition Damages Directive contains any provisions on interim relief, as in terms of substantive remedies these two legal acts are concerned exclusively with actions for damages.

124 On actions for injunctions generally, see section 7.02 above.

125 Art. 9(1)(a) IPR Enforcement Directive 2004/48.

126 Art. 2(1)(a) Consumer Injunctions Directive 2009/22.

127 On actions for damages generally, see section 7.A above.

128 Cf. e.g. CoJ joined cases C-143/88 and C-92/89, *Zuckerfabrik Süderdithmarschen*, para 29: '*purely financial damage cannot, as the Court has held on numerous occasions, be regarded in principle as irreparable*'.

129 E.g. CoJ Order case C-278/13 P(R), *Pilkington*, para 50: '*Damage of a pecuniary nature cannot, otherwise than in exceptional circumstances, be regarded as irreparable since, as a general rule, pecuniary compensation is capable of restoring the aggrieved person to the situation that obtained before he suffered the damage*'.

It is less clear where to place *contractual remedies* in this respect.[130] *A priori* there seems to be no reason to presume that the continuous application of a contract could inherently not lead to serious and irreparable damage. In that sense contractual remedies differ from damages claims. From this perspective the granting of a contractual remedy by means of an interim measure therefore need not be excluded. Yet this question remains largely unaddressed in the legislation under consideration here. This is arguably related to the flexibility that is mostly left to the Member States in determining the precise effects of invoking the contractual remedies in question.[131] It may not always be possible to invoke or establish these effects by means of measures that only apply provisionally. Where this is otherwise, the aforementioned provision on interim relief laid down in the Procurement Remedies Directives could, given its broad formulation, conceivably also be applied in principle in relation to the contractual remedy for which these directives provide.[132] The Unfair Terms Directive, in contrast, does not contain any provisions on interim relief, while it does provide for a contractual remedy.[133] Still, one could well imagine a situation where a consumer would suffer serious and irreparable damage if he were to continue to be bound by such a term during the full duration of ordinary court proceedings. Also under this latter directive, interim measures might thus be called for. It appears that in this case a solution would need to be found primarily on the basis of the applicable national law, subject, however, to the principles of equivalence, effectiveness and effective judicial protection.[134]

2. Measures on the disclosure of evidence

8.19 The IPR Enforcement Directive and the Competition Damages Directive are the natural points of reference when discussing measures on the disclosure of evidence and other relevant information in the context of private enforcement proceedings.[135] The former directive sets out three types of measures in this regard.[136] To begin with, it provides that a defendant may be ordered by the competent national court to *present* (that is, disclose) certain evidence lying within its control.[137] In this connection the communication of banking, financial or commercial documents may be ordered in cases of infringements

130 On contractual remedies generally, see section 8.A above.

131 See in particular subsection 8.A.2 above.

132 Art. 2d Procurement Remedies Directives 89/665 and 92/13. See subsection 3.B.3 above.

133 Art. 6(1) Unfair Terms Directive 93/13. See subsection 5.C.1 above.

134 Cf. CoJ case C-415/11, *Aziz*, para 57–63. As regards the above-mentioned principles, see subsections 2.A.2 (equivalence) and 2.A.3 (effectiveness) and section 2.C (effective judicial protection) above.

135 Cf. also Art. 3(6) International Bar Association ("IBA"), Rules on the taking of evidence in international commercial arbitration, 1 June 1999.

136 See subsection 4.B.1 above.

137 Art. 6 IPR Enforcement Directive 2004/48.

committed on a commercial scale. In the second place, it must be possible for a court to order certain measures to *preserve* relevant evidence.[138] This may include the detailed description, taking of samples or physical seizure of goods or the materials or implements used to produce or distribute them. Finally, defendants and certain third parties can be ordered under this directive to *provide information* on the origin of the infringing goods or services and the distribution networks used, such as the name of the producers and distributors, the quantities produced or the prices obtained.[139]

The Competition Damages Directive's disclosure regime has been inspired by the one found in the IPR Enforcement Directive.[140] It is comparable in several respects. The Competition Damages Directive establishes the main rule that national courts must be able to order the defendant or a third party to disclose evidence.[141] This is to be done upon request by either the applicant or the defendant. There are specific limitations concerning the disclosure of evidence included in the file of a competition authority and corresponding restrictions on the use of that evidence.[142] This directive also addresses the issue of preserving evidence.[143] But it does so in a different manner than the IPR Enforcement Directive. Rather than relying on court orders to ensure preservation, it requires the possibility of imposing penalties where a party destroys relevant evidence.

The above two directives are exceptional. Neither the Procurement Remedies Directives, the Consumer Injunctions Directive, the Unfair Terms Directive nor the Product Liability Directive contains provisions that are even remotely similar. Neither does any other act of secondary EU law appear to provide for measures on the disclosure of evidence *inter partes* that are comparable to the regimes on this subject matter set out in the two above-mentioned directives.

That raises the question of why the fields of intellectual property and com- **8.20**
petition law have been *singled out* for particular EU legislative action, whereas the other private enforcement-related directives under consideration remain entirely silent on this point. This question comes all the more to the fore in light of the generally rather positive assessment by stakeholders of the IPR Enforcement Directive's regime on the disclosure of evidence, which suggests that it

138 Art. 7(1) Enforcement Directive 2004/48.

139 Art. 8 IPR Enforcement Directive 2004/48.

140 See subsection 6.C.3 above. Cf. Commission, White paper on damages actions for breach of the EC antitrust rules, COM(2008) 165, p. 5; Commission, Proposal for Competition Damages Directive 2014/104, COM(2013) 404, p. 14.

141 Art. 5 Competition Damages Directive 2014/104.

142 Art. 6 and 7 Competition Damages Directive 2014/104.

143 Art. 8 Competition Damages Directive 2014/104.

might also be helpful for the purposes of private enforcement in other fields.[144] The answer to this question is essentially that access to evidence is generally deemed to be of particular importance in private enforcement proceedings relating to the two above-mentioned fields, more so than in relation to other infringements of substantive EU law. With respect to EU intellectual property law, the EU legislature has called this importance '*paramount*'.[145] In this connection reference is often made to the fact that the evidence and information that are crucial to a private party wishing to initiate private enforcement proceedings for an infringement of its intellectual property right are typically only in the possession of the infringer. The infringements in question are, moreover, regularly committed on a commercial scale and involving organised crime.[146] Therefore, unless the (potential) applicant is given access in one way or another, he may well experience very considerable difficulties when trying to take legal action pursuant to an alleged infringement. It seems that these difficulties can in certain cases be such that the private party concerned is practically barred from doing so. Largely similar arguments have been made in connection with competition law infringements. Here the EU legislature held that evidence is an '*important element*' for bringing actions for damages, in particular in light of the complexity and fact-intensity of competition cases, while such litigation is also said to be '*characterised by an information asymmetry*', meaning that relevant evidence and information are often only in the possession of the infringer or a third party.[147] In this field, infringements can also be committed in a professional and secretive manner.[148]

8.21 Is this reasoning convincing, in the sense that it sets these two fields of law apart from other infringements of EU law? An obvious objection is that many (potential) private party applicants tend to be confronted with the above-mentioned evidence-related difficulties, regardless of the specific subject matter of the case at hand.[149] It may, for example, be equally important and equally difficult for a private party that suspects that a public contract has been directly awarded to a competitor in violation of the EU public procurement rules or that its bid has not been evaluated in an objective and impartial manner to obtain the evidence necessary to substantiate its claim.[150] That said, contracting authorities will normally be under an obligation to act in a transparent manner and to

144 See para 4.17 above.
145 Recital 20 IPR Enforcement Directive 2004/48. See para 4.13 above.
146 See para 4.03 above.
147 Recitals 13 and 14 Competition Damages Directive 2014/104. See para 6.31 above.
148 See para 6.06 above.
149 Cf. Bruns (2011), p. 130. See e.g. also Grassie (2014), p. 682, where the absence of any rules in this regard in Commission, Proposal for a trade secrets directive, COM(2013) 813, is seen as a notable missing element.
150 Cf. CoJ case C-538/13, *eVigilo*, para 43.

provide reasons for their decisions.[151] Moreover, a private party that wishes to bring a claim under, say, the Unfair Terms Directive or the Product Liability Directive may – at least as compared with the aforementioned infringements in competition or intellectual property cases – often indeed be less dependent on the infringer. The content of a term in a consumer contract is plain for all parties concerned to see. The assessment of whether or not that term is unfair may certainly not always be easy, but it would seem that it does not typically depend on evidence or information that is solely in the possession of the alleged infringer or a third party. Similarly, while it may be far from easy to determine and demonstrate the defectiveness of a product (and the damage caused as a consequence of that defect), there is no reason to believe that this generally cannot be done without involving the alleged infringer or a third party.[152] Infringements of these latter rules are probably also to a lesser extent typically committed in a professional and concealed manner.

The above reasoning evidently involves a considerable degree of generalisation.[153] Nonetheless, it would appear that there are, therefore, grounds for distinguishing intellectual property and competition law from the other fields of EU law mentioned above. Whether or not these differences are such that EU interference and the "fragmenting" effect on national procedural law that will almost inevitably be the consequence of these sector-specific regimes are to be taken for granted remains a matter for (political) debate.[154] The outcome of that debate depends mainly on the respective weight that one attaches to accommodating the (perceived) needs of private parties in certain particular fields of EU law, on the one hand, and retaining a coherent and uniform set of rules on disclosure at national level, on the other hand. It may also be worth noting in this connection that, while the "ordinary" rules of national law that apply in the absence of such specific EU legislative measures on the disclosure

151 Cf. Art. 2 Public Sector Procurement Directive 2004/18 and Art. 10 Utilities Procurement Directive 2004/17. Cf. e.g. also CoJ case C-406/08, *Uniplex*, para 30–32; CoJ case C-538/13, *eVigilo*, para 42–4.

152 See, however, CoJ case C-310/13, *Novo Nordisk Pharma*, para 32, where the CoJ referred to '*the significant imbalance*' that exists between the two parties concerned to the detriment of consumers as regards access to information relating to the allegedly defective product.

153 There seems, for example, no reason to presume that *all* (or even most) infringements of intellectual property or competition law are committed in a secretive and professional manner. In addition, in many instances the applicants in fact may well have certain relevant pieces of evidence either in their possession or can have access thereto. That particularly applies as regards "follow-on" competition actions, where the private enforcement action is brought pursuant to a finding of an infringement by a public enforcement authority and where the applicant can thus benefit at least to some extent from the efforts made by the competent public enforcement authorities (if not through obtaining access to their file, then at least through these authorities' decisions finding an infringement of the substantive rules at issue).

154 Doubts on these points were expressed, for instance, in the context of the consultations relating to a possible initiative in the field of EU competition law, referred to in para 6.19 above. On issues of coherence and fragmentation at national level more generally, see subsection 10.D.2 below.

of evidence and information can differ considerably,[155] EU law requirements can occasionally still play a significant role. In such cases a national court may in particular be required to order certain measures of inquiry provided for by national law, including imposing an obligation on the defendant or a third party to produce a particular document, under the EU law principle of effectiveness.[156]

8.22 The importance for a private party that claims to be affected by an infringement of EU law of being able to obtain access to all relevant evidence and information is thus generally rather clear. But there is also another side to this matter, which relates to the resulting *burden* as well as the *risk of abuse* associated with rules on the disclosure of evidence of the type discussed above. For any such disclosure obligations almost inevitably constitute a burden on the parties that are subject to them, whereas overly broad disclosure rules can also lead to abuses. The parties that are potentially subject to such disclosure orders may well have a legitimate interest in keeping certain information to themselves or at least in preventing the opposing party in private enforcement proceedings from being granted access thereto. That applies especially where the parties involved in the dispute are competitors. Giving insight into an undertaking's internal production process, distribution channels, pricing policy or other commercially sensitive information can obviously be problematic. More generally, there can be a risk of "fishing expeditions", that is, non-specific and overly broad searches in the hope that some relevant information might be found. Concerns of this kind were raised particularly in relation to the Competition Damages Directive.[157] Yet they may well apply more generally, for instance in public procurement cases.[158] Also in relation to the IPR Enforcement Directive's regime, the risk of abuse has been noted.[159] Here the difficulties connected to involving third parties have in particular become visible.[160]

The IPR Enforcement Directive and the Competition Damages Directive both seek to address these concerns by establishing a *balance* between the various interests at stake. They do so in various ways. A first – and fundamental – safeguard comes in the form of judicial oversight. An order by the national court

155 According to Commission, Impact assessment report on damages actions for breach of the EU antitrust rules, SWD(2013) 203, p. 19, national rules regarding access to evidence are '*the primary example of divergence*'. See also European Parliament, Study on collective redress in antitrust, June 2012, p. 29.

156 E.g. CoJ case C-526/04, *Laboratoires Boiron*, para 55. See para 2.08 above.

157 See e.g. Commission, Staff working paper accompanying the white paper on damages actions for breach of the EC antitrust rules, SEC(2008) 404, pp. 23–4. See also recital 23 Competition Damages Directive 2014/104.

158 See e.g. CoJ case C-450/06, *Varec*.

159 Commission, Responses to the report on IPR Enforcement Directive 2004/48, July 2011, p. 19. See para 4.17 above.

160 See para 4.18 above.

seised is required before any evidence or information is to be disclosed. These courts are thus expected to exercise strict control,[161] which is in line with the legal traditions of most Member States.[162] Second, under both directives it is for the party seeking such a disclosure order to first present reasonably available evidence supporting its claim ("fact pleading").[163] In other words, the national court seised must be satisfied that there is a reasonable case before ordering disclosure. Third, both regimes require confidential information (and in competition cases also information covered by legal professional privilege) to be protected.[164] Fourth, in light of the aforementioned concerns, the Competition Damages Directive expressly limits the scope of disclosure orders to either specified items or relevant categories of evidence circumscribed as precisely and as narrowly as possible and it requires a national court to make a proportionality assessment, *inter alia* in light of the scope and costs of disclosure, especially for third parties.[165] Although more implicitly, similar requirements would appear to apply under the IPR Enforcement Directive.[166] Finally, the Competition Damages Directive requires that the parties subject to the possible disclosure order are given an opportunity to be heard.[167] This latter safeguard is, however, not provided for in the IPR Enforcement Directive. Quite the contrary, one could say, for where measures relating to the *preservation* of evidence are concerned, this latter directive expressly provides that such measures can in some situations be ordered without the other party having been heard, subject to certain additional requirements.[168] On the whole, it would thus appear that these two directives provide for adequate safeguards in this respect.

3. Recurring penalty payments

Regardless of what a national court decides in a private enforcement case (or in any other case for that matter), this decision will only have effect in practice where it is complied with effectively. An instrument to ensure compliance with **8.23**

161 Recital 16 Competition Damages Directive 2014/104.

162 Commission, Proposal for Competition Damages Directive 2014/104, COM(2013) 404, p. 14. See also Bruns (2011), p. 129.

163 See Art. 6(1) and 7(1) IPR Enforcement Directive 2004/48; Art. 5(1) Competition Damages Directive 2014/104. Art. 8(1) IPR Enforcement Directive 2004/48 requires a '*justified request*'.

164 Art. 6(1) and (2), 7(1) and 8(3)(e) IPR Enforcement Directive 2004/48; Art. 5(4) and (6) Competition Damages Directive 2014/104. See also Art. 5(3)(c) and Art. 8(1)(c) Competition Damages Directive 2014/104.

165 Art. 5(3) Competition Damages Directive 2014/104.

166 Art. 6(1) IPR Enforcement Directive 2004/48 refers more generally to '*specified evidence*', while its Art. 8 refers to '*a justified and proportionate request*'. See also Art. 3(2) IPR Enforcement Directive 2004/48, discussed in para 4.06 above, which requires among other things proportionality and safeguards against abuses when applying the measures set out in that directive.

167 Art. 5(7) Competition Damages Directive 2014/104.

168 Art. 7(1) IPR Enforcement Directive 2004/18. See para 4.15 above.

such decisions is a penalty payment, typically imposed on a recurring basis, for instance per day that the non-compliance continues. Granting this remedy means that a certain sum will be due if and when the party to the proceedings concerned does not comply with the judgment rendered within a set time period. Recurring penalty payments thus seek to ensure the (timely) compliance with the judgment in question. Unlike damages awards, they therefore do not aim to compensate any loss or damage caused by the infringement itself. That is illustrated by the fact that no payment will be due if the party subject to this measure complies with the judgment in a correct and timely manner. As the Court of Justice has held, the aim is to place the defendant under '*economic pressure which induces it to put an end to the breach established*'.[169]

8.24 Provision is made for this remedy in two legal acts considered in Part B above. The most detailed arrangement has been laid down in the Consumer Injunctions Directive. One of the remedies to be made available pursuant to that directive is:

> an order against the losing defendant for payments into the public purse or to any beneficiary designated in or under national legislation, in the event of failure to comply with the decision within a time limit specified by the courts or the administrative authorities, of a fixed amount for each day's delay or any other amount provided for in national legislation, with a view to ensuring compliance with the decisions.[170]

The IPR Enforcement Directive also refers to recurring penalty payments on two particular points, namely in relation to interlocutory and permanent injunctions.[171] In the latter case it is specified that this is to be done '*with a view to ensuring compliance*'.

Whereas the other directives assessed in the foregoing do not make provision for this remedy, the Procurement Remedies Directives illustrate that the same subject matter can also be addressed in a different manner. These latter directives require more generally that the Member States ensure that the decisions taken by the national courts (and other review bodies) can be effectively enforced.[172] This probably does not mean that recurring penalty

---

169 CoJ case C-177/04, *Commission v France*, para 91. This statement was made in relation to Article 260(2) TFEU, pursuant to which a (recurring) penalty payment can be imposed on Member States that have not taken the necessary measures to comply with an earlier finding of an infringement by the CoJ. For another example of recurring penalty payments in a public enforcement context, see Art. 5 and 24 Competition Regulation 1/2003.

170 Art. 2(1)(c) Consumer Injunctions Directive 2009/22. See para 5.08 above.

171 Art. 9(1)(a) and 11 IPR Enforcement Directive 2004/48. See para 4.20 and 4.24 above, respectively. See also Commission, Proposal for a trade secrets directive, COM(2013) 813, p. 25 (Art. 15).

172 Art. 2(8) Procurement Remedies Directives 89/665 and 92/13. See para 3.29 above.

payments must necessarily be provided for, but it would seem that doing so is one of the manners in which effect could be given to that provision. Comparable provisions can be found elsewhere in EU law.[173] On a similar note, the Commission's Collective Redress Recommendation refers to penalty payments as one of several types of possible measures to be issued against a losing defendant with a view to ensuring that the court's ruling in question will be complied with.[174]

It follows that, although this is not necessarily the only possible measure to this effect, the inclusion of EU legislative provisions on recurring penalty payments can offer a solution where there are concerns as to the compliance of losing parties with judgments issued in private enforcement cases.

For the present purposes, three further comments can be made in this regard. **8.25** First, this remedy is *ancillary* in nature, in that it is not a proper free-standing measure. As was set out above, it serves to ensure that a national court's decision is complied with. A recurring penalty payment can therefore not be imposed if the applicant does not also bring another, free-standing claim, that is upheld by that court. More specifically, the aforementioned provisions of the Consumer Injunctions Directive and the IPR Enforcement Directive make clear that these payments are typically ancillary to actions for injunctions. As was the case with interim measures,[175] they are not connected to actions for damages. Again, that also explains why neither the Product Liability Directive nor the Competition Damages Directive makes any mention of recurring penalty payments, given that in terms of substantive remedies these two directives focus exclusively on actions for damages.

Second, the legislative history of the Consumer Injunctions Directive in particular suggests that EU involvement with this remedy can be a rather *sensitive* affair.[176] Most notably, at the insistence of the Member States, the above-mentioned reference to penalty payments laid down in that directive is preceded by the phrase '*in so far as the legal system of the Member State concerned so permits*'. This remedy therefore must only be provided for under this directive to the extent that the domestic legal system of a Member State allows this. Largely comparably, the IPR Enforcement Directive stipulates in this respect that

173 See e.g. Art. 102 Community Trade Mark Regulation 207/2009. On this provision, see CoJ case C-235/09, *DHL Express*, para 59. See e.g. also Commission, Proposal for a regulation on the protection of individuals with regard to the processing of personal data and on the free movement of such data, COM(2012) 11, p. 90 (Art. 74(5)).

174 Point 20 Collective Redress Recommendation. See para 5.38 above.

175 See para 8.18 above.

176 See para 5.08 above.

recurring penalty payments must be available '*where appropriate*' and '*where provided for under national law*'.[177] The use of phrases of this kind would seem to make the provisions in question in effect rather non-committal. That can mean in turn that their effects in practice can be uncertain and that difficulties with respect to the enforcement of court rulings under these directives remain.[178] This might thus significantly reduce this remedy's potential as an instrument to ensure compliance.

Third, related to the previous point is the fact that recurring penalty payments are viewed very *differently* in the respective domestic legal systems of the Member States.[179] A clear majority of Member States provide for this remedy in one form or another. But English domestic law, for instance, does not provide for a remedy of this type (although the rules of "contempt of court" can to some extent fulfil a comparable function). Both French and German law do, but there are significant differences between these two legal systems in this regard. Under German law a (recurring) penalty payment is due to the *state*, whereas in France it is normally to be paid to the *private party applicant*. Most other jurisdictions in the EU largely follow one of these three basic models. It appears that, where the EU legislation at issue touches upon recurring penalty payments, the provisions in question have been drafted in such a manner that all three of these models can be retained. As was explained above, there is mostly no requirement to introduce this remedy where domestic law does not already provide for it. The Consumer Injunctions Directive further refers to '*payments into the public purse or to any beneficiary designated in or under national legislation*', meaning that neither the German nor the French approach is precluded under this directive. Without addressing this matter expressly, the IPR Enforcement Directive also seems to leave it open to whom the penalty payments are to be made. Therefore, not only do the above provisions leave some flexibility as to whether recurring penalty payments are to be made available in the first place, they do the same with respect to the question of what this remedy entails precisely.

4. Publicity measures

8.26 The term "publicity measures" refers to the possibility for the national court competent to rule on a private enforcement action to order the publication of

177 Note that this latter phrase has been included in Art. 11, but not in Art. 9(1)(a) IPR Enforcement Directive 2004/48.

178 Cf. Study, University of Leuven (2007), pp. 341; Commission, Second report on Consumer Injunctions Directive 2009/22, COM(2012) 635, pp. 13–14.

179 See further Jongbloet (2003), pp. 198–242; Study, University of Bielefeld (2008), pp. 611 and 622–4; Commission, Staff working document accompanying the report on IPR Enforcement Directive 2004/48, SEC(2010) 1589, p. 13.

either its decision in the case before it or of other relevant texts giving publicity to the infringement that was established. While no such measures have been set out in either the Procurement Remedies Directives or the Competition Damages Directive, in the two other fields of EU law discussed above, provision has been made for this remedy.

This remedy features most prominently in the IPR Enforcement Directive. This directive requires the Member States to ensure that the competent national courts can order '*appropriate measures for the dissemination of information concerning the decision, including displaying the decision and publishing it in full or in part*'.[180] These measures are to be imposed at the request of the applicant and implemented at the expense of the party found to have infringed the intellectual property right at issue. On an optional basis the Member States may under this directive also make provision for '*additional publicity measures which are appropriate to the particular circumstances, including prominent advertising*'. A largely similar regime has been included in the Commission's proposal for a trade secrets directive.[181]

The Consumer Injunctions Directive also contains rules on publicity measures, which are to be ordered '*where appropriate*'.[182] Apart from the publication of the decision itself, this directive also refers to the possibility of '*the publication of a corrective statement with a view to eliminating the continuing effects of the infringement*' being ordered. Comparable (optional) arrangements can be found in other consumer protection directives, such as the Unfair Commercial Practices Directive.[183]

The recitals of the IPR Enforcement Directive explain that the purpose of these publicity measures is to act as a '*supplementary deterrent*' and to '*contribute to the awareness of the public at large*'.[184] This makes two things clear. In the first place, this remedy is essentially meant to fulfil only a *supplementary function*. Although such publication can be of relevance, a private party will not initiate private enforcement proceedings merely to have a judgment published. The object of the legal proceedings will typically be a substantive claim of some sort, whether it is for compensation in damages, injunctive relief or at least a declaration by the court seised that an infringement occurred.[185] **8.27**

180 Art. 15 IPR Enforcement Directive 2004/48.

181 Commission, Proposal for a trade secrets directive, COM(2013) 813, p. 24 (Art. 14).

182 Art. 2(1)(b) Consumer Injunctions Directive 2009/22.

183 Art. 11(2) Unfair Commercial Practices Directive 2005/29. See e.g. also Art. 5(4) Misleading Advertising Directive 2006/114.

184 Recital 12 IPR Enforcement Directive 2004/48.

185 On declaratory relief, see also subsection 8.B.6 below.

In the second place, this remedy serves a dual purpose of *informing and deterring*. It can accordingly be expected to be normally most effective where the general public is directly affected by the infringements at issue or where the infringing party is sensitive to the harm to its reputation that may result from the publication. This explains its inclusion in the IPR Enforcement Directive and in the aforementioned consumer protection directives, as in these two fields these two conditions will generally often be met. This also explains why no such remedy has been laid down in the Procurement Remedies Directives. In public procurement cases infringements can certainly affect the public at large, but this occurs mostly only in an indirect manner. Moreover, the (semi-)public bodies that are subject to these rules are on the whole probably not sensitive to negative publicity in the same manner as commercial, consumer-oriented undertakings may be. This logic also suggests that publicity measures could be a relevant remedy in relation to at least certain infringements of EU competition law.[186] This remedy has so far not been part of the Commission's private enforcement agenda in this field, however. It therefore does not feature in the Competition Damages Directive.

8.28 To the foregoing one should add that this remedy tends to play only a rather modest role in practice. It generally receives little attention in relation to the IPR Enforcement Directive.[187] In respect of the Consumer Injunctions Directive it appears not to be used very frequently.[188] This may be due in part to the generally rather vague and seemingly non-committal wording of the above-mentioned provisions. The use of terms such as "appropriate measures", "including" and "where appropriate" and of optional provisions means that much is left to be determined by the Member States and their courts.[189] The situation might have been different had the possibility for a court to order "prominent advertising" or the publication of a "corrective statement" been imposed as a matter of EU law rather than leaving this to the Member States on an optional basis.

Having said that, it also seems fair to acknowledge that there are on the whole few indications that publicity measures can make more than a modest contribution to the private enforcement of EU law. Crucially, the interest in this remedy

---

186 On the possible relevance of reputational effects in a competition law context, cf. Study, CEPS, Erasmus University Rotterdam and LUISS (2007), pp. 152–3.

187 See para 4.32 above.

188 Study, University of Leuven (2007), pp. 341–2.

189 For an application by the EU courts, see GC case T-19/07, *Systran*, para 331 (annulled for reasons that are not of relevance here in CoJ case C-103/11 P, *Systran*). Here the GC held that the issuing of a press release by the GS itself should suffice in response to the applicant's request for an order to have the judgment published, at the defendant's expense, in specialist journals and reviews and on specialist websites.

from the side of the private parties concerned seems mostly limited.[190] This may well be connected to its aforementioned dual purpose of informing and deterring, which may generally be of only limited interest to a private party that is being confronted with an infringement of EU law. Especially in light of this dual purpose, publicity measures are arguably more suitable as a public enforcement instrument.[191] It seems therefore that this remedy can play a relevant, largely supplementary role in certain specific cases, but it is unlikely to be of major importance across the board for the private enforcement of EU law.

5. Measures on legal costs

Stakeholders, practitioners, legal scholars and the Commission have all regularly noted that high legal costs can be an important obstacle in practice for the application of the EU legislative measures discussed in the foregoing. These costs generally entail especially lawyers' fees, but they can also arise in the form of court fees or deposits and costs for involving experts. High legal costs have been observed to be a significant discouraging factor for initiating legal proceedings under the Procurement Remedies Directives, the IPR Enforcement Directive and the Product Liability Directive.[192] In relation to the enforcement of intellectual property rights, this has even been called a '*key deterring factor*' for initiating private enforcement proceedings, particularly for small and medium-sized enterprises.[193] Similar observations have been made in connection with the Consumer Injunctions Directive[194] and EU competition law,[195] as well as the private enforcement of consumer protection law[196] and civil litigation more generally.[197] Financial considerations have also been identified as an important element in the discussions on collective redress.[198] **8.29**

The EU courts, from their side, have also regularly acknowledged the importance of legal costs in relation to the private enforcement of EU law. A good

190 See, however, Commission, Second report on Consumer Injunctions Directive 2009/22, COM(2012) 635, p. 15.

191 Cf. e.g. Art. 30 Competition Regulation 1/2003.

192 See para 3.17 (concerning Procurement Remedies Directives 89/665 and 92/13), 4.21 and 4.31 (concerning IPR Enforcement Directive 2004/48) and 5.33 (concerning Product Liability Directive 85/374) above, respectively.

193 Commission, Responses to the public consultation on the civil enforcement of intellectual property rights, July 2013, p. 9.

194 Commission, Second report on Consumer Injunctions Directive 2009/22, COM(2012) 635, p. 11. See para 5.12 above.

195 E.g. Study, Ashurst (2004), pp. 8–9 and 92–6; Riley and Peysner (2006), p. 750; Vrcek (2010), p. 292; Danov and Becker (2013), p. 77.

196 E.g. Loos (2011), p. 491. See also para 5.04 above.

197 E.g. Tulibacka (2009), p. 1533; Hodges, Vogenauer and Tulibacka (2010), p. 7.

198 E.g. Civic Consulting (2008b), p. 4. See also para 5.36 and 5.37 above.

example is the *Océano Grupo* case law issued in relation to the Unfair Terms Directive, where the Court of Justice noted that (relatively) high legal costs can deter consumers from raising the unfairness of a term in a consumer contract for themselves.[199] The Court of Justice has at times also taken account of this element in its assessments of rules of national law under the principles of equivalence, effectiveness and effective judicial protection.[200] This latter principle can in certain cases also require the provision of legal aid to a party to the proceedings.[201]

These kinds of concerns related to high legal costs emerge, most notably, although certainly not exclusively, in relation to the EU law provisions seeking to facilitate the bringing of actions for damages. This is obviously the case where the Product Liability Directive and the initiative leading to the Competition Damages Directive are concerned, given that both directives concentrate on this remedy. But also with respect to the EU legal acts that provide for several (substantive) remedies, such as the Procurement Remedies Directives and the IPR Enforcement Directive, have the above-mentioned concerns mostly been raised in relation to their provisions on actions for damages. Indeed, high legal costs were amongst the reasons why in the context of the 2007 revision of the Procurement Remedies Directives the Commission decided not to focus on (further) facilitating damages claims for breaches of the EU public procurement rules, but rather to concentrate on other remedies instead.[202] The underlying reason is that the bringing of actions for damages tends to lead to rather complex and lengthy proceedings. This often translates into high legal costs. Another regularly heard complaint is that, even when damages are awarded, the sums in question tend to be relatively modest. When a substantial part of those sums is needed to cover lawyers' bills and other legal expenses, this can of course significantly reduce the attractiveness of this remedy.

8.30 Although the situation can differ considerably between the Member States,[203] there can therefore be little doubt that, generally speaking, legal costs can be a

199 CoJ joined cases C-240/98 and C-244/98, *Océano Grupo*, para 26, where reference is made specifically to lawyers' fees. Later rulings in this connection refer more generally to the costs of legal proceedings. See e.g. CoJ case C-618/10, *Banco Español de Crédito*, para 54. See para 5.19 and 5.20 above.

200 E.g. CoJ case C-78/98, *Preston*, para 60; CoJ case C-63/01, *Evans*, para 53–5 and 76–8; CoJ case C-268/06, *Impact*, para 51; CST Order case F-55/08 DEP, *De Nicola*, para 36. See, however, also CoJ case C-567/13, *Baczó*, para 47, where it was held (in the context of an assessment under the principle of equivalence) that costs are not the sole decisive factor. On the above-mentioned principles more generally, see subsections 2.A.2 (equivalence) and 2.A.3 (effectiveness) and section 2.B (effective judicial protection) above.

201 CoJ case C-279/09, *DEB*, para 36.

202 See para 3.18 above.

203 Cf. e.g. Opinion AG Kokott case C-260/11, *Edwards*, para 21. See further Hodges, Vogenauer and Tulibacka (2010).

significant obstacle to the private enforcement of EU law. One would thus expect this issue to be addressed at least to some extent in the EU legislation under consideration. But that is generally not the case; that legislation is mostly silent on the issue of legal costs.

There is one notable exception, however. The IPR Enforcement Directive addresses this issue in a general as well as in a specific manner. It stipulates that, generally, the measures, procedures and remedies to ensure the enforcement of the intellectual rights covered by this directive may not be '*unnecessarily complicated or costly*'.[204] More specifically, this directive also requires Member States to ensure that '*reasonable and proportionate legal costs and other expenses incurred by the successful party shall, as a general rule, be borne by the unsuccessful party, unless equity does not allow this*'.[205] The Court of Justice has clarified that this latter provision implies that the infringer '*must generally bear all the financial consequences of his conduct*'.[206]

To this one should add, however, that, notable as it may be, it cannot be said that the IPR Enforcement Directive's regime on legal costs is an unqualified success.[207] The continuing complaints by stakeholders about high legal costs in intellectual property cases suggest that it has not been very effective in addressing the aforementioned concerns related to high legal costs. In all likelihood this is related to the broad way in which the above provision has been formulated. The term "reasonable and proportionate legal costs and other expenses" obviously provides only limited clarity as to the sorts and the level of the costs to be compensated. That provision is also expressly (merely) a "general rule", which allows for deviations for reasons of equity. Indeed, this formulation is so broad that, although there are certain exceptions and it remains in the end for the Court of Justice to establish whether or not this position is correct, most Member States did not consider it necessary to amend their pre-existing rules of national law in order to comply with it. It is therefore hardly surprising that its effects in practice have mostly been limited. This broad formulation is largely a consequence of the objections raised during the legislative process by certain Member States as well as the European Parliament against too far-reaching EU involvement with rules on legal costs.

Comparable discussions have taken place in fields other than intellectual **8.31**
property law, especially in relation to what was to become the Competition Damages Directive. Initially, the Commission raised the option of providing for

204 Art. 3(1) IPR Enforcement Directive 2004/48. See para 4.06 above.
205 Art. 14 IPR Enforcement Directive 2004/48. See para 4.31 above.
206 CoJ case C-406/09, *Realchemie*, para 49.
207 See para 4.31 above.

a rule that would limit the legal costs to be paid by the unsuccessful applicant (one-way fee-shifting).[208] This suggestion received considerable criticism, however.[209] The Commission subsequently decided to exclude this issue entirely from its legislative initiative. Instead, its 2008 white paper merely "encouraged" the Member States to amend their domestic rules where necessary.[210] In line with the Commission's proposal, the Competition Damages Directive therefore does not contain any rules on legal costs.

The Commission's proposal in 2005 to include a (conditional) form of one-way fee-shifting in the Small Claims Regulation was similarly rejected by the EU legislature.[211] It is also noticeable that while the rules on civil redress set out in the Commission's 2013 proposal for a trade secrets directive are mostly comparable with those of the IPR Enforcement Directive, rules on legal costs are notably absent from this proposal.[212] It is furthermore true that the 2013 Collective Redress Recommendation, which is concerned with infringements of EU law more generally, does address the issue of legal costs.[213] It recommends that Member States ensure, first, that the party that loses a collective redress action reimburses necessary legal costs borne by the winning party and, second, that contingency fees are not permitted.[214] However, this recommendation is only that – a recommendation by the Commission. As such it is not an act of the EU legislature and it is not binding.[215] And even apart from that, in this case the wording used is in fact also rather broad and flexible. Most notably, the first recommendation mentioned above applies '*subject to the conditions provided for in the relevant national law*', while with respect to the latter recommendation it is said expressly that exceptions are permitted.

---

208 Commission, Green paper on damages actions for breach of the EC antitrust rules, COM(2005) 672, p. 9. Under the rule proposed there, an unsuccessful applicant would only have to pay legal costs where he acted in a manifestly unreasonable manner by bringing the case. Mentioned also is the option of granting the national court the discretionary power to order at the beginning of the proceedings that the applicant will not be exposed to any recovery of costs if the action proves unsuccessful.

209 Commission, Staff working paper accompanying the white paper on damages actions for breach of the EC antitrust rules, SEC(2008) 404, p. 74. Cf. Study, CEPS, Erasmus University Rotterdam and LUISS (2007), pp. 181–3.

210 Commission, White paper on damages actions for breach of the EC antitrust rules, COM(2008) 165, pp. 9–10. See also Commission, Staff working paper accompanying the white paper on damages actions for breach of the EC antitrust rules, SEC(2008) 404, p. 75.

211 Commission, Proposal for Small Claims Regulation 861/2007, COM(2005) 87, p. 16 (Art. 14(2)). See further Loos (2011), p. 507.

212 Commission, Proposal for a trade secrets directive, COM(2013) 813.

213 Collective Redress Recommendation 2013/396. See para 5.38 above.

214 Points 13 and 30 Collective Redress Recommendation 2013/396. Under a system based on "contingency fees" (or other forms of "success fees"), lawyers' fees are not charged independently from the outcome of the proceedings, but, for instance, as a percentage of the damages award if the action in question proves to be successful.

215 See para 5.39 above.

Consequently, while the importance of legal costs-related issues for the private enforcement of EU law is not in doubt, these issues are hardly addressed in a meaningful manner in EU legislation relating to private enforcement proceedings.[216] Only the Environmental Impact Assessment Directive provides for another scarce example of EU legislative action on this point, although this concerns not the allocation of costs between the parties but rather the costs of the proceedings *per se*.[217] In particular, according to this directive, the review procedures provided for therein may not be '*prohibitively expensive*'.[218] The CoJ has held that this implies that '*the costs of proceedings must neither exceed the financial resources of the person concerned nor appear, in any event, to be objectively unreasonable*'.[219] In this respect an objective analysis is required that takes account of a range of circumstances, including the situation of the persons concerned, the prospect of success, the importance of what is at stake, the complexity of the relevant law and procedure, the potentially frivolous nature of the claim and the existence of a legal aid scheme or a costs protection regime.[220]

Overlooking the foregoing, it appears that two factors are of particular relevance in explaining this paradoxical state of affairs. A first factor is that on the side of the EU legislature – not only the Council, but also the European Parliament – there appears to be a general feeling that these matters are best left to be regulated at *national* level. In this connection reference is regularly made to the principle of subsidiarity.[221] The aforementioned objections raised during the legislative process relating to the IPR Enforcement Directive's provision on legal costs were largely motivated on these grounds.[222] In relation to the Commission's competition law initiative, several respondents objected to EU interference that would lead to sector-specific rules on legal costs that would differ from those applicable in other civil cases.[223] As the European Parliament **8.32**

216 This does not necessarily exclude, however, the assessment of the compatibility of the applicable rules of national law on legal costs with the EU legislation at issue more generally. See CoJ case C-61/14, *Orrizonte Salute*, and CoJ case C-495/14, *Tita* (both pending), concerning the payment of certain fees as a precondition for access to the review procedures referred to in Procurement Remedies Directives 89/665 and 92/12.

217 For another form of EU legislative involvement with issues of legal costs, see Legal Aid Directive 2003/8. As regards legal costs related to the preliminary reference procedure set out in Art. 267 TFEU, see CoJ case C-472/99, *Clean Car Autoservice*, paras 23–32.

218 Art. 11(4) Environmental Impact Assessment Directive 2011/92.

219 CoJ case C-260/11, *Edwards*, para 40.

220 Ibid., para 40–48. See also CoJ case C-427/07, *Commission v Ireland*, para 92–4; CoJ case C-530/11, *Commission v UK*, para 33–72.

221 On this principle, see also para 10.08 below.

222 See para 4.31 above.

223 See e.g. the responses to the 2005 green paper submitted by the German, UK and Dutch authorities in the context of the consultations, referred to in para 6.19 above.

held with respect to a possible EU initiative on collective redress, '*Member States are to determine their own rules on the allocation of costs*'.[224]

A second factor is that the possibility of establishing EU rules on legal costs tends to be particularly sensitive where the contemplated rules are seen as capable of encouraging a "litigation culture". This term refers, broadly speaking, to a situation whereby litigation between private parties takes place to a degree that is considered unreasonable and undesirable.[225] Concerns of this kind tend to come to light especially where contemplated EU rules would entail a deviation from the "loser pays" principle. While the latter is certainly not absolute, it is widely accepted as the general point of departure for the allocation of legal costs between the parties to a dispute.[226] One of its key functions is to establish a threshold for unmeritorious litigation.[227] It does so mainly by creating a degree of financial risk for the (potential) applicant, which leads to a "case selection effect".[228] Thus the Commission held in 2008 that a possible judicial collective redress procedure should '*avoid elements which are said to encourage a litigation culture [...], such as [...] contingency fees*'.[229] This view found wide support in the subsequent consultation.[230] Along similar lines the European Parliament noted in 2012 that '*there can be no action without financial risk*' and that under the Member States' rules '*the unsuccessful party must bear the costs of the other party in order to avoid the proliferation of unmeritorious claims*'.[231] It has been observed that deviations from this "loser pays" principle, notably in the form of contingency fees, tend to be met with strong cultural resistance.[232] That

224 European Parliament, Resolution, Towards a coherent European approach to collective redress, P7_TA(2012)0021, para 20. See also European Parliament, Resolution on the white paper on damages actions for breach of the EC antitrust rules, P6_TA(2009)0187, para 20.

225 See para 11.26 below.

226 As regards the relevant rules established at EU level, see e.g. Art. 16 Small Claims Regulation 861/2007; Art. 138 CoJ Rules of procedure, OJ 2012, L 265/1; Art. 85(1) Community Trade Mark Regulation 207/2009; Art. 70(1) Community Designs Regulation 6/2002. As regards the rules applicable at national level, see e.g. Commission, Staff working paper accompanying the white paper on damages actions for breach of the EC antitrust rules, SEC(2008) 404, p. 17 (n. 26); Hodges, Vogenauer and Tulibacka (2010), p. 17; European Parliament, Study on collective redress in antitrust, June 2012, p. 31. See also UNIDROIT, Principles of Transnational Civil Procedure (Art. 25).

227 Cf. e.g. Commission, Public consultation towards a coherent approach to collective redress, SEC(2011) 173, p. 9.

228 Study, CEPS, Erasmus University Rotterdam and LUISS (2007), p. 222. Cf. e.g. also Andrews (2005), p. 181. On the relationship between this "loser pays" principle and the degree of litigation and the costs related thereto, see further Study, CEPS, Erasmus University Rotterdam and LUISS (2007), pp. 176–81. There it is explained, in essence, that, as compared with a situation where the parties bear their own costs, this principle can indeed reduce the likelihood of litigation, but that it can also discourage the bringing of meritorious suits and increase average total spending on legal costs by the parties.

229 Commission, Green paper on consumer collective redress, COM(2008) 794, p. 12.

230 Commission, Responses to the consultation and hearing on collective redress, October 2011, p. 15.

231 European Parliament, Resolution, Towards a coherent European approach to collective redress, P7_TA(2012)0021, para 20.

232 Hodges, Vogenauer and Tulibacka (2010), p. 25.

is the case despite the fact that such arrangements can also have certain positive effects, especially in terms of improved access to court for private parties who are affected by infringements of the substantive rules at issue.[233] In several Member States (for example Sweden and Germany) certain forms of contingency fees were therefore introduced in recent years, despite such resistance.[234] Against this background it is probably no coincidence that the aforementioned – adopted – provision of the IPR Enforcement Directive is largely consistent with this "loser pays" principle, whereas the rule that the Commission – unsuccessfully – suggested for competition law infringements and for small claims entailed a deviation from this principle. For similar reasons the Collective Redress Recommendation not only expressly refers to this principle,[235] it also states that '*the lawyer's remuneration and the method by which it is calculated [should] not create any incentive to litigation that is unnecessary from the point of view of the interest of any of the parties*'.[236] It also limits the above-mentioned recommendation not to permit contingency fees to situations where this would risk creating an incentive to such unnecessary litigation.[237]

In light of the above it would seem that, despite past and current concerns in this regard, there is at present at best only limited scope for adopting EU legislative measures on legal costs incurred in private enforcement proceedings before national courts, particularly where such measures are not in line with the "loser pays" principle and could be seen as leading to a litigation culture. An interesting question that remains, however, is what the outcome would be if the two above factors were found to be at odds, that is, in a situation where EU rules on legal costs might be deemed necessary precisely to address litigation culture-related concerns. It is for now an open question which of these two factors would carry more weight for the EU legislature in such a case.

6. "Unregulated" remedies: Declarations, unjust enrichment, restitution

At the end of this second and final chapter on the remedies set out in the rules of EU law assessed in the foregoing, it is appropriate to note that the domestic laws of the Member States tend to provide for remedies other than the ones discussed above, which can nonetheless also be of relevance for the purposes of the private enforcement of EU law before national courts. The answer to the **8.33**

233 See e.g. Opinion AG Poiares Maduro case C-94/04, *Cipolla*, para 94. See also Leskinen (2011), p. 87. For a broader assessment see Study, CEPS, Erasmus University Rotterdam and LUISS (2007), pp. 201–5, where it is concluded that the legal and economic literature is split as to the impact of contingency fees on litigation expenditure, settlement rates and the quality of the lawsuits filed.

234 Leskinen (2011), p. 89.

235 Point 19 Collective Redress Recommendation 2013/396.

236 Point 29 Collective Redress Recommendation 2013/396.

237 Point 30 Collective Redress Recommendation 2013/396.

question whether and to what extent such (seen from the perspective of EU law) "unregulated" remedies are provided for evidently depends on the domestic legal system of each individual Member State. Generally speaking, these remedies can include *declaratory relief*. This implies essentially that a private party applicant simply requests the national court to express itself on a particular legal question. This remedy is, for example, available in England and Wales, Italy, Spain and the Netherlands.[238] In addition, one could think of claims brought by private parties that are founded on the *unjust enrichment* of the infringer of EU law or for the *restitution* of unduly paid sums to or unfair profits made by the latter.[239] Actions of this kind can be available *inter alia* in Germany, the Czech Republic, England and Wales, the Netherlands and Spain.[240] They typically involve the payment of certain monetary sums, but they can nonetheless be distinguished from the actions for damages discussed earlier.[241] For they concentrate not on the *harm caused* on the side of the *applicant*, but on the *gains made* by the *defendant*. Whether or not the latter was at fault tends to be of lesser importance in this regard, if at all. German law also provides for a specific procedure for the "skimming-off" of profits made as a result of certain infringements in actions brought by designated third parties (business or consumer associations). Under that procedure the sums awarded flow to the public budget, which probably explains why this procedure is reportedly little used.[242] Whilst an in-depth assessment of these unregulated remedies and their potential in private enforcement proceedings falls outside the scope of this book, it can still be of relevance to note the following three points in this connection.

8.34 In the first place, in certain cases it may well be worth considering *including* the above-mentioned remedies in EU private enforcement-related legislation of the type at issue here. As regards declaratory relief, there admittedly appears to be generally limited "demand" on the part of stakeholders for this remedy where the private enforcement of EU law is concerned. Nonetheless, in certain cases a mere declaration that there has been an infringement can conceivably still be of importance to the private parties concerned. That may be so not only for

238 Barone and Amore (2010), p. 347; Callol (2010), p. 385; Lunsingh Scheurleer et al. (2010), p. 370; Smith, Maton and Cambell (2010), p. 311.

239 On occasion EU law can provide certain provisions on these matters. Concerning the restitution of "unfair profits" see e.g. Art. 97(1) Community Plant Variety Rights Regulation 2100/94 (where reference is made, however, to national law). See para 4.11 above. Similarly, Art. 26(2) Community Designs Regulation 6/2002 and Art. 55(3) Community Trade Mark Regulation 207/2009 refer to the possibility of claims based on unjust enrichment, yet again with reference to national law.

240 Callol (2010), p. 374; Lunsingh Scheurleer et al. (2010), p. 389; Smith, Maton and Cambell (2010), p. 310; Bejček (2011), pp. 49–50; Peyer (2012), p. 334.

241 See section 7.A above.

242 Commission, Impact assessment report on damages actions for breach of the EU antitrust rules, SWD(2013) 203, pp. 74–5. See also Micklitz (2011b), p. 115; Peyer (2012), p. 336.

symbolic reasons, but for instance also as a basis for subsequently negotiating a settlement between the parties to the dispute concerning the further consequences to be drawn from that finding. This can (either *de jure* or *de facto*) thus function as part of a two-stage procedure, whereby the illegality of the behaviour and the liability of the alleged infringer is first established, and thorny questions, such as the quantification of the damage,[243] can then either be left to be settled out of court or addressed at a later stage of the proceedings.[244] Declaratory relief sometimes also exists in a negative form, meaning that a private party requests the national court to state that certain behaviour is *not* contrary to a particular rule of law (or otherwise does not incur the liability of that undertaking).[245]

In relation to actions for unjust enrichment or restitution, two broad categories can be distinguished for the present purposes.[246] First, there is what could be called "pure" restitution. Such actions can typically be brought as a follow-up (or addition) to a successful contractual remedy of the type discussed above, for instance to recover sums paid under a contract that is automatically void within the meaning of Article 101(2) TFEU or pursuant to a term in a consumer contract that has been deemed to be unfair and therefore not binding on the consumer in question.[247] One could also think of actions brought by the customers of undertakings for the repayment of the overcharges that resulted from those undertakings having participated in a cartel.[248] Second, there is what is sometimes called "restitutory" (or gain-based) damages. Here the emphasis is not so much on the repayment of sums paid by the applicant, but rather on the gains made as a consequence of the infringements at issue. Actions of this kind may well be attractive private enforcement remedies, especially because they can involve fewer difficulties from a quantification point of view or because of the deterrent effects for the infringers concerned. There is research suggesting that the chances of success of actions for restitution can indeed be considerably higher than those of "classic" damages claims that concentrate on compensation for the harm caused.[249]

243 See subsection 7.A.4 above.

244 Cf. Commission, Green paper on damages actions for breach of the EC antitrust rules, COM(2005) 672, p. 8; Commission, Staff working paper accompanying the green paper on damages actions for breach of EC antitrust rules, SEC(2005) 1732, p. 42. See also Commission, Impact assessment report on damages actions for breach of the EU antitrust rules, SWD(2013) 203, p. 74 (concerning a proposed Austrian law).

245 Siragusa (2014), p. 248.

246 Cf. Van Gerven (2003b), pp. 63–4. See also Van Gerven, Lever and Larouche (2000), pp. 770–816 and 872.

247 See section 8.A above.

248 Cf. Hjelmeng (2013), p. 1011.

249 See Peyer (2012), p. 354. Here a 50 per cent success rate for restitution claims relating to competition law infringements in Germany is reported, which is considerably higher than for the actions for damages assessed in that study.

8.35 In the second place, the above examples already illustrate that these unregulated remedies can be *closely connected* to the remedies that are expressly provided for in the EU legislation on which this book concentrates. It may indeed not always be easy to draw a dividing line between them. This seems inevitable in a situation where the rules on some remedies are (to some extent) harmonised at EU level, whereas other remedies remain entirely unregulated as a matter of secondary EU law. Declaratory relief can, for example, resemble to some extent the publicity measures discussed earlier.[250] Or take the IPR Enforcement Directive. Its rules on actions for damages expressly stipulate that account can be taken of the "unfair profits" of infringers when setting the amount of damages due.[251] While this might thus seem to point to a restitutory element, it should still be seen in the light of the overall objective of ensuring that a rightholder can obtain '*damages appropriate to the actual prejudice suffered*', which thus corresponds to the "classic" compensatory function of damages awards.[252] It is this directive's provision on the '*recovery of profits*' as such that really appears to be amounting to restitutory damages of the type referred to above.[253] At present this latter provision is merely optional, however. Nonetheless, there are discussions as to whether these rules set out in the IPR Enforcement Directive could and should be extended so as to concentrate (even) more on the gains made by infringers rather than on the harm caused to the private parties concerned.[254]

The Competition Damages Directive provides another illustration of the questions that can arise in this connection. As its title ('*Directive [...] on certain rules governing actions for damages [...]*') already makes clear, this directive concentrates on actions for damages.[255] The scope of its regime on the disclosure – and on the non-disclosure – of evidence is expressly limited to these kinds of actions.[256] Should this be taken to mean that leniency applications are not necessarily barred from being disclosed in a private enforcement action in which restitution is claimed under national law? Or are these proceedings also covered by the directive? Judging by the wording of the provisions in question, one could be inclined to answer this last question in the negative. But that would mean that the directive's rules on the non-disclosure of these documents do not apply. That seems difficult to reconcile with the objectives of this directive generally and those rules specifically.[257] Similar questions can arise for

250 See subsection 8.B.4 above.
251 Art. 13(1)(a) IPR Enforcement Directive 2004/48. See para 4.28 above.
252 See Art. 13(1), first subparagraph and recital 26 IPR Enforcement Directive 2004/48.
253 Art. 13(2) IPR Enforcement Directive 2004/48.
254 See para 4.30 and 7.25 above.
255 For a definition of the term "actions for damages", see Art. 2(4) Competition Damages Directive 2014/104.
256 Art. 5(1) and 6(1) Competition Damages Directive 2014/104. See subsection 6.C.3 above.
257 See para 6.25 and 6.31 above, respectively.

instance in relation to the effects in proceedings for restitution before national courts of infringement decisions by national competition authorities and the directive's provisions on limitation periods.[258]

Lastly, the fact that the above-mentioned remedies are generally not expressly provided for in the secondary EU law at issue does not mean that *EU law generally* (notably primary EU law and the general principles of EU law) has no role to play in this respect. In particular, if private parties have an EU law right to damages in situations where their rights vested in that law are infringed, regardless of whether or not secondary EU law provides for such a right,[259] why would there not be an EU law right to restitution as well? A ruling such as *Muñoz* might well be understood as pointing in that direction.[260] That applies all the more so because there is already a considerable body of case law by the Court of Justice, pursuant to which the private parties concerned are entitled to the repayment of charges levied by public authorities contrary to EU law.[261] The Court has seemed careful in distinguishing this right to restitution from the right to damages under the principle of Member State liability.[262] This distinction has been criticised for being artificial and untenable,[263] which confirms that, as was noted above, it can indeed be difficult to draw a dividing line between the remedies at issue here. In any case it seems a comparatively limited step to transpose the logic underlying this case law to horizontal situations, that is, to apply it in legal proceedings where one private party claims restitution from another private party on the grounds that the original payment was made as a consequence of an infringement of EU law. After all, *Courage* is generally seen as a case where the principle of Member State liability, as developed in the Court's *Francovich* case law, was similarly transposed from a "vertical" to such a "horizontal" context.[264] **8.36**

Unjust enrichment may well be a particularly complex concept in this connection, however, essentially because it works in two ways. It is one thing to consider that it is unjustified for a party who, for instance, infringed EU law to

258 Art. 9 and 10 Competition Damages Directive 2014/104, respectively. See para 6.41 and 6.42 above, respectively.

259 See in particular para 2.27 above.

260 CoJ case C-253/00, *Muñoz*. See para 2.25 and 2.28 above.

261 See e.g. CoJ case 199/82, *San Giorgio*, para 12; CoJ case C-147/01, *Weber's Wine World*, para 93. See further Dougan (1999), p. 233; Milutinovic (2010), pp. 159–70.

262 See e.g. CoJ case C-66/95, *Sutton*, para 23–4; CoJ case C-591/10, *Littlewoods*, para 23. As regards the principle of Member State liability, see para 2.23 above.

263 Milutinovic (2010), p. 165. In a similar sense, see Dougan (1999), p. 262.

264 CoJ case C-453/99, *Courage*. See para 2.24, 2.27 and 6.14 above. In CoJ case C-242/95, *GT-Link*, para 58–9, the CoJ already appeared to take a step in that direction, although there it was also emphasised that it concerns a *public* undertaking, meaning that this was not evidently a proper horizontal situation as referred to above.

be enriched as a result of that infringement.[265] But it is quite another thing to determine whether it then also follows that it is justified that the private party affected by that infringement is awarded compensation that might go beyond the damage that it actually suffered as a consequence of that infringement. The latter would after all seem to entail unjust enrichment as well. The Court of Justice seems receptive to arguments of this kind. In its above-mentioned case law on unduly levied charges, it has essentially accepted that this could be a reason for not repaying those charges.[266] And in *Courage* it held that EU law does not prevent national courts from taking steps to ensure that the protection of rights guaranteed by EU law does not entail unjust enrichment.[267] The discussions concerning further restitution-related elements under the IPR Enforcement Directive referred to in the previous paragraph also largely turn around this point. In this connection it is also noteworthy that the Competition Damages Directive expressly precludes overcompensation, '*whether by means of punitive, multiple or other types of damages*'.[268]

Matters are complicated further where the private party requesting restitution may also be to blame to a greater or a lesser extent for the infringement in question.[269] Questions of this kind can arise in competition cases, for example when an undertaking that itself participated in the forbidden cartel requires restitution from a fellow cartel participant for payments made under a void contract. One could also think of restitution claims relating to public contracts that were illegally directly awarded (that is, without public tendering in violation of the applicable EU public procurement rules) and that can therefore be considered ineffective under the Procurement Remedies Directives.[270] Again, the Court's case law seems to suggest that it is permissible (although seemingly not necessarily required under EU law) to reject claims of this kind on the basis of the principle that a litigant should not profit from his own illegal behaviour.[271] This touches upon the issues of contributory negligence, which under the Product Liability Directive can be reason to reduce or disallow liability,[272] and of diligence and causality more generally.[273]

---

265 Note that unjust enrichment does not necessarily entail a prior infringement of EU or national law; the key is rather the absence of a valid legal basis for the enrichment. See e.g. CoJ case C-47/07 P, *Masdar*, paras 44–46.

266 E.g. CoJ case 199/82, *San Giorgio*, para 13; CoJ case C-309/06, *Marks & Spencer*, para 41.

267 CoJ case C-453/99, *Courage*, para 30. See also CoJ joined cases C-295/04 to C-298/04, *Manfredi*, para 94.

268 Art. 3(3) Competition Damages Directive 2014/104.

269 Cf. Van Gerven (2003b), pp. 83–4.

270 Art. 2d(1) Procurement Remedies Directives 89/665 and 92/13. See subsection 3.B.3 above.

271 CoJ case C-453/99, *Courage*, para 31.

272 Art. 8(2) Product Liability Directive 85/374. See para 5.31 above.

273 See further para 7.11 and 7.12 above.

9

PROCEDURAL ISSUES

This chapter continues the comparative and contextual analysis of the EU legislation and other relevant developments discussed in Part B that commenced in the two previous chapters. It does so by analysing in the four sections below the relevant provisions on a range of procedural issues that have either been set out in that legislation or that are otherwise of particular relevance in this connection, especially in light of the case law of the Court of Justice. This analysis also includes an issue that is not procedural in nature, strictly speaking, namely the scope of the legislation under consideration.

A. SCOPE AND LEGAL STANDING

This first section subsequently addresses the rules on the scope of the EU legislation facilitating the private enforcement of EU law before national courts under consideration in Part B above and on the legal standing of private parties wishing to initiate such private enforcement proceedings.

1. Scope

The importance of the rules on scope of the EU legislation at issue here lies first **9.01**
and foremost in the fact that they determine in respect of *which substantive rules* the remedies and procedures provided for in that legislation can be relied upon. In this connection the following two approaches can be distinguished.

The first approach is one whereby the scope of the particular private enforcement-related act of secondary EU law essentially *coincides* with that of the substantive rules of EU law in question. This approach is followed in cases where the said measures have been laid down in the substantive legal acts themselves, namely in the Unfair Terms Directive and the Product Liability Directive.[1] A similar logic underlies the Procurement Remedies Directives. For each of these two latter directives corresponds to one of the two directives with substantive rules on public procurement.[2] Yet the substantive EU public procurement rules laid down in the Defence Procurement Directive are not covered. Instead, the text of the Procurement Remedies Directives has essentially been "copied into" into this latter directive with some limited adaptations.[3] Slightly different is the Consumer Injunctions Directive. The annex to this directive lists a range of substantive EU consumer protection directives, the infringement of which could trigger legal action under the Consumer Injunctions Directive.[4] This approach should be understood against the background of the EU consumer protection *acquis* being scattered across many different legal acts.[5] Consequently, this directive does not come into play following *any* infringement of substantive EU consumer protection law. Particularly since this list has been gradually extended over the years, this directive now nonetheless covers a large proportion of substantive EU consumer protection law.

The second approach laid down in the IPR Enforcement Directive differs more substantially from the former. To begin with, the delimitation of the scope of this directive is wide, without, however, being very precise. This directive applies in essence to '*any infringement*' of intellectual property rights, to which the recitals add that the directive's scope should be as wide as possible.[6] More significant for the present purposes is, however, that the IPR Enforcement Directive applies not only to infringements of intellectual property rights provided for by *EU* law, but also those provided for by *national* law. Infringements of rights granted on the basis of rules of "purely" national laws (that is, rules of national laws other than those transposing EU directives) are therefore also covered as a matter of EU law. A comparable "mixed" approach is also provided for in the Competition Damages Directive, as it covers not only

1 See subsections 5.C.1 and 5.D.1 above.

2 Art. 1(1) Procurement Remedies Directives 89/665 and 92/13. These directives also cover infringements of the recently adopted Concessions Awards Directive 2014/23. See para 3.08 above.

3 Art. 55–64 Defence Procurement Directive 2009/81.

4 Art. 1(2) Consumer Injunctions Directive 2009/22. See para 5.09 above.

5 See para 5.03 above.

6 Art. 2(1) and recital 13 IPR Enforcement Directive 2004/48. The Commission's list of intellectual property rights covered may be helpful in practice, but it is neither legally binding nor exhaustive. The Commission's 2013 proposal for a trade secrets directive contains its own set of – largely similar – private enforcement-related rules to address unlawful acquisition, use and disclosure of trade secrets. See Commission, Proposal for a trade secrets directive, COM(2013) 813. See para 4.07 above.

infringements of EU competition law but also of certain provisions of national competition law.[7]

It would appear that, generally speaking, the former is the more logical approach. After all, the key objective of the EU legislation at issue here is generally facilitating the effective enforcement of *EU* law.[8] Although this need not be excluded, it may moreover not always be immediately evident that also covering rules of "purely" national law is justified from an internal market perspective, as is required under the legal basis that is relied upon in virtually all instances, namely Article 114 TFEU.[9] As the Commission held in its proposal for the IPR Enforcement Directive, the EU's involvement with enforcement-related issues can be seen as a '*logical extension*' of its involvement with the substantive law at issue.[10] Or, as the European Parliament noted in relation to consumer redress, '*the substantive rights conferred by [EU] legislation [...] must be supplemented by appropriate procedural mechanisms to ensure their enforcement*'.[11] The question is therefore, in particular, why that approach is not consistently followed. **9.02**

In this connection it can be noted that the Commission's proposal for the IPR Enforcement Directive was in fact only concerned with rights based on EU law. The provision pursuant to which infringements of intellectual property rights provided for by "purely" national law are also covered, referred to above, was introduced by the EU legislature.[12] Precisely the contrary had happened earlier, at the time of the adoption of the first of the two Procurement Remedies Directives. In the latter case the Commission had also proposed covering infringements of "purely" national laws on public procurement, but the EU legislature (then only the Council) did not take up this part of the proposal.[13] And in respect of the Competition Damages Directive, too, a change of approach can be observed. Originally the Commission's initiative was limited to infringements of EU law. The subsequent decision to also cover certain rules of national competition law might have been motivated at least in part by the fact that this provided a justification for involving the European Parliament in the legislative process as a proper co-legislator together with the Council, something on which it had long insisted.[14]

7 Art. 1(1) in conjunction with Art. 2(1) and (3) Competition Damages Directive 2014/104. See para 6.26 above.

8 See also para 10.03 and 11.05 below.

9 See para 10.02 below.

10 Commission, Proposal for IPR Enforcement Directive 2004/48, COM(2003) 46, p. 5.

11 European Parliament, Resolution on consumer redress, OJ 1987, C 99/203, recital C.

12 See para 4.07 above.

13 See para 3.08 above.

14 See para 6.26 above.

9.03 The foregoing indicates that it is not always easy to discern a clear and consistent line in relation to the scope of the EU legislation on private enforcement. While limiting the remedies and procedural rules provided for in that legislation to proceedings before national courts addressing (alleged) infringements of EU law is the general rule, in some cases this scope is broader in that certain infringements of "purely" national law can also be addressed under that legislation. It appears that considerations other than strictly legal ones can at times play a role in deciding which of these two approaches is to be followed in a particular case. Having said that, the practical significance of the above discussions should probably not be overstated either. The EU's involvement with substantive intellectual property law is very extensive.[15] That implies that relatively few intellectual property rights are provided for and regulated solely by "purely" national law. In that light, the decision to cover (virtually) *all* infringements of the substantive rules in this domain can be seen not only as a comparably modest but arguably also a sensible one, given that this ensures that the same private enforcement-related rules apply across the board.[16] It can further legitimately be argued that competition law is somewhat of a special case in this respect. For the Competition Damages Directive does not cover *all* infringements of the rules of substantive national competition law. Only covered are situations where, pursuant to the Competition Regulation, there is a requirement of the *parallel application* of substantive EU and national competition law.[17] That means that the extent to which this directive covers national law is restricted and, moreover, that this selected approach can be justified with reference to the need to avoid different remedial and procedural rules applying in one and the same action for damages brought by a private party pursuant to an (alleged) infringement.[18] In this sense these two exceptions to the above-mentioned general rule are indeed both rather limited and specific.

9.04 A separate and more specific issue regarding issues of scope is the question of infringement of *which provisions* of the rules of substantive law covered can lead to the remedies and procedural rules set out in the EU's private enforcement-related legislation being invoked by a private party. The role of the concept of a "right" is of particular importance in this regard.[19] For under that legislation it is not always evident that it is the infringement of a right, conferred on a private party by a rule of substantive EU (or national) law, that can "trigger" the

15 See para 4.02 above.

16 See also subsection 10.D.2 below.

17 Art. 3(1) Competition Regulation 1/2003. See para 6.04 above.

18 See recital 10 Competition Damages Directive 2014/104. See also Commission, Proposal for Competition Damages Directive 2014/104, COM(2013) 404, pp. 12–13.

19 As set out in para 2.04 above, the concept of a "right" is understood to refer to a legal position which a party recognised as such by the law may have and which in its normal state can be enforced by that party against others before a court of law.

application of this legislation. Under the IPR Enforcement Directive, the existence and subsequent infringement of an intellectual property *right* is clearly the central concept.[20] By contrast, the Procurement Remedies Directives and the Consumer Injunctions Directive do not make reference to the concept of a "right" at all.[21] The Procurement Remedies Directives stipulate essentially that it must be ensured that decisions taken by the contracting authorities may be reviewed on the grounds that they have infringed *EU law* in the field of public procurement.[22] The Consumer Injunctions Directive similarly defines the concept of an "infringement" as any act contrary to the *directives* listed in its annex which harms the collective interests of consumers.[23] These directives thus appear to "skip" the step whereby the question is asked whether the substantive rule of EU law that has been infringed actually confers a (legally enforceable) right on the private parties in question.[24]

That is remarkable because, ambiguous as the concept of a "right" may be in EU law,[25] it is a fundamental requirement for a rule of EU law to be enforceable by a private party before either a European or a national court. By concentrating on remedies without (explicitly) addressing the issue of rights, these directives seem to disregard the link that exists between both concepts. The general position is that each right conferred ought to be accompanied by a remedy ensuring that it is capable of being enforced (*ubi ius, ibi remedium*). Conversely, it seems to make little sense for the EU legislature to require the availability of certain remedies in the absence of the existence of a right. The importance of the question of conferral of rights is illustrated by the case law of the Court of Justice relating to the principle of Member State liability. One of the conditions for incurring such liability is that the rule of law that has been infringed was intended to confer rights on private parties.[26] Against this background it seems unlikely that in this respect the EU legislature meant to take a distinct line under the above directives. It seems that it has simply been *presumed* in those

20 See in particular Art. 2(1) IPR Enforcement Directive 2004/48.

21 Competition Damages Directive 2014/104 is somewhat ambiguous in this respect. It speaks generally of infringements of EU or national competition law, but it also places particular emphasis on private parties' right to full compensation. Its recital 3 explains that Art. 101 and 102 TFEU have direct effect and create rights and obligations for the private parties concerned. See also para 6.01 above.

22 Art. 1(1) Procurement Remedies Directives 89/665 and 92/13.

23 Art. 1(2) Consumer Injunctions Directive 2009/22. As from January 2016, this provision no longer refers to "directives" but instead to "EU acts", given that Annex I to Consumer Injunctions Directive 2009/22 also includes a regulation. See Art. 20 and 22 Consumer ODR Regulation 524/2013.

24 Note that this state of affairs is arguably somewhat more understandable where Consumer Injunctions Directive 2009/22 is concerned, given that, as discussed in para 5.06 above, this directive is exclusively concerned with the protection of the *collective* (and not the individual) interests of consumers (see its Art. 1(1)). Yet it would appear that these interests can nonetheless only be deemed to be affected where the rights that the substantive EU law at issue grants to these private parties are infringed.

25 See para 2.04 above.

26 See para 2.23 above.

cases that the substantive rules at issue confer rights on private parties that are capable of being enforced before national courts. Although this does not necessarily hold true in relation to all provisions set out in these directives,[27] this presumption mostly seems correct, as (subsequent) case law has made clear.[28]

2. Legal standing

9.05 Ensuring that private parties affected by an (alleged) infringement of EU law have the legal capacity to bring proceedings before the competent national courts is evidently a precondition for any effort to facilitate the private enforcement of EU law to be successful. Almost all legal acts under consideration therefore address the issue of legal standing (*locus standi*; that is, the rules on "who can sue") in some detail. This is testimony to the importance that is attributed to this issue in the present context. At first glance it might moreover appear that the provisions in question typically harmonise to a great extent the national laws concerned. In this sense these provisions signal both an understandable and an important inroad into the procedural autonomy of the Member States.[29]

Take, for instance, the Procurement Remedies Directives. There it is specified that '*any person having or having had an interest in obtaining a particular contract and who has been or risks being harmed by an alleged infringement*' has standing to bring a case.[30] The IPR Enforcement Directive is at least as detailed. It sets out four categories of persons having legal standing to initiate legal proceedings under that directive, namely rightholders, licensees, collective rights management bodies and professional defence bodies.[31] Issues of legal standing further lay at the very heart of the Consumer Injunctions Directive. This latter directive seeks to ensure that qualified entities (such as consumer associations) from one Member State can initiate legal actions in another Member State in cases of "intra-EU infringements" of the substantive consumer protection rules at

27 See e.g. Art. 75 Public Sector Procurement Directive 2004/18 and Art. 8a Unfair Terms Directive 93/13 on the provisions on the submission of information by the Member States to the Commission, or Art. 13 Unfair Commercial Practices Directive 2005/29 on the Member States' obligations to lay down penalties and to ensure that they are being enforced. Provisions of this type are unlikely to be qualified as conferring rights. Cf. e.g. CoJ case C-159/00, *Sapod*, para 61–62; CoJ case C-222/02, *Paul*, para 40–46.

28 See para 3.03 and 5.03 above.

29 In the absence of EU rules governing the matter, it is in principle for national law to determine a private party's standing and legal interest in bringing proceedings, subject to observance of the principles of equivalence and effectiveness and provided that the right to effective judicial protection is not undermined. See e.g. CoJ case C-12/08, *Mono Car Styling*, para 49.

30 Art. 1(3) Procurement Remedies Directives 89/665 and 92/13. See para 3.25 above.

31 Art. 4 IPR Enforcement Directive 2004/48. See para 4.33 above.

issue.[32] The Unfair Terms Directive also addresses the issue of legal standing. It specifies that persons or organisations having a legitimate interest in protecting consumers must be able to initiate legal proceedings under that directive.[33] Finally, pursuant to the Competition Damages Directive, '*anyone who had suffered harm caused by an infringement*' of the relevant competition rules is to be entitled to bring an action for damages.[34] This term "anyone" is to be understood broadly, covering consumers and undertakings, including indirect purchasers, as well as public authorities.[35]

However, the above-mentioned provisions nonetheless mostly continue to leave significant leeway to the Member States. This is ensured through the insertion of additional clauses that refer to national law in one way or another. These clauses mostly came about upon the insistence of the Member States represented in the Council. The Procurement Remedies Directives expressly stipulate, for example, that it is for the Member States to establish the applicable '*detailed rules*' in this regard. In relation to three out of four categories of persons having legal standing under the IPR Enforcement Directive (that is, licensees, collective rights management bodies and professional defence bodies), the phrase is added '*in so far as permitted by and in accordance with the provisions of the applicable law*'. In respect of the fourth category (that is, rightholders), only the latter part of this phrase has been added. This indicates arguably that (only) the latter private parties must in any case have legal standing on the basis of this directive, in which case the applicable detailed rules remain a matter of national law, whereas as regards the three other categories of potential applicants, even the question of *whether* they have legal standing as such seems to be determined by national law.[36] **9.06**

A largely similar picture emerges when the Consumer Injunctions Directive is considered in further detail. Under this directive it remains for the Member States to determine which "their" qualified entities are, meaning that it does not create a harmonised EU rule of legal standing for consumer associations and other similar entities.[37] It is true that this directive requires it to be ensured that "foreign" qualified entities (that is, entities considered qualified to initiate legal proceedings in accordance with the rules of a Member State other than the one where proceedings are brought) in principle have legal standing across the EU. However, the national court seised remains entitled to examine whether the

32 Art. 4 Consumer Injunctions Directive 2009/22. See para 5.06 and 5.07 above.
33 Art. 7(2) Unfair Terms Directive 93/13. See para 5.13 above.
34 Article 1(1) Competition Damages Directive 2014/104. See para 6.39 above.
35 Cf. recital 13 Competition Damages Directive 2014/104.
36 In this sense, see also Reinbothe (2010), p. 14; Lakits-Josse (2011), p. 527.
37 Cf. Betlem (1999), p. 414.

purpose of any such qualified entity justifies it in taking legal action in that specific case. The mutual recognition mechanism for the legal standing of these entities that this directive establishes is therefore not unqualified, but subject to an additional verification in concrete cases. It further follows from the above-mentioned provision in the Unfair Terms Directive that national law essentially determines which party has a legitimate interest. For here it is stated that having a legitimate interest '*under national law*' is required. Comparable statements can be found in other consumer protection directives and elsewhere in secondary EU law.[38] Only the Competition Damages Directive does not contain such an explicit reference to national law where matters of legal standing are concerned.[39]

9.07 It follows that the actual harmonising effect of the EU involvement with issues of legal standing is typically more modest than might appear at first sight. That applies even more so because, apart from the above-mentioned clauses, more often than not the above provisions mainly seem to *confirm* – rather than amend or otherwise affect – already existing national rules.[40] The Procurement Remedies Directives' requirement of the applicant having a (legitimate) interest was for instance inserted expressly with a view not to '*jeopardise*' the logic of the existing legal systems of the Member States.[41] Something similar can be said in relation to the IPR Enforcement Directive. As set out above, under this directive the legal standing of rightholders is regulated most extensively as a matter of EU law. But in the various domestic legal systems of the Member States precisely this category of private party applicants is normally capable of initiating legal proceedings under national law anyway.[42] A holder of an intellectual property right is after all evidently concerned by and will generally have a legitimate interest in acting upon an (alleged) infringement of their right. This may be less self-evident for the other categories listed in this directive, especially as regards collective rights management bodies and

38 E.g. Art. 11(2) Unfair Commercial Practices Directive 2005/29; Art. 5(1) Misleading Advertising Directive 2006/114; Art. 17(2) Gender Equality Directive 2006/54; Art. 3(2) Free Movement of Workers Enforcement Directive 2014/54.

39 Although this is different where actions for damages brought by a third party on behalf of the private party (allegedly) having suffered harm are concerned. See Art. 2(4) Competition Damages Directive 2014/104.

40 See e.g. also the statement made by the Commission and Greece at the time of the adoption of Public Sector Remedies Directive 89/665: '*the term "interest" in [the provision on legal standing of this directive] is equivalent in the Greek legal system to the concept of "legitimate interest" as consistently defined by the decisions of the Greek Council of State*'. See Council, doc. 7490/89, p. 10.

41 Council, doc. 7834/89 ADD 1, p. 7.

42 Cf. e.g. Cornish, Llewelyn and Aplin (2010), p. 58. A majority of Member States nonetheless reportedly amended their national laws in this regard pursuant to the adoption of IPR Enforcement Directive 2004/48. See Commission, Staff working document accompanying the report on IPR Enforcement Directive 2004/48, SEC(2010) 1589, p. 6.

professional defence bodies.[43] And precisely in relation to these categories this directive continues to leave a great deal of flexibility to the national legal systems.

It further follows from the foregoing that the Competition Damages Directive harmonises the relevant national rules on legal standing to a comparatively great extent. However, on this point this directive seems to do little more than codify the earlier case law of the Court of Justice.[44] For in cases such as *Courage* and *Manfredi* it has long been held that '*any individual*' must be able to claim compensation for the damage suffered as a consequence of an infringement of the EU competition rules.[45] In this case also the actual degree of harmonisation realised is thus in effect more limited than might appear at first sight. This probably also explains why legal standing-related issues generated relatively little debate when this directive was adopted.[46] At an earlier stage discussions in this connection focused especially on collective redress, but the Commission decided not to include this issue in its proposal. The EU legislature left this decision unaltered, meaning that it is not addressed in this directive.[47]

By way of a last comment, it is to be noted that, comparatively modest as some **9.08**
of the above-mentioned provisions on legal standing may thus be, this does not mean that they are of no practical importance. That applies especially when account is taken of the (potential) role of the Court of Justice in interpreting these provisions. This point is best illustrated with reference to the *Fritsch* case, which concerned the application of the aforementioned provision on legal standing laid down in the Procurement Remedies Directives.[48] Under the national law applicable in the case at hand, a dispute had first to be brought before a non-judicial conciliation committee for the applicant to have legal standing. The directives' provision being silent on this matter, the Court of Justice was asked whether such a rule is permitted. It answered in the negative. Specifically in relation to the express reference to national law made in this

---

43 Cf. e.g. Art. 47 Patent Court Agreement, pursuant to which the rightholder (that is, the patent proprietor) and the holder of an (exclusive) licence are entitled to bring actions, whereas for other persons and bodies reference is made to national law. On this agreement, see para 4.02 above. Cf. e.g. also Art. 104 Community Plant Variety Rights Regulation 2100/94, pursuant to which actions for infringements may be brought by the holder and in principle persons enjoying exploitation rights.

44 Cf. recital 12 Competition Damages Directive 2014/104.

45 CoJ case C-453/99, *Courage*, para 24; CoJ joined cases C-295/04 to C-298/04, *Manfredi*, para 59 and 61. See para 6.14 and 6.15 above, respectively.

46 As discussed in para 6.38 above, a legal standing-related issue that generated some debate in this connection at least at an earlier stage is the position of indirect purchasers.

47 See e.g. Commission, Staff working paper accompanying the white paper on damages actions for breach of the EC antitrust rules, SEC(2008) 404, pp. 13–22. Cf. recital 13 Competition Damages Directive 2014/104. See para 6.24 above. Instead, the issue of collective redress has been addressed in Collective Redress Recommendation 2013/396, discussed in para 5.38 above.

48 CoJ case C-410/01, *Fritsch*, para 28–34. See also the other CoJ case law relating to the provision on legal standing of Procurement Remedies Directives 89/665 and 92/13, discussed in para 3.25 above.

provision, it held that this '*does not authorise [the Member States] to give the term "interest in obtaining a public contract" an interpretation which may limit the effectiveness of that directive*'.[49] This suggests that the effects of such an explicit reference to national law are not absolute and it might well be interpreted in a restrictive manner where the Court considers that necessary to safeguard the effectiveness of the EU legal act in question.

It remains for now an open question whether reasoning similar to that set out in *Fritsch* is applicable in relation to the other provisions on legal standing discussed above. If so, that could obviously increase the degree of harmonisation actually achieved. There generally seems considerable potential to come to a rather extensive interpretation of these provisions on legal standing. Jurisprudential developments in relation to other fields of EU law, such as environmental law and state aid law, suggest that the Court might well be prepared to exploit this potential.[50] That could apply particularly when the provisions in question are interpreted in light of the principle of effective judicial protection, set out in the Charter.[51] Such Charter-consistent interpretation may well mean that the applicable legal standing requirements are not to be interpreted too restrictively.[52]

The Court's ruling in *Muñoz* is arguably of particular importance in this connection.[53] On the one hand, the Court appeared to signal in this case that it wished to allow a relatively broad category of private parties the possibility of bringing a case for an (alleged) infringement of certain quality standards for agricultural products set by EU law. It implicitly rejected Advocate General Geelhoed's suggestion to apply here the – restrictive – test of whether the applicant was directly and individually concerned, which applies to direct actions before the EU courts.[54] If that is the situation in a case where no specific private enforcement-facilitating EU legislation applies, it seems doubtful

---

49 Ibid., para 34.

50 In relation to Art. 11 Environmental Impact Assessment Directive 2011/92 see e.g. CoJ case C-263/08, *Djurgården*, para 40–52; CoJ case C-240/09, *Lesoochranárske zoskupenie*, para 51; CoJ case C-115/09, *Bund für Umwelt und Naturschutz Deutschland*, para 46; CoJ case C-72/12, *Altrip*, para 42–54. In relation to Art. 107 TFEU see e.g. CoJ case C-174/02, *Streekgewest Westelijk Noord-Brabant*, para 18–20. See also Metselaar (2014), p. 250.

51 Art. 47 Charter. See para 2.11 above.

52 On this Charter-consistent interpretation, see para 11.33 below.

53 CoJ case C-253/00, *Muñoz*. See para 2.25 above.

54 On these "direct actions" under Art. 263 TFEU, see para 1.02 above. See Opinion AG Geelhoed C-253/00, *Muñoz*, para 67–76. The CoJ's ruling in *Muñoz* on this point seems understandable not only considering the restrictiveness of the test under Art. 263 TFEU, but also given that if one wishes to make an analogy it might be more appropriate to instead apply the test for legal standing relating to the EU's non-contractual liability under Art. 340 TFEU. Under this latter provision no requirement of direct and individual concern applies. See e.g. Gutman (2011), pp. 703–8. For possible other analogies specifically in a competition law context, see Milutinovic (2010), pp. 222–8.

whether the Court would take a more restrictive line where such legislation does apply. On the other hand, in *Muñoz* the Court also seemed careful to stress that *competitors* of the infringing undertaking must be able to enforce the applicable rules by means of civil proceedings. Arguably this served to emphasise that as a matter of EU law not necessarily *any* third party is entitled to bring a private enforcement action.[55] Indeed, many understand this reference in *Muñoz* as hinting at a requirement for the applicant to have a sufficient *interest* to act.[56] There are also other rulings that appear to go in this direction,[57] although, as was noted above, in its *Courage* case law the Court has so far consistently emphasised that '*any individual*' is in principle entitled to bring such an action.[58]

The fact that there are certain, often somewhat ambiguously worded, rules of EU law in place implies that considerable scope for interpretation is left to the Court. While several issues remain to be clarified in this connection, the foregoing suggests that the Court may, generally speaking, be prepared to interpret provisions on legal standing of the type discussed above in a rather extensive manner, while at the same time seeking to prevent creating an *actio popularis*.[59]

---

55 This is related to the question of whether and if so in which cases as a matter of EU law a requirement exists pursuant to which an applicant must fall within the *protective scope* of the rule of law that is allegedly infringed for him to be able to rely thereon in the course of law (*Schutznorm*). Such a requirement exists, in various forms, in Member States such as Germany, Denmark, the Netherlands and Portugal. See Van Gerven (1995), p. 696. See further e.g. Prechal (2005), pp. 122, 238–9 and 284; Tridimas (2006), p. 480; Eilmansberger (2007), pp. 463–7; Leczykiewicz (2010a), pp. 278–9; Reich (2010), p. 127.

56 Biondi (2003), pp. 1248–9; Dougan (2004), p. 43. Cf. Temple Lang (2008), p. 98. In a similar sense, see Opinion AG Geelhoed C-253/00, *Muñoz*, para 63, 65 and 76.

57 E.g. CoJ joined case C-261/01 and C-262/01, *Van Calster*, para 64; CoJ case C-132/05, *Commission v Germany (Parmesan cheese)*, para 68–71; CoJ case C-426/05, *Tele2 Telecom*, para 38; CoJ case C-237/07, *Janecek*, para 39; CoJ joined cases C-165/09 to C-167/09, *Stichting Natuur en Milieu*, para 100. Note that also under Art. 263 TFEU a distinction is made between the tests for legal standing and for having an interest in bringing legal proceedings. The latter requires that there must be a vested and present interest, evaluated at the date on which the action is brought, which exists only if the action, if successful, is likely to procure an advantage for the party who has brought it. See e.g. GC case T-79/12, *Cisco systems*, para 34 and 35.

58 See in particular CoJ joined cases C-295/04 to C-298/04, *Manfredi*, para 62–4, discussed in para 6.15 above. There the CoJ added the phrase '*where there is a causal relationship*'. Whereas in practical terms the outcome may be similar, legally speaking, the question whether an applicant has a sufficient interest to be considered admissible in a particular case is, however, to be distinguished from the question whether this party, once having been considered admissible, can demonstrate that the harm suffered was caused by the alleged infringement. On the requirement of a causal link, see subsection 7.A.3 above.

59 Kornezov (2014), p. 258, where the prevention of *actio popularis* is linked with the separation of powers, at least in so far as legislative acts are concerned.

B. LIMITATION PERIODS AND RULES OF EVIDENCE

Two further procedural issues are discussed below, namely the limitation periods and the rules of evidence that may apply in private enforcement proceedings.

1. Limitation periods

9.09 Where a dispute emerges it is in the interest of all parties concerned to know by which date a possible legal action needs to be brought. For a (potential) applicant this evidently marks the moment before he must act if he wishes to do so. For the (potential) defendant as well as for any third parties that may be affected this marks the moment from which they are "safe" in the absence of an action having been brought. As the Court of Justice has consistently confirmed, it is in the interest of legal certainty to set reasonable limitation periods.[60] For that reason such periods also apply to litigation before the EU courts themselves. Actions for damages for the EU's non-contractual liability must, for example, be brought before those courts within five years from the occurrence of the event giving rise thereto.[61] This period begins to run at the moment at which the decision produces its effects *vis-à-vis* the parties concerned, that is, when the harm actually materialises in relation to these parties.[62]

The foregoing implies not only that limitation periods can be of considerable importance in the present context, it also underlines that setting rules on this subject matter is to a great extent a balancing act between the various interests at stake.[63] Just as setting too strict rules would be detrimental to the possibilities for private parties to initiate legal proceedings for infringements of EU law before the competent national courts, imposing excessively long limitation periods can cause disproportionate harm to the interests of the (potential) defendants and certain third parties. It would further be mistaken to concentrate only on the length of these periods. The question at which moment they begin to run can be at least as important, as can the precise nature of the periods in question and the circumstances in which they are to be applied. All of these issues come to light when considering the following legal acts.[64]

---

60 E.g. CoJ case C-30/02, *Recheio*, para 18. See para 2.08 above.

61 See Art. 46 of Protocol No 3 to the TFEU on the Statute of the Court of Justice of the European Union.

62 E.g. CoJ case C-460/09 P, *Inalca*, para 60.

63 Cf. Study, CEPS, Erasmus University Rotterdam and LUISS (2007), pp. 535–6.

64 Rules on limitation periods are notably absent from consumer protection directives such as Consumer Injunctions Directive 2009/22 and Unfair Terms Directive 93/13.

Take, to begin with, the IPR Enforcement Directive. This directive is very brief on this point. It only provides for a general reference to the need to avoid '*unreasonable time limits or unwarranted delays*'.[65] It does not set out any specific rules on limitation periods. This stands in marked contrast with the comparatively detailed manner in which this directive regulates many of the other remedial and procedural issues under discussion here. In part, this can probably be ascribed to the lack of a general and "inherent" urgency in the typical private enforcement disputes covered by this directive.[66] The interests of the parties wishing to enforce their intellectual property rights being the dominant policy concern here and existing limitation periods set on the basis of national law generally not being seen as an obstacle to be addressed, apparently no need was felt to impose any particular requirements in this respect at EU level. It is noticeable, however, that the Commission proposal for a directive on trade secrets, which provides for remedial and procedural rules that are largely similar to the ones set out in the IPR Enforcement Directive, does include a rule on limitation periods (of at least one year and at most two years; however, the Council wishes to replace this by a maximum of six years).[67] **9.10**

In contrast, limitation periods play a particularly important role in public procurement cases. Both the contracting authority and the selected bidder normally have a legitimate interest in concluding and executing the public contract in question as soon as possible and therefore in possible legal challenges by third parties (notably other bidders) being brought without delay.[68] The latter will nonetheless need some time to determine whether they can and wish to contest a contracting authority's decision and if so to prepare an application to this effect. Since their revision in 2007 the Procurement Remedies Directives therefore expressly allow for the setting of a range of limitation periods.[69] This is in line with earlier case law of the Court of Justice to this effect.[70] The length of these periods differs depending on the type of review sought, but they are generally very short. These directives provide for three types of limitation periods. First, there is a minimum period of 10 or 15 days (depending on the means of communication used) for requests for *review of the legality* of the contracting authority's decision, counting from its notification to the private party concerned.[71] Second, the minimum time period for actions **9.11**

65 Art. 3(1) IPR Enforcement Directive 2004/48. See para 4.06 above.

66 See also para 8.16 above.

67 Commission, Proposal for a trade secrets directive, COM(2013) 813, p. 20 (Art. 7). As to the Council's position, see Council, doc. 9870/14, p. 36.

68 See para 3.05 and 3.11 above. See e.g. CoJ case C-230/02, *Grossmann*, para 38, discussed in para 3.25 above.

69 See para 3.26 above.

70 E.g. CoJ case C-470/99, *Universale Bau*, para 71–9; CoJ case C-327/00, *Santex*, para 48–66; CoJ case C-241/06, *Lämmerzahl*, para 50–64.

71 Art. 2c Procurement Remedies Directives 89/665 and 92/13.

seeking the *ineffectiveness* of a concluded contract has been set at either 30 days (upon notification of the party concerned) or six months (upon the conclusion of the contract).[72] Third, in relation to *actions for damages* no specific limitation periods have been laid down as a matter of EU law. This is thus one of the other situations where the relevant limitation periods are expressly left to be determined by national law.[73]

Noticeable is further the explicit requirement laid down in the Procurement Remedies Directives that the above-mentioned notifications to the private party concerned must include the reasons for the decision in question. This reflects the thought that there can be no effective judicial protection – and the relevant limitation period may therefore not begin to run – until the private party concerned has been properly informed. Again, this is in line with earlier case law of the Court of Justice, both in respect of the principle of effective judicial protection generally and public procurement cases specifically.[74] In this manner this requirement to adequately inform the private parties concerned acts as a sort of counter-balance for the short limitation periods that can apply in public procurement cases.

9.12 Time periods are also of relevance in relation to proceedings brought under the Product Liability Directive. The main issue here is, however, one of limiting the effects in time of the no-fault ("strict") liability for which this directive makes provision and not so much ensuring rapid review as such.[75] Accordingly, this directive specifies two distinct types of time limits. In the first place, it sets out an "ordinary" *limitation period* for the bringing of actions for damages under the directive.[76] Its length is comparatively short for damages claims, namely three years. Unlike most of the other periods discussed in this subsection, this is moreover not a minimum period, which implies that national law cannot provide for a longer period. The directive specifies that this limitation period begins to run on the day on which the applicant becomes aware or should reasonably have become aware of the damage, the defect and the identity of the infringer. Issues relating to the suspension or interruption of this period are expressly left to national law.

72 Art. 2f(1) Procurement Remedies Directives 89/665 and 92/13.

73 Art. 2f(2) Procurement Remedies Directives 89/665 and 92/13.

74 See e.g. CoJ case 179/84, *Bozzetti*, para 17 (concerning the principle of effective judicial protection); CoJ case C-406/08, *Uniplex*, para 30–32 (concerning public procurement law). See e.g. also CoJ case C-19/13, *Fastweb*, para 58–60.

75 See para 5.30 above.

76 Art. 10 Product Liability Directive 85/374.

In the second place, the Product Liability Directive provides for another time period at the expiry of which the rights of the (potential) applicant are *extinguished*.[77] Differing from the aforementioned limitation period, this latter period starts to run from the moment that the product is put into circulation. Awareness on the part of injured private parties thus plays no role in this connection. The possible effects of this rather strict rule for these parties are offset to some extent by the longer duration of this period, namely ten years, and by the specification that no rights are extinguished if legal proceedings have been brought in the meantime. This latter rule ensures that at least in this respect the possible long duration of these legal proceedings does not come at the expense of a private party who has filed a damages claim under this directive.

Finally, one of the key objectives of the Competition Damages Directive is facilitating the bringing of actions for damages with a view to ensuring that injured private parties can obtain full compensation.[78] The aforementioned quest to establish an appropriate balance between the various interests at stake also underlies this directive's rules on limitation periods.[79] However, here the emphasis is on ensuring that these periods do not '*unduly hamper the bringing of actions for damages*', particularly in "follow-on" actions (that is, actions for damages brought pursuant to an earlier infringement decision by the competent public enforcement authority).[80] **9.13**

This directive's provision on limitation periods is, as a consequence, rather "claimant-friendly".[81] It stipulates that the applicable limitation periods shall not begin to run before the injured party knows or can reasonably be expected to know: (a) the behaviour and the fact that it constitutes an infringement; (b) that this infringement caused harm to that party; and (c) the identity of the infringer. A comparatively high threshold has been set in this manner. In particular, this requirement of knowledge of the fact that the behaviour in question qualifies as an infringement is an addition as compared with the above-mentioned rule of the Product Liability Directive. The wording used, moreover, seems to imply that (even) higher thresholds can in principle be set under national law. Another illustration of this directive's claimant-friendliness is the rule that limitation periods must have a length of at least five years. Not only is this period longer than the one set out in the Product Liability Directive (although in itself not unusually long), it is also a *minimum* period, meaning

77 Art. 11 Product Liability Directive 85/374.
78 Art. 1(1) Competition Damages Directive 2014/104. See para 6.25 above.
79 Cf. Commission, Proposal for Competition Damages Directive 2014/104, COM(2013) 404, p. 16.
80 Recital 36 Competition Damages Directive 2014/104.
81 Art. 10 Competition Damages Directive 2014/104. See para 6.42 above.

that longer periods may be provided for. Finally, specific to competition cases but therefore no less important is the rule that limitation periods are to be *suspended* (or interrupted) if a public enforcement authority initiates proceedings, for the duration of at least one year after those proceedings are terminated. This latter rule facilitates the bringing of "follow-on" actions, which can consequently be brought sometimes many years after the infringement was committed.

9.14 It follows that EU legislation on the private enforcement of EU law before national courts of the type at issue here not only regularly sets out harmonised rules on limitation periods, but also does so with a considerable degree of detail. While all these periods serve the interest of ensuring legal certainty for all parties concerned, the rules in question tend to be tailored each time to the specific characteristics and (perceived) needs of the typical situations in the fields of law at hand. This legislation therefore does not provide for a one-size-fits-all approach to limitation periods. Rather, the variety in dominant concerns means that the balance is struck each time in a somewhat different manner in each of the legal acts, leading to a variety of rules, particularly as regards the starting point, length and possible suspension of these periods.

2. Rules of evidence

9.15 It has already been discussed above which measures related to the *disclosure* of evidence that might be relevant in private enforcement proceedings are provided for in the EU legislation at issue.[82] The present subsection concentrates by contrast on the *rules of evidence*, which refers to the other evidence-related rules that may apply in this regard, notably those on the allocation of the burden of proof between the parties to the proceedings and the manner in which the national court seised is to assess the evidence presented to it. Although distinct, rules on disclosure and rules of evidence are related. Difficulties for a private party in obtaining the evidence needed to substantiate its claims are mainly problematic only when the burden of proof is on this party. Such difficulties may be a reason for the legislature to alleviate this burden, reverse it or provide for a lower standard of proof. It may also be a reason to empower national courts to take decisions of this kind in certain specific circumstances. Something similar applies with respect to the standard of proof. Measures on disclosure and on rules of evidence can thus be different ways to address comparable and often related challenges encountered in private enforcement proceedings. And also more generally, it is self-evident that rules of evidence can be crucial in determining the outcome of a private enforcement action, as they determine

82 See subsection 8.B.2 above.

essentially who needs to prove what and how the evidence submitted is weighed by the court.

When reviewing the legislation assessed in Part B above, it appears, however, that the (potential) importance of this subject matter has generally not been a reason for the EU legislature to address rules of evidence in any detail. Rules of this kind are mostly not provided for in that legislation. It seems for the most part to be simply presumed that in accordance with the relevant rules of national law it is for each party to substantiate its claims and for the national court seised to assess the evidence brought before it.[83] Few, if any, specific obligations tend to be imposed in this respect as a matter of EU law.[84] That does not mean that EU law is entirely irrelevant in this regard. For one thing, the rules of national law at issue may not be such as to prevent the objectives of the EU legislation in question from being achieved. The case law of the Court of Justice makes clear that this general rule can also have consequences for certain rules of evidence provided for in "purely" national law.[85] For another thing, the familiar boundaries flowing from the EU law principles of equivalence, effectiveness and effective judicial protection apply.[86] Also, on the basis of these principles the Court has already issued several rulings relating to rules of evidence.[87] But it does mean that the situation under the EU legislation at issue is largely similar to the one where no such legislation applies, meaning that in that sense it does little to alter the *status quo ante*. All the same, a more detailed assessment of this legislation reveals a number of noteworthy points concerning the rules of evidence that can apply in private enforcement proceedings as a matter of secondary EU law.

The first of these points is that the Product Liability Directive could be seen as **9.16**
deviating from the above general rule that this matter is mostly left to the domestic legal systems of the Member States. Its key provision holds that '*[t]he injured person shall be required to prove the damage, the defect and the causal relationship between defect and damage*'.[88] Here, therefore, EU law obviously determines the burden of proof. It would appear, however, that this is more a matter of drafting technique than one of substance. The essence of this provision is to lay down the principle of "strict" liability, which implies that it is

83 Cf. UNIDROIT, Principles of Transnational Civil Procedure (Art. 21).

84 See e.g. Art. 12 Unfair Commercial Practices Directive 2005/29.

85 See e.g. CoJ case C-479/12, *Gautzsch*, para 40–41 (concerning the burden of proof under Community Designs Regulation 6/2002); CoJ case C-405/03, *Class International*, para 73–4 (concerning Trade Marks Directive 2008/95 and Community Trade Mark Regulation 207/2009).

86 On these principles, see subsections 2.A.2 (equivalence) and 2.A.3 (effectiveness) and section 2.B (effective judicial protection) above.

87 See para 2.08 and 2.15 above.

88 Art. 4 Product Liability Directive 85/374.

not of relevance whether the producer of the defective product in question is at fault or not for liability in damages to be incurred under this directive.[89] In this case the EU legislature opted to formulate this in a positive manner by listing the elements that must be proved (and presumably first submitted, although the directive is notably silent on this point) by the applicant for liability to be incurred. A negative formulation, stating that no fault requirement applies, would seem to have been conceivable as well. The Unfair Commercial Practices Directive stipulates, for instance, that a remedy for which that directive provides (in that case injunctive relief) must be available '*even without proof of … intention of negligence on the part of the trader*'.[90] None of this appears as if it is meant to indicate a difference in substance.

In other words, the essence here seems not so much that the *applicant* must demonstrate the elements listed in the above provision. That seems generally presumed. The key is rather that the issue of whether the producer of the defective product is at fault is *irrelevant* and therefore need *not* to be proved (nor presumably first submitted) by the party that brings the private enforcement proceedings. It is similarly, of course, not without relevance that the Product Liability Directive specifies that the *defendant* must prove the existence of the possibly exonerating circumstances listed in this directive, such as the development risk defence.[91] Yet it would again probably be wrong to perceive this as a rule of evidence *per se*. The essence of this provision is rather that under this directive these defences are *available* to the defendant. It seems rather self-evident that it is then for that party to raise such a defence where it wishes to do so and to substantiate its claims in this regard.

9.17 Turning to EU competition law, the Competition Regulation contains a provision on the burden of proof that is relevant not only in public enforcement proceedings, but also for private enforcement cases.[92] It follows from this provision that in legal proceedings before national courts the burden of proving an alleged infringement of Articles 101 or 102 TFEU rests on the private party bringing the claim. It is also stipulated here that it is for the defendant to prove that the applicable conditions are fulfilled where he claims the benefit of Article 101(3) TFEU.[93] This is thus another rather scarce example of EU law providing for a rule of evidence where private enforcement proceedings are concerned. However, all that these rules appear to do is essentially confirm that it is in

89 See para 5.26 above.
90 Art. 11(2) Unfair Commercial Practices Directive 2005/29. See also para 7.31 above.
91 Art. 7 Product Liability Directive 85/374. See para 5.29 above.
92 Art. 2 Competition Regulation 1/2003. See para 6.04 above.
93 On Art. 101(3) TFEU, see further para 6.02 above.

principle for the applicant to demonstrate that there actually was an infringement, whereas the defendant must demonstrate the existence of an exonerating circumstance on which he may wish to rely in this regard. That hardly seems remarkable. That is illustrated by the fact that, although neither Article 102 TFEU itself nor the Competition Regulation expressly provides for such a rule, it remains possible for a defendant to demonstrate that there are objective justifications for an infringement of Article 102 TFEU or that the behaviour in question, on balance, benefits consumers.[94] It can further be noted that under the Competition Regulation, rules on the standard of proof remain to be determined by national law.[95]

Of greater interest for the present purposes are, therefore, the rules of evidence set out in the more recent Competition Damages Directive. This directive relies quite heavily on rules of evidence of various types, designed to alleviate the burden on a private party applicant. Three such rules stand out. First, there are the rules on the *effects of an infringement decision* of a national competition authority (or a review court), pursuant to which the infringements in question are either '*deemed to be irrefutably established*' or those decisions are '*at least prima facie evidence*' that they occurred.[96] Second, in relation to cartel infringements, the directive provides for a *rebuttable presumption* that this infringement caused harm.[97] Third, the directive addresses the issue of possible *passing-on* of the harm in part through establishing certain specific rules of evidence. In short, the passing-on defence is made available to alleged infringers, whereby it is stipulated that in such a case the burden of proof is on the party invoking it.[98] Indirect purchasers are also entitled to bring actions for damages under this directive, in which cases the burden of proving the existence and scope of such a passing-on rests with these parties, as the applicants.[99] However, in those cases an indirect purchaser is '*deemed to have proven*' that a passing-on to him occurred where he has shown that the defendant committed an infringement resulting in an overcharge (that is, a price increase resulting from the infringement) and that he purchased goods or services that were the subject of that infringement.[100] This rule is subject to a possibility for the defendant to '*demonstrate credibly to the satisfaction of the court*' that the overcharge was not or

94 See para 6.03 above.

95 Recital 5 Competition Regulation 1/2003.

96 Art. 9(1) and (2) Competition Damages Directive 2014/104 respectively. This difference depends on whether it concerns a decision by an authority of the same Member State as the one of the national court before which the private enforcement action is brought or rather a decision by an authority from another Member State. See para 6.41 above.

97 Art. 17(2) Competition Damages Directive 2014/104. See para 6.30 and 7.15 above.

98 Art. 13 Competition Damages Directive 2014/104. See para 6.37 above.

99 Art. 14(1) Competition Damages Directive 2014/104. See para 6.38 above.

100 Art. 14(2) Competition Damages Directive 2014/104.

not entirely passed on to the indirect purchasers concerned.[101] This is therefore essentially another (conditional) rebuttable presumption.

9.18 When the present subject matter is considered in a broader perspective, it becomes clear, on the one hand, that the above rules constitute a deviation from the aforementioned tendency of the EU legislature to leave it primarily to the Member States to determine the rules of evidence that apply in private enforcement proceedings before national courts. The IPR Enforcement Directive provides a good illustration of this tendency. In its 2003 proposal for this directive the Commission had, not unlike the Competition Damages Directive, suggested the inclusion of a rather innovative rule of evidence designed to tackle a particular problem, namely the quantification of the recoverable unfair profits made by an infringer.[102] Under this proposed rule the applicant would have had to provide evidence only with regard to the amount of the gross income achieved by the defendant. The latter would then be allowed to submit evidence of its deductible expenses and profits attributable to factors other than the infringement. The EU legislature did not retain this aspect of the proposal, however. As a consequence the IPR Enforcement Directive is largely silent both on this subject matter specifically and on rules of evidence more generally.[103]

On the other hand, it should be acknowledged that the above rules are for the most part not entirely exceptional. The Competition Damages Directive's rule on the passing-on defence resembles, for instance, the rule on the aforementioned development risk defence set out in the Product Liability Directive. As far as issues of evidence are concerned this seems primarily a specific expression of the general rule that the party wishing to rely on an exonerating circumstance must prove the existence thereof. Elsewhere in EU law many other such expressions can be found.[104] And also the manner in which the Product Liability Directive makes clear that a particular element does not need to be proved for liability to be incurred can be found elsewhere.[105] Neither are

101 Ibid.

102 Commission, Proposal for IPR Enforcement Directive 2004/48, COM(2003) 46, pp. 38–9 (Art. 17(2)). See para 4.27 and 7.16 above.

103 Apart from a sporadic reference, such as in Art. 9(3) IPR Enforcement Directive 2004/48.

104 E.g. Art. 23(2) Data Protection Directive 95/46; Art. 5(3) Air Passengers' Rights Regulation 261/2004; Art. 37(1) of Annex I to Rail Passengers' Rights Regulation 1371/2007. See e.g. also Art. 6(9) Consumer Rights Directive 2011/83 and Art. 5(4) Air Passengers' Rights Regulation 261/2004, pursuant to which the burden of proof that certain (information) obligations have been complied with is on the parties to which this obligation applies.

105 See e.g. Art. 2(7) Utilities Remedies Directive 92/13 concerning actions for damages for the costs of preparing the bid and participating in the contract award procedure, discussed in para 3.16 above. Also in this case the essence is not so much that the applicant must prove the elements listed (that is, infringement, real chance,

the above-mentioned rebuttable presumptions unique. Similar rules of EU law already exist in other domains, especially in relation to the issue of fault.[106] A particular example can be found in the Gender Equality Directive, which requires the Member States to ensure, in accordance with their national judicial systems, that when an applicant establishes '*facts from which it may be presumed that there has been direct or indirect discrimination, it shall be for the [defendant] to prove that there has been no breach of the principle of equal treatment*'.[107] It is arguably the Competition Damages Directive's rule on the effects of decisions by national competition authorities in private enforcement proceedings that is most remarkable, as no comparable provision of EU law appears to exist at present. It may therefore not be coincidence that it is precisely this latter rule that proved to be one of the most controversial elements of this directive and that was in the end considerably watered down by the EU legislature.[108]

C. FORUM AND RULES FACILITATING SETTLEMENTS

This third section of Chapter 9 is concerned with the private enforcement rules laid down in EU legislation relating to two additional procedural issues, namely forum (that is, the bodies competent to rule on the private enforcement actions in question) and out-of-court settlements and their facilitation.

1. Forum

It has been set out in Part A above that in the EU legal order the adjudication of claims brought by private parties for infringements of EU law by other private parties is primarily entrusted to national courts.[109] The Court of Justice has consistently held that, in the absence of specific EU rules, it is in principle for each Member State to designate the courts having jurisdiction to rule on such claims and to establish the applicable detailed rules (principle of national **9.19**

causal relationship), but rather what has *not* been listed (that is, that the applicant would actually have won the contract but for the infringement).

106 E.g. Art. 6(1) and (2) Electronic Signatures Directive 1999/93; Art. 20(3) Public Limited Liabilities Companies Directive 2012/30. See also para 7.07 above. Note that for competition cases the Commission had originally suggested providing for a similar rebuttable presumption of fault, allowing the defendant to demonstrate an excusable error. See Commission, White paper on damages actions for breach of the EC antitrust rules, COM(2008) 165, pp. 6–7. See para 7.06 above.

107 Art. 19 Gender Equality Directive 2006/54. See e.g. also Art. 8 Directive 2000/43/EC implementing the principle of equal treatment between persons irrespective of racial or ethnic origin, OJ 2000, L 180/22 ("Racial Equality Directive"). See e.g. CoJ case C-127/92, *Enderby*, para 13–19; CoJ case C-400/93, *Specialarbejderforbundet I Danmark*, para 24.

108 See para 6.41 above.

109 See subsection 1.A.1 above.

procedural autonomy).[110] In particular, the EU law principle of effectiveness can come into play in this connection, for example where a domestic system has been designed in such a manner that it might lead to procedural complications or other disadvantages making it impossible or excessively difficult for a private party to exercise its rights vested in EU law.[111] In addition, the fundamental right to effective judicial protection set out in the Charter implies a general requirement for the national courts concerned to be independent and impartial.[112] Nonetheless, the limits set by EU law in this regard are mostly rather broad.

It appears that the situation is for the most part not fundamentally different where EU legislation of the type assessed in Part B above applies. Issues related to forum generally and the designation of the body competent to decide on the cases brought under this legislation particularly are mostly left to be regulated by the Member States. None of the legal acts in question requires, for instance, the designation of specialised courts or the creation of specialised chambers within the competent national courts. This is the case despite the fact that such an approach is not uncommon at Member State level, for example for public procurement disputes or in relation to competition law infringements.[113] However, this does not mean that rules on forum are entirely absent. On the basis of an assessment of the EU legislation at issue, a distinction can be made between the following two groups of legal acts.

9.20 The first group of legal acts consists of the Product Liability Directive, the IPR Enforcement Directive and the Competition Damages Directive. The former does not touch upon the issue of which body is to rule on the product liability claims brought under this directive. This is, by implication, in principle left to the Member States. The situation is largely similar where the IPR Enforcement Directive is concerned. This directive is marginally more detailed, however, given that at various instances it speaks of '*judicial authorities*'.[114] It can be deduced that the competent bodies should at least be judicial in character, without this having been specified any further, however. The Competition Damages Directive is yet again somewhat more detailed, be it in an indirect manner. For under this latter directive the claims in question are to be brought before a '*national court*', which term has been defined there as a court or tribunal

---

110 See in particular CoJ case 33/76, *Rewe*, para 5. See subsection 2.A.1 above.

111 E.g. CoJ case C-63/01, *Evans*, para 44–58; CoJ case C-268/06, *Impact*, para 51–3. See para 2.08 above.

112 Art. 47 Charter. See para 2.11 and 2.13 above.

113 See para 3.28 and 6.40 above, respectively. See also CoJ joined cases C-295/04 to C-298/04, *Manfredi*, para 70–72.

114 See Art. 6–13 and 15 IPR Enforcement Directive 2004/48.

of a Member State within the meaning of Article 267 TFEU on the preliminary reference procedure.[115] This cross-reference implies that the case law of the Court of Justice regarding Article 267 TFEU is, as it were, "imported". Consequently, while the body competent to rule on the damages claims brought under this directive need not necessarily be judicial in character, when determining whether it qualifies as such, account is taken among other things of whether the body has been established by law, whether it is independent and whether the procedures before it are *inter partes*.[116]

Pursuant to all of the above-mentioned directives belonging to this first group, even if this is not expressly required as a matter of EU law, the presumption is that the actions brought are to be decided by the *civil* courts of the Member States. The Product Liability Directive and the Competition Damages Directive both focus on ensuring compensation in damages. As the Commission noted in connection with the latter directive, '*[a]warding compensation is [...] within the domain of national courts and of civil law and procedure*'.[117] While the IPR Enforcement Directive also provides for other forms of relief, the cases brought under this directive also typically concern disputes between two private parties regarding substantive law that is usually qualified as civil law.[118]

9.21 The second group of legal acts consists of the Procurement Remedies Directives and a number of consumer protection directives other than the Product Liability Directive, notably the Consumer Injunctions Directive, the Unfair Terms Directive and the Unfair Commercial Practices Directive. These directives differ from the above-mentioned ones in that they leave the Member States an express choice when designating the competent forum. They offer the Member States essentially two options.[119]

The first possibility is to designate a body that is *judicial* in character. Whilst this is again not specified in the directives in question, actions under the above-mentioned consumer protection directives are normally to be brought before the *civil* courts.[120] In cases covered by the Procurement Remedies Directives it is not uncommon for Member States to attribute competence to the *administrative* courts or to "split" the jurisdiction between these two types of

115 Art. 2(9) Competition Damages Directive 2014/104. See para 6.40 above.
116 See para 1.02 above.
117 Commission, Proposal for Competition Damages Directive 2014/104, COM(2013) 404, p. 2.
118 See para 4.34 above.
119 Art. 2(9) Procurement Remedies Directives 89/665 and 92/13; Art. 2(1) Consumer Injunctions Directive 2009/22; Art. 7(2) Unfair Terms Directive 93/13; Art. 11(1) Unfair Commercial Practices Directive 2005/29. See e.g. also Art. 5(1) Misleading Advertising Directive 2006/114.
120 See para 510 and 5.13 above.

courts.[121] Either way, again no further specific EU law requirements apply where a Member State decides to designate a judicial body.[122]

However, as an alternative, the above-mentioned directives also allow the Member States to designate a *non-judicial body*. The said consumer protection directives refer in this respect expressly to such a body being an administrative authority. The Procurement Remedies Directives leave it open what sort of body this should be. This can thus be a (non-judicial) administrative authority, but it could, for example, also be an arbitration board. This flexibility probably reflects the already existing wide variety at national level as regards the bodies competent to resolve public procurement disputes. Given that in public procurement cases the defendants are typically (semi-)public bodies and rapid review is a particular concern, in practice many Member States provide for a form of non-judicial review at first instance, mostly before an administrative authority of some sort.[123] The Unfair Terms Directive does not contain any further detailed rules that apply to these non-judicial bodies. But the Procurement Remedies Directives especially, as well as the Unfair Commercial Practices Directive, do go into further detail.[124] The rules set out in these latter directives differ to some extent from each other, yet they have in common that they essentially require that, if not at first instance then at least on appeal, the claims brought are decided by a body that is independent and impartial. They also provide for procedural safeguards such as the right of the parties to be heard and an obligation to provide reasons in writing for the board's decisions. Furthermore, they require that the possibility of making a preliminary reference to the Court of Justice is ensured, if only on appeal.[125] That means that in this case also the relevant requirements set by the Court are "imported" in an indirect manner, as was described in the previous paragraph.

9.22 It follows that in private enforcement-related matters the EU legislature tends to be involved only to a limited extent with issues of forum generally and the

121 See para 3.28 above. Such a "split" is expressly allowed under Art. 2(2) Procurement Remedies Directives 89/665 and 92/13.

122 Cf. CoJ case C-413/12, *ACICL*, para 28–30; CoJ case C-567/13, *Baczó*, para 40 (both concerning Unfair Terms Directive 92/13).

123 See para 3.28 above.

124 Art. 2(9) Procurement Remedies Directives 89/665 and 92/13; Art. 11(3) Unfair Commercial Practices Directive 2005/29. See para 3.28 and 5.13 above, respectively. See e.g. also Art. 5(5) Misleading Advertising Directive 2006/114. As to Consumer Injunctions Directive 2009/22, in light of its recital 9, it arguably requires equivalent standards in cases where a Member State opts to designate a non-judicial body. See para 5.10 above.

125 Under the Unfair Commercial Practices Directive 2005/29 this is implicit in the requirement that appeal to a judicial authority must be possible. In Procurement Remedies Directives 89/665 and 92/13 this requirement is made explicit (see their Art. 2(9)).

designation of the body competent to rule on the actions in question specifically. This is mostly left to be regulated by the Member States. However, it appears that in this context the need felt to regulate these issues varies depending principally on the type of body designated by the Member States to rule on the private enforcement actions in question. Whenever a *judicial body* is designated, regardless of whether it is a civil or an administrative court, the EU legislature appears not to be particularly concerned about the conduct of the proceedings, the precise judicial architecture or safeguards in terms of independence and impartiality and similar issues. Otherwise specific requirements would have been inserted on these points. In none of the instances assessed above was this even proposed, however. Neither did forum-related issues otherwise come up as a particular point of attention in the assessments by the Commission, academic studies or consultations of stakeholders concerning the EU legislation under consideration. This seems to imply that the parties concerned mostly have considerable confidence that these matters can in principle safely be left to be regulated by national law. Such confidence seems, in contrast, not always apparent when the Member States are given the possibility of designating a *non-judicial* body as the forum competent to rule on the private enforcement proceedings in question. In the latter case safeguards in terms of independence and impartiality and fairness of the proceedings are at times (although not always) prescribed as a matter of EU law with a considerable degree of detail.

2. Rules facilitating settlements

Few would contest that reaching an amicable settlement between the parties to a dispute will in many cases be preferable to litigation. Not only may this help save costs, time and energy on the part of the parties concerned, it is also attractive from the perspective of procedural economy.[126] For this reason many national legal systems have been structured in such a manner as to encourage out-of-court settlements to be reached before a final judgment is rendered.[127] Several of the acts of EU legislation on private enforcement under consideration here also seek to do this, with a view to avoiding unnecessary litigation.[128] This occurs essentially in two distinct ways. **9.23**

A first such way is to require the potential private party applicant to first address the opposing party before initiating legal proceedings. While the IPR **9.24**

126 Cf. e.g. European Parliament, Study on collective redress in antitrust, June 2012, p. 76.

127 See e.g. Van Rhee (2005), p. 187; European Parliament, Study on collective redress in antitrust, June 2012, p. 33. See e.g. also CoJ joined cases C-317/08 to C-320/08, *Alassini*, para 64 (regarding the Italian legal system); Bowsher and Moser (2006), p. 196 (regarding the English legal system). See also UNIDROIT, Principles of Transnational Civil Procedure (Art. 23).

128 See also para 11.11 below.

Enforcement Directive, the Product Liability Directive, the Unfair Terms Directive and the Competition Damages Directive do not contain any rules on *pre-trial contacts* of this kind, several of the other directives discussed in Part B above do. The Consumer Injunctions Directive speaks of the possibility of "prior consultation". It provides in essence that Member States may require, before injunction proceedings can be brought, the potential applicant to try to achieve the cessation of the alleged infringement in consultation with the potential defendant (with the possible further involvement of a qualified entity within the meaning of this directive).[129] The Unfair Commercial Practices Directive simply speaks of the possibility to '*require prior recourse to other established means of dealing with complaints*', including those established under industry codes of conduct.[130] Finally, under the Procurement Remedies Directives a private party applicant may be required to first notify the opposing party (that is, the contracting authority concerned) of its intention to seek review.[131]

It is noticeable that these directives providing for this possibility of requiring pre-trial contacts are mostly the same directives that expressly allow for *administrative* review in one form or another, as was discussed in the previous subsection.[132] Conversely, the directives that do not (expressly) contain rules on pre-trial review tend to presume that the cases brought on the basis thereof are to be adjudicated by the competent national *civil* courts.[133] This thus suggests a link between administrative review and requiring the establishment of pre-trial contacts, whereas in relation to proceedings before civil courts such a requirement appears generally not to be deemed appropriate.

9.25 Out-of-court settlements can also be encouraged by providing for mechanisms for *alternative dispute resolution*. This largely serves the same aims as the rules on pre-trial contacts referred to above, but here the presumption is that the parties concerned cannot resolve the dispute by themselves. The intervention of an outside entity, not being a court (or an administrative authority fulfilling a similar function), is thus required. On the whole the EU legislation at issue here touches upon this latter issue only very sparingly. None of the acts such as the IPR Enforcement Directive, the Consumer Injunctions Directive, the Unfair Terms Directive and the Product Liability Directive contains rules related to alternative dispute resolution. As regards public procurement law, the situation

129 Art. 5 Consumer Injunctions Directive 2009/22. See para 5.10 above.

130 Art. 11(1) Unfair Commercial Practices Directive 2005/29. See para 5.13 above.

131 Art. 1(4) Procurement Remedies Directives 89/665 and 92/13. In addition, pursuant to their Art. 1(5), the Member States may also require the private party concerned to first seek *review* with that contracting authority. This possibility of "internal review" is related to the fact that in public procurement disputes the defendant tends to be a (semi-)public body. See para 3.28 above.

132 See para 9.21 above.

133 See para 9.20 above.

is somewhat mixed. On the one hand, in 2007 the "conciliation procedure" for which one of the two Procurement Remedies Directives provided and which was meant to facilitate the out-of-court resolution of disputes was abolished.[134] On the other hand, as has been discussed above, these directives' rules on forum have been drafted in such a manner that, subject to certain conditions, they allow for cases to be decided by review bodies other than courts or administrative authorities, such as arbitration boards.[135]

The interest at EU level for facilitating alternative dispute resolution seems to be increasing, however. This is illustrated by two more recent developments. First, in 2013 the Consumer ADR Directive was adopted.[136] This directive seeks to ensure that EU-wide in all economic sectors alternative dispute resolution procedures are available for consumer disputes. These procedures are to be easily accessible and should offer adequate safeguards in terms of independence, impartiality and speed, among other things. Second, the 2014 Competition Damages Directive contains rules on consensual dispute settlement (covering alternative dispute settlement as well as out-of-court settlements between the parties). Yet while these rules clearly aim to encourage and facilitate these forms of dispute resolution, this directive does not require the establishment of nor regulate these mechanisms as such. Rather the Competition Damages Directive is concerned with the *effects* of such settlements and the attempts to reach them on the legal proceedings covered by the directive.[137]

As a first additional observation the *optional nature* of the above provisions of EU law can be noted. This comes to light in two distinct ways for each of the two types of measures discussed above. In the first place, where pre-trial contacts are concerned the said provisions essentially establish an option for the *Member States*. EU law does not require potential applicants to establish such contracts with a view to exploring the possibility of an amicable settlement. Rather this decision is left to each individual Member State, the EU legislation in question merely making it explicit that such a requirement is not precluded as a matter of EU law.[138] However, where a Member State has chosen to exercise **9.26**

134 See para 3.30 above.

135 See para 5.28 and 9.21 above.

136 Consumer ADR Directive 2013/11. See para 5.42 above.

137 Art. 18–19 Competition Damages Directive 2014/104. See para 6.43 above.

138 Note that this does not necessarily mean that, where this has *not* been made explicit in the EU legislation at issue, the Member States are *precluded* from imposing a requirement to establish pre-trial contacts between the parties on the basis of ("purely") national law. The main difference is that in the latter situation discussion could arise as to whether the requirement is compatible with the objectives of the EU legislation at issue and, where relevant, the principles of equivalence, effectiveness and effective judicial protection, discussed in subsections 2.A.2 and 2.A.3 and section 2.B above, respectively.

this option, the private party concerned will normally be bound by it in accordance with the applicable rules of national law.

In the second place, concerning alternative dispute resolution the Consumer ADR Directive does not leave the Member States any choice, however, in that they are required to take certain measures to facilitate the out-of-court settlement of disputes.[139] But under this directive the use of these mechanisms is optional for the *private party* concerned. The mechanisms established under this directive are to be used by consumers on a voluntary basis.[140] That is also the most common situation where ("purely") national law provides for procedural rules of this kind.[141] The outcome of the alternative dispute resolution process is, moreover, not necessarily binding on the parties concerned.[142] In connection with the Competition Damages Directive, the Commission similarly expressly rejected the option of *obliging* a private party to make an attempt to settle the dispute in an alternative manner.[143] As was noted above, the rules in question remain limited to encouraging and facilitating consensual dispute resolution.

It follows that EU legislation on private enforcement can seek to encourage and facilitate out-of-court settlements and alternative dispute resolution, *inter alia* through allowing for a legal requirement to first address the opposing party, but it does not provide for an obligation to first submit the matter to a third party such as an alternative dispute resolution body.[144]

9.27 A second additional observation is that the EU legislature appears to have been aware of some of the *possible disadvantages* associated with encouraging pre-trial contacts and alternative dispute resolution in the ways described above. Most notably, such efforts will inevitably lead to certain delays, which in turn could have further adverse consequences, particularly for potential applicants. Most of the above-mentioned directives seek to address the risks in this regard, albeit in different ways. The Consumer Injunctions Directive sets a maximum time period for the duration of the prior consultations between the parties. It provides that the private party concerned is free to bring an action without further delay if no cessation of the infringement has been achieved within two

139 Even if the Member States are left considerable discretion as regards the manner in which they give effect to their obligations under this directive. See e.g. Art. 5(3) and (4) Consumer ADR Directive 2013/11.

140 Art. 1 Consumer ADR Directive 2013/11.

141 See para 5.41 above.

142 See e.g. also points 25–26 Collective Redress Recommendation 2013/396. See para 5.38 above.

143 Commission, Impact assessment report on damages actions for breach of the EU antitrust rules, SWD(2013) 203, p. 35.

144 This is also what would appear to follow from CoJ case C-410/01, *Fritsch*, para 28–34; CoJ joined cases C-317/08 to C-320/08, *Alassini*, para 52–60. See para 3.25 and 2.08 above, respectively.

weeks after the reception of the request for consultation. The Procurement Remedies Directives seek especially to prevent delays that might allow the disputed public contract to be concluded in the meantime or which may lead to the applicant being time-barred. The aforementioned obligation to notify therefore does not affect the standstill period during which the contracting authority may not conclude the contract and neither does it affect any other time limits for review.[145] The Competition Damages Directive similarly provides that limitation periods for initiating legal proceedings are to be suspended for the duration of the consensual dispute resolution process.[146] The latter also empowers national courts to suspend the legal proceedings where they have already started, subject to a maximum of two years.[147]

These rules all essentially give effect to the view that a private party affected by an alleged infringement should not be adversely affected when making use of mechanisms that aim to facilitate an amicable settlement of the dispute at hand.[148] However, the EU legislature appears to still have a somewhat narrow perception of the possible disadvantages referred to above. Especially for consumers, it may not always be easy to prove that they contacted the opposing party before initiating legal proceedings and thus meet a requirement to this effect that may apply.[149] This concern remains unaddressed in the above-mentioned directives. In addition, it is noticeable the Court of Justice seems to take a broader view when assessing national rules providing for recourse to consensual dispute settlement procedures under the principles of effectiveness and effective judicial protection. In this context the Court has looked at whether any such arrangement leads to significant disadvantages for the applicant not only in terms of possible delays and the legal consequences that this may have, but also in light of other practical or legal factors that may be relevant, such as additional costs.[150]

To this one can also add that when this subject matter is considered more generally, it emerges that out-of-court settlements and alternative dispute resolution are not to be assessed necessarily only in positive terms.[151] Resolving

145 On these limitation periods and this standstill period, see para 3.26 and 3.27 above, respectively. Similarly, these directives require that the aforementioned prior "internal review" involves the immediate suspension of the possibility of concluding the contract.

146 Art. 18(1) Competition Damages Directive 2014/104. See e.g. also point 27 Collective Redress Recommendation 2013/396, discussed in para 5.38 above.

147 Art. 17(2) Competition Damages Directive 2014/104.

148 Cf. GC case T-407/07, *CMB Maschinenbau*, para 103.

149 Loos (2011), pp. 493–4.

150 CoJ case C-63/01, *Evans*, para 44–58; CoJ joined cases C-317/08 to C-320/08, *Alassini*, para 52–66. See para 2.08 and 2.13 above, respectively.

151 For a more detailed assessment from an economic perspective and for further references, see Study, CEPS, Erasmus University Rotterdam and LUISS (2007), pp. 138–50.

disputes in this manner typically relies on negotiations between the directly interested parties behind closed doors, whether or not with the help of a third party such as a mediator. That is, however, for instance generally at odds with the main aims of transparency and competition pursued by the EU public procurement rules.[152] The Procurement Remedies Directives would not reach their underlying aim of strengthening compliance with substantive EU public procurement law if an out-of-court settlement were to lead to an agreement, pursuant to which an aggrieved private party drops its claim in return for the contracting authority awarding it a future contract without competitive tendering. Likewise for the parties directly concerned by a competition law-related dispute, settling the dispute is the dominant objective and not ensuring compliance with the law or contributing to effective competition. There is, therefore, a risk that such settlements are not desirable from a competition policy point of view, if not outright anticompetitive.[153] In order to address these kinds of risks, the rules applicable to alternative dispute resolution in particular may include a requirement that any agreement reached must be in accordance with EU law or that interested third parties are allowed to intervene, as was the case for the "conciliation procedure" that used to be available at EU level for the amicable settlement of public procurement disputes.[154] However, this requirement may well have been among the reasons why this procedure generated so little interest in practice that it was abolished in 2007. The 2013 Collective Redress Recommendation now contains a comparable provision.[155] It is notable in this connection that "alternative dispute resolvers" are not necessarily obliged to apply the law when solving the dispute at hand.[156] And even when they do, it is not evident that they are always best placed to do so. For even where the amounts at issue may be small, the legal questions raised can be complex, while the option of referring preliminary questions to the Court of Justice under Article 267 TFEU in order to obtain guidance and ensure the uniform interpretation of EU law is in principle not available in those cases.[157] Finally, the fact that out-of-court settlements and the outcomes of alternative dispute resolution are almost by definition not transparent means that they generally do not act as precedents, do not contribute to the development of the law and do not serve purposes of general deterrence in the same manner as court judgments generally do.[158]

---

152 Cf. Trepte (2007), pp. 373–4 and 376–7. See also Arrowsmith (2005), p. 1435; Caranta (2011a), p. 84.

153 See further Wils (2003a), p. 483; Wilsher (2006), p. 35; Milutinovic (2010), pp. 242 and 356.

154 Art. 10(4) and Art. 11 Utilities Remedies Directive 92/13, as they stood before 2007. See para 3.30 above.

155 Point 28 Collective Redress Recommendation 2013/396. See para 5.38 above. See also Hondius (2009), p. 242.

156 Wagner (2014), p. 177 (concerning Consumer ADR Directive 2013/11, discussed in para 5.42 above).

157 Ibid., pp. 178–9. On Art. 267 TFEU, see para 1.02 above.

158 Cf. Jacobs and Deisenhofer (2003), p. 196.

D. JUDICIAL REVIEW

This fourth and last section of Chapter 9 addresses two issues related to the judicial review that the competent national courts are to exercise in private enforcement proceedings governed by EU law of the type at issue in this book. The first of these two issues is the standard of judicial review, whereas the second is the scope for those courts to assess certain elements of EU law of their own motion. Both issues are subsequently discussed in the two subsections below.

1. Standard of judicial review

In a sense, a discussion of the standard of judicial review to be applied by the national court in cases brought under the EU legislation assessed in Part B above can be very short indeed, given that no express requirements whatsoever have been set out therein. None of the legal acts in question expressly addresses this issue with any degree of detail. At most, some very general references can be found, for instance where the Competition Damages Directive refers to something having to be demonstrated '*credibly to the satisfaction of the court*'.[159] Neither have any provisions of EU law on this subject matter providing for a degree of detail been proposed or even seriously discussed in relation to this legislation. There is, however, some case law available from which certain indications might be deduced as to what is required from the national courts in this respect as a matter of EU law. **9.28**

Most notably, in *Hospital Ingenieure* the Court of Justice expanded on the standard of judicial review to be applied under the Procurement Remedies Directives.[160] In this case the defendant (a contracting authority) had decided to withdraw an invitation to tender after several private parties had already submitted a bid. One of these parties contested this decision, arguing that it was discriminatory. A question that emerged in the resulting litigation was whether the review exercised by the national court seised could be limited to whether or not the contested decision was arbitrary. The Court of Justice held that, in light of their objective, the scope of the judicial review exercised in cases brought under the Procurement Remedies Directives cannot be interpreted restrictively. Even where the contracting authority has a wide discretion, it must be possible to verify the compatibility of such a decision with the relevant substantive EU public procurement rules. According to the Court, in the absence of any indications to the contrary, the letter and the spirit of the Procurement **9.29**

159 Art. 14(2) Competition Damages Directive 2014/104. See para 6.38 above.

160 CoJ case C-92/00, *Hospital Ingenieure*, para 57–64. See also CoJ case C-440/13, *Croce Amica One Italia*, para 38–46.

Remedies Directives do not, therefore, permit the conclusion that the Member States can limit the review of the legality of a contested decision to whether or not it is arbitrary. Without using these words, the Court thus appeared to consider that these directives preclude what is sometimes referred to as "marginal" judicial review by the competent national court.

9.30 There is other case law that relates to situations where EU law is alleged to have been infringed but where no specific secondary EU law facilitating private enforcement applies. In these situations the standard of judicial review provided for under national law is to be assessed where relevant under the EU law principles of equivalence, effectiveness and effective judicial protection.[161] An example of a case where the Court of Justice made such an assessment is the 1999 *Upjohn* ruling.[162] This case concerned the judicial review of national decisions revoking marketing authorisation for certain medicinal products, which was a matter that was deemed to require complex assessments. The Court found in essence that a national rule providing that the decisions in question were not subject to "full" judicial review, whereby the national court seised substitutes its own assessment of the facts and of the scientific evidence for the contested assessment made by the competent national authorities, did not infringe the principle of effectiveness.

It is noticeable that in reaching this conclusion the Court drew a parallel with the review by the *EU courts* of decisions taken by the EU institutions and bodies involving complex assessments. In the latter context it has consistently been held that the judicial review exercised does not entail a "full" review in the aforementioned sense, at least as regards matters in relation to which the EU institutions concerned have discretion. In those cases the EU courts typically restrict themselves to examining the accuracy of the findings of facts and law as well as to verifying that the contested decision is not vitiated by a manifest error or a misuse of powers and that the bounds of discretion have not clearly been exceeded.[163] *Upjohn* thus seems to imply that the review exercised by the national courts seised in cases such as the ones at issue there need only be

161 On these principles generally, see subsections 2.A.2 (equivalence) and 2.A.3 (effectiveness) and section 2.B (effective judicial protection) above.

162 CoJ case C-120/97, *Upjohn*, para 30–37. See also CoJ case C-55/06, *Arcor*, para 170.

163 See ibid., para 34, for further references. As regards the standard of judicial review in relation to the principles of subsidiarity and proportionality and the fundamental rights guaranteed under the Charter, see also subsection 10.A.2 below. Note that, as was touched upon in para 2.13 above, a stricter test applies in legal proceedings involving the imposition of penalties for infringements of the EU competition rules.

modestly intrusive as a matter of EU law. Indeed this ruling has been understood as the Court having declined an invitation to raise the standards of judicial review across the EU.[164]

It is not immediately evident how the two above-mentioned rulings relate to each other and consequently which broader conclusions can be drawn from them. Whereas it appears to follow from *Hospital Ingenieure* that "marginal" review is insufficient, *Upjohn* implies that "full" judicial review is not required. The existence of discretion on the part of the body that had taken the contested decision might be a relevant factor, but this is unlikely to explain the difference in outcome in these two cases.[165] One view is therefore that what the Court of Justice required in *Hospital Ingenieure* was something more than a mere marginal (arbitrariness) review, but without necessarily entailing full review of the sort at issue in *Upjohn*. Such a "middle way" in terms of the intensity of the review exercised by a national court may well be conceivable. This is largely speculative, however, especially because any positive indication of what may be required under the Procurement Remedies Directives was entirely absent in *Hospital Ingenieure*. This also leaves open the question of whether it makes any substantial difference whether or not secondary EU law of the type at issue here applies. **9.31**

A possible alternative reading of these two rulings is that under the Procurement Remedies Directives a higher standard of judicial review is required than the one that would apply in "ordinary" cases where no secondary EU law of this kind applies and that are therefore to be assessed under the aforementioned EU law principles. If this latter reading is correct, it would basically seem to be the *mere existence* of such secondary EU law – and in particular the need to safeguard the objective that it seeks to achieve – that implies that such a higher standard is required. After all, the Procurement Remedies Directives do not contain any express provisions on the issue of the standard of judicial review. This reading would then also seem to suggest that the Court of Justice may well come to conclusions similar to the one reached in *Hospital Ingenieure* when interpreting the other EU legislation under consideration here. For none of these acts expressly addresses the issue of the standard of judicial review to be

164 Tridimas (2001), p. 82.

165 In *Hospital Ingenieure* the contested decision concerned a matter where, pursuant to national law, the contracting authority enjoyed a wide discretion, which the CoJ appeared to accept. This therefore does not seem to set this case apart from *Upjohn*. Moreover, according to the approach consistently followed by the EU courts, in cases where the EU institutions themselves act as contracting authorities, they enjoy a broad margin of assessment and the judicial review is consequently limited. See e.g. GC case T-407/07, *CMB Machinenbau*, para 115–16; GC case T-461/08, *Europaïki Dynamiki*, para 100 and 137.

applied either, whereas the overall objectives pursued by this legislation are largely comparable.[166]

Therefore, even if the EU legislature has thus far not expressly addressed the issue of the standard of judicial review that applies in a private enforcement case, the Court of Justice has occasionally acknowledged its importance. While the case law available to date seems insufficient to draw any firm conclusions as to the question of precisely which EU law requirements apply in this regard, it can safely be said that this absence of express EU rules does not necessarily mean that no such requirements apply.

2. Own-motion judicial review

9.32 Another judicial review-related question is whether as a matter of EU law a national court seised in a private enforcement action may or must raise of its own motion (*ex officio*) – thus without one of the parties to the dispute having done so – certain points of EU law that may be relevant for deciding the case at hand. An in-depth assessment of this complex and seemingly not yet fully settled matter falls outside the scope of this book.[167] Nonetheless, this question has come up regularly in relation to the EU legislation discussed in Part B above. Indeed, the Court's most remarkable line of case law on this subject matter has been issued in relation to some of this legislation. A brief consideration is therefore appropriate.

9.33 In this regard three general points should be noted at the outset. To begin with, under the domestic laws of most Member States national courts have generally been assigned a *passive role* in legal proceedings between private parties.[168] Although there are certain differences between these laws, it is principally left to the parties to the proceedings to "frame" the dispute and to submit the relevant legal arguments to support their respective claims. As the Court of Justice has noted, this reflects prevailing conceptions concerning the relations between the state and the individual, it safeguards the rights of defence and it

166 See in particular para 10.03 below. One such difference that may be relevant in this connection is that the review exercised under Procurement Remedies Directives 89/665 and 92/13 typically concerns acts by (semi-)public bodies and not acts of other private parties, which in turn can imply, depending on the domestic legal system, that the relevant cases are to be brought before administrative, rather than civil, courts. See also para 3.28 above.

167 For further references on this subject matter specifically in relation to Unfair Terms Directive 93/13, see para 5.19 above. On this subject matter more generally, see Ancery (2012); Lenaerts, Maselis and Gutman (2014), pp. 131–136; Snijders (2014), p. 95.

168 For an overview, see Van Rhee (2005), pp. 189–93. See also Stuyck (2011), p. 513. Cf. UNIDROIT, Principles of Transnational Civil Procedure (Art. 10(1)).

ensures the proper conduct of proceedings.[169] This does not mean that this passive role is absolute, however. Most notably, in many jurisdictions the courts seised are required to raise of their own motion points of law that are considered to be of fundamental importance and therefore a matter of public policy (*d'ordre public*). That is also the situation before the EU courts, where proceedings are also in principle *inter partes*. These latter courts are, however, required to raise of their own motion certain matters of public policy, such as a failure to state reasons for a contested decision. But unless the parties to the proceedings raise these points, they do not verify, for instance, whether an action brought is time-barred or whether a contested decision is compatible with EU competition law.[170]

A second preliminary remark is that the secondary EU law under consideration here does *not expressly oblige* these courts to deviate from the above-mentioned general rules established on the basis of the domestic laws of the Member States. The question of whether such own-motion judicial review is possible, precluded or obligatory as a matter of EU law is simply *not addressed* in any of the legal acts in question. It appears that the same applies for most (if not all) other acts of secondary EU law.[171]

A third and last point concerns the case law of the Court of Justice considered at a general level. It appears to follow from this case law that, as a general rule, EU law does *not require* national courts to abandon the predominantly passive role assigned to them on the basis of national law either.[172] However, the EU law principle of *equivalence* in particular can require a deviation from this general rule in certain cases.[173] It follows from this principle that, when a national court must raise certain rules of its own motion pursuant to national law, it must also raise comparable rules of EU law. Straightforward as this may sound, this principle has sometimes led to rather extensive interpretation in the present context. On occasion the Court has ruled that the particular role of the concept of public policy – which, as was noted above, in many national legal systems requires courts to abandon their passive role – can oblige these courts to

169 CoJ joined cases C-430/93 and C-431/93, *Van Schijndel*, para 21; CoJ joined cases C-222/05 and C-225/05, *Van der Weerd*, para 35.

170 Cf. e.g. CoJ case 20/88, *Roquette frères*, para 12; CoJ case C-386/10 P, *Chalkor*, para 64–6; CoJ case C-510/11 P, *Kone*, para 30–32; CoJ case C-224/12 P, *Netherlands v Commission*, para 97. See, however, also CoJ case C-530/12 P, *OHIM v National Lottery Commission*, para 44–5.

171 Cf. Storskrubb (2008), p. 232, who argues that the role assigned to national courts under Small Claims Regulation 861/2007 in assisting applicants fundamentally changes their traditionally passive role. See also point 9 Collective Redress Recommendation 2013/396.

172 CoJ case 70/77, *Simmenthal*, para 10; CoJ joined cases C-430/93 and C-431/93, *Van Schijndel*, para 16–22; CoJ joined cases C-222/05 and C-225/05, *Van der Weerd*, para 28; CoJ case C-2/06, *Kempter*, para 45.

173 On this principle, see further subsection 2.A.2 above.

intervene of their own motion where EU law is at stake. It reached this conclusion by stressing in particular the fundamental nature and importance of the EU rules at issue.[174] By insisting on a broad interpretation of the (national law) concept of public policy under the principle of equivalence, an "indirect" route to an obligation to raise certain points of EU law has thus been construed. This is necessarily limited, however, to situations where national law provides for an obligation for courts to raise issues of public policy of their own motion in the first place. Where national law does not provide for such a rule, there is no scope for reaching similar findings on the basis of the principle of equivalence.

9.34 Turning more in detail to the fields of law assessed in the foregoing, even if the rules of secondary EU law do not provide any express obligations in this regard, an assessment of three key cases relating to the present subject matter nonetheless exposes certain notable differences. First, there is the *GAT* case concerning EU public procurement law.[175] In this case the Court of Justice ruled in essence that it is for the domestic legal system of each Member State to determine whether and in which circumstances a national court seised in an action brought under the Procurement Remedies Directives may raise of its own motion an infringement of EU law. It was found that neither the objective of these directives nor any of their specific provisions precludes a rule of national law pursuant to which that court is to raise such points of its own motion. The Court added, however, that under these directives an action for damages *cannot be dismissed* on the ground, raised on the court's own motion, that the contract award procedure had anyway been unlawful (and that therefore no damages were due for lack of causality). For this would be incompatible with the directives' objectives of ensuring rapid and effective review for aggrieved private parties.

This ruling thus seems to contrast with the case law in the fields of EU consumer protection law (in particular the Unfair Terms Directive) and EU competition law (in particular Article 101 TFEU). As regards the former, the Court held in the *Océano Grupo* case law, in essence, that a national court seised is in principle *obliged* to raise of its own motion the unfairness of a term in a consumer contract, so as to ensure that consumers are given effective protection.[176] In this respect the Court pointed to the often weak position of consumers and the nature and importance of the public interest underlying consumer protection in the EU legal order. As regards the latter, even if at the

174 E.g. CoJ case C-126/97, *Eco Swiss*, para 36–9; CoJ case C-40/08, *Asturcom*, para 49–55. Underlying this issue is the question of how the CoJ approaches concepts of "public policy" (*d'ordre public*) and "mandatory rules". See further Prechal (1998), pp. 689–705; Snijders (2009), pp. 142–5; Schebesta (2010), pp. 864–77.

175 CoJ case C-315/01, *GAT*, para 46–55. See para 3.19 above.

176 CoJ joined cases C-240/98 and C-244/98, *Océano Grupo*, para 22–9. See para 5.19 and 5.20 above.

time no particular secondary EU law comparable with the above-mentioned directives applied (given that the Competition Damages Directives had not yet been adopted), in *Eco Swiss* the Court confirmed the existence of a similar obligation, at least in relation to the proceedings for the annulment of an arbitration award that were at issue in that case.[177] In this context the Court noted *inter alia* the fundamental importance attributed to the EU rules at issue, which contributed to the conclusion that the matters under consideration in that case were to be considered as constituting matters of public policy that, as was explained above, a national court may have to raise of its own motion.[178]

The next question is what *explains* the differences that seem apparent when comparing the above case law. It may be tempting to conclude that consumer protection law and competition law are to be considered of exceptional importance in the EU legal order and that therefore these points of law must be raised by a national court of its own motion, whereas the same would not – or at least not necessarily or to the same extent – apply in relation to other fields of law such as public procurement law. However, this view does not seem to provide a satisfactory explanation. To start with, even if the above case law certainly makes it clear that the nature and importance of the EU rules at issue can be a relevant factor, as it stands it hardly allows for such an unambiguous conclusion.[179] At least for now many uncertainties remain, especially in terms of the precise legal basis for imposing such an obligation on national courts in the said cases. Moreover, EU public procurement law is rooted in the EU Treaties' fundamental freedoms, notably those of establishment and to provide services.[180] This makes it unlikely that these rules should somehow be deemed "less fundamental" than EU law on consumer protection and competition. **9.35**

It is submitted that the different approaches and outcomes in the three above-mentioned rulings can probably be better explained in another way. Three points should be noted in this regard. First, the questions referred differed. In *GAT* the Court of Justice was asked whether EU law *precluded* review of the national court's own motion. Even if the subsequent considerations by the Court were formulated in general terms, they should arguably still be understood in that light. That means that it is not excluded that in other public procurement cases the Court will rule that EU law *requires* such

177 CoJ case C-126/97, *Eco Swiss*, para 36–41. See para 6.05 above.

178 It remains to be clarified whether this finding can simply be transposed to cases that do not concern proceedings for the annulment of an arbitration award, especially considering the different nature of the concept of public policy. See para 6.05 above. In this connection it can also be noted that in legal proceedings before the EU courts, possible infringements of EU competition law are not considered as a matter of public policy that must be raised of the court's own motion. See para 9.33 above.

179 Cf. Opinion AG Poiares Maduro, joined cases C-222/05 to C-225/05, *Van der Weerd*, para 27–9.

180 See para 3.02 and 3.03 above.

own-motion review, as it did in *Océano Grupo* and *Eco Swiss*. Second, in *GAT* the Court may have stressed that this question is to be settled primarily in accordance with national law, but it nonetheless superimposed certain EU law requirements, derived from the need to safeguard the objective of the EU legislation in question. In that sense the difference between *GAT*, on the one hand, and *Océano Grupo* and *Eco Swiss*, on the other hand, might be more cosmetic than fundamental. Third and probably most importantly, in each of the three above-mentioned cases the relevant EU law requirements appeared to serve primarily the protection of the rights of the private parties initiating the legal proceedings. From this perspective, the principal difference between these cases is that this very same consideration argued *in favour* of active judicial intervention as a matter of EU law in *Océano Grupo* and *Eco Swiss*, whereas in the specific factual circumstances of *GAT* it argued *against* it (given that in this latter case an *ex officio* finding of an *earlier* infringement could mean that the damages claim at issue was to be dismissed).

The fact that the reasoning and the conclusions reached differed in the three above-mentioned rulings should therefore not distract from the fundamental objective that the Court of Justice consistently seeks to achieve, namely the *effective protection of rights* that private parties derive from EU law in proceedings before national courts. The Court has long insisted on this being one of the key tasks of the national courts in the EU legal order.[181] This consideration also underpins its position that, where national law provides for discretion for the court to raise points of its own motion, this should be understood as an obligation where points of EU law are concerned.[182] This reading is moreover consistent with other cases where similar issues emerged. Most notably, in *Heemskerk* it was found that, at least in situations where the principle of no *reformatio in pejus* is enshrined in national procedural law, a national court is not obliged to raise issues of EU law of its own motion where this would have the effect of leaving the private party applicant worse off than if he had not done so.[183] The Court made it clear in this case that this applies even where this may lead to negative consequences for certain matters of general interest protected by EU law (in the case at hand: animal welfare and the EU's financial interests).

181 E.g. CoJ case 106/77, *Simmenthal*, para 16; CoJ Opinion 1/09, *Patent Court Agreement*, para 66 and 68. Note that here the emphasis tends to be on the rights of the private party *applicant*. Where the *defendant* is also a private party, the latter's rights (which may or may not derive from EU law) typically receive less attention. See para 11.22 below.

182 CoJ joined cases C-430/93 and C-431/93, *Van Schijndel*, para 13–14; CoJ case C-72/95, *Kraaijeveld*, para 58; CoJ joined cases C-222/05 and C-225/05, *Van der Weerd*, para 29–32; CoJ case C-40/08, *Asturcom*, para 54.

183 CoJ case C-455/06, *Heemskerk*, para 44–8. See further Geursen (2009), p. 131. See e.g. also CoJ case C-87/90, *Verholen*, para 11–16; CoJ case C-18/13, *Maks Pen*, para 33–9.

The conclusion here is therefore to some extent comparable with the one formulated with respect to the judicial review-related issues considered in the previous subsection. That is to say, while it is clear that the EU legislation under consideration does not expressly address the question of whether and, if so, in which circumstances a national court may or must raise certain points of EU law of its own motion (*ex officio*), it is equally clear from the relevant case law that at least in some instances this issue can nonetheless be of considerable importance. Also in this regard this case law tends to be casuistic and not always unambiguous, however, meaning that several issues still remain to be fully clarified. It would nonetheless appear that it is not primarily the nature or importance of the EU law at stake that underlies the imposition of certain EU law requirements relating to own-motion judicial review. Rather, apart from applications of the principle of equivalence, the central unifying factor behind the Court's case law appears to be its desire to ensure the effective protection of the rights of private parties derived from EU law in private enforcement proceedings before national courts. **9.36**

Part D

BROADER ASPECTS, PERSPECTIVES AND CONCLUSIONS

10

THE HOW, WHEN AND WHY OF EU LEGISLATION ON PRIVATE ENFORCEMENT

One could say that the three foregoing chapters that together made up Part C of this book were essentially concerned with the question of how the private enforcement of EU law is facilitated by the EU legislature in terms of remedies and procedural provisions. The present chapter, as the first of the three chapters of the final part of this book, considers a number of broader aspects that emerge in this connection. The questions addressed here can be summarised as the how (understood more broadly), when and why EU legislation facilitates private enforcement of EU law. More specifically, it is first assessed from a *legal* perspective what is the EU legislature's scope to enact secondary law of the type at issue here. Attention then turns to the *political* and *policy* aspects and facilitating factors that can be of relevance in this respect. The questions addressed are thus essentially whether the EU has the legal empowerment and a sufficient policy reason as well as the necessary political will to enact legislative measures related to the private enforcement of EU law. Next, the added value of these legislative measures is considered, particularly as compared with legislative inaction at EU level. In the last subsection of this chapter, the how of the EU legislation at issue is re-assessed, this time particularly in terms of coherence and fragmentation. Chapter 11 seeks to "zoom out" even further and put in perspective the phenomenon of private enforcement generally and EU legislation on this subject matter specifically. Finally, Chapter 12 summarises the main findings and conclusions based on the foregoing.

A. THE EU'S LEGAL SCOPE TO ACT

An important question from a legal perspective when considering the EU legislation on private enforcement at issue here, more generally, is that of the EU legislature's scope to act under the EU Treaties. In this connection, three specific issues are addressed in the subsections below. First, there is the question of the legal basis for the EU to act in this regard. Second, the legal constraints on the EU associated with the principles of subsidiarity and proportionality and the fundamental rights guaranteed in the Charter are assessed. Finally, the significance of the principle of national procedural autonomy in the present context is (re-)considered.

1. Legal basis issues

10.01 Of fundamental – and indeed constitutional[1] – importance in relation to the EU's scope to legislate on a particular subject matter is the question of whether and, if so, to what extent the EU Treaties contain a sufficient legal basis for the intended act. That applies for the adoption of secondary EU law generally and it certainly also applies in the present context. The importance and sensitivity of this question in relation to private enforcement-related EU legislation is illustrated by the critical comments that have been made in relation to possible legislative action on matters such as collective redress and the private enforcement of EU competition law.[2]

The requirement of a legal basis derives from the principle of conferral. Pursuant to this principle, the EU can act only within the competences conferred upon it by the Member States in the EU Treaties to attain the objectives set out therein.[3] Competences not conferred upon the EU remain with the Member States.[4] The EU Treaties list and categorise the areas of EU competence.[5] In accordance with this general distribution of competences, many particular legal bases have been set out throughout these Treaties. Each act of secondary EU law needs to be rooted in such a legal basis. In most cases the legal bases provided for concern a specific sector or subject matter, such as the protection of personal data, the establishment of a common agricultural policy or the pursuit of certain environmental objectives.[6] Where a legal basis for a particular legal act is lacking or where it is exceeded, that act is open to

1 See e.g. GC joined cases T-458/10 to T-467/10 and T-471/10, *McBride*, para 25.
2 See para 5.37 and 6.19 above, respectively.
3 Art. 4(1) TEU.
4 Art. 5(2) TEU.
5 Art. 2–5 TFEU.
6 See Art. 16(2), Art. 43(2) and Art. 192 TFEU, respectively.

being annulled by the Court of Justice.[7] It is settled case law that the choice of legal basis must be based on objective factors that are amenable to judicial review and that include in particular the aim and the content of the intended legislative measure in question.[8]

Two partial exceptions aside, the legal basis used for all private enforcement-related EU legislation assessed in Part B above is Article 114 TFEU. The Procurement Remedies Directives, the IPR Enforcement Directive, the Consumer Injunctions Directive and the Unfair Terms Directive have all been adopted on the basis of this article.[9] The first partial exception is the Product Liability Directive, which has been adopted under Article 115 TFEU. This does not constitute a divergence that is of further relevance here, however, as the differences in terms of substance between Article 114 and 115 TFEU are limited and the use of this latter article is because of the fact that Article 114 TFEU did not exist at the time that the Product Liability Directive was proposed and adopted.[10] That is illustrated by the fact that the subsequent amendment of this directive in 1999 was based on Article 114 TFEU.[11] The other partial exception is the Competition Damages Directive, as this directive rests on a dual legal basis, namely not on Article 114 alone but also on Article 103 TFEU. The background of the addition of this latter article in this particular case has already been discussed.[12] **10.02**

Article 114 TFEU empowers the EU legislature to '*adopt the measures for the approximation of the provisions laid down by law, regulation or administrative action in Member States which have as their object the establishment and functioning of the internal market*'. This illustrates that, notwithstanding the fact that the EU is mostly empowered to enact secondary law in relation to specific sectors or subject matter, the EU Treaties sometimes confer powers in a more broadly formulated manner. That does not imply, however, that the powers conferred on the EU under this article are unlimited. As is evident from its wording, Article 114 TFEU requires in particular a link with the EU's internal market. In its

7 See Art. 263 TFEU as regards "direct actions" before the EU courts. Its second subparagraph specifies that one of the grounds for annulment is a lack of competence. An "indirect" route for establishing the invalidity of secondary EU law is the preliminary reference procedure set out in Art. 267 TFEU, discussed in para 1.02 above.

8 E.g. CoJ case C-155/91, *Commission v Council*, para 7; CoJ case C-440/05, *Commission v Council*, para 61; CoJ case C-301/06, *Ireland v Parliament and Council*, para 60.

9 See para 3.05, 3.06, 4.06, 5.05 and 5.14 above, respectively.

10 Article 114 TFEU was not inserted in the EU Treaties until 1987 (through the Single European Act). To the extent relevant in the present context, Art. 114 and 115 TFEU are mostly worded in a similar manner, a key difference being that the former article allows for the adoption of legislation by qualified majority voting instead of the unanimity required under the latter article.

11 See Product Liability Amending Directive 1999/34.

12 See para 6.27 above. In relation to Art. 103 TFEU, see also para 10.05 below.

landmark *Tobacco Advertising* judgment dating from 2000, the Court of Justice elaborated on this requirement.[13] This case concerned a challenge brought by Germany to the legality of a directive on tobacco advertising that had been adopted on the basis of Article 114 TFEU.[14] The Court held that this article did not vest in the EU legislature a general power to regulate the internal market. A mere finding of certain disparities between the relevant laws of the Member States and of an abstract risk of obstacles to the exercise of the EU Treaties' fundamental freedoms or of distortions of competition liable to result therefrom does not suffice to justify its use. The Court underlined that instead EU legislation adopted on the basis of Article 114 TFEU must genuinely have as its object the improvement of the conditions for the establishment and functioning of the internal market. Any alleged distortion of competition that the legislation concerned seeks to eliminate must be appreciable. This does not necessarily exclude the use of this article to prevent the emergence of future obstacles, provided, however, that this emergence is likely and that the EU legislative measures in question are designed to prevent these obstacles from emerging. In the case at hand the Court found that these conditions had not been met. It therefore annulled the directive. In subsequent case law the Court dealt with similar questions, essentially confirming and expanding on the line set out in *Tobacco Advertising*.[15]

10.03 In this light all legal acts considered in Part B above rely in essence on two key considerations. In the first place, they all highlight – be it to a greater or lesser extent – the existence of certain *divergences* between the relevant laws of the Member States. It is then typically noted that this leads to a distortion of competition and a fragmentation of the internal market, which in turn is the justification for the EU to take legislative action with a view to reducing these divergences. While the Procurement Remedies Directive and the Product Liability Directive do not go into much detail on this point, this logic has for instance been set out quite extensively in the IPR Enforcement Directive. Its recitals speak of the existence of '*major disparities as regards the means of enforcing intellectual property rights*', which are said to be prejudicial to the functioning of the internal market and to make it impossible to ensure that these rights enjoy an equivalent level of protection throughout the EU.[16] The IPR Enforcement Directive therefore aims '*to approximate legislative systems so as to ensure a high,*

13 CoJ case C-376/98, *Germany v Parliament and Council (Tobacco advertising)*, para 83–86 and 106–7.

14 Directive 98/43/EC on the approximation of the laws, regulations and administrative provisions of the Member States relating to the advertising and sponsorship of tobacco products, OJ 1998, L 213/9.

15 E.g. CoJ case 491/01, *British American Tobacco*; CoJ case C-217/04, *UK v Parliament and Council*; CoJ case C-380/03, *Germany v Parliament and Council (Tobacco advertising II)*; CoJ case C-155/04, *Alliance for National Health*; CoJ case C-301/06, *Ireland v Parliament and Council*; CoJ case C-58/08, *Vodafone*; CoJ case C-270/12, *UK v Parliament and Council*.

16 Recital 7 and 8 IPR Enforcement Directive 2004/48. See para 4.06 above.

equivalent and homogeneous level of protection in the internal market'.[17] Likewise, in the recitals of the Competition Damages Directive it is said that '*marked differences*' exist between the relevant laws of the Member States, which lead to an '*uneven playing field*'.[18] This directive seeks to '*reduce*' and to '*prevent the increase*' of such differences.[19] Considerations of this kind can also be found in the Unfair Terms Directive. After having observed that there are '*marked divergences*' between the relevant laws of the Member States, it is noted there that '*uniform rules of law in the matter of unfair terms*' should be adopted.[20]

A second key consideration is the justification of the harmonised rules in terms of *effectiveness*. The IPR Enforcement Directive recalls for example the need for '*effective means of enforcing intellectual property rights*' and for ensuring that the substantive law on intellectual property is '*applied effectively*'.[21] Along the same lines the Competition Damages Directive states that the said divergences '*affect the substantive effectiveness*' of the EU right to compensation for infringements and leads to the '*uneven enforcement*' of this right.[22] As the Commission noted in its proposal, this directive '*seeks to ensure the effective enforcement of the EU competition rules*', against the background of the idea that such private enforcement contributes to ensuring compliance with these rules.[23] It similarly follows from the recitals of the Procurement Remedies Directives that these directives aim to ensure the '*effective application*' of the substantive rules at issue, whereby the importance of the availability of '*effective remedies*' at the national level is also stressed.[24] The purpose of the measures provided for in the Consumer Injunctions Directive is essentially to ensure that '*the effectiveness of national measures transposing the [substantive EU consumer protection directives concerned] [...] is [not] thwarted*' in cross-border situations.[25] Such a focus on effectiveness may be somewhat less clearly articulated in the Product Liability Directive and the Unfair Terms Directive, probably because these directives contain substantive as well as remedial and procedural rules, but they nonetheless also make it

17 Recital 10 IPR Enforcement Directive 2004/48. See para 4.06 above.

18 Recital 7 Competition Damages Directive 2014/104. See para 6.23 and 6.27 above.

19 Recital 9 Competition Damages Directive 2014/104.

20 Recitals 3 and 10 Unfair Terms Directive 93/13. See para 5.15 above.

21 Recital 3 IPR Enforcement Directive 2004/48.

22 Recitals 7 and 8 Competition Damages Directive 2014/104.

23 Commission, Proposal for Competition Damages Directive 2014/104, COM(2013) 404, p. 2.

24 Recitals 1 and 4 Public Sector Remedies Directive 89/665 and recitals 1 and 3 Utilities Remedies Directive 92/13. See also recital 81 Concessions Awards Directive 2014/23, which explains that the scope of the Procurement Remedies Directives must be extended so as to also cover infringements of that directive by pointing to the need '*to ensure adequate judicial protection of candidates and tenderers in the concession award procedures, as well as to make effective the enforcement of this Directive*'.

25 Recital 4 Consumer Injunctions Directive 2009/22.

clear that the overarching aim is to contribute to the effective protection of consumers.[26]

10.04 The fact that Article 114 TFEU is the legal basis for virtually all EU legislation considered in the foregoing does not mean that its use has always been accepted in an unquestioned manner. The first of the two types of concerns and points of discussion that occasionally emerged in particular in this connection relates to the above-mentioned requirement of a sufficient link with the *internal market*. Such concerns were raised especially in relation to the Unfair Terms Directive and the Product Liability Directive during the legislative process[27] and occasionally also in the legal literature.[28] This has, however, on the whole not been a topic of debate of a substantial nature. Considering the central importance of this internal market requirement under Article 114 TFEU, it can in fact be seen as remarkable that this issue has been raised so sparingly in relation to the EU legislation at issue. Neither have any legal challenges been brought before the EU courts for any alleged failure to meet this requirement. This can be explained by the fact that the link between the internal market and the *substantive* rules of EU law to which the said legislation relates is rather evident.[29] That being so, even if one thing does not necessarily follow from the other, the adoption of additional EU rules relating to the *enforcement* of those substantive rules – by means of a '*logical extension*'[30] of or a '*corollary*'[31] to those substantive rules – may also generate comparatively little debate on this point.[32]

The second type of concern relates in essence to the question of whether Article 114 TFEU can be used as a basis for EU legislative measures that harmonise national law on *(civil) procedure*. The issue here is not so much whether the EU is competent at all, but rather whether either Article 114 TFEU or another provision of the EU Treaties is the most appropriate legal basis for any such intended legislative intervention. Concerns of this type emerged in 2003 in

26 Cf. recital 13 Product Liability Directive 85/374; recital 10 Unfair Terms Directive 93/13.

27 As regards Unfair Terms Directive 93/13 see Council, doc. 4176/91, pp. 2–3; Council, doc. 4904/91, p. 2 and its annex. As regards Product Liability Directive 85/374, critical comments in this regard were initially voiced from the side of the European Parliament. See European Parliament, doc. 246/78, pp. 6–9. However, this position was subsequently reversed; see European Parliament, doc. 71/79.

28 As regards Product Liability Directive 85/374, see e.g. Whittaker (2005), p. 439. Cf. Weatherill (2012), pp. 1306–10 (in relation to a number of other (substantive) consumer protection directives).

29 See para 3.01–3.03 (concerning substantive EU public procurement law), para 4.02 (concerning substantive EU intellectual property law), para 5.01–5.03 (concerning substantive EU consumer protection law) and para 6.01–6.03 (concerning substantive EU competition law).

30 Commission, Proposal for IPR Enforcement Directive 2004/48, COM(2003) 46, p. 5.

31 Reinbothe (2010), p. 6.

32 Cf. e.g. also European Parliament, Resolution on consumer redress, OJ 1987, C 99/203, recital C: '*the substantive rights conferred by [EU] legislation on the consumer must be supplemented by appropriate procedural mechanisms to ensure their enforcement*'.

relation to the proposal for the IPR Enforcement Directive. Several Member States raised the question of whether that draft directive should not (also) be based on Article 81 TFEU concerning judicial cooperation in civil matters, given that many of its provisions relate to matters of civil procedural law.[33] The Commission had already answered this question in the negative, as it had based its proposal solely on Article 114 TFEU.[34] The legal service of the Council subsequently agreed. In essence, the latter pointed out that the draft directive did not seek to establish harmonised rules eliminating cross-border obstacles to the good functioning of civil proceedings in general.[35] It rather sought to harmonise remedies and procedures only in so far as necessary to achieve a particular sectoral aim, namely to ensure that intellectual property rights enjoy effective and equivalent protection throughout the EU.[36] This intervention proved sufficient to settle the matter within the Council. Comparable discussions with comparable outcomes took place in connection with the Consumer Injunctions Directive[37] and the Competition Damages Directive.[38]

This modest degree of debate and the absence of legal challenges do not necessarily mean in and of themselves that the legality of the use of Article 114 TFEU for the present purposes is established beyond doubt. That is, after all, only for the Court of Justice to decide. The foregoing nonetheless seems to allow for the conclusion that the parties concerned mostly agree on the use that can be made of this article so as to adopt EU legislation facilitating the private enforcement of EU law. Although this must always be assessed on a case-by-case basis in light of the aim and the content of each intended legislative measure, legal basis issues therefore certainly need not be an absolute bar on the EU enacting legislation on private enforcement-related matters. **10.05**

That applies all the more so because Article 114 TFEU is not necessarily the *only* possible legal basis for the adoption of EU legislation of the type at issue here, its frequent use in the present context notwithstanding. Depending on the case at hand, other articles of the EU Treaties may offer more specific (and therefore in principle preferable[39]) alternatives. Article 103 TFEU provides an

33 See Council, doc. 6052/04, p. 7. The relevant provision of the EU Treaties at the time was Art. 65 EC. This provision is not exactly identical to its successor, Art. 81 TFEU, further discussed in para 10.49 below, but these differences are only of limited relevance here. Cf. para 4.34 above.

34 See further Commission, Proposal for IPR Enforcement Directive 2004/48, COM(2003) 46, pp. 16–17.

35 Cf. recital 11 IPR Enforcement Directive 2004/48.

36 Council, doc. 6299/04, p. 2.

37 See Council, doc. 7562/98. In this case the UK made a statement on this matter, accepting the outcome that this directive was to be based on Art. 114 TFEU, while underlining that '*it does not accept [EU] competence in the field of civil judicial procedure*'.

38 See Council, doc. 16176/13; Council, doc. 15983/13, p. 2. See para 6.19 and 6.27 above.

39 Cf. e.g. CoJ case C-48/14, *Parliament v Council*, para 36.

example of such an alternative in so far as EU legislative measures giving effect to EU competition law are concerned. It has been widely agreed that Article 103 TFEU is, generally speaking, the most obvious legal basis for the adoption of an act of secondary EU law that is specifically concerned with the private enforcement of EU competition law.[40] The Competition Damages Directive demonstrates that the Commission as well as the EU legislature essentially concurred with this view, even though in this particular case Article 103 has been used together with Article 114 TFEU in light of the fact that the directive also relates to infringements of certain rules of national competition law.[41] The possible relevance of articles other than Article 114 TFEU is further illustrated by other acts of secondary EU law that address private enforcement-related matters. The Gender Equality Directive has, for example, been based on Article 157(3) TFEU concerning social policy, whereas the Environmental Impact Assessment Directive has been established under Article 192(1) TFEU concerning the environment.[42]

10.06 As a final point it is to be noted that in the EU legal order, the choice of legal basis is not only decisive for the question of whether the EU is competent to act, but that it also determines the applicable *legislative procedure* for the adoption of the proposed legal act in question. Of particular importance in this connection are the relative powers granted to the EU's two main institutions where the adoption of secondary EU law is concerned: the Council and the European Parliament.[43] Under the ordinary legislative procedure, these two institutions essentially decide jointly.[44] As its name indicates, this procedure is prescribed most commonly in the EU Treaties. But the latter can also require a "special" legislative procedure to be followed in certain specific cases.[45] That is, for example, the case under Article 103 TFEU. This article demands only to consult the European Parliament, thus leaving it to the Council to adopt the acts established on this basis. As such, the choice of legal basis can affect the balance between these two institutions – and consequently it can be a cause of

40 See para 6.27 above.
41 Ibid.
42 Gender Equality Directive 2006/54; Environmental Impact Assessment Directive 2011/92.
43 In addition, the choice of legal basis can be of importance for the applicable *voting requirements* in the Council, including whether a qualified majority or unanimity is required. It may be assumed that this latter issue played a role in the above-mentioned discussions on whether IPR Enforcement Directive 2004/48 and Consumer Injunctions Directive 2009/22 should be based either on Art. 81 or 114 TFEU (although since the revision of Art. 81 TFEU (former Art. 65 EC) this distinction is no longer equally relevant in this regard).
44 See Art. 289(1) and 294 TFEU.
45 See Art. 289(2) TFEU.

inter-institutional differences of opinion and potential conflicts at EU level, as the developments relating to the Competition Damages Directive illustrate.[46]

2. Subsidiarity, proportionality and fundamental rights

Apart from the principle of conferral that underlies the requirement of a sufficient legal basis for the EU to be able to adopt private enforcement-related acts of secondary EU law, as was set out in the previous subsection, there are two other noteworthy principles that can constrain the EU's capacity to act, namely the principles of subsidiarity and proportionality. In this regard Article 5 TEU provides for what could be called a three-step test in relation to the existence and exercise of EU competences, addressing in essence first the question of whether the EU Treaties *allow* the EU to act (principle of conferral, discussed above), then the question of whether the EU is *better placed* to act than the Member States individually (principle of subsidiarity) and finally the question of whether the intended EU measure is a *suitable means* in relation to the objective sought (principle of proportionality). **10.07**

More specifically, pursuant to the principle of *subsidiarity*, in areas which do not fall within its exclusive competence,[47] the EU can act '*only if and in so far as the objectives of the proposed action cannot be sufficiently achieved by the Member States, either at central level or at regional and local level, but can rather, by reason of the scale or effects of the proposed action, be better achieved at [EU] level*'.[48] It follows that, even where the necessary powers have been conferred on the EU, the intended EU action must essentially still have added value as compared with action at national level before these powers can be exercised. **10.08**

In legal terms the importance of this principle is rather limited, however. The EU courts tend not to employ a high standard of judicial review in this regard when deciding on the legality of acts of secondary EU law.[49] This means that the legal relevance of the principle of subsidiarity is mainly procedural. It implies, among other things, an obligation to consult widely,[50] to involve

46 See para 6.19 and 6.27 above.

47 See Art. 3 TFEU, which contains a (relatively short) list of the areas where the EU has exclusive competence. It includes '*establishing of the competition rules necessary for the functioning of the internal market*' (point b).

48 Art. 5(3) TEU. See further Tridimas (2006), pp. 183–8; Craig and De Búrca (2011), pp. 94–100; Craig (2012), p. 72.

49 E.g. CoJ case C-84/94, *UK v Council*, para 55; CoJ case C-377/98, *Netherlands v Parliament and Council*, para 32–3; CoJ case C-491/01, *British American Tobacco*, para 177–85; GC case T-526/10, *Inuit*, para 80–85 (appeal pending; see CoJ case C-398/13 P, *Inuit*).

50 Cf. Art. 2 Protocol (No 2) to the EU Treaties on the application of the principles of subsidiarity and proportionality.

national parliaments[51] and to explain why it is considered to have been complied with in a particular case.[52] This principle has therefore been called '*par excellence a political principle, which seeks to influence the legislative process ex ante [and which has had] virtually no impact as a ground for [judicial] review*'.[53]

In connection with the EU legislation and other private enforcement-related initiatives discussed in Part B above, interested parties, including some Member States, have regularly invoked the principle of subsidiarity when objecting to certain suggested or proposed measures. This occurred, for example, in relation to the IPR Enforcement Directive, both in general and in relation to its rules on legal costs.[54] Subsidiarity-related concerns were also voiced in connection with possible EU legislative involvement with issues of collective redress and the initiative that led to the Competition Damages Directive.[55] It follows from the foregoing that concerns of this kind are probably best understood as expressions of political or policy-related concerns as to whether or not it is seen as appropriate or desirable for the EU to exercise its competences concerning the matters in question.[56] That is not to suggest that concerns of this type are not to be taken seriously. Quite to the contrary, there is no question that the existence or absence of a solid policy justification or sufficient political will and support by stakeholders is a crucial requirement for the adoption of any legislation.[57] The point here is rather that this is not a matter of the legality of the exercise of the EU's competences in a strict sense.

10.09 In accordance with the principle of *proportionality*, the content and form of EU action may not exceed what is necessary to achieve the objectives of the EU Treaties.[58] This proportionality test, which also extends to the EU's law-making activities, thus essentially concerns the issue of how the EU makes use of its power to act once it has been established that it is both competent and best placed to do so. It appears that, contrary to the two aforementioned principles of conferral and subsidiarity, proportionality does not emerge as an issue that tends to be frequently invoked in connection with the private enforcement-related EU legislation at issue here.

Suffice to note, therefore, that the Court of Justice allows the EU legislature a broad discretion in this regard at least in areas that involve political, economic

51 Cf. Protocol (No 1) to the EU Treaties on the role of national parliaments in the EU.
52 Cf. e.g. recital 31 IPR Enforcement Directive 2004/48.
53 Tridimas (2006), p. 183.
54 See para 4.10 and 4.31 above, respectively. On these rules on legal costs, see also subsection 8.B.5 above.
55 See para 5.37 and 6.19 above, respectively.
56 In a similar sense, see Komninos (2008), pp. 46–8.
57 See also subsection 10.B.1 below.
58 Art. 5(4) TEU. See further Tridimas (2006), pp. 177–80; Craig and De Búrca (2011), pp. 526–33.

and social choices and where complex assessments are to be made, limiting its review to verifying the absence of any manifest errors, misuse of power or manifest excess of the bounds of that discretion.[59] The EU legislature must base its choices on objective criteria and, where relevant, examine whether the objectives pursued by the measure chosen are such as to justify even substantial negative economic consequences for certain undertakings.[60] Yet the Court does not substitute its own assessment for that of the appropriateness or otherwise of these measures, but rather limits itself to verifying that the EU legislative measures in question are not manifestly inappropriate for achieving the objective pursued.[61] The standard of judicial review is thus limited. That applies especially where divergent interests are to be reconciled and options are thus to be selected within the context of the policy choices which are the legislature's responsibility.[62]

A different kind of legal constraint for the EU legislature when enacting private enforcement-related legislation of the type at issue here concerns the need to respect *fundamental rights* guaranteed in the EU legal order.[63] It has already been noted earlier that the role, and especially the visibility, of fundamental rights in EU law has considerably increased since the Charter became legally binding in 2009.[64] The general obligation for the EU to respect the rights set out in the Charter implies that also the secondary law adopted by its legislature must comply with the Charter.[65] **10.10**

The Court of Justice has also confirmed, however, that the fundamental rights that are typically at issue here – such as, as the case may be, the protection of personal data, the freedom to conduct a business, the protection of intellectual property and the right to an effective remedy and a fair trial[66] – are not absolute.[67] In the words of the Court, they '*do not constitute unfettered prerogatives*'.[68] In its Article 52(1), the Charter expressly allows for the limitation of the exercise of the rights laid down therein in the general interest or to protect

59 E.g. CoJ case C-84/94, *UK v Council*, para 58; CoJ case C-491/01, *British American Tobacco*, para 123; CoJ case C-344/04, *IATA*, para 80; CoJ case C-58/08, *Vodafone*, para 52. See also, more generally, e.g. CoJ case C-127/07, *Arcelor Atlantique*, para 57–9; CoJ case C-601/11 P, *France v Commission*, para 142.

60 E.g. CoJ case C-58/08, *Vodafone*, para 53.

61 E.g. CoJ case C-150/94, *UK v Council*, para 83.

62 E.g. ibid., para 89.

63 As regards a number of more specific fundamental rights-related issues that can emerge in the present context, see also subsections 11.B.5 and 11.B.6 below.

64 See para 2.11 above.

65 Cf. CoJ opinion 2/13, *ECHR*, para 169.

66 See Art. 8, 16, 17(2) and 47 Charter, respectively.

67 E.g. CoJ case C-275/06, *Promusicae*, para 61–9; CoJ joined cases C-92/09 and C-93/09, *Schecke*, para 48; CoJ case C-283/11, *Sky Österreich*, para 45 and 60; CoJ case C-399/11, *Melloni*, para 49.

68 E.g. CoJ joined cases C-317/08 to C-320/08, *Alassini*, para 63; CoJ case C-418/11, *Texdata*, para 84.

the rights of others, provided that the limitation is laid down in law, the essence of the fundamental right concerned continues to be respected and the restriction is proportional to the objective pursued.

It remains to be fully clarified how "strict" the Court of Justice's review is when verifying whether acts of secondary EU law are consistent with the Charter. On the one hand, the Court has acknowledged in this context that the EU legislature can enjoy a wide margin of appreciation.[69] On the other hand, the case law available to date suggests that this margin can actually be rather limited in practice and that the judicial review exercised by the Court can in fact be rather strict. This will depend on factors such as the area concerned, the nature of the rights at issue and the seriousness of the interference with those rights.[70] That being so, although it remains difficult to determine this in the abstract and further clarification in the case law will need to be awaited, as it stands the overall impression is that acts of secondary EU law are generally more likely to be annulled for lack of respect for fundamental rights than for an insufficient legal basis or incompatibility with the principles of subsidiarity and proportionality.[71]

3. National procedural autonomy revisited

10.11 A further question that can arise in relation to the foregoing is what role is left, if any, for the principle of national procedural autonomy. This principle has already been introduced in Part A above.[72] The findings of Part B above confirm that the Member States have no proper autonomy as regards matters related to remedies and procedures applicable in proceedings before national courts, in the sense that the EU would necessarily be barred from legislating on these matters.[73] As this book illustrates, over the decades a broad range of EU legislative measures relating to precisely these matters have been adopted. These measures touch upon matters as diverse as the requirements for liability

69 CoJ joined cases C-402/05 P and C-415/05 P, *Kadi*, para 360.

70 CoJ joined cases C-293/12 and C-594/12, *Digital Rights Ireland*, para 47–8.

71 For example, whereas annulments for lack of a sufficient legal basis or infringements of the principles of subsidiarity and proportionality generally remain scarce, in the above-mentioned rulings in *Kadi*, *Schecke* and *Digital Rights Ireland*, the CoJ annulled the acts in question for failure to respect the applicable fundamental rights (in the latter case it had ruled earlier that the legal basis chosen for the act in question was sufficient; see CoJ case C-301/06, *Ireland v Parliament and Council*). Cf. Craig and De Búrca (2011), pp. 372–8.

72 See subsection 2.A.1 above.

73 For this reason the use of the term "national procedural autonomy" has often been criticised. See e.g. Kakouris (1997), p. 1408; Milutinovic (2010), p. 308; Lindholm (2011), p. 472; Bobek (2012), p. 305. Alternative terms have therefore been suggested, such as "procedural competence" of the Member States or "a combination of national procedural competence and European procedural primacy". See Van Gerven (2000), p. 502; Delicostopoulos (2003), pp. 599–613, respectively. The term "national procedural autonomy" nonetheless continues to be generally used.

in damages to be incurred, the availability of interim relief, rules on legal costs, the limitation periods that apply to the bringing of legal proceedings and the forum competent to hear the private enforcement actions brought under this legislation.[74] That the EU need not be barred from acting is also confirmed by the discussion in the two preceding subsections, where it was found that neither the requirement of a sufficient legal basis nor the principles of subsidiarity and proportionality nor the requirement to respect fundamental rights need be insurmountable obstacles. In that sense the principle of national procedural autonomy has no further role to play. Nonetheless, against this background three further comments can be made on this principle and its relevance in this context.

10.12 In the first place, it may be helpful to distinguish between two types of EU activities in private enforcement-related matters, namely *law-making* and *judiciary* activities. To begin with the latter, the Court of Justice must evidently provide an answer on the basis of the law as it stands when a preliminary question is referred to it concerning the rules that regulate the enforcement of EU law at national level. Although the foregoing might seem to suggest otherwise, the fact remains that in many instances no particular rule of secondary EU law applies that addresses in any degree of detail the remedial and procedural matters that may arise in this respect. In those cases, by default as it were, national law takes centre stage.[75] In that sense, the Member States possess a degree of "autonomy" concerning these matters, subject to the limits resulting from the EU law principles of equivalence and effectiveness. It is in this context that the Court of Justice regularly refers to the principle of national procedural autonomy.[76]

This should not be misunderstood to mean, however, that – where there is a sufficient legal basis and the principles of subsidiarity and proportionality are respected – the EU is barred from *legislating* on private enforcement-related matters. The 1976 *Rewe* judgment itself, which laid the legal foundations of the principle of national procedural autonomy, has already made this clear. For there the Court held that this principle applied in the absence of rules of EU law, while noting that '*[w]here necessary, Articles [114 to 117 and 352 TFEU] enable appropriate measures to be taken to remedy differences between the provisions laid down by law, regulation or administrative action in Member States if they are likely to distort or harm the functioning of the internal market*'.[77] The Court thus indicated that harmonisation relating to the remedies and procedures available

74 See section 7.A and subsections 8.B.1, 8.B.5, 9.B.1 and 9.C.1 above, respectively.

75 Cf. Milutinovic (2010), p. 312. See also para 2.02 above.

76 See section 2.A above.

77 CoJ case 33/76, *Rewe*, para 5. See para 2.01 above.

in private enforcement proceedings before national courts is possible in principle, provided that the conditions of the relevant legal basis are met.[78] The Court has since made this (even) more explicit. In 1994 it was asked to rule on the distribution of competences between the EU and the Member States in relation to the conclusion of the TRIPS Agreement, which touches upon many of the issues that are also addressed in the IPR Enforcement Directive.[79] In that context several Member States had argued that, given that the TRIPS Agreement includes various measures relating to remedies and procedures applicable in proceedings before their respective national courts, this is a Member State competence. The Court held, however, that '*[i]f that argument is to be understood as meaning that all those measures are within some sort of domain reserved for the Member States, it cannot be accepted. The [EU] is certainly competent to harmonise national rules on those matters, in so far as, in the words of Article [115 TFEU], they "directly affect the establishment or functioning of the internal market"*'.[80]

Therefore, with respect also to possible EU legislative measures, the principle of national procedural autonomy can probably best be understood as a default rule. The essence here is not so much one of the autonomy of the *Member States*. The key question is rather whether or not the *EU* is competent to act and if so to what extent it has exercised these competences. This is not fundamentally different from any other intended or actual EU legislative activity, regardless of whether it concerns matters that are substantive or procedural in nature.[81] When the EU legislature has not (or not yet) acted, it is for the Member States to take all necessary measures to enable the private parties concerned to effectively exercise their rights based on EU law.[82] As was the case with the principle of subsidiarity,[83] opposition to possible EU legislative action on private enforcement-related matters expressed in terms of national procedural autonomy is perhaps better understood as a policy or a political concern than as a strictly legal one.

10.13 In the second place, in many respects "purely" national rules (that is, rules of national law other than those transposing directives) on remedial and procedural matters continue to be of considerable importance even where EU legislation facilitating the private enforcement of EU law before national courts has been adopted. For this legislation often leaves considerable space for what could

78 On legal basis issues, see subsection 10.A.1 above.

79 See para 4.12 above.

80 CoJ Opinion 1/94, *WTO*, para 104. Although reference is made here to Art. 115 TFEU, there can be no doubt that this observation also extends in principle to Art. 114 TFEU. On the relationship between these two articles, see also para 10.02 above.

81 Cf. Art. 4(1) and 5(2) TEU; Art. 2(2) TFEU.

82 Cf. Art. 4(3) and 19(1) TEU.

83 See para 10.08 above.

be called *"residual" autonomy* on the part of the Member States. That is to say, the scope of this EU legislation and the level of detail provided for on the matters covered may mean that the degree of EU involvement can be seen as remarkable and far-reaching when compared with most other fields of EU law. But the degree of EU involvement with the applicable remedial and procedural rules generally still remains rather modest when compared with the bodies of written and unwritten rules on these matters that apply at the domestic level. It is evident that this EU legislation by no means amounts to a complete and exhaustive procedural code. In that sense, significant scope for autonomous decision-making at national level typically remains even where such EU legislation applies.

It is to be noted in this connection that all EU legal acts discussed in the foregoing are *directives*. That implies that the Member States are inherently left with some leeway. For in the EU legal order a directive is binding as to the result to be achieved, but it leaves the choice of form and methods to the Member States when transposing the EU rules concerned into national law.[84] It is true that this does not mean that directives cannot set out extensive, detailed and exhaustive rules and thus limit the Member States' scope for manoeuvre to a great extent. However, this has on the whole not been the approach followed in the directives under consideration here. The Unfair Terms Directive states, for instance, that '*as they now stand, national laws allow only partial harmonisation to be envisaged*'.[85] Similarly, the Consumer Injunctions Directive declares rather modestly that '*some degree of approximation of national provisions*' is needed.[86] The IPR Enforcement Directive may be comparatively ambitious in seeking to ensure a high, equivalent and homogeneous level of protection across the EU, but it also provides that the Member States remain free to establish national rules on the matters covered that are more favourable to rightholders.[87] The Commission has therefore described this directive as '*a minimum but standard toolbox*'.[88] Similarly, it has held that its initiative concerning the private enforcement of EU competition law aims to achieve '*effective minimum protection*'.[89]

84 Art. 288, third subparagraph TFEU. According to the CoJ's case law, it follows from this provision that when the Member States transpose a directive they have an obligation to ensure that it is fully effective, whilst retaining a broad discretion as to the choice of methods. See e.g. CoJ case C-389/08, *Base*, para 24–5.

85 Recital 12 Unfair Terms Directive 93/13.

86 Recital 7 Consumer Injunctions Directive 2009/22.

87 Art. 2(1) IPR Enforcement Directive 2004/48.

88 Commission, Report on IPR Enforcement Directive 2004/48, COM(2010) 779, p. 5.

89 Commission, White paper on damages actions for breach of the EC antitrust rules, COM(2008) 165, p. 2.

The Product Liability Directive may be somewhat of an outlier in this regard, given that the Court of Justice has held that it entails "maximum" harmonisation.[90] This implies that Member States cannot adopt diverging measures concerning issues falling within its scope. It that sense, this directive is more prescriptive and significantly limits the Member States' flexibility. It is questionable, however, whether this finding corresponds with the EU legislature's intention when adopting the directive.[91] More importantly, in this particular case this hardly means that the Member States no longer have any scope for manoeuvre. For one thing, the Product Liability Directive contains several optional provisions, for example on the availability of the development risk defence and the possibility of capping the amount of damages due.[92] By leaving it to the Member States to decide whether or not they wish to enact these provisions in their respective national laws, those laws will almost inevitably continue to differ; at best only the margins are narrowed. For another thing, the number of issues exhaustively regulated by this directive is rather limited. This means that, on many other relevant private enforcement-related matters that could arise in this connection and that fall outside the scope of this directive, the Member States remain in principle at liberty to set their own rules.

Although the scope and intensity of the EU involvement thus differs by directive, the EU legislation at hand thus generally leaves the Member States a significant degree of flexibility. It does so in three ways in particular. The first way is *not to deal* with a given issue at all, or not in any detail. For example, contrary to the Commission's earlier intentions and apart from an occasional reference in its recitals, the Competition Damages Directive does not address issues of fault, collective redress or legal costs.[93] And despite earlier suggestions by the Commission to include more specific rules on this subject matter, the Procurement Remedies Directive largely leaves it open as to which heads of damages are to be compensated.[94] The second way is to include an *express reference to national law*. One could think of the IPR Enforcement Directive's rules on legal standing. The reference to national law contained therein leaves many issues to be decided at the level of the Member States.[95] The Unfair Terms Directive similarly refers to national law in connection with the contractual remedy for which it provides.[96] The third way is the inclusion of *optional*

90 E.g. CoJ case C-52/00, *Commission v France*, para 14–24. See para 5.25 above.

91 Cf. Council, Resolution on amendment of the liability for defective products directive, OJ 2002, C 26/2. At the time of adoption of Product Liability Directive 84/374, the Council was the sole legislator.

92 Art. 15(1)(b) and Art. 16 Product Liability Directive 85/374, respectively. See para 5.29 and 5.32 above, respectively.

93 See para 6.24 above.

94 See para 3.16 above. See also subsection 7.A.5 above.

95 Art. 4 IPR Enforcement Directive 2004/48. See para 4.33 above. See also subsection 9.A.2 above.

96 Art. 6(1) Unfair Terms Directive 93/13. See para 5.16–5.18 above. See also section 7.B above.

provisions. It has already been noted above that the Product Liability Directive contains several such provisions. The Consumer Injunctions Directive offers another example where it leaves it to the Member States to decide whether or not they wish to impose a requirement of pre-trial contacts between the parties to disputes that fall within that directive's scope.[97]

In the third place, EU legislation facilitating the private enforcement of EU law before national courts may thus often leave the Member States considerable residual autonomy, but as soon as a particular issue is considered to fall within the scope of this legislation, it is no longer covered by the principle of national procedural autonomy. The aforementioned residual autonomy therefore only constitutes "procedural autonomy" within the meaning of the Court's *Rewe* case law, where the issue in question is not covered by that legislation. In all other cases there is, to use the Court's words in *Rewe*, no longer an '*absence of [EU] rules on the subject*'.[98] Accordingly, in the latter cases the rules of national law concerned are not subject to the comparatively (although by no means always[99]) more "lenient" test under the principles of *equivalence and effectiveness*,[100] but rather to the principle of *primacy of EU law*. Put differently, while the EU legislation at issue here may be concerned with remedial and procedural issues, it still concerns EU law. As such, it is not to be treated any differently from EU law that addresses issues of substantive law. Whether or not EU legislation of this kind applies can therefore be of considerable importance, even if it leaves the Member States a degree of flexibility on certain issues. In concrete terms, the application of such legislation means in particular that the main test applied in cases falling within its scope is whether the exercise of the discretion that may be left to the Member States is such as to ensure the effectiveness and the objectives of this legislation (as opposed to the test under the "*Rewe* principles" of equivalence and effectiveness).[101] **10.14**

It is unfortunately not always clear whether or not a particular issue falls within the scope of EU legal acts such as the ones at issue here, meaning that uncertainty can exist as to the test that is to be applied. For instance, the Court has held that the Unfair Terms Directive regulates neither which court is to

97 Art. 5 Consumer Injunctions Directive 2009/22. See para 5.11 above. See also subsection 9.C.2 above.

98 CoJ case 33/76, *Rewe*, para 5. See para 2.01 above.

99 See subsections 2.A.2 and 2.A.3 above.

100 Cf. Jacobs and Deisenhofer (2003), pp. 216–17; Schebesta (2010), p. 856. See also Trstenjak and Beysen (2011), p. 103.

101 It is settled case law that the objectives pursued are particularly important when interpreting provisions of EU law and the scope of any discretion that it may leave to the Member States. See e.g. CoJ case C-323/03, *Commission v Spain*, para 23; CoJ case C-145/10, *Painer*, para 107; CoJ case C-306/12, *Spedition Welter*, para 17.

have territorial jurisdiction nor the number of instances of jurisdiction.[102] Both issues were therefore considered to fall within the Member States' procedural autonomy and were assessed under the EU law principles of equivalence and effectiveness.[103] Yet while this same directive does not (expressly) regulate the question of own-motion review either, in *Océano Grupo* this latter issue was assessed and decided in light of the objective of this directive and its particular provision at issue.[104] The Procurement Remedies Directives similarly do not expressly regulate in any way the standard of judicial review to be applied in cases brought under these directives. But in *Hospital Ingenieure* the Court nonetheless did not consider this issue to fall within the Member States' procedural autonomy. Instead it formulated an answer on the basis of the spirit and objective of these directives.[105]

It is further true that in cases such as the ones referred to above it sometimes actually seems to matter little which test is applied. The Court has, for example, come to the conclusion that either way EU law requires in principle full compensation of any damage caused as a consequence of an infringement of EU law.[106] Yet in other cases the mere existence of a specific rule of EU law does appear to be of relevance. For instance, as was noted above, the Unfair Terms Directive expressly refers to national law where it stipulates that unfair terms in consumer contracts are not binding on the consumer. But, while acknowledging that the Member States consequently have a certain degree of autonomy in this respect, the Court has insisted all the same that any outcome must be such so as to ensure the full effectiveness and achieve the objective of this rule of EU law.[107] Furthermore, in the aforementioned rulings in *Océano Grupo* and *Hospital Ingenieure*, the Court drew rather far-reaching conclusions.[108] In the former it held that under the Unfair Terms Directive own-motion review is in

---

102 CoJ case C-413/12, *ACICL*, para 28 and 30; CoJ case C-567/13, *Baczó*, para 40. See e.g. also CoJ case C-479/12, *Gautzsch*, para 39–42. In this latter ruling it is noted that Community Designs Regulation 6/2002 contains express rules neither on the burden of proof nor on the production of evidence. That first issue is then, nonetheless, considered to be regulated by EU law, so as to ensure that the objective of that regulation can be entailed, whereas the latter issue is left to be determined by national law, subject to the principles of equivalence and effectiveness.

103 On these principles, see section 2.A above.

104 CoJ joined cases C-240/98 and C-244/98, *Océano Grupo*, para 26. Note, however, that in some subsequent cases this same question is assessed under the principles of equivalence and effectiveness. See para 5.19 and 5.20 above.

105 CoJ C-92/00, *Hospital Ingenieure*, para 57–64. See para 9.29 above.

106 Cf. e.g. CoJ case C271/91, *Marshall*, para 26 (relating to Gender Equality Directive 2006/54); CoJ case C-203/99, *Veedfald*, para 25–8 (relating to Product Liability Directive 85/374); CoJ joined cases C-295/04 to C-298/04, *Manfredi*, para 92–7 (relating to EU competition law, without any further specific rules of EU law being applicable, given that this case pre-dates the adoption of Competition Damages Directive 2014/104).

107 CoJ case C-618/10, *Banco Español de Crédito*, para 62 and 72.

108 CoJ joined cases C-240/98 and C-244/98, *Océano Grupo*; CoJ C-92/00, *Hospital Ingenieure*. See para 5.19 and para 9.29 above, respectively.

principle required, whereas in the latter it found that the judicial review exercised under the Procurement Remedies Directives cannot be limited to the question of whether or not the contested decision is arbitrary. This could be taken to suggest that the *mere existence* of specific EU legislation of the type under consideration can imply that a higher threshold to be met by national law is set, even in cases where that legislation does not expressly touch upon that particular issue.

B. POLITICAL ASPECTS AND POLICY-RELATED FACTORS

The EU having, within certain limits, the legal capacity to take legislative action on private enforcement-related matters is one (important) thing, as was discussed above. Quite another thing, however, is the extent to which there is also the required *political will* and there are deemed to be sufficient *policy* reasons to propose and adopt such legislation. Although these matters largely fall outside the scope of a legal study such as the present one, they are nonetheless worth considering here. The relevant political aspects are therefore first briefly discussed below. Attention then turns to the three factors of a political and policy nature that can affect the chances of EU legislation facilitating the private enforcement of EU law being adopted.

1. Political aspects

The prospect of adopting EU legislation of the type at issue here can be **10.15** politically sensitive and the process of establishing such legislation can (therefore) be lengthy and cumbersome. Many of the Commission suggestions and proposals discussed in Part B above proved to be controversial. It took, for example, almost two decades and several revisions of the Commission proposal to reach agreement on the Unfair Terms Directive.[109] Furthermore, not only did it take nine years of discussions by the EU legislature for it to adopt the Commission's proposal for the Product Liability Directive, it also required the insertion of various exceptions, limitations and optional provisions.[110] In the case of the Competition Damages Directive, while discussions had already started at an earlier stage, even between the publication of the Commission's 2005 green paper and the adoption of this directive almost a decade elapsed filled with studies, official documents, discussions and consultations.[111] And even then it seems questionable whether this directive would have been

109 See para 5.14 above.
110 See para 5.25 above.
111 See section 6.B above.

proposed and adopted in the absence of additional rulings by the Court (notably *Pfleiderer*) and the exclusion of controversial issues, such as collective redress, fault requirements and legal costs.[112] The discussions related to a possible EU legislative initiative on collective redress provide yet another example of the controversies that can arise in this regard.[113] In the latter case, these controversies and resulting delays were such that fears were expressed that the initiative had got '*lost in consultation*'.[114] In the end the Commission decided to limit itself, at least for the time being, to adopting a recommendation rather than submitting a proposal for a legally binding act of secondary EU law.[115]

Arguably a further illustration of the sensitivity of EU legislative involvement with private enforcement-related matters are the efforts that the Commission typically makes to emphasise that the domestic legal systems and traditions of the Member States will continue to be respected as much as possible. In relation to the Procurement Remedies Directives, the Commission held, for instance, that '*[c]onsiderable flexibility is left for the Member States to implement the directive's requirements in accordance with their particular approaches to administrative and judicial review*'.[116] And in its proposal for the Consumer Injunctions Directive it highlighted that '*historical and legal traditions will be in no way compromised*' and that '*the proposed text in no way prejudices established remedies at national level*'.[117] When proposing the IPR Enforcement Directive the Commission similarly declared that '*[a]ccount must be taken of the legal traditions and situation of each Member State*' and that the enforcement in question is to take place '*within the existing national frameworks*'.[118]

These findings are in line with other observations. Other commentators have noted that EU legislative measures of the type at issue here tend to be inherently '*politically sensitive*'[119] and that their adoption can thus be '*an extremely challenging process*'.[120] That is probably the case because national rules on remedies and (civil) procedure often reflect considerations that are fundamental to a Member State's political organisation, social and economic structure, constitutional and social identity and its arrangements for wealth distribution. This has therefore been described as '*a complex area of policy-driven*

112 See para 6.24 above.
113 See para 5.37 above.
114 Jeffries (2011), p. 1.
115 Collective Redress Recommendation 2013/396. See para 5.38 and 5.39 above.
116 Commission, Proposal for Utilities Remedies Directive 92/13, COM(90) 297, p. 15. See para 3.10 above
117 Commission, Proposal for Consumer Injunctions Directive 2009/22, COM(95) 712, p. 8. See para 5.05 above.
118 Commission, Proposal for IPR Enforcement Directive 2004/48, COM(2003) 46, p. 15. See para 4.09 above.
119 Jacobs and Deisenhofer (2003), p. 216. See e.g. also Adinolfi (2012), p. 286.
120 Tulibacka (2009), p. 1527.

rules, the application of which is irrevocably linked to legal cultures and judicial practices'.[121] In this light it has been submitted that EU legislative interference with remedies and procedures for the private enforcement of EU law before national courts is '*more taboo*' than with substantive law.[122]

However, the above point should not be overstated either. The mere fact that the EU legislation assessed in the foregoing has in fact been adopted demonstrates that one cannot speak of a taboo. There can furthermore be no question that adopting secondary EU law on matters of substantive law can sometimes be highly controversial as well.[123] EU legislation on private enforcement-related matters therefore certainly does not have a monopoly on controversy. Most important for the present purposes is, however, the observation that adopting this latter type of EU legislation is *not always* particularly sensitive or difficult. It rather appears that the degree of controversy that the various EU legal acts discussed in Part B above generate tends to vary considerably. **10.16**

More specifically it has been seen in the foregoing that the Unfair Terms Directive, the Product Liability Directive, the Competition Damages Directive and a possible legislative initiative on collective redress all proved to be controversial.[124] However, although some discussions and controversies certainly emerged, particularly in the legal literature, the process leading to the adoption of the IPR Enforcement Directive has in contrast been on the whole relatively smooth and speedy.[125] Arguably the main bone of contention during the legislative process leading to the adoption of this latter directive, namely the possible inclusion of EU rules on criminal measures, was moreover essentially of a public enforcement nature rather than concerning a private enforcement-related matter strictly speaking.[126] In addition, the IPR Enforcement Directive stands out for the rather rare example that it offers of a case where the EU legislature (and in particular the Member States represented in Council) enacted further-reaching harmonisation than the Commission had proposed. For the scope of this directive was extended so as to also cover infringements of

121 Ibid., p. 1533. In a similar sense, see Dougan (2011), p. 410.

122 Komninos (2008), p. 144 (n. 19) (although this author also acknowledges the gradual emergence at EU level of a '*positive integration drive*' in relation to rules on remedies and procedures; see pp. 142–4).

123 See e.g. the difficulties in establishing secondary EU law on patents, referred to in para 4.02 above. See e.g. also Services Directive 2006/123, which has been described as '*one of the most controversial and disputed pieces of European legislation in recent years*'. See Flower (2007), p. 217.

124 Controversy is, of course, not easy to measure in a clear and objective manner. For the present purposes, this is assessed based on the overall picture that emerges in light of the following elements in particular: the duration of the legislative process and its preparatory stages; the discussions by the EU legislature; the degree to which the Commission proposal underwent substantial changes in the course of that process; and the extent, content and tone of the public and academic debate relating to the acts in question.

125 See para 4.05 above.

126 See para 4.38 above.

intellectual property rights provided for by ("purely") national law, and the general restriction on infringements committed for commercial purposes or causing significant harm that the Commission has proposed was deleted and instead applied only with respect to certain specific measures.[127]

Neither was the Consumer Injunctions Directive overly controversial.[128] In relation to the Procurement Remedies Directives, some controversy certainly arose.[129] However, in this case also the single most hotly debated issue concerned essentially a matter of public rather than of private enforcement, namely the powers for the Commission to intervene directly at national level.[130] It can further be noted that the legislative process leading to the revision of these directives in 2007 did not prove to be exceptionally problematic.[131] Finally, despite the aforementioned controversies that it generated, it should not be forgotten that the actual legislative process leading to the adoption of the Competition Damages Directive was rather smooth and speedy.[132] Once more the main bones of contention during this process were essentially public enforcement-related matters, particularly the extent to which evidence included in the file of a public enforcement authority should be shielded from disclosure and the effects of infringement decisions by those authorities in private enforcement proceedings.[133]

10.17 The obvious next question is what *explains* these differences in terms of controversy arising in relation to the various legal acts under consideration here. There are clearly limits to the extent that the above-mentioned directives and the fields of law at issue can be compared. Having said that, the main point that emerges from the foregoing is that – contrary to what one might perhaps expect – the degree of controversy that a given private enforcement-related legislative proposal generates does *not* seem primarily related to the "intrusiveness" (seen from the viewpoint of national law) of the measures it contains. On many accounts the IPR Enforcement Directive probably contains the most extensive EU legislative measures in this regard, yet this directive proved relatively uncontroversial during the law-making process. Something similar can be said of the Procurement Remedies Directives, which also touch upon a considerable number of remedial and procedural matters that had hitherto mostly been left to the Member States. Still these directives appeared not to be excessively

127 See para 4.07 above. See also subsection 9.A.1 above.
128 See para 5.05 above.
129 See para 3.05 above.
130 See para 3.05 and 3.33 above.
131 See para 3.09 above.
132 See para 6.24 above.
133 See para 6.33 and 6.41 above, respectively.

controversial. That is all the more noticeable given that the Procurement Remedies Directives were among the first free-standing EU legal acts of this type.[134]

This is not to suggest of course that the content of a private enforcement-related act of secondary EU law is of no significance whatsoever in this respect. But what the foregoing does seem to indicate is that other factors can play a role that can be at least as important. It appears that these factors often relate more to the *context* of the initiative at issue than to its *content*. Three of the political and policy-related factors that can affect the chances of EU legislation facilitating the private enforcement of EU law being adopted are identified and discussed in the following three subsections.

2. Overall enforcement framework

The first of these factors can be summarised as the overall enforcement framework. This refers to the influence that the existence of certain public enforcement mechanisms and considerations related to the interaction between public and private enforcement can have on discussions concerning EU legislation facilitating the private enforcement of EU law before national courts. It appears that while in legal-procedural terms both forms of enforcement mostly function independently of each other, matters relating to public and private enforcement of EU law can nonetheless be linked in some respects. That can be explained as follows. **10.18**

It is appropriate to first briefly consider the relationship between public and private enforcement of EU law generally. Where public enforcement takes the form of infringement proceedings, both forms of enforcement are in principle distinct in legal-procedural terms. That is to say, while the Court of Justice has long seen private enforcement ("the vigilance of individuals") as a possible supplement to this form of public enforcement,[135] this does not mean that it considers both forms of enforcement to be inherently linked or interchangeable. Indeed, as the Court noted as far back as in 1968, '*the guarantees given to individuals under the Treaty to safeguard their individual rights and the powers granted to the [EU] institutions with regard to the observance by the [Member] States of their obligations [under EU law] have different objects, aims and effects*'.[136] Here the Court added that legal actions brought by private parties are '*intended to protect individual rights in a specific case, whilst intervention by the [EU] authorities* **10.19**

134 See subsection 1.2.1 above.

135 See para 1.01 above.

136 CoJ case 28/67, *Firma Molkerei*, p. 153.

has as its object the general and uniform observance of [EU] law'.[137] The fact that an allegedly infringed provision of EU law is directly effective and that at national level certain remedies are available to the private party concerned is therefore generally not a relevant argument in the context of infringement proceedings.[138] Conversely, although this can of course be helpful in practice, it is not legally required that the Court of Justice first establishes in infringement proceedings that there is an infringement of EU law for a private party to be able to successfully bring an action for damages against a Member State.[139]

It is further noticeable that in cases such as *Courage* and *Muñoz*, in which the Court articulated the (nascent) principle of private party liability for infringements of EU law,[140] certain public enforcement mechanisms were in place,[141] but that the Court's rulings in these cases contain no indication that this plays a particular role in this regard, other than the observation that private enforcement can be a useful supplement to public enforcement. These rulings rather suggest that private parties must be able to enforce their rights in private enforcement proceedings before national courts regardless of whether EU or national law provides for a certain form of public enforcement of the EU rules in question. There is in other words no "enforcement monopoly" on the side of public authorities.[142] On a similar note, the Court has held that legal proceedings that permit an undertaking that has been fined by the Commission for a competition law infringement to contest that penalty do not serve to facilitate

137 Ibid.

138 Cf. e.g. CoJ case 29/84, *Commission v Germany*, para 29; CoJ case C-508/03, *Commission v UK*, para 71. Note also that in cases such as CoJ case 68/88, *Commission v Greece (Greek maize)*, discussed in para 2.19 above, no indications to this effect were made. CoJ case C-132/05, *Commission v Germany (Parmesan cheese)*, para 68–81, can arguably be seen as an exception to this general rule. There the CoJ did take account of the fact that the domestic legal system of the Member State concerned provided legal instruments designed to ensure the effective protection of the rights that private parties derive from the regulation in question. It would appear, however, that this ruling should be seen in light of the specifics of the case at hand, particularly the fact that the Commission had seemingly not submitted that that Member State had infringed its duty of sincere cooperation (Art. 4(3) TEU; see para 2.03 above) and that the regulation in question itself placed the burden of ensuring enforcement on the Member State where the goods at issue were produced rather than the one where they were consumed. See also Prete and Smulders (2010), p. 23, who suggest that a pragmatic acknowledgment on the part of the CoJ that it may be impossible for the Member States to act of their own motion against all possible infringements of EU law occurring in their territory may (also) have played a role here.

139 See CoJ case C-445/06, *Danske Slagterier*, para 37–9. See e.g. also CoJ case 39/72, *Commission v Italy (slaughtered cows)*, para 11. Cf. Craig and De Búrca (2011), pp. 414–15. On these actions for damages pursuant to the principle of Member State liability generally, see para 2.23 above.

140 See CoJ case C-453/99, *Courage*; CoJ case C-253/00, *Muñoz*. See subsections 2.D.2 and 2.D.3 above.

141 In *Courage* this is not expressly mentioned, but that being a case involving EU competition law there can be no doubt that specific public enforcement mechanisms were in place (see also subsection 6.D.2 above). In *Muñoz* it is expressly stated that public enforcement penalties could be imposed, but that the competent national authority refused to act upon the complaints (see its para 16 and 19). See also Opinion AG Geelhoed case C-253/00, *Muñoz*, para 50–55; Betlem (2003), p. 213.

142 Cf. Opinion AG Geelhoed case C-253/00, *Muñoz*, para 55.

the bringing of actions for damages by private parties for that same infringement.[143] Although also in this case the finding in one type of proceedings may in practice well have a bearing on the other type of proceedings, and although the 2014 Competition Damages Directive formalises this interrelationship to some extent,[144] the fact remains that in legal-procedural terms public and private enforcement largely remain two separate worlds.

Against this background let us first consider the fields where public enforcement generally plays a *limited role*, at least in so far as EU law is concerned. This is particularly the case in the fields of EU public procurement and intellectual property law.[145] In these two fields there is no obligation for the Member States to designate a public authority that is charged with enforcing the substantive rules in question and that is granted significant supervisory, investigatory and punitive powers for that purpose. Although the Commission has in the past sought to obtain certain powers for itself to address infringements of EU public procurement law at national level, is it not empowered to fulfil such a public enforcement role in this regard.[146] At the same time, it is precisely in these two fields that relatively ambitious and detailed EU private enforcement-related measures have been enacted, namely the Procurement Remedies Directives and the IPR Enforcement Directive. **10.20**

As a matter of EU law, public enforcement has furthermore historically played only a rather modest role in relation to the enforcement of EU consumer protection law.[147] And also in this field has a considerable body of secondary EU law on private enforcement been adopted, as the Consumer Injunctions Directive, the Unfair Terms Directive and the Product Liability Directive illustrate. Conversely, the EU has more recently considerably strengthened the public enforcement framework in this field, notably through the adoption of the CPC Regulation in 2004.[148] It has been observed that since the adoption of that regulation the public enforcement authorities of the Member States mostly prefer to cooperate between themselves rather than to initiate legal proceedings under the Consumer Injunctions Directive, as they can also be entitled to do.[149]

---

143 CoJ case C-596/11 P, *Schenker*, para 23.

144 For example, by regulating the effects of findings of infringements in the context of public enforcement proceedings on any possible subsequent private enforcement proceedings brought under Competition Damages Directive 2014/104. See its Art. 9, discussed in para 6.41 above. On this interrelationship and interaction more generally, see further para 6.51 above.

145 See subsections 3.D.2 and 4.D.2 above, respectively.

146 See para 3.33 above.

147 See subsection 5.E.4 above.

148 CPC Regulation 2006/2004. See para 5.44 above.

149 See Commission, Second report on Consumer Injunctions Directive 2009/22, COM(2012) 635, p. 7. On the possibility of empowering certain public authorities to act under Consumer Injunctions Directive 2009/22, see para 5.06 above.

It is noticeable that over roughly same period of time the Commission has consistently decided against (substantially) amending the above-mentioned consumer protection directives to improve the possibilities for private enforcement provided for therein.[150] Neither were any significant new legislative initiatives on this point developed.[151]

10.21 All this contrasts markedly with the developments with respect to the enforcement of EU competition law, where public enforcement generally plays a *key role*.[152] There is probably no other field of EU law where public enforcement mechanisms have been so well established. There is certainly no other field where the Commission itself has such far-reaching powers to supervise and enforce compliance with the relevant rules of EU law *vis-à-vis* private parties. At the same time it has been seen that it has been difficult to enact private enforcement-related EU legislative measures in this field. Although several factors play a role in this regard, there can be little doubt that concerns relating to the potential harmful effects of increased private enforcement on the existing public enforcement mechanisms featured prominently among them. Indeed, for some the very existence of a robust and effective public enforcement framework may perhaps not entirely eliminate, but nonetheless significantly qualify and reduce the need for EU legislative measures facilitating the private enforcement of EU competition law.[153] At the very least the existence of these public enforcement mechanisms may well limit the sense of urgency when considering such measures.

The fact that in 2014 the Competition Damages Directive was adopted does not imply that the above-mentioned concerns no longer existed. Quite to the contrary, while it is evident that this directive contains a range of private enforcement-facilitating measures, there is a good case to be made that the fact that this directive was in the end proposed and adopted owes at least as much to a desire to protect public enforcement, particularly in light of the Court's

150 See para 5.12, 5.22 and 5.33 above.

151 As discussed in subsections 5.E.2 and 5.E.3 above, the EU has in recent years taken certain measures with respect to collective redress (notably Collective Redress Recommendation 2013/396) and alternative dispute resolution (notably Consumer ADR Directive 2013/11), respectively. This illustrates that public enforcement is not the EU's *sole* focus where infringements of EU consumer protection law are concerned. However, it does not substantially affect the above-mentioned observation that in recent years the EU legislature tends to place less emphasis on private enforcement in this field. Collective Redress Recommendation 2013/396 is not specifically concerned with infringements of EU consumer protection law, but rather with infringements of EU law generally and it is moreover not legally binding. No EU legislation on collective redress has been adopted or even proposed to date. Furthermore, alternative dispute resolution is by definition an alternative to and not a type of private enforcement (at least as this term is understood here).

152 See subsection 6.D.2 above.

153 Cf. e.g. Wils (2003a), p. 473; Eilmansberger (2007), p. 478; Hjelmeng (2013), p. 1033.

Pfleiderer case law, as it was driven by a desire to facilitate private enforcement.[154] As the Commission noted when submitting its proposal for this directive, '*the EU right to compensation can sometimes be at odds with the effectiveness of public enforcement of the EU competition rules*'.[155] The protection of public enforcement was therefore elevated to an objective of this directive in its own right, on a par with – and in some respects taking precedence over – the original (sole) objective of the Commission's initiative, namely to facilitate the bringing of actions for damages by private parties for competition law infringements (whereby the interaction between both types of enforcement was merely one point of focus among many others).[156]

It thus appears that, while public and private enforcement remain largely separate in legal-procedural terms, the existence or absence of well-established and robust public enforcement mechanisms can nonetheless be an important factor when determining whether EU law measures relating to private enforcement are enacted in a given field and, if so, what type of measures are provided for. This works essentially in two ways. On the one hand, the absence of such public enforcement mechanisms may reinforce the "demand" for private enforcement and thus for secondary EU law of the type under consideration here. As such, it can act as a facilitating factor. On the other hand, in situations where public enforcement mechanisms of this kind are already "on offer" there may not only be less "demand" for private enforcement-facilitating measures, but there can also be concerns about the possible negative consequences of the latter on the former. These two latter elements can act as a barrier to the adoption of EU legislation of the type at issue here, both in terms of its coming into being and of its objectives and content. **10.22**

3. International dimension

A second factor that can affect the chances of secondary EU law facilitating private enforcement being adopted is what is referred to here as the international dimension. At the heart of this argument lies the fact that both the Procurement Remedies Directives and the IPR Enforcement Directive, which, as was noted above, are noticeable for the degree of detail and "intrusiveness" in respect of matters of remedies and procedures for private enforcement purposes, should be understood against the background of two international agreements concerning these two fields of law, namely the GPA (Agreement on **10.23**

154 CoJ case C-360/09, *Pfleiderer*. See subsection 6.B.4 and para 6.24 above. In this sense, see also Cauffman (2015), p. 128.

155 Commission, Impact assessment report on damages actions for breach of the EU antitrust rules, SWD(2013) 203, p. 5.

156 See para 6.23 and 6.25 above.

Government Procurement) and the TRIPS (Trade-Related Aspects of Intellectual Property) Agreement. All Member States as well as the EU are party to these two agreements.[157] They are, moreover, both exceptional compared with other international agreements in that they make provision for the private enforcement of the substantive rules at issue rather than leaving issues of compliance and enforcement solely to the states concerned.[158] The content of the above directives reflects to a great extent those of the international agreement to which they correspond, although the former are typically more detailed than the latter. This makes it tempting to conclude that the fact that the EU and the Member States were already bound by these international agreements is an important element explaining the adoption of these acts of secondary EU law.

Things are not as straightforward as that, however. As regards the IPR Enforcement Directive there can be little doubt that the above logic has indeed been at work. As has been noted elsewhere, the TRIPS Agreement in effect '*paved the way*' for the EU harmonisation measures in question.[159] The Commission itself spoke of a '*TRIPS plus approach*' when it submitted its proposal for this directive.[160] However, the same cannot be said of the Procurement Remedies Directives. These latter directives were adopted in 1989 and 1992. Although negotiations had started as early as 1986, the GPA was only concluded several years later, namely in 1994. Already the timing of events therefore suggests that the influence of the latter on the former has probably been limited at best. This is confirmed by the legislative history of the Procurement Remedies Directives, which reveals no indications that either the GPA itself or the ongoing negotiations on this international agreement had a substantial influence on the coming into being and the content of these directives. It is in fact more likely that – conversely – the GPA was modelled at least in part upon the Procurement Remedies Directives.[161] For the EU can of course contribute to the "production" of international law as much as it can be a "consumer" thereof.

10.24 Yet that does not mean that the potential relevance of this international dimension in the present context is therefore limited to the IPR Enforcement Directive only. There are also other instances where this has proven to be a relevant factor. Influences stemming from international law appear to have been

---

157 Regarding these two agreements, see further para 3.12 and 4.12 above, respectively.

158 These agreements are, however, in principle not directly effective in the EU legal order. As regards the GPA, see Anderson and Arrowsmith (2011), p. 32. As regards the TRIPS Agreement, see CoJ case C-135/10, *SCF*, para 46.

159 Reinbothe (2010), p. 5.

160 Commission, Press release on the proposal for IPR Enforcement Directive 2004/48, IP/03/144, p. 1.

161 Footer (1995), p. 88; Zhang (2011), p. 485.

largely absent in relation to the Consumer Injunctions Directive, the Unfair Terms Directive and the Competition Damages Directive. But the situation is different where the Product Liability Directive is concerned. In 1977 the Council of Europe established a Convention on product liability in regard to personal injury and death.[162] The legislative history of this directive shows that this international agreement served as a valuable point of reference and offered some necessary common ground during the long and difficult negotiations at EU level that preceded its adoption.[163]

Similar influences can be observed as regards certain other acts of secondary EU law than those discussed in Part B above. A good example is the Environmental Impact Assessment Directive. This directive also contains a number of measures facilitating the private enforcement of the environmental rules in question, most notably with respect to measures on legal costs and the legal standing of the private parties concerned.[164] The provisions in question were introduced in 2003 in order to give effect to the United Nation's "Århus Convention" on access to information, public participation in decision-making and access to justice in environmental matters.[165] Similarly, the Rail Passengers' Rights Regulation, for instance, expressly builds on the relevant international law instrument.[166]

4. Temporal aspect

A third factor that can be of relevance in this regard concerns what could be called the temporal aspect. One could perhaps also speak of the political climate or, if you will, the *Zeitgeist*. Either way this refers to the evolution over time of the mainly political but to some extent also legal considerations that affect the scope for adopting EU legislation of the type at issue here. This aspect is inherently difficult to measure or pin down. There are nevertheless several **10.25**

162 Council of Europe, Convention on product liability in regard to personal injury and death, 27 January 1977. See also Whittaker (2005), pp. 433–5; Micklitz, Reich and Rott (2009), p. 220.

163 See e.g. Council, doc. 5555/80, pp. 4–5, 9 and 11; Council, doc. 7772/80, pp. 8–11 and 13; Council, doc. 9976/80, pp. 10–11 and 13–17; Council, doc. 4161/81, p. 4; Council, doc. 7945/81, p. 6 and annex (p. 7). In a similar sense, see also Whittaker (2005), pp. 433–5; Micklitz, Reich and Rott (2009), p. 220.

164 Art. 11 Environmental Impact Assessment Directive 2011/92. See para 8.31 and 9.08 above, respectively.

165 See Decision 2005/370/EC on the conclusion, on behalf of the European Community, of the Convention on access to information, public participation in decision-making and access to justice in environmental matters, OJ 2005, L 124/1. The above-mentioned provision was inserted into Environmental Impact Assessment Directive 2011/92 by Directive 2003/35/EC providing for public participation in respect of the drawing up of certain plans and programmes relating to the environment, OJ 2003, L 156/17. On this convention and its impact on EU law, see further Oliver (2013), p. 1423; Eliantonio (2014), p. 257.

166 Recital 6 Rail Passengers Rights' Regulation 1371/2007. See the Convention concerning international carriage by rail (COFIT), 9 May 1980, concluded in the framework of the Intergovernmental Organisation for International Carriage by Rail (OTIF).

indications that suggest that, put simply, it may well be that EU legislation that was adopted, say, two decades ago may not have been adopted today, or at least not in a similar form or under similar conditions.

10.26 The first of the three such indications that stand out in this regard can be derived from the dates of adoption of the legal acts assessed in Part B. The Product Liability Directive was adopted in 1985, the two Procurement Remedies Directives in 1989 and 1992, the Unfair Terms Directive in 1993, the Consumer Injunctions Directive in 1998 (codified in 2009), while the IPR Enforcement Directive dates from 2004. It follows that these six legal acts are all over a decade old and most are considerably older. Only one of the legal acts under consideration is more recent, namely the Competition Damages Directive, which was adopted in November 2014. Also, several other, comparable EU legal acts are of a respectable age. The 2006 Gender Equality Directive is, for example, a recast of directives that originally date from 1976 and 1980.[167]

A second indication emerges when the developments related to the Product Liability Directive are assessed in further detail. Despite the controversy that it generated at the time, it was adopted (unanimously, as its legal basis, Article 115 TFEU, required[168]) in 1985. Over the years various shortcomings in the functioning of this directive have been identified.[169] Yet the Commission has thus far consistently decided against proposing to amend this directive.[170] The references that it made in this connection with the above-mentioned controversies and its stated fear of upsetting the existing "delicate balance" between the various interests at stake seem to suggest that the Commission believes that it may not be possible to reach an agreement again. If it were to propose an amendment, it is not inconceivable that certain Member States would seek to use the opportunity to reduce the degree of harmonisation currently provided for.[171] Whatever the merit of the Commission's argument that it has not sufficiently been demonstrated that the aforementioned shortcomings constitute a problem from an internal market perspective,[172] it seems questionable

167 Gender Equality Directive 2006/54. See para 1.09 above.

168 See para 10.02 above.

169 See para 5.33 above. See also para 7.04 above.

170 Commission, Second report on Product Liability Directive 85/374, COM(2000) 893, p. 28; Commission, Third report on Product Liability Directive 85/374, COM(2006) 496, pp. 11–12; Commission, Fourth report on Product Liability Directive 85/374, COM(2011) 547, p. 4.

171 Cf. Council, Resolution on amendment of the liability for defective products directive, OJ 2002, C 26/2. Here it was in effect suggested to amend this directive so as to allow more scope for the application of national rules. Note that, pursuant to Art. 17(2) TEU, the Commission has the virtually exclusive right to propose secondary EU law, including amendments thereof, but that once the Commission has made a proposal the EU legislature is, within certain limits, at liberty to amend it.

172 As was noted in para 7.04 above, the Commission does not appear to have made much effort to obtain such evidence.

whether this directive would have been proposed and adopted in the first place had a similar standard been applied at that time. Indeed, this Commission position has been described elsewhere as *'overly complacent'*.[173] As a consequence of this position, the Product Liability Directive has remained substantially unaltered for an unusually long period of time, namely almost three decades.[174]

Third and more generally, account can be taken of the more recent consultations and other public statements regarding some of the directives and initiatives discussed in Part B above. The responses generated suggest that several Member States may have become increasingly vocal in expressing hesitations as regards possible EU legislative intervention on the matters under consideration here.[175] As was noted earlier, the fact that such objections are often formulated in legal terms (for example alleged non-respect for the principles of subsidiarity or national procedural autonomy) and that as such these arguments seem not always entirely convincing should not distract from the apparent underlying political uneasiness about the initiatives in question.[176] Perhaps more surprising is that this development also seems to extend to the European Parliament. In the late 1970s and 1980s this institution called for a range of EU legislative measures harmonising national law concerning consumers' access to court, including measures on collective redress.[177] In 2000 in relation to the Product Liability Directive, it still contemplated addressing as a matter of EU law remedial and procedural issues such as burden of proof, limitation periods, non-material damage and quantification of damages.[178] All this contrasts with the seemingly more cautious positions that it has taken more recently, at least in some cases. For instance, in 2008 it stated that *'safeguarding effective enforcement of rights originating from [EU] legislation is principally an obligation of the Member States'* and that *'the [EU] is not competent to prescribe rules for national procedural law'*.[179] A year later it also took the view that rules on

173 Fairgrieve and Howells (2007), p. 978.

174 A limited amendment, which led to agricultural products being brought within the scope of this directive, was enacted in 1999 as a consequence of exceptional circumstances, namely the "mad cow" crisis. See para 5.33 above.

175 See para 5.37 and 6.19 above.

176 See para 10.08 and 10.12 above.

177 See e.g. the 1977 report and resolution by the European Parliament, cited in Commission, Memorandum on consumer redress, COM(84) 629, p. 7; European Parliament, Resolution on consumer redress, OJ 1987, C 99/203.

178 European Parliament, Resolution on the Commission green paper on liability for defective products, A5–0061/2000.

179 European Parliament, Resolution on the EU consumer policy strategy 2007–2013, P6_TA(2008)0211, para 34.

limitation periods and the allocation of legal costs should in principle be left to be set by the Member States.[180]

10.27 This is by no means to suggest that, politically speaking, there is no longer scope for the EU to adopt or amend secondary law on private enforcement. For one thing, this would risk overlooking that neither did all relevant Commission initiatives in the past actually lead to EU legislation of this kind being adopted. The Commission's draft directive on the liability of suppliers of services, proposed in 1990, encountered, for example, so much resistance that it was withdrawn a few years later.[181] Around the same time the Commission also unsuccessfully proposed EU rules establishing (no-fault) civil liability in relation to waste.[182] For another thing, it is evident, too, that in more recent times legislation of the type at issue here does get adopted. The 2007 amendment of the Procurement Remedies Directives is a case in point. This amendment involved the introduction of several new private enforcement-facilitating measures, most notably a new contractual remedy.[183] Another evident example is the adoption of the Competition Damages Directive in 2014. Besides, several other private enforcement-related measures have also been proposed and adopted at EU level in recent years.[184]

What the foregoing does appear to indicate is that there is a case to be made that, generally speaking, the *threshold* for the EU to act may well have been *raised*. Although all this is to a considerable extent a matter of political appreciation, it also has a legal side to it. The 2000 *Tobacco Advertising* judgment on the use of Article 114 TFEU as a legal basis can be seen as a turning point in this regard.[185] This case did not concern private enforcement-related legislation as such. Nonetheless, already the very fact that this legal challenge was brought (and several other actions for annulment of EU legislation brought by Member States for alleged lack of a sufficient legal basis or infringements of the principle of subsidiarity in the same period[186]) can be seen as a symptom of the increasing uneasiness referred to above. Moreover, the resulting judgment underlines that,

---

180 European Parliament, Resolution on the white paper on damages actions for breach of the EC antitrust rules, P6_TA(2009)0187, para 19–20.

181 Commission, Proposal for a services liability directive, COM(90) 482. See para 5.34 above.

182 Commission, Proposal for a directive on civil liability for damage caused by waste, COM(89) 282; Commission, Proposal for a Council directive on the landfill of waste, COM(91) 102. This latter proposal was eventually adopted in 1999, but without the provision on liability referred to above. See Directive 1999/31/EC on the landfill of waste, OJ 1999, L 182/1.

183 See para 3.09 and 3.21 above.

184 See para 1.11 above.

185 CoJ case C-376/98, *Germany v Parliament and Council (Tobacco advertising)*. See para 10.02 above.

186 E.g. CoJ case C-84/94, *UK v Council*; CoJ case C-377/98, *Netherlands v Parliament and Council*; CoJ case C-217/04, *UK v Parliament and Council*; CoJ case C-380/03, *Germany v Parliament and Council (Tobacco advertising II)*.

despite its rather broad wording, there are limits to the extent to which Article 114 TFEU can be relied upon. This latter point – the first such finding in relation to this article – is of evident importance also in the present context, considering that almost all of the legislation at issue here is based on this article.[187] It appears that the EU legislature has taken good note of the message that the Court of Justice thus conveyed. Whereas justifications of this kind are generally brief in the legal acts such as the Procurement Remedies Directives and the Product Liability Directive that *pre*-date this judgment, legal acts such as the IPR Enforcement Directive and the Competition Damages Directive that *post*-date it tend to extensively explain this link between the internal market and the harmonisation measures at hand.[188]

At a more abstract level it appears that various phases can be discerned in the activities of the EU legislature relating to matters of remedies and procedures for the private enforcement of EU law in proceedings before national courts.[189] There is a first phase, running roughly up until the late 1980s, that is characterised by *relative inactivity* on the part of the EU legislature. The second phase, which runs from the late 1980s roughly until the early 2000s, marks the period where the EU is increasingly *active and ambitious* in this respect. And subsequently there is a third phase, extending to the present, where EU legislative action of the type at issue here is certainly not excluded *per se*, but where its *limits* become more clearly visible. **10.28**

The parallel with the evolution of the case law of the Court of Justice on this very same subject matter is striking, albeit that the phases in the activities of the EU legislature appear to trail those of its judiciary by a few years.[190] In both cases this evolution in EU activity can arguably be traced back to the same underlying broader developments. One can distinguish in particular: (a) an initial focus on the part of the EU on substantive matters and getting the European project "up and running" and EU law established and generally accepted at national level; (b) a period of relative "euro-enthusiasm", particularly in the context of the 1992 internal market project, accompanied by increased concerns about the effective implementation, application and enforcement of

187 See para 10.02 above.

188 See para 10.03 above.

189 See also the overview set out in subsection 1.B.1 above.

190 See para 2.07 above. As was explained there, the relevant case law has evolved over time, whereby three phases are typically distinguished, namely a prudent initial phase (up to the early 1980s), a significantly bolder and more "interventionist" period (mid-1980s–early 1990s) and a phase characterised by a more balanced and selective approach (mid-1990s onwards).

EU law at national level;[191] (c) a period characterised by a more balanced and selective approach, reflecting the increased maturity of EU law and the EU as a political system, but also increasing concerns and resistance in some corners related to a perception of "Brussels" being overly intrusive.

C. THE ADDED VALUE OF EU LEGISLATION ON PRIVATE ENFORCEMENT

In the foregoing subsections it has been discussed which elements can drive, constrain and facilitate the adoption of EU legislation on private enforcement. In order to complement the picture that thus emerges, a further relevant question is what, generally speaking, is the "added value" of adopting such legislation.[192] Two points stand out in this connection. The first concerns the added value as compared to leaving the matters in question to the judiciary. The second relates to the relevance of factors other than remedial and procedural rules. These two points are subsequently discussed below.

1. Legislative v judicial action

10.29 The first point that could be seen as questioning the added value of EU legislative measures on the matters and of the type under consideration here is essentially founded on the fact that, as construed by the Court of Justice, the principles of effectiveness and effective judicial protection in particular, as well as considerations related to the effectiveness of EU law generally, can be powerful forces where the private enforcement of this law before national courts is concerned. This has already been discussed above.[193] The Court has, for instance, ruled that in proceedings before national courts there can be an obligation to ensure that interim relief is available,[194] that actions for damages for infringements of EU law can be brought against both Member States and private parties,[195] that national rules of evidence are applied in a particular manner[196] and that unreasonable limitation periods set by national law are to be

---

191 Cf. e.g. Council, Resolution on the effective uniform application of Community law and on the penalties applicable for breaches of Community law in the internal market, OJ 1995, C 188/1: '*in the field of the internal market the [EU] has moved from an intensively legislative phase to a phase focusing on the effective operation of common rules*'.

192 As this section is meant to complement the foregoing, the focus is not on the circumstances that may justify taking legislative action at EU level in an individual case, but rather on its possible "added value" considered at a more abstract level.

193 See subsection 2.A.3 and sections 2.B and 2.D above.

194 E.g. CoJ case C-213/89, *Factortame*, para 21; CoJ case C-416/10, *Križan*, para 107. See para 2.22 above.

195 E.g. CoJ joined cases C-6/90 and C-9/90, *Francovich*; CoJ case C-453/99, *Courage*. See para 2.23 and 2.24 above, respectively.

196 E.g. CoJ case C-228/98, *Dounias*, para 71; CoJ case C-526/04, *Laboratoires Boiron*, para 55. See para 2.08 above.

disapplied.[197] Taken together this constitutes a considerable body of "judge-made law" on the remedies and procedures that apply in private enforcement proceedings before national courts.[198] It is, moreover, by no means excluded that (even) more far-reaching requirements can be deduced from the above-mentioned principles. For example, it has been argued that on this basis duties to facilitate collective redress actions, enable the ordering of the disclosure of evidence or depart from certain evidential presumptions under national law can be construed.[199]

This judge-made law being already quite well elaborated and there arguably being scope for its being extended further, one might wonder to what extent there is still a need for "legislature-made law" facilitating the private enforcement of EU law before national courts of the type under consideration here. Why not simply leave these matters to be dealt with by the national courts seised? These courts can refer preliminary questions to the Court of Justice where required. Such an approach may seem all the more attractive given that the EU legislation in question often leaves the Member States a significant degree of flexibility anyway and that enacting it can be a politically sensitive and cumbersome affair.[200] Leaving the matters under consideration to be decided only on the basis of the aforementioned principles in so far as EU law is concerned can also have the advantage of leaving time in the national courts seised for case-by-case assessments.

It is interesting to see how on this point a degree of ambiguity appears to exist **10.30**
on the part of the EU institutions concerned and especially the Commission. On the one hand, it has been seen in the foregoing chapters that the latter generally tends to advocate the adoption of secondary EU law on private enforcement. Its efforts to this effect in relation to consumer collective redress and in the field of competition law are but two recent examples thereof.[201] On the other hand, the Commission has also frequently stressed the potency of the above-mentioned EU law principles that underpin the said judge-made law referred to above. Indeed, it has sometimes done so to such an extent that it actually seems to matter little whether or not any such secondary EU law applies. For instance, in the field of public procurement law the Commission has deduced from the principle of effectiveness a rule on legal standing that it

197 E.g. CoJ case C349/07, *Sopropé*, para 44. CoJ case C-69/10, *Samba Diouf*, para 66–67. See para 2.08 and 2.15 above.

198 Micklitz (2012), p. 366.

199 Temple Lang (2008), pp. 101 and 107. These views are based on a combined reading of the principles of effectiveness and sincere cooperation.

200 See in particular para 10.13 and 10.15 above, respectively.

201 See subsection 5.E.2 and section 6.B above, respectively.

believes should apply in cases not covered by the Procurement Remedies Directives, which is in effect precisely the same as the one laid down in these directives.[202] And in the Court of Justice also it has sometimes seemed to make little difference in this connection whether these directives apply or whether the case is to be adjudicated under the principle of effective judicial protection.[203]

The Commission has further suggested that, pursuant to the principle of effectiveness, an applicant cannot be required to prove the exact amount of damage suffered in competition cases.[204] Yet it has nonetheless deemed it necessary to issue detailed (non-legally binding) guidance for the parties concerned and for the national courts as to how to quantify this damage and to include rules on this subject matter in the Competition Damages Directive.[205] Other provisions of this directive, especially those on the concept of "damage" and on legal standing, are expressly presented as mere "reaffirmations" of EU law as it already stood before its adoption.[206] While this presentation was probably aimed at facilitating the adoption of the directive in that it underlines that some of the rules provided for in that directive apply anyway, they also beg the question why – if those rules indeed apply anyway – it is necessary to include them in an act of secondary law such as the Competition Damages Directive. This comment applies not least with respect to the literal codification of the principles of equivalence and effectiveness that this directive also contains.[207]

10.31 While these are generally all legitimate comments, it should not to be overlooked, however, that legislation and the legislature have certain inherent advantages as compared with judge-made solutions and the courts respectively. The EU courts are neither formally charged nor particularly well placed to

---

202 See Commission, Interpretative communication on the Community law applicable to contract awards not or not fully subject to the provisions of the Public Procurement Directives, OJ 2006, C 179/2, para 2.3.3. Cf. Dahlgaard Dingel (1999), p. 228. On these directives' rules on legal standing, see para 3.25 above. See also subsection 9.A.2 above.

203 Cf. CoJ case C-129/04, *Espace Trianon*, para 20 (regarding Procurement Remedies Directive 89/665 and 92/12); CoJ joined cases C-145/08 and C-149/08, *Club Hotel Loutraiki*, para 65–80 (regarding the principle of effective judicial protection).

204 Commission, Staff working paper accompanying the white paper on damages actions for breach of the EC antitrust rules, SEC(2008) 404, p. 60.

205 Commission, Practical guide on quantifying harm in actions for damages based on breaches of Article 101 and 102 TFEU, SWD(2013) 205; Art. 17 Competition Damages Directive 2014/104. See para 6.30 above.

206 Recital 12 Competition Damages Directive 2014/104. See para 6.29 and 6.39 above, respectively. See also Commission, White paper on damages actions for breach of the EC antitrust rules, COM(2008) 165, p. 7.

207 Art. 4 Competition Damages Directive 2014/104. The Commission's proposal on this point contained slightly divergent wording with respect to the principle of effectiveness. See Commission, Proposal for Competition Damages Directive 2014/104, COM(2013) 404, p. 31 (Art. 3).

establish quasi-legislative measures.[208] Obviously courts can only act in response to a case having been brought before them. That implies that case-law-driven solutions are by definition reactive and often also time-consuming as well as casuistic. In addition, such jurisprudential solutions in principle entail "negative integration". That is to say, the Court of Justice is empowered to indicate how EU law should be interpreted and therefore clarify either expressly (in infringement proceedings) or by implication (in preliminary reference proceedings) which particular rules of national law are considered to be inconsistent with EU law and should thus be disapplied. But it has at best only limited scope to "positively" indicate which rules or mechanisms should be applied instead.

The political difficulties that may arise in this regard notwithstanding, on most of these issues the EU legislature is in a considerably better position. The latter can be proactive, set out a more detailed and structured approach and positively require certain measures to be taken at national level. Matters of remedies and procedures also often concern points of a rather technical nature, which are generally probably better dealt with by the legislature. For the latter can benefit from the involvement of experts, consult stakeholders, issue studies and carry out impact assessments. Democratic legitimacy also mitigates in favour of having these matters primarily dealt with by the legislature.[209] Some also believe that, as compared with the "judicial law-making" of the Court of Justice, involving the EU legislature might better "protect" the interests of the Member States against too much EU "intrusion" into their domestic legal systems.[210]

The adoption of secondary EU law can furthermore contribute to legal **10.32**
certainty and the development of the law. Increasing legal certainty can in itself be of considerable importance. Concerns about legal uncertainty in the absence of EU legislation featured prominently, for example, in relation to the Competition Damages Directive.[211] It can further be recalled that many have criticised the aforementioned judge-made law on remedies and procedures for

208 See further e.g. Snyder (1993), p. 50; Fernández Martín (1996), pp. 202–3 and 228; Jacobs and Deisenhofer (2003), p. 223; Nazzini (2012), p. 1001. See also para 1.08 above.

209 Cf. Opinion AG Trstenjak case C-101/08, *Audiolux*, para 108: '*Rule-making generally involves a choice between different political and social interests which are represented by the institutions and bodies participating in the rule-making procedure. In addition to the relevant democratic legitimation, those bodies possess the necessary expertise to fulfil the political responsibility conferred on them*'.

210 Lindholm (2007), p. 273.

211 See e.g. Commission, Impact assessment report on damages actions for breach of the EU antitrust rules, SWD(2013) 203, pp. 14 and 17.

its unpredictability.[212] This unpredictability can evidently be reduced by enacting secondary EU law. And particularly through a dynamic interplay between the legislature and the judiciary, the law can further develop where secondary EU law applies. Regardless of whether it is fully "autonomous" or concerns in whole or in part a codification of pre-existing case law, the adoption of secondary EU law typically leads to further interpretations thereof by the EU courts, as has been illustrated throughout this book. As a consequence, the law evolves. This certainly occurs given the Court's tendency to sometimes interpret the EU legislation under consideration (and perhaps EU law generally) in a rather extensive manner. As was noted above, the Court has, for instance, also derived certain requirements from this legislation in cases where it does not address a particular issue or where it expressly leaves a margin of manoeuvre to the Member States.[213] It follows that even where these acts are comparatively modest in the degree of harmonisation that they establish, their mere existence can be a "stepping stone" for the Court to address certain issues as a matter of EU law.

Somewhat paradoxically, perhaps, this interplay can thus reduce to some extent the above-mentioned advantages that adopting EU legislation can have in terms of providing legal certainty and "protection" against EU "intrusion". While that is important to bear in mind, this seems neither entirely avoidable nor peculiar to EU law, however. In any case, it would not seem to follow that it is therefore preferable not to adopt such secondary EU law in the first place. Any such extensive interpretations by the Court of Justice may, moreover, often be as much due to the scope for interpretation that the legislation in question leaves, as it is due to any "activism" on the part of the Court, which is in principle bound to rule on the cases brought before it.[214] Leaving certain issues unaddressed or regulating them only in vague or general terms in secondary EU law may thus increase the scope for manoeuvre not only of the Member States,[215] but also of the EU courts.

10.33 Therefore, it cannot be maintained that EU legislative action on private enforcement-related matters of the type at issue here generally does not provide any added value as compared with leaving matters to the courts. The more important point that emerges on the basis of the foregoing is rather that there can be *alternatives* to the "legislative route" that takes central stage in this book. The Commission and the EU legislature could thus decide (or in effect be forced to decide, for example in light of political objections to EU legislative

212 See para 2.03 above.
213 See para 10.14 above.
214 See para 1.08 above.
215 See in particular para 10.13 above.

action) to leave certain matters to be settled by the judiciary rather than to address them in EU legislation. Notwithstanding the aforementioned disadvantages of this judicial route, over time, effects that are at least to some extent similar to those of adopting secondary EU law may well emerge. The appeal of this alternative route may increase in relation to the (arguably increasing) difficulties encountered when seeking to enact legislative measures.[216]

The potential importance of this "judicial route" generally and the preliminary reference procedure in particular to address private enforcement-related difficulties is already evident from the fact that all the aforementioned landmark rulings with a particular importance in the present context (that is, *Simmenthal*, *Factortame*, *Francovich*, *Courage* and *Muñoz*) concerned preliminary rulings relating to situations where no secondary EU law facilitating the private enforcement of EU law before national courts of the type at issue here applied.[217] Another illustration is the fact that to date no secondary EU law has been adopted to facilitate the bringing of actions for damages by private parties for infringements of EU law under the principle of Member State liability.[218] In terms of origin, rationale and (at least to some extent) content, this principle is closely related to the (nascent) principle of private party liability that is of particular relevance in the present context.[219] Despite this absence, a range of EU law requirements with a considerable level of detail have nonetheless been developed in the Court's case law.[220] This may admittedly not lead to a situation that leaves nothing to be desired. Many private parties indeed still encounter difficulties when trying to obtain compensation in damages from Member States.[221] But that is an unfair standard; neither does adopting secondary EU law on private enforcement necessarily lead to optimal solutions.[222] The

216 See subsections 10.B.1 and 10.B.4 above.

217 CoJ case 106/77, *Simmenthal*; CoJ case C-213/89, *Factortame*; CoJ joined cases C-6/90 and C-9/90, *Francovich*; CoJ case C-453/99, *Courage*; CoJ case C-253/00, *Muñoz*. See subsections 2.D.1 and 2.D.2 above.

218 On this principle, see para 2.23 above. Note that, at least where their provisions on actions for damages are concerned, Procurement Remedies Directives 89/665 and 92/13 could be seen as codifications of this principle, particularly in light of CoJ case C-568/08, *Combinatie Spijker*, para 87, discussed in para 3.19 above. However, these directives pre-date the above-mentioned *Francovich* ruling that articulated the principle of Member State liability. It can therefore be ruled out that when adopting these directives the EU legislature aimed to codify the case law on this principle.

219 See para 2.27 above.

220 See para 2.23 above.

221 See e.g. Van Dam (2006), p. 40; Lock (2012), p. 1675.

222 See e.g. para 7.03 above concerning the difficulties that private parties who wish to bring actions for damages under the secondary EU law at issue here tend to experience.

absence of specific EU legislation facilitating the bringing of private enforcement actions pursuant to the principle of Member State liability thus illustrates that taking legislative action is not necessarily the only way forward in this regard.

The Commission, moreover, has the possibility of trying to accelerate and "steer" jurisprudential developments by initiating infringement proceedings in selected cases.[223] Rulings in cases concerning public enforcement-related matters such as *Greek Maize* demonstrate that this can be a way to clarify the obligations on the Member States in this respect.[224] It is remarkable that in relation to the private enforcement-related matters at issue here infringement proceedings tend to play only a very limited role, if at all.[225] Although in legal terms there are obvious limits to what can be achieved in this manner, this state of affairs seems in large part the result of a policy choice. To give a concrete example, it would probably be difficult to establish through infringement proceedings that as a matter of primary EU law a finding of a competition law infringement by a national competition authority must necessarily have binding effect on a national court seised in a private enforcement case. For this to be achieved, the adoption of secondary EU law seems required.[226] However, where the Commission finds that the laws of certain Member States set the threshold for proving the extent of damages too high or provide for too limited disclosure possibilities, thus making it impossible or excessively difficult for a private party to obtain full compensation for an infringement of EU law, there seems, legally speaking, nothing to prevent it from initiating infringement proceedings against those Member States. This could be done either instead of or in addition to proposing secondary EU law on the subject matter in question. The general absence of infringement proceedings for private enforcement-related matters suggests, however, that the Commission often tends to prefer the "legislative route" to address private enforcement-related difficulties that it identifies.

2. Other relevant factors

10.34 The second set of considerations that could be seen as questioning the added value of secondary EU law facilitating the private enforcement of EU law is more practical in nature. The central point here is that litigation patterns

223 See subsection 2.C.1 above.

224 CoJ case 68/88, *Commission v Greece (Greek maize)*. See para 2.19 above.

225 EU public procurement law is to some extent an exception, given that in this field the Commission has at times brought infringement proceedings concerning private enforcement-related matters, notably as regards concluded contracts and standstill periods. See para 3.20 and 3.27 above, respectively.

226 Cf. Art. 9 Competition Damages Directive 2014/104. See para 6.41 above.

typically depend on a broad range of factors, only a limited number of which can conceivably be addressed through adopting legislation. As has been seen in the foregoing chapters, this legislation is typically concerned with the applicable remedial and procedural rules in legal proceedings for (alleged) infringements of EU law before national courts. But there can be little doubt that many other factors can play a role that may be at least as important as those rules when a private party must decide whether or not to initiate or continue to pursue such proceedings. In other words, there can also be certain "unwritten obstacles" to the success of private enforcement claims.[227]

As far back as in 1984 the Commission noted, for instance, the relevance of '*psychological barriers*'.[228] A more recent survey speaks in this connection of a '*significant emotional component*'.[229] These findings typically relate to consumer disputes.[230] Presumably factors of this kind tend to play less of a role where the private parties concerned are undertakings, which are parties that act in a professional capacity. But also for the latter parties factors other than strictly legal considerations can be of relevance. They may, for example, fear harming the commercial relationship with the opposing party or certain forms of retaliation. Such concerns play a role particularly in public procurement cases in light of some undertakings' dependence on public contracts and fears of being "blacklisted".[231] Yet they can also be relevant in other fields, including in competition cases.[232] And even apart from that, both consumers and undertakings may simply prefer to spend their time, energy and resources on things other than litigation (opportunity costs; rational apathy).[233]

The awareness of the existence and applicability of the relevant rules of EU law and the rights that these rules may confer on the private parties concerned can be another important element in this connection, as has frequently been noted in relation to several of the fields of law at issue here.[234] This does not

227 Cf. Heinemann (2011), p. 219.

228 Commission, Memorandum on consumer redress, COM(84) 629 final, p. 6, where it is noted that consumers may be '*overawed or intimidated by the atmosphere of the courthouse or the courtroom, by the formality of the proceedings and of the legal language and even by the judges' and advocates' robes*'.

229 Eurobarometer, Consumer redress in the EU, August 2009, pp. 7 and 42.

230 See e.g. also Loos (2011), p. 491.

231 See para 3.17 above.

232 See e.g. Commission, Impact assessment report on damages actions for breach of the EU antitrust rules, SWD(2013) 203, pp. 28–9. See also Basedow (2003), p. 37; Peysner (2006), p. 97; Eilmansberger (2007), p. 447; Milutinovic (2010), p. 125; Van den Bergh (2013), pp. 13–20.

233 See e.g. para 3.17 and 5.36 above.

234 E.g. Commission, Green paper on public procurement in the EU, COM(96) 583, p. 17; Brown (1998), p. 93; Study, Lovells (2003), p. x; Eurobarometer, Consumer redress in the EU, August 2009, pp. 9 and 39; Loos (2011), p. 490. See also CoJ joined cases C-240/98 and C-244/98, *Océano Grupo*, para 26, discussed in para 5.19 above, where consumers' '*ignorance of the law*' was considered a relevant factor in concluding that in certain cases national courts must act on their own motion.

necessarily only concern awareness on the part of (potential) private party applicants. The training, expertise and attitudes of other actors involved – such as legal representatives, judges and potential infringers – as well as the structure of the legal market, may all be relevant as well.[235]

It is moreover widely agreed that parties' willingness to litigate tends to be influenced by social and cultural factors.[236] The "claim-consciousness" of private parties can differ significantly between Member States.[237] Some speak therefore of differences in '*procedural DNA*' or the '*procedural culture*'.[238] Even within one and the same Member State, litigation habits can vary across various fields of law.[239] Considerations of this kind can also affect the extent to which the competent national courts are inclined to make use of the procedural possibilities that may be provided for "in the books", for instance to estimate the harm caused by an infringement of EU law or to order the disclosure of certain items of evidence that may be needed to prove that such an infringement occurred or to quantify the harm caused as a consequence thereof.[240]

10.35 Taken together the above factors can be seen as putting in doubt the added value of the EU legislation at issue, given that this legislation generally does not – and often cannot – address these factors. Yet again matters are not black and white. Most of the above-mentioned observations do not constitute *absolute* arguments against the adoption of EU legislation facilitating private enforcement of the type under consideration here. The fact that psychological and emotional factors, commercial and pragmatic considerations as well as social and cultural attitudes play a role does not mean therefore that EU legislation has no role to play. Indeed, this could equally be seen precisely as a reason for arguing in favour of enacting such legislation. For in this manner the factors that *are* capable of being influenced by legislation will be influenced to the greatest extent possible. Most of the above-mentioned factors, moreover, are unlikely to be static. They can be expected to evolve over time at least to some

---

235 E.g. Jones (2003), p. 107; Kur (2004), pp. 825–6; Cafaggi and Micklitz (2009), pp. 426–7 and 436–7; Loos (2011), p. 490.

236 E.g. Van Gerven (2003b), pp. 74 and 213; Dougan (2002), p. 157; Wolf (2003), p. 422; Arrowsmith (2005), pp. 1436–7; Drake (2006), p. 862; Howells (2008), pp. 121 and 133. See also Commission, Impact assessment report on remedies in the field of public procurement, SEC(2006) 557, p. 16.

237 Study, Lovells (2003), pp. ix and 23.

238 Fairgrieve and Lichère (2011), p. 194; Opinion AG Geelhoed joined cases C-295/04 to C-298/04, *Manfredi*, para 31, respectively.

239 E.g. where one study (Study, Lovells (2003)) singled out the UK as a particularly "claim-conscious" jurisdiction in relation to product liability, other reports (Wood Report (2004); Fairgrieve and Lichère (2011), p. 192) noted that in the UK private parties are very hesitant in bringing claims for breaches of the public procurement rules.

240 Heinemann (2011), p. 219. As was noted in para 6.30 and 6.31 above, national law does sometimes provide for possibilities of this sort, which tend, however, to be used only to a limited extent in practice.

extent. There is no reason to presume that EU legislation could not play a role in that process.

It would further appear that EU legislation of the type at issue here can in fact fulfil a particularly important function in raising awareness. Although it reportedly has not had a substantial effect in terms of increased litigation, the Product Liability Directive has for example been accredited with contributing towards '*an increased awareness of and emphasis on product safety*'.[241] The introduction of the Procurement Remedies Directives has similarly been found to have contributed to improved awareness on the part of aggrieved tenderers of their rights conferred by EU public procurement law,[242] just as the IPR Enforcement Directive has been said to have "sensitised" courts and legal practitioners.[243] This "awareness-raising" potential of EU legislation has not been lost on the Commission. It has repeatedly invoked it as an important argument in favour of adopting EU legislative measures of the type at issue here, *inter alia* in relation to the revision of the Procurement Remedies Directives.[244] Another example is the Commission's statement concerning its proposal for the Competition Damages Directive that '*[r]aising awareness is necessary in order to ensure that victims of competition law infringements make use of their right to full compensation and, hence, contribute to achieving the purpose of an effective private enforcement of competition law*'.[245] Earlier the Commission had held that private parties would also be '*brought closer*' to the EU competition rules through its initiative in this field[246] and that codifying some of the relevant case law could lead to '*greater awareness*'.[247]

In fact, it may well be that even merely *discussing* possible legislative action can already have certain effects in practice. Over the past period damages litigation for infringements of competition law has on the whole gradually increased in the EU.[248] This has happened largely in parallel to the discussions on a possible EU legislative initiative in this field, meaning that this increase occurred before the Competition Damages Directive was adopted and transposed into national

241 Commission, First report on Product Liability Directive 85/374, COM(95) 617, p. 2. This conclusion is based on Study, McKenna (1994).

242 Study, Herbert Smith (1996), p. 21.

243 Geiger, Raynard and Rodà (2011), p. 546.

244 Commission, Impact assessment report on remedies in the field of public procurement, SEC(2006) 557, p. 34.

245 Commission, Impact assessment report on damages actions for breach of the EU antitrust rules, SWD(2013) 203, p. 26. See e.g. also Commission, Staff working paper accompanying the white paper on damages actions for breach of the EC antitrust rules, SEC(2008) 404, p. 98.

246 Commission, Green paper on damages actions for breach of the EC antitrust rules, COM(2005) 672, p. 4.

247 Commission, Staff working paper accompanying the green paper on damages actions for breach of EC antitrust rules, SEC(2005) 1732, p. 7.

248 See para 6.23 above.

law. Although several factors are likely to have played a role in this connection,[249] it appears that the years of discussions, studies, official documents, academic publications and consultations on a possible legislative initiative in this field have certainly helped "sensitise" the private parties concerned, their legal representatives and the national courts.[250] Furthermore, it may well be that these discussions have also played a role in bringing about legislative change at the national level with respect to the private enforcement of competition law.[251] The national legislator may thus also have been "sensitised". Whatever its precise cause, this increased degree of litigation can, moreover, have self-reinforcing effects, especially where it leads to additional, well-published and broadly debated preliminary rulings by the Court of Justice.

10.36 Therefore, again, the main point is not that the above-mentioned factors necessarily argue against the adoption of EU legislation facilitating the private enforcement of EU law before national courts of the type under consideration here. The foregoing has rather served to underline that the remedial and procedural matters addressed in this legislation should not be assessed *in isolation*. It is submitted that account ought to be taken of the broader context in which this legislation operates or is to operate when considering the question of whether or not to adopt or amend such EU legislation or when assessing the effects in practice of EU legislative action or inaction in this respect. This argues against an approach whereby the need for EU legislative action is principally determined in light of the number of cases brought in a given field of law. Not only would few consider litigation to be an end in itself;[252] too many factors would also seem to be at work for this to be an adequate measure to be able to determine such a need.

D. COHERENCE AND FRAGMENTATION

This final section of Chapter 10 takes as its point of departure that the adoption of EU legislation facilitating the private enforcement of EU law is deemed both feasible and necessary in light of the relevant legal, political and policy considerations. On that basis the question essentially addressed is *how* to legislate in such a case. It is first shown that the legislation analysed in the foregoing

---

249 The CoJ's *Courage* case law has e.g. undoubtedly been another relevant factor. See para 6.14–6.16 above.

250 See e.g. Kammin and Becker (2013), p. 61.

251 See e.g. Commission, Impact assessment report on damages actions for breach of the EU antitrust rules, SWD(2013) 203, p. 17 (see also its pp. 74–5). Here it is noted that several Member States had already adopted or amended their legislation or were considering doing so with a view to facilitating the bringing of actions for damages for breaches of the competition rules.

252 Cf. Cafaggi and Micklitz (2009), p. 443.

chapters can lead to concerns in terms of coherence and fragmentation both when they are considered from the perspective of EU law (first subsection) and national law (second subsection). The third subsection then assesses to what extent there is scope for a more coherent approach at EU level.

1. Coherence and fragmentation at EU level

In light of the foregoing, it seems fair to say that EU legislation facilitating the private enforcement of EU law before national courts leaves much to be desired in terms of *internal coherence*. On the whole, neither in this legislation itself nor in the preparatory and explanatory documents relating thereto can indications be found that these legal acts are underpinned by an approach that seeks to address the remedial and procedural matters in question in a coherent and consistent manner. These acts and documents have instead been mostly tailored to the perceived needs and specifics of the sector at issue. Little account is taken of the state of play in other fields of EU law, let alone that much consideration seems to be given to the possible future development of EU law concerning private enforcement seen in its entirety. **10.37**

Hardly any attention appears to have been paid, for instance, to ensuring a coherent and consistent approach where EU rules on actions for damages are concerned, even if this remedy takes an important place in most directives under consideration and similar concerns often arise in several fields of law.[253] There can of course be good reasons for addressing certain particular concerns in a particular manner. But it is difficult to see why one should not at least try to depart from a common position, for example on points such as the applicable causality requirements and the quantification and qualification of the harm caused.[254] It has similarly already been seen above that, notwithstanding certain relevant differences, in respect of the contractual remedies provided for there appears to be scope for improving the internal coherence of the rules of EU law at issue.[255] It is also not immediately evident why the EU legislative measures in question tend to be drafted in a different manner every time where provision is made for recurring penalty payments or for publicity measures.[256] The rules on the *inter partes* disclosure of evidence set out in the Competition Damages Directive are in a sense a positive exception, as they are expressly inspired by the corresponding arrangement of the IPR Enforcement Directive.[257] This would,

253 See subsection 7.A.1 above.
254 See subsections 7.A.3, 7.A.4 and 7.B.5 above, respectively.
255 See subsection 8.A.1 above.
256 See subsections 8.B.3 and 8.B.4 above, respectively.
257 See Commission, Proposal for Competition Damages Directive 2014/104, COM(2013) 404, p. 14.

however, seem to make it all the more regrettable that these provisions have been drafted and structured in a slightly diverging manner.[258]

In this light it is unsurprising that many commentators have cast a harsh verdict on the EU's legislative involvement with the remedies and procedures applicable in private enforcement proceedings before national courts generally and with issues such as non-contractual liability (tort) and contract law specifically. The relevant bodies of EU law have been criticised for their '*piecemeal nature*',[259] their '*ad hoc*' character[260] and '*compartmentalisation*'.[261] EU law relating to non-contractual liability has been called a '*rather ramshackle creation*',[262] while in this connection it has also been held that it is '*hard to identify any consistency of approach at all*'.[263] EU law on consumer contracts has similarly been described as '*wildly unsystematic*'.[264] It has rightfully been observed that when addressing these kinds of matters, the EU legislature is mostly interested in solving certain particular problems rather than in securing legal integrity or doctrinal coherence.[265]

10.38 An obvious but therefore no less relevant point to make in this connection is that each of the legal acts and initiatives assessed in Part B above relates to one particular sector of economic activity regulated by EU law. The Procurement Remedies Directives are limited to the enforcement of the EU rules in the field of public procurement, the IPR Enforcement Directive is primarily linked to EU legislation in the field of intellectual property, and so on. In fact, hardly ever is an *entire* sector or field of law covered.[266] The two aforementioned directives may be comparatively ambitious in so far as their scope is concerned, but they do not provide "full" coverage of the substantive rules of EU law at issue, even at sectoral level. The Procurement Remedies Directives do not apply to infringements of the Defence Procurement Directive, for instance. Instead, the latter contains a set of (largely but not entirely similar) private enforcement-related rules of its own.[267] This thus adds to the differentiation that already results from the fact that the EU legislature found it necessary to adopt not one but two Procurement Remedies Directives that also differ slightly from each other. As

---

258 Cf. Art. 6 and 7(1) IPR Enforcement Directive 2004/18; Art. 5 Competition Damages Directive 2014/104. See subsection 8.B.2 above.
259 Van Gerven (1995), p. 525
260 Dougan (2004), p. 15
261 Milutinovic (2010), p. 341.
262 Kellner (2009), p. 151.
263 Oliphant (2008), p. 271 (regarding the qualification and quantification of damages).
264 Weatherill (2012), p. 1280.
265 Collins (2011), p. 453. See e.g. also Curtin (1993), p. 17.
266 As regards the scope of the EU legislation at issue more generally, see subsection 9.A.1 above.
267 Art. 55–64 Defence Procurement Directive 2009/81. See para 3.08 above.

to the IPR Enforcement Directive, the Commission decided to lay down a separate set of rules on civil redress in its proposal for a trade secrets directive rather than to amend the IPR Enforcement Directive.[268] And even apart from that, at present certain private enforcement-related provisions concerning intellectual property law infringements can already be found in legal acts other than the IPR Enforcement Directive, for example in the Infosoc Directive.[269] The Competition Damages Directive's scope may furthermore be relatively broad in that it covers in principle all infringements of Articles 101 and 102 TFEU (but not infringements of EU law on state aid, for example), yet its scope is narrow in the sense that it concentrates on actions for damages, leaving other possibly relevant substantive private enforcement remedies entirely unregulated.

It follows that none of these directives regulate private enforcement-related matters in an entire field of EU law in a more or less complete manner, let alone that they cover several or even all fields covered by substantive EU law. This is evidently different to many national legal systems. Particularly in Member States with a civil law (as opposed to common law) system, rules on remedies and procedures typically apply much more broadly, regardless of which types of substantive rules are infringed.[270]

The resulting "compartmentalisation" is in part inherent in the manner in which competences have been vested in the EU. As was explained earlier, pursuant to the principle of conferral, the EU cannot legislate as it sees fit.[271] The EU Treaties mostly confer powers on a sector-specific basis, notably with a view to addressing issues with a transnational dimension. Also, Article 114 TFEU does not vest in the EU a general power to regulate the internal market.[272] That being so, it can hardly come as a surprise that secondary EU law is mostly sector-specific. That applies for the *substantive* rules in question and, by extension, also for the rules on remedies and procedures that seek to facilitate the *enforcement* of those substantive rules by private parties before national courts. It is true that in and of itself this need not lead to incoherence and inconsistencies. The reality is, however, that the latter is typically the result of such a "stand-alone" approach. That tends already to be the case where the private enforcement-related rules relate to the same sector, as is illustrated by the generally limited, but nonetheless noticeable, differences between the 10.39

268 Commission, Proposal for a trade secrets directive, COM(2013) 813, pp. 19–24 (Art. 5–14). See para 4.07 above. Unlike IPR Enforcement Directive 2004/48, this proposal includes e.g. rules on limitation periods, whereas it does not provide for rules on the disclosure of evidence or on legal costs.

269 Art. 8 Infosoc Directive 2001/29. See para 4.11 above.

270 On the impact at national level, see further subsection 10.D.2 below.

271 See para 10.01 above.

272 See para 10.02 above. See also para 10.47 below.

Defence Procurement Directive and the Procurement Remedies Directives and between the proposal for a trade secrets directive and the IPR Enforcement Directive. And it certainly applies where entirely different sectors are concerned. Diversity of legal bases may therefore result in equally fragmented mindsets among administrators, decision-makers and stakeholders.[273]

One could well imagine establishing an underlying programme or framework of some sort in light of which the EU's private enforcement-related legislation could be drafted, regardless of the sector or subsector concerned.[274] It could set out certain guiding principles, standardised approaches, rules on uniform terminology, and so on. Generally speaking, neither the need for tailor-made solutions in certain specific cases nor constraints related to the legal basis of a particular proposed act of secondary EU law need stand in the way of such an approach. In that sense, more can and indeed should be expected from the Commission and the EU legislature.[275] Yet there are also reasons for not being overly optimistic in this regard. The everyday reality of Brussels-based law-making is likely to continue to lead to situations where issues related to internal coherence and consistency play (at best) only a secondary role, whether or not a "horizontal" programme or framework of some kind exists. When discussing a draft legal act that is only concerned with, say, private enforcement in the field of competition law, the parties involved (not only the EU institutions concerned, but also experts, academics, private sector stakeholders and other interested parties) may well have concerns other than ensuring consistency with the EU rules that already apply, for instance, in the field of intellectual property law. Account should further be taken of the political sensitivity of many of the matters under consideration.[276] Things tend to be complicated further by the need to reconcile different legal cultures, mentalities and linguistic issues in the process of EU law-making.[277] All this may well necessitate innovative rather than standardised solutions for a draft act to be adopted or even proposed. This almost inevitably comes at the expense of well-intended and in themselves laudable ambitions in terms of coherence and consistency.

10.40 Another – more fundamental – point to be made in this connection is that the current sector-specific approach also implies a differentiation in *enforcement possibilities* within the broader category of rights of private parties vested in EU law. While the EU legislation and initiatives at issue here typically seek to make

273 Dawson and Muir (2014), p. 222.

274 Cf. European Parliament, Council and Commission, Interinstitutional agreement on better law-making, OJ 2003, C 321/1.

275 Cf. Art. 7 TFEU. See also Van Gerven (2008a), p. 42.

276 See subsection 10.B.1 above.

277 Cf. Van Gerven (2008a), p. 43.

it easier for these parties to enforce their rights based on substantive EU law on public procurement, intellectual property, consumer protection and competition law, in many other instances where EU law grants rights to private parties, no comparable legislation exists. Here the issue of coherence thus does not relate so much to the differences between the various legal acts at issue, but rather to the difference that exists between the fields of law where such acts have been adopted, on the one hand, and the fields where that is not the case, on the other hand. As a result of this differentiation, in certain fields private parties can rely on private enforcement-facilitating measures, which can make it easier, for instance, to claim damages, have interim measures granted, obtain evidence or ensure that judgments are complied with, whereas in other fields no such measures are available.

Not without reason has the appropriateness of the resulting sector-specific privileging of certain fields of EU law and the rights derived from that law over others been questioned.[278] Such an approach can raise issues of fairness and equal treatment. To illustrate this point, it is evident that, further to the Court's ruling in *Courage*, the Commission and subsequently the EU legislature have sought to ensure that a private party affected by a competition law infringement can receive full compensation by proposing and adopting the Competition Damages Directive.[279] But it is not immediately clear why no such legislative follow-up has been given to the Court's finding in *Muñoz* that private parties should be able to bring civil proceedings to address infringements of certain agricultural rules.[280] Similarly, the Procurement Remedies Directives seek to facilitate the private enforcement of the Substantive Public Directives, which give expression to the EU Treaties' fundamental freedoms (particularly the freedoms of establishment and to provide services).[281] Yet one could wonder why no such measures exist, for example, in respect of the rights that private parties can derive from the Services Directive, which was also adopted on the basis of these provisions.[282]

Once more the point here is not that there cannot be good grounds for differentiating between the enforcement possibilities that exist with respect to various substantive rules of EU law or in particular situations.[283] It may well be that one sector is considered to be of greater economic importance than 10.41

278 E.g. Wolf (2003), pp. 422–3; Van Dam (2006), p. 345; Reich (2007), p. 738.

279 CoJ case C-453/99, *Courage*. See subsections 6.B.2, 6.B.3, 6.B.4 and 6.C.1 above.

280 CoJ case C-253/00, *Muñoz*. See para 2.25 above.

281 See para 3.02 and 3.03 above.

282 Services Directive 2006/123.

283 Cf. also the discussion of certain sector-specific measures on the disclosure of evidence in subsection 8.B.2 above.

another, that certain rules are singled out as a political priority, that the enforcement-related difficulties encountered by private parties differ, and so on. Likewise, there can also be reasons for such differentiation between the various substantive rules that apply within a particular field of law.[284] The main point here is rather that the question of whether or not there are such grounds does not seem to receive much attention, if at all, when EU legislation of the type at issue here is being prepared, discussed and adopted. It is in particular often far from clear on the basis of *which criteria* these choices are made or indeed whether the question on what basis certain particular domains are singled out has been asked at all. It may only be human for individual observers to sometimes seem to assume rather easily that their own field of specialisation is exceptional and worthy of special treatment. It is remarkable, however, how little attention is generally paid at institutional level to the question of whether and why a particular field of EU law requires special legislative measures so as to facilitate the private enforcement of the substantive rules in question.

In relation to the Competition Damages Directive, some attention has been given to this issue, presumably in response to earlier critical comments by stakeholders.[285] In 2008 the Commission argued that the fact that similar private enforcement-related problems might exist in other fields is in and of itself not a reason for the EU not to act in this particular field. This seems a valid point to make. But it would have been considerably more convincing had the following statements about competition cases being '*unusually difficult*', given their '*particular complexity*' and the '*particularly high*' and '*unevenly distributed*' evidential burden been properly explained and substantiated.[286] At least some of these submissions may well be less self-evident than seems to be presumed. Competition cases can undoubtedly be complicated. But are they inherently more complex than other forms of commercial litigation, especially considering that in some ("follow-on") competition cases applicants can build on the findings of unusually powerful public enforcement authorities? It has already been seen in the foregoing that low levels of damages litigation and the problems typically cited in this connection (such as high costs, lengthy proceedings, difficulties in meeting the standard of proof and difficulties in quantifying the harm) are by no means unique to competition cases.[287] In 2013 the Commission also highlighted another element, namely that the amount of uncompensated harm caused by competition law infringements would be

284 Cf. e.g. Hüschelrath and Peyer (2013), p. 585.

285 See para 6.19 above. See e.g. also European Parliament, Resolution on the white paper on damages actions for breach of the EC antitrust rules, P6_TA(2009)0187, para 3 and 5.

286 Commission, Staff working paper accompanying the white paper on damages actions for breach of the EC antitrust rules, SEC(2008) 404, pp. 95–6.

287 See in particular para 7.03 above.

'*particularly big*'.[288] That might be true. However, again this statement seems largely speculative. The estimate of the harm caused by the infringements at issue is no more than a very rough approximation.[289] And again there are no indications whatsoever that a quantitative comparison has been made to underpin this statement.

2. Coherence and fragmentation at national level

Even if they take a somewhat different form, it is important to note that concerns related to coherence and fragmentation emerge not only at EU, but also at *national* level. A particular concern in this regard is that EU legislative measures of the type at issue can lead to *fragmentation* (that is, a lessening of the internal coherence) of the respective domestic legal systems of the Member States. Adopting specific remedial and procedural provisions for, say, the enforcement of rights based on the EU public procurement rules can cause a degree of disruption of the national legal systems, in as much as these provisions of EU law do not cover rights based on "purely" national procurement law (that is, rules of national law other than those transposing a directive). As is perhaps to be expected, concerns along these lines have regularly been expressed, especially by the Member States in relation to the EU legislation discussed above, either with respect to an intended EU legislative initiative generally or a particular provision of a proposal.[290] Yet it is noticeable that especially in more recent years the European Parliament has highlighted them as well.[291] Concerns of this kind have also been widely acknowledged in the legal literature.[292] **10.42**

288 Commission, Impact assessment report on damages actions for breach of the EU antitrust rules, SWD(2013) 203, p. 18 (n. 42).

289 Cf. ibid., p. 22, where it is observed that '*the absence of reliable empirical data makes precise quantification impossible*', but that '*there is general agreement that the infringements of competition law cause substantial harm*'. The subsequent estimates give a somewhat more concrete indication, but the ranges remain very wide (between €5.7 and €23.3 billion a year EU-wide) and the costs cited do not coincide with the size of the uncompensated harm as a consequence of the infringements that the proposal seeks to address. A comparison with other fields of law is entirely absent.

290 See e.g. para 3.28 (concerning the possibility under Procurement Remedies Directives 89/665 and 92/13 of designating several separate review bodies), para 4.10 (concerning the legislative initiative leading to IPR Enforcement Directive 2004/48), para 5.28 (concerning a provision on compensation for non-material damage under Product Liability Directive 85/374), para 5.37 (concerning a possible legislative initiative on collective redress) and para 6.19 (concerning the legislative initiative leading to Competition Damages Directive 2014/104) above.

291 E.g. European Parliament, Resolution on the white paper on damages actions for breach of the EC antitrust rules, P6_TA(2009)0187, para 5; European Parliament, Resolution, Towards a coherent European approach to collective redress, P7_TA(2012)0021, para 15.

292 See e.g. Van Gerven (1995), p. 700; Cornish et al. (2003), p. 448; Dougan (2011), p. 416; Weatherill (2012), p. 1315.

This fragmenting effect at national level – the "dark side of EU harmonisation", as it has been called[293] – may not be unique to EU legislation of the type at issue here. Yet this concern arguably features more prominently in the present context for two reasons. First, matters related to the remedies and procedures applicable in private enforcement proceedings before national courts have traditionally mostly been left to be regulated by the domestic legal systems of the Member States.[294] This means that these legal systems have on the whole been able to retain a considerable degree of internal coherence in this respect, certainly as compared to many matters of substantive law. Second, at least in most Member States with a civil law tradition, the national bodies of law regulating these matters (for example regarding legal standing, damages claims or legal costs) have typically been designed to apply across the board, regardless of the nature or origin of the rule of substantive law at issue. The EU's sector-specific manner of legislating tends to necessitate a deviation from this point of departure. This effect is aggravated by the fact that, as was pointed out in the previous subsection, the EU rules in question tend to differ from each other.

10.43 This fragmenting effect can be looked upon in different ways. One view is to see it simply as an unfortunate but necessary evil that results from the supranational structure of the EU and the position of EU law in relation to national law.[295] There is certainly some truth in this. The manner in which powers have been conferred on the EU makes it, generally speaking, impossible to cover all situations, including situations without an internal market relevance or another cross-border dimension, in a single act of secondary EU law and thus to ensure coherence across the board.[296] It naturally follows that national law tends to be harmonised on a selective basis, which necessarily implies that rules of national law *other* than the ones to which that act of secondary EU law relates remain unaffected. A degree of fragmentation at national level may therefore indeed be a necessary and often unavoidable evil.

However, it is submitted that this is not – or at least this should not be – the last word to be said on the matter. It would in particular be incorrect to perceive the above-mentioned concerns about fragmentation at national level as being mainly a matter of national legislative design and elegance. For the fragmentation referred to above can have significant "real-world" consequences. The rules of national law that are affected by this EU legislation are often the result of centuries of legal evolution and – more importantly – they may well reflect

293 Van Gerven (2003a), p. 401.
294 See in particular para 1.06 and 2.01 above.
295 Komninos (2008), p. 181.
296 See also subsection 10.D.3 below.

certain legitimate political, social and cultural preferences.[297] In accordance with these preferences, most of these rules, moreover, perform a useful function.[298] Although none of this constitutes an absolute bar to EU legislative action in this domain, it may well be a reason not to set these rules aside too easily. Indeed, while it may be true that procedural idiosyncrasy, unlike national costume or regional cuisine, is not to be nurtured for its own sake,[299] neither is this merely a question of easily "transferable technology".[300] There is a balance to be struck.

That applies all the more so given that in this context also EU legislative interference tends to imply preferential treatment in terms of enforcement possibilities in certain fields of law and of certain rights in others.[301] The rights, the enforcement of which the EU legislation at issue seeks to facilitate, are after all mostly rights conferred by substantive EU law.[302] The result of EU legislative action facilitating private enforcement can therefore be more favourable treatment in terms of enforcement of certain rights vested in *EU* law as compared with rights vested in ("purely") *national* law. There is, however, no reason to assume that the former, simply by virtue of being EU rights, are of greater importance than the latter.[303] It is not evident that a private party seeking to enforce a right vested in, for instance, EU consumer protection law ought to be treated more favourably than the party that seeks to enforce such a right vested in "purely" national consumer protection law. In this context, also, issues of fairness and equal treatment can thus arise.[304]

A final point to note in this connection is the *spillover effect* that EU legislation **10.44** of the type at issue here can have. This refers to the phenomenon that, pursuant to the adoption of this legislation (or indeed the case law of the Court of Justice[305]), Member States regularly decide to apply the requirements set out in that legislation more broadly. For instance, the Procurement Remedies Directives only cover infringements of the substantive *EU* public procurement

---

297 Cf. Storme (1994), p. 38; Van Gerven (2008b), p. 409; Storskrubb (2008), p. 21; Dougan (2011), p. 410.

298 Cf. CoJ case C-413/12, *ACICL*, para 38: '*[national] procedural rules relating to the structure of internal legal remedies and the number of instances of jurisdiction pursue a general interest in the sound administration of justice and foreseeability*'. In a similar sense, see Dougan (2004), p. 28; Prechal (2005), p. 173.

299 Storskrubb (2008), p. 13 (citing English case law).

300 Harlow (2000), pp. 80–83.

301 See also para 10.40 above.

302 See subsection 9.A.1 above.

303 Cf. Opinion AG Jacobs joined cases C-430/93 and C-431/93, *Van Schijndel*, para 27.

304 Cf. CoJ case C-279/09, *DEB*, para 56. In this ruling (concerning national rules on legal aid) the CoJ held that applicants relying on EU law should not be favoured over other applicants.

305 See Hartmann (2012), p. 620, where it is noted that, pursuant to CoJ joined cases C-6/90 and C-9/90, *Francovich*, several Member States "implemented" the principle of Member State liability articulated in that ruling in purely domestic situations too. On this ruling and this principle, see para 2.23 above.

rules.[306] Nonetheless, when transposing these directives many Member States decided to apply the same remedial and procedural rules to infringements of rules of "purely" national substantive public procurement law.[307] Such a spill-over effect has also been observed to occur with respect to the Consumer Injunctions Directive[308] and the Product Liability Directive.[309] Of course these Member States are not *legally obliged* under EU law to take such steps. Strictly speaking this is no more than harmonisation on a voluntary basis. But the fact that the Member States nonetheless regularly do so underlines the sincerity of the above-mentioned concerns regarding the fragmentation of their respective national legal systems, as this is often the only way to retain a degree of internal coherence and ensure equal treatment. Moreover, this spillover effect can also lead to questions as regards the practical effects of the principle of conferral, which is of fundamental importance in the EU legal order.[310]

10.45 In many respects the conclusion to be drawn concerning matters of coherence and fragmentation considered from the perspective of national law is therefore comparable to the one set out in the previous subsection that concentrated on the EU perspective. In legal terms none of the foregoing constitutes an absolute bar to the adoption of EU legislation facilitating the private enforcement of EU law. There may, moreover, well be valid and convincing policy reasons for taking such legislative action at EU level. It is submitted, however, that, although this may be the outcome, concerns related to fragmentation at national level should not be simply shrugged off *a priori* as an unfortunate but necessary evil. For the reasons set out above, the possible consequences for the domestic legal systems of the Member States merit being given appropriate weight in the EU decision-making process, as a matter of good law-making and respect for the principles of subsidiarity and proportionality.[311]

---

306 See para 3.08 above.

307 Commission, Report on the impact and effectiveness of EU public procurement legislation, SEC(2011) 853, p. 67.

308 Study, University of Bielefeld (2008), p. 610.

309 Van Gerven, Lever and Larouche (2000), p. 648. For another example, outside the scope of Part B above, see the (proposed) application of the provisions of Mediation Directive 2008/52 not only in cross-border but also in "purely" national disputes under Netherlands and Italian law. See European Parliament Policy Department (2011), p. 67; Davies and Szyszczak (2011), p. 702.

310 See para 10.01 above.

311 In a similar sense, see Opinion AG Jacobs joined cases C-430/93 and C-431/93, *Van Schijndel*, para 27; De Búrca (1997), p. 45; Van Gerven (2008a), p. 43; Milutinovic (2010), p. 328.

3. Towards a more coherent approach?

It is understandable in light of the foregoing that calls for a more coherent EU legislative approach on the matters under consideration here have often been made.[312] It should be acknowledged in this connection that more recently there have been some (modest) signs of a "de-compartmentalisation", or at least certain attempts thereto. As was noted above, despite certain (regrettable) differences between the two regimes, the Competition Damages Directive at least acknowledges the existence of and seeks to build on the arrangement in the IPR Enforcement Directive on the *inter partes* disclosure of evidence.[313] At an earlier stage, when this competition law initiative was still expected to include rules on collective redress, account was also taken of the approach involving qualified entities set out in the Consumer Injunctions Directive.[314] This collective redress aspect has since developed from a "competition-only" into a broader initiative that also covers infringements of consumer protection law and other rules of substantive EU law from which private parties can derive rights.[315] The Commission explained this decision to opt for a broader approach with reference to the fact that competition law is not the only field where infringements may lead to "scattered" damages and the wish to avoid the unnecessary fragmentation of the civil laws of the Member States.[316] **10.46**

Also, elsewhere in EU law attention to ensuring a more coherent and consistent approach appears to be increasing. Ambitions in this regard were expressed, for instance, in relation to the enforcement of EU rules on passengers' rights.[317] In the field of contract law a number of further initiatives were also taken towards this aim.[318] These include involving academics so as to establish a "common frame of reference".[319] In due time this academic work may contribute to the creation of more extensive and more coherent EU legislation on the

312 E.g. Van Gerven (2004a), pp. 527–32; Koziol and Schulze (2008a), p. 608; Lukas (2008), p. 102; Storskrubb (2008), p. 305; Kellner (2009), p. 152; Zippro (2009a), p. 220; Tulibacka (2009), p. 1557.

313 See subsection 8.B.2 above.

314 Commission, Staff working paper accompanying the white paper on damages actions for breach of the EC antitrust rules, SEC(2008) 404, p. 19. See Art. 3 Consumer Injunctions Directive 2009/22, discussed in para 5.06 above.

315 Collective Redress Recommendation 2013/396. See subsection 5.E.2 above.

316 Commission, Impact assessment report on damages actions for breach of the EU antitrust rules, SWD(2013) 203, p. 55.

317 Commission, White paper on a roadmap on a single European transport area, COM(2011) 144, p. 23.

318 See e.g. Commission, Green paper on policy options towards a European contract law for consumers and businesses, COM(2010) 348.

319 Von Bar and Clive (2010). For a discussion and further references, see e.g. Hondius (2011), p. 531. For other academic contributions see e.g. Lando and Beale (2000); Lando et al. (2003); Hartkamp et al. (2011). More specifically on the topic of the law of non-contractual liability (tort), see also Van Gerven, Lever and Larouche (2000); Van Dam (2006); Koziol and Schulze (2008b). See also the work of the European Group on tort law.

aforementioned issues,[320] although for now that seems still a rather distant and uncertain prospect.[321] The said initiatives also include legislative proposals, most notably for a consumer rights directive and for a regulation on a European sales law.[322] Without going into detail here it can, however, be noted that these proposals have been received rather critically.[323] Whereas the proposal for a regulation on a European sales law is currently still pending, the Consumer Rights Directive was adopted in 2011.[324] In the course of the legislative process, substantial amendments to the Commission's proposal were made, including a significant reduction of its scope. Many find the resulting directive disappointing.[325] Indeed, it has led to the observation that '*there are limits to what is politically palatable in the name of "coherence"*'.[326]

It thus seems that a coherent approach, while laudable, is often more easily called for and dreamt up in the abstract than brought into EU legislative practice.[327]

10.47 A similar conclusion is likely to emerge – perhaps *a fortiori* – when considering the scope for considerably more *ambitious* legislative arrangements, which would cut across various sectors and regulate national remedial and procedural rules for the private enforcement of EU law before national courts in a more coherent manner. Leaving political, policy and practical issues aside for a moment, as the law stands, the main legal constraint seems once more the requirement for a sufficient legal basis.[328] It has for example been suggested that the EU might take legislative action to address differences between national laws on remedies and procedures in a more general manner under Article 114 TFEU. To this effect it has been submitted that '*the harmonisation of procedural rules [is] a sine qua non for market integration*' and that '*the Member States of the*

---

320 Some of the academic work referred to above is at times invoked in opinions of certain AGs. See further Basedow (2010a), p. 465 (n. 103); Gutman (2011), p. 748.

321 Cf. Commission Decision 2010/233/EU setting up the expert group on a common frame of reference in the area of European contract law, OJ 2010, L 105/109; Study, Expert group on European contract law (2011).

322 Commission, Proposal for Consumer Rights Directive 2011/83, COM(2008) 614; Commission, Proposal for a regulation on a common European sales law, COM(2011) 635.

323 On the proposed directive, see e.g. Micklitz and Reich (2009), p. 471; Ackermann (2010), p. 587; Hondius (2010), p. 103. In relation to the proposed regulation, see e.g. Lando (2011), p. 717; Samoy, Dang Vu and Jansen (2011), p. 855; Heideman (2012), p. 119.

324 Consumer Rights Directive 2011/83.

325 E.g. Stuyck (2012), p. 69.

326 Weatherill (2012), pp. 1311.

327 See further e.g. Weitenberg (2008), p. 309; Basedow (2010a), p. 443.

328 Apart from the articles discussed above, Art. 352 TFEU could also be considered here. This article provides a legal basis where EU action is necessary to attain one of the objectives set out in the EU Treaties. However, this provision has important limitations of its own. Most notably, it is residual in nature, as it can only be applied '*if the [EU] Treaties have not provided the necessary powers*', and it requires that the Council acts unanimously in adopting the proposed legislative measure.

European Union, having created an internal market, are obliged to correct … unwanted effects which stem from procedural differences'.[329] Others have argued that:

> [i]f a market is to flourish, disputes arising out of business conducted in the market must be resolved consistently with one another, and that requires more than uniform substantive law. Distortion is bound to occur if the mode of litigation, with all that that implies by way of procedural techniques and by way of their implications for costs, delays, appeals, enforcement of judgments and so on, varies substantially from one place to another.[330]

Claims of this type may not be untrue. Yet it is another matter whether that suffices for the present purposes, particularly in light of their level of abstraction. It has already been noted above that the use of a legal basis can only be determined in light of the aim and the content of a concrete intended legislative measure and that Article 114 TFEU does not grant the EU a general power to regulate the internal market.[331] A real, appreciable effect of the identified disparities on the internal market is required. It seems questionable whether broad claims such as the ones set out above can be sufficiently substantiated so as to withstand scrutiny by the Court of Justice if and when challenged. In practice it would generally seem difficult to meet this standard where the intended legislative measures relate to matters of remedies and procedures to be applied across the board. The Court of Justice has held, for instance, that the possibility that undertakings would hesitate to sell goods in another Member State because they are subject to different procedural rules '*is too uncertain and indirect for that national provision to be regarded as liable to hinder trade between Member States*'.[332] While this case did not concern the use of Article 114 TFEU as a legal basis, it nonetheless seems to illustrate the mostly indirect or subsidiary effects that national rules on remedies and procedures have. Adopting private enforcement-related EU legislation based on this article therefore seems difficult to conceive without making the argument that the intended measures are required in order to ensure the effectiveness of certain *specific* substantive rules of EU law (as opposed to those rules *generally*).[333] In other

329 Storskrubb (2008), pp. 78–9. In a similar sense, see e.g. Van den Bossche (2003), pp. 52–4.

330 Jolowicz (1994), p. xiii. See also Storme (1994), pp. 43–53.

331 See para 10.02 above.

332 Cf. CoJ case C-412/97, *ED*, para 11. See e.g. also CoJ case 811/79, *Ariete*, para 16. See also Dougan (2004), pp. 23 and 100; Van Dam (2006), pp. 133–8; Study, Cauffman, Faure and Hartlief (2009), p. 308.

333 Cf. Commission, Impact assessment report on damages actions for breach of the EU antitrust rules, SWD(2013) 203, p. 41. Here it is said that '*[e]ffective redress, fair competition and the proper functioning of the internal market would [...] require comparable exposure to damages claims, which can be brought about only by similar procedural rules governing actions for damages*'. This also seems a rather broad and abstract claim, even if here it evidently relates only to national rules relating to EU (and in some cases national) competition law.

words, for the present purposes enforcement rules mostly "follow" the substantial rules to which they relate.[334]

10.48 It is further important not to misunderstand the meaning of issues of *uniformity* that can arise in the present context. It is true that the Court of Justice has held the uniform application of EU law to be a fundamental requirement of the EU legal order.[335] However, it has also ruled that the existence of certain differences between jurisdictions is inevitable where national law is relied upon for remedial and procedural matters (which continues to be the "default" position under EU law[336]) or where the harmonisation at EU level in this respect is limited (which is mostly the case here[337]).[338] The fundamental requirement of uniform *application*, therefore, does not necessarily involve (fully) uniform rules on *enforcement* at national level.[339] In relation to (private) enforcement-related matters, a certain degree of diversity can and often must be accepted. As Advocate General Reischl observed in 1980, the fact that '*the legal position of the individual may […] differ in the various Member States is simply a consequence of the implementation of [EU] law by the Member States, which is accepted by the [EU] legal system*'.[340] There can be no doubt that EU law has since evolved further, but, as a general rule, this would seem to be no less true today.[341]

It has also been observed that the Court of Justice does not regard uniformity as an all-embracing principle that does not allow for any national differences. Advocate General Van Gerven (writing extrajudicially) has noted that '*the requirement of universal application is fundamental, but does not override other principles, such as, in particular, the principle of the Member States' competence in "procedural" matters*'.[342] More specifically in relation to EU legislative measures, he added that:

> [w]ithin the EU, uniformity of laws, or even far-reaching harmonisation, must not be an objective in itself, as it is not of itself a higher good than diversity. The diversity between the legal families within the EU is so huge (not only with regard to content but also, and even more so, with regard to style and mentalities), and the task to achieve

334 Cf. CoJ case C-60/03, *Wolff and Müller*, para 36–7.
335 E.g. CoJ joined cases C-143/88 and C-92/89, *Zuckerfabrik Süderdithmarschen*, para 26.
336 See in particular para 2.01 and 10.12 above.
337 See in particular para 10.13 above.
338 E.g. CoJ joined cases 205/82 to 215/82, *Deutsche Milchkontor*, par. 21; CoJ case C-570/08, *Simvoulio*, para 37.
339 Cf. Micklitz (2012), p. 395.
340 Opinion AG Reischl case 61/79, *Denkavit*, p. 1233.
341 Cf. Opinion AG Jacobs joined cases C-430/93 and C-431/93, *Van Schijndel*, para 45.
342 Van Gerven (2000), p. 505. See also Dougan (2002), p. 162, where it is held that uniformity is neither a general principle nor a primary goal in the EU legal order.

unity so daunting and time and resources-consuming, that unification and harmonisation should occur only when there is a good justification for it.[343]

It has also been observed that the degree of EU involvement with substantive law can vary significantly from one field to another. This might in turn well be seen as a reason for '*selectively matching the required level of remedial-procedural harmonisation to the actual degree of substantive approximation achieved within any given policy area*'.[344]

A certain degree of increased uniformity may therefore well be the *consequence* of the adoption of EU legislation of the type assessed in the foregoing, but it is not its (main) *purpose*.[345] Some may see the resulting state of affairs as objectionable, whereas others may deem it entirely appropriate. The key point here is, however, that this is principally looked upon in a "neutral" manner as a matter of EU law, in the sense that in and of itself a quest for uniformity cannot be a basis for the EU to act in this regard. For that to be the case a sufficient legal basis in the EU Treaties is required. Indeed, whereas increased uniformity across the EU may be likely to be beneficial for the enforcement of rights vested in EU law by private parties, it cannot readily be assumed that – conversely – a degree of diversity in the applicable national rules as such necessarily leads to weak private enforcement.[346]

Finally, the question can arise as to the relevance in this regard of Article 81 **10.49**
TFEU concerning judicial cooperation in civil matters. Questions relating to this article have occasionally been voiced in relation to the EU legislation at issue.[347] Moreover, over the past decade or so an increasing body of secondary EU law has been adopted on the basis of this article. This latter legislation is mostly of an international private-law type, but it also goes further by addressing various specific procedural issues.[348] Of particular relevance here is that Article 81 TFEU allows for the adoption of EU legislative measures aimed at ensuring '*effective access to justice*' or at '*the elimination of obstacles to the proper functioning of civil proceedings, if necessary by promoting the compatibility of the rules on civil procedure applicable in the Member States*'.[349] Both "access to justice" and the "proper functioning of civil proceedings" are – or at least can be – rather

343 Van Gerven (2008b), p. 409.
344 Dougan (2002), p. 162. See also Dougan (2004).
345 Cf. Prechal (2005), p. 178.
346 Cf. Milutinovic (2010), p. 97.
347 See para 10.04 above.
348 See para 1.12 above.
349 Art. 81(2) TFEU, points (e) and (f), respectively. Note that the above reference to effective access to justice was only introduced in 2009 (Treaty of Lisbon).

broad concepts. This suggests that a range of legislative private enforcement-related measures could conceivably be adopted on this basis.[350] This legal basis, moreover, inherently deals with procedural issues. It is therefore not "subsidiary" in nature. Indeed, it can be said that more generally developments in relation to the EU's "area of freedom, security and justice" mean that it '*reaches beyond economic integration and disconnects individually enforceable rights from the market logic*'.[351] It follows that Article 81 TFEU undeniably has potential as a possible legal basis for broader EU legislative measures on many of the issues under consideration here.[352]

However, as it stands, Article 81 TFEU also contains several important limitations. It includes an internal market requirement of its own, which is, however, formulated somewhat loosely as compared with both its formulation as it stood before 2009 (Treaty of Lisbon) and with Article 114 TFEU.[353] More important, therefore, seems the requirement that the measures to be adopted on this basis must concern matters having cross-border implications.[354] The interpretation of this requirement has been particularly contentious. The Commission has sought to interpret it in an extensive manner.[355] However, the Council in particular has consistently rejected any interpretation other than the one pursuant to which this requirement excludes situations internal to a Member State from the scope of the intended EU legal act.[356] A further limitation is that the measures adopted under Article 81 TFEU must be limited to cooperation in civil matters. Rules regarding proceedings under administrative law – which can be of relevance, for instance, in relation to infringements of EU public procurement or consumer protection law[357] – are thus excluded. Where it refers to civil procedure, it also seems doubtful that in this context the

350 In a similar sense, see Lindholm (2011), p. 470. Legal Aid Directive 2003/8 has been adopted on the basis of Article 81(2)(f) TFEU.

351 Micklitz (2012), p. 370 (in relation to the CoJ case law on citizenship).

352 Cf. Tulibacka (2009), p. 1561; Dougan (2011), pp. 436–7; Kuipers (2011), p. 545; Leskinen (2011), p. 114; Van Schagen (2012), p. 37.

353 Art. 81(2) TFEU. Here it is stated here that the measures in question shall be adopted '*particularly when necessary for the proper functioning of the internal market*'. The use of the word "particularly" suggests that this is not necessarily the case. Before the entry into force of the Treaty of Lisbon (2009) it read '*in so far as necessary*' for the proper functioning of the internal market. On this requirement and its relation to Art. 114 TFEU, see further Bariatti (2011), pp. 23–5; Stuyck (2011), pp. 527–8.

354 Art. 81(1) TFEU.

355 Most notably, in its 2005 proposal for Small Claims Regulation 861/2007 the Commission argued that '*procedural law by its nature may have cross-border implications*' and that '*[a] measure which is necessary for the proper functioning of the internal market has necessarily cross-border implications*'. On this reading the "internal market requirement" and the "cross-border requirement" set out in Art. 81 TFEU would thus basically coincide. See Commission, Proposal for Small Claims Regulation 861/2007, COM(2005) 87, p. 6.

356 See further e.g. Storskrubb (2008), pp. 42, 173–4, 185, 206–7 and 220–21; Stuyck (2009), p. 67; Tulibacka (2009), pp. 1562–3; Bariatti (2011), pp. 29–30.

357 See in particular para 9.21 above.

term "procedure" is to be interpreted in a manner equally as broad as the term "procedural" when used in relation to the principle of national procedural autonomy.[358] Finally, certain Member States "opted out" of this part of the EU Treaties, meaning that they are not (or at least not necessarily) bound by any of the measures adopted on this basis.[359]

All in all it thus appears that, despite its apparent potential and the scope for possible future developments in this domain, as it stands Article 81 TFEU does not allow an approach whereby all aforementioned concerns related to fragmentation and coherence emerging in a private enforcement context are a thing of the past.

---

358 See para 2.01 above.

359 Namely Denmark, Ireland and the UK. See Protocols Nos 21 and 22 to the EU Treaties.

11

TWO PERSPECTIVES ON PRIVATE ENFORCEMENT

With a view to further deepening the understanding of EU legislation facilitating the private enforcement of EU law before national courts, the present penultimate chapter seeks to "take a step back" and assess the concept of private enforcement generally and EU legislation thereon specifically at a more fundamental level. It does so by assessing these matters from two different angles. The first section below focuses on considerations related to effectiveness. While it has already been seen that ensuring effectiveness is an important "driver" behind the EU legislation at issue, it is shown below that the concept of effectiveness in EU law is neither unambiguous nor unproblematic for the present purposes. The second section of this chapter subsequently assesses this legislation from the perspective of the "horizontalisation" of the enforcement of EU law. There it is explained what is meant by this term and what its implications are, particularly at the practical level and in so far as the various relevant fundamental rights are concerned.

A. THE EFFECTIVENESS PERSPECTIVE

Considerations related to effectiveness lie in many ways at the heart of the issues discussed in the foregoing chapters. It is explained below that in this context a distinction can be made between two different "expressions" of the principle of effectiveness as it exists in EU law. They often coincide and reinforce each other, but that is not always the case. It is further demonstrated that tensions, if not outright conflicts, can and do exist between these two forms of effectiveness where the private enforcement of EU law is concerned. On that basis three additional remarks are made.

1. Two expressions of effectiveness

In the foregoing many references have been made to considerations of effectiveness. Most notably, considerations of this kind have been identified as central elements in justifying the EU legislation considered in Part B above.[1] This is consistent with the crucial role that effectiveness-related considerations tend to play in underpinning the key legal doctrines of EU law regarding the enforcement of EU law at national level. The clearest example may be the principle of effectiveness, as articulated in the *Rewe* case law, pursuant to which, as regards matters falling within their procedural autonomy, Member States may not make it impossible or excessively difficult for private parties to exercise their rights conferred by EU law.[2] Effectiveness is obviously also a consideration that is central to the principle of effective judicial protection laid down in Article 47 Charter.[3] Considerations of effectiveness moreover underpin landmark rulings concerning matters of both public and private enforcement before national courts, such as *Greek Maize* (regarding penalties for infringements of EU law), *Simmenthal* (regarding the setting aside of national law that infringes EU law), *Francovich* (regarding the principle of Member State liability for infringements of EU law) and *Courage* and *Muñoz* (regarding the liability of private parties for infringements of EU law).[4] **11.01**

There can therefore be little doubt as to the crucial importance of considerations of effectiveness when discussing the topic of private enforcement of EU law before national courts. However, while it is all very well to speak of "effectiveness" generally, this is of limited importance if one does not answer the question of effectiveness *of what* precisely. **11.02**

The case law of the Court of Justice in this respect has been said to be '*strewn with intermittent and inconsistent references to "effectiveness", "effective protection" and "effective judicial protection"*'.[5] Others have criticised the Court for its '*almost chronic inability to adhere to any consistent legal terminology*' where matters of

1 See in particular para 10.03 above.

2 See subsection 2.A.3 above.

3 See section 2.B above.

4 CoJ case 68/88, *Commission v Greece (Greek maize)*; CoJ case 106/77, *Simmenthal*; CoJ joined cases C-6/90 and C-9/90, *Francovich*; CoJ case C-453/99, *Courage*; CoJ case C-253/00, *Muñoz*. See subsections 2.C.2, 2.D.2 and 2.D.3 above.

5 Drake (2006), pp. 843–4.

effectiveness are concerned.[6] Largely, as a consequence, the concept of "effectiveness" in EU law has been described as '*multifunctional and double-edged*' and '*a handy device for best result instrumentalism*',[7] as a '*moving target*'[8] and as '*a kind of jack-in-the-box instrument*'.[9] This suggests that in this context the concept of "effectiveness" can be as hard to capture as it can be of crucial importance. For the present purposes, it is nonetheless necessary to make a distinction in relation to the broader concept of effectiveness as it manifests itself in EU law. That distinction boils down to the following.[10]

On the one hand, there are situations where the (subjective) *right of a private party* conferred by EU law is the main interest that is being protected. This notion of effectiveness inherently underlies the principle of effective judicial protection laid down in Article 47 Charter. It also largely corresponds with the principle of effectiveness, as developed in the aforementioned *Rewe* case law.[11] On the other hand, there are situations where the emphasis is on the protection of the interests associated with the effective application and enforcement of (objective) *EU law per se*. This expression of effectiveness was particularly clearly articulated in *Simmenthal*, where the Court of Justice insisted that rules of EU law must have '*full force and effect*'.[12] In this ruling it emphasised the constitutional character of these considerations by noting the importance of safeguarding the effectiveness of the obligations of the Member States under the EU Treaties, so as not to '*imperil the very foundations of the [EU]*'.[13] Similarly, in *Courage* it was made clear that considerations of this kind can also be essential in relation to specific policy objectives that the rules of EU law at issue seek to achieve, *in casu* the full effectiveness of the EU competition rules.[14]

11.03 Before discussing the significance of drawing the above distinction in the following, two preliminary remarks should be made. To begin with, making a

6 Oliver (2011), p. 2038.

7 Ross (2006), pp. 480 and 486.

8 Lindholm (2007), p. 297.

9 Micklitz (2012), p. 398.

10 Comparable distinctions have been made elsewhere. See e.g. Snyder (1993), p. 46 (who speaks of a "bottom up" perspective providing judicial protection for the individual and a "top down" perspective performing an essentially political function of social control); Prechal (2005), p. 304 (referring to "the need for effective judicial protection" and "the desire to give full effect to EU rules"); Nebbia (2008b), pp. 28–34 (distinguishing between "effective judicial protection" and "effective enforcement"); Dougan (2011), p. 427 and 431 (distinguishing between "the principle of effectiveness in its narrow *Rewe/Comet* sense" and "independent manifestations of some broader concept of effectiveness", complemented by the principle of effective judicial protection as a "distinct EU right in and of itself"); Bobek (2012), p. 316 (referring to the "protection of an individual" as compared with the "protection of all individuals within the EU").

11 On the relationship between these two principles, see para 2.12 above.

12 CoJ case 106/77, *Simmenthal*, para 22. See para 2.21 above.

13 Ibid., para 17–20.

14 CoJ case C-453/99, *Courage*, para 25. See para 2.24 and 6.14 above.

distinction such as the one referred to above inevitably involves a degree of *simplification*. In practice, things are not always as clear-cut. This is at least in part due to the manner in which the Court of Justice tends to employ the concept of effectiveness; as was noted above, many have found clarity and consistency to be lacking. To give a concrete example, under the "*Rewe* principle" of effectiveness, the protection of rights that private parties derive from EU law does not always take centre stage. This principle occasionally "transforms" into a requirement not to make the application and enforcement of EU law *per se* impossible or excessively difficult.[15] And while in *Simmenthal* the emphasis was placed on the above-mentioned "constitutional" considerations related to the effectiveness of EU law *per se*, this line of argumentation was nonetheless blended in that ruling with a rights-based narrative, as the Court of Justice also noted there that national courts must '*protect rights which the latter confers on individuals*'.[16] More generally, it should not be forgotten that the distinction between the individual and the general interest that underlies the above-mentioned distinction is not a matter of black and white, but rather one of degree. For every legal rule and its correct application in an individual case can be considered to be in the general interest.[17] Put differently, the full effectiveness of EU law can be achieved only if private parties can assert before their national courts the rights that they derive from EU law.[18] And, conversely, objective law will generally serve to give effect to the subjective entitlements of the parties concerned.[19]

That leads to the second preliminary remark. The two forms of effectiveness identified above are generally understood in the case law of the Court of Justice to be vectors pointing in the same direction. This implies that these two expressions of effectiveness and the interests that underlie them often *coincide*. The Court's ruling in *Francovich* offers perhaps the best illustration. In that case it was held that the '*full effectiveness of [EU] rules would be impaired and the*

15 Cf. e.g. CoJ joined cases C-430/93 and C-431/93, *Van Schijndel*, para 17 and 19; CoJ case C-443/03, *Leffler*, para 49–52 and 65. See also CoJ case C-226/99, *Siples*, para 17–20. By contrast, e.g. in CoJ case C-536/11, *Donau Chemie*, para 27, both issues were kept expressly separate. For a view insisting on keeping the test applied under the "*Rewe* principle" of effectiveness restricted to the enforcement of rights rather than the enforcement of EU law *per se*, see Opinion AG Bot case C-455/06, *Heemskerk*, para 121–30. Note that some argue that the "*Rewe* principle" of effectiveness is or should be primarily concerned with the enforcement of (objective) EU law *per se*. See Dougan (2011), p. 425; Prechal and Widdershoven (2011), p. 31; Parret (2012), p. 159. It is, however, submitted that as the law stands this view seems difficult to maintain in light of the CoJ's case law, discussed in subsection 2.A.3 above.

16 CoJ case 106/77, *Simmenthal*, para 21.

17 Prechal (2005), p. 119.

18 Lenaerts, Maselis and Gutman (2014), p. 108.

19 Cf. e.g. Opinion AG Tesauro joined cases C-46/93 and C-48/93, *Brasserie du Pêcheur*, para 32, where it is observed that the central value articulated in the *Francovich* ruling on Member State liability is the effectiveness of EU law '*and hence*' complete judicial protection.

protection of the rights which they grant would be weakened' if private parties were unable to obtain compensation in cases of infringements of EU law attributable to Member States.[20] Both the effective protection of the (subjective) rights of private parties and the effectiveness of (objective) EU law *per se* were thus seen as arguing in favour of acknowledging the existence of a principle of Member State liability. A similar logic is apparent, for instance, in *Courage* concerning the liability of private parties for breaches of EU law.[21] As construed by the Court of Justice, these two expressions of effectiveness are therefore generally used in a '*two-fold sense*'.[22] Put differently, they are of a '*dual nature*'.[23] The underlying concerns are thus intimately linked and in effect mostly treated as two sides of the same coin.[24]

2. From dual nature to dual vigilance

11.04 The two expressions of effectiveness identified above may not only *coincide*, but often actually *reinforce* each other. That is already evident from the relevant case law. Let us return, for instance, to the aforementioned *Courage* ruling. Here the Court found not only that the full effectiveness of the rule of EU competition law at issue would be put at risk if it were not open for a private party to claim damages for loss caused by the infringement of that rule. It also highlighted that the existence of such a right for private parties would '*strengthen the working*' of that rule and would '*discourage infringements*' thereof, thus making a '*significant contribution to the maintenance of effective competition*' in the EU.[25] As has been noted with reference to *Courage*, '*[w]hile pursuing his private interest, a plaintiff in such proceedings contributes at the same time to the protection of the public interest*'.[26] Comparable considerations are apparent in *Muñoz*, which was concerned with the enforcement of EU rules that set quality standards and encouraged fair competition in the agricultural field. There the Court held that civil proceedings to enforce the rights that can be derived from those rules '*strengthens [their] practical working*' and, as a supplement to the existing public enforcement mechanisms, '*helps to discourage practices [...] which distort competition*'.[27]

20 CoJ joined cases C-6/90 and C-9/90, *Francovich*, para 33. See para 2.23 above.
21 CoJ case C-453/99, *Courage*, para 25.
22 Steiner (1995), p. 57.
23 Prechal (1998), p. 706.
24 Prechal (2005), pp. 132 and 215.
25 CoJ case C-453/99, *Courage*, para 25–7.
26 EFTA Court case E-14/11, *Schenker*, para 132.
27 CoJ case C-253/00, *Muñoz*, para 31. See para 2.25 above.

These cases thus echo the "dual vigilance"[28] logic that was already apparent in the Court's 1963 ruling in *Van Gend en Loos*. As was noted at the outset of this book, the Court held in that ruling that '*[t]he vigilance of individuals concerned to protect their rights amounts to an effective supervision in addition to the supervision entrusted … to the diligence of the Commission and the Member States*'.[29] The thought that the general and the individual interest can coincide and that, moreover, legal actions brought by private parties in their individual interest can also contribute to reaching certain policy objectives in the general interest – as a matter of the "dual vigilance" exercised by those parties as well as the competent public enforcement authorities – has thus been crucial in underpinning the principle of direct effect and the private enforcement model that emerged from that basis.[30]

As regards more specifically the private enforcement-related EU legislation assessed in Part B, it appears that this legislation relies typically on a mix of considerations related to ensuring the effectiveness of EU law *per se*, on the one hand, and the effective protection of the rights of private parties, on the other hand. Where the emphasis is placed precisely can vary somewhat in the directive concerned, but a common theme is always the "dual vigilance" philosophy referred to above. **11.05**

Of that legislation, the Procurement Remedies Directives are probably most outspoken in their desire to strengthen the compliance with – and thus the effectiveness of – the relevant rules of substantive EU law. In its proposal for the first of these two directives the Commission stated that the underlying aim was '*to ensure that the rules of public contracts are correctly applied*'.[31] This objective is also reflected in the recitals of these directives.[32] It has subsequently been echoed in the Court's case law, where the objective of these directives has been held to be '*to guarantee the existence of effective remedies for infringements of [EU] law in the field of public procurement or of the national rules implementing that law, so as to ensure the effective application of the [Substantive Procurement Directives]*'.[33] The Consumer Injunctions Directive is also rather explicit in this respect, in particular where its recitals state that its aims to address concerns that

28 Cf. Weatherill (2000), p. 92; Tridimas (2006), p. 546.
29 CoJ case 26/62, *Van Gend en Loos*, p. 13.
30 See para 1.01 above.
31 Commission, Amended proposal for Public Sector Remedies Directive 89/665, COM(88) 733, p. 10. See para 3.05 above.
32 See in particular recital 2 Procurement Remedies Directives 89/665 and 92/13.
33 CoJ case C-406/08, *Uniplex*, para 26. See para 3.07 above.

'*the effectiveness of national measures transposing the [substantive consumer protection directives concerned] ... may be thwarted*'.[34] It is indeed noticeable that neither the Procurement Remedies Directives nor the Consumer Injunctions Directive even address the issue of "rights" of private parties expressly, but instead refer to infringements of the relevant substantive law generally.[35] By contrast, the IPR Enforcement Directive in particular places more emphasis on the protection of the rights of the private parties concerned. It aims to ensure a high level of protection for holders of intellectual property rights.[36] Yet this directive also makes it clear that this objective should be understood in light of the necessity '*to ensure that the substantive law on intellectual property [...] is applied effectively*'.[37]

The Competition Damages Directive further illustrates how over time the emphasis can sometimes shift somewhat from one expression of effectiveness to another.[38] In relation to this initiative the emphasis was initially largely on the "general interest function" (deterrence, punishment) of damages claims that is associated with ensuring the effectiveness of the relevant EU rules *per se*. It was only subsequently that the "private interest" function (compensation for loss and damage suffered by private parties) associated with the effective enforcement of rights of private parties conferred by those EU rules was articulated more forcefully.[39] All the same there can be no doubt, however, that it is essentially the thought that the *combining* of both functions and the mutually reinforcing effect that can then emerge that underpins this initiative. As the Commission noted in its proposal, '*if the likelihood increases that infringers of Articles 101 and 102 [TFEU] have to bear the costs of their infringement, this will not only shift the costs away from the victims of the illegal behaviour, but will also be an incentive for better compliance with the EU competition rules*'.[40] Against that background the proposed directive '*seeks to ensure the effective enforcement of the*

34 Recital 4 Consumer Injunctions Directive 2009/22. See para 5.07 above.

35 See para 9.04 above.

36 See in particular recital 10 IPR Enforcement Directive 2004/48. See also CoJ case C-406/09, *Realchemie*, para 49. See para 4.06 above.

37 Recital 3 IPR Enforcement Directive 2004/48. See also para 4.04 above.

38 It appears that there has been a (somewhat) comparable "shift" where Procurement Remedies Directives 89/665 and 92/13 are concerned, in the sense that in this connection the objective of effective judicial protection of the private parties concerned has recently been given increased attention. See in particular recital 81 Concessions Awards Directive 2014/23, where it is explained that the scope of the Procurement Remedies Directives must be extended so as also to cover infringements of that directive, with reference to the need '*to ensure adequate judicial protection of candidates and tenderers in the concession award procedures, as well as to make effective the enforcement of this Directive*'. See para 3.02 above.

39 See in particular para 6.18 above.

40 Commission, Proposal for Competition Damages Directive 2014/104, COM(2013) 404, p. 4.

EU competition rules by [...] ensuring that victims of the EU competition rules can obtain full compensation for the harm they suffered'.[41]

The duality referred to above also comes to light in many *specific provisions* of the EU legislation assessed in the foregoing. It is evident that many of those provisions serve first and foremost to facilitate the enforcement of the rights of the private parties concerned. These parties are, for example, the prime beneficiaries of the EU rules at issue on obtaining compensation in damages or injunctive relief.[42] Yet the "general interest function" of private enforcement actions can also be detected here. Take for instance the IPR Enforcement Directive, which stipulates in a general manner that the remedies and procedures provided for therein must be '*effective, proportionate and dissuasive*'.[43] This is a phrase that is normally used in relation to the penalties for which the Member States must make provision as a matter of public enforcement of EU law.[44] Particularly dissuasiveness, to which also the Procurement Remedies Directives refer,[45] is something that is generally of little direct interest to a private party seeking to enforce its rights. It rather points to a desire for prevention, so as to ensure that the infringement will not occur again.[46] As such, it is closely related to the interests associated with the effective enforcement of EU law *per se*. Something similar can be said of the publicity measures provided for in the IPR Enforcement Directive, the Consumer Injunctions Directive and certain other consumer protection directives, which serve the dual purpose of informing the public at large and deterring infringers.[47] Deterrence is also closely related to the interests associated with the effective enforcement of EU law *per se*.[48] Another illustration is the Commission's express aim to ensure that the Procurement Remedies Directives' provisions on actions for damages serve as a '*genuine incentive to compliance*'.[49] **11.06**

41 Ibid., pp. 2–3. See also recitals 3 and 4 Competition Damages Directive 2014/104.

42 See sections 7.A and 7.B above, respectively.

43 Art. 3(2) IPR Enforcement Directive 2004/48. See para 4.06 above.

44 See para 2.20 above.

45 See Art. 2(1)(c) and (5) Utilities Remedies Directive 92/13. This provision offers the possibility, as an alternative for the setting aside of a decision taken in breach of the applicable procurement rules, of paying a particular sum set at a level high enough to "dissuade" the contracting authority from committing or persisting in an infringement. See para 3.15 above.

46 Cf. Prechal (1997), p. 10.

47 Art. 15 IPR Enforcement Directive 2004/48; Art. 2(1)(b) Consumer Injunctions Directive 2009/22. See also Art. 11(2) Unfair Commercial Practices Directive 2005/29; Art. 5(4) Misleading Advertising Directive 2006/114. See para 8.27 above.

48 Cf. Hodges (2011), p. 438.

49 Commission, Proposal for Utilities Remedies Directive 92/13, COM(90) 297, pp. 12–13. See e.g. also the Commission's remark in the context of the 2007 revision of these directives that amending the provisions on actions for damages so as to further facilitate the bringing of such actions would have '*few benefits*' in terms of corrective effects on the award procedure and the contract signed. This suggests that in this connection no attention was paid to the possible benefits of such an amendment in terms of the possibilities for the private

The Court of Justice has further noted, for instance, that the injunctions and the contractual remedy provided for in the Unfair Terms Directive also serve purposes of deterrence and dissuasion.[50] And elsewhere in EU law too the Court regularly emphasises the deterrent effect of the civil law remedies, notably those set out in the Gender Equality Directive.[51] Similarly, in relation to the Consumer Injunctions Directive, the Commission has referred to injunctions as a '*succesful tool for policing markets*' and as a '*governance tool [which] can be used as a deterrent*'.[52] A further illustration is the regular use of the term "penalty" in connection with the remedies set out in the EU legislation at issue here. This term is normally associated with general interests related to punishment and deterrence and thus with ensuring the effectiveness of the EU law *per se* rather than the enforcement of a right of a private party.[53] The Commission has called the contractual remedy set out in the Unfair Terms Directive a '*civil penalty*'.[54] The Court of Justice has similarly referred to the remedies set out in the Procurement Remedies Directives as penalties.[55] More specifically in relation to the contractual remedy of ineffectiveness set out in these latter directives, provision is made for "alternative penalties".[56] This term not only suggests a penalising element where this provision is concerned, the word "alternative" also implies that the EU legislature saw this contractual remedy itself as a sort of penalty. Indeed, the Commission spoke in this connection of '*sanctions intended not to leave unpunished the conclusion of a contract*'.[57] The term "penalties" is also used in relation to provisions on civil liability in some other provisions of secondary EU law.[58]

11.07 It follows that the relevant case law and the EU legislation on private enforcement seek to ensure that the private parties concerned can effectively enforce their rights vested in EU law before national courts both as a means to

---

parties concerned to obtain compensation for the harm suffered as a consequence of the infringements of EU law at issue. See Commission, Impact assessment report on remedies in the field of public procurement, SEC(2006) 557, p. 26. See para 3.18 above.

50 As regards these injunctions, see CoJ case C-372/99, *Commission v Italy*, para 15; CoJ case C-472/10, *Invitel*, para 37; CoJ case C-470/12, *Pohotovost*, para 44. As regards this contractual remedy, see CoJ case C-618/10, *Banco Español de Crédito*, para 69.

51 Art. 18 Gender Equality Directive 2006/54. See e.g. CoJ case 14/83, *Von Colson*, para 23; CoJ case C-177/88, *Dekker*, para 23–6; CoJ case C-54/07, *Feryn*, para 38–9. See e.g. CoJ case C-174/12, *Hirmann*, para 43.

52 Commission, Second report on Consumer Injunctions Directive 2009/22, COM(2012) 635, p. 7.

53 Cf. the third of the three *Engel* criteria, referred to in para 11.36 below. Cf. e.g. Opinion AG Sharpston case C-174/12, *Hirmann*, para 47.

54 Commission, Report on Unfair Terms Directive 93/13, COM(2000) 248, p. 19.

55 CoJ case C-315/01, *GAT*, para 55.

56 Art. 2e(2) Procurement Remedies Directives 89/665 and 92/13. See para 3.23 above.

57 Commission, Proposal for Procurement Remedies Amending Directive 2007/66, COM(2006) 195, p. 18 (Art. 2f(4)).

58 See e.g. Art. 39 Directive 2005/60/EC on the prevention of the use of the financial system for the purpose of money laundering and terrorist financing, OJ 2005, L 309/15.

safeguard the effective judicial protection of those parties and as a way to ensure that EU law is effectively applied and enforced at national level. This duality in effect constitutes the *very essence* of the concept of private enforcement as it exists in the EU legal order.[59] Although this study has not sought to quantify this, there seems generally little reason to doubt that the overall effect on both the individual interest of the private parties concerned and the general interest is often positive. The idea of private parties pursuing their own interests and in so doing furthering the general interest also is obviously attractive. It is moreover by no means unique to the present context. Adam Smith observed in 1776 that:

> every individual necessarily labours to render the annual revenue of the society as great as he can. He generally, indeed, neither intends to promote the public interest, nor knows how much he is promoting it. [...] [H]e intends only his own gain, and he is in this, as in many other cases, led by an invisible hand to promote an end which was no part of his intention. Nor is it always the worse for the society that it was no part of it. By pursuing his own interest he frequently promotes that of the society more effectually than when he really intends to promote it.[60]

The adoption of EU legislation facilitating the private enforcement of EU law before national courts can be seen as an instance where this famous "invisible hand" becomes visible to some extent and is given some guidance by the EU legislature.

3. Tensions and potential conflicts

On the basis of the foregoing one might be tempted to conclude that the individual and the general interests at stake when enforcing EU law before national courts make a "perfect match". But situations can and do arise where the said interests underlying these two expressions of effectiveness *collide* rather than *collude*, or where there is at least a certain tension between them. Given the centrality of both expressions of effectiveness in private enforcement-related matters, this can lead to pressing questions of various sorts. This is illustrated by the following four examples. **11.08**

59 There is also a semantic side to this discussion. It has been argued that the term "private enforcement" is semantically biased towards the idea of ensuring compliance with EU law *per se*, while terms such as "claims for damages" or "effective protection" connote more strongly the idea of compensating a victim of a wrong and safeguarding his subjective rights. See Nebbia (2008b), p. 24. See also Ottervanger (2014), pp. 18–19. Whereas this latter statement is undoubtedly correct, it is submitted that in EU law generally there is, however, not necessarily such a bias where the term "private enforcement" is concerned. For this term leaves open the key question, namely *what* is being "privately enforced": EU law *per se* or the rights that private parties derive therefrom?

60 Adam Smith, cited in Cambell and Skinner (1976), p. 456. Cf. Ottervanger (2010), p. 5.

11.09 First, tensions and potential conflicts of this kind can emerge in relation to the question of how to deal with *leniency applicants* in relation to the private enforcement of EU competition law. The difficulties that can arise in this connection have already been discussed rather extensively above, particularly where the possible disclosure of leniency applications and other relevant evidence in the file of a competition authority is concerned.[61] Suffice to note, therefore, that from the perspective of an injured private party wishing to claim compensation the disclosure of such documents could be highly beneficial, whereas too permissive disclosure rules are by contrast widely seen as putting at risk the effectiveness of the leniency programmes and therefore public enforcement as such. Thus, as the Commission observed, '*the EU right to compensation can sometimes be at odds with the effectiveness of public enforcement of the EU competition rules*'.[62] After considerable debate the EU legislature eventually cut the knot by opting for absolute protection from disclosure for certain documents (the "black list"), temporal protection until the public enforcement proceedings are terminated for a larger category of documents (the "grey list") and, in principle, disclosability for all other documents in a competition authority's file.[63] As was explained above, while there certainly seem grounds to argue that in this manner a reasonable and tenable balance has been struck between the inherently conflicting interests at stake, some scope for discussion remains.[64]

A related issue is whether successful leniency applicants should be granted a "rebate" on any damage claim brought against them. This was one of the options outlined in the Commission's 2005 green paper on actions for damages for competition law infringements.[65] This would clearly make leniency programmes more attractive. But this would evidently also be at odds with the ambition to ensure full compensation for private parties who suffered harm as a consequence of such infringements. This option was therefore not retained in the subsequent white paper, which instead focused on a less far-reaching option, namely limiting the civil liability of successful leniency applicants to claims brought by their direct and indirect purchasers.[66] This means that in cartel cases the undertakings in question would not be jointly and severally

61 See in particular subsections 6.B.4 and 6.C.3 above.

62 Commission, Impact assessment report on damages actions for breach of the EU antitrust rules, SWD(2013) 203, p. 5.

63 Art. 5 and 6 Competition Damages Directive 2014/104. See para 6.32 and 6.33 above.

64 See para 6.34 above.

65 Commission, Green paper on damages actions for breach of the EC antitrust rules, COM(2005) 672, p. 10. For a discussion of those options, see Milutinovic (2010), pp. 274–8.

66 Commission, White paper on damages actions for breach of the EC antitrust rules, COM(2008) 165, p. 10. See further Commission, Staff working paper accompanying the white paper on damages actions for breach of the EC antitrust rules, SEC(2008) 404, pp. 81–9.

liable for the entire damage caused. On the one hand, such a rule might make it more difficult for an injured party to obtain full compensation. On the other hand, without such a rule these undertakings would be the most likely of all co-infringing undertakings to be addressed by a damages claim for the entire damage (given that they will generally not contest the decision by the competent competition authority finding an infringement, as they obtained leniency). This can also constitute a threat to the attractiveness of the leniency programmes and a form of '*undue exposure to damages claims*'.[67] For that reason this suggestion made its way into the Commission's proposal and subsequently also into the Competition Damages Directive itself.[68] Illustrative of the effort to strike a balance between the various interests at stake is the addition in this directive of a rule pursuant to which this limitation of joint and several liability does not apply where full compensation cannot be obtained from the co-infringing undertakings that did not obtain leniency.

Second, the distinction between the two expressions of effectiveness referred to above can have a bearing on discussions on how to assess the issue of *punitive damages*, which are damages awards that go beyond mere compensation for the harm suffered with a view to punishing and deterring infringers. Seen from an individual rights perspective, there appears to be no justification for making provision for this type of damages. Full compensation for the loss or damage caused by the infringement is the general rule; no less, but also no more.[69] But the aims of punishment and deterrence associated with punitive damages fit in well with a perspective whereby the main concern is the effectiveness of EU law *per se*. From which angle this matter is assessed consequently determines to a large extent the views on the appropriateness of punitive damages as a matter of EU law. Where the view is taken that compensation is not a sanction[70] and that deterrence and punishment are tasks better left to public enforcement,[71] it logically follows that there is no place for punitive damages. However, in the alternative view, whereby the effectiveness of EU law *per se* takes centre stage, there is a "deficit" if damages are regarded as purely compensatory[72] and the idea of limiting damages to compensation for the harm suffered can be dismissed as '*formal(istic)*' and something that is to be abolished.[73] The tension **11.10**

67 Recital 38 Competition Damages Directive 2014/104. See also Commission, Proposal for Competition Damages Directive 2014/104, COM(2013) 404, p. 16.

68 Art. 11(3) Competition Damages Directive 2014/104. See para 6.36 above. This reasoning does not explain, however, why in relation to the infringing undertakings concerned the right to obtain a contribution from the undertaking that successfully applied for leniency is limited too.

69 See in particular para 7.20 above.

70 Van Gerven (2000), p. 530.

71 Wils (2009), p. 22.

72 Komninos (2008), p. 211.

73 Milutinovic (2010), p. 221.

between these two fundamentally differing views lies at the heart of the discussions referred to above on whether or not punitive damages are an appropriate private enforcement instrument to be provided for in secondary EU law.[74]

11.11 Third, take the topic of *out-of-court settlements*, reached either after a form of alternative dispute resolution or simply through direct negotiations between the parties concerned. At first sight it might appear that reaching such a settlement – as opposed to litigating a case until a final judgment is rendered – is both attractive for the private parties concerned and in the general interest. Both interests are after all generally served where disputes are terminated faster and with lower legal and administrative costs, as will typically be the case where disputes are settled. Several directives considered in Part B above therefore contain provisions that aim to facilitate pre-trial contacts between the parties to the dispute and to otherwise encourage out-of-court settlements between them.[75] However, these kinds of provisions can also have disadvantages.[76] To what extent they emerge and how they are to be assessed may again vary depending upon which of the two above-mentioned perspectives one places the emphasis.

On the one hand, concerning such rules that aim to *facilitate settlements*, there can be certain disadvantages, particularly for the (potential) private party applicants concerned. One could think of delays and the associated risk of limitation periods expiring. In these cases the general interest could thus argue in favour of encouraging settlements, while the individual interests of the private parties concerned can point in a different direction. The latter interests can be safeguarded to some extent by taking specific legislative measures (for example, the suspension of limitation periods for the duration of the settlement attempt), but this is unlikely to address all possible disadvantages (for example, in terms of additional costs and complexities). On the other hand, the situation can be largely reversed where *out-of-court settlements as such* are concerned (as opposed to the rules facilitating them referred to above). Then settling the dispute may be advantageous for the private parties concerned, while from the perspective of the effectiveness of EU law *per se* there may also be some notable disadvantages. Settlements tend, after all, to be primarily based on considerations of convenience for the parties concerned and not – or at least not necessarily – on considerations of legality or effectiveness of the law.[77] This means that there can be a real risk that these parties will settle a dispute in a

74 See subsection 7.A.6 above.
75 See in particular para 9.24 above.
76 See para 9.27 above.
77 Cf. Jacobs and Deisenhofer (2003), p. 196 (see also p. 221).

manner that is not compatible with, for example, the applicable EU rules on public procurement or competition. Settlements and arbitration awards are, moreover, often not published. The parties concerned may well find this attractive. Yet this also means that no contribution is made to the clarification and development of the law nor to establishing general deterrence in the same manner as court judgments generally do.

Finally, addressing the issue of *collective redress* can also involve tensions and trade-offs between the two aforementioned expressions of effectiveness and the interests that underlie them.[78] Take the Commission's Collective Redress Recommendation which was adopted in 2013.[79] The stated main aim of this initiative is ensuring private parties' access to court and the effective enforcement of their rights vested in EU law.[80] This thus suggests an approach concentrating on the enforcement of the right of the private parties concerned. However, at the same time many of the arguments that have been put forward in this connection to justify the possible introduction of special rules on collective redress are of a "general interest nature". They relate for instance to contributing to the overall level of enforcement, the aggregate loss that "scattered" damages can cause to society, procedural efficiency and the risk of abuse.[81] Indeed, the Commission's remark in 2011 that '*careful consideration must be given as to whether and in which area an EU initiative would bring added value for improving the enforcement of EU law*' suggests that it found ensuring the effectiveness of EU law *per se* at least equally important as the protection of rights of private parties.[82] **11.12**

The aforementioned distinction can again have important consequences in this regard. Arguably only where "scattered" damages are at stake (that is, a situation where many parties each individually suffered relatively low amounts of damage resulting from the same or similar unlawful behaviour) can an enforcement of rights rationale convincingly be invoked for justifying the introduction of special rules on collective redress. In other cases of mass damages, where the damage suffered results from the same or similar unlawful behaviour but the

78 Various proposals have been made in the legal literature with a view to finding the correct balance in this connection. See e.g. Cafaggi and Micklitz (2009), p. 444 (opt-in for private applicants and opt-out for public applicants); Micklitz, Reich and Rott (2009), p. 361 (opt-in for small claims, opt-out for bigger ones).

79 Collective Redress Recommendation 2013/396. See para 5.38 above.

80 See e.g. recital 10 and point 1 Collective Redress Recommendation 2013/396. See e.g. also Commission, Public consultation towards a coherent approach to collective redress, SEC(2011) 173, p. 7; Commission, Communication towards a European horizontal framework for collective redress, COM(2013) 401, p. 2.

81 See e.g. Commission, Public consultation towards a coherent approach to collective redress, SEC(2011) 173, pp. 3 and 9; Commission, Communication towards a European horizontal framework for collective redress, COM(2013) 401, pp. 7 and 9.

82 Commission, Public consultation towards a coherent approach to collective redress, SEC(2011) 173, p. 5.

damage to each individual party concerned is nonetheless significant, each of these parties normally has individually a sufficient incentive to take legal action. The Commission's Collective Redress Recommendation is, however, not limited to such cases of "scattered" damages.[83] In these other cases rules on collective redress are first and foremost about ensuring efficient administration of justice.[84] This can of course also be a perfectly legitimate reason to enact legislation. However, it then seems confusing or even misleading to justify suggestions to this effect in terms of access to justice and the enforcement of rights. This is of particular importance, given that identifying the objective at stake can be crucial when assessing whether the EU has the required legal basis to act and, if so, whether the principles of subsidiarity and proportionality are complied with.[85]

The same tension can come to light in relation to a more specific collective redress-related issue, namely whether an opt-in or opt-out approach is preferable.[86] It is common ground that most private parties do not make the effort to opt in to a collective redress scheme even where it is available.[87] Seen from a perspective that is primarily concerned with the enforcement of rights, this need not be overly problematic, in particular not where legal aid, specific small claim procedures and alternative dispute resolution mechanisms are available where necessary. After all, the principle of party autonomy implies that parties can also decide *not* to initiate legal proceedings, for example because they consider that the amounts at stake are not worth even the modest effort of opting in. In such cases these parties' "rational apathy" can seem very rational

83 See the definition of "mass harm situation" in point 3 Collective Redress Recommendation 2013/396. The Commission specifically referred to "scattered low-value damage" in its earlier work on collective redress in a competition law context. However, in that case also the argumentation brought forward seemed to blur points related to individual rights (access to court, right to compensation) and the effective enforcement of EU law *per se* (procedural economy, undesirability of illegal gains remaining in the hands of the infringer). See Commission, Staff working paper accompanying the white paper on damages actions for breach of the EC antitrust rules, SEC(2008) 404, pp. 15–16.

84 Cf. Stadler (2009), p. 307; Cupa (2012), p. 511.

85 Cf. e.g. points (e) and (f) of Art. 81(2) TFEU, discussed in para 10.49 above. On issues of legal basis and the principles of subsidiarity and proportionality, see subsections 10.A.1 and 10.A.2 above, respectively. For example, where the effective enforcement of EU law *per se* is identified as the main objective at stake, one might argue in favour of establishing or reinforcing *public* enforcement mechanisms. In a sense public enforcement is after all the ultimate form of collective redress. Public enforcement might well then be seen as preferable to and more proportionate than meddling with the basic principles of the legal systems of the Member States (with respect to legal standing, the role of the courts, party autonomy, and so on) to facilitate collective redress in an attempt to achieve a result that seems inherently difficult to reach via civil law means. Cf. e.g. Frese (2011), p. 410.

86 In short, an opt-in system implies that any party allegedly having suffered damage must explicitly indicate that it wishes to participate in the collective redress procedure, whereas under an opt-out system consent is assumed and the party concerned has instead the opportunity to expressly indicate that it does not want to participate.

87 Study, Civic Consulting (2008a), p. 9; Nazzini (2009), pp. 426–7; Miller (2009), p. 280; Tzakas (2011), p. 1136–7; Buccirossi and Carpagnano (2013), p. 5; Van den Bergh (2013), p. 23; Jones (2014), p. 301.

indeed.[88] As the Court of Justice held in another context, the effective protection of rights vested in EU law may find its limits in the '*total inertia*' of the private party concerned.[89] But legislative intervention may then still be required to safeguard the effectiveness of EU law *per se*. Scattered or not, collectively the negative effects of the infringements can still be very significant. Seen from this latter perspective, the limited appeal of opt-in collective redress schemes may well be considered problematic therefore and thus a reason to introduce opt-out mechanisms.[90] On that view an express opt-in requirement would '*hamper the effectiveness and deterrent effect*'[91] of the collective redress scheme and has been said to be '*excessive and formalistic*'.[92] Additionally, the loss of influence of the individual parties concerned on the course of the litigation or the undermining of these parties' right to be heard under an opt-out collective redress scheme will then not be seen as much of a concern.[93] Yet what are excess and formalism to some, are to others constitutionally protected fundamental rights and therefore convincing reasons to reject opt-out schemes,[94] as occurred in Germany and Sweden.[95]

4. Three final remarks

A first final remark in relation to the issues assessed in the foregoing subsections is that it is probably no exaggeration to say that in many respects the above discussions go to the *very heart* of EU law. Few will dispute that the finding in *Van Gend en Loos* in 1963 that EU law can confer rights directly upon private parties which are enforceable before national courts laid the basis for '*one of the great achievements of EU law*'.[96] This has, in the words of Advocate General Jacobs (writing extrajudicially), '*clearly proved fundamental in creating the EU legal order and, indeed, in transforming the [EU Treaties] from a classical instrument* **11.13**

88 Cf. Eurobarometer, Consumer redress in the EU, August 2009, p. 12, where it is found that the majority of consumers prefer their small claims to be fully handled by a consumer organisation or a public enforcement authority. Collective alternative dispute resolution emerges as the second-best option. Only where higher-value claims are at stake do consumers generally favour collective redress proper.

89 CoJ case C-40/08, *Asturcom*, para 47.

90 Nazzini (2009), pp. 426–8; Andreangeli (2012), p. 529.

91 Cf. Tzakas (2011), p. 1136.

92 Ibid., p. 1137. See also Tzakas (2014), p. 236.

93 Stadler (2009), pp. 315 and 317.

94 See e.g. European Parliament, Study on collective redress in antitrust, June 2012, p. 65, where it is argued that a ("pure") opt-out system is incompatible with the fundamental right to a fair trial guaranteed under Art. 6 ECHR and Art. 47 Charter, discussed in section 2.B above.

95 Stadler (2009), p. 317.

96 Reich (2010), p. 118. For critical comments (but not a denial of the importance of this finding), see e.g. Lindholm (2007), p. 256.

of international law into (or towards) the constitution of a quasi-federal organism'.[97] Since then both the EU judiciary and the EU legislature have been rather "generous" in conferring rights on private parties.[98] This has occurred to such an extent that it has been said that the '*language of rights permeated every aspect of EU law*'.[99]

This does not mean, however, that an "individual rights perspective" as described above necessarily prevails. The above remark by Advocate General Jacobs was followed by the observation that:

> the Court's approach, historically at any rate, has not been to promote the rights of individuals for their own sake or as a matter of ideology; its approach has essentially been pragmatic and the recognition of individual rights has almost been instrumental, being seen as necessary to ensure the effectiveness of the legal order.[100]

In a similar vein, it has been held elsewhere that '*the case law suggests that the principle of full effectiveness of [EU] law is a leading theme in the conferral on individuals of a right to damages for breach of [EU] law*'.[101] Although there is certainly no consensus on this point,[102] many understand the Court's "language of rights" primarily in such an "instrumentalist" manner, meaning that the rights of private parties vested in EU law are at least in part instruments to help achieve the underlying objective of ensuring the effectiveness of EU law *per se*.[103] Put differently, in this latter view the "ethos of individual rights" in EU law is little more than an '*inevitable by-product*' of the underlying quest to ensure the effective application and enforcement of EU law at national level.[104] It follows that in this view the private parties in question could and should be seen primarily as "private policemen", "private attorneys general" or "law enforcers acting in the public interest".[105]

97 Jacobs (2004b), p. 307. This statement was made in relation to direct effect, of which the conferral of rights upon private parties is a consequence (see p. 306; see also para 2.04 above). In a similar sense, see e.g. Weatherill (2000), p. 99–101; Drake (2005), p. 329.

98 Eilmansberger (2004), p. 1205.

99 Wakefield (2009), p. 410.

100 Jacobs (2004b), p. 308.

101 Nazzini (2009), p. 405. See also Nazzini (2011), p. 131.

102 While recognising the importance that the CoJ often attaches to safeguarding the effectiveness of EU law *per se*, some consider that at least in certain cases '*the response of the Court suggests rather unambiguously that priority should be given to effective judicial protection*'. See Nebbia (2008b), p. 33. In a similar sense, see also e.g. Leczykiewicz (2010a), p. 282; Dougan (2011), pp. 425 and 431. For yet another approach, see e.g. Becker (2007), pp. 1051–6.

103 E.g. Prechal (2005), p. 111: '*it is more often the case that full application of [EU] law provisions as such is what matters, as opposed to the protection of any specific rights*'. In a similar sense, see e.g. Caranta 1995), p. 725; Kilpatrick (2000), p. 2; Geursen (2009), p. 136; Dougan (2011), p. 425; Micklitz (2011a), p. 563.

104 Dougan (2004), p. 76.

105 See Drake (2006), p. 843; Kilpatrick (2000), p. 2; Gyselen (2001), p. 144, respectively.

This leads to the second remark, which concerns the question of what the position of the *Court of Justice* would be if and when it must choose between prioritising either the interests associated with safeguarding the rights of private parties vested in EU law or those associated with the effectiveness of this law *per se*. This has been described earlier as '*the real hard case*', whereby it is '*not easy to predict what the choice of the Court will be*'.[106] The existence of the diverging views outlined above can be seen as testimony to the ambiguity of the case law available to date and the aforementioned tendency of the Court of Justice to underline the symmetry and the synergy between both interests rather than to make an explicit choice between them. It consequently remains disputed whether, put simply, EU law serves individual rights or these rights serve EU law.[107] While acknowledging the resulting uncertainty and the fact that this question is hard to answer in the abstract, it is submitted here that a purely "instrumentalist" view, whereby the interests associated with the enforcement of EU law *per se* would take precedence where a choice is unavoidable, is unlikely to be upheld. This can be explained as follows. **11.14**

This results, to begin with, from a further assessment of the origin and purpose of the Court's frequent insistence on safeguarding the effectiveness of EU law *per se*. Court of Justice Judge Pescatore (writing extrajudicially) noted in this respect that '*[e]ffectiveness is the very soul of legal rules*', given that '*the purpose of any legal rule … is to achieve some practical aim and it would be running counter to its essential purpose if one handled it in such a way as to render it practically meaningless*'.[108] This highlights that at least in its origin any such reference to effectiveness is an application of an *interpretative technique*.[109] This implies that the effectiveness of EU law is not an end in itself; the end in question depends on the content of the rule of EU law at issue. It is rather a means to an end, namely ensuring that that rule is meaningful in practice.[110] Against this background it should come as no surprise that Advocate General Jacobs found on another occasion that '*the proper application of the law does not necessarily mean that there cannot be any limits on its application [but rather that] the interest in full application may need to be balanced against other considerations, such as legal certainty, sound administration of justice and the orderly and proper conduct of proceedings*'.[111] As Judge Pescatore reminded us, the rule at issue should *not be*

---

106 Prechal (1997), p. 13.

107 Cf. Milutinovic (2010), p. 89.

108 Pescatore (1983), p. 177.

109 Tridimas (2006), p. 419. In a similar sense, see Jacobs (2004b), p. 315; Prechal (2005), p. 219; Ross (2006), p. 497.

110 Van den Bogaert (2002), p. 136. See also Leczykiewicz (2010a), p. 274; Temple Lang (2008), p. 95. For a good example of the application of this interpretative technique, see CoJ case C-105/03, *Pupino*, para 38 and 42.

111 Opinion AG Jacobs joined cases C-430/93 and C-431/93, *Van Schijndel*, para 31. See also Jacobs (1997), pp. 26–7.

meaningless – which is not quite the same thing as saying that it can never yield to some extent to another interest that is considered to be of fundamental importance.[112] Particularly if we add to this the above-mentioned consistent emphasis placed by the Court of Justice on the conferral upon and effective protection of rights of private parties vested in EU law, including the rise to prominence of the principle of effective judicial protection,[113] the conclusion seems justified that a purely "instrumentalist" interpretation is not (or perhaps no longer[114]) likely to be upheld.[115] Therefore, as the law stands there seems to be no reason to presume *a priori* that the effectiveness of EU law *per se* must and will always prevail over the rights of private parties should a conflict emerge.

It appears that rather than establishing a clear hierarchy, the Court of Justice is more likely to insist on *balancing* the two fundamental interests at issue on a case-by-case basis. This was the essence of its approach in the aforementioned *Pfleiderer* case law.[116] There the Court had an opportunity to prioritise the interest related to the effective public enforcement of EU competition law (no access to leniency documents) over the interest related to the right to obtain full compensation of the private parties concerned (full and unconditional access to these documents), or vice versa. However, it did not do so. It instead insisted on a case-by-case balancing of the interests at stake, without establishing a clear hierarchy between them. This case law, moreover, does not stand on its own. The Court seems inclined to follow a comparable approach, emphasising the need to find a balanced solution, also in other cases where it is confronted with (potentially) conflicting principles and interests of a fundamental nature. One example is the *Van Schijndel* case law, where the Court allowed in essence for a balancing of the interests of EU law and the protection of rights vested therein, on the one hand, and the basic principles of the legal systems of the Member States, on the other hand.[117] The Court typically also insists on a balancing approach in cases where various fundamental rights of private parties are in

---

112 Cf. e.g. Opinion AG Léger case C-66/95, *Sutton*, para 71: '*Thus, national rules clearly may not be applied in such a way as to wholly negate the exercise of a right based on [EU] law*'.

113 See para 2.11 above. Broadly speaking, this rise went hand in hand with the expansion of EU competences beyond purely economic issues covering also matters such as social policy and consumer protection, as well as the creation of the concept of EU citizenship, which the CoJ has referred to as '*destined to be the fundamental status of nationals of the Member States*'. See CoJ case C-184/99, *Grzelczyk*, para 31. Cf. Dougan (2004), pp. 75–82.

114 Note that the above words of AG Jacobs referring to the CoJ's "instrumentalist" approach included the qualification '*historically at any rate*'.

115 As a subsidiary point, it can also be noted that EU law allows for other means to protect the EU's interest, most notably through infringement proceedings *ex* Art. 258 TFEU (and in competition cases also public enforcement exercised by the Commission). See Opinion AG Jacobs joined cases C-430/93 and C-431/93, *Van Schijndel*, para 26.

116 CoJ case C-360/09, *Pfleiderer*. See para 6.21 above.

117 CoJ joined cases C-430/93 and C-431/93, *Van Schijndel*, para 19. See para 2.09 and 6.05 above.

conflict with each other, as was the case, for example, in *Promusicae*.[118] And it did so again in *Smidberger*, where the EU law provisions on the free movement of goods conflicted with the freedoms of expression and of assembly of certain private parties.[119] A further illustration is the *Atlanta* case law on the possibilities for national courts to grant interim relief with respect to the application of secondary EU law whose validity is in doubt.[120] There the Court of Justice established as an important condition in this context the balancing between the interests of the EU related to ensuring the full effect of EU law, on the one hand, and the interests of the private parties at issue, on the other hand.

It is, of course, true that the situations and the interests at stake in each of the above-mentioned cases all differ to a greater or lesser extent. Still, it is suggested that the positions are sufficiently comparable to be able to consider that in the present context also the interests involved can be essentially "too fundamental" to be forced into a hierarchical relationship.[121] If that view is correct, this approach should arguably be seen as a consequence of the increased maturity of EU law over time.[122] Now that EU law is established more firmly than in the early decades of the process of European integration, there may be less of a need to "instrumentalise" concepts such as rights of private parties to ensure its effectiveness. It can then also more easily "afford" to give way to some extent to other legitimate interests where appropriate, such as those related to the effective enforcement of those very same rights.[123]

The third and last remark concerns the implications of the foregoing specifically for the *EU legislature* in relation to legislation on private enforcement. The institutions involved in the EU's law-making process do not necessarily need to follow the same approach as the Court of Justice with respect to the issues discussed above. The balancing and prioritising of the various interests at stake in a particular situation are the very essence of law-making (which in itself may be an additional argument as to why the Court could be expected to take a nuanced approach). Generally speaking, there is no rule of law that precludes the EU legislature from letting what it sees as the general interest prevail over the interests of certain private parties when regulating a particular situation, or vice versa. In so doing the EU legislature must of course respect certain boundaries. These come in the form of procedure (for example consulting **11.15**

118 CoJ case C-275/06, *Promusicae*, para 68. See para 4.18 above. See e.g. also CoJ case C-461/10, *Bonnier*, para 56–60; CoJ case C-283/11, *Sky Österreich*, para 59–60.

119 CoJ case C-112/00, *Smidberger*, para 81. See e.g. also CoJ case C-438/05, *Viking Line*, para 79.

120 CoJ case C-465/93, *Atlanta*, para 42–4 and 50. See para 2.22 above.

121 Cf. Reich (2010), pp. 140–41.

122 For a detailed overview and discussion of the relevant developments over time, see Eilmansberger (2004), pp. 1201–31. Cf. Tridimas (2001), p. 77.

123 Cf. Prechal (1998), p. 686; Bengoetxea (2008), p. 22.

widely, stating reasons)[124] as well as substance (for example proportionality, fundamental rights).[125] Procedural requirements by definition do not amount to an absolute bar, however. Moreover, in relation to issues of substance, the EU legislature tends to enjoy broad discretion when making political, economic and social choices and complex assessments.[126] Subject to certain conditions, this may also involve restricting the exercise of fundamental rights of certain private parties.[127]

The EU legislature therefore generally has, not unrestricted, but nonetheless considerable freedom to legislate in a manner that it deems appropriate on the above-mentioned matters involving tensions and conflicts between the two expressions of effectiveness that are of particular importance here. In other words, this is to a considerable extent a matter of policy choices. The discussion in the foregoing subsections has highlighted in particular the importance – when making these policy choices – of clearly identifying the objectives that an EU legislative initiative related to private enforcement seeks to achieve and the effects that this can have on establishing the approach to be followed. It has been illustrated especially how one's views on the objective that is primarily to be achieved determine to a great extent the answers to questions such as whether and, if so, to what extent and in what manner leniency applicants are to be shielded from private enforcement litigation; punitive damages are desirable or objectionable as a private enforcement instrument; out-of-court settlements between the private parties to an EU law-related dispute are to be encouraged or a reason for concern; and whether and, if so, in which form collective redress mechanisms are to be provided for.

B. THE HORIZONTALISATION PERSPECTIVE

In Chapter 1 it was recalled how the Court of Justice has made it clear that the EU legal order is essentially triangular in nature, in that EU law is not exclusively a matter between the Member States and the EU institutions but that it can also grant private parties a legal position in their own right, which – largely driven by considerations related to effectiveness – led to the creation and elaboration of a private enforcement model.[128] In the present section the emphasis is on another aspect of this model. It builds on the point that over the

124 See e.g. Art. 11(3) and 296 TFEU.
125 See subsection 10.A.2 above.
126 Cf. para 10.08–10.09 above.
127 See para 10.10 above.
128 See para 1.01 above.

years it has become clear that private parties can invoke their rights vested in EU law not only in "vertical" legal relationships (that is, *vis-à-vis* the Member States and the EU institutions), but also in "horizontal" legal relationships (that is, *vis-à-vis* other private parties). The present section thus looks at private enforcement from a "horizontalisation" perspective. Below, the main aspects of this development are first sketched in relation to EU law generally and the private enforcement of this law specifically. Attention then turns to the most important implications in terms of enforcement, costs, concerns related to creating a "litigation culture" and situations where "diffuse" interests are at stake. Next, the three categories of "hybrid" enforcement are outlined, followed by an assessment of the main fundamental rights-related implications of this horizontalisation.

1. The horizontalisation of EU law and its enforcement

A first issue to be elaborated on in this regard is whether the provisions of EU law in question are capable of having *horizontal direct effect*, that is, whether they can be relied upon directly in legal proceedings between two private parties. As was noted earlier, in this respect a distinction must be made between various legal instruments that exist in EU law.[129] On the one hand, provisions of the EU Treaties, regulations and decisions that are sufficiently clear and unconditional can be directly effective in horizontal legal relationships, whereas, on the other hand, the Court of Justice has consistently refused to construe directives as being capable of having such effect. In the case of directives, transposition by the Member States into national law is required before the rules in question can have direct legal effects between private parties. **11.16**

This latter limitation is obviously an important one in the present context. For one thing, the substantive EU law to which the legal acts discussed in Part B above relate have often been laid down in directives. That is the case for substantive EU public procurement law, EU consumer protection law and, in part, substantive EU intellectual property law.[130] Another part of substantive EU intellectual property law has been laid down in regulations, whereas substantive EU competition law is founded by the EU Treaties (that is, Articles 101 and 102 TFEU).[131] For another thing, all private enforcement facilitating legal acts assessed in the foregoing are themselves directives. Transposition into national law is thus generally required for them to have effect in disputes

129 See para 1.04 above.

130 See para 3.02 (concerning public procurement law), 4.02 (concerning intellectual property law) and 5.03 (concerning consumer protection law) above.

131 See para 4.02 (concerning intellectual property law) and 6.02 and 6.03 (concerning competition law) above.

between two private parties. In the absence thereof, the provisions in question have no direct effect in such horizontal legal relationships.

While therefore undoubtedly important, the practical implications of this lack of horizontal direct effect of directives should at the same time probably not be overstated either. Although there is certainly scope for improvement, especially in terms of the speed with which transposition takes place, the Member States mostly still transpose directives into national law in a timely and adequate manner.[132] The private parties concerned can therefore normally invoke their rights vested in EU law *vis-à-vis* other private parties too, on the basis of the national laws transposing the directives in question. And even where transposition is late or inadequate, national law must be interpreted in so far as possible in light of the wording and the purpose of the directives at issue, pursuant to the EU law principle of consistent interpretation.[133] In this manner a directive can thus still have important "indirect" effects in legal relationships between private parties.[134] Finally, in certain cases directives give expression to a general principle of EU law. When certain rules of national law are incompatible with that principle, they may therefore still need to be disapplied, in disputes between two private parties as much as in any other dispute.[135] Some understand this to boil down to all but the same thing as granting horizontal direct effect to directives.[136]

11.17 A second important issue is whether the provisions of EU law in question actually *confer rights* on which a private party can rely in respect to another private party. It has been explained earlier that the issues of direct effect and conferral of rights may often coincide, but that they are not identical.[137] Whether a provision confers a right on a given private party depends on its content. When the content of a provision of EU law is such as to confer rights and how that is to be determined is regrettably not always entirely clear, however. Yet this does not appear to be overly problematic for the present purposes. For the substantive EU law, the private enforcement of which the legal acts under consideration here seek to facilitate, generally does confer rights

---

132 Cf. Commission, 31st Annual report on monitoring the application of EU law (2013), COM(2014) 612, pp. 3–4.

133 See para 1.04 above.

134 In addition, a private party who suffers damage as a consequence of a lack of timely and adequate transposition of a directive can seek to obtain compensation from the Member State in question under the principle of Member State liability, discussed in para 2.23 above.

135 See e.g. CoJ case C-555/07, *Kücükdeveci*, para 50–51. For a case where the CoJ expressly refused to apply similar reasoning, see CoJ case C-176/12, *Association de médiation sociale*, para 41–7.

136 E.g. Thüsing and Horler (2010), p. 1161. For a more nuanced analysis, see Peers (2010), p. 849. On the possible horizontal direct effects of general principles of EU law more generally, see further e.g. Groussot and Lindgard (2008), p. 173; De Mol (2010), p. 293; Hartkamp (2010b), p. 250; Azoulai (2012), p. 215.

137 See para 2.04 above.

on which private parties can rely, against other private parties also.[138] Indeed, if that were otherwise there would be little point in adopting these private enforcement-facilitating legal acts in the first place. And also more generally EU law, as construed by the Court of Justice, tends to be rather "generous" in conferring rights on private parties.[139]

This "generosity" at times also extends to the related issue of the identification of the *addressee* of a particular provision of EU law. This determines who is bound by the obligation in question and consequently against whom the rights that private parties may be able to derive from that provision can be invoked. The most notable example is probably Article 157 TFEU concerning gender equality in relation to which the Court of Justice has held that '*the fact that certain provisions of the Treaty are formally addressed to the Member States does not prevent rights from being conferred at the same time on any individual who has an interest in the performance of the duties thus laid down*'.[140] This provision therefore applies not only to the action of public authorities, but also to agreements between private parties.[141] Although the relevant case law is still evolving and this may not apply to all these provisions to the same extent, the EU Treaties' provisions on the fundamental freedoms (that is, Articles 34, 45, 49 and 56 TFEU) are generally subject to a certain degree of horizontalisation as well. It has become clear that, even if these provisions are also formally addressed only to the Member States, private parties can also in certain situations rely on the rights that they derive from them against parties that may be functionally rather closely related to the state but that are nevertheless not themselves public authorities.[142]

In light of the foregoing, one can therefore speak of a perhaps not universal and unrestricted, but nonetheless clearly apparent, development towards the *horizontalisation* of substantive EU law. In many ways the development of the concept of private enforcement of that law both in the enforcement-related case law discussed in Part A and in the EU legislation on private enforcement discussed in Part B above can be seen as an *expression* and *extension* of this horizontalisation of substantive EU law. For where substantive law is increasingly "horizontalised", attention logically also turns to the remedies and procedures that seek to ensure that the enforcement of the rights of private parties derived from that law is a realistic possibility. This is well illustrated by the **11.18**

138 See in particular para 9.04 above.

139 See para 11.13 above.

140 CoJ case 43/75, *Defrenne*, para 31.

141 Ibid., para 39.

142 See e.g. CoJ case C-438/05, *Viking Line*, para 33; CoJ case C-171/11, *Fra.bo*. See further Van den Bogaert (2002), p. 123; Krenn (2012), p. 177; Van Harten and Nauta (2013), p. 677; Verbruggen (2014), p. 201.

aforementioned provision on gender equality, which was first substantially horizontalised, what in turn led to EU involvement – by its judiciary as well as by its legislature – with the rules of national law relating to the enforcement of this provision.[143]

Accordingly, it has been observed that a ruling such as *Muñoz* – where the Court of Justice held that national law cannot preclude the private parties concerned from relying in a horizontal relationship on the rules laid down in two EU regulations on common quality standards for certain agricultural products[144] – '*transposes the principle of horizontal direct effect to the procedural and remedial plain*'.[145] In other words, this ruling clarified the practical consequences of that principle.[146] Similar observations have been made in a competition law context in relation to the Court's rulings in *BRT* and *Courage*.[147] In this latter context Advocate General Van Gerven had in 1993 already spoken of '*the logical conclusion of the horizontal direct effect*' of the rules of substantive EU law concerned.[148] The (nascent) principle of private party liability articulated in *Courage* and *Muñoz* can thus be seen as the corollary of the principle of direct effect and the granting of rights by EU law directly to private parties, which underlines once more that the legal order established under the EU Treaties is truly triangular in nature.[149]

Some caution is admittedly in place when drawing conclusions on the basis of the above case law. In *Muñoz*, the rights in question derived from regulations. Similarly, in *Courage*, where the same principle of private party liability for infringements of EU law was articulated, they derived from the EU Treaties, namely Article 101 TFEU. It therefore does not necessarily follow that this principle can also be applied to directives, which, as was recalled above, have no horizontal direct effect.[150] There seems no reason, however, to presume that in principle the same logic could not be applied to provisions of national law transposing a directive.[151] That is certainly the presumption underlying the EU legislation facilitating the private enforcement of EU law before national courts at issue here. After all, as was also noted above, in many instances this legislation

143 This resulted in what is now Gender Equality Directive 2006/54. See e.g. CoJ case 43/75, *Defrenne*, para 40; CoJ case 14/83, *Van Colson*, para 23–8.

144 CoJ case C-253/00, *Muñoz*. See para 2.25 above.

145 Tridimas (2006), p. 546.

146 Biondi (2003), p. 1243.

147 CoJ case 127/73, *BRT*; CoJ case C-453/99, *Courage*. See para 6.01 (concerning *BRT*) and para 2.24 and 6.14 (concerning *Courage*) above. See Milutinovic (2014), p. 346.

148 Opinion AG Van Gerven case C-128/92, *Banks*, para 44.

149 Cf. Kelliher (2008), p. 7.

150 Cf. Tridimas (2006), p. 546.

151 Cf. Prechal (1997), p. 5; Betlem (2003), pp. 215–16.

seeks to facilitate the enforcement of rights vested in rules of substantive EU law that have been laid down in directives. It may therefore be presumed that this principle of private party liability can, as a general rule, be applied in all situations where provisions of EU law that confer rights on private parties are infringed by other private parties.[152]

There can be little doubt also that the secondary EU law considered in Part B above focuses primarily on the horizontalised private enforcement of EU law. The legal acts assessed generally set out rules on remedies and procedures that can be relied upon by private parties in cases of (alleged) infringements of EU substantive law by another private party. It can be noted in this connection that the infringements to be addressed in legal acts such as the IPR Enforcement Directive, the Consumer Injunctions Directive, the Product Liability Directive and the Competition Damages Directive are typically committed by *private parties*. There is one notable exception, however. For the Procurement Remedies Directives are typically concerned with private enforcement actions to be brought against *(semi-)public bodies*, and not against other private parties.[153] **11.19**

This exception serves to underline that the EU legislation facilitating private enforcement at issue may have *mostly* been designed to apply to disputes between two private parties, but it does not *necessarily* remain limited to such situations. Put differently, this legislation can give effect not only to the principle of *private* party liability for infringements of EU law, but also to that of *public* party (that is, Member State) liability for such infringements.[154] One could say that it may in effect be the other way round. *Van Gend en Loos*, where the Court of Justice laid the foundations for the private enforcement model, concerned a case brought by a private party against a public body.[155] Since then the Court's enforcement-related case law has evolved by first articulating the principle of Member State liability and only subsequently that of private party liability. Likewise, where secondary EU law on this subject matter is concerned, it would seem that in some respects the Procurement Remedies Directives "led the way" and subsequently "spilled over" from the vertical to the horizontal domain.

152 In a similar sense, see e.g. Dougan (2004), p. 386; Drake (2006), pp. 858 and 861; Van Dam (2006), p. 345; Komninos (2008), pp. 176–9; Milutinovic (2010), p. 76. Cf. Ward (1998), p. 70. See also Opinion AG Geelhoed case C-253/00, *Muñoz*, para 2–3. Tridimas (2006), p. 547, appears, however, to take the view that the scope of application of this principle is limited to the internal market.

153 See in particular para 3.02 above.

154 See also para 2.27 above.

155 CoJ case 26/62, *Van Gend en Loos*, p. 1. See para 1.01 above. The public body in question was the Netherlands Inland Revenue Administration.

It is further important to note that this distinction between vertical and horizontal situations is far from absolute. Private undertakings can in certain situations be bound by rules of substantive EU public procurement law as well, which implies that the Procurement Remedies Directives can also apply to disputes between two private parties.[156] Indeed in the domestic legal systems of certain Member States procurement law is generally considered as a matter of civil law, considering that the bodies that are subject to these rules act in a private rather than a public capacity where they procure goods or services on the market.[157] Conversely, it is not excluded that legal proceedings are brought under the IPR Enforcement Directive against a public body. After all, public bodies can at times also infringe intellectual property rights. The same applies to the Competition Damages Directive, considering that public bodies can sometimes also be subject to (and therefore be infringers of) the substantive EU competition rules to which this directive relates.[158] Indeed, these latter two directives could theoretically even apply to disputes between two public bodies, given that public bodies can not only be defendants but also be applicants in the cases covered by these directives.[159]

11.20 Finally, the IPR Enforcement Directive in particular takes this process of horizontalisation one step further in some respects. Under this directive certain *third parties* (that is, private parties who are not themselves accused of having infringed any intellectual property right) can be required to disclose information on the origin and distribution network used for an alleged infringement of the relevant rules of EU law.[160] Covered by this provision are, most notably, intermediaries whose services were used by alleged infringers. This directive also allows for injunctions to be imposed on these third-party intermediaries.[161] In practice these obligations tend to play a particularly important role in the online sphere, for instance with respect to internet service providers who may be required to disclose certain information concerning their customers who have been found to be infringing intellectual property rights or to block the latter's internet access. Bringing these third parties within the directive's scope has been justified on the basis of their role as "gatekeepers" and the relevant information and means to act that they often possess. This is also one of the IPR Enforcement Directive's most controversial aspects, however. Critics see this as

156 See para 3.08 and 3.11 above.

157 See para 3.11 above.

158 See para 6.01 and 6.26 above.

159 Cf. e.g. recital 13 Competition Damages Directive 2014/104.

160 Art. 8 IPR Enforcement Directive 2004/48. See para 4.16 above.

161 Art. 9(1)(a) and 11 IPR Enforcement Directive 2004/48. See para 4.20 above. See also Art. 8(3) Infosoc Directive 2001/29.

the undue "privatisation" of enforcement that forces these third parties to act as a sort of "internet police".[162]

The Court of Justice has highlighted certain limitations that are to be respected in connection with the above-mentioned provisions of the IPR Enforcement Directive. These limitations relate in particular to the fundamental rights that may be at stake. Depending on the case at hand, it concerns not the only fundamental rights of the persons who make use of the services provided by these intermediaries (for example the right to protection of personal data and the freedom to receive and impart information) and the persons affected by the infringements at issue (for example the right to the protection of intellectual property), but also the freedom to conduct a business of the intermediaries themselves.[163] It is noticeable, however, that the Court has so far not expressed any objections in principle to the involvement of these third parties as such. Quite to the contrary, it has interpreted the provision of the IPR Enforcement Directive on these injunctions rather extensively, particularly where it held that this remedy can be relied upon with a view not only to terminating ongoing infringements but also to prevent future ones from occurring.[164] In relation to certain (online) copyright infringements, the Court has further expressly held that '*intermediaries are, in many cases, best placed to bring such infringing activities to an end*'.[165] The only differentiation between actual infringers and these third-party intermediaries that indisputably did not engage in any infringing activity seems thus far the Court's recognition that in this context the latter cannot be required to '*make unbearable sacrifices*'.[166]

It is true that the above-mentioned remedies that are available with respect to third parties under the IPR Enforcement Directive are limited in several respects. In terms of personal scope, they remain limited to *certain categories* of (and therefore not just any) third parties. Moreover, in terms of substance they only concern the issuing of *injunctions* (and not other remedies) as well as the possible disclosure of rather narrowly *specified information* (as opposed to all information that might be relevant). The very existence of these provisions nonetheless illustrates how far the horizontalisation of the enforcement of EU law can extend. It is furthermore not inconceivable that this approach will be taken a step further in due time. Although at present there appear to be no specific plans to this effect, one could think of making other remedies available

162 See para 4.21 above.

163 E.g. CoJ case C-70/10, *Scarlet Extended*, para 46–52.

164 E.g. CoJ case C-324/09, *L'Oréal v eBay*, para 128–34. See para 4.24 above.

165 CoJ case C-314/12, *UPC Telekabel Wien*, para 27 (relating to the injunctions referred to in Art. 8(3) Infosoc Directive 2001/29).

166 Ibid., para 53.

with respect to certain third parties deemed to be implicated in infringements of EU law, such as actions for damages.[167] Indeed, this tendency to involve third parties in private enforcement proceedings already appears to be spreading to other sectors. Most notably, the Competition Damages Directive also provides for the possibility of third parties being ordered to disclose evidence that may be of relevance in private enforcement proceedings.[168] It is noticeable that, unlike under the IPR Enforcement Directive, this latter regime covers in principle *all* third parties that may have relevant evidence that lies within their control and that also the *sort of evidence* in question has not been circumscribed in any detail here. This means that in this respect the scope of the Competition Damages Directive's provision on disclosure is wide and that the third parties concerned are in fact treated hardly any differently to defendants.[169]

2. Private enforcement implications

11.21 What does the foregoing mean in practical terms? When considering the private enforcement implications of this horizontalisation, it is once more important to distinguish between the two different expressions of effectiveness identified in the foregoing.[170] To begin with, seen from an *individual rights perspective* the implications seem quite straightforward. Generally speaking, the more the enforcement of EU law is horizontalised, the better the possibilities for private parties to enforce the rights that they derive from that law. Horizontalised EU law may occasionally offer these parties an entirely new legal venue, as was the case for the private parties affected by the (alleged) infringement of the EU competition and agricultural rules at issue in *Courage* and *Muñoz* respectively.[171] More often the improvement of the enforcement possibilities of the private parties concerned is, however, more gradual, for instance by clarifying specific matters such as the terms under which they are to be given access to evidence lying within the control of the opponent or can claim compensation in damages pursuant to infringements.[172]

---

167 Cf. Commission, Responses to the public consultation on the civil enforcement of intellectual property rights, July 2013, p. 17.

168 Art. 5 Competition Damages Directive 2014/104. See para 6.32 above.

169 Only in the context of the proportionality assessment referred to in Art. 5(3) Competition Damages Directive 2014/104 is (limited) attention paid to the specific interests of third parties. There it is stipulated that the factors relating to the scope and costs of the requested disclosure as well as the protection of confidential information apply '*especially for any third parties concerned*'.

170 See para 11.02 above.

171 CoJ case C-453/99, *Courage*; CoJ case C-253/00, *Muñoz*. See para 2.24 and 6.14 (*Courage*) and 2.25 (*Muñoz*) above.

172 See subsection 8.B.2 and section 7.A above, respectively.

The requirements in this respect that flow from secondary EU law can be rather modest in terms of the level of detail that they provide or the standard that they establish,[173] but it can nonetheless safely be assumed that no single Member State already complied with all remedial and procedural requirements discussed in the foregoing chapters before they were imposed on them by the EU legal acts under consideration. In most cases, the Member States have thus been obliged to amend their respective national laws, at least to some extent. Overall, the position of private parties wishing to bring a private enforcement claim has improved as a consequence. From this perspective, the practical implications resulting from the EU legislative action at issue are thus generally to be assessed positively.

But there is also another side to this coin. The case law and the legislative measures discussed above typically reduce the burden on the (potential) *applicant* in private enforcement proceedings. It is primarily this private party that benefits from the availability under EU law of remedies such as actions for damages, contractual remedies, interim relief, the disclosure of evidence and recurring penalty payments.[174] The EU law provisions on procedural issues such as legal standing, limitation periods and forum have mostly also been established with the interests of the applicants in mind.[175] Although, legally speaking, these provisions may affect all parties to the dispute, in practice they primarily benefit the applicants.[176] This raises the question of the position of the (potential) *defendant* in the disputes covered by the EU legislation at issue. **11.22**

It is true that improving the legal position of the applicant in a horizontal context does not *necessarily* mean that the defendant's position deteriorates in a manner that is to be deemed unfair or legally problematic. It is hard to see which legitimate reasons a defendant could invoke for arguing that he is unduly affected by EU legislative measures that seek, for instance, to safeguard and improve an applicant's access to court so as to allow this party to obtain a fair, timely and enforceable ruling on the lawfulness of certain behaviour on the part of the defendant. That can indeed actually also be in the interest of the latter. In that sense, there is no "one-to-one" relationship between an improvement of the position of the applicant and a deterioration of that of the defendant. Nonetheless, it remains striking that in the present context at best very limited attention

173 See in particular para 10.13 above.

174 See sections 7.01 and 7.03 and subsections 8.B.1 and 8.B.3 above, respectively.

175 See subsections 9.A.2, 9.B.1 and 9.C.1 above, respectively.

176 In specific cases there are certain exceptions, however, such as the rules on (very short) limitation periods for bringing actions set out in Art. 2c and 2f Procurement Remedies Directives 89/665 and 92/13, the possible cap on the liability of procedures laid down in Art. 16(1) Product Liability Directive 85/374 or the passing-on defence in Art. 13 Competition Damages Directive 2014/104. See para 3.26, 5.32 and 6.37 above, respectively.

tends to be paid to the position of the latter. That applies all the more so because, at the stage when the relevant measures are applied for, it often still remains to be determined whether an infringement of EU law has actually been committed. At that stage one can often only speak of an *alleged* infringement of EU law. In a *vertical* context such a generally rather one-sided focus on improving the position of the applicant might normally not be much of a concern. In that case the defendant (which is by definition the state or one of its entities) is generally not considered to be in need of any special protection.[177] But this is considerably less evident in *horizontal* legal relationships, which concern disputes between two private parties who are, as a general rule, presumed to be equals.[178]

Even when leaving the possible fundamental rights-related implications aside for now,[179] the question can therefore arise why certain measures are not made available to the defendant as well. Take, for instance, the IPR Enforcement Directive. This directive facilitates the enforcement of the intellectual property rights of private parties. But a private party who wishes to *challenge* the existence or validity of such a right cannot benefit from the measures for which it provides.[180] Furthermore, the wording of this directive's provisions on the preservation of evidence and on obtaining information from certain third parties seems to suggest that these measures are only available to private party applicants.[181] Yet private party defendants may also wish to rely on those provisions in order to be able to demonstrate that they did not act in an infringing manner. The Competition Damages Directive similarly regulates the effects of decisions by national competition authorities (and of the national courts reviewing those decisions) in private enforcement proceedings only where it concerns findings of *infringements*.[182] Although under EU law these authorities cannot establish that no infringement occurred, they may still find that in certain cases there are *no grounds for action* on their part.[183] Or a review court might *annul* a decision by these authorities finding an infringement. Defendants in private enforcement cases may sometimes wish to rely on decisions of this type. But the Competition Damages Directive leaves the legal effects of these decisions entirely unaddressed. Comparable questions can arise in relation to certain rules on the allocation of legal costs, particularly if they were to amount to one-way fee shifting.[184]

---

177 Cf. Himsworth (1997), p. 310; Dougan (2004), pp. 13–14.

178 Cf. Jacobs and Deisenhofer (2003), p. 205.

179 See in particular para 11.34 below.

180 CoJ case C-180/11, *Bericap*, para 77. See also CoJ case C-435/12, *ACI Adam*, para 62.

181 Art. 7 and 8 IPR Enforcement Directive 2004/48. See para 4.15 and 4.16 above.

182 Art. 9 Competition Damages Directive 2014/104. See para 6.41 above.

183 Art. 5 Competition Regulation 1/2003. See e.g. CoJ case C-375/09, *Tele 2 Polska*, para 19–30.

184 See subsection 8.B.5 above.

An assessment of the private enforcement implications of the process of horizontalisation referred to above is altogether rather different if we consider them from the perspective of ensuring the *effectiveness of EU law per se*.[185] Then the main consequence in practical terms of private parties being facilitated in bringing their actions for (alleged) infringements of EU law before national courts is that this helps draw private resources into the overall "enforcement mix".[186] Private parties who consider that they have a reasonable prospect of obtaining, for instance, an injunction or a damages award for such infringements can be expected to monitor more closely the behaviour of their (commercial) counterparts and initiate legal proceedings where they deem this necessary. This in turn should act as an incentive for the parties that are subject to these rules to improve compliance and avoid acting in an infringing manner. It has already been seen that this "dual vigilance" logic was an important consideration when adopting the legislation assessed in Part B above.[187] The resulting beneficial effect in terms of overall compliance and enforcement can be particularly important, given that the resources available for public enforcement (where such mechanisms exist in the first place) are often limited, certainly in times of budgetary constraints.[188] **11.23**

It would further be wrong to see this as only a matter of financial means to be employed for enforcement purposes. In many cases private parties also possess considerable expertise and inside knowledge of the practical workings of a given sector, which public enforcement authorities may not possess or at least not to the same extent. Moreover, these authorities may sometimes not wish to pursue certain infringements in light of their policy of prioritisation or under political influence. Constraints of this latter type will normally not apply to private parties affected by infringements of EU law.

Seen from this latter perspective, a private enforcement model also has certain important *limitations*, however, which can reduce the effectiveness and deterrent effect of possible private enforcement actions and therefore of a model that relies on "regulation through litigation" as such.[189] First and foremost, it should not be forgotten that (potential) private party applicants inevitably act primarily **11.24**

185 See further Benedict (1995), p. 250; Jacobs and Deisenhofer (2003), p. 191; Jones (2004), p. 21; Hodges (2006), p. 1395; Eilmansberger (2007), p. 443; Wils (2009), p. 6; Milutinovic (2010), pp. 17 and 352; Peyer (2011), p. 635; Canenbley and Steinvorth (2011), p. 321; Lock (2012), p. 1675; Whish and Bailey (2012), p. 295; Möschel (2013), pp. 4–6; Van den Bergh (2013), pp. 13–20.

186 Jones (2004), p. 21.

187 See in particular para 10.03 and 11.05 above.

188 Cf. Commission, Staff working paper accompanying the white paper on damages actions for breach of the EC antitrust rules, SEC(2008) 404, p. 11. See e.g. also Heads of the European competition authorities, Resolution on competition authorities in the EU: the continued need for effective institutions, 16 November 2010.

189 Cf. Hodges (2006), p. 1394.

in accordance with what they see as their own interests. These private parties decide for themselves if, when and how they wish to initiate legal proceedings to address alleged infringements of the applicable rules of EU law. As the Court of Justice has put it, '*in a civil suit, it is for the parties to take the initiative*', which '*reflects fundamental conceptions prevailing in most Member States as to the relations between the State and the individual*'.[190] National law on civil procedure is largely based on the concept of party autonomy, which is reflected *inter alia* in the principle of judicial passivity.[191] This also implies that no party can be forced to initiate litigation when it does not want to do so.[192] Private parties will typically base their decisions in this regard on a cost/benefit analysis that takes account only of their own individual interests. No account is normally taken of broader considerations in the general interest, such as the overall benefits in terms of effective enforcement of the law or the optimal level of enforcement. In a competition case, private enforcement can consequently easily lead to a focus on protecting the competitor, rather than competition as such.[193] This distinction might perhaps be less apparent in other fields of law, but the main point is not fundamentally different.

In addition, the investigative and evidence-gathering powers of private parties are normally rather limited.[194] That is certainly the case when these powers are compared with those attributed to the competent public enforcement authorities.[195] It is evident, for instance, that, unlike competition authorities, private parties cannot carry out "dawn raids" on undertakings suspected of having infringed the EU competition rules.[196] The IPR Enforcement Directive and the Competition Damages Directive particularly seek to address this issue by providing for specific measures on the disclosure of evidence by the parties to the dispute.[197] However, the resulting possibilities for the private parties

190 CoJ joined cases C-430/93 and C-431/93, *Van Schijndel*, para 21. See e.g. also Opinion AG Geelhoed joined cases C-295/04 to C-298/04, *Manfredi*, para 31.

191 Ebers (2010), p. 826. See also Opinion AG Jacobs joined cases C-430/93 and C-431/93, *Van Schijndel*, para 33–7.

192 Cf. Jacobs and Deisenhofer (2003), p. 191.

193 Cf. Hjelmeng (2013), pp. 1024 and 1032.

194 See e.g. Commission, Green paper on combating counterfeiting and piracy in the single market, COM(98) 569, p. 18, where the Commission noted that one of the advantages of addressing infringements of intellectual property law through public enforcement (and more specifically through criminal measures) is the '*more effective gathering of evidence*'. Cf. Whish (1994), p. 4; Wils (2003a), p. 480; Jones (2004), p. 17; Frese (2011), p. 410; Canenbley and Steinvorth (2011), p. 321.

195 It should be noted, however, that the powers of the public enforcement authorities concerned under EU law can differ significantly depending on the field of law at issue. See subsections 3.D.2, 4.D.2, 5.E.4 and 6.D.2 above.

196 See para 6.47 above.

197 See in particular subsection 8.B.2 above. See also the *ex parte* search order procedure provided for in Art. 7 IPR Enforcement Directive 2004/48. See para 4.15 above. See also para 11.22 above and 11.37 below.

concerned in terms of investigation and evidence-gathering remain comparatively limited. There are clear limits to the extent to which private parties are and indeed can be granted such powers, essentially for the simple reason that they are private parties. As such, granting these parties too far-reaching powers in this regard inevitably raises concerns in terms of risk of abuse, fairness and equality of arms.[198] The relevant provisions set out in the two above-mentioned directives therefore include a whole range of safeguards.[199] These safeguards include in particular judicial oversight, meaning that one could say that these powers have in fact been attributed primarily to the national courts rather than to the private parties concerned directly.

3. Costs, litigation culture and diffuse interests

Although private enforcement can thus help increase overall levels of enforcement without extra expenditure on public enforcement, it would be a mistake to think that private enforcement and the measures taken to facilitate it do not also entail certain *costs*.[200] The most visible costs relate directly to the litigation before national courts resulting from the legal claims the enforcement of which the legislation assessed above seeks to facilitate. This involves expenditure on the part of the courts before which the proceedings are brought as well as legal costs for the parties to the dispute.[201] **11.25**

But there can also be other costs that are sometimes less immediately apparent, such as costs related to possible "over-deterrence". Facilitating private enforcement actions may lead to a risk that potential defendants adapt their behaviour not so much because there is a clear-cut case of them infringing EU law, but rather simply out of fear of being sued. A private party could, for example, decide not to bring an innovative product onto the market for that reason. There can thus be a "chilling effect". A related matter is the possibility of strategic litigation and the harassment of innocent parties, known as "nuisance cases". For even when a legal action is unlikely to be successful, the mere fact that it is brought can be problematic for the defendant, for example because of the legal costs and other resources that the latter may have to spend on its defence or the reputational damage that may result from the fact that such litigation is pending.

198 See para 11.24 above and 11.34 below.
199 See in particular para 8.22 above.
200 See further e.g. Wils (2003a), pp. 479 and 484; Kur (2004), p. 829; Hodges (2006), p. 1395; Eilmansberger (2007), p. 459; Milutinovic (2010), pp. 16–17; Peyer (2011), pp. 635–41.
201 On legal costs, see also subsection 8.B.5 above.

The above may lead to costs not only for the (potential) defendants in a private enforcement action, but also for society as a whole.[202] These negative effects are to some extent an inevitable by-product of any legal system or legislative measure that aims to offer effective judicial protection to private parties and at least in part also to punish and deter infringers. However, that should not distract from the fact that the more these objectives are pursued through particular private enforcement-facilitating measures of the type at issue here, the bigger these risks and the associated costs generally become.

11.26 That brings us to the concerns about creating or encouraging what is often called a "*litigation culture*". Concerns of this type have been expressed regularly in connection with private enforcement-related EU legislation, whether in the form of fears of "cowboy tenderers" bringing "nuisance cases" under the Procurement Remedies Directives,[203] a perceived risk of the Product Liability Directive leading to "excessive litigation"[204] or more general concerns about creating or encouraging such a culture through an EU initiative on collective redress or the private enforcement of EU competition law.[205] In this connection reference is often made to the – presumed[206] – private enforcement-related excesses in the United States.[207] This term "litigation culture" refers, broadly speaking, to a situation where litigation between private parties takes place to a degree that is considered to be undesirable, harmful or even abusive.[208] Understood in this manner there are obviously few people who will argue in favour of creating or encouraging such a culture. This presumes that a clear dividing line can be drawn between an "excessive" and a "healthy" degree of litigation. Making such a distinction may be far from easy in practice, however. Views on where this line is to be drawn tend to depend not only on whether or not the party concerned is likely to be an applicant or a defendant in private enforcement proceedings, it also typically involves a value judgement of sorts. It may

---

202 Cf. European Parliament, Study on collective redress in antitrust, June 2012, p. 41.

203 See para 3.05 and 3.09 above.

204 See para 5.25 and 5.28 above.

205 See para 5.37 and 6.19 above, respectively. See e.g. also Hodges (2006), p. 1398.

206 Whether or not this perception actually rests on a realistic understanding of the US system is another matter. As noted by Micklitz (2011b), p. 114 (in relation to collective redress), observations made in this regard tend to be based on the unquestioned assumption that the situations in the EU and the US are comparable and on rather superficial knowledge of the situation in the US. In a similar sense, see e.g. also Lande (2010), p. 11; Gavil (2014), p. 12.

207 Cf. e.g. Commission, Public consultation towards a coherent approach to collective redress, SEC(2011) 173, p. 9; European Parliament, Resolution, Towards a coherent European approach to collective redress, P7_TA(2012)0021, p. 2; Commission, Communication towards a European horizontal framework for collective redress, COM(2013) 401, p. 3.

208 Commission, Communication towards a European horizontal framework for collective redress, COM(2013) 401, p. 7: '*Litigation can be considered abusive when it is intentionally targeted against law-abiding businesses in order to cause reputational damage or to inflict an undue financial burden on them*'. See also e.g. Garben (2013), pp. 42–3.

well vary according to whether the enforcement of EU law *per se* or safeguarding the rights of private parties is seen as the principal objective. In any case, it is not difficult to spot the inherent tension between the ambition to see more private enforcement claims being brought and the desire to avoid a litigation culture. Also, the EU might not be able to have its cake and eat it too.[209]

Having said that, there are good reasons to believe that, at least as matters stand at present, there are generally few litigation culture-related risks. To begin with, the impact of the relevant EU legislation in practice should probably generally not be overstated.[210] And even apart from that, it is broadly agreed that EU law does not provide for what the Commission has called a '*toxic cocktail*'[211] of rules on issues such as class action, punitive (treble) damages, intrusive pre-trial discovery and legal costs (contingency fees) that is deemed to have led to excesses in the United States.[212] Indeed, on none of these issues are there currently similar rules in place in the EU legal system, let alone would such rules apply in combination.[213] It can further be noted that the above-mentioned concerns tend to arise especially in connection with the facilitation of actions for damages under EU law. However, despite the more recent increase observed in several fields, precisely these types of private enforcement actions remain for now typically rather scarce in practice, even where EU legislative action has been taken.[214] The Commission thus may well be correct in its assessment that in the EU, under-compensation is at present generally more of a concern than possible overcompensation.[215]

Besides, if required, the EU legislature has several instruments at its disposal to help avoid creating situations that are deemed harmful and undesirable.[216] The Product Liability Directive offers one example in this regard, where it sets a financial threshold of €500 for damages awards.[217] This threshold has been

209 Cf. Keyte (2014), p. 203.

210 See subsection 10.D.2 above.

211 Commission, Questions and answers regarding the green paper on consumer collective redress, MEMO/08/741, p. 4.

212 E.g. Commission, Green paper on consumer collective redress, COM(2008) 794, pp. 12–14; European Parliament, Study on collective redress in antitrust, June 2012, p. 11; recital 15 Collective Redress Recommendation 2013/396. See e.g. also Hodges (2011), pp. 438–9; Van den Bergh (2013), p. 13.

213 See subsections 5.E.2 (collective redress), 7.A.6 (punitive damages), 8.B.2 (measures on the disclosure of evidence) and 8.B.5 (measures on legal costs) above.

214 See in particular para 7.03 above.

215 Commission, Impact assessment report on damages actions for breach of the EU antitrust rules, SWD(2013) 203, p. 18.

216 More generally, in a different context the CoJ has made it clear that EU law cannot be relied upon for abusive or fraudulent ends. See e.g. CoJ case C-153/13, *SICES*, para 29–34; CoJ joined cases C-58/13 and C-59/13, *Torresi*, para 42–6.

217 Art. 9 Product Liability Directive 85/375. See para 5.28 above.

expressly designed to '*avoid litigation in an excessive number of cases*'.[218] Even if this could conceivably be seen as objectionable, especially from the perspective of a private party's right to full compensation, the Court of Justice has so far not expressed any objections in principle to this measure.[219] Another possible instrument is the regulation of legal costs and, in particular, rules on their allocation between the parties to the dispute. The "loser pays" principle in particular can and does act as a threshold against unmeritorious claims and excessive litigation.[220] A further example can be found in the IPR Enforcement Directive, which requires in general terms that safeguards against abuse are provided for.[221] The proposal for a trade secrets directive contains a rule that would take this one step further where it seeks to address litigation that is '*intimidating or harassing*'.[222]

11.27 Finally, it has already been seen that the concept of a "right" is an indispensable element for a private enforcement model to function, as it essentially links the relevant objective law to the subjective entitlement of a given private party.[223] However, the interests that substantive EU law seeks to protect can sometimes be "*diffuse*" in nature and therefore hard to capture in terms of individual rights that private parties can derive from EU law.[224] One could think of EU environmental law, where legal protection '*generally serves not only the individual interest of claimants, but also, or even exclusively, the public*'.[225] Although in this domain also EU law, as construed by the Court of Justice, appears to have been as "generous" as possible in conferring legally enforceable rights on private parties,[226] the fact remains that in these types of cases it is not always evident that such rights are at issue and consequently that private parties (even where they have an incentive to do so) have the required interest and legal standing to initiate proceedings to address alleged infringements.[227] The issue here is

218 Recital 9 Product Liability Directive 85/374.

219 CoJ case C-52/00, *Commission v France*, para 29–32; CoJ case C-154/00, *Commission v Greece*, para 29–32.

220 See para 8.32 above.

221 Art. 3(2) IPR Enforcement Directive 2004/48. See para 4.06 above.

222 Commission, Proposal for a trade secrets directive, COM(2013) 813, pp. 19–20 (Art. 6(2)). See also Commission, Proposal for Competition Damages Directive 2014/104, COM(2013) 404, p. 35 (Art. 8(1)(d)), where the Commission proposed providing for penalties for cases of abuse relating to the rules on the disclosure of evidence laid down in Competition Damages Directive 2014/104. This aspect of the proposal was, however, not retained by the EU legislature.

223 See para 2.04, 9.04 and 11.17 above.

224 Even if there are certain similarities, this situation where the interests at stake are "diffuse" is to be distinguished from the situation where substantive EU law grants "individual" rights to private parties, but where these parties may not be inclined to enforce them for other reasons, such as the low monetary value of the issue at stake. The latter situation is discussed in the context of collective redress. See subsection 5.E.2 above.

225 Opinion AG Kokott case C–260/11, *Edwards*, para 40.

226 See e.g. CoJ case C-131/88, *Commission v Germany*, para 7; CoJ case C-72/95, *Kraaijeveld*, para 56; CoJ 1996, case C-298/95, *Commission v Germany*, para 16; CoJ case C-420/11, *Leth*, para 32.

227 On legal standing, see also subsection 9.A.2 above.

therefore not so much that the private parties concerned might be discouraged from bringing a legal action in light of potential practical drawbacks such as costs or other risks involved, but rather that there might be no such parties who are, legally speaking, in a position to bring an action in the first place.[228] In the latter case the vigilance of these private parties will be of no relevance in terms of private enforcement.

This particularity can be addressed at least to some extent by providing for particular rules on legal standing that allow certain specific parties to bring legal proceedings. One could think of consumer associations, trade unions or non-governmental organisations which aim to protect the environment. As the Court of Justice noted in an environmental case, this can be seen as appropriate precisely because the rules of substantive EU law in question mostly address the public interest and not merely the protection of the interests of individual private parties as such.[229] Yet even where such specific parties are entitled to initiate legal proceedings, and valuable as such actions may be in certain cases, this still means that the group of potential applicants is significantly reduced as compared with a situation where in principle *any* interested private party affected by an infringement of EU law can bring a case. It is debatable whether such "general interest litigation" amounts to private enforcement at all.[230] It is at least not private enforcement in a "pure" sense, given that the category of potential applicants is by definition limited to parties that seek to defend the public – or at least not only a strictly individual – interest. Certain private enforcement remedies, such as actions for damages, moreover, seem less suitable in these cases. For where diffuse interests are at stake, the damage caused by an infringement may not be "individual" either.

A private enforcement model therefore generally does not seem particularly well suited to the types of situations referred to above.[231] Indeed, the EU legislature itself appears to be of the view that persons invoking a general or public interest (as taxpayers) can be prevented from relying on the remedies and procedural provisions set out in the Procurement Remedies Directives.[232] In such situations public enforcement may well be a more appropriate and

228 Cf. Eliantonio (2014), pp. 259–60.

229 CoJ case C-115/09, *Bund für Umwelt und Naturschutz Deutschland*, para 46.

230 The above arguably constitutes a form of "hybrid" enforcement, discussed in subsection 11.B.4 below. The legal systems of several Member States provide for certain forms of "public interest litigation", whereby legal actions are brought by entities seeking to protect fragmented, diffuse or collective interests. See further e.g. Jacobs and Deisenhofer (2003), p. 192; Wilsher (2006), p. 34; Eliantonio (2014), pp. 260–61.

231 See further Weatherill (2000), p. 87; Micklitz (2011a), p. 568.

232 See recital 122 New Public Sector Directive 2014/24; recital 128 New Utilities Procurement Directive 2014/25.

effective means of enforcement. It is probably no coincidence that the Environmental Liability Directive does not provide for "classic" liability in damages,[233] nor that it was precisely in the field of environmental law that criminal sanctions were (controversially) introduced as a matter of EU law.[234] This point seems to be further underscored by the fact that alleged violations of EU environmental law tend to top the list of fields about which private parties complain to the Commission with a view to the latter exercising its public enforcement powers under the EU Treaties.[235]

4. Hybrid enforcement

11.28 It has already been seen in the foregoing that, while public and private enforcement can supplement each other, both forms of enforcement are largely unconnected in legal-procedural terms.[236] Nonetheless, certain "hybrid" forms of enforcement, which mix elements of both enforcement mechanisms, have emerged in the EU legislation at hand, in Commission proposals and in the legal literature related thereto.[237] The following three types of such hybrid enforcement can be distinguished.

11.29 A first way in which this can occur concerns the granting of certain *quasi-public powers to private parties*. An example of such an approach is the *ex parte* search order procedure provided for in the IPR Enforcement Directive.[238] Under this (optional) regime certain investigatory powers – notably to enter premises for the description or physical seizure of infringing goods, materials used for their production or documents relating thereto – can be granted to a private party, which this party can exercise in relation to another private party that allegedly infringed its intellectual property rights. It has been pointed out in the legal literature that this entails a remarkable measure of "privatisation".[239] Indeed, many Member States consider that this measure is more common in the context of criminal proceedings than in civil ones and therefore did not make use of

233 Environmental Liability Directive 2004/35. See also Art. 11 Environmental Impact Assessment Directive 2011/92, pursuant to which private parties are to be given access to review procedures for challenging the legality of decisions, acts or omissions subject to public participation under that directive. However, this latter directive does not in principle confer a right to compensation in damages. See CoJ case C-420/11, *Leth*, para 46–7.

234 See CoJ case C-176/03, *Commission v Council*.

235 See Commission, 31st Annual report on monitoring the application of EU law (2013), COM(2014) 612, pp. 7–8. Cf. Rawlings (2000), p. 278. On infringement proceedings, see subsection 2.C.1 above.

236 See para 10.19 above.

237 The term "hybrid enforcement" is used (only in relation to the qualified entity approach discussed below) by Cupa (2012), p. 528, with reference to Basedow (2010b), p. 16. See also Collins (2011), p. 460; Hodges (2011), p. 440.

238 Art. 7 IPR Enforcement Directive 2004/48. See para 4.15 above. See also para 11.22 above and 11.37 below.

239 Cornish, Llewelyn and Aplin (2010), pp. 89–90 (regarding the English law equivalent of this procedure).

this option offered under the directive.[240] ACTA offers another example, where it creates the possibility for a national court to order an Internet service provider to disclose *to certain private parties* information to identify alleged infringers of intellectual property rights that use the provider's services.[241] Had the EU ratified this international agreement, this would arguably have entailed a further step in the above-mentioned process of horizontalisation. For even if under EU law as it stands the Member States are not necessarily *precluded* from providing for a possibility of disclosing this information in the context of legal proceedings between private parties under national law,[242] that law (more specifically the E-Commerce Directive[243]) currently only provides for the possibility of this kind of disclosure *to public authorities*.

The second type of hybrid enforcement relates to the involvement of **11.30** *(quasi-)public authorities in civil proceedings*. This involvement can, for instance, take the form of the Commission being involved in proceedings before national courts. Proposals to this effect were made at the time of the adoption of the two Procurement Remedies Directives. There the Commission unsuccessfully suggested it be granted the power to intervene directly by submitting *amicus curiae* observations in national legal proceedings or by suspending ongoing contract award procedures.[244] Years later a somewhat comparable arrangement did find its way into the Competition Regulation, however. It entitles both the Commission and national competition authorities to submit *amicus curiae* observations in legal proceedings before national courts, either upon request or on their own initiative. The Commission may do so whenever it considers that the coherent application of EU competition law so requires.[245] In addition, more recently the Competition Damages Directive took a few steps further in this direction. It allows the Commission and national competition authorities to intervene in pending private enforcement proceedings by submitting observations on the proportionality of a disclosure request concerning evidence included in the authority's file and by providing assistance on the determination of the quantum of damages.[246] It is noticeable that neither of these two

240 Commission, Staff working document accompanying the report on IPR Enforcement Directive 2004/48, SEC(2010) 1589, p. 9.

241 Art. 27(4) ACTA. ACTA is the international treaty that aimed to step up the fight against infringements of intellectual property rights worldwide, which the EU signed but eventually did not ratify. See para 4.12 above.

242 See CoJ case C-275/06, *Promusicae*, para 58–69. See para 4.18 above.

243 Art. 15(2) E-Commerce Directive 2000/31.

244 See para 3.33 above.

245 Art. 15 Competition Regulation 1/2003. See para 6.04 above.

246 Art. 6(11) and 17(3) Competition Damages Directive 2014/104 respectively. See para 6.33 and 6.30 above, respectively. Reference can further be made to the provisions on the effects of decisions by national competition authorities (and the courts reviewing these decisions) in private enforcement proceedings. See Art. 9 Competition Damages Directive 2014/104, discussed in para 6.41 above.

provisions was included in the Commission's proposal. The effects in practice of these rules will largely depend on the position taken by the authorities concerned, however, as in both cases they are *entitled* but not *obliged* to intervene.[247] More radical suggestions have been made in the legal literature, such as the possibility for certain public authorities to bring actions for damages *themselves* in the general interest to obtain compensation for the harm suffered by all consumers or by society as a whole.[248]

A somewhat distinct form of hybrid enforcement that also falls into this second category is litigation brought by qualified entities under the Consumer Injunctions Directive.[249] This directive empowers both certain public authorities (for example an ombudsman or a consumer protection authority) and certain private parties (for example a consumer association) to initiate legal proceedings before national courts with a view to bringing an infringement of EU consumer protection law to an end. Strictly speaking, the parties may not be exercising public powers when they do so.[250] Yet they can still be said to act in a quasi-public – or at least not in a fully "private" – capacity. After all, these qualified entities take legal action not in their own interest, but in the interest of all consumers collectively.[251] They do so moreover pursuant to some form of *ex ante* designation or approval by the Member State concerned. In some jurisdictions these associations are also (co-)financed by public means.[252] After having initially contemplated following a similar approach with respect to collective redress specifically for competition law infringements,[253] this approach relying on qualified entities has since become an important element of the Commission's broader Collective Redress Recommendation.[254]

11.31 The third and last category of hybrid enforcement is essentially the mirror image of the one discussed in the previous paragraph. Instead of introducing a

247 Concerning assistance on the quantification of the harm, the European Parliament unsuccessfully argued for such an obligation. See European Parliament, Report on the proposal for Competition Damages Directive 2014/104, A7–0089/2014, p. 29 (Art. 16).

248 E.g. Milutinovic (2010), p. 135; Tzakas (2011), p. 1150. The suggestions described here are to be distinguished from the situation where a public authority claims compensation for injury that it suffered *itself* as a consequence of an infringement of EU law. In this latter case the authority acts in a private capacity and will thus essentially be in the same position as any private party. Cf. e.g. CoJ case C-199/11, *Otis*. The actions referred to above would be similar to *parens patriae* actions known in several national jurisdictions, such as in France. See Komninos (2008), p. xv

249 Art. 3 Consumer Injunctions Directive 2009/22. See para 5.06 above.

250 Cf. CoJ 1 case C-167/00, *Henkel*, para 30.

251 See also para 11.27 above with respect to actions by third parties where "diffuse" interests are at stake.

252 See e.g. Rott (2001), pp. 418 (regarding Germany) and 430 (regarding England). In Italy provision is made for consumer associations to be (co-)financed by the proceeds of fines imposed by the national competition authority. See Komninos (2008), p. 237.

253 See para 6.18 and 6.24 above.

254 Points 4 and 6 Collective Redress Recommendation 2013/396. See para 5.38 above.

(quasi-)public element in civil litigation, it concerns the introduction of a *"private" element in public enforcement* proceedings. Most notably, in its 2006 proposal on criminal measures for infringements of intellectual property rights, which did not get adopted for reasons largely unrelated to this particular aspect of the proposal, the Commission suggested allowing rightholders to form "joint investigation teams" with the competent national public enforcement authorities.[255] The involvement of the latter prevents this from being a proper "privatisation" of typically public prerogatives. Yet granting private parties such a formal and active role in criminal investigations would still have been a remarkable development. Elsewhere in EU law the term "joint investigation teams" refers only to the cooperation between several *public* authorities.[256] This proposal would also have implied a significant step beyond the already existing cooperation arrangements between the private and public parties concerned as regards intellectual property-related customs matters, where the former can (only) *request* the latter to take action.[257]

Other suggestions made in the legal literature (typically relating to competition law infringements) seek to integrate damages claims in public enforcement proceedings.[258] This could involve private parties intervening in these proceedings, whereby they would be allowed to bring actions for damages in their own name. This connects with the possibility under the national laws of some Member States allowing private parties to benefit from the efforts made by the competent public enforcement authorities, for instance in criminal proceedings.[259] Alternatively, it has been suggested that (part of) the proceeds of the fines imposed by the public authorities could be used to compensate the private parties that suffered harm as a consequence of the established infringement or that the granting of leniency would be made subject to compensation having been paid. Once more the 2014 Competition Damages Directive takes a step in this direction, as it provides that competition authorities may consider any compensation payments made as part of consensual settlements as a mitigating factor when setting the fines for the infringements at issue.[260] This provision did not feature in this Commission's proposal, however. And again this step is a

255 Commission, Proposal for a directive on criminal measures for the enforcement of intellectual property rights, COM(2006) 168, p. 11 (Art. 7). See para 4.38 above.

256 See Framework Decision 2002/465/JHA on joint investigation teams, OJ 2002, L 162/1. See also Art. 88(2)(b) TFEU.

257 See in particular Customs Enforcement Regulation 608/2013, discussed in para 4.11 above.

258 E.g. Van Gerven (2003b), p. 77; Wolf (2003), p. 423; Canenbley and Steinvorth (2011), pp. 324–6; Heinemann (2011), p. 225. These suggestions sometimes draw on the possibilities that exist in some national jurisdictions (e.g. in Germany) to integrate damages claims into criminal proceedings.

259 See e.g. Hodges (2013), p. 80.

260 Art. 18(3) Competition Damages Directive 2014/104. See para 6.43 above.

rather modest one, in that this concerns merely a (seemingly already existing) *possibility* for and not an *obligation* on those authorities.

11.32 The above legislative provisions, proposals and academic suggestions have in common that they essentially all seek in one way or another to bridge the divide between public and private enforcement. They illustrate that hybrid solutions of various kinds are conceivable and have also to some extent actually been enacted in EU law to address specific enforcement-related concerns touched upon above. With an optimistic reading this indicates that (also) in legal-procedural terms the division between these two forms of enforcement need not be absolute. With some creativity, optimal use can be made of the relative advantages that the public and private parties involved may offer in terms of the enforcement of EU law and the rights that can be derived from that law. Through hybrid enforcement mechanisms of the type discussed above, it may thus be possible to optimise the aforementioned "enforcement mix".[261]

A less optimistic reading is also possible, however. It is clear that comparatively few of the hybrid enforcement arrangements outlined in the foregoing paragraphs are current law or even stand a reasonable chance of becoming law. And where this is otherwise, the provisions in question tend to be formulated in a rather non-committal manner. Particularly the measures of the first category referred to above (that is, granting quasi-public powers to private parties) seem to generate resistance, as the controversy related to ACTA illustrates.[262] Moreover, some of those suggestions can be understood not so much as creative solutions, but rather as testimony to the inherent *limitations* of a private enforcement model. For instance, if in respect of actions for damages the intervention by a public enforcement authority is structurally required for such actions to be dealt with successfully by national courts, this would seem to highlight the difficulties associated with these actions as much as it highlights their potential for private enforcement purposes.[263] Involving public enforcement authorities in private enforcement proceedings or, conversely, involving private parties in public enforcement proceedings may not be a feasible option anyway in many fields other than competition law, for the simple reason that no comparable public enforcement mechanisms exist. It further appears that an approach relying on qualified entities has shortcomings of its own, notably in terms of incentives and capacity to act, funding, possible principal/agent

261 See para 11.23 above.

262 See para 4.12 above. See also subsections 11.B.5 and 11.B.6 below for an assessment of these types of measures from a fundamental rights perspective.

263 On these difficulties, see in particular para 7.03 above.

problems and the distribution of any possible damages awards.[264] The more such shortcomings are addressed through increased public involvement with these entities (in terms of regulation, public funding, oversight, and so on), the more the question can arise what the added value is as compared with ("traditional") public enforcement.

In addition, from the perspective of the public enforcement authorities concerned, one of the key features of a private enforcement model is that it can *supplement* public enforcement and as such lighten the burden on – and to some extent perhaps even replace – the competent public enforcement authorities in a given field. Blurring the two forms of enforcement may well be seen as being at odds with that philosophy. To give a concrete example, there may well be better ways to contribute to the effective enforcement of the law than using the public enforcement authorities' scarce resources to quantify the harm suffered by a private party or to otherwise be involved in private enforcement litigation.[265] The Commission has stated in relation to its aforementioned possibility of making *amicus curiae* interventions in proceedings before national courts that it has '*no intention to serve the private interests of the parties involved in the case pending*'.[266] Even if it had the necessary resources to do so (which it considers it has not[267]), the Commission does not wish to '*transform into an investigator for the benefit of national litigation at the request of national courts*'.[268] It has therefore thus far used this possibility rather sparingly, to the disappointment of certain stakeholders.[269] This hesitance probably lies behind the fact that it was not the Commission that proposed the above-mentioned provisions on possible interventions by competition authorities in private enforcement proceedings, just as it is reflected in the care that has been taken to emphasise in those provisions that the authorities concerned cannot be obliged to provide such assistance. Indeed, in this connection even the mere possibility of having to disclose evidence in their files was seen as too much of a burden on these authorities. This can therefore only be required under the Competition Damages Directive where no party or other third party is reasonably able to provide that evidence.[270]

---

264 See para 5.12 above. See e.g. also Hodges (2006), p. 1388 and 1391; Leskinen (2011), p. 90; European Parliament, Study on collective redress in antitrust, June 2012, p. 40; Commission, Second report on Consumer Injunctions Directive 2009/22, COM(2012) 635, p. 6. Cf. CoJ case C-413/12, *ACICL*, para 37.

265 Cf. Study, CEPS, Erasmus University Rotterdam and LUISS (2007), pp. 200–201.

266 Commission, Cooperation notice, OJ 2004, C 101/54, para 19.

267 See Hodges (2013), p. 73.

268 Statement by Commission officials, reported in Komninos (2003), p. xxx.

269 Commission, Report on Competition Regulation 1/2003, COM(2009) 206, pp. 8–9.

270 Art. 6(10) Competition Damages Directive 2014/104. See para 6.35 above.

It therefore appears that, while there is evidently nothing against seeking to optimise the interaction between public and private enforcement also in legal-procedural terms and some creativity and innovation may well be called for in this respect, there are limits in principle and in practicce as to what can be sensibly achieved by blurring the distinction between the two.

5. Fundamental rights (1): Horizontal effects and "civil" rights

11.33 The horizontalisation of the enforcement of EU law also raises issues with a fundamental rights dimension. As a first and general issue there is the question whether the rights set out in the Charter can have horizontal *direct* effect, meaning that they can be invoked directly in legal relationships between private parties. On this issue the case law is still evolving.[271] Some caution is therefore required. That said, the Charter is expressly addressed only to the institutions and other bodies of the EU as well as to the Member States when they are implementing EU law.[272] It moreover stipulated that it does not extend the field of application of EU law and does not establish new powers or tasks for the EU.[273] Many commentators take the view that to consider that the provisions of the Charter are directly effective in horizontal relationships would in effect bypass these important delimitations and that therefore such effect should be considered excluded.[274]

In any case the foregoing does not mean that the Charter is not of relevance in the horizontal legal relationships under consideration here. For one thing, where there is some form of involvement by public or quasi-public bodies, this can still be reason to apply the Charter directly to the case at hand. There may thus be some margin of interpretation when determining precisely what constitutes a horizontal relationship.[275] For another thing, and more importantly for the present purposes, it is clear that the fundamental rights set out in the Charter can have *indirect* effects in such relationships.[276] In this regard the

271 See e.g. CoJ case C-176/12, *Association de médiation sociale*, para 40–48.

272 Art. 51(1) Charter. On the meaning of this term "implementing EU law", see para 2.11 above.

273 Art. 51(2) Charter.

274 See e.g. Opinion AG Trstenjak case C-282/10, *Dominguez*, para 80–83, with further references. See also Craig (2010), pp. 206–7; Leczykiewicz (2010b), p. 332; Ladenburger (2012), p. 35. Inclined to the same view, but somewhat more hesitant, are Rosas and Armanti (2010), pp. 160–62. As regards the formal addressees of provisions of EU law, see, however, also CoJ case 43/75, *Defrenne*, para 31, discussed in para 11.17 above. Furthermore, an open question remains to what extent the fundamental rights, in their capacity as general principles of EU law (see para 2.10 above), could in some cases be applied in horizontal situations. On the horizontal direct effect of those principles, see para 11.16 above. On these issues, see also Nauta (2012), p. 19; Leczykiewicz (2013), p. 479.

275 For a range of such conceivable situations, see Rosas and Armanti (2010), pp. 160–62; Ladenburger (2012), pp. 35–7. See also Craig (2010), pp. 207–8.

276 Cf. Craig (2010), pp. 209–10; Ladenburger (2012), p. 16.

Court of Justice has held that '*the Member States must not only interpret their national law in a manner consistent with [EU] law, but also make sure they do not rely on an interpretation of an instrument of secondary legislation which would be in conflict with the fundamental rights protected by the [EU] legal order or with the other general principles of [EU] law*'.[277] It has further ruled that '*under a general principle of interpretation, [an EU] measure must be interpreted, as far as possible, in such a way as not to affect its validity and in conformity with primary law as a whole and, in particular, with the provisions of the Charter*'.[278] Thus, as a particular form of the general EU law principle of consistent interpretation,[279] provisions of both secondary EU law and national law implementing that law may, where relevant, need to be interpreted in a Charter-consistent manner. The Court of Justice has already in many cases interpreted provisions of EU law in light of the principle of effective judicial protection set out in Article 47 Charter.[280] Considering the importance of this latter principle in the present context, there may well be considerable scope to interpret also the EU legislation at issue here in light of especially (but certainly not exclusively) this Charter provision.[281] It would appear, however, that also in this case the principle of consistent interpretation is limited, in that it cannot lead to an interpretation *contra legem*.[282]

The Charter can also be of importance in litigation between two private parties involving matters of EU law in other, more specific manners. Seen from the perspective of the state, the primary objective of the relevant (typically civil law) proceedings is to settle the dispute at hand in a fair manner, whereby the state and particularly the national courts normally remain neutral and passive.[283] Accordingly, in terms of fundamental rights, the focus is on ensuring that everyone can have a fair and public hearing within a reasonable time by an independent and impartial court, as is guaranteed under Article 47 Charter.[284] This involves, among other things, respect for the principle of *equality of arms*, **11.34**

277 CoJ joined cases C-411/10 and C-493/10, *N.S.*, para 77–8. See e.g. also CoJ case C-275/06, *Promusicae*, para 68; CoJ case C-277/11, *M.M.*, para 93; CoJ joined cases C-356/11 and C-357/11, *Maahanmuuttovirasto*, para 78.

278 CoJ case C-579/12 RX-II, *Strack*, para 40. See e.g. also CoJ case C-400/10 PPU, *McB.*, para 52 and 60; CoJ case C-426/11, *Alemo-Herron*, para 30.

279 See para 1.04 above.

280 E.g. CoJ case C-459/99, *MRAX*, para 101–2; CoJ case C-50/00 P, *UPA*, para 42; CoJ case C-506/04, *Wilson*, para 45; CoJ case C-268/06, *Impact*, para 54; CoJ case C-240/09, *Lesoochranárske zoskupenie*, para 51; CoJ case C-300/11, *ZZ, para 50–51.*

281 See e.g. para 9.08 above on the interpretation of some of the provisions on legal standing laid down in this legislation.

282 See e.g. CoJ case C-583/11 P, *Inuit*, para 97.

283 Cf. e.g. Cadiet (2005), pp. 57–58. On the passive role of courts in civil proceedings and the own-motion application of EU law, see also subsection 9.4.2 above.

284 On Art. 47 Charter generally, see para 2.11 above. As was noted there, in contrast to Art. 6(1) ECHR, Art. 47 Charter applies to proceedings that are civil as well as administrative in nature.

which requires a fair balance between the parties, and the right to *adversarial proceedings*, which requires that all parties have knowledge of and can comment on all evidence adduced and observations filed.[285] This in turn brings us back to a point made earlier, namely that the EU legislation at issue tends to focus rather one-sidedly on improving the position of the applicant, while little attention appears generally to be paid to that of the defendant.[286]

This can be illustrated with reference to the IPR Enforcement Directive's regime on an applicant's right of information, which can involve the disclosure of certain information held by third parties.[287] Judging by its wording, it appears that only applicants (and not also defendants) are able to rely on the provision in question. If that reading is correct, it would contrast markedly with the Competition Damages Directive's disclosure regime, which is expressly also available to defendants.[288] The Commission noted in this latter context that in private enforcement proceedings the defendant may also need to have access to evidence in so far as the burden of proof falls on him.[289] The Competition Damages Directive explains the choice of making the measures on the disclosure of evidence also available to defendants in terms of equality of arms.[290] Furthermore, the possibility under the IPR Enforcement Directive to order measures to *preserve* evidence may lead to questions not only from the perspective of equality of arms, but also from that of the right to adversarial proceedings.[291] For these measures, which also appear to be available to the applicant only, can also be ordered without the defendant having been heard. Again, this stands in clear contrast with the more recent Competition Damages Directive, which expressly requires the party concerned to be heard before that party can be ordered to disclose evidence.[292] The fact that these measures can also affect third parties can lead to additional fundamental rights-related questions, for instance as regards the protection of privacy and personal data, the freedom of expression and information as well as the freedom to conduct a business.[293]

11.35 Does this mean that the aforementioned fundamental rights are or will be infringed in the cases referred to above, particularly where the aforementioned

---

285 See para 2.14 and 2.15 above. Cf. Hodges (2006), pp. 1400–1401.

286 See para 11.22 above.

287 Art. 8 IPR Enforcement Directive 2004/48. See para 4.16. See also para 11.22 above.

288 Art. 5 Competition Damages Directive 2014/104. See para 6.32 above.

289 Cf. Commission, Proposal for Competition Damages Directive 2014/104, COM(2013) 404, p. 13.

290 Recital 15 Competition Damages Directive 2014/104.

291 Art. 7 IPR Enforcement Directive 2004/48. See para 4.15 above.

292 Art. 5(7) Competition Damages Directive 2014/104. See para 6.35 above.

293 Art. 7, 8, 11, and 16 Charter, respectively. In addition to the above-mentioned fundamental rights, in specific cases other fundamental rights can also be of relevance, such as those relating to the protection of intellectual property (Art. 17(2) Charter) and consumer protection (Art. 38 Charter). See in particular para 4.18 and 4.24 above.

provisions of the IPR Enforcement Directive are concerned? It is submitted that this is, generally speaking, probably not the case. The fundamental rights of the type at issue here are not unfettered prerogatives.[294] The Court of Justice has repeatedly held that they may need to be balanced against the other fundamental rights that can be at issue in a particular case.[295] The Charter expressly allows the restriction of the exercise of these rights in the general interest and to protect the rights of other parties.[296] In this connection, it must be acknowledged that the EU legislation under consideration, including the IPR Enforcement Directive, provides for several limitations and safeguards. This latter directive stipulates, for example, that any measure granted must be fair, equitable and proportionate.[297] It also contains more specific requirements concerning the possibility of ordering the disclosure of evidence and other relevant information,[298] as well as the specific substantive and procedural safeguards attached to the above-mentioned possibility of granting preservation measures without hearing the opposing party.[299] Added to the fact that these provisions of EU law are to be interpreted in a Charter-consistent manner where necessary, that further safeguards may apply as a matter of national law and that the fairness of the proceedings as a whole is what matters in this regard, there appears to be generally little reason to believe that the aforementioned EU legislative measures as such necessarily involve the infringement of the fundamental rights referred to above. As has been discussed earlier, although some scope for debate remains, there appear to be grounds for coming to a similar conclusion with respect to the absolute bar to the disclosure (and use) of certain pieces of evidence that the Competition Damages Directive establishes.[300]

Yet it is evident that in this respect a certain *tension* can nonetheless exist. Ensuring the fundamental right to a fair trial generally and to equality of arms and adversarial proceedings specifically may well need to be a point of special attention in relation to the type of private enforcement-facilitating measures referred to above. That applies to the EU legislature at the stage of the adoption of such measures, as well as to the national legislatures when transposing them into national law and the national courts when they are being called upon to apply and interpret these measures in individual cases.[301] Particularly if the remedial and procedural rights of private party applicants in horizontal legal

294 E.g. CoJ case C-418/11, *Texdata*, para 84. See para 10.10 above.
295 E.g. CoJ case C-275/06, *Promusicae*, para 68. See para 4.18 above. See e.g. also CoJ case C-461/10, *Bonnier*, para 56–60; CoJ case C-283/11, *Sky Österreich*, para 59–60.
296 Art. 52(1) Charter. See also para 10.10 above.
297 Art. 3(1) and (2) IPR Enforcement Directive 2004/48. See para 4.06 above.
298 Art. 7 and 8 IPR Enforcement Directive 2004/48. See in particular para 8.22 above.
299 Art. 7(1) IPR Enforcement Directive 2004/48. See para 4.15 above.
300 Art. 6(6) and 7(1) Competition Damages Directive 2014/104. See para 6.34 above.
301 Cf. e.g. CoJ case 125/79, *Denilauler*, para 13 and 15; CoJ case C-450/06, *Varec*, para 44–55.

contexts were to be further reinforced, there might well be a point where the above assessment leads to a different conclusion. In other words, the balance to be struck can be a delicate one and a degree of caution on this point is therefore called for.

6. Fundamental rights (2): "Criminal" rights

11.36 Fundamental rights can also come into play in another manner in the present context. Put crudely, fundamental rights are rights of defence enjoyed by private parties in respect of public authorities.[302] These rights are of particular relevance in the context of *criminal* proceedings. In those cases the private parties concerned may benefit, for instance, from the presumption of innocence, the privilege against self-incrimination (*nemo tenetur*), the principle of legality and the principle that one cannot be punished twice for the same offence (*ne bis in idem*).[303] These rights function, as it were, as a counterbalance to the powers vested in the competent public enforcement authorities to detect, punish and deter infringements in the general interest.[304] Whether or not proceedings are criminal in nature is for the present purposes to be determined on the *substance*. Decisive are the three so-called *Engel* criteria, namely: (a) the classification of the measure under national law; (b) the nature of the offence; and (c) the nature and severity of the possible penalty.[305]

The foregoing implies that the above-mentioned fundamental rights can *inter alia* also be invoked in proceedings for the imposition of fines under competition law where those proceedings are nominally a matter of *administrative* law, as is typically the case in the EU.[306] In contrast, these rights do not apply in legal relationships between private parties in proceedings that are truly *civil* in

302 Opinion AG Trstenjak case C-101/08, *Audiolux*, para 77.

303 Art. 48–50 Charter. More specifically, under the Charter the "triggers" for the application of the above rights are the existence of a "charge" (Art. 48), "criminal offences and penalties" (Art. 49) and "criminal proceedings" (Art. 50). Under Art. 6(2) and (3) ECHR the existence of a "criminal charge" is the (corresponding) central element. Other examples are full jurisdiction of the competent courts, the proportionality of sanctions and retro-application of the more lenient penalty. See e.g. CoJ case C-386/10 P, *Chalkor*, para 53–67; CoJ case C-17/10, *Toshiba*, para 64. See further Zippro (2009b), pp. 450–59.

304 See e.g. CoJ joined cases 100/80 to 103/80, *Musique Diffusion Française*, para 105–6; GC case T-13/03, *Nintendo*, para 73; CoJ case C-429/07, *Inspecteur van de Belastingdienst v X*, para 36–7 (all concerning the Commission's powers in relation to infringements of EU competition law).

305 See e.g. ECtHR case 5100/71, *Engel v Netherlands*, para 82; ECtHR case 73053/01, *Jussila v Finland*, para 30–31. These criteria have since been applied by the EU courts. See e.g. CoJ case C-489/10, *Bonda*, para 37; CoJ case C-617/10, *Åklagaren*, para 35.

306 E.g. CoJ case C-301/04 P, *SGL Carbon*, para 42; CoJ case C-352/09 P, *ThyssenKrupp*, para 80; CoJ case C-17/10, *Toshiba*, para 94. On the public enforcement of EU competition law, see subsection 6.4.2 above.

nature, which is also determined on the substance.[307] That means that these rights may generally be of no importance in the context of horizontalised enforcement, that is, in disputes between two private parties. But this distinction between typical criminal (that is, vertical) and typical civil (that is, horizontal) cases sometimes becomes blurred as a consequence of the legislative measures discussed above. That means in turn that it is not excluded that the above-mentioned "criminal" fundamental rights might also come into play in the present context of horizontalised enforcement. This can be illustrated through the following three examples.

First, consider again the *ex parte search order procedure* set out in the IPR Enforcement Directive.[308] This (optional) provision creates the possibility for a private party whose intellectual property rights have allegedly been infringed to enter certain premises for the description or physical seizure of infringing goods, materials used for their production or documents relating thereto. With respect to the similar procedure provided for in English law (on which this directive's regime has been inspired) the national courts initially took the view that the privilege against self-incrimination could be invoked. This view was only reversed after it had been ensured that any statement obtained from the defendant in this manner could not be used in criminal proceedings.[309] It is furthermore true that as part of this procedure a national court must first decide whether or not to grant this order. This thus ensures a degree of objective control and constitutes an important safeguard. Nonetheless, it has been pointed out in the legal literature that the fact remains that the *execution* of such an order entails a private party that can arguably least be expected to preserve a measure of objectivity and sense of proportion acting in a manner that may amount to a direct infraction of personal liberties of the private party that is subject to the search.[310] **11.37**

This is by no means merely an academic discussion. In 1989 the Court of Human Rights highlighted certain concerns with respect to the said procedure, as provided for under English law.[311] In the case at hand no breach of the right to a private and family life was found,[312] it being noted that the order in question was a necessary step in the effective pursuit by private parties of their

307 E.g. ECtHR case 6232/73, *Köning v Germany*, para 88–90; ECtHR case 21522/93, *Georgiadis v Greece*, para 34. On the non-applicability, as a general rule, of the privilege against self-incrimination in civil proceedings concerning EU competition law, see also CoJ case C-60/92, *Otto v Postbank*, para 11–17.

308 Art. 7 IPR Enforcement Directive 2004/28. See para 4.15 above. See also para 11.22 above.

309 Cornish, Llewelyn and Aplin (2010), pp. 92–93.

310 Ibid., pp. 89–90 (regarding the English law equivalent of this procedure).

311 On the ECtHR, see also para 2.10 above.

312 Art. 8 ECHR. Cf. Art. 7 Charter.

intellectual property rights and that the scope of that order was limited so as to keep its impact within reasonable bounds.[313] Yet the Court of Human Rights also held that such an order is '*capable of producing damaging and irreversible damage*' for the private party defendant and that it is '*essential that this measure should be accompanied by adequate and effective safeguards against arbitrary interference and abuse*'.[314] Along similar lines, many Member States associate this *ex parte* search order more with criminal proceedings than with civil ones and therefore chose not to transpose it into national law.[315] Comparable concerns came to light in the more recent Patent Court Agreement, which contains a provision that gives effect to the above-mentioned provision of the IPR Enforcement Directive.[316] This agreement contains additional safeguards, however, in that it provides that the order to inspect certain premises can only be executed by a person appointed by the court and it expressly prohibits the applicant being present during the search.[317]

All this shows that, while a procedure of this kind is not *per se* problematic from a fundamental rights perspective, it can certainly lead to some concerns in this respect. Certain particular safeguards may therefore be required to address these concerns.

11.38 Second, questions of this kind can also emerge in connection with the measures on the *disclosure of evidence* that were discussed above.[318] In a competition law context, the Commission has held that the privilege against self-incrimination cannot be invoked to prevent the disclosure of unfavourable evidence in private enforcement proceedings.[319] Advocate General Jääskinen similarly took the view in his opinion in *Donau Chemie* that this privilege '*does not apply in private law contexts*'.[320] While these statements are, generally speaking, undoubtedly correct, they may nonetheless require a degree of nuance in light of the

313 ECtHR case 10461/83, *Chappell v UK*, para 59–60. These limitations related to the duration of order, the times at which and the number of persons by whom the applicant's search could be effected as well as the purposes for which any materials seised could be used. Reference is further made to the undertakings given by the applicants or their solicitors and the remedies available to the defendant. See also para 61 of this judgment on the role of the solicitor under English law, as an officer to the court.

314 Ibid., para 57.

315 Commission, Staff working document accompanying the report on IPR Enforcement Directive 2004/48, SEC(2010) 1589, p. 9.

316 On this agreement and its relationship to IPR Enforcement Directive 2004/48, see para 4.02 above.

317 Cf. e.g. Art. 60(3) and (4) Patent Court Agreement. The applicant can only be represented by an independent legal practitioner.

318 See subsection 8.B.2 above.

319 Commission, Staff working paper accompanying the white paper on damages actions for breach of the EC antitrust rules, SEC(2008) 404, p. 37.

320 Opinion AG Jääskinen case C-536/11, *Donau Chemie*, para 56.

foregoing.[321] This is again illustrated by the more cautious line in this respect that was taken by the drafters of the Patent Court Agreement. This agreement provides expressly that a court order to disclose evidence may not result in an obligation of self-incrimination.[322] A similar concern is echoed in the IPR Enforcement Directive's provision on the right of information, pursuant to which infringers and certain third parties can be required to disclose certain information. There it is said that this right is without prejudice to other statutory provisions that '*afford an opportunity for refusing to provide information which would force the person [concerned] to admit to his/her own participation or that of his/her close relatives in an infringement*'.[323]

A third and final example concerns the possibility of awarding *punitive damages*, for which EU law does not provide at present but which has repeatedly been debated in the present context.[324] By definition, punitive damages seek to penalise. Pursuant to the aforementioned *Engel* criteria, the existence of a punitive element is an important aspect in determining whether – in substance – the proceedings are criminal in nature and hence whether the aforementioned fundamental rights can be relied upon.[325] Accordingly, it is at least conceivable that in civil proceedings involving punitive damages the defendant must be deemed to be entitled to invoke the privilege against self-incrimination or the principle of *ne bis in idem*.[326] Opinions differ especially on the possible application of this latter principle in such cases.[327] Also, this is by no means merely an academic discussion. Whether or not this principle of *ne bis in idem* applies can be of considerable practical importance, given the possible concurrent imposition of fines and award of punitive damages for the same anti-competitive behaviour.[328] As was the case with *ex parte* search orders mentioned earlier, this question has already been the topic of debates and litigation, **11.39**

321 Note that, unlike the AG, the CoJ left this issue untouched in its ruling in *Donau Chemie*. See CoJ case C-536/11, *Donau Chemie*, discussed in para 6.22 above.

322 Art. 59(1) Patent Court Agreement. On this agreement, see para 4.02 above.

323 Art. 8(3)(d) IPR Enforcement Directive 2004/48. See para 4.16 above.

324 See in particular subsection 7.A.5 above. See also para 11.10 above.

325 See para 11.36 above.

326 Cf. Zippro (2009b), p. 450. Specifically in relation to penalties and the privilege against self-incrimination, see CoJ case C-60/92, *Otto v Postbank*, para 16.

327 Cf. e.g. Milutinovic (2010), p. 131 (who argues that punitive damages do not breach the said principle); Wils (2009), p. 22 (who argues essentially the contrary).

328 Note that, even where it can be assumed that this principle applies, its application may not always be straightforward. In particular, only in retrospect can it be said with certainty that both types of punishment were imposed in a concrete case. At the time of a punitive damages award, public enforcement proceedings may still be pending or not even have been initiated, or vice versa. Cf. Zippro (2009b), pp. 457–8.

especially in England.[329] For now it largely remains an open question as to how the Court of Justice would address it.[330]

11.40 In light of the foregoing there seems no reason to believe that the EU legislative measures discussed here are such that the fundamental rights referred to above have been or will be infringed. With the possible exception of punitive damages, for which EU law at present does not provide, however, these measures are unlikely to insert a "criminal" element in horizontalised enforcement proceedings to such an extent that, as a counterbalance, fundamental rights such as the presumption of innocence, the privilege against self-incrimination and the *ne bis in idem* principle ought to be available to a defendant. It would seem that this nonetheless remains an important point of attention when discussing EU legislation facilitating the private enforcement of EU law. Generally speaking, the more a "dual vigilance" logic translates into particular powers or prerogatives being granted to a private party applicant, the less "civil" in substance the proceedings are and the more likely it becomes that these "criminal" fundamental rights can be relied upon. Put differently, one cannot equip a private party with the powers to act as a "private policeman" or "private attorney general" without equipping the party that may be subject to the exercise of these powers with the fundamental rights safeguards that would have been available to the latter had he been prosecuted by a "real" policeman or attorney general.

329 For a discussion, see e.g. Frese (2011), pp. 425–6.

330 It may be possible to derive some indications from GC case T-59/02, *Archer Daniels Midlands*, para 349–51 (where it was held that there is no need to take account of punitive damages paid in a non-Member State jurisdiction when setting fines in competition cases) and CoJ case C-301/04 P, *SGL Carbon*, para 32–4 (where it was found that the *ne bis in idem* principle is not applicable in relation to competition fines imposed by a non-Member State).

12

SUMMARY AND CONCLUSIONS

This final chapter summarises the main findings that emerge on the basis of the foregoing and brings together the most important general lines running through the earlier chapters. It concentrates on the questions of what EU legislation facilitating the private enforcement of EU law before national courts entails, particularly in terms of remedies and procedural provisions, and how legislation of this kind should be understood more generally, notably as regards its typical characteristics and underlying objectives as well as the advantages and drawbacks of and the limits to the choices made by the EU legislature in this connection. To that end this chapter consists of three parts. In the first section a number of general remarks are made with respect to the EU's legislative activities relating to private enforcement. The second section then focuses more specifically on the remedies and procedural provisions for private enforcement purposes set out in the EU legislation at issue. The last section outlines the main findings with respect to the nature, limits and effects of private enforcement generally and EU legislative action in this regard in particular.

A. PRIVATE ENFORCEMENT BETWEEN INTERFERENCE AND AUTONOMY

A central theme in this section is the tension that can exist between EU "interference" and the Member States' "autonomy" in relation to the (possible) adoption of EU legislation facilitating the private enforcement of EU law. This is of course a common theme in almost all instances where secondary EU law is being established. However, it is arguably of particular importance in the present context, especially given that the remedial and procedural issues under consideration have traditionally largely been left to be regulated by the Member States. In the first subsection below the relative value of the "autonomy" referred to above as well as the possibility for the EU to act on these matters are highlighted. The second subsection then explains that there are nonetheless limits to the EU's scope to act on private enforcement-related matters and that the Member States tend to retain considerable "residual" autonomy in this regard. The further consequences of this tension are also discussed.

1. The scope for enacting EU legislation on private enforcement

12.01 In the foregoing chapters it has been seen how over the past decades the EU legislature has enacted a range of legislative measures that facilitate the private enforcement of EU law before national courts. These measures can touch upon issues of civil as well as administrative law, substance as well as procedure, and remedies as well as procedures. This book has concentrated on seven acts of secondary EU law that provide – to varying degrees and in different ways – for measures of this kind, namely the two Procurement Remedies Directives, dating from 1989 and 1992 and revised in 2007;[1] the 2004 IPR Enforcement Directive;[2] the Consumer Injunctions Directive, which was adopted in 1998 and codified in 2009;[3] the 1993 Unfair Terms Directive;[4] the Product Liability Directive, which dates from 1985;[5] and the Competition Damages Directive which was adopted in 2014.[6] Several other private enforcement-related provisions and developments have also been assessed, most notably the provision of primary EU law that anticompetitive agreements are automatically void[7] and the Commission's 2013 Collective Redress Recommendation.[8]

12.02 It is evident that EU legislative measures of this kind affect national rules on remedies and procedures applicable in such private enforcement proceedings. As the Court of Justice has consistently held ever since its 1976 judgment in *Rewe*, pursuant to the principle of national procedural autonomy, it is for the

1 Procurement Remedies Directives 89/665 and 92/13, discussed in Chapter 3 above.
2 IPR Enforcement Directive 2004/48, discussed in Chapter 4 above.
3 Consumer Injunctions Directive 2009/22, discussed in section 5.A above.
4 Unfair Terms Directive 93/13, discussed in section 5.C above.
5 Product Liability Directive 85/374, discussed in section 5.D above.
6 Competition Damages Directive 2014/104, discussed in Chapter 6 above.
7 Art. 101(2) TFEU, discussed in subsection 6.A.3 above.
8 Collective Redress Recommendation 2013/396, discussed in subsection 5.E.2 above.

Member States to set these rules.[9] The Member States have considerable discretion in this regard, although they remain bound to respect EU law, in particular the principles of equivalence and effectiveness.[10] The very existence of the above-mentioned EU legislation already indicates, however, that this principle should not be misunderstood as constituting an *absolute bar* on the EU to act on these matters. As the Court already held in *Rewe*, this principle only applies in the absence of EU rules. It later clarified that rules on remedies and procedures applicable in private enforcement proceedings are not '*within some sort of domain reserved for the Member States*'.[11] Quite to the contrary, the Court has held that the EU is '*certainly competent to harmonise national rules on those matters*' in so far as the EU Treaties provide for a sufficient legal basis.[12] It follows that in fact the key question is not one of autonomy of the *Member States*. This is approaching the matter from the wrong angle. As is generally the case, where possible acts of secondary EU law are concerned, the key issue is rather whether or not the *EU* is competent to act. Where the EU legislature has not (yet) acted, it is for the Member States to take all necessary measures to enable the private parties concerned to effectively exercise their rights based on EU law.[13]

In the present context the significance of the principle of national procedural autonomy is therefore threefold. First, it highlights the importance of the question of whether and if so to what extent the EU is *competent to act* on private enforcement-related matters. Second, where EU legislation on those matters of the type at issue here has also been adopted, this principle can continue to be of relevance with respect to issues falling *outside the scope* of that legislation. In those cases there is, after all, still an absence of EU rules. Third, it can also serve a function that is not strictly legal. This principle can in particular function as a means to *signal political unease or opposition* (as opposed to a proper legal concern) in relation to an intended private enforcement-related EU legislative initiative. As such, it serves as a reminder that it is one thing for the EU to be competent to act on certain private enforcement-related matters, but that it can be quite another thing to determine whether it is also seen as appropriate or desirable for the EU to actually exercise those competences. As is further discussed below, EU legislative involvement with the matters at issue here can indeed be a sensitive affair.

9 CoJ case 33/76, *Rewe*, para 5. See subsection 2.A.1 above.

10 See subsections 2.A.2 and 2.A.3 above, respectively.

11 CoJ Opinion 1/94, *WTO*, para 104.

12 Ibid.

13 Cf. Art. 4(3) and 19(1) TEU.

12.03 Legally speaking, the key question is therefore, first and foremost, that of the EU's competence to adopt secondary law facilitating the private enforcement of EU law. In this respect it is to be noted that Article 114 TFEU on harmonisation for the establishment and the functioning of the EU's internal market constitutes the legal basis for virtually all above-mentioned EU legal acts.[14] There has been comparatively little debate on this point at the time of adoption of these acts. Neither have there to date been any legal challenges concerning the use of this legal basis. Although this might certainly be taken as an indication to that effect, in and of itself this does not allow for the conclusion that the EU is competent to enact legislation of this type on the basis of this article. An express ruling by the Court of Justice would be required for drawing any definitive conclusions. Moreover, in relation to possible future EU legislative measures of this type, it will always need to be assessed whether the legal basis that this article offers suffices in light of the aim and the content of those particular measures. In specific cases there may furthermore be other, more specific legal bases available. Article 103 TFEU is one example thereof in so far as EU legislative measures that give effect to substantive EU competition law are concerned. This article would indeed generally seem the most logical legal basis for secondary EU law on the private enforcement of EU competition law, even if (perhaps somewhat less self-evidently) the Competition Damages Directive had been adopted on a dual legal basis, namely Article 103 as well as Article 114 TFEU.[15] The above qualifications notwithstanding, it appears therefore that Article 114 TFEU is not only a commonly used legal basis for EU legislation facilitating the private enforcement of EU law before national courts, but also that – to the extent that this can be said in the abstract – there also seems little reason to doubt that it can legitimately be used for those purposes.

2. The limits to the EU's scope to act and its consequences

12.04 The foregoing evidently does not mean that there are no limits to the EU's scope to act in relation to private enforcement. In particular, Article 114 TFEU does not empower the EU to regulate the internal market generally. The EU can act on this basis only if and to the extent that that is *demonstrably required* for internal market purposes in accordance with the conditions set out in this article. Generally speaking, these conditions can be expected to be met where the EU legislative measures in question are necessary to ensure the effective enforcement of certain internal market-related rules of substantive EU law. Indeed, that is precisely what the EU legislation under consideration here essentially seeks to achieve. Each of those directives is primarily concerned with

14 See subsection 10.A.1 above.

15 See subsection 6.C.1 above.

harmonising the provisions of national law so as to facilitate the enforcement of the rights that private parties derive from the rules of substantive EU law in question – namely on public procurement, intellectual property, consumer protection and competition law, which are all closely connected to the EU's internal market – with a view to improving overall levels of compliance and enforcement of those rules.[16]

Yet these limits inherent in Article 114 TFEU reduce the possibility of – and may in practice even preclude – adopting EU legislation that is of broader application, covering the enforcement of *all* substantive rules of EU law that confer rights on private parties or even all legal proceedings before national courts generally. That applies all the more so when account is taken of the additional constraints on the EU's legislative activities resulting from the principles of subsidiarity and proportionality.[17] It would seem that as the law stands, neither does any Treaty provision other than Article 114 TFEU constitute a sufficient legal basis for the adoption of EU legislation of the type referred to above that can apply across the board. Article 81 TFEU on judicial cooperation in civil matters undeniably has some potential to serve as such, as it empowers the EU to take measures to ensure "effective access to justice" and to eliminate "obstacles to the proper functioning of civil proceedings".[18] Yet this provision has certain important limits of its own. Most notably, not only does it also require a link with the internal market (although arguably a looser one than under Article 114 TFEU), any EU action on this basis is also to remain limited to '*civil matters having cross-border implications*'.

For the foreseeable future the private enforcement-related issues under consideration here are therefore likely to continue to be regulated on a sector-specific basis. On the one hand, this should not prevent the Commission and the EU legislature from improving the internal coherence and consistency of the legislation that they propose and adopt to this effect respectively. It has been shown that more can and indeed should be expected in this regard.[19] On the other hand, this implies that a degree of fragmentation of the legal systems of the Member States may prove unavoidable.[20] For where the EU legislative interference relates only to certain situations but not to others (for example addressing infringements of the EU rules on public procurement but not those of "purely" national rules in this domain or infringements of substantive rules in other fields), the effects in the domestic legal sphere are necessarily uneven. At

16 See subsections 10.A.1 and 11.A.2 above.

17 Art. 5(3) and (4) TEU. See subsection 10.A.2 above.

18 See subsection 10.D.3 above.

19 See subsection 10.D.1 above.

20 See subsections 10.D.2 and 10.D.3 above.

the same time that does not mean that this possible "fragmenting" effect should not be given serious consideration when adopting EU legislation facilitating the private enforcement of EU law before national courts. That is the case not only because many of the affected national rules tend to fulfil a useful and legitimate function, but also because those rules tend to apply across the board, regardless of the sector or the origin of the rights concerned. Careful consideration and a degree of constraint on the part of the EU legislature therefore seem to be in place in this regard.

12.05 The EU legislature may thus have considerable scope to adopt legislation of the type under consideration and it may already have exercised these competences on several occasions, but this should not distract from the fact that many remedial and national rules applicable in private enforcement proceedings are still determined by "purely" national law (that is, national law other than that transposing a directive). This is a point that risks being overlooked in a study such as this one, which concentrates on EU legislative action in this domain. In other words, the above-mentioned legislation may imply increased EU involvement with private enforcement proceedings before national courts, a point that is further underlined by the fact that comparable acts apply in certain other fields of EU law.[21] However, for the time being as well as for the foreseeable future, this development remains not only gradual and far from linear,[22] but in many respects also incomplete. This results in particular from the following four considerations.

In the first place, many sectors governed by substantive EU law other than the ones assessed in the foregoing remain mostly or even entirely unaffected by EU legislation of the type at issue here. In the second place, even if this legislation touches upon a considerable number of important remedial and procedural matters, it certainly does not regulate all matters that can be of relevance in private enforcement proceedings. There are many other important issues that often remain largely unaddressed, such as the applicable rules of evidence and the standard of judicial review to be exercised by the national courts seised.[23] In the third place, the EU involvement also tends to be uneven in the sense that, when taken together, the above-mentioned legislation may address many private enforcement-related issues, but not all legal acts in question touch upon all matters discussed here. In fact, far from it. Just to give one example, while only the IPR Enforcement Directive deals with the allocation of legal costs

21 E.g. Gender Equality Directive 2006/54.
22 See subsection 10.B.4 above.
23 See subsections 9.B.2 and 9.D.2 above, respectively.

between the parties,[24] this is also one of the few legal acts under consideration that does not contain any rules on limitation periods.[25] Finally, the level of detail provided for in the provisions of this EU legislation is often rather limited. With respect to damages claims, the Procurement Remedies Directives stipulate for instance little more than that it must be possible to award damages to private parties injured as a result of an infringement.[26] The Unfair Terms Directive similarly provides little more than the bare minimum where it lays down a contractual remedy, while expressly referring to national law in this connection.[27]

Consequently, without putting into question the (potential) importance of any of these legal acts and the provisions laid down therein individually, let alone the above-mentioned development more generally, it remains important to see these EU legislative measures in their proper perspective. The EU's involvement may be remarkable, especially as compared with the general rule that remedial and procedural matters relating to legal proceedings for the private enforcement of EU law before national courts are in principle left to be regulated by the Member States, but as it stands there is no question of something resembling an EU code of civil or administrative proceedings being established. There is thus still a considerable degree of "residual" autonomy to be exercised by the Member States.

That leads to a last general remark, which relates to the degree of controversy **12.06**
generated by EU legislative action related to private enforcement. The foregoing indicates, on the one hand, that, contrary to what is sometimes presumed, there is no reason to believe that such EU involvement is generally and necessarily politically sensitive.[28] The relatively smooth adoption of the IPR Enforcement Directive, which contains some of the most far-reaching private enforcement-related measures available to date, is a case in point. Here a number of *contextual* factors (upcoming EU enlargement, absence of adequate public enforcement, existence of the TRIPS Agreement) appear to have carried at least as much weight during the law-making process as the *content* of the proposal as such.[29] On the other hand, it has also been found that EU involvement with private enforcement-related issues can indeed be a sensitive matter. As is discussed in further detail in the following two sections, that is the

24 Art. 14 IPR Enforcement Directive 2004/48. See subsection 8.B.5 above.

25 See subsection 9.B.1 above.

26 Art. 2(1)(c) Public Sector Remedies Directive 89/665; Art. 2(1)(d) Utilities Remedies Directive 92/13. See subsection 3.B.2 above.

27 Art. 6(1) Product Liability Directive 93/13. See subsection 5.C.1 above.

28 See subsection 10.B.1 above.

29 See subsections 10.B.2 and 10.B.3 above.

case most notably where national rules on non-contractual liability (tort), contract law, penalty payments, legal costs and legal standing are affected. The fact that, as was noted above, not few of the provisions of EU law under consideration are broadly – not to say vaguely or ambiguously – worded is at least in part a result of this sensitivity. For leaving a degree of flexibility or ambiguity allows political compromises to be made. This can at times be the only manner in which agreement can be reached at EU level on a legislative proposal.

All the same, this manner of drafting the provisions concerned can have important consequences beyond the sphere of political compromises made in the context of the EU's decision-making process. These consequences need not be negative. In particular, this tends to leave the Member States a margin of manoeuvre when transposing the provisions at issue into national law, as is required considering that all of the above-mentioned acts are directives. That facilitates the embedment of those provisions in the domestic legal systems in which they are to function and therefore limits the "fragmenting" effect referred to above. This sometimes occurs to the point that no transposition at all is considered to be needed, because the domestic legal system of a given Member State is already deemed to be compliant.[30] It should further be noted that even broadly or ambiguously worded provisions of EU law can have an important impact in practice. Among other things, such provisions can help make all parties concerned (that is, private parties affected by infringements, but also possible infringers, lawyers and judges) aware of the rights and enforcement possibilities that may exist as a matter of EU law. Largely independent of their content, the EU rules at issue therefore tend to fulfil an important "awareness-raising" function.[31] Awareness is obviously a necessary precondition for the rights derived from EU law to be of relevance in practice.

Having said that, enacting broadly worded provisions of EU law and leaving flexibility to the Member States often also comes at a price. For the private parties concerned this can result in legal uncertainty and a degree of unequal treatment as a consequence of diverging rules of national law. Seen from the perspective of the EU, the main disadvantage is the continuing differences between the laws of the Member States and the related risk of the objectives of the harmonisation aimed for not being achieved. But for the Member States

30 Although the correctness of this assessment remains subject to review by the CoJ, such a position has, for instance, been taken by (almost) all Member States with respect to the transposition of Art. 14 IPR Enforcement Directive 2004/48 on legal costs. See subsection 4.B.5 above. As regards the possibility for Member States not to transpose directives when they deem their domestic legal system to be already compliant generally, see e.g. CoJ case C-151/12, *Commission v Spain*, para 26–8.

31 See subsection 10.D.2 above.

too there can be such a price. There can in particular be a certain loss of control and risk of unanticipated consequences when this EU legislation is applied and interpreted after its adoption. Over time this uncertainty and ambiguity are likely to lead to preliminary questions being referred to the Court of Justice. The Court being bound in principle to answer such questions and the wording of the rules of EU law in question providing only limited guidance, the Court tends to attach particular weight to the objectives of the legislation at hand. This can in turn sometimes lead to expansive and (for some) unexpected interpretations. An example is the *Océano Grupo* case law, pursuant to which national courts seised under the Unfair Terms Directive must in principle raise the unfairness of a term in a "standard" consumer contract – and consequently the related contractual remedy – of their own motion, that is, even where the private party applicant has not done so.[32] Another example is the finding that the Procurement Remedies Directives preclude judicial review exercised by the national courts seised from being limited to a test of whether or not the contested decision is arbitrary.[33] EU legislation facilitating the private enforcement of EU law before national courts of the type at issue here can thus also play an important role as a "stepping stone" for Court rulings, even – or perhaps: particularly – in relation to matters that are not expressly or extensively addressed in that legislation.

B. REMEDIES AND PROCEDURES FOR PRIVATE ENFORCEMENT PURPOSES

This second section looks more in detail at what the EU legislation at issue might entail in terms of the instruments that it offers to private parties for pursuing private enforcement actions. To this end the three "main" (substantive) private enforcement remedies laid down in this legislation – namely actions for damages, actions for injunctions and contractual remedies – are first subsequently discussed. Attention then turns to the other remedies, which are not necessarily any less important. However, these latter remedies are generally less widely provided for, they tend to be concerned with certain more specific issues and they are mostly not "free-standing" but instead dependent on a "main" claim of some sort being brought as well. Attention is also briefly paid to the remedies that remain unregulated in the EU legislation at issue. At the end of this section the findings with respect to that legislation's most important provisions of a procedural nature (including their rules on the scope of the EU legislative measures in question) are outlined.

32 CoJ joined cases C-240/98 and C-244/98, *Océano Grupo*, para 22–9. See subsections 5.C.2 and 9.D.2 above.

33 CoJ C-92/00, *Hospital Ingenieure*, para 57–64. See subsection 9.D.1 above.

1. Actions for damages

12.07 For some the very term "private enforcement" typically connotes private parties bringing actions for damages before national courts for infringements of EU law. Where competition law infringements are concerned, this seems to hold true for the Commission, given that it decided to concentrate the Competition Damages Directive exclusively on this substantive remedy.[34] While acknowledging that other remedies can be of relevance too, in its wake certainly in a competition law context, most attention in academic publications on private enforcement tends to go to this particular remedy. In a sense, it also appears to hold true for the Court of Justice. The Court is evidently constrained by the cases brought before it, but it is nonetheless noticeable that, for instance, both in its competition law-related case law (*Courage*, *Manfredi*, *Pfleiderer*[35]) and in its case law concerning infringements of EU law committed by the Member States (*Francovich*, *Brasserie du Pêcheur*[36]), the emphasis tends to be on compensation in damages. To a considerable extent the same applies for the EU legislature. For actions for damages are not only central to the Competition Damages Directive, this is also an important remedy provided for in other private enforcement-related EU legislation such as the Procurement Remedies Directives, the IPR Enforcement Directive and the Product Liability Directive.

Generally speaking, the above directives all aim to ensure that private parties that suffer loss or damage as a consequence of an infringement of EU law can obtain compensation, which in turn is expected to contribute to strengthening compliance with the substantive rules at issue. At the more detailed level there are several thorny issues, however. *Causality* generally leads to few structural difficulties.[37] In contrast, the issue of *fault* requirements is certainly one of them.[38] The approaches found in the above-mentioned legislation in this regard range from the "strict" (no-fault) liability provided for in the Product Liability Directive[39] to the IPR Enforcement Directive which requires that the infringer acted '*knowingly or with reasonable grounds to know*'.[40] Matters are complicated further when account is taken of the case law of the Court of Justice on matters of fault. Most notably the Court has interpreted the Procurement Remedies Directives' silence in this regard as implying that no

34 See subsection 6.C.2 above.

35 CoJ case C-453/99, *Courage*; CoJ joined cases C-295/04 to C-298/04, *Manfredi*; CoJ case C-360/09, *Pfleiderer*. See subsections 6.B.2 and 6.B.4 above.

36 CoJ joined cases C-6/90 and C-9/90, *Francovich*; CoJ joined cases C-46/93 and C-48/93, *Brasserie du Pêcheur*. See subsection 2.D.1 above.

37 See subsection 7.A.3 above.

38 See subsection 7.A.2 above.

39 Art. 4 Product Liability Directive 85/374. See subsection 5.D.1 above.

40 Art. 13(1) IPR Enforcement Directive 2004/48. See subsection 4.B.4 above.

fault requirement can be applied in the cases brought under these directives.[41] It cannot be excluded that the Court would come to a similar conclusion with respect to the Competition Damages Directive. After all, despite earlier suggestions to this effect,[42] this directive does not expressly address this issue. That will, however, largely depend on the importance that the Court attaches to the relevant statements in the directive's recitals.[43] More generally, it also appears that, while the reasons for these differing approaches are not always clear and a no-fault approach can have considerable disruptive effects at national level, in practice the approach chosen as a matter of EU law has at most only a limited effect on the degree of successful damages litigation.

Quantifying the harm suffered tends to be an important practical bottleneck for successfully bringing damages claims.[44] The Commission has therefore proposed EU rules on this subject matter on several occasions. The EU legislature mostly rejected these proposals, however. Yet the more recent adoption of the Competition Damages Directive, which contains several limited but nonetheless noteworthy provisions on quantification, illustrates that this is not always the case. It especially appears that rules that are not overly rigid but instead allow the national court seised a degree of flexibility, for instance to estimate the extent of the harm caused, can be both acceptable to the EU legislature and helpful in practice. It has on the whole proven less difficult to adopt common rules on the *qualification* of damages, which specify the heads of damages to be compensated. Here the EU's involvement is typically more substantial than where matters of quantification are concerned.[45] Certainly when read together with the relevant case law (referred to below) these rules indicate that a general rule of EU law is emerging according to which – subject to possible deviations or precision in the EU legislation at hand – any harm caused by infringements of EU law must be compensated in full. That means that costs and lost profits as well as interest and non-material damage must, as a general rule, be compensable. Although extensively debated, EU law currently does not provide for the award of punitive damages, however.[46] Neither is the award of punitive damages at present considered to be necessarily precluded as a matter of EU law, although more recently there appears to be a development towards their prohibition.

---

41 CoJ case C-314/09, *Stadt Graz*, para 30–45.

42 See in particular Commission, White paper on damages actions for breach of the EC antitrust rules, COM(2008) 165, pp. 6–7.

43 Recital 11 Competition Damages Directive 2014/104.

44 See subsection 7.A.4 above.

45 See subsection 7.A.5 above.

46 See subsection 7.A.6 above.

12.08 When considered more generally, one of the main findings of this study is that harmonising national laws relating to actions for damages for private enforcement purposes is often a problematic affair, with, in many cases, disappointing results in practice.[47] To begin with, agreeing at EU level on the rules to be provided for is often difficult. EU interference with issues of non-contractual liability (tort) remains a sensitive matter. This can translate into the relevant provisions of EU law being worded in a broad and minimalistic manner (for example the Procurement Remedies Directives' damages regime generally[48]), the Member States being left several options (for example the IPR Enforcement Directive's rules on setting damages[49]), the inclusion of express references to national law (for example the Product Liability Directive's provision on non-material damage[50]) or EU law simply not addressing certain issues at all (for example the issue of fault under the Competition Damages Directive). The "net harmonising effect" of these provisions of EU law is therefore often rather limited indeed. Furthermore, in all fields of law at issue here where legislative measures of this kind have been taken, private parties often continue to be hesitant to initiate damages claims. This is in part due to (anticipated) difficulties associated with these claims, such as lengthy proceedings, high legal costs and problems in demonstrating and quantifying the harm suffered. But even apart from that it appears that these parties might prefer spending their time, energy and financial resources on more forward-looking activities rather than seeking to obtain *ex post* compensation. Other considerations can also play a role in specific cases, such as the fear of "biting the hand that feeds you" in procurement cases, the difficulty of identifying infringers in intellectual property cases or the "rational apathy" of consumers in "mass damage" situations where the harm suffered is modest for each of these private parties individually.

All this thus puts in perspective the finding that there is '*astonishing diversity and total underdevelopment*' as regards actions for damages for infringements of EU competition law.[51] To the extent that the number of cases successfully brought is to be considered an appropriate indicator in the first place (which seems debatable, considering that many disputes may be settled and that anyway litigation would not appear to be an end in itself), the Commission had already concluded three decades earlier that '*[s]cant use has yet been made of the possibility of actions for damages for breaches of the [EU] competition rules*'.[52] More

47 See in particular subsection 7.A.1 above.

48 Art. 2(1)(c) Public Sector Remedies Directive 89/665; Art. 2(1)(d) Utilities Remedies Directive 92/13. See subsection 3.B.2 above.

49 Art. 13(1) IPR Enforcement Directive 2004/48. See subsection 4.B.4 above.

50 Art. 9 Product Liability Directive 85/374. See subsection 5.D.1 above.

51 Study, Ashurst (2004), p. 1.

52 Commission, Thirteenth report on competition policy, 1984, p. 136.

importantly, the situation is often largely similar in many other fields of EU law. For instance, although the degree of litigation seems to have increased somewhat since then, after the Procurement Remedies Directives' regime had been in force for several years it was reported that '*no more than a handful*' of damages cases had been brought EU-wide.[53] Likewise, roughly a decade after its adoption, a study found that '*almost no cases have been reported*' under the Product Liability Directive.[54] And in 2010 the Commission observed in relation to the IPR Enforcement Directive that in intellectual property cases damages awards '*are not requested [...] as a matter of course*'.[55] This limited degree of damages litigation for (alleged) infringements of EU law in these fields other than EU competition law is all the more remarkable, given that there the EU legislature enacted specific measures meant to facilitate the bringing of this kind of private enforcement actions years or even decades ago.

There are reasons to doubt whether the Commission and the EU legislature are willing and able to alter this situation by substantially "beefing up" the applicable rules of EU law on this point. These doubts seem to result at least as much from political or policy constraints as from any strictly legal considerations. The Product Liability Directive has, for example, been left substantially unaltered for almost three decades, despite there being broad agreement that this directive has done relatively little to alleviate the burden on private parties wishing to obtain compensation in damages.[56] The Commission similarly seems hesitant to propose amending the IPR Enforcement Directive's damages regime.[57] But probably the best illustration is the 2007 revision of the Procurement Remedies Directives.[58] In that context the problems encountered by private parties having suffered harm as a consequence of infringements of EU public procurement law were expressly acknowledged. However, the Commission – and with it the EU legislature – saw this as a reason for introducing another remedy (namely a contractual remedy, discussed below) rather than for attempting to improve and further elaborate these directives' rules on damages claims. This evidently contrasts with the extensive efforts that the Commission especially has made over the past decade to seek EU legislation that gives effect to the right to compensation in damages for competition law infringements, which eventually led to the adoption of the Competition Damages Directive.[59] And on many points (also) this latter directive is only limitedly prescriptive. Moreover, the **12.09**

53 Study, Herbert Smith (1996), p. 18.

54 Study, McKenna (1994), p. 45.

55 Commission, Staff working document accompanying the report on IPR Enforcement Directive 2004/48, SEC(2010) 1589, p. 21.

56 See subsection 5.D.2 above.

57 See subsection 4.A.2 above.

58 See subsection 3.A.3 above.

59 See subsection 6.B.3 above.

fact that it was eventually proposed and adopted is arguably more due to a desire to protect the existing public enforcement mechanism (particularly leniency programmes) than to a broadly shared ambition to facilitate the private enforcement of EU competition law as such.[60]

It may therefore well be that some of the most noticeable legal developments with respect to actions for damages in a private enforcement context are still to come from Luxembourg rather than from Brussels. For instance, as was noted above, the Court of Justice has already held that the absence of an express fault requirement in the Procurement Remedies Directives implies that the application of such a requirement under national law is precluded.[61] As a consequence, liability under these directives is probably more "strict" even than under the no-fault Product Liability Directive. For the latter contains a range of exonerating circumstances and other moderating provisions on which a defendant can seek to rely, which are evidently entirely absent in the former.[62] There is also case law suggesting that, unless expressly provided otherwise, non-material damage is also to be compensated, and indeed that the harm caused must be compensated in full, including costs, lost profits and interests.[63] In this connection the scope for dynamic interplay between the EU's judiciary and its legislature is not to be overlooked. As was noted earlier, almost irrespective of their precise content, the above directives can fulfil a function in terms of "awareness-raising" for all parties concerned and as a "stepping stone" for the Court of Justice. Put crudely, for it to be able to issue rulings, the Court needs cases to be brought before it and EU law to interpret. On both accounts these directives can play an important role, notwithstanding their sometimes only modestly prescriptive rules on actions for damages (perhaps even to the contrary). And the Court's rulings can in turn also lead to further legislative developments. That is illustrated by the Competition Damages Directive, which in many respects codifies and builds on the Court's earlier *Courage* case law.[64]

2. Actions for injunctions

12.10 The story of the second main remedy discussed above, namely actions for injunctions, is altogether rather different. This remedy is a common one, especially in the field of EU consumer protection law. Not only the Consumer

60 CoJ case C-360/09, *Pfleiderer*. See subsections 6.B.4 and 6.C.1 above.

61 CoJ case C-314/09, *Stadt Graz*, para 30–45. See subsections 3.B.2 and 7.A.2 above.

62 E.g. Art. 7 and 16(1) Product Liability Directive 85/374. See subsection 5.D.2 above.

63 E.g. CoJ case C271/91, *Marshall*, para 26; CoJ case C-203/99, *Veedfald*, para 25–28; CoJ case C-168/00, *Leitner*, para 21–3; CoJ joined cases C-295/04 to C-298/04, *Manfredi*, para 92–7. See subsection 7.A.4 above.

64 CoJ case C-453/99, *Courage*. See subsections 2.D.2 and 6.B.2 above.

Injunctions Directive, but also several other directives, including the Unfair Terms Directive, contain provisions in this regard.[65] This remedy further plays an important role under the IPR Enforcement Directive[66] and, although perhaps to a somewhat lesser extent, the Procurement Remedies Directives.[67] In EU legislative terms this remedy is therefore by and large as widely provided for as actions for damages. Together with actions for damages, it is also one of the two key remedies addressed in the Commission's Collective Redress Recommendation.[68]

And yet injunctive relief arguably still remains an undervalued possible course of action in the present context. This remedy tends to receive only limited attention both in the private enforcement-related legal literature and in the case law of the Court of Justice. More than a decade after *Courage* it still remains to be clarified if the reasoning set out in that case can also be extended to remedies other than actions for damages, particularly with respect to actions for injunctions.[69] As compared with the academic and institutional attention and follow-up given to *Courage*, the Court's ruling in *Muñoz* – based on similar reasoning but relating to the civil law consequences of EU law infringements generally – went almost unnoticed.[70] This remedy is also notably absent from the Competition Damages Directive, for reasons that seem not immediately evident and that have in any case to date regrettably not been properly explained.

It appears that injunctive relief can in fact be an important remedy in private enforcement proceedings, including in competition cases. In particular, although this will obviously depend on the circumstances of the case at hand, private parties confronted with EU law infringements are often most interested in a "quick fix", that is, (relatively) uncomplicated, speedy and not overly costly proceedings that serve to determine whether or not the relevant rules of substantive EU law have been infringed and that oblige the defendant to stop acting in that manner in case of an affirmative answer. To a considerable extent actions for injunctions can satisfy this need. **12.11**

65 Art. 2(1)(a) Consumer Injunctions Directive 2009/22; Art. 7(1) Unfair Terms Directive 93/13. See subsections 5.2.1 and 5.2.2 above, respectively.

66 Art. 9(1) and 11 IPR Enforcement Directive 2004/48. See subsections 4.2.2 and 4.2.3 above, respectively.

67 Art. 2(1)(b) Procurement Remedies Directives 89/665 and 92/13. See subsection 3.2.1 above.

68 See in particular section IV Collective Redress Recommendation 2013/396, discussed in subsection 5.5.2 above.

69 Cf. Opinion AG Jacobs joined cases C-264/01, C-306/01, C-354/01 and C-355/01, *AOB Bundesverband*, par. 105.

70 CoJ case C-253/00, *Muñoz*. See subsection 2.4.2 above. For a broader assessment of *Courage* and *Muñoz*, see subsection 2.4.3 above.

With respect to the EU legislation under consideration, two factors stand out in this regard, namely the (likely) absence as a matter of EU law of a requirement to demonstrate, in order for injunctive relief to be granted, that the defendant was *at fault* when committing the infringement at issue and that the infringement caused (sufficiently quantified) *harm* to the private party applicant.[71] Even if there can be significant differences between the domestic legal systems of the Member States in this regard, as a consequence proceedings for injunctive relief are typically less complex, faster and less costly, at least as compared with actions for damages. That applies all the more so because, as is further discussed below, unlike actions for damages, injunctions can often be granted as interim relief. The above-mentioned directives regularly expressly require certain forms of injunctive relief to be made available by means of interim measures.[72] In addition, in many instances the provisions of EU law in question also leave a degree of flexibility to the Member States and, by extension, to the national courts seised. That can allow the latter to issue orders tailored to the specifics of the case at hand.

Taken together, the above probably goes a long way in explaining the relative success in practice of injunctive relief as a private enforcement remedy, despite this remedy often receiving only a limited degree of broader attention.[73] It is mostly positively assessed in consumer cases, for instance. And in relation to infringements of intellectual property law, stakeholders have even identified this as the '*main enforcement remedy*'.[74] There also may well be considerable "demand" for providing for the possibility of granting injunctive relief in competition cases.[75] The forward-looking (relatively) "quick fix" that injunctive relief can offer can thus be more attractive for many private parties than the inherently backward-looking remedy of compensation for past harm.[76] This remedy therefore deserves to be taken seriously in a private enforcement context. Although this will always need to be assessed on a case-by-case basis, there may well be grounds for making it available and facilitating it more broadly as a possible way for private parties to address infringements of EU law in proceedings before national courts.

---

71 See subsection 7.B.2 above.

72 E.g. Art. 9(1)(a) IPR Enforcement Directive 2004/48; Art. 2(1)(a) Consumer Injunctions Directive 2009/22.

73 See subsection 7.B.2 above.

74 Commission, Staff working document accompanying the report on IPR Enforcement Directive 2004/48, SEC(2010) 1589, p. 14 (regarding preliminary injunctions).

75 See subsection 7.B.3 above.

76 Cf. CoJ case C-169/14, *Sánchez Morcillo*, para 43, where it is held that in certain cases the purely compensatory nature of a damages award might mean that the protection conferred on the private party concerned is incomplete and insufficient.

The foregoing does not mean, however, that EU law on injunctive relief as it stands does not leave room for improvement. Two points are to be noted in particular. In the first place, the provisions in question are arguably *too unclear and too lenient* in some respects. Most notably, the EU legal acts under consideration do not stipulate expressly that no requirements of fault or harm can apply for injunctive relief to be granted.[77] This means that there remains scope for debate – and for deviating approaches at national level – on these two important points. The possibility offered by both the Procurement Remedies Directives and the IPR Enforcement Directive to allow in certain cases a defendant to "buy off" an injunction that might otherwise have been granted can also be seen as an example of too far-reaching flexibility.[78] These provisions essentially allow injunctive relief to be "transformed" into compensatory relief, thus possibly denying a private party applicant the possibility of obtaining the former where required. **12.12**

In the second place, it appears that this remedy generally functions in an unsatisfactory manner where *cross-border infringements* are at stake.[79] The Consumer Injunctions Directive, which specifically seeks to address these kinds of infringements, is a case in point. It has thus far largely failed to address the pre-existing difficulties that it was meant to address, considering that the system it established to this effect has been used only very sporadically. Similar shortcomings have been observed in connection with the IPR Enforcement Directive. These difficulties are probably not peculiar to this specific remedy, however. It would appear that they come to light here mainly because injunctive relief is otherwise relatively frequently applied for and granted. The Commission may therefore well be correct in treating this concern as an expression of more general difficulties connected to cross-border litigation relating to infringements of EU law. Nonetheless, it remains to be seen whether the improvements that may result from measures of broader application, such as the Brussels I Regulation and the Rome II Regulation, will lead to significant improvements in this respect.[80] Additional measures might be called for.

3. Contractual remedies

Contractual remedies (that is, private enforcement actions intended to make good infringements of EU law by seeking to nullify or to otherwise make **12.13**

77 For two exceptions, see Art. 11(2) Unfair Commercial Practices Directive 2005/29; Art. 5(3) Misleading Advertising Directive 2006/114.

78 Art. 12 IPR Enforcement Directive 2004/48; Art. 2(1)(c) and 2(5) Utilities Remedies Directive 92/13.

79 See subsection 7.B.3 above.

80 Brussels I Regulation 1215/2012; Rome II Regulation 864/2007.

ineffective contractual arrangements entered into in relation to those infringements) can be found in three of the four selected fields of EU law discussed above. Article 101(2) TFEU stipulates that contracts that are contrary to the prohibition of anticompetitive behaviour (notably cartels) are "automatically void".[81] Under the Unfair Terms Directive, unfair terms in "standard" consumer contracts are "not binding" on the consumers concerned.[82] And the Procurement Remedies Directives stipulate that contracts concluded pursuant to certain infringements of the EU public procurement rules are to be considered "ineffective".[83]

12.14 This remedy can play an important role where the EU law infringements to be addressed have a contractual dimension of some sort.[84] The precise nature of this dimension can differ. In competition cases the conclusion of the *contract as such* essentially constitutes the infringement of EU law. By contrast, in public procurement cases the conclusion of the contract is a *consequence* of an infringement committed at an earlier stage, namely during the preceding contract award procedure. And under the Unfair Terms Directive it is the inclusion of a *particular term* that can have implications for the contract in question. Despite these differences, these contractual remedies have in common that they essentially all seek to prevent private parties from being confronted with a *fait accompli* in the form of a concluded contract when they try to address an infringement of EU law. In the absence of this remedy being expressly provided for as a matter of EU law, primary EU law may arguably still require the contract to be terminated in certain cases.[85] Considerable uncertainty exists in this regard, however. It would moreover seem that in those cases the outcome is likely to depend to a great extent on the circumstances of the case at hand and the applicable provisions of national law.

It follows that this remedy is more selective in nature than the other two "main" (substantive) remedies discussed earlier. After all, by no means *all* infringements of EU law typically have a contractual dimension of the type referred to here. The IPR Enforcement Directive does not provide for this remedy, for instance. And neither does EU law expressly provide for a contractual remedy in relation to abuses of a dominant position within the meaning of Article 102 TFEU. This selectiveness is further illustrated by the fact that the contractual remedy set out in the Procurement Remedies Directives is available only with

81 See subsection 6.A.3 above.

82 Art. 6(1) Unfair Terms Directive 93/13. See subsection 5.C.1 above.

83 Art. 2d(1) Procurement Remedies Directives 89/665 and 92/13. See subsection 3.B.3 above.

84 See subsection 8.A.1 above.

85 See subsection 8.A.3 above.

respect to what are considered to be the most serious infringements of substantive EU public procurement law. The possible contractual consequences of other infringements of that law remain unaddressed in these directives. This appears to imply that in these latter cases the contracts in question can in principle remain effective in so far as EU law is concerned.

Furthermore, the fact that each of the three above-mentioned provisions uses a different term ("automatically void", "not binding", "ineffective") suggests a *lack of coherence* at EU level where this remedy is provided for. This remark applies all the more so because consumer protection directives other than the Unfair Terms Directive use different terms yet again in this regard.[86] It is important to note that this is not merely a matter of terminology. There are notable differences as regards the legal effects that result from this remedy being awarded. The Court of Justice has, for instance, long held that the effects under Article 101(2) TFEU are absolute (that is, they apply *vis-à-vis* all contracting parties as well as third parties) and that they work retroactively (*ex tunc*).[87] By contrast, the wording of the Unfair Terms Directive makes it clear that here the effects are relative (that is, they only affect certain parties),[88] while the Procurement Remedies Directives expressly allow for this remedy having effects only for future purposes (*ex nunc*).[89] In addition, the effects of this remedy being invoked on the remaining, "non-infringing" provisions of the contracts in question can vary too. Competition law is largely neutral on this point, as it leaves questions of severability in principle to national law.[90] The Unfair Terms Directive's approach can be described as one of restraint, in that it seeks to leave the other provisions of the contract unaffected as much as possible.[91] Although this remains to be clarified, under the Procurement Remedies Directives there would generally seem to be little scope for severance. For in procurement cases the *entire* contract will normally result from the infringement of EU law during the earlier contract award procedure. Under these directives this thus seems more of an all-or-nothing type of issue. 12.15

86 E.g. Art. 3(2), (5) and (6) Consumer Sales Directive 1999/44 speaks of contracts being '*rescinded*'. Elsewhere reference is made to the possibility of "withdrawal" from a contract, whereby this term is moreover used in different legal acts with two apparently distinct meanings (cf. e.g. Art. 4(5) and (6) Package Travel Directive 90/314 and Art. 9 Consumer Rights Directive 2011/83).

87 E.g. CoJ joined cases C-295/04 to C-298/04, *Manfredi*, para 57.

88 Art. 6(1) Unfair Terms Directive 93/13 provides that the unfair contract term shall not be binding "on the consumer".

89 Art. 2d(2) Procurement Remedies Directives 89/665 and 92/13. However, in that case provision must be made for the "alternative penalties" set out in Art. 2e of these directives.

90 E.g. CoJ case 56/65, *Société Technique Minière*, p. 250.

91 E.g. CoJ case C-453/10, *Pereničová*, para 31–5.

These differences are to some extent understandable, given that the objectives of the above three contractual remedies and the contexts in which they operate differ. A one-size-fits-all approach on the matters discussed above is therefore not always in place. For example, absolute effects generally seem entirely appropriate for breaches of the relevant competition rules. But that is certainly not the case for breaches of the rules on unfair terms in consumer contracts, as the latter are meant only to protect the interests of the consumer concerned. The above-mentioned distinct approaches as regards the non-infringing provisions also seem understandable, in light of the different nature of the contractual dimension at issue as explained above. But this explains by no means all these differences in terms of the legal effects of the contractual remedies provided for in the EU legislation at issue. It would seem that, even when allowing for the required relative effects, the Unfair Terms Directive could have set out these effects more specifically as a matter of EU law. From a legal perspective, it is also far from evident why, while Article 101(2) TFEU stipulates that anticompetitive contracts are "automatically void", in the Procurement Remedies Directives the legally much less distinct term "ineffectiveness" is used. Under these latter directives the contract in question must, moreover, first be *considered* ineffective, which implies that in this case there are no "automatic" effects.[92]

12.16 That leads to the last point to be made in this connection. If, as was noted above, EU legislative interference with matters relating to non-contractual liability (tort) tends to be sensitive, this surely also holds true – and indeed perhaps even more so – where contract law is concerned. Contract law has traditionally been left to be regulated by the Member States. Even the Court of Justice can seem hesitant to venture too deeply into this domain.[93] This tension between the EU wishing to take certain contract-law-related legislative measures to facilitate the private enforcement of EU law before national courts, on the one hand, and the Member States wishing to avoid too much EU involvement regarding matters of contract law, on the other hand, goes a long way in explaining why this remedy has been regulated in such an incoherent and unspecific manner, as already touched upon above. Indeed, the legislative histories of both the Unfair Terms Directive and the Procurement Remedies Directives show that the legally rather indistinct terms "not binding" and "ineffective" were introduced at the behest of the EU legislature. The Commission had proposed using more specific wording (namely "void" and "invalid", respectively). In contrast to what the Commission had proposed, these two

92 Cf. recital 13 Procurement Remedies Amending Directive 2007/66.

93 Cf. e.g. CoJ case C-159/00, *Sapod*, para 52; CoJ case C-91/08, *Wall*, para 63–5; CoJ case C-215/08, *Friz*, para 45.

directives now also expressly refer to national law for the precise legal consequences of this remedy.[94] The complex system of possible "alternative penalties" and judicial discretion for which the Procurement Remedies Directives provide in this regard is also testimony to the compromises that sometimes need to be struck when enacting secondary EU law of the type at issue here.[95]

It is therefore unsurprising that the laws of the Member States provide for a range of legal concepts when transposing the terms "not binding" and "ineffectiveness", such as non-existence, revocability, voidability and unenforceability. As was noted earlier, this flexibility can help to ensure an optimal "fit" with the domestic legal systems of the Member States in which these provisions of EU law are to be embedded. However, when taken too far, as is arguably at times the case here, it can also put at risk the very harmonised and effective enforcement possibilities that the EU legislative measures in question seek to achieve. This very same tension is also reflected in the case law of the Court of Justice. It has, for example, acknowledged that under the Unfair Terms Directive the Member States have '*a certain degree of autonomy*' to define the applicable legal arrangements, while at the same time insisting on the need to guarantee the full effectiveness of the objectives of this provision of EU law.[96] Although more factors are likely to play a role in this respect, this ambiguity may well be an important element in explaining why the practical effects of the contractual remedies at issue here are not always assessed in a positive manner.

4. Interim relief, measures on the disclosure of evidence and penalty payments

Turning to the other remedies found in the EU legislation assessed above, a first **12.17**
remedy is *interim relief*.[97] The Court of Justice has held that this remedy serves in essence '*to ensure the full effectiveness of the judgment to be given on the existence of the rights claimed under [EU] law*'.[98] Without interim relief being available, the situation "on the ground" may well evolve in such a manner pending a definitive ruling in the dispute at hand that this latter ruling becomes devoid of practical effects. One could think of a public contract that is awarded and executed while the contract award decision is still being contested in court. As the Court of Justice observed, in these cases the granting of interim measures can prevent a *lacuna* in the legal protection of the private parties concerned from

94 Art. 6(1) Unfair Terms Directive 93/13; Art. 2d(2) Procurement Remedies Directives 89/665 and 92/13.
95 Art. 2d(3) and Art. 2e Procurement Remedies Directives 89/665 and 92/13. See subsection 3.B.3 above.
96 CoJ case C-618/10, *Banco Español de Crédito*, para 62 and 72.
97 See subsection 8.B.1 above.
98 CoJ case C-416/10, *Križan*, para 107.

occurring.[99] Although there can be significant differences between the laws of the Member States, proceedings for interim measures are therefore typically (relatively) uncomplicated and speedy. The resulting measures, however, apply only provisionally; they do not finally determine the legal situation in the dispute at hand.[100] The latter can be achieved only through legal proceedings on the merits of the case.

Therefore the availability of this remedy under the EU legislation at issue principally depends on whether the typical disputes in question are deemed to require judicial intervention at short notice. At one end of the spectrum are the Procurement Remedies Directives, where interim measures take an important place.[101] As the above example relating to the award and execution of a public contract illustrates, disputes arising in that context often need to be addressed quickly.[102] At the other end of the spectrum are the Product Liability Directive and the Competition Damages Directive. These latter two directives do not provide for this remedy at all, because in terms of substantive remedies they are exclusively concerned with actions for damages, which are generally not seen as urgent.[103] Somewhere in between these two "extremes" lies the IPR Enforcement Directive. This directive requires interim relief to be made available for two specific purposes, namely to prevent imminent infringements from occurring and to preserve relevant evidence.[104] The consumer protection directives at issue here in turn take a somewhat different route. For they tend to leave it principally to the Member States to ensure speedy legal proceedings, leaving it open whether or not these proceedings should be interlocutory in nature.[105]

The above directives mostly establish a link between the possibility of granting interim relief, on the one hand, and injunctive relief of some sort, on the other hand. Generally speaking, interim measures lend themselves well to bringing an (alleged) infringement to a (provisional) halt or to prevent damage from occurring. It is noticeable, however, that the EU legislation under consideration here mostly only provides for limited details on the functioning of these proceedings. Only the Procurement Remedies Directives are to some extent an exception, as they go some way in specifying what these interim measures are to

99 CoJ Order case C-278/13 P(R), *Pilkington*, para 36.

100 Cf. CoJ case C-568/08, *Combinatie Spijker*, para 61.

101 Art. 2(1)(a) Procurement Remedies Directives 89/665 and 92/13. See subsection 3.B.1 above.

102 Cf. Art. 1(1) Procurement Remedies Directives 89/665 and 92/13, which specify that these directives aim to ensure that decisions taken in relation to contract award procedures can be reviewed '*as rapidly as possible*'.

103 Cf. e.g. CoJ joined cases C-143/88 and C-92/89, *Zuckerfabrik Süderdithmarschen*, para 29; CoJ Order case C-278/13 P(R), *Pilkington*, para 50.

104 Art. 7(1) and Art. 9(1)(a) IPR Enforcement Directive 2004/48. See subsections 4.B.1 and 4.B.2 above.

105 Art. 2(1)(a) Consumer Injunctions Directive 2009/22. See subsection 5.B.1 above. See e.g. also Art. 11(2) Unfair Commercial Practices Directive 2005/29; Art. 5(3) Misleading Advertising Directive 2006/114.

entail. These directives refer to the suspension of the contract award procedure or of the implementation of a decision taken by the contracting authority concerned. Even if such an exercise often takes place in this connection more generally, they are also alone in expressly allowing for the balancing of the various interests at stake by the competent national court.[106] The Court of Justice has further held that the Procurement Remedies Directives preclude making the filing of an application for interim measures dependent on a requirement that proceedings on the merits must first have been brought, even where the latter are a mere formality.[107] As regards this latter point, the situation seems largely similar under the IPR Enforcement Directive. There it is stated that the said provisional measures to preserve evidence are to be made available even before the commencement of proceedings on the merits of the case.[108]

Another relevant private enforcement remedy is concerned with measures on **12.18** the *disclosure of evidence* and other relevant information.[109] Certain general EU law requirements in this respect can be derived from the principles of equivalence and effectiveness.[110] Over and above these general requirements there are two EU legal acts that contain specific rules on this remedy, namely the IPR Enforcement Directive and the Competition Damages Directive.[111] Both regimes essentially aim to ensure that in the private enforcement proceedings concerned, applicants (and where relevant also defendants) can obtain access to evidence that is in the possession or that lies within the control of either the opposing party in the dispute at hand or a third party. They also seek to ensure that this evidence is preserved, either by means of a court order to this effect (IPR Enforcement Directive) or by means of sanctions if evidence is destroyed (Competition Damages Directive). The practical effects of the disclosure possibilities offered under the IPR Enforcement Directive are assessed mostly favourably. Many also agree that measures were called for in relation to competition law infringements. According to the Commission the national laws pre-dating the Competition Damages Directive not only varied considerably, but could also mean that there was '*no effective access to evidence for victims of a competition law infringement*'.[112]

---

106 Art. 2(5) Public Sector Remedies Directive 89/665; Art. 2(4) Utilities Remedies Directive 92/13.

107 CoJ case C-214/00, *Commission v Spain*, para 99–100.

108 Art. 7(1) IPR Enforcement Directive 2004/48.

109 See subsection 8.B.2 above.

110 E.g. CoJ case C-526/04, *Laboratoires Boiron*, para 55. See subsection 2.A.3 above.

111 Art. 6–8 IPR Enforcement Directive 2004/48; Art. 5–7 Competition Damages Directive 2014/104. See subsections 4.B.1 and 6.C.3 above, respectively.

112 Commission, Impact assessment report on damages actions for breach of the EU antitrust rules, SWD(2013) 203, p. 19 (regarding competition cases).

It has nonetheless been seen in the foregoing that two issues of broader relevance tend to arise in this connection. In the first place, this is an example of a situation where in relation to the EU's legislative intervention several questions of *coherence and fragmentation* come to light. Even if the Competition Damages Directive was inspired by the IPR Enforcement Directive, there are certain differences between the two disclosure regimes. Some of these differences are understandable, such as the special rules on the disclosure of evidence included in the files of public enforcement authorities that the former directive provides for. For these rules are to a great extent specific to the manner in which competition law is being enforced in the EU, namely through strong public enforcement and with heavy reliance on leniency programmes. Other differences between these two regimes are more difficult to understand and are to be regretted, however. This includes the manner in which the requests for disclosure must be specified and the formulation of the standard to be met before disclosure can be ordered. A further – and more fundamental – question is why these two fields of law have been singled out for EU legislative action, while no such action has been taken in other fields. This decision implies that the enforcement possibilities of the private parties concerned by (alleged) infringements of EU intellectual property and competition law are increased, while those of private parties affected by infringements of other rules of EU law or of "purely" national law remain unaltered. This also implies that there is a fragmenting effect on the national legal systems concerned, as the latter tend to address matters of disclosure across the board, regardless of the field of law at issue. On balance it would seem that there are grounds for arguing that the concealed and professional manner in which intellectual property and competition law infringements tend to be committed sets these two fields of law apart, at least when compared to typical infringements of public procurement and consumer protection law. Whether or not these differences are such that the aforementioned consequences of this sector-specific approach are to be taken for granted remains, however, a matter for (political) debate.[113]

The second issue is the risk of *conflicting interests and abuse*. Concerns of this kind have been expressed in relation to the disclosure regimes set out in both the IPR Enforcement Directive and the Competition Damages Directive, for instance concerning the possible high costs of complying with these disclosure orders, the possibility of confidential information or personal data being disclosed and abuse through overly broad "fishing expeditions". A balance is therefore to be struck between the legitimate interests of the applicants, the

113 Doubts on these points were expressed, for example, in the context of the consultations relating to Competition Damages Directive 2014/104, discussed in subsection 6.B.3 above. On issues of coherence and fragmentation at national level more generally, see also subsection 10.D.2 above.

defendants and the third parties that may be involved. At a more abstract level this also concerns a balancing between the interests served by private enforcement of EU law generally and the risk associated with a "litigation culture". Several safeguards have therefore been included in the two above-mentioned directives. They include the requirement of a court order, thus ensuring judicial oversight; the obligation to first present reasonably available evidence supporting the claims in question ("fact pleading"); a requirement to delineate the disclosure orders in a specific, narrow and proportionate manner, especially under the Competition Damages Directive; and rules on the protection of confidential information. It would appear that in this manner these directives strike a reasonable balance, although the effects in practice may depend in part on the precise manner in which the above rules are transposed into national law and subsequently applied at national level. In particular, the possible involvement of third parties seems an aspect that may require special attention in this regard.

Turning to *recurring penalty payments*, the Consumer Injunctions Directive describes this as: **12.19**

> an order against the losing defendant for payments into the public purse or to any beneficiary designated in or under national legislation, in the event of failure to comply with the decision within a time limit specified by the courts or the administrative authorities, of a fixed amount for each day's delay or any other amount provided for in national legislation, with a view to ensuring compliance with the decisions.[114]

It follows that this remedy serves to ensure that the defendant takes the necessary measures to comply with a ruling by a national court issued in a private enforcement case.[115] It does so by imposing a financial penalty, often on a recurring basis, for instance for each day that the non-compliance persists after a certain date. The aim is thus, in the words of the Court of Justice, to place the defendant under '*economic pressure which induces it to put an end to the breach established*'.[116] No payment will be due, however, if timely compliance with the judgment at issue is ensured. It follows that this remedy can be especially useful in situations where there is reason to doubt the defendants' commitment to comply with a court's ruling in private enforcement proceedings. Apart from the Consumer Injunctions Directive, of the legal acts under consideration only the IPR Enforcement Directive also provides for this remedy.[117]

114 Art. 2(1)(c) Consumer Injunctions Directive 2009/22. See subsection 5.B.1 above.

115 See subsection 8.B.3 above.

116 CoJ case C-177/04, *Commission v France*, para 91 (concerning Article 260(2) TFEU).

117 Art. 9(1)(a) and Art. 11 IPR Enforcement Directive 2004/48. See subsections 4.B.2 and 4.B.3 above.

That leads to the question of what explains the rather limited availability under EU law of this remedy for private enforcement purposes. Two points stand out in this regard. In the first place, the two above-mentioned directives make this remedy available specifically in relation to the *injunctive relief* that may be granted under the legislation at hand. Much like interim measures, this remedy is thus not available in relation to actions for damages. This explains why it has not been laid down in acts such as the Product Liability Directive and the Competition Damages Directive, which concentrate exclusively on compensation in damages. In the second place, it appears that this is another subject matter where EU legislative intervention tends to be seen as particularly *sensitive*. This is likely to be connected to the differences between the national laws in this respect. While some domestic legal systems of the Member States are entirely unfamiliar with this remedy, where that is otherwise, differences exist particularly as to whether any such penalty payments are due to the state or rather to the private party applicant concerned. At the insistence of the Member States represented in Council, the above-mentioned reference to this remedy in the Consumer Injunctions Directive is therefore preceded by the phrase '*in so far as the legal system of the Member State concerned so permits*'. The IPR Enforcement Directive similarly contains phrases qualifying the Member States' obligations in this respect, namely '*where appropriate*' and '*where provided for under national law*'.[118] Further, both directives leave open who is the beneficiary of the payment. The fact that the Procurement Remedies Directives do not provide for this remedy, but instead require the Member States in a more general manner to ensure that decisions by the competent national courts are effectively enforced should probably also be seen in light of this sensitivity.[119] The provisions of these latter directives further illustrate that there are also means other than providing for penalty payments when the need is felt to take EU legislative measures to ensure that judgments issued in private enforcement proceedings are complied with.

5. Publicity measures, legal costs and "unregulated" remedies

12.20 Another remedy that is provided for in only some of the acts of secondary EU law assessed above is the possibility for the national court seised to order *publicity measures*. The IPR Enforcement Directive speaks of '*appropriate measures for the dissemination of information concerning the decision, including displaying the decision and publishing it in full or in part*'.[120] This directive adds that the Member States may in addition make provision for the ordering of '*additional*

118 This latter phrase has been included in Art. 11 IPR Enforcement Directive 2004/48 (on "permanent" injunctions), but not in its Art. 9(1)(a) (on interlocutory injunctions).

119 Art. 2(8) Procurement Remedies Directives 89/665 and 92/13. See subsection 3.C.3 above.

120 Art. 15 IPR Enforcement Directive 2004/48. See subsection 4.B.5 above.

publicity measures which are appropriate to the particular circumstances, including prominent advertising'. These publicity measures are to be imposed at the request of the applicant and implemented at the expense of the infringer. The Consumer Injunctions Directive and certain other consumer protection directives contain a largely similar remedy, which is to be ordered '*where appropriate*'.[121]

This remedy serves a dual purpose, namely deterring infringers and contributing to the awareness of the public at large.[122] It can therefore be expected to be normally most effective where the general public is directly affected by the infringements of EU law at issue and where the infringing party is sensitive to the reputational damage that may result from the publication. This explains its inclusion in the above-mentioned directives, just as it probably explains its absence from acts such as the Procurement Remedies Directives. It might also mean that, although it has not been included in the Competition Damages Directive, this remedy might well be of relevance at least in certain competition cases. Having said that, where EU law requires this remedy to be made available, it mostly appears to play only a modest role in practice. The often rather non-committal manner in which it has been set out may be part of the explanation for this. It appears, however, that even apart from that this remedy generally tends to generate only limited interest on the part of private parties who are being confronted by infringements of EU law. Particularly in light of its above-mentioned dual purpose (that is, deterrence and awareness-raising), it is arguably more suitable as a public enforcement instrument.[123]

Although both are evidently concerned with different subject matter, there is a **12.21** remarkable degree of similarity between the EU law measures on the disclosure of evidence discussed above and those on *legal costs*.[124] Both issues are of considerable practical importance to private parties who may wish to initiate private enforcement proceedings, especially (but not exclusively) where actions for damages are concerned. And both issues have been singled out for EU legislative action, in particular in relation to infringements of EU intellectual property and competition law, although in the end no binding measures on legal costs have been set out in the Competition Damages Directive.[125] Of the EU

121 Art. 2(1)(b) Consumer Injunctions Directive 2009/22. See subsection 5.B.1 above. See e.g. also Art. 11(2) Unfair Commercial Practices Directive 2005/29; Art. 5(4) Misleading Advertising Directive 2006/114.

122 Recital 12 IPR Enforcement Directive 2004/48.

123 Cf. e.g. Art. 30 Competition Regulation 1/2003.

124 See subsection 8.B.5 above.

125 For earlier discussions on this subject matter, see in particular Commission, Green paper on damages actions for breach of the EC antitrust rules, COM(2005) 672, p. 9; Commission, White paper on damages actions for breach of the EC antitrust rules, COM(2008) 165, pp. 9–10; Commission, Staff working paper accompanying the white paper on damages actions for breach of the EC antitrust rules, SEC(2008) 404, pp. 74–5.

legislation under consideration, only the IPR Enforcement Directive contains, therefore, measures on legal costs. This latter directive provides that '*reasonable and proportionate legal costs and other expenses incurred by the successful party shall, as a general rule, be borne by the unsuccessful party, unless equity does not allow this*'.[126] That implies that the infringer must generally bear all the financial consequences of their conduct.[127] Exceptional as it may be,[128] this provision has been drafted in a very broad manner, to the extent that most Member States did not even consider it necessary to amend their pre-existing rules of national law to comply with it. Although it cannot be excluded that the Court of Justice will develop more ambitious requirements on the basis of this provision, it is therefore unsurprising that its introduction so far seems to have done little to alleviate stakeholders' concerns related to the legal costs involved in bringing private enforcement actions for infringements of EU intellectual property law. In a similar manner, the Commission's (non-legally binding) Collective Redress Recommendation also leaves the Member States a large margin of manoeuvre when setting rules on legal costs.[129]

The result is therefore somewhat of a paradox. On the one hand, the importance of legal costs for the private enforcement of EU law is generally not in doubt. On the other hand, as it stands this subject matter is hardly addressed in a meaningful manner in EU law. This state of affairs can probably be explained by two considerations in particular. First, many find that EU "interference" is undesirable in this domain. There appears to be a general preference to leave this subject matter to be regulated by the Member States, as a matter of subsidiarity and so as to avoid fragmentation at national level. Second, as was the case in relation to the aforementioned measures on the disclosure of evidence, concerns about creating or encouraging a "litigation culture" are frequently voiced in this connection. That applies especially where possible rules of EU law would entail a deviation from the generally accepted "loser pays" principle. In this light, it is probably no coincidence that the above-mentioned rule set out in the IPR Enforcement Directive, which is broadly consistent with this principle, did get adopted, whereas the Commission's earlier suggestion to include a rule on legal costs in the Competition Damages

126 Art. 14 IPR Enforcement Directive 2004/48. See subsection 4.B.5 above. See also the "general rules" set out in Art. 3(1) IPR Enforcement Directive 2004/48, discussed in subsection 4.A.2 above, pursuant to which the measures, procedures and remedies for the enforcement of the intellectual rights set out in this directive may not be '*unnecessarily complicated or costly*'.

127 CoJ case C-406/09, *Realchemie*, para 49.

128 For another (scarce) example of EU involvement in this domain, see Art. 11(4) Environmental Impact Assessment Directive 2011/92. Cf. CoJ case C-260/11, *Edwards*, para 40–48; CoJ case C-427/07, *Commission v Ireland*, para 92–4; CoJ case C-530/11, *Commission v UK*, para 33–72.

129 Points 13 and 30 Collective Redress Recommendation 2013/396. See subsection 5.E.2 above.

Directive, which could have implied a deviation from this principle, received considerable criticism and was eventually dropped.

It might therefore seem unlikely that the EU will take additional private enforcement-related legislative measures on legal costs in the foreseeable future. That applies all the more so because not only the Member States represented in Council mostly tend to be of the above views, as is perhaps to be expected, but also its co-legislator, the European Parliament. The watering down of the IPR Enforcement Directive's rule on legal costs largely occurred at the insistence of the two EU co-legislators. And in 2012 the European Parliament declared that '*Member States are to determine their own rules on the allocation of [legal] costs*', while also insisting that '*there can be no action without financial risk*'.[130] Nonetheless, it is uncertain whether this means that this matter is therefore to be considered entirely "settled" at EU level. For one thing, legal costs remain of considerable practical importance in the present context. For another thing, the two above-mentioned considerations can be at odds with each other. It remains an open question for the time being what would carry more weight for the EU legislature: its opposition against EU legislative involvement with rules of legal costs (which implies that no EU legislative measures are to be taken) or its desire to ensure that the applicable rules are such as to avoid creating or encouraging a litigation culture (which could imply that certain measures are to be taken, for example prohibiting contingency fees as a matter of EU law). Debates on possible EU legislative measures regarding rules of legal costs applicable in private enforcement proceedings before national courts may therefore well continue.

Finally, it should not be forgotten that the above overview is not exhaustive. **12.22**
That is to say, although this can naturally vary significantly by Member State, the national laws of the Member States regularly also provide for *other* remedies, which remain unregulated as a matter of secondary EU law but which can nonetheless also be of importance for the purposes of the private enforcement of EU law before national courts.[131] One could think in particular of actions for declaratory relief, actions based on unjust enrichment and actions for restitution. This latter remedy, especially, can be relevant here, not least because on this point there is already a well-established body of case law concerning "vertical" situations, pursuant to which private parties can claim the repayment of charges levied contrary to EU law by the Member States' authorities.[132] In its

130 European Parliament, Resolution, Towards a coherent European approach to collective redress, P7_TA(2012)0021, para 20. See also European Parliament, Resolution on the white paper on damages actions for breach of the EC antitrust rules, P6_TA(2009)0187, para 20.

131 See subsection 8.B.6 above.

132 E.g. CoJ case 199/82, *San Giorgio*, para 12; CoJ case C-147/01, *Weber's Wine World*, para 93.

"pure" form restitution can involve an action for the repayment of sums paid from one private party to another as a consequence of an infringement of EU law. As such, an action for restitution could serve as a follow-up to a successful contractual remedy. Actions for "restitutory damages" can be used to claim the *gains made* by the infringer, as opposed to claiming compensation for the *harm caused* by the infringement on the part of the private party applicant through the "classic" actions for damages discussed earlier. These (in so far as secondary EU law is concerned) "unregulated" remedies could therefore conceivably play a role in the EU's broader approach on private enforcement.

Furthermore, noting the existence and the private enforcement potential of the above remedies is not only of relevance with a view to possible future legislative action at EU level in this regard; these remedies can also be of relevance in other ways. In particular, it may not always be easy to clearly distinguish those remedies from the ones that are at present already regulated by the EU legislation facilitating the private enforcement of EU law before national courts at issue here. That is illustrated by the fact that, under the IPR Enforcement Directive's regime on actions for damages, account can be taken of the "unfair profits" made by the infringer. This points to a restitution-related element, even though this directive's overall emphasis remains on the compensatory function of damages awards.[133] Likewise, views can differ as to whether and if so in which cases actions for restitution brought under national law qualify as "actions for damages" within the meaning of the Competition Damages Directive. This latter question is of practical relevance, especially because it determines whether or not this directive's rules on matters such as the non-disclosure of certain items of evidence apply to the legal proceedings in question.[134] Finally, the concept of unjust enrichment can lead to particular complexities of its own, mainly because it can be a double-edged sword. For unjust enrichment may serve as a ground for reclaiming payments made to a party that infringed EU law, but it can also be an argument for rejecting such claims for restitution where they would lead to the overcompensation of the private party applicant.

6. Scope, legal standing, limitation periods and rules of evidence

12.23 A first point to notice when assessing issues of *scope* relating to EU legislation facilitating the private enforcement of EU law before national courts is that the remedies and procedures provided for in the legislation assessed have in principle been made available on a sector-specific basis.[135] Accordingly, the

133 Art. 13(1)(a) and (2) IPR Enforcement Directive 2004/48. See also its recital 26.

134 See in particular Art. 2(4) and Art. 6 Competition Damages Directive 2014/104.

135 See subsection 9.A.1 above.

Procurement Remedies Directives relate to infringements of substantive public procurement law,[136] the IPR Enforcement Directive can be relied upon with respect to infringements of substantive intellectual property law,[137] the Consumer Injunctions Directives correspond to substantive consumer protection law[138] and the Competition Damages Directive is available to private parties wishing to address an infringement of substantive competition law.[139] The Unfair Terms Directive and the Product Liability Directive are somewhat more specific, in that the private enforcement-related rules set out in these two directives only address possible infringements of the substantive rules for which these same directives provide.[140] However, even when leaving these latter two directives aside, the "match" that has thus been established between remedial and procedural rules, on the one hand, and the substantive rules, on the other hand, is far from clear-cut, for several reasons.

First, the above-mentioned legislation tends not to extend to *all* rules of substantive EU law in the particular sector at issue. The Procurement Remedies Directives cover infringements of the rules set out in the two main Substantive Procurement Directives as well as the Concessions Awards Directive, but not the Defence Procurement Directive.[141] Likewise, the Consumer Injunctions Directive lists in its annex many but not all acts of substantive EU consumer protection law, just as the Competition Damages Directive only addresses infringements of competition law in a narrow sense, namely Articles 101 and 102 TFEU (thus excluding for example EU rules on state aid). And while the scope of the IPR Enforcement Directive is wide (if rather unspecific),[142] in the field of intellectual property law other private enforcement-related rules have been included in certain more specific acts of secondary EU law (such as the Infosoc Directive[143]), whereas in 2013 the Commission moreover proposed a *lex specialis* concerning trade secrets.[144] Second – and more remarkably perhaps

136 Art. 1(1) Procurement Remedies Directives 89/665 and 92/13. See subsection 3.A.2 above.

137 Art. 2(1) IPR Enforcement Directive 2004/48. See subsection 4.A.2 above.

138 Art. 1(2) and Annex I Consumer Injunctions Directive 2009/22. See subsection 5.B.2 above.

139 Art. 1(1) read in conjunction with Art. 2(1) and (3) Competition Damages Directive 2014/104. See subsection 6.C.1 above.

140 See subsections 5.C.1 and 5.D.1 above.

141 Instead, the text of Procurement Remedies Directives 89/665 and 92/13 has, with some limited adaptations, essentially been "copied into" Defence Procurement Directive 2009/81 (see its Art. 55–64).

142 See recital 13 IPR Enforcement Directive 2004/48. See also Commission, Statement concerning Article 2 IPR Enforcement Directive 2004/48, OJ 2005, L 94/37.

143 See Art. 8 Infosoc Directive 2001/29.

144 Also the enforcement-related provisions of this proposed directive on trade secrets are essentially, yet not entirely, the same as the ones set out in IPR Enforcement Directive 2004/48. See Commission, Proposal for a trade secrets directive, COM(2013) 813.

– both the IPR Enforcement Directive and the Competition Damages Directive cover not only infringements of the relevant rules of *EU* law, but also of certain rules of *national* substantive law applicable in the field of law at issue. While this can arguably be explained with reference to the specifics of these two fields of law, this nonetheless demonstrates that the EU legislature can in certain cases also be concerned with the effective private enforcement of national law before national courts. Third and finally, it is noticeable that in this legislation the point that private enforcement is only possible where the provisions of substantive law at issue confer *rights* on the private parties concerned is not always clearly articulated. The Procurement Remedies Directives and the Consumer Injunctions Directive do not make reference to the concept of a "right" at all. The former essentially refer to infringements of *EU law* in the field of public procurement generally, whereas the latter similarly defines the concept of an "infringement" as any act contrary to the *directives* listed in its annex which harms the collective interests of consumers. It appears, however, that here the intention has not been to break the link between rights and remedies (*ubi ius, ibi remedium*). The better view is probably that when drafting these directives it was simply presumed – on the whole seemingly correctly – that in these cases also the relevant rules of substantive law confer rights on private parties on which they can rely before national courts and that it is in relation to infringements of those rights that the remedial and procedural rules set out therein can be invoked.

12.24 One of the most important procedural issues touched upon in the foregoing is that of *legal standing* (*locus standi*), which refers to the rules that determine which parties are entitled to initiate private enforcement proceedings under the applicable EU legislation.[145] In many respects the EU's involvement with this issue echoes the more general tendencies touched upon earlier. For private enforcement to be a realistic option for private parties affected by infringement of certain rules of substantive EU law, it is evidently of crucial importance to ensure that these parties are not precluded from bringing a case. All EU legal acts under consideration therefore contain rules on legal standing. The IPR Enforcement Directive specifies, for example, which four categories of parties should in principle be allowed to bring a case.[146] It is even one of the main aims of the Consumer Injunctions Directive to specify which entities are entitled to act upon (alleged) infringements of the relevant EU consumer protection rules.[147] One might thus be inclined to conclude that EU law typically regulates this subject matter to a great extent.

145 See subsection 9.A.2 above.

146 Art. 4 IPR Enforcement Directive 2004/48. See subsection 4.C.1 above.

147 Art. 4 Consumer Injunctions Directive 2009/22. See subsection 5.B.2 above.

However, the provisions of EU law in question have often been drafted in such a way that the Member States did not need to take any action to comply with them. The express statement by the EU legislature (at the time only the Council) in relation to the Procurement Remedies Directives' rule on legal standing that it did not wish to '*jeopardise*' the logic of the existing domestic legal systems of the Member States seems illustrative.[148] Mostly at the insistence of the Member States, almost all provisions in question therefore contain express references to national law. These references are sometimes limited to the applicable detailed rules, as is the case under the Procurement Remedies Directives. But in other instances they appear to relate to the more fundamental question as to which parties are entitled to initiate private enforcement proceedings in the first place. For example, three of the four categories of potential applicants specified in the IPR Enforcement Directive (only) have legal standing '*in so far as permitted by and in accordance with the rules of the applicable law*'. The degree of harmonisation provided for is thus often more limited than might appear at first sight. In many respects the relevant provisions of EU law tend to confirm the pre-existing rules of national law as much as they may lead to these rules being altered.

It would seem therefore that this is another situation where the dynamic interplay between the EU legislature and the EU judiciary might be of particular importance. For the Court of Justice may well derive from the above provisions more ambitious requirements as a matter of EU law. With respect to the Procurement Remedies Directives, the Court has already signalled that, while the inclusion of an express reference to national law may allow the Member States a certain margin of manoeuvre, the exercise thereof should not endanger the effectiveness of these directives.[149] Conversely, the Competition Damages Directive, where an express reference to national law is notably absent in relation to the issue of legal standing, is an example of a case where the EU legislature codified and built on earlier case law.[150] More generally, even if much remains to be clarified, when seen in light of the Court's other case law on legal standing-related issues[151] as well as the need for an interpretation that is consistent with the fundamental right to an effective remedy guaranteed under

148 Council, doc. 7834/89 ADD 1, p. 7.

149 CoJ case C-410/01, *Fritsch*, para 28–34.

150 See in particular Art. 1(1) and recitals 12 and 13 Competition Damages Directive 2014/104. Cf. CoJ case C-453/99, *Courage*, para 24; CoJ joined cases C-295/04 to C-298/04, *Manfredi*, para 59 and 61. See subsection 6.C.5 above.

151 See e.g. CoJ case C-253/00, *Muñoz*, para 32; CoJ case C-174/02, *Streekgewest Westelijk Noord-Brabant*, para 18–20; CoJ case C-132/05, *Commission v Germany (Parmesan cheese)*, para 68–71; CoJ case C-240/09, *Lesoochranárske zoskupenie*, para 51.

the Charter,[152] the Court may well be inclined to interpret the above provisions rather extensively, without, however, creating an *actio popularis*.

12.25 Another procedural issue that is often of particular importance in a private enforcement context is that of *limitation periods*.[153] These periods determine before which date an aggrieved private party must initiate legal proceedings to address an (alleged) infringement of EU law, should it wish to do so. Rules of this kind serve to ensure legal certainty, particularly for possible defendants and affected third parties. At the same time, their length and application in specific cases should not be such as to deprive the private parties concerned from a reasonable opportunity to bring a private enforcement action. In particular, the Procurement Remedies Directives, the Product Liability Directive and the Competition Damages Directive all contain relatively detailed rules in this regard.[154] When considering these rules in their totality, it appears that the EU legislature tends not to rely on a one-size-fits-all approach where limitation periods are concerned. Instead, the balance between the various interests at stake is often struck in a slightly different manner in light of the specific objectives that the directives in question seek to achieve and the particularities of the field of law at issue.

The rules on limitation periods set out in the three above-mentioned directives accordingly each have certain specific characteristics. Although this depends on the form of relief sought, the Procurement Remedies Directives provide for limitation periods that are generally very short (as little as ten days in certain cases). This is consistent with these directives' aim to ensure that the judicial review is not only effective, but also – and in particular – rapid. By contrast the time periods set out in the Product Liability Directive primarily serve as a sort of temporal "counterbalance" against the "strict" liability provided for in this directive. This directive therefore not only provides for a relatively short limitation period for damages claims (three years), but it also lays down an additional period after which all relevant rights are extinguished in any case. The Competition Damages Directive's rules on limitation periods relating to possible damages claims brought under this directive stand out as being "claimant-friendly". These rules seek to ensure that any limitation period has a considerable length (five years), while allowing the Member States to set longer periods. These rules also determine, in a manner that is rather "generous" to

152 Art. 47 Charter. See section 2.B and subsection 11.B.5 above.

153 See subsection 9.B.1 above.

154 Art. 2c and Art. 2f(1) and (2) Procurement Remedies Directives 89/665 and 92/13; Art. 10 and 11 Product Liability Directive 85/374; Art. 10 Competition Damages Directive 2014/104. IPR Enforcement Directive 2004/48 addresses this issue only in a very general manner (see its Art. 3(1)). See subsections 3.C.2, 5.D.2, 6.C.5 and 4.C.2 above, respectively.

(potential) private party applicants, the moment at which the limitation period begins to run and they specify that these periods are to be suspended until after the completion of any relevant public enforcement investigations and proceedings.

Turning to *rules of evidence*, the main conclusion to be drawn here is that the EU legislation assessed here only sporadically specifies which party has the burden of proof in private enforcement proceedings and how the available evidence is to be assessed.[155] For the most part it seems to be simply presumed that in accordance with the relevant rules of national law it is for the private party applicant to substantiate their claims and for the national court seised to assess the evidence brought before it. It is true that the Product Liability Directive specifies what applicants must demonstrate for liability in damages to be incurred and what defendants must demonstrate to be able to rely on the defences set out in this directive, including what is known as the "development risk defence".[156] However, the point here seems more one of making clear that the liability provided for is "strict" and that the said defences are available rather than one of addressing the burden of proof proper. The same essentially applies with respect to the Competition Regulation, which stipulates that it is for the applicant to prove that an infringement occurred, while the defendant must prove that the conditions of Article 101(3) TFEU have been met if it wishes to rely on this provision by means of a defence.[157] **12.26**

Even if the Commission eventually did not pursue its earlier suggestion to provide for a rebuttable presumption of fault in competition cases,[158] the Competition Damages Directive is still comparatively ambitious where rules of evidence are concerned. Most notably, it regulates the effects in private enforcement proceedings of infringement decisions taken by public enforcement authorities (and the national court reviewing these decisions) as either irrefutable or *prima facie* evidence, it includes particular rules of evidence regarding cases where the harm may have been "passed on" to a third party and it provides for a rebuttable presumption that certain infringements caused harm.[159] While these rules go further than the ones set out in the other EU legislation looked at

155 See subsection 9.B.2 above.

156 Art. 4 and 7 Product Liability Directive 85/374. See subsections 5.D.1 and 5.D.2 above, respectively.

157 Art. 2 Competition Regulation 1/2003. See subsection 6.A.1 above.

158 See in particular Commission, White paper on damages actions for breach of the EC antitrust rules, COM(2008) 165, pp. 6–7.

159 Art. 9 (effects infringement decisions), Art. 13 and 14(1) and (2) (passing-on) and Art. 17(2) (quantification of harm) Competition Damages Directive 2014/104. See subsections 6.C.5, 6.C.4 and 6.C.2 above, respectively.

here, elsewhere in EU law comparable rules of evidence can be found, particularly rebuttable presumptions and reversals of the burden of proof.[160] Seen in this broader perspective, the above rules on the effects of infringement decisions appear to be the most innovative and perhaps for that reason also the most controversial.

7. Forum, rules facilitating settlements and judicial review

12.27 This study indicates that detailed EU rules on *forum* (that is, the national courts or other bodies before which the private enforcement proceedings at issue are to be brought) are unusual at least so far as the EU legislation assessed in the foregoing is concerned.[161] In fact, hardly any such rules are provided for regarding situations where the private enforcement claims in question are presumed to be brought before a *civil* court, as is the case under the Product Liability Directive, the IPR Enforcement Directive and the Competition Damages Directive (although the reference in this latter directive to Article 267 TFEU on the preliminary reference procedure implies that indirectly certain requirements apply[162]). The situation is more heterogeneous, however, under the Procurement Remedies Directives and consumer protection directives such as the Consumer Injunctions Directive and the Unfair Terms Directive.[163] Probably in light of the differences existing at national level, these latter directives leave the Member States the choice of whether to designate a judicial or a non-judicial body to rule on the claims brought on the basis of these directives. These *judicial* bodies can be either civil or administrative courts. In those cases, again, no further requirements have been specified. But this can be different where these bodies are *non-judicial* in character, such as an administrative appeal board or an ombudsman. In particular, the Procurement Remedies Directives illustrate that in those cases additional and rather detailed requirements can apply, which essentially aim to ensure that the review exercised is independent and impartial.[164] These requirements include rules on the composition of the review bodies concerned, the parties' right to be heard, decisions being reasoned and in writing as well as the possibility of making preliminary references to the Court of Justice.

160 See e.g. Art. 6(1) and (2) Electronic Signatures Directive 1999/93; Art. 8 Racial Equality Directive 2000/43; Art. 5(3) and (4) Air Passengers' Rights Regulation 261/2004; Art. 19 Gender Equality Directive 2006/54; Art. 6(9) Consumer Rights Directive 2011/83; Art. 20(3) Public Limited Liabilities Companies Directive 2012/30.

161 See subsection 9.C.1 above.

162 See Art. 2(9) Competition Damages Directive 2014/104. See subsection 6.C.5 above.

163 Art. 2(9) Procurement Remedies Directives 89/665 and 92/13; Art. 2(1) Consumer Injunctions Directive 2009/22; Art. 7(2) Unfair Terms Directive 93/13. See subsections 3.C.3, 5.B.2 and 5.C.2, respectively.

164 See e.g. also Art. 11(1) Unfair Commercial Practices Directive 2005/29; Art. 5(1) Misleading Advertising Directive 2006/114.

It thus appears that often a considerable degree of "residual" procedural autonomy remains for the Member States where rules of forum are concerned. As the Court of Justice has consistently held ever since *Rewe*, it is, in the absence of specific EU rules, in principle for each Member State to designate the national courts having jurisdiction to rule on private enforcement actions and to specify the detailed rules that apply in this respect.[165] The assessment in the foregoing suggests that secondary EU law on private enforcement of the type at issue mostly leaves this general rule unaffected, particularly where the Member States designate bodies that are judicial in character. Put simply, the EU legislature appears to trust that the (civil or administrative) courts of the Member States will do their work in an independent, impartial and fair manner. Yet it tends to be less inclined to do so where the task of ruling on the private enforcement actions in question is attributed to administrative authorities or other non-judicial bodies.

The EU legislation under consideration aims to encourage the *out-of-court settlement* of disputes involving alleged infringements of EU law essentially in two distinct ways.[166] In the first possible way, rules on *pre-trial contacts* do so by obliging potential applicants to first contact the alleged infringers before initiating legal proceedings. Rules of this kind are typically found in the acts that expressly allow for review by administrative courts, notably the Consumer Injunctions Directive and the Procurement Remedies Directives.[167] A second possible way is the provision of rules on *alternative dispute resolution*, which in contrast presume that the parties concerned are unable to resolve the dispute between them and therefore provide for the involvement of (non-judicial) outside entities of some sort. Leaving aside the Procurement Remedies Directives' aforementioned broadly formulated rules on forum mentioned above (which could entail arbitration) and the "conciliation mechanism" for which one of these directives provided until their revision in 2007,[168] it has been seen that the EU legislation at issue does not set out rules on alternative dispute resolution as such. The focus is squarely on facilitating *judicial* redress. However, the Competition Damages Directive nonetheless includes certain rules that expressly seek to *encourage* attempts at settling disputes out-of-court, especially by specifying the effects thereof on legal proceedings brought under this directive (suspension of limitation periods and possibly also of legal **12.28**

165 CoJ case 33/76, *Rewe*, para 5.

166 See subsection 9.C.2 above.

167 Art. 1(4) and (5) Procurement Remedies Directives 89/665 and 92/13; Art. 5 Consumer Injunctions Directive 2009/22. See subsections 3.C.3 and 5.B.2 above, respectively. See e.g. also Art. 11(1) Unfair Commercial Practices Directive 2005/29.

168 Art. 9–11 Utilities Remedies Directive 92/13, as it stood before the 2007 amendment. See subsection 3.D.1 above.

proceedings; reduction of claims for compensation and contribution).[169] This illustrates that the EU legislature does not see judicial redress and alternative dispute resolution as being entirely unrelated. It also illustrates more generally that interest at EU level in alternative dispute resolution appears to be increasing, as the adoption in 2013 of the Consumer ADR Directive also illustrates.[170]

Two additional points merit being noticed here. In the first place, the above-mentioned provisions of EU law are characterised by their *optional nature*. The rules on pre-trial contacts can be binding on the parties concerned, but they are mere options available to the Member States. The reverse is true for the rules on alternative dispute resolution referred to above. These latter rules are binding on the Member States, but they are optional for the parties concerned. Neither the Competition Damages Directive nor the Consumer ADR Directive obliges private party applicants to have recourse to alternative dispute resolution mechanisms. In the second place, there is generally little doubt that out-of-court settlements and alternative dispute resolution can have certain advantages, notably in terms of lower costs, informality and speed. This is therefore potentially an interesting way to resolve disputes involving infringements of EU law. Yet there can also be certain *disadvantages*, especially for (potential) applicants. The above directives mostly address these disadvantages in so far as possible delays and the associated risks during attempts to reach a settlement (such as the expiry of limitation periods) are concerned. However, the EU legislature seems to take a narrower view than the EU judiciary on this point, given that the latter also tends to take account of possible additional costs and practical complications for the private parties concerned.[171] Another, more general, potential disadvantage that tends to receive only limited attention is how to safeguard the general interest associated with issues such as the legality of any settlement reached between the parties and the lack of transparency of settlements.[172]

12.29 Finally, two procedural issues that both relate to the *judicial review* to be exercised by national courts seised in private enforcement proceedings are to be considered, namely the standard of judicial review and the question of whether those courts are required to raise certain points of EU law of their own motion (*ex officio*, that is, without any of the parties to the proceedings having raised these points). Both issues have in common that none of the private enforcement-related EU legislation assessed in the foregoing addresses them expressly. But in both instances certain requirements have nonetheless been

169 Art. 18–19 Competition Damages Directive 2014/104. See subsection 6.C.5 above.

170 Consumer ADR Directive 2013/11. See subsection 5.E.3 above.

171 CoJ case C-63/01, *Evans*, para 44–58; CoJ joined cases C-317/08 to C-320/08, *Alassini*, para 52–66.

172 See also subsection 11.A.3 above.

developed in the case law. As regards the *standard* of judicial review the Court has held in particular that it is not compatible with the objective of the Procurement Remedies Directives if the test to be applied is limited to whether or not the defendant acted in an arbitrary manner.[173] For now it remains to be clarified what standard is then required under these directives and whether – and if so, to what extent – this ruling can be applied more broadly. There is other case law suggesting that EU law generally (especially the principle of effectiveness) does not require "full" judicial review, that is, the empowerment of a national court to substitute its own assessment for that of the defendant.[174] Consequently, the required standard arguably lies somewhere in between a test of arbitrariness and full review. Yet it cannot be excluded that a higher standard applies in cases brought under secondary EU law of the type at issue here, as compared with cases where no such legislation applies and which therefore fall within the procedural autonomy of the Member States.

At least as many questions can arise with respect to EU law requirements regarding the possible *own-motion review* by a national court in private enforcement litigation.[175] Such an obligation implies a deviation from the predominantly passive role of those courts, particularly in legal proceedings between private parties, under the domestic laws of the Member States, which the Court of Justice has accepted as a general rule.[176] In a remarkable line of case law the Court has, however, also clarified that under the Unfair Terms Directive an *obligation* of own-motion review exists in principle, in light of the often weak position of consumers and the nature and importance of the public interest underlying consumer protection in the EU legal order.[177] The Court has further held that in competition cases a similar obligation can exist, at least where the possible annulment of arbitration awards is concerned, whereby the importance of the EU rules in question has again been highlighted, without, however, making it clear precisely in which situations and on which grounds such an obligation exists in this field of law.[178] By contrast, in relation to the Procurement Remedies Directives the Court has left this question primarily to be determined by national law, while noting at the same time that these directives

173 CoJ C-92/00, *Hospital Ingenieure*, para 57–64. See subsection 9.D.1 above.

174 CoJ case C-120/97, *Upjohn*, para 30–37.

175 See subsection 9.D.2 above.

176 E.g. CoJ joined cases C-430/93 and C-431/93, *Van Schijndel*, para 21; CoJ joined cases C-222/05 and C-225/05, *Van der Weerd*, para 28.

177 See in particular CoJ joined cases C-240/98 and C-244/98, *Océano Grupo*, para 22–9. See subsection 5.C.2 above.

178 See CoJ joined cases C-430/93 and C-431/93, *Van Schijndel*, para 13–14 and 22; CoJ case C-126/97, *Eco Swiss*, para 36–41; CoJ joined cases C-295/04 to C-298/04, *Manfredi*, para 31; CoJ case C-8/08, *T-Mobile Netherlands*, para 49. See subsection 6.A.1 above.

can *preclude* own-motion review.[179] The overall picture that thus emerges is therefore far from clear. Further clarification is awaited. Nonetheless, it would appear that the nature or importance of the rules of substantive EU law at stake in the above-mentioned cases is not the decisive element in explaining these differing outcomes. The crucial issue seems rather a desire on the part of the Court to ensure the effective protection of the rights that the private parties concerned derive from EU law. While in some cases this consideration can argue in favour of own-motion review, in other instances it can argue against it.

C. PRIVATE ENFORCEMENT IN PERSPECTIVE

In many respects a central theme running through the two preceding sections has been the tension between EU "interference" and the Member States' "autonomy" where the possible adoption of EU legislation facilitating the private enforcement of EU law before national courts is concerned. This last section, where the emphasis is more on private enforcement generally, has a somewhat different central theme, namely the relevance of the distinction and interaction between "public" and "private" in private enforcement-related matters in the present context. A question that is of particular importance in this connection is whether and, if so, to what extent private enforcement can and should be understood as an enforcement instrument in the general interest. This distinction and interaction between "public" and "private" further plays a role in relation to the concluding remarks on the matters assessed in the foregoing, together with a number of other inherent limitations and points of particular attention that arise in connection with EU legislation of the type under consideration here. These two issues are subsequently addressed in the two final subsections of this book.

1. Private enforcement as a supplementary enforcement instrument

12.30 The foregoing has shown that the relationship between public and private enforcement is both an important and a complex issue in the present context. Just as the enforcement of the rights that private parties derive from EU law normally takes place in proceedings before national courts, public enforcement also mostly takes place at national level.[180] The Commission itself is only exceptionally empowered to address (alleged) infringements of rules of substantive EU law by private parties, notably in the field of EU competition law.[181]

179 CoJ case C-315/01, *GAT*, para 46–55. See subsection 3.B.2 above.

180 See in particular subsections 1.A.1 and 2.C.2 above.

181 See subsections 2.C.2 and 6.D.2 above.

Consequently, the responsibility for ensuring public enforcement normally lies with the Member States where compliance with EU law by private parties is concerned. In this respect EU law typically requires the Member States to provide for effective, proportionate and dissuasive penalties. The Member States can also be required to designate public enforcement authorities to exercise certain powers to investigate, terminate and punish infringements. However, the extent of these requirements and these powers tends to differ significantly between the various fields of EU law.

When considering these public enforcement-related obligations under EU law and the EU legislation facilitating the private enforcement of EU law before national courts discussed above in their totality, the starting point is that these are to a great extent two largely *unrelated* matters.[182] These two sets of obligations exist for the most part independently from each other. A Member State will, for instance, generally not be deemed to have fulfilled its duties under EU law to ensure public enforcement of the substantive rules in question merely because it has permitted or facilitated private enforcement. Similarly, whereas for an assessment under the principle of effective judicial protection regard can be had to the entirety of the remedies available to the private party concerned in a given legal system, the availability or absence of certain public enforcement mechanisms does not appear to be a relevant factor in this respect, however.[183] And while private parties can seek to "trigger" public enforcement proceedings by filing complaints, that does not mean that they become a party to the legal proceedings to which their complaint may (or may not) lead.[184] **12.31**

It is true that especially in the field of EU competition law there is a degree of interaction. The Competition Regulation provides for the possibility of *amicus curiae* interventions by the competent public enforcement authorities, including the Commission, in private enforcement proceedings.[185] The Competition Damages Directive further provides for the possibility of such interventions specifically in relation to requests for the disclosure of evidence included in their files and to the quantification of damages.[186] This directive also regulates the effects of findings of infringements in public enforcement proceedings, and the

182 See subsection 10.B.2 above.

183 See also subsection 2.B.1 above.

184 See subsections 2.C.1 (concerning infringement proceedings) and 6.D.2 (concerning the public enforcement of EU competition law) above.

185 Art. 15 Competition Regulation 1/2003. See subsection 6.A.1 above.

186 Art. 6(11) and 17(3) Competition Damages Directive 2014/104. See subsections 6.C.3 and 6.C.2 above, respectively.

suspension of limitation periods until after the termination of public enforcement proceedings, as well as the possibility for the public enforcement authorities concerned, when determining the appropriate penalty for an infringement, to take account of compensation paid to injured private parties pursuant to an out-of-court settlement.[187] But these are on the whole rather limited exceptions. That is already illustrated by the optional nature of most of the abovementioned rules set out in the Competition Damages Directive. Moreover, no comparable rules exist (and to some extent cannot even exist, in the absence of any significant public enforcement obligations under EU law) in other fields of EU law. It is noticeable that both in the field of EU competition law and in the other fields of law under consideration several suggestions and proposals that aimed to connect more closely the two enforcement mechanisms were not taken over by the EU legislature.[188] In legal-procedural terms, public and private enforcement therefore remain for the most part two separate worlds.

12.32 Yet in several other respects public and private enforcement ought not to be considered entirely in isolation from each other. When assessed at a more general level the most evident link between the two is that both forms of enforcement can help increase overall levels of enforcement of and eventually compliance with EU law. Private enforcement is frequently seen as a means to *supplement* (or complement) public enforcement. Broadly speaking, this view rests on the idea that private enforcement can help to draw important resources into the overall "enforcement mix". That can be all the more important given that the resources of the competent public enforcement authorities tend to be limited. This is not only a matter of human and financial resources. Private parties can also have specific expertise and inside knowledge of the practical workings of a particular sector, which might make it easier for them to detect and pursue infringements of EU law than it is for public enforcement authorities.

This insight is by no means a recent one. The possible beneficial effects in terms of increasing the overall enforcement capacity that might result from the "vigilance of individuals" has already played an important role in the Court of Justice's 1963 landmark judgment in *Van Gend en Loos*, which articulated the principle of direct effect of EU law that is a necessary prerequisite for a private enforcement model to function.[189] Similarly, the Commission has already observed over three decades ago that damages awards to injured private parties

187 Art. 9, 10(4) and 18(3) Competition Damages Directive 2014/104. See subsection 6.C.5 above.

188 See subsection 11.B.4 above.

189 CoJ case 26/62, *Van Gend en Loos*. See subsection 1.A.1 above.

'*would render [EU] law more effective*' and might therefore have to be facilitated.[190] More recently, the same thought has been echoed in rulings such as *Courage* and *Muñoz*, where the Court stressed the beneficial effects of private parties being able to address other private parties' (alleged) infringements of EU law in terms of strengthening the working of the substantive rules of EU law in question and discouraging infringements of those rules.[191]

Although the degree to which this has been articulated differs somewhat by the legal act at issue, there can be no doubt that the EU legislation under consideration builds on this insight. The Procurement Remedies Directives, for instance, ultimately aim '*to ensure that the rules of public contracts are correctly applied*'.[192] The Consumer Injunctions Directive similarly seeks to prevent the effectiveness of substantive EU consumer protection law from being '*thwarted*'.[193] Although this "general interest function" of private enforcement litigation is less clearly articulated in the IPR Enforcement Directive, this directive too should be understood against the background of a desire '*to ensure that the substantive law on intellectual property [...] is applied effectively*'.[194] Likewise, the Commission stated in its proposal for the Competition Damages Directive that that directive is meant to act as '*an incentive for better compliance*'.[195] It added that '*[t]he overall enforcement of the EU competition rules is best guaranteed through complementary public and private enforcement*'[196] and that public and private enforcement are '*complementary tools serving the objective of an effective enforcement of the EU competition rules*'.[197] The private enforcement-facilitating measures introduced by this directive should therefore also be seen in light of the desire to further the full effectiveness and practical effects of the substantive EU competition law at issue.[198] The Collective Redress Recommendation similarly declares that '*[t]he possibility for private persons to pursue claims based on violations of such rights supplements public enforcement*'.[199] **12.33**

---

190 Commission, Thirteenth report on competition policy, 1984, p. 136.

191 CoJ case C-453/99, *Courage*, para 25–7; CoJ case C-253/00, *Muñoz*, para 31. See subsections 2.D.2 and 2.D.3 above.

192 Commission, Amended proposal for Public Sector Remedies Directive 89/665, COM(88) 733, p. 10. Cf. recital 2 Procurement Remedies Directives 89/665 and 92/13. See e.g. also CoJ case C-406/08, *Uniplex*, para 26.

193 Recital 4 Consumer Injunctions Directive 2009/22.

194 Recital 3 IPR Enforcement Directive 2004/48.

195 Commission, Proposal for Competition Damages Directive 2014/104, COM(2013) 404, p. 4.

196 Ibid., p. 3.

197 Commission, Impact assessment report on damages actions for breach of the EU antitrust rules, SWD(2013) 203, p. 12.

198 Cf. recital 3 Competition Damages Directive 2014/104.

199 Recital 2 Collective Redress Recommendation 2013/396.

This "general interest function" of private enforcement is also echoed in several of the *specific provisions* on remedial and procedural issues that have been included in the EU legislation at issue. An example is the reference in the IPR Enforcement Directive to the measures, procedures and remedies set out therein being '*effective, proportionate and dissuasive*'.[200] As was noted above, this is what EU law normally requires with respect to the penalties to be provided for by national law as a matter of public enforcement. The Court of Justice has further clarified that the provisions on injunctions and the contractual remedy provided for in the Unfair Terms Directive serve a purpose in terms of deterrence and dissuasion.[201] Along similar lines, the Commission has noted that the injunctive relief available under the Consumer Injunctions Directive can be a '*successful tool for policing markets*' and a '*governance tool [which] can be used as a deterrent*'.[202] Other illustrations are the Procurement Remedies Directives' provisions on "alternative penalties"[203] and the publicity measures for which the IPR Enforcement and the Consumer Injunctions Directive provide, which serve as a "supplementary deterrent" and to inform the public at large.[204]

12.34 The underlying idea is thus essentially to co-opt and "instrumentalise" interested private parties so as to encourage them to play their role as '*the "real guardians" of the legal integrity of [EU] law*'.[205] On this view private enforcement involves private parties as '*law enforcers acting in the public interest, rather than as holders of subjective rights*', as a Commission official argued in 2001 in a competition law context.[206] Others speak of these parties acting as "private policemen"[207] or "private attorneys general".[208] Although these effects have not been investigated or quantified here, there seems little reason to doubt that in this manner the vigilance of interested private parties can indeed make an important contribution to improving overall levels of enforcement of and compliance with the rules of EU law. In all likelihood that applies even more so where private enforcement-facilitating EU legislation of the type at issue here is in place. Nonetheless, the foregoing also indicates that the view whereby private enforcement is primarily or even solely seen in such an "instrumental" manner is

200 Art. 3(2) IPR Enforcement Directive 2004/48.

201 Cf. CoJ case C-372/99, *Commission v Italy*, para 15; CoJ case C-618/10, *Banco Español de Crédito*, para 69.

202 Commission, Second report on Consumer Injunctions Directive 2009/22, COM(2012) 635, p. 7.

203 Art. 2e(2) Procurement Remedies Directives 89/665 and 92/13.

204 Art. 15 IPR Enforcement Directive 2004/48; Art. 2(1)(b) Consumer Injunctions Directive 2009/22. See subsection 8.B.4 above.

205 Weiler (1991), pp. 2413–14.

206 Gyselen (2001), pp. 144–5 (this author was at the time head of unit in the Commission's Directorate General for Competition; this paper was written as a personal title, however).

207 E.g. Drake (2006), p. 843.

208 E.g. Kilpatrick (2000), p. 2.

incorrect or at least incomplete. In this connection the following points in particular can be noted.

To begin with, considering private enforcement primarily as a supplement to public enforcement seems to presuppose that public enforcement mechanisms are in place. In some fields this certainly is the case. Especially in relation to EU competition law infringements, robust and well-entrenched public enforcement mechanisms exist both at EU and at national level.[209] However, in many other fields of law, public enforcement plays at best only a limited role as a matter of EU law. These latter fields include EU public procurement and intellectual property law.[210] It is noticeable that in these two fields precisely have some of the most elaborated EU legal acts facilitating private enforcement been enacted, namely the Procurement Remedies Directives and the IPR Enforcement Directive, respectively. Initially the same held true where the EU's law-making activities in the field of consumer protection law are concerned. The EU's involvement with public enforcement in this field has historically been limited,[211] while several private enforcement-related acts were adopted (Consumer Injunctions Directive, Unfair Terms Directive, Product Liability Directive). Yet more recently attention has focused on strengthening public enforcement, which appears to have come at the expense of the EU's long-standing ambition to facilitate private enforcement in this field. **12.35**

All this suggests that seeing the relationship between public and private enforcement merely in complementary or supplementary terms risks overlooking that – as a matter of policy rather than in strictly legal terms – there can be what rather appears to be a *substitution* effect.[212] That is to say, at least some private enforcement-related EU legal acts of the type under consideration here appear to have been established at EU level not so much as a supplement, but rather as a substitute for weak or even almost entirely absent public enforcement mechanisms under EU law. Put differently, the absence of robust and well-entrenched public enforcement mechanisms as a matter of EU law in a given field may well be an important factor in determining the "demand" for private enforcement-related EU legislation. The considerable difficulties encountered in establishing the Competition Damages Directive seem to confirm this. Many of the concerns expressed in connection with this initiative relate to the negative effects that it might have on the public enforcement already "supplied" in this field. The existence of the latter can thus not only lessen "demand", but it

209 See subsection 6.D.2 above.
210 See subsections 3.D.2 and 4.D.2 above, respectively.
211 See subsection 5.E.4 above.
212 See subsection 10.B.2 above.

might in effect also act as a *barrier* to the adoption of private enforcement-related measures. It is noticeable in this regard that this competition law initiative transformed over time from one that wholeheartedly sought to encourage private enforcement to one that is as much driven by a desire to shield the existing public enforcement structures from the (potential) negative effects of increased private enforcement in this field.[213]

12.36 A second point is that seeing private enforcement principally as a supplement to public enforcement and considering private parties essentially as law enforcers in the general interest places the emphasis squarely on the interests associated with ensuring the effectiveness of EU law *per se*. This largely neglects that ensuring the effective enforcement of the *rights* that private parties may derive from this law can be an objective in its own right. There is no reason to presume that this latter objective is of secondary importance in the EU legal order.[214] As Advocate General Jääskinen observed, applicants in private enforcement proceedings are essentially simply seeking legal protection in relation to a private law claim rather than enforcing a public policy.[215] It can be noted in this connection that, although the Court may at times have seemed ambiguous on this point, it has held that the purpose of the EU law principle of Member State liability is not punishment or deterrence, but rather to ensure that the parties having suffered damage are compensated.[216] In light of the parallelism between these two principles, the situation is unlikely to be fundamentally different where the principle of private party liability, which underlies the concept of private enforcement, is concerned.[217] Moreover, an overly one-sided emphasis on the "general interest function" of damages claims and, by extension, private enforcement actions more generally would seem to sit uncomfortably with the predominant views that the rules of national law of this kind aim to punish and deter only as a *secondary* objective, if at all.[218]

While the EU legislation at issue may therefore have to be seen against the background of a desire to supplement or even substitute public enforcement and thus to improve the effectiveness of the relevant rules of substantive EU law, at the same time it also aims to help the private parties concerned to enforce their (subjective) rights derived from that law.[219] Those parties are obviously the prime beneficiaries, for instance, of the '*high, equivalent and homogeneous level of*

213 See subsection 6.C.1 above.
214 See subsection 11.A.4 above.
215 Opinion AG Jääskinen case C-536/11, *Donau Chemie*, para 48.
216 CoJ case C-470/03, *AGM-COS.MET*, para 88.
217 See in particular subsections 2.D.2 and 2.D.3 above.
218 See subsection 7.A.6 above.
219 See subsection 11.B.2 above.

protection' that the IPR Enforcement Directive aims to establish.[220] The Unfair Terms Directive seeks among other things '*to safeguard the citizen in his role as consumer*',[221] just as the Product Liability Directive makes it clear that '*injured person[s] should be able to claim full compensation*'.[222] The Competition Damages Directive likewise also aims to ensure that the '*Union right to compensation*' can be exercised effectively, in accordance with the principle of effective judicial protection.[223] While (as was the case with the contribution of private enforcement to improving overall levels of enforcement of and compliance with EU law, referred to above) these effects for the private parties concerned have not been investigated or quantified in the foregoing either, it can safely be assumed that the possibilities of enforcing their rights derived from EU law have generally improved as a consequence of the introduction of the specific EU rules on remedies and procedures for private enforcement purposes discussed above.

All this argues for not distinguishing too rigidly between the objectives of ensuring the effectiveness of EU law *per se* and the effective enforcement of the rights that private parties derive from that law. They are intertwined. This distinction also matters little in practice where the two underlying interests (that is, the general interest and the individual interests of the private parties concerned) coincide, as is often the case. A private party who is affected by an infringement of, say, the EU public procurement rules may find it entirely in its own individual interest to initiate legal proceedings so as to have a discriminatory provision struck out from the tender documents, a contract award procedure annulled or damages awarded. At the same time, bringing private enforcement actions of this kind – or indeed already the mere realistic *risk* of such actions being brought – can be an incentive for the parties that are subject to these rules to ensure compliance, which is evidently in the general interest. The thought that both objectives can be reached at the same time and that there can, moreover, be mutual beneficial effects in fact lies at the very heart of the private enforcement model generally and the EU legislation assessed in this book specifically. Concentrating only on the "general interest function" thereof thus risks overlooking the *duality* that is central to the concept of private enforcement as it exists in the EU legal order.

Lastly, the above distinction between ensuring the effectiveness of EU law *per se* **12.37**
and ensuring the effective enforcement of the rights that private parties derive from this law can also be of importance in the present context considering that the two interests involved may at times *collide* rather than *collude* or there can at

220 Recital 10 IPR Enforcement Directive 2004/48.

221 Recital 6 Unfair Terms Directive 93/13.

222 Recital 5 Product Liability Directive 85/374.

223 Recital 4 Competition Damages Directive 2014/104. See also its Art. 1(1).

least be a certain tension between them. This can occur, for instance, in relation to issues such as whether and to what extent infringers who applied for leniency for competition law infringements should be protected from being held liable in private enforcement actions; whether punitive damages are required or to be rejected at EU level; whether out-of-court settlements should be encouraged or treated with some caution; and whether collective redress mechanisms ought to be provided for as a matter of EU law and, if so, in which cases and in what form.[224] As the Commission once put it, in this context there can be an '*[inevitable] trade-off between justice [...] and efficiency*'.[225]

It is submitted that in situations of this kind the Court of Justice is, generally speaking, likely to insist on both interests being *balanced* rather than placing them in a hierarchical relationship.[226] It would appear that both are, in principle, equally fundamental in the EU legal order. In and of itself that does not necessarily mean that the EU legislature is barred from prioritising one interest over the other when it acts in this respect. If and when it does so it must, however, respect certain boundaries, notably in terms of procedural requirements, proportionality and fundamental rights. The aforementioned distinction is important for the present purposes, given that the assessment of an (intended) EU legislative measure on private enforcement, for instance on any of the above-mentioned issues (that is, protection of leniency applicants, punitive damages, settlements, collective redress), often largely depends on which of the two objectives in question is identified as the principal one that the legislature wishes to achieve. For this may well have a bearing on the need for and the specific design of those measures. It can also be of relevance when determining whether and, if so, to what extent the EU's intended action meets the "three-step test" under the principles of conferral, subsidiarity and proportionality.[227]

2. Concluding remarks

12.38 A first concluding remark relates to the conceived role of private parties as "law enforcers in the general interest" mentioned above. Implicit in the foregoing is that these parties can generally be expected to act as such only *up to a certain point*, namely the point at which the general interest and the individual interests of the private parties concerned no longer coincide. In many instances this point might never be reached, considering the parallelism that often exists between

224 See subsection 11.A.3 above.

225 Commission, Staff working paper accompanying the green paper on damages actions for breach of EC antitrust rules, SEC(2005) 1732, pp. 49–50.

226 See subsection 11.A.4 above.

227 See also subsections 10.A.1 and 10.A.2 above.

the two interests. But even apart from the above-mentioned situations where these two interests may fundamentally be at odds with each other, it should not be overlooked that many other factors can also lead a private party to conclude that its interests are not served by initiating or continuing to pursue legal proceedings for an (alleged) infringement of EU law before a national court.

An evident and particularly important factor in practice is the costs involved, seen in light of the possible gains of a private enforcement action for the private party affected by an (alleged) infringement of EU law.[228] Yet in the overall cost/benefit analysis that these parties will typically make in this connection, several other factors can play a role too. These factors include, as the case may be, a fear of harming an existing business relationship or of retaliatory measures; a possible general preference for investing in more forward-looking matters rather than in litigation; limited awareness of the law; emotional or psychological considerations (stress, distraction, uncertainty); and culturally determined views on litigation.[229] Many of these factors can inherently be difficult or even impossible to influence through the adoption of legislation. While it is therefore important to acknowledge and take account of such factors in relation to possible EU legislative measures of the type discussed here, the (potential) importance of factors of this kind should not be taken to mean that a private enforcement model cannot properly function or that these measures are necessarily ineffective. In many respects these measures can be understood as attempts to prevent the aforementioned point from being reached. For instance, the easier it is for a private party to have access to relevant evidence, to quantify the harm suffered or to have its legal costs reimbursed, the more likely it is that this party will deem it in its interest to bring an infringement of EU law to the attention of a national court.

It is, moreover, important to acknowledge that the private parties concerned are autonomous when taking their decisions in this respect. As the Court of Justice has observed, '*in a civil suit, it is for the parties to take the initiative*', which is a reflection of '*fundamental conceptions prevailing in most Member States as to the relations between the State and the individual*'.[230] That implies that the EU legislature may seek to encourage, lure or facilitate private parties into bringing and continuing to pursue private enforcement proceedings before national courts, but that these parties can in the end not be guided, instructed or forced to do so if and when – for whatever reason – they do not deem this opportune. Therefore, just as in a public enforcement context the Commission '*has a*

228 See subsection 11.B.3 above.

229 See subsection 10.C.2 above.

230 CoJ joined cases C-430/93 and C-431/93, *Van Schijndel*, para 21. See e.g. also Opinion AG Geelhoed joined cases C-295/04 to C-298/04, *Manfredi*, para 31.

discretion which excludes the right for individuals to require that institution to adopt a specific position'[231] as regards the bringing of infringement proceedings, which implies that in this connection one can thus at most speak of "privately triggered public enforcement";[232] conversely private parties have such discretion in relation to the bringing of private enforcement proceedings and in the latter context one can thus at most speak of "publicly triggered private enforcement". All this evidently limits the extent to which private enforcement can be used as an instrument for the enforcement of EU law in the general interest.

12.39 In the second place, not all *fields of EU law* may be equally well suited for private enforcement, in light of practical as well as legal considerations. To start with the former (and building on the previous point), in certain fields it can be particularly difficult to provide incentives for the private parties concerned to initiate private enforcement proceedings. A good example is EU consumer protection law. Here the private parties concerned (that is, consumers) by definition do not act in a professional capacity.[233] That means that their resources and expertise might be relatively limited. Some of the other aforementioned factors may also carry particular weight for these parties, such as a lack of awareness of the law and emotional and psychological considerations. At least as important is that in practice the harm caused by infringements of EU consumer protection law may well be comparably modest when considered at the level of the individual consumer ("scattered" damage). This can thus tilt the aforementioned cost/benefit analysis in favour of not taking legal action when an infringement occurs. Distinct yet related issues can arise for legal reasons. It has already been seen how a private enforcement model essentially seeks to build on the parallelism between the general interest and the individual interests of the parties concerned. The concept of a "right" constitutes a crucial link between the two. A private party will normally only be able to bring a private enforcement case where the rule of EU law at issue is capable of conferring rights.[234] If not, there may simply be nothing to "privately enforce". It follows that there may be limited or no scope for private enforcement in situations where the interests at stake are "diffuse" in nature and hard or even impossible to capture in terms of individual rights, as can be the case, for instance, with EU environmental law.[235]

---

231 CoJ case 247/87, *Star Fruit Company*, para 11.

232 See subsection 2.C.1 above.

233 In EU consumer protection law the term "consumer" is normally defined as a natural person acting for purposes falling outside his trade, business, craft or profession. See subsection 5.A.2 above.

234 Cf. recitals 6 and 7 Collective Redress Recommendation 2013/396, where the question of whether or not EU law grants rights to private parties is put at the forefront when indicating in which fields private enforcement could take place.

235 See subsection 11.B.3 above.

It is true that certain particular rules and approaches could help address difficulties of this kind. One could think of facilitating collective redress, notably in situations where EU law does confer rights on private parties but where the damage caused by the infringements at issue is "scattered". The Collective Redress Recommendation suggests that in such cases legal proceedings could be brought either by "representative entities" or by certain public authorities.[236] This approach is comparable with the one found in the Consumer Injunctions Directive, which relies on qualified entities or public authorities to initiate legal proceedings in the collective interest of consumers.[237] Relatively broad rules on legal standing can similarly empower certain non-governmental organisations, trade unions or other third parties to act upon infringements. It appears that this possibility tends to enjoy increasing interest at EU level.[238] However, relying on these third parties can lead to certain complications of its own, for example as regards their funding, case selection, oversight and the distribution of any possible damages awards. Indeed, views can differ as to whether this actually constitutes private enforcement properly speaking. After all, these parties may generally act through civil law means, but they essentially do so in the public – or at least not in a strictly individual – interest. The more these parties are made subject to specific rules and public oversight to address the possible complications referred to above, the less this constitutes private enforcement in a "pure" sense and the more it becomes a sort of "public enforcement by private means".

A third concluding remark is that, while private enforcement might in some cases lead to less expenditure on public enforcement, it is certainly *not cost-free*.[239] There evidently are direct costs, particularly in the form of expenditure on the part of the national courts seised as well as the legal and other costs incurred by the parties to the dispute. In addition there may also be more indirect costs, which tend to be less visible, such as opportunity costs for the parties concerned and costs related to possible "over-deterrence" and "chilling effects" on parties who may decide not to engage in certain not evidently illegal activity out of fear of being sued nonetheless. Costs of this kind are not only borne by the parties directly concerned, but to some extent also by society as a whole. This underlines that private enforcement should not be "over-facilitated". **12.40**

236 Points 5–7 Collective Redress Recommendation 2013/396.

237 Art. 1(1) and Art. 3 Consumer Injunctions Directive 2009/22.

238 See e.g. Art. 3(2) Free Movement of Workers Enforcement Directive2014/54; Art. 11(3) Posting of Workers Enforcement Directive 2014/67. See e.g. also Commission, Proposal for a regulation on the protection of individuals with regard to the processing of personal data and on the free movement of such data, COM(2012) 11, p. 90 (Art. 76(1) and (2)).

239 See subsection 11.B.3 above.

Against this background, concerns regarding the creation or encouragement of a "litigation culture", where private enforcement litigation takes place to an extent that is deemed to be undesirable, harmful or even abusive, have over the decades regularly been voiced in relation to EU legislative measures of the type at issue, particularly by parties who might be defendants in private enforcement actions and by the European Parliament.[240] There can evidently be a degree of tension between the ambition to facilitate a "healthy" degree of private enforcement and the fear that this may lead to "excessive" litigation (even if it were possible to capture both forms of litigation in neat, commonly agreed categories of this kind, which seems unlikely). This tension may to some extent be unavoidable. It results in particular from the aforementioned autonomy of the private parties concerned and the related, in the end rather limited, scope for the EU legislature to guide or control these parties' actions in this respect.

Having said that, it would appear that there generally seems little reason for "litigation culture"-related concerns of this kind. Both as it now stands and for the foreseeable future, EU law is far from providing for the '*toxic cocktail*'[241] of private enforcement-related measures (punitive damages, intrusive pre-trial discovery, class action, contingency fees) that are deemed to have led to excesses in this regard in the United States. Indeed, practical experience with acts such as the Procurement Remedies Directives, the IPR Enforcement Directive and the Product Liability Directive shows that – certainly where damages claims are concerned – the degree of private enforcement litigation in the EU can by no means be called excessive.[242] The Commission therefore seems largely correct in its assessment that under-compensation is at present probably more of a concern than possible overcompensation.[243] And where this is nonetheless deemed a realistic concern, the EU legislature has certain measures at its disposal to address it. Examples of such measures assessed in the foregoing include the threshold amounts for damages set out in the Product Liability Directive,[244] the inclusion of rules on the allocation of legal costs based on the "loser pays" principle,[245] the Competition Damages Directive's rule prohibiting

240 E.g. European Parliament, Resolution on the white paper on damages actions for breach of the EC antitrust rules, P6_TA(2009)0187, para 9; European Parliament, Resolution, Towards a coherent European approach to collective redress, P7_TA(2012)0021, para 2. See also subsections 5.E.2 and 6.B.2 above.

241 Commission, Questions and answers regarding the green paper on consumer collective redress, MEMO/08/741, p. 4.

242 See subsection 7.A.1 above.

243 Commission, Impact assessment report on damages actions for breach of the EU antitrust rules, SWD(2013) 203, p. 18.

244 Art. 9 Product Liability Directive 85/374.

245 See subsection 8.B.5 above.

overcompensation[246] and the IPR Enforcement Directive's general rules requiring safeguards against abuse.[247]

By way of a fourth remark it can be noted that private enforcement typically – although by no means necessarily, as especially the Procurement Remedies Directives illustrate – takes place "*horizontally*" (that is, in legal relationships between private parties). This is thus a difference as compared to public enforcement, which normally works "vertically" (that is, in legal relationships between the state, on the one hand, and a given private party, on the other hand). As such, the increased and increasing possibilities for the private enforcement of EU law created in private enforcement-facilitating EU legislation of the type at issue here both exemplify and extend a gradual trend towards the "horizontalisation" of EU law.[248] This can be seen as transposing and giving further effect to the principle of horizontal direct effect in the procedural and remedial sphere. In the words of the Commission, this can be seen as a '*logical extension*' of the EU's involvement with the substantive law that applies in these horizontal legal relationships.[249] **12.41**

This point can in turn have several important implications in the present context. For one thing, the point of departure in civil litigation is the equality of the parties to the dispute. As a matter of fundamental rights (more specifically, the "civil" right to a fair trial), in private enforcement proceedings the principles of *equality of arms* and *adversarial proceedings* must be respected.[250] This means, for instance, that a private party can only be allowed to carry out searches at the premises of an alleged infringer, as the IPR Enforcement Directive permits, where adequate safeguards have been provided for.[251] For another thing, the more private enforcement is made akin to public enforcement by granting the private party applicants concerned certain powers to investigate or to penalise (alleged) infringements of EU law, the more likely it is that the parties who are subject to these powers may be able to rely on fundamental rights that apply in criminal proceedings, such as the privilege against self-incrimination and the *ne bis in idem* principle.[252] Given that the question of whether or not proceedings

246 See Art. 3(3) Competition Damages Directive 2014/104. See also its Art. 12(1) and (2).

247 Art. 3(2) IPR Enforcement Directive 2004/48. See also Commission, Proposal for a trade secrets directive, COM(2013) 813, pp. 19–20 (Art. 6(2)).

248 See subsection 11.B.1 above.

249 Commission, Proposal for IPR Enforcement Directive 2004/48, COM(2003) 46, p. 5. Cf. e.g. also European Parliament, Resolution on consumer redress, OJ 1987, C 99/203, recital C: '*the substantive rights conferred by [EU] legislation on the consumer must be supplemented by appropriate procedural mechanisms to ensure their enforcement*'.

250 Art. 47 Charter. See section 2.B and subsection 11.B.5 above.

251 Art. 7 IPR Enforcement Directive 2004/28.

252 Art. 48–50 Charter. See subsection 11.B.6 above.

are "criminal" in nature is to be determined on the substance, the fact that private enforcement proceedings are often qualified as "civil" under national law does not necessarily mean that these latter rights cannot be invoked. Therefore, these latter fundamental rights can also conceivably come into play here, for instance in relation to the aforementioned *ex parte* search orders, measures on the disclosure of evidence or possible punitive damages.[253]

Generally speaking, there currently seems little reason to believe, however, that the EU legislation facilitating the private enforcement of EU law before national courts assessed above is such as to raise serious concerns in terms of fundamental rights. Seemingly adequate safeguards tend to be provided for to ensure respect for the right to a fair trial that applies in civil proceedings, while the nature and effects of the measures under consideration do not appear to justify the conclusion that the proceedings in which they are applied must be qualified as criminal in nature. Still, the foregoing implies that there are limits to the extent to which the EU legislature can seek to facilitate private enforcement, in particular where this consists of granting private party applicants certain special powers to fulfil their role as "law enforcers in the general interest". Too strong and too one-sided a focus on improving the position of the applicant might well lead to concerns as regard the position of the defendant in these horizontal situations. This arguably applies even more so where the private enforcement proceedings also involve certain *third parties* (which may for example have relevant information concerning the infringement or whose services are being used in committing the infringement). While it seems that generally little attention tends to be paid to questions of this kind when EU legislation of the type at issue here is enacted, this therefore remains a point of particular attention.

12.42 That brings us to the last concluding remark, which concerns *EU policy* on private enforcement. It departs from the observation that at present no such policy to speak of exists. It has been seen in the foregoing that only very few general lines can be discerned where the EU's law-making activities in this regard are concerned. It is evident that in some instances the EU legislature has deemed it necessary to take measures to facilitate private enforcement, for reasons relating to the effectiveness of EU law *per se* as well as the effective judicial protection of the private parties concerned. It also seems to be accepted that these measures can entail the introduction of a range of remedial or procedural provisions applicable in proceedings before national courts, which generally still leave the Member States considerable flexibility. But beyond that

253 See subsections 8.B.2 (measures on the disclosure of evidence) and 7.A.5 (punitive damages) above, respectively.

there is limited common ground. One of the few better articulated points of general application is that anything that might lead to the excesses which are perceived to exist in the United States is considered something that is to be rejected. To the extent that the EU has a policy on private enforcement it thus seems to be characterised mainly by agreement on what it should *not* entail.

It is submitted that there are nonetheless good reasons for establishing such an EU policy that is worthy of the name. Concerns relating to compliance with and the enforcement of EU law at national level continue to be a matter of particular concern in the EU legal order.[254] Notwithstanding its inherent limits, private enforcement can – and indeed already does – play a particularly important role in addressing these concerns. The coherence, acceptance and practical effects of any EU legislative measures adopted under this aim are likely to increase when they are underpinned by a proper policy. The more frequently and extensively the EU legislature acts on private enforcement-related matters, the more reason there is for developing such a policy. While for legal as well as political reasons the EU may not have a free hand in designing and implementing an all-encompassing policy on the enforcement by private parties of their rights derived from EU law before national courts, establishing an overarching policy regarding the situations where it does act (or contemplates acting) is arguably the best manner to address and reconcile the complex and sometimes contradictory issues that can arise in this connection. This is not only a matter of ensuring a coherent and consistent – and therefore probably more credible and effective – approach at EU level, it also relates to fundamental questions of differentiation in terms of enforcement possibilities for private parties and therefore to questions of fairness and equal treatment, which inevitably arise where private enforcement-related action is taken in certain sectors but not in others. These questions extend to the situation at national level, notably in relation to differences that may exist between national jurisdictions in the absence of EU legislative action on this point and to the fragmentation caused within the domestic legal systems of the Member States where EU action of this type is taken on a selective basis.

While this is not the place to expand in detail on the content of any such policy **12.43** on the EU's legislative activities relating to private enforcement before national courts, it would appear that in light of the foregoing, five points merit being noted in particular. First, establishing a general policy does not necessarily mean that a *uniform* (one-size-fits-all) approach should be adopted. Full uniformity in terms of private enforcement-related measures is not required as a matter of EU law and would probably also not do justice to the complexities and the

254 See subsection 1.A.2 above.

specificities of the EU legal order as it stands.[255] Establishing an overarching policy does not preclude addressing certain specific challenges through specific solutions.

Second, an issue to be addressed is the *scope* of the EU legislative action in this regard. There especially appears to be a need to formulate criteria that provide guidance when deciding which substantive rules of EU (or national) law are to be supplemented by specific remedial and procedural rules set out in secondary EU law. These criteria could include, for instance, the enforcement difficulties experienced by private parties, the impact of the infringements in question on the EU's internal market or on other key EU policies, the anticipated effectiveness of private enforcement-related measures and the possible existence of alternative courses of action. Careful consideration and explanation on this point are in place, not only in light of the inevitable fragmenting effects at national level, but also because this choice implies giving preferential status to certain private parties who derive rights from EU law while denying it to other private parties whose rights happen to derive from other, non-selected provisions of substantive EU law (or from "purely" national law).

Third, any such policy should more clearly establish *which objective* (or objectives) the EU wishes to achieve by facilitating private enforcement. This may sound self-evident, but, as has already been seen, there still appears to be considerable ambiguity on this point. That relates particularly to the objectives of strengthening overall levels of compliance with and enforcement of EU law *per se*, on the one hand, and helping the private parties concerned to effectively enforce the rights derived from that law as such, on the other hand. The parallelism that often (although by no means always) exists between these interests is no reason for rather lazily or confusingly mixing and blurring both rationales and the arguments related thereto when addressing the matters at issue here. Clearly and correctly identifying the objective(s) pursued by each EU legislative initiative related to private enforcement is not only important for its own sake, it also determines to a great extent which measures are to be enacted precisely and which not. And it can further be of importance for correctly identifying the required legal basis for the intended EU legal act in question and for an assessment under the principles of subsidiarity and proportionality. Providing for analytical clarity is therefore also a prerequisite for establishing the correct balance between EU "interference" and Member States' "autonomy" discussed earlier.

---

255 See subsection 10.D.3 above.

Fourth, in relation to the objective(s) pursued, a clear line ought to be formulated as regards the *means employed*, especially in terms of the remedies and procedural provisions for private enforcement purposes set out in the EU legislation at issue. This is not merely a matter of "technicalities", such as the manner in which the relevant provisions of EU law are drafted, although that certainly is an important aspect as well. It also extends to more fundamental matters, notably the basic principles and assumptions underlying those provisions (for example, concerning the possible deterrent or punitive function of damages awards, the importance attached to the fact that a contract may already have been concluded pursuant to an infringement, the degree to which national courts are expected to be active in private enforcement proceedings, and so on). Another aspect is outlining the criteria on the basis of which it is decided which remedies and procedural rules are to be provided for in which situations – which is yet another issue in respect of which there currently seems scope for improvement. In other words, this is a matter of deciding as well as properly explaining which "tool" from the private enforcement "toolbox" is to be used in particular cases.

Finally, it is suggested that an EU policy on private enforcement should address the matters discussed above from an *overall enforcement perspective*. This involves, in particular, elaborating on the relationship and interaction between public and private enforcement. One aspect is the need to address in a balanced manner the aforementioned tensions that can exist between the two forms of enforcement. But also more generally the possible existence of and suitability and scope for public enforcement in a given situation can be a relevant factor in determining in which cases the EU is to enact which types of private enforcement-related measures, and vice versa. As has been set out above, the relationship between the two can be as much one of substitution as one of supplementation, particularly where private enforcement is (in part) seen as an enforcement instrument in the general interest. Another aspect is the scope that may exist in certain cases for optimising the relationship between public and private enforcement in legal-procedural terms (for example by allowing public enforcement authorities to intervene in private enforcement proceedings in one form or another). Having said that, it seems equally important, however, to also acknowledge that there are clear limits to the extent to which the distinction between the two forms of enforcement can and should be blurred. For all the possible parallelism in the interests at stake and the mutual reinforcing effects that might exist in this regard, public and private enforcement mostly have different objects, aims and effects. The vigilance of private parties might '*amount to an effective supervision*' in addition to the relevant public enforcement mechanisms, as the Court of Justice held over half a century ago in *Van Gend en Loos*, but in that very same judgment the Court has already made clear that this only applies with respect to the private parties '*concerned*' and, moreover, that the vigilance of these parties serves only '*to protect their rights*'.[256] Indeed, around the same time the Court observed that legal actions brought by private parties under EU law are '*intended to protect individual rights in a specific case*', whereas an action in infringement proceedings – and by extension public enforcement more generally – '*has as its object the general and uniform observance of [EU] law*'.[257] Therefore, while private parties can undoubtedly make a valuable contribution to achieving this latter objective, the fact remains that their vigilance concerns, first and foremost, their own individual interests.

256 CoJ case 26/62, *Van Gend en Loos*, p. 13.
257 CoJ case 28/67, *Firma Molkerei*, p. 153.

BIBLIOGRAPHY

LEGAL LITERATURE

P Aalto, 2011, *Public liability in EU law: Brasserie, Bergaderm and beyond*, Hart.

T Ackermann, 2010, 'Buying legitimacy? The Commission's proposal on consumer rights', *EBLR* 21, pp. 587–602.

R Ackrill and A Kay, 2006, 'Historical-institutionalist perspectives on the development of the EU budget system', *JEPP* 13, pp. 113–33.

D Adamov, B Fazekas and K Tivadar, 2009, 'Damages in trade mark infringements litigation: a comparative analysis of the Hungarian, other European and US jurisdictions,' *JIPLP* 4, pp. 341–6.

A Adinolfi, 2012, 'The "procedural autonomy" of Member States and the constraints stemming from the ECJ's case law: is judicial activism still necessary?', in: HW Micklitz and B De Witte (eds), *The European Court of Justice and the autonomy of the Member States*, Intersentia, pp. 281–304.

J Alfaro and T Reher, 2010, 'Towards the directive on private enforcement of EC competition law: is the time ripe?', *EAR*, pp. 43–6.

A Ancery, 2012, *Ambtshalve toepassing van EU-recht*, Kluwer.

R Anderson, 2012, 'The conclusion of the renegotiation of the World Trade Organization Agreement on Government Procurement: what it means for the Agreement and for the world economy', *PPLR* 21, pp. 83–94.

R Anderson, 2014, 'The coming in force of the revised WTO Agreement on Government Procurement, and related developments', *PPLR* 23, pp. NA160–NA163.

R Anderson and S Arrowsmith, 2011, 'The WTO regime on government procurement: past, present and future', in: S Arrowsmith and R Anderson, *The WTO regime on government procurement: challenge and reform*, Cambridge University Press, pp. 3–58.

A Andreangeli, 2004, 'Courage Ltd v Crehan and the enforcement of Article 81 EC before the national courts', *ECLR* 25, pp. 758–64.

A Andreangeli, 2009, 'From complainant to "private attorney general": the modernisation of EU competition enforcement and private antitrust actions before national courts', in: M Dougan and S Currie (eds), *50 Years of the European Treaties: looking back and thinking forward*, Hart, pp. 229–54.

N Andrews, 2005, 'The new English civil procedure rules (1998)', in: CH Van Rhee (ed.), *European traditions in civil procedure*, Intersentia, pp. 161–84.

A Arnull, 2011, 'The principle of effective judicial protection in EU law: an unruly horse?', *ELRev* 36, pp. 51–70.

S Arrowsmith, 2003, *Government procurement in the WTO*, Kluwer Law International.

S Arrowsmith, 2005, *The law of public and utilities procurement*, Sweet & Maxwell.

S Arrowsmith, J Linarelli and D Wallace, 2000, *Regulating public procurement*, Kluwer Law International.

MJ Azar-Baud, 2010, 'Les actions en cessation en matière de protection des intérêts des consommateurs: á propos de la directive 2009/22/EC', *REDC*, pp. 199–223.

L Azoulai, 2012, 'The case of fundamental rights: a state of ambivalence', in: HW Micklitz and B De Witte (eds), *The European Court of Justice and the autonomy of the Member States*, Intersentia, pp. 207–18.

RM Babirad, 2013, 'The Commission's proposal for a Directive on damages for anti-competitive infringements: an increase in evidentiary accessibility, disclosure and legal certainty for private litigants', *GCLR* 6, pp. 155–60.

D Bailey, 2007, 'Damages actions under the EC Merger Regulation', *CMLRev* 44, pp. 101–39.

SH Bailey, 2015, 'Reflections on standing for judicial review in procurement cases', *PPLR* 24, pp. 122–132.

D Baker, 2014, 'Trying to use criminal law and incarceration to punish participants and deter cartels raises some broad political and social questions in Europe', in: P Lowe and M Marquis (eds), *European competition law annual 2011: integrating public and private enforcement of competition law – implications for courts and agencies*, Hart, pp. 41–62.

S Bariatti, 2011, *Cases and materials on international private law*, Hart.

G Barone and R Amore, 2010, 'Italy', in: A Foer and J Cuneo (eds), *The international handbook on private enforcement of competition law*, Edward Elgar, pp. 346–67.

J Basedow, 2003, 'Who will protect competition in Europe? From central enforcement to authority networks', in: T Einhorn (ed.), *Spontaneous order, organization and the law: roads to a European civil society (Liber amoricum Ernst-Joachim Mestmäcker)*, Asser Press, pp. 15–40.

J Basedow, 2010a, 'The Court of Justice and private law: vacillations, general principles and the architecture of the European judiciary', *ERPL* 18, pp. 443–74.

J Basedow, 2010b, *Enforcing European competition law: harmonising private and public approaches in a more differentiated enforcement model*, Nomos.

J Basedow, J Terhechte and L Tichý (eds), 2011, *Private enforcement of competition law*, Nomos.

B Batchelor, R Pike and M Ghiorghies, 2013, 'Collective distress: European Commission proposal on antitrust damages actions', GCLR 6, pp. 161–6.

F Becker, 2007, 'Application of Community law by Member States' public authorities: between autonomy and effectiveness', *CMLRev* 44, pp. 1035–56.

R Beetz and E Tremmel, 2010, 'Austria', in: J Busche, M Trimborn and B Fabry (eds), *Patent infringement worldwide: claim interpretation, infringement, damages*, Carl Heymanns Verlag, pp. 9–26.

J Bejček, 2011, 'Economic and legal substance of damages', in: J Basedow, J Terhechte and L Tichý (eds), *Private enforcement of competition law*, Nomos, pp. 47–66.

N Bel, 2008, 'Aanscherping van rechtsbescherming in aanbestedingszaken: een bespreking van Richtlijn 2007/66/EG', *NTER* 14, pp. 106–12.

F Benedict, 1995, 'Subsidiarity and antitrust: the enforcement of European competition law in the national courts of the Member States', *LPIB* 27, pp. 247–76.

Y Benhamou, 2009, 'Compensation of damages for infringements of intellectual property rights in France, under Directive 2004/48/EC and its transposition law: new notions?', *IIC* 40, pp. 125–52.

J Bengoetxea, 2008, 'Is direct effect a general principle of European law?', in: U Bernitz, J Nergelius and C Cardner (eds), *General principles of EC law in a process of development*, Wolters Kluwer, pp. 3–24.

P Bentley and D Henry, 2014, 'Antitrust damages actions: obtaining probative evidence in the hands of another party', *WComp* 37, pp. 271–92.

G Betlem, 1999, 'Cross-border private enforcement of Community law', in: J Vervaele (ed.), *Compliance and enforcement of European Community law*, Kluwer, pp. 391–418.

G Betlem, 2003, 'Private handhaving van EG-recht na Muñoz: dat moet kunnen', *NTER* 9, pp. 212–17.

G Betlem, 2007, 'Public and private transnational enforcement of EU consumer law', *EBLR* 18, pp. 683–708.

AE Beumer and A Karpetas, 2012, 'The disclosure of files and documents in EU cartel cases: fairy tale or reality?', *ECJ* 8, pp. 123–51.

A Biondi, 2003, 'Case C-253/00, Antonio Muñoz y Cia, Superior Fruiticola SA v Frumar Ltd, Redbridge Produce Marketing Ltd, Judgment of the Full Court of 17 September 2002, [2002] ECR I-7289', *CMLRev* 40, pp. 1241–50.

A Biondi and M Farley, 2009, *The right to damages in EU law*, Wolters Kluwer.

M Bobek, 2012, 'Why there is no principle of "procedural autonomy" of the Member States', in: HW Micklitz and B De Witte (eds), *The European Court of Justice and the autonomy of the Member States*, Intersentia, pp. 305–24.

M Bogdan, 1998, 'Some reflections regarding the new EU directive on injunctions for the protection of consumers' interests', *CLJ* 6, pp. 369–75.

E Bonadio, 2008, 'Remedies and sanctions for the infringements of intellectual property rights under EC law', *EIPR* 30, pp. 320–27.

C Bovis, 2005, *Public procurement in the European Union*, Palgrave Macmillan.

C Bovis, 2007, *EU public procurement law*, Edward Elgar.

M Bowsher and P Moser, 2006, 'Damages for breach of the EC public procurement rules in the United Kingdom', *PPLR* 15, pp. 195–210.

P Boylan, 2009, 'Draft damages directive: off the agenda for now', *PLC* 28 October.

J Bridge, 1984, 'Procedural aspects of the enforcement of European Community law through the legal systems of the Member States', *ELRev* 9, pp. 28–42.

J Brinkhof, M Van Gardingen and R Hermans, 2010, 'The Netherlands', in: J Busche, M Trimborn and B Fabry (eds), *Patent infringement worldwide: claim interpretation, infringement, damages*, Carl Heymanns Verlag, pp. 163–84.

M Bronckers and NM McNelis, 2012, 'Is the EU obliged to improve the protection of trade secrets? An inquiry into TRIPS, the European Convention on Human Rights and the EU Charter of Fundamental Rights', *EIPR* 34, pp. 673–88.

A Brown, 1998, 'Effectiveness of remedies at national level in the field of public procurement', *PPLR* 11, pp. 89–97.

A Brown, 2015, 'When will publication of a voluntary *ex ante* transparency notice provide protection against the remedy of contract ineffectiveness? Case C-19/13 Ministero dell'Interno v Fastweb SpA', PPLR 24, pp. NA10–NA16.

A Bruns, 2011, 'Private enforcement of competition law: evidence', in: J Basedow, J Terhechte and L Tichý (eds), *Private enforcement of competition law*, Nomos, pp. 127–42.

P Buccirossi and M Carpagnano, 2013, 'Is it time for the European Union to legislate in the field of collective redress in antitrust (and how)?', *JECLP* 4, pp. 3–16.

FW Bulst, 2011, 'Passing-on', in: J Basedow, J Terhechte and L Tichý (eds), *Private enforcement of competition law*, Nomos, pp. 67–82.

M Burgi, 2011, 'EU procurement rules: a report about the German remedies system', in: S Treumer and F Lichère (eds), *Enforcement of the EU public procurement rules*, DJØF, pp. 105–54.

J Burrichter and E Ahlenstiel, 2014, 'Integrating public and private enforcement in Europe, legal and jurisdictional issues: the German perspective', in: P Lowe and M Marquis (eds), *European competition law annual 2011: integrating public and private enforcement of competition law – implications for courts and agencies*, Hart, pp. 95–108.

H Butz, 2014, 'Integrating public and private enforcement of competition law: issues for courts', in: P Lowe and M Marquis (eds), *European competition law annual 2011: integrating public and private enforcement of competition law – implications for courts and agencies*, Hart, pp. 327–34.

L Cadiet, 2005, 'The new French code of civil procedure (1975)', in: CH Van Rhee (ed.), *European traditions in civil procedure*, Intersentia, pp. 49–68.

F Cafaggi and HW Micklitz, 2009, 'Administrative and judicial enforcement in consumer protection: the way forward', in: F Cafaggi and HW Micklitz (eds), *New frontiers of consumer protection: the interplay between private and public enforcement*, Intersentia, pp. 401–46.

D Calisti and L Haasbeek, 2013, 'The proposal for a directive on antitrust damages actions: the European Commission sets the stage for private enforcement in the European Union', *CPI Antitrust Chronicle* August, pp. 1–9.

D Calisti and L Haasbeek, 2015, 'The Directive on antitrust damages actions and its role in the future enforcement of the EU antitrust rules', *CPI Antitrust Chronicle*, January, pp. 2–8.

P Callol, 2010, 'Spain', in: A Foer and J Cuneo (eds), *The international handbook on private enforcement of competition law*, Edward Elgar, pp. 380–94.

R Cambell and A Skinner (ed.), 1976, *The Glasgow edition of the Works and Correspondence of Adam Smith* (volume 2a), Clarendon Press.

S Campbell and T Feunteun, 2014, 'Designing a balanced system: damages, deterrence, leniency and litigants' rights: a claimant's perspective', in: P Lowe and M Marquis (eds), *European competition law annual 2011: integrating public and private enforcement of competition law – implications for courts and agencies*, Hart, pp. 27–40.

C Canenbley and T Steinvorth, 2011, 'Effective enforcement of competition law: is there a solution to the conflict between leniency programmes and private damages actions?', *JECLP* 2, pp. 315–26.

R Caranta, 1995, 'Judicial protection against Member States: a new ius commune takes shape', *CMLRev* 32, pp. 702–26.

R Caranta, 2011a, 'Many different paths, but are they all leading to effectiveness?', in: S Treumer and F Lichère (eds), *Enforcement of the EU public procurement rules*, DJØF, pp. 53–94.

R Caranta, 2011b, 'Damages: causation and recoverable losses', in: D Fairgrieve and F Lichère (eds), *Public procurement law: damages as an effective remedy*, Hart, pp. 167–84.

R. Caranta, 2015, 'The changes to the public contract directives and the story they tell about how EU law works', *CMLRev* 52, pp. 391–460.

C Cauffman, 2010, 'Injunctions at the request of third parties in EU competition law', *MJECL* 17 2010, pp. 58–86

C Cauffman, 2011a, 'The interaction of leniency programmes and actions for damages', *CompLRev* 7, pp. 181–220.

C Cauffman, 2011b, 'Access to leniency-related documents after *Pfleiderer*', *WComp* 34, pp. 597–614.

C Cauffman, 2012, 'The impact of voidness for infringements of Article 101 TFEU on related contracts', *ECJ* 8, pp. 95–121.

C Cauffman, 2013, 'The European Commission proposal for a directive on antitrust damages: a first assessment', *MJECL* 20, pp. 623–34.

C Cauffman, 2015, 'De Richtlijn betreffende schadevorderingen wegens inbreuken op het mededingingsrecht', *SEW* 63, pp. 116–125.

K Chellel, 2009, 'Competition class actions suffer setback as EU shuns directive', *The Lawyer*, 6 October.

M Chisholm, 1997, 'Some observations on the use of injunctions and interdicts in the enforcement of EU law', in: J Lonbay and A Biondi (eds), *Remedies for breach of EC law*, John Wiley & Sons, pp. 73–84.

M Clifton, 2009, 'Ineffectiveness, the new deterrent: will the new remedies directive ensure greater compliance with the substantive procurement rules in the classical sectors?', *PPLR* 18, pp. 165–83.

J Cohen and A Mottet Haugaard, 2010, 'Monetary compensation for trade mark infringements in the European Union', *JIPLP* 5, pp. 372–7.

H Collins, 2011, 'The hybrid quality of European private law', in: R Brownsword et al. (eds), *The foundations of European private law*, Hart, pp. 453–64.

M Comba, 2011, 'Enforcement of EU procurement rules: the Italian system of remedies', in: S Treumer and F Lichère (eds), *Enforcement of the EU public procurement rules*, DJØF, pp. 235–54.

W Cornish, J Drexl, R Hilty and A Kur, 2003, 'Procedures and remedies for enforcing IPRs: the European Commission's proposed directive', *EIPR* 25, pp. 447–9.

W Cornish, D Llewelyn and T Aplin, 2010, *Intellectual property: Patents, copyright, trademarks and allied rights*, Sweet & Maxwell.

P Craig, 2010, *The Lisbon Treaty: law, politics and Treaty reform*, Oxford University Press.

P Craig, 2012, 'Subsidiarity: a political and legal analysis', *JCMS* 50, pp. 72–87.

P Craig, 2013, 'EU accession to the ECHR: competence, procedure and substance', *FILJ* 36, pp. 1114–50.

P Craig and G De Búrca, 2011, *EU law: text, cases and materials*, Oxford University Press.

R Craven, 2014, 'The EU's 2014 Concessions Directive', *PPLR* 23, pp. 188–200.

L Crofts, 2013, 'Legal advice casts doubt on EU damage-claim law', MLex 31 October.

K Cseres, M Schienkel and F Vogelaar (eds), 2006, *Criminalization of competition law enforcement: economic and legal implications for the EU Member States*, Edward Elgar.

B Cupa, 2012, 'Scattered damages: a comparative study about the enforcement deficit of low-value damage and the class actions approach', *ERPL* 20, pp. 507–39.

D Curtin, 1993, 'The constitutional structure of the Union: a Europe of bits and pieces', *CMLRev* 30, pp. 17–69.

K Daele, 2004, 'Regulation 1383/2003: a new step in the fight against counterfeit and pirated goods at the borders of the European Union', *EIPR* 26, pp. 214–24.

D Dahlgaard Dingel, 1999, *Public procurement: a harmonization of the national judicial review of the application of Community law*, Kluwer Law International.

M Danov and F Becker, 2013, 'Concluding remarks on promoting regulatory competition: issues to be addressed', in: M Danov, F Becker and P Beaumont (eds), *Cross-border EU competition law actions*, Hart, pp. 81–95.

M Danov and S Dnes, 2013, 'Cross-border EU competition litigation: new evidence from England and Wales', in: M Danov, F Becker and P Beaumont (eds), *Cross-border EU competition law actions*, Hart, pp. 33–60.

J Davies and E Szyszczak, 2011, 'ADR: effective protection of consumer rights?', *ELRev* 36, pp. 695–706.

M Dawson and E Muir, 2014, 'One for all and all for one? The collective enforcement of EU law', *LIEI* 41, pp. 215–24.

G De Búrca, 1997, 'National procedural rules and remedies: the changing approach of the Court of Justice', in: J Lonbay and A Biondo (eds), *Remedies for breach of EC law*, John Wiley & Sons, pp. 37–46.

PA De Miguel Asensio, 2014, 'Regulation (EU) No 542/2014 and the International Jurisdiction of the Unified Patent Court', *IIC* 45, pp. 868–888.

M De Mol, 2010, 'Kücükdeveci: *Mangold* revisited – horizontal direct effect of a general principle of EU law', *EuConst* 6, pp. 293–308.

J De Werra, 2012, 'Can alternative dispute resolution mechanisms become the default method for solving international intellectual property disputes?', *CWILJ* 43, pp. 39–75.

J Delicostopoulos, 2003, 'Towards procedural primacy in national legal systems', *ELJ*, pp. 599–613.

L Devigne, P Velasco-Martins and A Iliopoulou, 2010, 'Where is ACTA taking us? Policies and politics', in: I Stamatoudi (ed.), *Copyright enforcement and the Internet*, Wolters Kluwer, pp. 29–42.

M Döring and F van Velsen, 2006, 'Is cross-border relief in European patent litigation at an end?', *JIPLP* 1, pp. 858–60.

M Dougan, 1999, 'Cutting your losses in the enforcement deficit: a Community right to the recovery of unlawfully paid charges?', in: A Dashwood and A

Wards (eds), *Cambridge Yearbook of European legal studies 1998*, Hart, pp. 233–67.
M Dougan, 2002, 'Enforcing the single market: the judicial harmonisation of national remedies and procedural rules', in: C Barnard and J Scott, *The law of the single European market*, Hart, pp. 153–80.
M Dougan, 2004, *National remedies before the Court of Justice: issues of harmonisation and differentiation*, Hart.
M Dougan, 2010, 'Who exactly benefits from the Treaties? The murky interaction between Union and national competence over the capacity to enforce EU law', in: C Barnard and O Odudu (eds), *Cambridge yearbook of European legal studies 2009–2010*, Hart, pp. 73–120.
M Dougan, 2011, 'The vicissitudes of life at the coalface: remedies and procedures for enforcing Union law before the national courts', in: P Craig and G De Búrca (eds), *The evolution of EU law*, Oxford University Press, pp. 407–38.
M Dougan, 2012a, 'Judicial activism or constitutional interaction?', in: HW Micklitz and B De Witte (eds), *The European Court of Justice and the autonomy of the Member States*, Intersentia, pp. 113–48.
M Dougan, 2012b, 'From the velvet glove to the iron fist: criminal sanctions for the enforcement of Union law', in: M Cremona, *Compliance and the enforcement of EU law*, Oxford University Press, pp. 74–131.
S Douglas-Scott, 2006, 'A tale of two courts: Luxembourg, Strasbourg and the growing European human rights *acquis*', *CMLRev* 43, pp. 629–65.
D Dragos, B Neamtu and R Veliscu, 2011, 'Remedies in public procurement in Romania', in: S Treumer and F Lichère (eds), *Enforcement of the EU public procurement rules*, DJØF, pp. 155–200.
S Drake, 2005, 'Twenty years after "Von Colson": the impact of "indirect effect" on the protection of the individual's Community rights', *ELRev* 30, pp. 329–48.
S Drake, 2006, 'Scope of Courage and the principle of "individual liability" for damages: further development of the principle of effective judicial protection by the ECJ', *ELRev* 31, pp. 841–64.
BJ Drijber and H Stergiou, 2009, 'Public procurement and internal market law', *CMLRev* 46, pp. 805–46.
I Durant, 2008, 'Causation', in: H Koziol and R Schulze (eds), *Tort law of the European Community*, Springer, pp. 47–79.
M Ebers, 2010, 'From *Océano* to *Asturcom*: mandatory consumer law, *ex officio* application of European law and res judicata', *ERPL* 18, pp. 823–46.
C Ehlermann, 2000, 'The modernisation of EC antitrust policy: a legal and cultural revolution', *CMLRev* 37, pp. 537–90.

C Ehlermann, 2008, 'Foreword', in: A Komninos, *EC private antitrust enforcement: decentralised application of EC competition law by national courts*, Hart, pp. vii–xii.

C Ehlermann and I Atanasiu (eds), 2003, *European competition law annual 2001: effective private enforcement of EC antitrust law*, Hart.

H Eidenmuller, F Faust, H Grigoleit, N Jansen, G Wagner and R Zimmermann, 2011, 'Towards a revision of the consumer *acquis*', *CMLRev* 48, pp. 1077–1123.

T Eilmansberger, 2004, 'The relationship between rights and remedies in EC law: in search of the missing link', *CMLRev* 41, pp. 1199–1246.

T Eilmansberger, 2007, 'The green paper on damages actions for breach of EC antitrust rules and beyond: reflections on the utility and feasibility of stimulating private enforcement through legislative actions', *CMLRev* 44, pp. 431–78.

D Eklöf and L Pehrson, 2008, 'General principles in private law', in: U Bernitz, J Nergelius and C Cardner (eds), *General principles of EC law in a process of development*, Wolters Kluwer, pp. 191–8.

M Eliantonio, 2014, 'Collective redress in environmental matters in the EU: a role model or a "problem child"?', *LIEI* 41, pp. 257–74.

C Esteva Mosso, 2013, 'The European Commission's role: main achievements and next steps', in: N Charbit (ed.), *New frontiers of antitrust 2013*, Bruylant, pp. 133–42.

European academics, 2011, 'Opinion on Anti-Counterfeiting Trade Agreement', *JIPITEC* 2, pp. 65–72.

D Fairgrieve and G Howells, 2007, 'Rethinking product liability: a missing element in the European Commission's third review of the European Product Liability Directive', *MLR* 70, pp. 962–78.

D Fairgrieve and F Lichère, 2011, 'EU: procedures and access to justice in damages claims for public procurement breaches', in: D Fairgrieve and F Lichère (eds), *Public procurement law: damages as an effective remedy*, Hart, pp. 185–96.

M Farley and N Pourbaix, 2015, 'The EU Concessions Directive: building (toll) bridges between competition law and public procurement?', *JECLP* 6, pp. 15–25.

J Fernández Martín, 1996, *The EC public procurement rules: a critical analysis*, Clarendon Press.

D Fields, 2011, 'Injunctions granted in one EU Member State have pan-European effect', *JIPLP* 6, pp. 597–8.

J Fitzgerald and A Firth, 2014, 'Is Article 13 of the Enforcement Directive a redundancy notice for the accounts of profits remedy in the UK?', *JIPLP* 9, pp. 737–41.

J Flower, 2007, 'Negotiating European legislation: the Services Directive', in: C Barnard (ed.), *Cambridge yearbook of European legal studies 2006–2007*, Hart, pp. 217–38.

L Flynn, 2008, 'When national procedural autonomy meets the effectiveness of Community law, can it survive the impact?', *ESA Forum* 9, pp. 245–58.

M Footer, 1995, 'Remedies under the new GATT Agreement on Government Procurement', *PPLR* 4, pp. 80–90.

N Forwood, 2008, 'The Court of First Instance, its development and future role in the legal architecture of the European Union', in: A Arnull, P Eeckhout and T Tridimas (eds), *Continuity and change in EU law: essays in honour of Sir Francis Jacobs*, Oxford University Press, pp. 34–47.

M Frabboni, 2010, 'File-sharing and the role of intermediaries in the market-place: national, European Union and international developments', in: I Stamatoudi (ed.), *Copyright enforcement and the Internet*, Wolters Kluwer, pp. 119–46.

M Frese, 2011, 'Fines and damages under EU competition law: implications of the accumulation of liability', *WComp* 34, pp. 397–432.

D Galetta, 2010, *Procedural autonomy of EU Member States: paradise lost?*, Springer.

AM Galvin, 2015, 'Collective redress and the EU Directive on actions for antitrust damages on parallel paths – where are we now?', *CPI Antitrust Chronicle* February, pp. 2–6.

R Gamble, 2013, 'Whether neap or spring, the tide turns for private enforcement: the EU proposal for a Directive on damages examined', *ECLR* 34, pp. 611–20.

R Gamble, 2014, 'The European embrace of private enforcement: This time with feeling', *ECLR* 35, pp. 469–479.

S Garben, 2013, 'Sky-high controversy and high-flying claims? The Sturgeon case law in light of judicial activism, euroscepticism and eurolegalism', *CMLRev* 50, pp. 15–46.

A Gardella, 2008, 'Torpedoes and actions for negative declarations in international IP litigation', in: A Nuyts (ed.), *International litigation in intellectual property and information technology*, Wolters Kluwer, pp. 181–206.

N Gardner, 2014, 'Mediation and its relevance to intellectual property disputes', *JIPLP* 9, pp. 565–74.

A Gavil, 2014, 'Designing private rights of action for competition policy systems: the role of interdependence and the advantages of a sequential approach', in: P Lowe and M Marquis (eds), *European competition law annual 2011: integrating public and private enforcement of competition law – implications for courts and agencies*, Hart, pp. 3–16.

C Geiger, 2009, 'Intellectual property shall be protected!? Article 17(2) of the Charter of Fundamental Rights of the European Union: a mysterious provision with an unclear scope', *EIPR* 31, pp. 113–17.

C Geiger, 2010, 'Of ACTA, "pirates" and organised criminality: how "criminal" should the enforcement of intellectual property be?', *IIC* 41, pp. 628–32.

C Geiger, J Raynard and C Rodà, 2011, 'What developments for the European framework on enforcements of intellectual property rights? A comment on the evaluation report dated December 22, 2010', *EIPR* 33, pp. 543–9.

W Geursen, 2009, 'Handhaving van het objectieve gemeenschapsrecht via het effectiviteits-beginsel vs subjectieve rechtsbescherming via het nationaal-rechtelijke verbod op reformatio in peius', *NTER* 15, pp. 131–9.

J Giandomenico, 2009, 'Path dependency in EU enlargement: Macedonia's candidate status from a historical-institutionalist perspective', *EFAR* 14, pp. 89–112.

G Gibbons, 2014, 'Trade mark remedies in the United Kingdom and Ireland: recent developments', *EIPR* 36, pp. 22–8.

C Gielen, 2005, 'De Richtlijn handhaving IE-rechten', *NTER* 11, pp. 6–11.

J Golding and P Henty, 2008, 'The new Remedies Directives of the EC: standstill and effectiveness', *PPLR* 17, pp. 146–54.

L Gormley, 1997, 'Remedies in EU public procurement: Community provisions and the United Kingdom', in: J Lonbay and A Biondi (eds), *Remedies for breach of EC law*, John Wiley and Sons, pp. 155–64.

P Gragl, 2014, 'A giant leap for European human rights? The final agreement on the European Union's accession to the European Convention on Human Rights', *CMLRev* 51, pp. 13–58.

M Granger, 2007, 'National applications of Francovich', *ELRev* 32, pp. 157–92.

G Grassie, 2014, 'Trade secrets: the new EU enforcement regime', *JIPLP* 9, pp. 677–83.

S Greer, 2008, 'Choosing paths in European Union health services policy: a political analysis of a critical conjuncture', *JESP* 18, pp. 219–31.

X Groussot and H Lindgard, 2008, 'Are the general principles of Community law affecting private law?', in: U Bernitz, J Nergelius and C Cardner (eds), *General principles of EC law in a process of development*, Wolters Kluwer, pp. 155–76.

B Grzeszick, 2011, 'Case C-440/07 P, *Schneider Electric SA v* Commission, Judgment of the European Court of Justice (Grand Chamber) of 16 July 2009, [2009] ECR I-6413', *CMLRev* 48, pp. 907–23.

K Gutman, 2011, 'The evolution of the action for damages against the European Union and its place in the system of judicial protection', *CMLRev* 48, pp. 695–750.

L Guttuso, 2014, 'The enduring question of access to leniency materials in private proceedings: one draft Directive and several court rulings', *GCLR* 7, pp. 10–22.

L Gyselen, 2001, 'Comment from the point of view of EU competition law', in: J Wouters and J Stuyck (eds), *Principles of proper conduct for supranational, state and private actors in the European Union: towards a ius commune*, Intersentia, pp. 135–54.

B Haar, 2014, 'Civil liability of credit rating agencies after CRA 3: regulatory all-or-nothing approaches between immunity and over-deterrence', *EBLR* 25, pp. 315–34.

D Hadroušek and M Somlek, 2015, 'Solving the European Union's General Court', *ELRev* 40, pp. 188–206.

KM Halonen, 2015, 'Shielding against damages for ineffectiveness: The limitations of liability available for contracting authorities: a Finnish approach', *PPLR* 24, pp. 111–121.

B Hanotiau, 2010, 'L'arbitrabilité des litiges de propriété intellectuelle', in: J de Werra (ed.), *La résolution des litiges de propriété intellectuelle*, Schulthess Médias Juridiques, pp. 155–74.

G Harbottle, 2006, 'The implementation in England and Wales of the European Enforcement Directive', *JIPLP* 1, pp. 719–27.

C Harlow, 2000, 'A common European law of remedies?', in: C Kilpatrick, T Novitz and P Skidmore (eds), *The future of remedies in Europe*, Hart, pp. 69–83.

A Harmathy, 2010, 'The impact of the practice of the European Court of Justice on the civil and commercial law of the Member States of the European Union', *ERPL* 18, pp. 429–41.

A Hartkamp, 2010a, 'The effect of the EC Treaty in private law: on direct and indirect horizontal effects of primary Community law', *ERPL* 18, pp. 527–48.

A Hartkamp, 2010b, 'The general principles of EU law and private law', *RabelsZ* 75, pp. 241–59.

A Hartkamp, M Hesselink, E Hondius, C Mak and E du Perron (eds), 2011, *Towards a European civil code*, Kluwer.

B Hartmann, 2012, 'Alignment of national government liability law in Europe after *Francovich*', *ERA Forum* 12, pp. 613–24.

S Hassan, 2010, 'Damage compensation for infringements of industrial property rights in Italy', *IIC* 41, pp. 753–79.

M Hazelhorst, 2010, 'Private enforcement of EU competition law: why punitive damages are a step too far', *ERPL* 18, pp. 757–72.

JM Hebly (ed.), 2011, *European Public Procurement: legislative history of the 'Remedies' Directives 89/665/EEC and 92/13/EEC*, Kluwer Law International.

J Hebly and F Wilman, 2010, 'Schadevergoeding wegens schending van het aanbestedingsrecht', *BR* 8, pp. 326–34.

J Hebly, E De Boer and F Wilman, 2007, *Rechtsbescherming bij aanbesteding*, Uitgeverij Parijs.

M Heideman, 2012, 'European private law at the crossroads: the proposed European sales law', *ERPL* 20, pp. 1119–38.

A Heinemann, 2011, 'The rise of a private competition law culture: experience and vision', in: J Basedow, J Terhechte and L Tichý (eds), *Private enforcement of competition law*, Nomos, pp. 218–29.

B Hess, 2008, 'Preservation and taking of evidence in cross-border proceedings: comparative remarks in the context of IP litigation', in: A Nuyts (ed.), *International litigation in intellectual property and information technology*, Wolters Kluwer, pp. 289–301.

C Hilson, 2005, 'The role of discretion in EC law on non-contractual liability', *CMLRev* 42, pp. 677–95.

R Hilty, A Kur and A Peukert, 2006, 'Statement of the Max Planck Institute for intellectual property, competition and tax law on the proposal for a directive of the European Parliament and of the Council on criminal measures aimed at ensuring the enforcement of intellectual property rights', *IIC* 37.

C Himsworth, 1997, 'Things fall apart: the harmonisation of Community judicial protection revisited', *ELRev* 22, pp. 291–311.

AL Hinds, 2014, 'All settled? Some six years of cartel settlement', *ECLR* 35, pp. 292–8.

E Hjelmeng, 2013 'Competition law remedies: striving for coherence or finding new ways?', *CMLRev* 50, pp. 1007–37.

C Hodges, 2006, 'Competition enforcement, regulation and civil justice: what is the case?', *CMLRev* 43, pp. 1381–407.

C Hodges, 2011, 'Public and private enforcement: the practical implications for policy architecture', in: R Brownsword, HW Micklitz, L Niglia, S Weatherill (eds), *The foundations of European private law*, Hart, pp. 437–52.

C Hodges, 2013, 'Collective redress: a breakthrough or a *damp squib*?', *JCP*, pp. 67–89.

C Hodges, S Vogenauer and M Tulibacka (eds), 2010, *The costs and funding of civil litigation: a comparative perspective*, Hart.

M Hohler, 2012, 'Private enforcement of state aid law: problems of guaranteeing EU rights by means of national (procedural) law', *EStAL* 3, pp. 369–87.

E Hondius, 2009, 'Public and private enforcement in consumer protection: a Dutch perspective', in: F Cafaggi and HW Micklitz, *New frontiers of consumer protection: the interplay between private and public enforcement*, Intersentia, pp. 235–61.

E Hondius, 2010, 'The proposal for a European directive on consumer rights: a step in the right direction', *ERPL* 18, pp. 103–27.

E Hondius, 2011, 'From "toolbox" to academic standard: the current and future status of the draft common frame of reference', in: R Brownsword et al. (eds), *The foundations of European private law*, Hart, pp. 531–54.

M Honoré and N Eram Jensen, 2011, 'Damages in state aid cases', *EStAL* 2, pp. 265–86.

A Howard, 2014, 'The draft directive on competition law damages: what does it mean for infringers and victims?', *ECLR* 35, pp. 51–5.

G Howells, 2008, 'Is European product liability harmonized?', in: H Koziol and R Schulze (eds), *Tort law of the European Community*, Springer, pp. 121–34.

C Hummer and M Cywinski, 2014, 'ECJ judgments in "EnBW" and "Donau Chemie" and the unresolved problems of access to the file', *GCLR* 7, pp. 115–18.

K Hüschelrath and S Peyer, 2013, 'Public and private enforcement of competition law: a differentiated approach', *WComp* 36, pp. 585–613.

M Husovec and M Peguera, 2015, 'Much ado about little: Privately litigated internet disconnection injunctions', *IIC* 46, pp. 10–37.

S Iglesias Sánchez, 2012, 'The Court and the Charter: the impact of the entry into force of the Lisbon Treaty on the ECJ's approach to fundamental rights', *CMLRev* 49, pp. 1565–1611.

J Izquierdo Peris, 1999, 'Liability for defective products in the European Union: developments since 1995: the European Commission's green paper', *CLJ* 7, pp. 9–22.

P Jabaly, 2010, 'IP litigation or ADR: costing out the decision', *JIPLP* 5, pp. 730–35.

J Jacob, 1987, *The fabric of English civil justice*, Stevens & Sons.

F Jacobs, 1983, 'Damages for breach of Article 86 EEC', *ELRev* 8, pp. 353–62.

F Jacobs, 1997, 'Enforcing Community rights and obligations in national courts: striking the balance', in: J Lonbay and A Biondi (eds), *Remedies for breach of EC law*, John Wiley & Sons, pp. 25–36.

F Jacobs, 2004a, 'Recent and on-going measures to improve the efficiency of the European Court of Justice', *ELRev* 29, pp. 823–30.

F Jacobs, 2004b, 'The evolution of the European legal order', *CMLRev* 41, pp. 303–16.

F Jacobs and T Deisenhofer, 2003, 'Procedural aspects of the effective private enforcement of EC competition rules: a Community perspective', in: C Ehlermann and I Atanasiu (eds), *European competition law annual 2001: effective private enforcement of EC antitrust law*, Hart, pp. 185–226.

N Jalabert-Doury, 2010, 'France', in: A Foer and J Cuneo (eds), *The international handbook on private enforcement of competition law*, Edward Elgar, pp. 316–29.

A Jeffries, 2011, 'EU proposals on collective redress: lost in consultation?', *CPI Antitrust Chronicle* April, pp. 1–6.

J Jolowicz, 1994, 'Preface', in: J Storme (ed.), *Approximation of judiciary law in the European Union*, Kluwer, pp. xiii–xiv.

C Jones, 1999, *Private enforcement of antitrust law in the EU, UK and US*, Oxford University Press.

C Jones, 2003, 'A new dawn for private competition law remedies in Europe? Reflections from the US', in: C Ehlermann and I Atanasiu (eds), *European competition law annual 2001: effective private enforcement of EC antitrust law*, Hart, pp. 95–108.

C Jones, 2004, 'Private antitrust enforcement in Europe: a policy analysis and reality check', *WComp* 27, pp. 13–24.

A Jongbloet, 2003, 'De dwangsom als een speciale sanctie in het Europese privaatrecht', in: M Storme (ed.), *Procedural laws in Europe: towards harmonisation*, Maklu, pp. 193–255.

P Joseph, 2006, 'The rise and fall of cross-border jurisdiction and remedies in IP disputes', *JIPLP* 1, pp. 850–57.

T Kadner Graziono and C Oertel, 2008, 'EC tort law and the German legal family', in: H Koziol and R Schulze (eds), *Tort law of the European Community*, Springer, pp. 439–87.

C Kakouris, 1997, 'Do Member States possess judicial procedural "autonomy"?', *CMLRev* 34, pp. 1389–1412.

SL Kaleda, 2014, 'Claims for damages in EU procurement and effective protection of individual rights', *ELRev* 39, pp. 193–209.

J Kammin and F Becker, 2013, 'Cross-border EU competition litigation: qualitative interviews from Germany', in: M Danov, F Becker and P Beaumont (eds), *Cross-border EU competition law actions*, Hart, pp. 61–80.

A Kay, 2003, 'Path dependency and the CAP', *JEPP* 10, pp. 405–20.

B Keirsbilck, 2013, 'The *erga omnes* effect of the finding of an unfair contract term: *Nemzeti*', *CMLRev* 50, pp. 1467–78.

M Kellerbauer, 2014, 'The recent case law on the disclosure of information regarding EU competition law infringements to private damages claimants', *ECLR* 35, pp. 56–62.

D Kelliher, 2008, 'Aims and scope', in: H Koziol and R Schulze (eds), *Tort law of the European Community*, Springer, pp. 1–22.

M Kellner, 2009, 'Tort law of the European Community: a plea for an overarching pan-European framework', *ERPL* 17, pp. 133–54.

C Kersting, 2014, 'Removing the tension between public and private enforcement: disclosure and privileges for successful leniency applicants', *JECLP* 5, pp. 2–5.

J Keyte, 2014, 'Collective redress: perspectives from the US experience', in: P Lowe and M Marquis (eds), *European competition law annual 2011: integrating public and private enforcement of competition law – implications for courts and agencies*, Hart, pp. 195–204.

C Kilpatrick, 2000, 'The future of remedies in Europe', in: C Kilpatrick, T Novitz and P Skidmore (eds), *The future of remedies in Europe*, Hart, pp. 1–34.

C Kilpatrick, T Novitz and P Skidmore (eds), 2000, *The future of remedies in Europe*, Hart.

A Komninos, 2002, 'New prospects for private enforcement of EC competition law: Courage v Crehan and the Community rights to damages', *CMLRev* 39, pp. 447–87.

A Komninos, 2003, 'Introduction', in: C Ehlermann and I Atanasiu (eds), *European competition law annual 2001: effective private enforcement of EC antitrust law*, Hart, pp. xxxi–xlii.

A Komninos, 2006, 'Public and Private Antitrust Enforcement in Europe: Complement? Overlap?', *CompLRev* 3, pp. 5–26.

A Komninos, 2007, 'Effect of Commission decisions on private antitrust enforcement litigation: setting the story straight', *CMLRev* 44, pp. 1387–1428.

A Komninos, 2008, *EC private antitrust enforcement: decentralised application of EC competition law by national courts*, Hart.

A Komninos, 2009, 'Civil antitrust remedies between Community and national law', in: C Barnard and O Odudu (eds), *The outer limits of European Union law*, Hart, pp. 363–400.

A Komninos, 2014, 'The relationship between public and private enforcement: *quod Dei Deo, quod Ceasaris Ceasari*', in: P Lowe and M Marquis (eds), *European competition law annual 2011: integrating public and private enforcement of competition law – implications for courts and agencies*, Hart, pp. 141–58.

A Kornezov, 2014, 'Shaping the new architecture of the EU system of judicial remedies: comment on *Inuit*', *ELRev* 29, pp. 251–63.

T Kotsonis, 2011a, 'Green paper on the modernisation of EU public procurement policy towards a more efficient European procurement market', *PPLR* 20, pp. NA51–NA58.

T Kotsonis, 2011b, 'The basis on which the remedy of damages must be made available under the Remedies Directive: Stadt Graz v Strabag AG (C-314/09)', *PPLR* 20, pp. NA59–NA63.

T Kotsonis, 2014, 'The 2014 Utilities Directive of the EU: codification, flexibilisation and other misdemeanours', *PPLR* 23, pp. 169–87.

H Koziol and R Schulze, 2008a, 'Conclusion', in: H Koziol and R Schulze (eds), *Tort law of the European Community*, Springer, pp. 589–610.

H Koziol and R Schulze (eds), 2008b, *Tort law of the European Community*, Springer.

C Krenn, 2012, 'A missing piece in the horizontal effect "jigsaw": horizontal direct and the free movement of goods', *CMLRev* 49, pp. 177–215.

J Kuipers, 2011, 'The legal basis for a European optional instrument', *ERPL* 19, pp. 545–64.

A Kumar Singh, 2014, '*Pfleiderer*: assessing its impact on the impact of the European leniency programme', *ECLR* 35, pp. 110–23.

A Kur, 2004, 'The Enforcement Directive: rough start, happy landing?', *IIC* 35, pp. 821–30.

A Kur, 2006, 'A farewell to cross-border injunctions? The ECJ decisions in *GAT v LUK* and *Roche Nederland v Primus and Goldenberg*', *IIC* 37, pp. 844–55.

C Ladenburger, 2012, 'The interaction between the Charter of Fundamental Rights, the European Convention of Human Rights and national constitutions', Institutional report to the 2012 FIDE Conference.

A Lakits-Josse, 2011, 'Directive 2004/48/EC of the European Parliament and of the Council of 29 April 2004 on the enforcement of intellectual property rights', in: T Cottier and P Véron (eds), *Concise international and European IP law: TRIPS, Paris Convention, European enforcement and transfer of technology*, Wolters Kluwer, pp. 515–54.

R Lande, 2010, 'Benefits of private enforcement: empirical background', in: A Foer and J Cuneo (eds), *The international handbook on private enforcement of competition law*, Edward Elgar, pp. 3–11.

O Lando, 2011, 'Comments and questions relating to the European Commission's proposal for a regulation on a common European sales law', *ERPL* 19, pp. 717–28.

O Lando and H Beale (eds), 2000, *Principles of European contract law: parts I and II*, Kluwer.

O Lando, E Clive, A Prüm and R Zimmermann (eds), 2003, *Principles of European contract law: part III*, Kluwer.

H Laurila and T Kalliokoski, 2014, 'Developments in Finnish private antitrust litigation: Finland fast-forward into the future?', *ECLR* 35, pp. 519–524.

D Leczykiewicz, 2010a, 'Private party liability in EU law: in search of the general regime', in: C Barnard and O Odudu (eds), *Cambridge yearbook of European legal studies 2009–2010*, Hart, pp. 257–82.

D Leczykiewicz, 2010b, '"Effective judicial protection" of human rights after Lisbon: should national courts be empowered to review EU secondary law?', *ELRev* 35, pp. 326–48.

D Leczykiewicz, 2013, 'Horizontal application of the charter of fundamental rights', *ELRev* 38, pp. 479–97.

H Leffler, 2003, 'Damages liability for breach of EC procurement law: governing principles and practical solutions', *PPLR* 12, pp. 151–74.

K Lenaerts, D Arts and I Maselis, 2006, *Procedural law of the European Union*, Sweet & Maxwell.

K Lenaerts, I Maselis and K Gutman, 2014, *EU Procedural law*, Oxford University Press.

C Leskinen, 2011, 'Collective actions: rethinking funding and national cost rules', *CompLRev* 7, pp. 87–121.

F Lichère, 2006, 'Damages for violation of the EC public procurement rules in France', *PPLR* 15, pp. 171–8.

F Lichère and N Gabayet, 2011, 'Enforcement of the public procurement rules in France', in: S Treumer and F Lichère (eds), *Enforcement of the EU public procurement rules*, DJØF, pp. 299–330.

J Lindholm, 2007, *State procedure and Union rights*, Iustus Förlag.

J Lindholm, 2011, 'DCFR, please meet national procedure: enforcing the frame of reference using national procedural law', in: R Brownsword, HW Micklitz, L Niglia, S Weatherill (eds), *The foundations of European private law*, Hart, pp. 465–86.

T Lock, 2010, 'EU accession to the ECHR: implications for the judicial review in Strasbourg', *ELRev* 35, pp. 777–98.

T Lock, 2012, 'Is private enforcement of EU law through State liability a myth? An assessment of 20 years of *Francovich*', *CMLRev* 49, pp. 1675–1702.

M Loos, 2011, 'Individual private enforcement of consumer rights in civil courts in Europe', in: R Brownsword, HW Micklitz, L Niglia and S Weatherill (eds), *The foundations of European private law*, Hart, pp. 487–512.

F Louis, 2014, 'Promoting private enforcement: remember Article 102 TFEU', in: P Lowe and M Marquis (eds), *European competition law annual 2011: integrating public and private enforcement of competition law – implications for courts and agencies*, Hart, pp. 85–94.

P Lowe and M Marquis (eds), 2014, *European competition law annual 2011: integrating public and private enforcement of competition law – implications for courts and agencies*, Hart.

M Lukas, 2008, 'Fault liability', in: H Koziol and R Schulze (eds), *Tort law of the European Community*, Springer, pp. 81–102.

R Lundgren and S Ulfsdotter, 2010, 'Sweden', in: J Busche, M Trimborn and B Fabry (eds), *Patent infringement worldwide: claim interpretation, infringement, damages*, Carl Heymanns Verlag, pp. 205–22.

D Lunsingh Scheurleer, H Speyart, F Wijers and J Fanoy, 2010, 'The Netherlands', in: A Foer and J Cuneo (eds), *The international handbook on private enforcement of competition law*, Edward Elgar, pp. 368–79.

M Marquis, 2014, 'Perchance to dream: well-integrated public and private antitrust enforcement in the European Union', in: P Lowe and M Marquis (eds), *European competition law annual 2011: integrating public and private enforcement of competition law – implications for courts and agencies*, Hart, pp. xiii–lxxxi.

C Massa and A Strowell, 2004, 'The scope of the proposed IP enforcement directive: torn between the desire to harmonise and the need to combat piracy', *EIPR* 26, pp. 244–53.

D Matthews, 2010, 'The Lisbon Treaty, trade agreements and the enforcement of intellectual property rights', *EIPR* 32, pp. 104–12.

D Matthews and P Žikovská, 2013, 'The rise and fall of the Anti-Counterfeiting Trade Agreement (ACTA): lessons for the European Union', *IIC* 44, pp. 626–55.

P Meier-Beck, 2004, 'Damages for patent infringement according to German law: basic principles, assessment and enforcement', *IIC* 35, pp. 327–52.

A Meij, 2013, 'Courts in transition: administration of justice and how to organise it', *CMLRev* 50, pp. 3–13.

A Metselaar, 2014, 'Who can invoke state aid law before national judges? That floating question of legal interest in the case law of the Dutch courts', *EStAL* 13, pp. 250–60.

HW Micklitz, 2001, 'Efficacité internationale de l'action en suspension des clauses abusives: le point de vue allemand', *RIDC* 52, pp. 867–73.

HW Micklitz, 2011a, 'Administrative enforcement of private law', in: R Brownsword, HW Micklitz, L Niglia and S Weatherill (eds), *The foundations of European private law*, Hart, pp. 563–92.

HW Micklitz, 2011b, 'Collective private enforcement in antitrust law – what is going wrong in the debate?', in: J Basedow, J Terhechte and L Tichý (eds), *Private enforcement of competition law*, Nomos, pp. 101–19.

HW Micklitz, 2012, 'The ECJ between the individual citizen and the Member States: a plea for a judge-made European law on remedies', in: HW Micklitz and B De Witte (eds), *The European Court of Justice and the autonomy of the Member States*, Intersentia, pp. 349–400.

HW Micklitz and N Reich, 2009, 'Crónica de una muerte anunciada: the Commission proposal for a "directive on consumer rights"', *CMLRev* 46, pp. 471–519.

HW Micklitz, N Reich and P Rott, 2009, *Understanding EU consumer law*, Intersentia.

G Miller, 2009, 'Compensation and deterrence in consumer class actions in the United States and Europe', in: F Cafaggi and HW Micklitz, *New frontiers of consumer protection: the interplay between private and public enforcement*, Intersentia, pp. 263–82.

V Milutinovic, 2010, *The 'right to damages' under EC competition law: from Courage v Crehan to the white paper and beyond*, Wolters Kluwer.

V Milutinovic, 2014, 'The "right to damages" in a "system of parallel competences": a fresh look at *BRT v SABAM* and its subsequent interpretation', in: P Lowe and M Marquis (eds), *European competition law annual 2011: integrating public and private enforcement of competition law – implications for courts and agencies*, Hart, pp. 341–76.

V Milutinovic, 2015, 'The antitrust damages directive: the ideal of just compensation and the primacy of public enforcement', *CPI Antitrust Chronicle* January, pp. 2–18.

M Monti, 2003, 'Effective private enforcement of EC antitrust law', in: C Ehlermann and I Atanasiu, *European competition law annual 2001: effective private enforcement of EC antitrust law*, Hart, pp. 3–8.

W Möschel, 2013, 'Should private enforcement of competition law be strengthened?', *GCLR* 6, pp. 1–6.

A Mowbray, 2012, *Cases, materials and commentary on the European Convention on Human Rights*, Oxford University Press.

F Murphy, 2014, 'EU Commission proposes new measures re private actions for damages and collective actions', *ECLR* 35, pp. 223–6.

C Nagy, 2011, 'The new Hungarian rules on damages caused by horizontal hardcore cartels: presumed price increase and limited protection for whistleblowers', *ECLR* 31, pp. 63–7.

B Nascimbene, 2013, 'Interaction between leniency programmes and damages actions in antitrust law: perspectives for collective redress', *WComp* 36, pp. 269–83.

T Nauta, 2012, 'De inroepbaarheid van het Handvest voor de Europese en nationale rechter', *NTER* 18, pp. 19–25.

R Nazzini, 2009, 'Potency and act of the principle of effectiveness: the development of competition law remedies and procedures in Community law', in: C Barnard and O Odudu (eds), *The outer limits of European Union law*, Hart, pp. 401–36.

R Nazzini, 2011, 'The objective of private remedies in EU competition law', *GCLR* 4, pp. 131–46.

R Nazzini, 2012, 'Administrative enforcement, judicial review and fundamental rights in EU competition law: a comparative contextual-functionalist perspective', *CMLRev* 49, pp. 971–1005.

P Nebbia, 2008a, 'Do the rules on state aids have a life of their own? National procedural autonomy and effectiveness in the *Lucchini* case', *ELRev* 33, pp. 427–38.

P Nebbia, 2008b, 'Damages actions for the infringement of EC competition law: compensation or deterrence?', *ELRev* 33, pp. 23–36.

R Neruda, 2011, 'Private or public enforcement of competition law?', in: J Basedow, J Terhechte and L Tichý (eds), *Private enforcement of competition law*, Nomos, pp. 230–50.

L Neville Brown, 1997, 'National protection of Community rights: reconciling autonomy and effectiveness', in: J Lonbay and A Biondi (eds), *Remedies for breach of EC law*, John Wiley & Sons, pp. 67–72.

P Nielsen, 2013, 'The new Brussels I Regulation', *CMLRev* 50, pp. 503–28.

K Nordlander and M Abenhaïm, 2014, 'The "discoverability" of leniency documents and the proposed directive on damages actions for antitrust infringements', *CPI Antitrust Chronicle* February, pp. 1–8.

M Norrgård, 2005, 'The role conferred on the national judge by Directive 2004/48/EC on the enforcement of intellectual property rights', *ERA Forum* 6, pp. 503–14.

A Nuyts (ed.), 2008, *International litigation in intellectual property and information technology*, Wolters Kluwer.

K Oliphant, 2008, 'The nature and assessment of damages', in: H Koziol and R Schulze (eds), *Tort law of the European Community*, Springer, pp. 241–71.

P Oliver, 2011, 'Case C-279/09, *DEB v Germany*, Judgment of the European Court of Justice (Second Chamber) of 22 December 2010, nyr', *CMLRev* 48, pp. 2023–40.

P Oliver, 2013, 'Access to information and to justice in EU environmental law: the Aarhus Convention', *FILJ* 36, pp. 1423–70.

A Ortega González, 2014, 'De moeilijke balans tussen het clementieprogramma en schadevergoedingsvorderingen: *Where do we come from, where do we go?*', *SEW* 62, pp. 117–134.

T Ottervanger, 2010, 'Maatschappelijk verantwoord concurreren: mededingingsrecht in een veranderende wereld', *Oratie* Leiden University, 19 March.

T Ottervanger, 2014, 'Designing a balanced system: damages, deterrence, leniency and litigants' rights', in: P Lowe and M Marquis (eds), *European competition law annual 2011: integrating public and private enforcement of competition law – implications for courts and agencies*, Hart, pp. 17–26.

L Parret, 2012, 'Effectieve rechtsbescherming: eindeloos potentieel, ongeleid projectiel?', *NTER* 18, pp. 157–68.

S Peers, 2010, 'Supremacy, equality and human rights: comments on "Kücükdeveci" (C-55/07)', *ELRev* 35, pp. 849–56.

M Pérez, A Rabadán and E Serano, 2010, 'Spain', in: J Busche, M Trimborn and B Fabry (eds), *Patent infringement worldwide: claim interpretation, infringement, damages*, Carl Heymanns Verlag, pp. 185–204.

P Pescatore, 1983, 'The doctrine of "direct effect": an infant disease of Community law', *ELRev* 8, pp. 155–77.

S Peyer, 2011, 'Cartel members only: revisiting private antitrust policy in Europe', *ICLQ* 60, pp. 627–57.

S Peyer, 2012, 'Private antitrust litigation in Germany from 2005 to 2007: empirical evidence', *JCLE* 8, pp. 331–59.

S Peyer, undated, 'Injunctive relief and private antitrust enforcement', *CCP Working Paper* 11-7 (marked as "work in progress").

J Peysner, 2006, 'Costs and financing in private third party competition damages actions', *CompLRev* 5, pp. 97–115.

W Pfenningstorf, 1991, 'Uniform liability rules for service providers: a preliminary comment', *GPRI* 16, pp. 493–9.

S Pietrini, 2014, 'The future of collective damages actions in Europe', in: P Lowe and M Marquis (eds), *European competition law annual 2011: integrating public and private enforcement of competition law – implications for courts and agencies*, Hart, pp. 257–68.

E Pijnacker Hordijk, G Van der Bend and J Van Nouhuys, 2009, *Aanbestedingsrecht: handboek van het Europese en het Nederlandse aanbestedingsrecht*, Sdu Uitgevers.

E Pistoa, 2014, 'Enhanced cooperation as a tool to … enhance cooperation? *Italy and Spain v Council*', *CMLRev* 51, pp. 247–60.

C Poncibò, 2009, 'The reform of Directive 98/27/EC', in: F Cafaggi and HW Micklitz (eds), *New frontiers of consumer protection: the interplay between private and public enforcement*, Intersentia, pp. 283–304.

S Prechal, 1997, 'EC requirements for an effective remedy', in: J Lonbay and A Biondi (eds), *Remedies for breach of EC law*, John Wiley & Sons, pp. 3–14.

S Prechal, 1998, 'Community law in national courts: the lessons from Van Schijndel', *CMLRev* 35, pp. 681–706.

S Prechal, 2001, 'Judge-made harmonization of national procedural rules: a bridging perspective', in: J Wouters and J Stuyck (eds), *Principles of proper conduct for supranational, state and private actors in the European Union: towards a ius commune*, Intersentia, pp. 39–58.

S Prechal, 2005, *Directives in EC law*, Oxford University Press.

S Prechal, 2006, 'Member State liability and direct effect: what's the difference after all?', *EBLR* 17, pp. 299–316.

S Prechal and R Widdershoven, 2011, 'Redefining the relationship between "Rewe-effectiveness" and effective judicial protection', *REAL* 4, pp. 31–50.

L Prete and B Smulders, 2010, 'The coming of age of infringement proceedings', *CMLRev* 47, pp. 9–61.

H Pries and P Friton, 2011, 'Designing effective challenge procedures: the EU's experience with remedies', in: S Arrowsmith and R Anderson, *The WTO regime on government procurement: challenge and reform*, Cambridge University Press, pp. 511–31.

H Rasmussen, 2000, 'Remedying the crumbling EC judicial system', *CMLRev* 37, pp. 1071–1112.

J Ratliff, 2014, 'Integrating public and private enforcement of competition law: implications for courts and agencies', in: P Lowe and M Marquis (eds), *European competition law annual 2011: integrating public and private enforcement of competition law – implications for courts and agencies*, Hart, pp. 271–94.

R Rawlings, 2000, 'Engaged elites: citizen action and institutional attitudes in Commission enforcement', in: C Kilpatrick, T Novitz and P Skidmore (eds), *The future of remedies in Europe*, Hart, pp. 267–96.

R Rebhahn, 2008, 'Non-contractual liability in damages of Member States for breach of Community law', in: H Koziol and R Schulze (eds), *Tort law of the European Community*, Springer, pp. 179–211.

N Reich, 1986, 'Product safety and product liability: an analysis of the EEC Council Directive of 25 July 1985 on the approximation of the laws, regulations and administrative provisions of the member States concerning liability for defective products', *JCP* 9, pp. 133–54.

N Reich, 2010, 'The interrelation between rights and duties in EU law: reflections on the state of liability law in the multilevel governance system of the Union: is there a need for a more coherent approach in European private law?', in: P Eeckhout and T Tridimas (eds), *Yearbook of European law 2010*, Oxford University Press, pp. 112–63.

A Reich and O Shabat, 2014, 'The remedy of damages in public procurement in Israel and the EU: a proposal for reform', *PPLR* 23, pp. 50–77.

J Reinbothe, 2010, 'The EU IPR Enforcement Directive 2004/48/EC as a tool for copyright enforcement', in: I Stamatoudi (ed.), *Copyright enforcement and the internet*, Wolters Kluwer, pp. 3–28.

A Riley and J Peysner, 2006, 'Damages in EC antitrust actions: who pays the piper?', *ELRev* 31, pp. 748–61.

J Rivas and G Eclair-Heath, 2012, 'Striking the balance between public and private enforcement: the case for consensual compensation as a mitigating circumstance in setting fines for violations of EU competition law', *RDC* 9, pp. 1–7.

F Rizzuto, 2012, 'Leniency and damages actions: the impact of recent European Union court jurisprudence', *GCLR* 5, pp. 1–13.

O Rognstad, 2011, 'Compensation and restitution in EU intellectual property law', in: M Andenas and K Lilleholt (eds), *Remedies and substantive law: European dimensions of economic and private law*, University of Oslo Faculty of Law Legal Studies Research Paper Series No 2011-18, pp. 49–58.

N Roland, 2014, 'Calculating damages in copyright infringement actions under Belgian law', *JIPLP* 9, pp. 292–7.

A Rosas and L Armanti, 2010, *EU constitutional law: an introduction*, Hart.

JT Rosch, 2014, 'Designing a private remedies system for antitrust cases: lessons learned from the US experience', in: P Lowe and M Marquis (eds), *European competition law annual 2011: integrating public and private enforcement of competition law – implications for courts and agencies*, Hart, pp. 179–94.

M Ross, 2006, 'Effectiveness in the European legal order(s): beyond supremacy to constitutional proportionality?', *ELRev* 31, pp. 476–98.

P Rott, 2001, 'The protection of consumers' interests after the implementation of the EC Consumer Injunctions Directive into German and English law', *JCP* 24, pp. 399–439.

A Ruch-Larsen, 2006, 'Damages under German law for infringement of EU public procurement law', *PPLR* 15, pp. 179–94.
J Rüggeberg and M Schinkel, 2006, 'Consolidating antitrust damages in Europe: a proposal for standing in line with efficient private enforcement', *WComp* 29, pp. 395–420.
M Safjan and P Miklaszewicz, 2010, 'Horizontal effect of the general principles of EU law in the sphere of private law', *ERPL* 18, pp. 475–86.
MA Saias, 2014, 'Unlawful acquisition of trade secrets by cyber theft: between the proposed directive on trade secrets and the directive on cyber attacks', *JIPLP* 9, pp. 721–9.
I Samoy, T Dang Vu and S Jansen, 2011, 'Don't find fault, find a remedy', *ERPL* 19, pp. 855–72.
M Schaffner, 2010, 'Two years on: the French experience of the Enforcement Directive', *JIPLP* 5, pp. 178–85.
H Schebesta, 2010, 'Does the national court know European law? A note on *ex officio* application after *Asturcom*', *ERPL* 18, pp. 847–80.
K Schiemann, 2008, 'The functioning of the Court of Justice in an enlarged Union and the future of the Court', in: A Arnull, P Eeckhout and T Tridimas (eds), *Continuity and change in EU law: essays in honour of Sir Francis Jacobs*, Oxford University Press, pp. 3–19.
M Schneider and O Vrins, 2006, 'The EU offensive against IP offences: should rightholders be offended?', *JIPLP* 1, pp. 173–6.
S Schnell, 2011, 'The Community trade mark: unitary EU right, EU-wide injunction?', *EIPR* 33, pp. 210–26.
C Seville, 2009, *EU intellectual property law and policy*, Edward Elgar.
L Silva Morais, 2014, 'Integrating public and private enforcement in Europe: legal issues', in: P Lowe and M Marquis (eds), *European competition law annual 2011: integrating public and private enforcement of competition law – implications for courts and agencies*, Hart, pp. 109–40.
M Siragusa, 2014, 'Options for collective redress in the EU', in: P Lowe and M Marquis (eds), *European competition law annual 2011: integrating public and private enforcement of competition law – implications for courts and agencies*, Hart, pp. 235–56.
M Slavicek, 2006, 'Damages for breach of the EC public procurement rules in Sweden', *PPLR* 15, pp. 223–40.
H Smith, 1992, 'The *Francovich* case: state liability and the individual's right to damages', *ECLR* 13, pp. 129–32.
V Smith, A Maton and S Cambell, 2010, 'England and Wales', in: A Foer and J Cuneo (eds), *The international handbook on private enforcement of competition law*, Edward Elgar, pp. 296–315.
H Snijders, 2009, 'Interpretation of national rules for *ex officio* raising of points of Community law by national courts', in: H Snijders and S Vogenauer (eds),

Content and meaning of national law in the context of transnational law, Sellier, pp. 133–56.

H Snijders, 2014, 'New developments in national rules for *ex officio* raising of points of Community law by national courts', in: A Hartkamp et al. (eds), *The influence of EU law on national private law*, Kluwer, pp. 95–118.

F Snyder, 1993, 'The effectiveness of European Community law: institutions, processes, tools and techniques', *MLR* 56, pp. 19–54.

H Speyart, 2005, 'Tien jaar doorwerking van het EG-recht in het IE-recht: van externe factor naar interne motor', *NTER* 11, pp. 267–76.

A Stadler, 2009, 'Group actions as a remedy to enforce consumer interests', in: F Cafaggi and HW Micklitz, *New frontiers of consumer protection: the interplay between private and public enforcement*, Intersentia, pp. 305–28.

A Stadler, 2013a, 'The Commission's recommendation on common principles of collective redress and private international law issues', *NiPR* 32, pp. 483–8.

A Stadler, 2013b, 'Practical obstacles in cross-border litigation and communication between (EU) courts', *ErLRev* 6, pp. 151–67.

P Stauber, 2014, 'The European draft directive on antitrust damages claims and its potential consequences for German law', *GCLR* 7, pp. 23–38.

J Steiner, 1987, 'How to make the action suit the case: domestic remedies for breach of EEC law', *ELRev* 12, pp. 102–12.

J Steiner, 1995, *Enforcing EC law*, Blackstone Press.

J Storme, 1994, 'General introductory report', in: J Storme (ed.), *Approximation of judiciary law in the European Union*, Kluwer, pp. 37–70.

M Storme, 2007, 'Freedom of contract: mandatory and non-mandatory rules in European contract law', *ERPL* 15, pp. 230–50.

E Storskrubb, 2008, *Civil procedure and EU law: a policy area uncovered*, Oxford University Press.

E Storskrubb, 2011, 'Civil justice: a newcomer and an unstoppable wave?', in: P Craig and G De Búrca (eds), *The evolution of EU law*, Oxford University Press, pp. 299–322.

J Stuyck, 2001, 'Joined cases C-240/98 to C-244/98, *Océano Grupo Editorial SA v Rocio Murciano Quintero* and *Salvat Editore SA v José M Sànchez Alcón Prades et al*, Judgment of the Full Court of 27 June 2000, nyr', *CMLRev* 38, pp. 719–37.

J Stuyck, 2009, 'Public and private enforcement in consumer protection: general comparison EU–USA', in: F Cafaggi and HW Micklitz (eds), *New frontiers of consumer protection: the interplay between private and public enforcement*, Intersentia, pp. 63–90.

J Stuyck, 2010, 'Case C-243/08, *Pannon GSM Zrt V Erzsébet Sustikné Györfi*, judgment of the Court (Fourth Chamber) of 4 June 2009, not yet reported and Case C-40/08, *Asturcom Telecomunicationes SL v Maria Cristiba*

Rodriguez Nogueira, judgment of the Court (First Chamber) of 6 October 2009, not yet reported', *CMLRev* 47, pp. 879–98.

J Stuyck, 2011, 'Enforcement and compliance: an EU law perspective', in: R Brownsword, HW Micklitz, L Niglia, S Weatherill (eds), *The foundations of European private law*, Hart, pp. 513–30.

J Stuyck, 2012, 'La nouvelle directive relative aux droits des consommateurs', *JDE* 20, pp. 69–75.

E Szyszczak and J Delicostopoulos, 1997, 'Intrusion into national procedural autonomy: the French paradigm', *ELRev* 22, pp. 141–9.

H Taschner, 2002, 'Case C-203/99, *Henning Veedfald v Arhus Amtskommune*, judgment of the Court (Fifth Chamber) of 10 May 2001, nyr', *CMLRev* 39, pp. 385–92.

J Temple Lang, 1981, 'Community antitrust law: compliance and enforcement', *CMLRev* 18, pp. 335–62.

J Temple Lang, 1984, 'EEC competition actions in member states' courts: claims for damages, declarations and injunctions for breach of Community antitrust law', in: B Hawk (ed.), *Annual proceedings of the Fordham Corporate Law Institute 1983*, Matthew Bender, pp. 219–304.

J Temple Lang, 1985, 'Injunctions and damages in national courts under European Community competition law', *ILP* March, pp. 29–32.

J Temple Lang, 2008, 'Article 10 EC: the most important "general principle" of Community law', in: U Bernitz, J Nergelius and C Cardner (eds), *General principles of EC law in a process of development*, Wolters Kluwer, pp. 75–114.

S Theurich, 2010, 'Designing tailored alternative dispute resolution in intellectual property: the experience of WIPO', in: J de Werra (ed.), *La résolution des litiges de propriété intellectuelle*, Schulthess Médias Juridiques, pp. 175–93.

G Thüsing and S Horler, 2010, 'Case C-555/07, *Seda Kücükdeveci v Swedex*, Judgment of the Court (Grand Chamber) of 19 January 2010, not yet reported', *CMLRev* 47, pp. 1161–72.

L Tichý, 2008, 'EC tort law and the Eastern-European legal family', in: H Koziol and R Schulze (eds), *Tort law of the European Community*, Springer, pp. 513–38.

U Till, 2010, 'Great Britain', in: J Busche, M Trimborn and B Fabry (eds), *Patent infringement worldwide: claim interpretation, infringement, damages*, Carl Heymanns Verlag, pp. 99–139.

A Toth, 1978, *Legal protection of individuals in the European Communities Volume II: remedies and procedure*, North Holland Publishing Company.

P Trepte, 2007, *Public procurement in the EU: a practitioner's guide*, Oxford University Press.

S Treumer, 2006, 'Damages for breach of the EC public procurement rules: changes in European regulation and practice', *PPLR* 15, pp. 159–70.

S Treumer, 2011a, 'Basis and conditions for a damages claim for breach of the EU public procurement rules', in: D Fairgrieve and F Lichère (eds), *Public procurement law: damages as an effective remedy*, Hart, pp. 149–66.

S Treumer, 2011b, 'Enforcement of the EU public procurement rules: the state of law and current issues', in: S Treumer and F Lichère (eds), *Enforcement of the EU public procurement rules*, DJØF, pp. 17–52.

S Treumer, 2011c, 'Enforcement of the EU public procurement rules: Danish regulation and practice', in: S Treumer and F Lichère (eds), *Enforcement of the EU public procurement rules*, DJØF, pp. 255–98.

S Treumer and F Lichère (eds), 2011, *Enforcement of the EU public procurement rules*, DJØF.

T Tridimas, 1996, 'The ECJ and judicial activism', *ELRev* 21, pp. 199–210.

T Tridimas, 2001, 'Judicial review and the Community judicature: towards a new European constitutionalism?', in: J Wouters and J Stuyck (eds), *Principles of proper conduct for supranational, state and private actors in the European Union: towards a ius commune*, Intersentia, pp. 71–84.

T Tridimas, 2006, *The general principles of EU law*, Oxford University Press.

S Troiano, 2008, 'EC tort law and the Romanic legal family', in: H Koziol and R Schulze (eds), *Tort law of the European Community*, Springer, pp. 395–438.

V Trstenjak and E Beysen, 2011, 'European consumer protection law: *curia semper dabit remedium*?', *CMLRev* 48, pp. 95–124.

M Trybus, 2011, 'An overview of the United Kingdom public procurement review and remedies system with an emphasis on England and Wales', in: S Treumer and F Lichère (eds), *Enforcement of the EU public procurement rules*, DJØF, pp. 201–34.

M Trybus, 2013, 'The tailor-made EU Defence and Security Procurement Directive: limitation, flexibility, descriptiveness and substitution', *ELRev* 38, pp. 3–29.

M Tulibacka, 2009, 'Europeanization of civil procedures: in search of a coherent approach', *CMLRev* 46, pp. 1527–65.

DP Tzakas, 2011, 'Effective collective redress in antitrust and consumer protection matters: a panacea or a chimera?' *CMLRev* 48, pp. 1125–74.

DP Tzakas, 2014, 'Collective redress in the field of EU competition law: the need for an EI remedy and the impact of the recent Commission Recommendation', *LEIE* 41, pp. 225–42.

H Ullrich, 2015, 'The European patent and its courts: an uncertain prospect and an unfinished agenda', *IIC* 46, pp. 1–9.

H Unberath and A Johnston, 2007, 'The double-headed approach of the ECJ concerning consumer protection', *CMLRev* 44, pp. 1237–84.

G Urbanchuk and J Tumbridge, 2008, 'Patent damages: the European landscape', *JIPLP* 3, pp. 576–9.

M Uřičař, 2011, 'Evidence in competition law cases: problems in Czech law', in: J Basedow, J Terhechte and L Tichý (eds), *Private enforcement of competition law*, Nomos, pp. 143–52.
C van Dam, 2006, *European tort law*, Oxford University Press.
R van den Bergh, 2013, 'Private enforcement of European competition law and the persisting collective action problem', *MJECL* 20, pp. 12–34.
S van den Bogaert, 2002, 'Horizontality: the court attacks?', in: C Barnard and J Scott, *The law of the single European market*, Hart, pp. 123–52.
A Van den Bossche, 2003, 'Europees Gemeenschapsrecht: bron van en reden voor toenadering', in: M Storme (ed.), *Procedural laws in Europe: towards harmonisation*, Maklu, pp. 25–54.
P Van Doorn, 1989, 'Réflexions sur l'effet direct des directives communautaires à propos de la Directive sur la responsabilité du fait des produits', *GP* April, pp. 11–14.
P Van Eecke, 2011, 'Online service providers and liability: a plea for a balanced approach', *CMLRev* 48, pp. 1455–1502.
W Van Gerven, 1995, 'Bridging the gap between Community and national law: towards a principle of homogeneity in the field of legal remedies?', *CMLRev* 32, pp. 679–702.
W Van Gerven, 2000, 'Of rights, remedies and procedures', *CMLRev* 37, pp. 501–36.
W Van Gerven, 2003a, 'European political integration, comparative law and private enforcement of competition law', in: T Einhorn (ed.), *Spontaneous order, organization and the law: roads to a European civil society (Liber amoricum Ernst-Joachim Mestmäcker)*, Asser Press, pp. 393–412.
W Van Gerven, 2003b, 'Substantive remedies for the private enforcement of EC antitrust rules before national courts', in: C Ehlermann and I Atanasiu (eds), *European competition law annual 2001: effective private enforcement of EC antitrust law*, Hart, pp. 53–94.
W Van Gerven, 2004a, 'Harmonisation of private law: do we need it?', *CMLRev* 41, pp. 505–32.
W Van Gerven, 2004b, 'The emergence of a common European tort law: the EU contribution', in: S Moreira de Sousa and W Heusel (eds), *Enforcing Community law from Francovich to Köbler: twelve years of the state liability principle*, Bundesanzeiger, pp. 225–41.
W Van Gerven, 2008a, 'Two twin-principles of EU law: democracy and accountability, consistency and convergence', in: U Bernitz, J Nergelius and C Cardner (eds), *General principles of EC law in a process of development*, Wolters Kluwer, pp. 25–46.
W Van Gerven, 2008b, 'About rules and principles, codification and legislation, harmonisation and convergence, and education in the area of contract law',

in: *Continuity and change in EU law: essays in honour of Sir Francis Jacobs*, Oxford University Press, pp. 400–414.

W Van Gerven, J Lever and P Larouche, 2000, *Cases, materials and text on national, supranational and international tort law*, Hart.

H Van Harten and T Nauta, 2013, 'Towards horizontal direct effect of the free movement of goods? Comment on *Fra.bo*', *ELRev* 38, pp. 677–94.

P Van Malleghem and N Baeten, 2014, 'Before the law stands a gatekeeper, or what is a "regulatory act" in Article 263(4) TFEU? *Inuit Tapiriit Kanatami*', *CMLRev* 51, pp. 1187–1216.

CH Van Rhee, 2005, 'Specific topics: introduction', in: CH Van Rhee (ed.), *European traditions in civil procedure*, Intersentia, pp. 185–96.

E Van Schagen, 2012, 'More consistency and legal certainty in the private law *acquis*: a plea for better justification for the harmonisation of private law', *MJECL* 19, pp. 37–63.

B Vandermeulen, 2005, 'Harmonisation of IP litigation practices: still a long road ahead', *JIPLP* 1, pp. 30–35.

A Vaquer, 2008, 'Damage', in: H Koziol and R Schulze (eds), *Tort law of the European Community*, Springer, pp. 23–45.

P Verbruggen, 2014, 'The impact of primary law on private relationships: horizontal direct effect under the free movement of goods and services', *ERPL* 22, pp. 201–16.

M Vitoria, 2006, 'Mediation in intellectual property disputes', *JIPLP* 1, pp. 398–405.

SB Völcker, 2012, 'Case C-360/09 *Pfleiderer AG v Bundeskarlelamt*, Judgment of the Court of Justice (Grand Chamber) of 14 June 2011, nyr', *CMLRev* 49, pp. 695–720.

C Von Bar and E Clive (eds), 2010, *Principles, definitions and model rules of European private law: draft common frame of reference (DCFR) Volumes I–VI*, Oxford University Press.

B Vrcek, 2010, 'Overview of Europe', in: A Foer and J Cuneo (eds), *The international handbook on private enforcement of competition law*, Edward Elgar, pp. 277–95.

C Vrendenbarg, 2013, 'De "volledige" proceskostenveroordeling in IE-zaken: een kritische bespreking van de implementatie en interpretatie van artikel 14 Handhavingsrichtlijn in Nederland', *BIE* 6, pp. 160–68.

O Vrins and M Schneider, 2006, *Enforcement of intellectual property rights through border measures: law and practice in the EU*, Oxford University Press.

G Wagner, 2014, 'Private law enforcement through ADR: wonder drug or snake oil', *CMLRev* 51, pp. 165–94.

J Wakefield, 2009, 'Retrench and reform: the action for damages', in: P Eeckhout and T Tridimas (eds), *Yearbook of European law 2009*, Oxford University Press, pp. 390–434.

A Ward, 1998, 'New frontiers in private enforcement of EC directives', *ELRev* 23, pp. 65–78.
A Ward, 2009, 'National and EC remedies under the EU Treaty: limits and the role of the ECHR', in: C Barnard and O Odudu (eds), *The outer limits of European Union law*, Hart, pp. 329–62.
S Weatherill, 2000, 'Addressing problems of imbalanced implementation in EC law: remedies in an institutional perspective', in: C Kilpatrick, T Novitz and P Skidmore (eds), *The future of remedies in Europe*, Hart, pp. 87–116.
S Weatherill, 2005, *EU consumer law and policy*, Edward Elgar.
S Weatherill, 2011, 'Consumer policy', in: P Craig and G De Búrca (eds), *The evolution of EU law*, Oxford University Press, pp. 837–8.
S Weatherill, 2012, 'The Consumer Rights Directive: how and why a quest for "coherence" has (largely) failed', *CMLRev* 49, pp. 1279–1317.
CF Weidt, 2014, 'The directive on actions for damages after passing the European Parliament', *ECLR* 35, pp. 438–44.
J Weiler, 1981, 'The Community system: the dual character of supranationalism', in: F Jacobs (ed.), *Yearbook of European law*, Oxford University Press, pp. 267–306.
J Weiler, 1991, 'The transformation of Europe', *YLJ* 100, pp. 2403–83.
F Weiss, 1993, *Public procurement in European Community law*, Athlone Press.
M Weitenberg, 2008, 'Terminology', in: H Koziol and R Schulze (eds), *Tort law of the European Community*, Springer, pp. 309–40.
R Whish, 1994, 'The enforcement of EC competition law in the domestic courts of the Member States', *EBLR* 5, pp. 3–9.
R Whish and D Bailey, 2012, *Competition law*, Oxford University Press.
S Whittaker, 2005, *Liability for products: English law, French law and European harmonisation*, Oxford University Press.
R Williams, 2008, 'A new Remedies Directive for the European Community', *PPLR* 17, pp. NA19–NA25.
R Williams, 2012, 'Commission proposals to modernise public procurement', *PPLR* 21, pp. NA101–NA105.
R Williams, 2014, 'European Parliament consent to the conclusion of the revised World Trade Organization's Government Procurement Agreement', *PPLR* 23, pp. NA29–NA30.
F Wilman, 2008, 'Stilstand is vooruitgang: herziening van de rechtsbescherm-ingsrichtlijnen voor de "klassieke" sectoren', *TA* 2, pp. 115–30.
W Wils, 2003a, 'Should private antitrust enforcement be encouraged in Europe?', *WComp* 26, pp. 473–88.
W Wils, 2003b, 'Does the effective enforcement of Articles 81 and 82 EC require not only fines on undertakings, but also individual penalties, and in particular imprisonment?', in: C Ehlermann and I Atanasiu (eds), *European*

competition law annual 2001: effective private enforcement of EC antitrust law, Hart, pp. 409–50.

W Wils, 2005, 'Is criminalisation of EU competition law the answer?', *WComp* 28, pp. 117–59.

W Wils, 2008, *Efficiency and justice in European antitrust enforcement*, Hart.

W Wils, 2009, 'The relationship between public antitrust enforcement and private actions for damages', *WComp* 32, pp. 3–26.

W Wils, 2013, 'Ten years of Regulation 1/2003: a retrospective', *JECLP* 4, pp. 293–301.

D Wilsher, 2006, 'The public aspects of private enforcement in EC law: some constitutional and administrative challenges of a damages culture', *CompLRev* 3, pp. 27–45.

S Wisking, K Dietzel and M Herron, 2014, 'European Commission finally publishes measures to facilitate competition law private actions in the European Union', *ECLR* 35, pp. 185–93.

D Wolf, 2003, 'European political integration, comparative law and private enforcement of competition rules', in: T Einhorn (ed.), *Spontaneous order, organization and the law: roads to a European civil society (Liber amoricum Ernst-Joachim Mestmäcker)*, Asser Press, pp. 421–4.

X Zhang, 2011, 'Constructing a system of challenge procedures to comply with the Agreement on Government Procurement', in: S Arrowsmith and R Anderson, *The WTO regime on government procurement: challenge and reform*, Cambridge University Press, pp. 483–510.

E Zippro, 2009a, 'The white paper on damages actions for breach of the EC antitrust rules', in: H Snijders and S Vogenauer (eds), *Content and meaning of national law in the context of transnational law*, Sellier European Law Publishers, pp. 213–22.

E Zippro, 2009b, *Privaatrechtelijke handhaving van mededingingsrecht*, Kluwer.

M Zuleeg, 2003, 'Criminal sanctions to be imposed on individuals as enforcement instruments in European competition law', in: C Ehlermann and I Atanasiu (eds), *European competition law annual 2001: effective private enforcement of EC antitrust law*, Hart, pp. 451–60.

STUDIES AND REPORTS

Ashurst, 2004, 'Conditions of claims for damages in case of infringement of EC competition rules', 31 August.

C Cauffman, M Faure and T Hartlief, 2009, 'Harmonisatie van het consumentenrecht in Europa: consequenties voor Nederland', 26 March.

CEPS, Erasmus University Rotterdam and LUISS, 2007, 'Making antitrust damages actions more effective in the EU: welfare impact and potential scenarios', 21 December.

Civic Consulting, 2007, 'Analytical report on the green paper on the review of the consumer acquis', 6 November.

Civic Consulting, 2008a, 'Evaluation of the effectiveness and efficiency of collective redress mechanisms in the European Union', August.

Civic Consulting, 2008b, 'The problems faced by consumers in obtaining redress for infringements of consumer protection legislation and the economic consequences of such problems', August.

Civic Consulting, 2009, 'The use of alternative dispute resolution in the European Union', 16 October.

Civic Consulting, Van Dijk and ICF GHK, 2012, '(External) evaluation of the Consumer Protection Cooperation Regulation', 17 December.

Cleary Gottlieb, Steen and Hamilton, 1988, 'Extraits de l'analyse des moyens de la regularité des procedures de passation des marchés publics dans les Etats Membres de la C.E.', doc. CCO/88/73, 22 June.

European Communities Trade Mark Association (ECTA), undated, 'Monetary compensation for trade mark infringement as applied in the courts of the European Union'.

European Competition Network (ECN), 2012a, Working group cooperation issues and due process, 'Investigative powers report', 31 October.

European Competition Network (ECN), 2012b, Working group cooperation issues and due process, 'Decision-making powers report', 31 October.

European Observatory on Counterfeiting and Piracy, undated a, 'Evidence and right of information in intellectual property rights'.

European Observatory on Counterfeiting and Piracy, undated b, 'Injunctions in intellectual property rights'.

European Observatory on Counterfeiting and Piracy, undated c, 'Corrective measures in intellectual property rights'.

European Observatory on Counterfeiting and Piracy, undated d, 'Damages in intellectual property rights'.

Expert group on European contract law, 2011, 'Feasibility study for a future instrument in European contract law', 3 May.

Fondazione Rosselli, 2004, 'Analysis of the economic impact of the development risk clause as provided by Directive 85/374/EEC on liability for defective products'.

Herbert Smith, 1996, 'Procurement Remedies', CCO/97/13.

High-level group on the functioning of the internal market, 1992, 'The internal market after 1992: meeting the challenge', 28 October.

Italian Authority for the Supervision of Public Contracts, 2010, 'The comparative survey on the national public procurement systems across the PPN'.

Lovells, 2003, 'Product liability in the European Union'.
McKenna, 1994, 'Report on the application of Directive 85/374/EEC on liability for defective products', May.
Oxera Consulting, 2009, 'Quantifying antitrust damages: towards non-binding guidance for courts', December.
J Pelkmans and A Correia de Brito, 2012, 'Enforcement in the EU single market'.
UK government, 2013, 'Review of the balance of competences between the United Kingdom and the European Union: the single market', July.
University of Bielefeld, 2008, 'EC consumer law compendium: comparative analysis', February.
University of Leuven, 2007, 'An analysis and evaluation of alternative means of consumer redress other than redress through ordinary judicial proceedings', 17 January.
View, 2004, 'Comparative analysis of national liability systems for remedying damages caused by defective consumer services', April.
G Westkamp, 2007, 'The implementation of Directive 2001/29/EC in the Member States', February.
A Wood, 2004, supported by the Office of Government Commerce, 'Investigating UK business experiences of competing for public contracts in other EU countries', November.

INDEX